Educational Foundations

An Anthology
Second Edition

Edited by

ROSELLE K. CHARTOCK
Massachusetts College of Liberal Arts

PEARSON

Merrill
Prentice Hall

Upper Saddle River, New Jersey
Columbus, Ohio

Library of Congress Cataloging-in-Publication Data

Educational foundations: an anthology / edited by Roselle K.
Chartock.—2nd ed.
   p.   cm.
Includes bibliographical references and index.
   ISBN 0-13-098746-8 (pbk.)
   1. Education—Study and teaching (Higher)—United States.   2. Educational sociology.   3. Education—
History.   4. Education—United States—History.   5. Teaching. I. Chartock, Roselle.
   LB17.E393   2004
   370'.71'1—dc21

                                                                                    2003008202

Vice President and Executive Publisher: Jeffery W. Johnston
Acquisitions/Executive Editor: Debra A. Stollenwerk
Editorial Assistant: Mary Morrill
Development Editor: Daniel J. Parker
Production Editor: Kris Robinson-Roach
Production Coordination: *The GTS Companies*/York, PA Campus
Design Coordinator: Diane C. Lorenzo

Photo Coordinator: Valerie Schultz
Cover Designer: Ali Mohrman
Cover image: Superstock
Production Manager: Pamela D. Bennett
Director of Marketing: Ann Castel Davis
Marketing Manager: Darcy Betts Prybella
Marketing Coordinator: Tyra Poole

This book was set in ACaslon Regular by *The GTS Companies*/York, PA Campus. It was printed and bound by R. R. Donnelley & Sons Company. The cover was printed by Phoenix Color Corp.

Photo Credits: Scott Cunningham/Merrill, p. 259; Laima Druskis/PH College, p. 205; Library of Congress, pp. 1, 63; BJ Pendergast, The Independent, p. 315; Anne Vega/Merrill, p. 133.

Pearson Education Ltd.
Pearson Education Singapore Pte. Ltd.
Pearson Education Canada, Ltd.
Pearson Education—Japan

Pearson Education Australia Pty. Limited
Pearson Education North Asia Ltd.
Pearson Educación de Mexico, S.A. de C.V.
Pearson Education Malaysia Pte. Ltd.

10 9 8 7 6 5
ISBN: 0-13-098746-8

For all those teachers who love what they do.

Educator Learning Center:
An Invaluable Online Resource

Merrill Education and the Association for Supervision and Curriculum Development (ASCD) invite you to take advantage of a new online resource, one that provides access to the top research and proven strategies associated with ASCD and Merrill—the Educator Learning Center. At **www.EducatorLearningCenter.com** you will find resources that will enhance your students' understanding of course topics and of current educational issues, in addition to being invaluable for further research.

How the Educator Learning Center will help your students become better teachers
With the combined resources of Merrill Education and ASCD, you and your students will find a wealth of tools and materials to better prepare them for the classroom.

Research
- More than 600 articles from the ASCD journal *Educational Leadership* discuss everyday issues faced by practicing teachers.
- A direct link on the site to Research Navigator™ gives students access to many of the leading education journals, as well as extensive content detailing the research process.
- Excerpts from Merrill Education texts give your students insights on important topics of instructional methods, diverse populations, assessment, classroom management, technology, and refining classroom practice.

Classroom Practice
- Hundreds of lesson plans and teaching strategies are categorized by content area and age range.
- Case studies and classroom video footage provide virtual field experience for student reflection.
- Computer simulations and other electronic tools keep your students abreast of today's classrooms and current technologies.

Look into the value of Educator Learning Center yourself
Preview the value of this educational environment by visiting **www.EducatorLearningCenter.com** and clicking on "Demo." For a free 4-month subscription to the Educator Learning Center in conjunction with this text, simply contact your Merrill/Prentice Hall sales representative.

Preface

This is not a traditional foundations of education text. While it does cover all of the traditional themes of the history, philosophy, politics, and sociology of education as well as the nature of school environments and the teaching profession, it does so in a different way. Through excerpts from novels, biographies, memoirs, lectures, essays, plays, and poetry, and through songs and paintings, this anthology brings traditional themes to life within meaningful contexts.

Theoretical Framework and Rationale

I really love these works and the artists and writers who have created them. Perhaps this is too personal a tribute to make in the preface of a textbook. But that is precisely the point of *this* text: to personalize and humanize the education courses for which this material is intended. At its very core, education is about people, that is, students, teachers, and others, who operate in a number of diverse environments. And this text is about bringing those people, processes, and environments to life for your students. Future educators will learn from many of the teachers and others described in these pages. They will identify with some; they'll disagree with others. They will likely wish they could meet a few of the more inspiring ones. But in all cases, students will be stimulated to think deeply about the ideas and actions they are reading about, and they will want to compare them with their own practices and beliefs about teaching and education.

This anthology unites liberal education with traditional teacher education by drawing from a number of liberal arts disciplines, including history, literature, and art. By using this interdisciplinary approach, students will be able to experience firsthand a valuable model that they, too, can emulate once they become teachers. As they are motivated by these resources and make emotional connections to them, they will also be learning how to integrate curriculum in new and meaningful ways. "Showing the connections between things"—as one teacher in this anthology describes her way of teaching (Freedman, 1991)—is the approach taken here.

In addition, the literature included in this text will enable students to come face to face with the fact that education is characterized by controversies of many sorts. They've been there in the past, they're facing us now, and they will be with us in the 21st century. And even though each chapter focuses on a different traditional theme, students will soon notice that many of the same controversies appear again and again throughout the book and are not always resolved. That is the nature of education, and students need to be aware of such realities within their field.

The rationale for choosing these particular selections from among so many others was based, in part, on their emotional and intellectual appeal for readers. Each selection represents an exemplary work of literature, art, or poetry and is clearly representative of the chapter theme. Foundations students need facts, yes. But they also need to be inspired. These readings provide that inspiration. Students will be able to view aspects of human behavior or thought that are universal in nature and that, in many cases, transcend cultures as well as time. Some of the excerpts will literally have the students laughing (e.g., Kaufman, 1991) and crying (Gibson, 1980). A few will arouse anger (Johnson, 1990); others, feelings of satisfaction (Taylor, 1951). And all will provide springboards to discussion and instruction by offering realistic situations around which students can solve problems, gain knowledge, and identify personally.

While the readings within a particular chapter have implications for that particular chapter's topic or theme, nearly all of the selections relate to more than one theme and could have been placed just as appropriately within the contexts of other chapters. For example, the José Calderon poem in chapter 3 ("Philosophical Foundations") and the excerpt from *All-of-a-Kind Family* in chapter 2 ("Historical Perspectives") are relevant to the multicultural theme of chapter 6 ("Living and Learning in a Diverse Society: Sociology of Education"). The *Bakke* decision on affirmative action (chapter 4; "The Politics of Education") certainly has implications for the minority issues discussed in chapter 6 as well as links to the history of education (chapter 2). And nearly all of the readings have connections to the first chapter, on "Teacher Behavior, Teacher Roles." So there can be some flexibility in the ways you use these selections. If one selection in a chapter seems to be better suited for illustrating another theme, there is no reason why its use can't be broadened. There are nine new readings in this second edition, and they, too, reflect more than one theme.

Organization and Pedagogical Features of the Text

The anthology is divided into six thematic chapters, each containing several selections. Each chapter begins with a comprehensive instructional narrative explaining the theme of the chapter along with useful, factual background information. Brief introductions to each selection explain to the student its particular connection to the chapter. To help students visualize the themes, a different Norman Rockwell painting appears as the first selection in each chapter. These six paintings can stimulate questions among the students as they begin their investigation of each of the major topics in the text.

Because this text is a pedagogical tool, there are a number of activities, including discussion questions and research projects, some of which involve interviewing, dramatization, and debate (see Appendix A "Debate Format"); all of them enable students to explore in more depth the concepts that compose the traditional content of a foundations course. Students may engage in some of the activities individually or with peers, in the library or in the field. Many of the questions and projects incorporate terms, concepts, and other data that students are likely to encounter in other education courses, thus allowing them to make connections to those courses and to educational theory and practice. The anthology can be used as a supplement to a traditional expository text or can satisfy the objectives of a foundations course on its own (see Appendix B, "How to Use This Text: Two Suggested Approaches").

A list of suggested Additional Readings appears at the end of each chapter, along with a list of references cited in the chapter. These sources will allow students to do more research on the people, ideas, and topics contained in the personal and literary accounts. To complete several of the activities and projects suggested after each reading, students will need to use the library as well as the Internet, newspapers, and education journals. Therefore, they should become familiar with reference facilities available in their area and on their campus.

At the end of the anthology is a Concluding Activity you may want to have the students begin working on now: their own fiction or nonfiction account of teaching based on their personal educational experiences as participants-observers in schools for at least 12 years. This exercise should remind them that they already have useful knowledge about schooling, pedagogy, and all of the themes presented herein. By recognizing that they, too, have a personal scenario to reflect upon and learn from, students will be able to make better use of the scenarios in this anthology. In fact, you may want to have students do the activity twice, once at the beginning of the course and then again at the conclusion. It is hoped that when their personal narratives are viewed together with the textual narratives, the students' educational journey will become more meaningful.

What's New in This Edition?

This second edition features several additions and some changes that strengthen it conceptually and facilitate its use by instructors.

First, the Contents now contains a brief description of each of the selections in the text so that you can determine immediately its relevance to your course aims and objectives.

The text begins with the chapter "Teacher Behavior, Teacher Roles: Teacher Ethics and Experiences" rather than with "Historical Perspectives." This change enables students to encounter contemporary scenarios with which they may more easily identify before going on to the real and fictional teachers of the past (chapter 2).

Besides updating the time line, "Influential People and Events in the History of American Education" (in chapter 2), eight selections have been added that either provide another perspective not included in the first edition or provide useful information that expands the depth and breadth of certain chapters.

In chapter 1, two selections, "Professional Standards for Teachers" (2001) and "Attention, Class!!! 16 Ways to Be a Smarter Teacher" (2001), provide students with excellent guidelines for effective teaching behavior as they begin to establish their own styles of teaching. One of the readings added to chapter 2, "Historical Perspectives," portrays the educational legacy of the Puritans—still observable in schools today—and the second, the more progressive legacy of the pioneering educator Johann Heinrich Pestalozzi. In chapter 3, "Philosophical Foundations," an excerpt from the writing of Diane Ravitch (2000), a "liberal traditionalist," and the views of a number of educators and a judge (Archibold, 2001) round out some of the perspectives addressing the central philosophical question, "What Kind of Education Is Adequate?" Two radically different views emanate from E. D. Hirsch, Jr. (1996), and Paulo Freire (1985), who, despite their political differences, agree that education can transform society. Their work expands the depth and breadth of chapter 4 ("The Politics of Education"). Chapter 6 ("Living and Learning in a Diverse Society") now includes an excerpt from a work of children's literature (Little, 2000) that takes the chapter's definition of diversity beyond that related to race, ethnicity, and religion to include children with learning and physical disabilities.

Additions to the appendixes include one for the instructor of the course and one for the students. For the instructor's benefit, two approaches for using this text are suggested; one describes how the book can serve as the primary vehicle of instruction, and the other suggests how the text can be used as a supplementary source. Because so many of the activities in the text involve the students in preparing presentations with and for their peers, an outline of a lesson plan along with a sample plan is included for their use. The appendixes still provide the "Debate Format: Learning through Teamwork and Formal Argument" so that students can address the many controversial issues raised in the text.

Acknowledgments

One of the frustrations of being a teacher is that teachers frequently do not receive immediate gratification. That is, we don't always know if our efforts in the classroom are having the desired outcome. It is likely that every teacher has experienced hearing from at least one former student about some statement that greatly affected the student, although the teacher had no idea it was even penetrating the surface! Education is, indeed, a cumulative experience, and the influences on my own thinking and education are products of literally thousands of people who unfortunately go unrecognized, although I hope that they were aware at the time that they had had an impact. Among them is the late Jack Shepard at Skidmore College.

Next, I want to thank the authors, artists, poets, and writers whose works appear in this anthology. They have greatly inspired me and the students with whom I have shared them. Those foundations of education students at the Massachusetts College of Liberal Arts have also inspired me with their open and insightful responses to these creative works.

The reviewers of this text made many significant suggestions, and I want to thank all of them for their experience in the field and their honesty and kindness: Judy Arnold, Lincoln Memorial University; Rick A. Breault, University of Indianapolis; Erin Brumbaugh, Marietta College; Tina Dawson, Antioch University, Seattle; Martin Eigenberger, University of Wisconsin—Parkside; and Stephen D. Oates, Northern Michigan University.

Sounding boards Bonnie Silvers, Cheryl Nelsen, Margaret Chang, and Sharon Clark, all educators and friends, were there when I needed them, as were Linda Pero and other staff members at The Norman Rockwell Museum at Stockbridge, Massachusetts.

Christina Kelly was invaluable as former student, information gatherer, advisor, permissions assistant, friend, and rock.

Penelope Lord's contribution as typist cannot be measured in terms of her technical expertise. It was not merely her hands that made a difference. She was there with head and heart.

I also want to thank Kris Robinson-Roach and Kathy Termeer for their dedication and hard work in preparing the manuscript for publication.

My editor at Prentice Hall, Debbie Stollenwerk, was empathetic and supportive from the beginning to the end of the process, and I have so much respect for her professional wisdom and dedication *and* her disposition! Embarking on revisions for a second edition can be a daunting task. Debbie made it a rewarding and fulfilling one. My thanks also go to her assistants, Mary Morrill and Dan Parker, who always followed through on my various questions without hesitation.

Finally, I thank my children, Jonas and Sarah, for the pride, joy, and beauty they bring to my life. They are among the wisest of my teachers. And for the greatest inspiration of all, I thank my husband, Alan, who is all things to me.

Brief Contents

Contents

Chapter 1
Teacher Behavior, Teacher Roles: Teacher Ethics and Experiences   1

---

* New selection (not in first edition).

Chapter 2
Historical Perspectives   63

Chapter 4
The Politics of Education: School Governance, School Funding, and Legal Issues   205

4.3 ***The Water Is Wide* (1972), Pat Conroy 214**
Conroy shares his real-life experience teaching on a small island off the coast of South Carolina and what happens when he appeals to the board of education to get his job back after he is fired.
Questions for Discussion and Debate 220
Activities and Projects 220

4.4 ***The Thread That Runs So True* (1949), Jesse Stuart 221**
This realistic and poignant look at Stuart's many professional positions in rural schools also sheds light on his difficulties surviving financially in those positions.
Questions for Discussion and Debate 224
Activities and Projects 225

This ONE

4.5 ***Death at an Early Age* (1967), Jonathan Kozol 225**
This excerpt is from a classic exposé about the problems and politics in an urban school system presented through the eyes of a white teacher among African American children.
Questions for Discussion and Debate 232
Activities and Projects 233

4.6 School-to-Work Opportunities Act of 1994, 103rd Congress of the United States 234
Section 2 of the act contains the rationale for this federal law that promotes programs to educate students about careers and the working world.
Questions for Discussion and Debate 237
Activities and Projects 237

***4.7** ***The Politics of Education* (1985), Paulo Freire 239**
The noted Brazilian educator argues that education is political and, as such, can be the vehicle for transforming society.
Questions for Discussion and Debate 240
Activities and Projects 241

***4.8 "Test Evasion" (1996), E. D. Hirsch, Jr. 242**
A theorist who calls himself both an educational conservative and a political liberal argues for high-stakes testing.
Questions for Discussion and Debate 245
Activities and Projects 246

4.9 "Bakke Syllabus": ***Regents of the University of California*** **v.** ***Bakke*** **(1978), Supreme Court of the United States 248**
The landmark Supreme Court decision on affirmative action establishes support for both sides of the issue.
Questions for Discussion and Debate 251
Activities and Projects 252

Chapter 6
Living and Learning in a Diverse Society: Sociology of Education   315

NOTE: Every effort has been made to provide accurate and current Internet information in this book. However, the Internet and information posted on it are constantly changing, it is inevitable that some of the Internet addresses listed in this textbook will change.

Chapter 1

Teacher Behavior, Teacher Roles

Teacher Ethics and Experiences

—Helen Keller with her teacher, Annie Sullivan. See excerpt from *The Miracle Worker* in chapter 5.

The tragic events that took place on the morning of September 11, 2001, changed people's lives and behavior forever, teachers included. In the immediate aftermath of the terrorist attacks, teachers all around the country were faced with the challenge of what to say and do with their students, at a time when they themselves were reeling from the news. And that morning there were teachers, principals, and staff members who, without prior training in emergency rescue operations, skillfully and compassionately evacuated some 8,000 students from the schools nearest the World Trade Center (Sandham, 2001). Events had redefined their roles and had turned them into what New York State Education Commissioner Richard Mills called "quiet heroes" (New York State United Teachers, 2001, p. 7). "They led the children to safety through falling debris and black smoke so thick that only the person directly ahead was visible. One teacher saw the plane hit the World Trade Center building right

1

where he knew his brother worked. Yet he stayed with his colleagues and the students until every child was taken home" (Feldman, 2001, p. 5).

While teachers may sometimes appear to be superhuman, as in the preceding case, they are, indeed, all too human. Yet they are often viewed in terms of two extremes: as godlike noble creatures without the same bodily functions and needs shared by other mortals or as elevated babysitters with salaries to match. Because teachers are charged with the awesome responsibility of transferring the "wealth of tradition" from one generation to the next and preparing "thinking individuals" who will serve their communities (Einstein, 1954, p. 60), society wants, or expects, them to be better, smarter, cleverer, wiser. But are they?

Not necessarily. Teachers are not always heroes; they make mistakes like everyone else because they are human beings, not machines. Teachers' behavior, like that of other groups, cannot be stereotyped. Suffice it to say that there are no two alike. They, indeed, represent a cross section of the society as a whole, although they may not be representative in terms of gender and race because the profession is still increasingly White, 90.7% in 1996, and female, 74.4% (National Education Association [NEA], 1997).

There are, of course, certain teacher behaviors that studies have shown to be effective, behaviors for which teachers are praised and respected, among them the ability to motivate students and use diverse instructional strategies (Hunter & Russell, 1981; Johnson & Johnson, 1991; Perrone, 1991; Shulman, 1987). However, the task of measuring the actual impact of these effective behaviors is nearly impossible since such effects are often not revealed until years after the students have left the teacher's classroom. True, the student's grades may reflect short-term instructional success, but more often than not, teachers will never know the long-term effects unless the student returns to tell them, and few do. If they do, however, and they say, "Thank you," that is perhaps the best measure teachers have regarding the effectiveness of their behavior. On the other hand, some teachers never learn about the damage they have done to some students who may carry psychic scars with them forever.

Are teachers really all that powerful, however? Powerful enough both to inspire and to scar? Can their behavior make a difference in a child's life, or are teachers peripheral at best compared to all of the other influences on a child, from his or her peers, to parents, to the media, and, perhaps most significant, to the child's own disposition? The answers to these questions likely fall along a broad spectrum of *all* of the above possibilities to a greater or lesser extent, depending on the child and teacher. One thing is fairly certain, however: All of us can think of at least one teacher whose behavior profoundly affected us in one way or another. Hopefully, along the way you have encountered a few who teach because they want the chance to make a student's life more meaningful and the world a better place as well as to experience the indescribable feeling that comes at the end of a perfect lesson.

While this kind of positive power is exhilarating for both the teacher and the student, there remains the nitty-gritty question of just how much real power teachers have, not just in terms of their influence on students but in terms of their role within the field of education and in the community in general. If teachers' salaries are any reflection of their power and worth, then there is certainly some inconsistency across the country within different states and school systems. The same inconsistency exists also in terms of teachers' power to choose curriculum content and materials. Ideally, the teacher should be a "kind of artist in his province . . . and given extensive liberty in the selection of the material to be taught and the methods of teaching" (Einstein, 1954, p. 63). But all too often that "pleasure in the shaping of his work is killed by force and external pressure" (p. 63). And while teaching gives one inner satisfaction, the teacher's satisfaction cannot "fill the stomachs of his children" (p. 66). Although we may be living at a time when most families have two incomes and teachers' associations or unions have secured better wages for teachers, the fact is that they are still undervalued and underpaid.

Speaking of the community, teachers' roles are interestingly a microcosm of the roles seen within the community as a whole. For example, teachers are white-collar workers since their minds are their major tool, but they play the blue-collar worker when they put their hands and feet to work on the playground, during lunch duty, or when cleaning up their rooms. They are bookkeepers, storytellers, humorists, psychologists, evaluators, technologists, parents, and more! Although the scenery doesn't always change, the actor–teacher must take on different personas, often in the space of just a few minutes. Indeed, there are few professions in which just one role, that of teacher, is inclusive of so many others. But, alas, the roles played by teachers are among the least understood and often least respected by the public who pays them (Lortie, 1975). Teachers might benefit from the services of a few public relations experts to help inform their constituents about what many of them do all day long, after school, and, frequently, into the night and on weekends (NEA, 1997).

Yet, ironically, little of what the average teacher does do is central to instruction! "Few teachers are employed in schools as researchers, instructional leaders, or curriculum developers. And even when principals create opportunities for teachers to define a new role, too many teachers return to given roles [those the public expects of them], and do not maintain an image of themselves as instructional leaders" (Fischer & Kiefer, 1994, pp. 41–42). Many of the roles given to teachers by the public may be the result of the images of teachers conveyed in song, in film, on television, and in children's literature, many of which are stereotypical and run the gamut from the permissive Mr. Kotter, in television's "Welcome Back, Kotter," to the traditional authoritarian teacher in Marc Brown's (1986) *Arthur's Teacher Trouble* (Kantor, 1994, p. 181; Trousdale, 1994, p. 201). These images can often act to stifle or limit the role that individual teachers might otherwise construct for themselves. The challenge teachers continue to face is how ultimately to become liberated from restraining roles in order to "begin to actively create their own images of their work . . . something of their [own] person" (Joseph & Burnaford, 1994, p. 42).

Brief Background

There does not yet exist a set of national standards for teacher behavior. However, the "Code of Ethics of the Education Profession" of the National Education Association (NEA, 1975) and its affiliates does indicate in its Preamble and Principles a number of roles, behaviors, and "aspirations of all educators" as well as some standards by which to judge conduct. Like any document of this kind, the provisions appear rational but very general and thus open to broad interpretation. For example, such statements as "The educator . . . shall not intentionally expose the student to embarrassment or disparagement" are clearly descriptive of teacher behavior that happens thousands of times each day! What constitutes disparaging, embarrassing behavior is, of course, clearly debatable. This brings to mind two relevant questions: What, then, is the value of such general standards? and How is it possible to enforce them? These questions continue to challenge school administrations, teachers, and everyone else concerned about education, including government.

As stated in chapter 4, nearly all branches and levels of government have played a role in defining the nature of a teacher's job and behavior. And historically, public education leaders such as Horace Mann (1891) have played key roles in establishing many of those standards. State education departments continue to define teacher certification proficiencies and charge local education authorities with enforcing them. And school committees expect administrators to evaluate teachers' adherence to locally devised standards of performance. However, administrators and other authorities don't always carry out this charge, and such inaction may account, in part, for the low esteem with which the public regards the profession in general. Perhaps it is as a result of this problem that some states have passed reforms—if that is the right word—that are trying to address the difficulty of assessing teacher behavior in a more accountable fashion. Massachusetts, for example, has repealed the tenure law and replaced it with a system of 5-year evaluations (Massachusetts Education Reform Act, 1994).

The jury is still not in as to whether or not this approach will make it easier to remove incompetent and unprofessional teachers. Nevertheless, with or without tenure, a teacher's rights are protected by a number of legislative and judicial decisions. The hundreds of U.S. Supreme Court cases that affect or dictate teachers' roles, behavior, and rights make education one of the most complex and exciting areas of study for any teacher. For example, court decisions might influence and define the extent of a teacher's academic freedom, whether or not a teacher is free to speak an opinion contrary to his or her school's policy, or the extent of a teacher's right to a personal lifestyle contrary to community standards. The Court's decisions will often reflect any changes in public attitudes about such issues that take place over time (Alexander & Alexander, 1992).

Research has shown that what students tend to care about and remember most about their favorite teachers years later is not so much what they taught them, but who the teachers were—their humanity, their character. Albert Einstein (1954) put it this way: "The only rational way of educating is to be an example . . ." (p. 57), and he noted that there was "too much education altogether, especially in American schools. [T]he wit was not wrong who defined education in this way: 'Education is that which remains, if one has forgotten everything he learned in school'" (p. 63).

Janusz Korczak (1878–1942), the Polish–Jewish educator and pediatrician, agreed that the teacher's role should be characterized by restraint. During his work as teacher trainer at two pedagogical institutions in Warsaw, Poland, during the first half of the 20th century, Korczak advised student teachers not to offer too many explanations to children but, rather, to step back sometimes and allow the child freedom. In his book, *How to Love a Child,* he wrote, "The child's mind [is like] a forest in which the tops of trees gently sway, the branches mingle, and the shivering leaves touch. Sometimes a tree grazes its neighbor and receives the vibrations of a hundred or a thousand trees—of the whole forest. Whenever any of us says, 'right—wrong—pay attention—do it again,' it is like a gust of wind that plays havoc with the child" (Lifton, 1989, p. 83).

Korczak's life as an educator exemplifies the meaning of the teacher as role model. He established progressive orphanages for Polish workers' children in the 1920s and 1930s, and later, institutions for war orphans. The Nazis were liquidating the Warsaw ghetto in 1942, and on August 6, Korczak was forced to evacuate his Jewish orphanage there, gather together some 200 children, and march them to the trains to be taken to the death camp, Treblinka. While he did not have to go with them, Korczak chose not to abandon them but to die with the orphans under his care (Lifton, 1989, p. 5). Although his example may be a rather extreme one—certainly few of us will be tested in this way—his life inspires and instructs:

> Don't try to become a teacher overnight with psychological bookkeeping in your heart and educational theory in your head. (Lifton, 1989, p. 144)

Selections

The excerpts in this chapter portray teachers in a number of roles they are expected to fulfill, and they are shown behaving in ways that reflect the fact that they are, indeed, all too human and, at times, inhuman. In Norman Rockwell's portrayal of the schoolteacher, you'll see the stereotypical old-maid schoolteacher, a concept that no longer conveys an accurate image, and perhaps never did. The painting presents a springboard for discussion about the roles and behaviors of teachers. Three nonfictional selections focus on real teachers. One of them is put into a position of considering her role as mandated reporter in the case of suspected child abuse (Johnson, 1990), another is seen in her role as a cooperating teacher (Kidder, 1990), and the third simply in her role as an excellent instructor and leader (Freedman, 1990). Miss Dove (Patton, 1954) and Mr. Chips (Hilton, 1963) will remind you of the fact that a traditional teacher can be as endearing and effective as more progressive ones, and that there are no "supposed-to's" in education! You will be able to compare and contrast the behavior of teachers in two fictional excerpts (*The Chocolate War*, 1974, and *A Tree Grows in Brooklyn*, 1943), in terms of their character, their motivations, and their personalities.

Two sets of standards will guide you as you establish your own ideas about appropriate professional behavior. The first set, established by the Massachusetts Department of Education (2001) in its *Regulations for Educator Licensure and Preparation Program Approval*, conveys the standards that teachers are required to meet. "Attention, Class!!! 16 Ways to Be a Smarter Teacher" (Salter, 2001) provides a comprehensive list of behaviors that are universal to excellent teaching in any context.

As you encounter these standards and these real and fictional teachers, reflect on your own evolving teaching style and behavior. Are you more acquainted now with the variety of roles you will be taking on and the many choices you'll need to make as you assume your place in the profession? It is my hope that this chapter will help you as you move toward achieving your goals.

> Teaching is not something one learns to do, once and for all, and then practices, problem-free, for a lifetime. . . . Teaching depends on growth and development, and it is practiced in dynamic situations that are never twice the same.   (Ayers, 1993, p. 127)

1.1   Work of Art: *The School Teacher* (1956)

Norman Rockwell

Norman Rockwell's painting of Miss Jones standing in front of her class is perhaps the most famous—and most stereotypical—of all paintings depicting a schoolteacher. Following its publication on the cover of *The Saturday Evening Post* (March 17, 1956), Rockwell received many letters from schoolteachers complaining bitterly that he had insulted them. Schoolteachers were not drab, funny-looking old maids, they said. Responded Rockwell, "I still don't understand why a picture of one old-maid schoolteacher implies that I think all schoolteachers are drab old maids" (*Norman Rockwell Album*, [NRA], 1961). In fact, Rockwell said that he painted the cover as a sort of tribute to schoolteachers, in particular, his favorite, Miss Julia M. Smith, his eighth-grade teacher "who taught me all the history, arithmetic, grammar and geography I know and encouraged me to draw" (*NRA*, 1961). What he wanted to express in the portrait was the "selfless devotion of teachers, willing to work long hours for their students" (*NRA*, 1961).

The fact is, however, that this stereotype of the "old-maid schoolteacher" is, in part, historically sound. During the second half of the 19th century and up to the present, the majority of teachers have been women, particularly for grades K–6. And before the 1950s, many women teachers were, indeed, unmarried. Women were seen as nurturers and more suited than men for teaching children. They were also a cheap and abundant workforce. On the other hand, teaching and administrative positions in the secondary schools, colleges, and universities were dominated by men, who were considered more intellectually capable. And those women who did succeed in gaining access to the secondary schools were paid less than men for equal work. This editor recalls talking to female colleagues who protested in the 1950s and 1960s for the right to earn the same salary as their male counterparts.

Historically, most of the women who went into teaching were unmarried. Those with families were home caring for their own children, as tradition kept women at home once they were married. It was common for unmarried women to teach and then to leave the profession once they got married. An unspoken but well-known rule in hiring teachers was to avoid hiring a married woman because she might become pregnant and leave soon after being hired. With that point in mind, it was once totally acceptable to ask a young woman applying for a teaching job if she *was* married. Now such a question is considered discriminatory. Before the age of women's liberation, many schools were known to dismiss a teacher if she did get married, and most dismissed her if she became pregnant.

Suffice it to say that the legacy of discrimination against women in American education reflects the long history of the treatment of women in general. (See also chapters 2 and 6.) Fortunately, we now rightfully consider the term *old maid* pejorative, and marriage and family no longer prevent women from entering the teaching profession. Nevertheless, there is still a need to continue the struggle for gender equity even though laws now exist that prevent and/or punish such discrimination.

Underneath the surface of Rockwell's painting, also known as *Happy Birthday, Miss Jones,* is this story of the role of the unmarried female schoolteacher who derives joy from her surrogate children—although it's likely that not all of these teachers loved children. Like all stereotypes, that one, too, is flawed.

On the surface of this painting, as with most of Rockwell's work, there is a story waiting to be discovered through the details he includes. "This technique of insisting on a story told with correct details appealed to his audience. Details and precision are something that one can see and comment on in a painting" (Rockwell, 1990, p. 24). Notice every detail in this painting and develop in your mind a narrative of the events that might have taken place before the scene you see, what is happening in the scene itself, and what you think will happen next.

Rockwell's paintings appear in all six chapters of this anthology. There are reasons for this, apart from their clear relationship to the themes of the chapters. In an article about his father's paintings, Peter Rockwell noted that his father had an unspoken agreement with his public that his pictures could be understood by anyone. "These were pictures for a democratic, anti-elitist society . . . capable of conveying their story to both rich and poor, city and country dwellers" (Rockwell, 1990, p. 24). Thus these paintings are representative of America's system of public education, both striving for democracy, striving to serve and meet the needs of rich and poor, city and country dweller. And such ideas permeate the chapters in this anthology.

Norman Rockwell was both praised and criticized for this particular Rockwellian appeal, his detractors accusing him of destroying Americans' taste for contemporary or more modern, abstract work. But, responds Peter Rockwell (1990) to this accusation, his father's work—and the man himself—was "neither so unthinking nor unquestioning as both his admirers and detractors presumed" (p. 25), and the other Rockwell paintings in this anthology clearly confirm that point.

Questions for Discussion and Debate

1. Study this painting and all of the details therein, including the postures of the students and the eraser on one of their heads. Then share your perceptions of the story this painting conveys. Include in your story all the before, during, and after details of the events and feelings involved. Do you and your colleagues perceive the same scenario? Likely there will be differences since we usually bring our own personal experiences and stories to our interpretations of art—or anything else for that matter, including how we perceive our students.

2. Debate this point: Stereotypes like that of old-maid schoolteacher seriously affect the image the public has of the profession and cause negative responses.

3. Debate this statement: Stereotypes of teachers have always been misleading and distort the truth about America's teachers.

4. Compare this painting of Miss Jones to the painting in chapter 2 of Ichabod Crane. How are they the same or different in terms of content *and* painting style?

5. Do you like this painting? Why, or why not?

6. Is this scene, painted in 1956, dated? That is, are there details in the painting that convey facts and conditions different from those you would see in a classroom today? Discuss your view.

Activities and Projects

1. What stereotypes of teachers besides that of the old-maid schoolteacher exist in art, literature, poetry, or drama? Do research on this question and share your findings. Consult libraries and also the text, *Images of Schoolteachers in Twentieth-Century America* (Joseph & Burnaford, 1994). Which of the stereotypes are most offensive? Which do you believe have some validity? What are the origins of these stereotypes? Their effects?

2. Prepare a dramatic portrayal of one or more of the class's interpretations of what is happening in the painting, as well as what may be happening before and what might happen after this scene.

happen after this scene.

3. Draw a classroom scene, or find pictures that will portray your view of the *typical* teacher. If there is no generalization in your mind, then by all means portray the diversity of teachers and teacher roles in your work of art. You might want to do a three-dimensional portrayal (i.e., with puppets or toy figures) or a photographic one. Give your work a title, as Rockwell did for his painting. Bring your version of a classroom scene or teacher to your peers so they can tell you the story they see in your work of art.

1.2   *Goodbye, Mr. Chips* (1963)

James Hilton

Chips, his students called him affectionately, instead of his real name, Mr. Chipping. And "Goodbye, Mr. Chips" were the words he had heard spoken by hundreds and hundreds of his students as they left the halls of Brookfield, an elite boarding school outside of London, to enter adulthood and, in some cases, as they went off to fight in World War I.

James Hilton, an English-born novelist who lived the later part of his life in California, created this extraordinary teacher, Chips, who has been loved as much by the readers and movie watchers who have come to know him as he was loved by the boys at Brookfield.

In this excerpt from the novel, you indirectly meet Chips's wife, who, it turns out, greatly influences the kind of teacher he becomes. Chips had been a bachelor until the age of 48, "an age at which a permanence of habits begins to be predictable" (Hilton, 1963, p. 19). As housemaster and teacher of Latin and Greek, he had been known as a "decent fellow and a hard worker" (p. 30). Then one summer while on vacation in the Lake District, he meets a young woman, Kathie, falls in love, and marries her. His life and his teaching are transformed, and at the same time, traditions at Brookfield become somewhat less predictable.

As you read the excerpt, notice the nature of Chips's transformation. Decide if he is the kind of teacher you would like to have and, more important, if he is the kind of teacher you would like to become.

There had followed then a time of such happiness that Chips, remembering it long afterward, hardly believed it could ever have happened before or since in the world. For his marriage was a triumphant success. Katherine conquered Brookfield as she had conquered Chips; she was immensely popular with boys and masters alike. Even the wives of the masters, tempted at first to be jealous of one so young and lovely, could not long resist her charms.

But most remarkable of all was the change she made in Chips. Till his marriage he had been a dry and rather neutral sort of person; liked and thought well of by Brookfield in general, but not of the stuff that makes for great popularity or that stirs great affection. He had been at Brookfield for over a quarter of a century, long enough to have established himself as a decent fellow and a hard worker; but just too long for anyone to believe him capable of ever being much more. He had, in fact, already begun to sink into that creeping dry rot of pedagogy which is the worst and ultimate pitfall of the profession; giving the same lessons year after year had formed a groove into which the other affairs of his life adjusted themselves with insidious ease. He worked well; he was conscientious; he was a fixture that gave service, satisfaction, confidence, everything except inspiration.

And then came this astonishing girl-wife whom nobody had expected—least of all Chips himself. She made him, to all appearances, a new man; though most of the newness was really a warming to life of things that were old, imprisoned, and unguessed. His eyes gained sparkle; his mind, which was adequately if not brilliantly equipped, began to move more adventurously. The one thing he had always had, a sense of humor, blossomed into a sudden richness to which his years lent maturity. He began to feel a greater sureness; his discipline improved to a point at which it could become, in a sense, less rigid; he became more popular. When he had first come to Brookfield he had aimed to be loved, honored, and obeyed—but obeyed, at any rate. Obedience he had secured, and honor had been granted him; but only now came love, the sudden love of boys for a man who was kind without being soft, who understood them well enough, but not too much, and whose private happiness linked them with their own. He began to make little jokes, the sort that schoolboys like—mnemonics and puns that raised laughs and at the same time imprinted something in the mind. There was one that never failed to please, though it was only a sample of many others. Whenever his Roman History forms came to deal with the Lex Canuleia, the law that permitted patricians to marry plebeians, Chips used to add: "So that, you see, if Miss Plebs wanted Mr. Patrician to marry her, and he said he couldn't, she probably replied: 'Oh yes, you can, you liar!'" Roars of laughter.

And Kathie broadened his views and opinions, also, giving him an outlook far beyond the roofs and turrets of Brookfield, so that he saw his country as something deep and gracious to which Brookfield was but one of many feeding streams. She had a cleverer brain than his, and he could not confute her ideas even if and when he disagreed with them; he remained, for instance, a Conservative in politics, despite all her radical-socialist talk. But even where he did not accept, he absorbed; her young idealism worked upon his maturity to produce an amalgam very gentle and wise.

Sometimes she persuaded him completely. Brookfield, for example, ran a mission in East London, to which boys and parents contributed generously with money but rarely with personal contact. It was Katherine who suggested that a team from the mission should come up to Brookfield and play one of the School's elevens at soccer. The idea was so revolutionary that from anyone but Katherine it could not have survived its first frosty reception. To introduce a group of slum boys to the serene pleasaunces of better-class youngsters seemed at first a wanton stirring of all kinds of things that had better be left untouched. The whole staff was against it, and the School, if its opinion could have been taken, was probably against it too. Everyone was certain that the East End lads would be hooligans, or else that they would be made to feel uncomfortable; anyhow, there would be "incidents," and everyone would be confused and upset. Yet Katherine persisted.

"Chips," she said, "they're wrong, you know, and I'm right. I'm looking ahead to the future, they and you are looking back to the past. England isn't always going to be divided into officers and 'other ranks.' And those Poplar boys are just as important—to England—as Brookfield is. You've got to have them here, Chips. You can't satisfy your conscience by writing a check for a few guineas and keeping them at arm's length. Besides, they're proud of Brookfield—just as you are. Years hence, maybe, boys of that sort will be coming here— a few of them, at any rate. Why not? Why ever not? Chips, dear, remember this is eighteen-ninety-seven—not sixty-seven, when you were up at Cambridge. You got your ideas well stuck in those days, and good ideas they were too, a lot of them. But a few—just a few, Chips—want unsticking. . . ."

Rather to her surprise, he gave way and suddenly became a keen advocate of the proposal, and the *volte-face* was so complete that the authorities were taken unawares and found themselves consenting to the dangerous experiment. The boys from Poplar arrived at Brookfield one Saturday afternoon, played soccer with the School's second team, were honorably defeated by seven goals to five, and later had high tea with the School team in the Dining Hall. They then met the Head and were shown over the School, and Chips saw them off at the railway station in the evening. Everything had passed without the slightest hitch of any kind, and it was clear that the visitors were taking away with them as fine an impression as they had left behind.

They took back with them also the memory of a charming woman who had met them and talked to them; for once, years later, during the War, a private stationed at a big military camp near Brookfield called on Chips and said

he had been one of that first visiting team. Chips gave him tea and chatted with him, till at length, shaking hands, the man said: "And 'ow's the missus, sir? I remember her very well."

"Do you?" Chips answered, eagerly. "Do you remember her?"

"Rather. I should think anyone would."

And Chips replied: "They don't, you know. At least, not here. Boys come and go; new faces all the time; memories don't last. Even masters don't stay forever. Since last year—when old Gribble retired—he's—um—the School butler—there hasn't been anyone here who ever saw my wife. She died, you know, less than a year after your visit. In ninety-eight."

"I'm real sorry to 'ear that, sir. There's two or three o' my pals, anyhow, who remember 'er clear as anything, though we did only see 'er that wunst. Yes, we remember 'er, all right."

"I'm very glad. . . . That was a grand day we all had—and a fine game, too."

"One o' the best days aht I ever 'ad in me life. Wish it was then and not nah—straight, I do. I'm off to Frawnce to-morrer."

A month or so later Chips heard that he had been killed at Passchendaele.

▬▬▬▬ Questions for Discussion and Debate ▬▬▬▬

1. Describe Chips's transformation. That is, what was Chips like *before* marriage? After marriage? Which traits appeared or were further developed? Which of the new traits do you consider to be most important? Why?

2. Chips used mnemonics and puns. What do those terms mean? What is the example of the pun given in the excerpt? Why are these effective teaching devices?

3. What were the outcomes of the soccer game between Brookfield and the East End kids, the "slum boys"?

   a. What was the significance of this event?

   b. Are there any similarities between the traditional attitudes at Brookfield and the attitudes of schools, educators, and/or students in America's cities? In other words, does America have its Brookfields and its Poplars? Explain.

(Refer to chapter 6, "Living and Learning in a Diverse Society.")

c. Are you familiar with any "dangerous experiments" that have taken place in American schools?

4. Is Chips a teacher you would want to have? And is he someone whose style you would want to emulate? Why or why not?

5. Kathie provided a form of professional development for Chips. That is, she indirectly taught him to think and behave differently as a teacher, and he and his students were all the better for it. The implication here is that people *can* change if exposed, in a meaningful way, to new ideas. Share professional development ideas and other influences you may have learned at conferences or from mentors that have changed the way you originally thought or acted as a teacher or student teacher.

6. There are teachers who, like Chips (before his marriage), teach the same lessons year after year, having fallen into that "creeping dry rot of pedagogy" (Hilton, 1963, p. 30). Brainstorm what actions might be taken by schools or administrators to pull these teachers out of their holes. Then take sides on this statement: Some teachers are unsalvageable and simply can't be changed and should thus be removed from the classroom.

Activities and Projects

1. The environment of the private school differs from that of the public school as chapter 5 indicates. Public schools in America, for example, have traditionally been places where students of all socioeconomic classes can come together to learn, whereas private schools, usually affordable only by the upper and upper-middle classes, have traditionally segregated students from "the real world." Frequently, teachers' behaviors and roles differ as a result of the differences between these two environments.

   a. Visit one or more private schools in your area and interview some teachers about why they chose to teach there and what their attitudes are about public versus private education. Then interview some public schoolteachers with the same questions. Compare and contrast their responses and share your findings with the class. Lead a discussion about the similarities and differences between public and private education as well as the advantages and disadvantages of teaching within each type of school. How do the roles vary as related to the differences in each of the two environments? (This research can also be done in the library if you are unable to do interviews.)

   b. Find out if there have been any successful collaborations between inner-city schools and suburban or other schools. Describe them and discuss what value these connections had for both groups.

2. Watch three or more of the films listed below, in which there is a considerable amount of dialogue between teachers and their students. Do a study of the nature of these dialogues using a checklist of desirable dialogue characteristics that you and the class devise ahead of time. That way you can watch the films for those characteristics and document the kinds of teacher behaviors

you and the class would like to emulate with students—and which ones to avoid. Share the data from your film research with your peers. Consider acting out those scenes from the movies in which the communications between teacher and student were constructive and authentic.

Possible films to use in your research besides *Goodbye, Mr. Chips:*

- *Conrack* (based on *The Water is Wide*)
- *Dead Poets' Society*
- *Good Morning, Miss Dove*
- *Lean on Me*
- *Stand and Deliver*
- *Up the Down Staircase*
- *Dangerous Minds*
- *Ferris Bueller's Day Off*
- *The Breakfast Club*
- *To Sir, With Love*
- *Teachers*
- *Mr. Holland's Opus*
- *Good Will Hunting*
- *Blackboard Jungle*
- *Rushmore*
- *Fifty Violins*
- *The Emperor's Club*
- *Slam*
- *Finding Forrester*

3. You can "visit" another private school by reading a portion of *The Catcher in the Rye* by J. D. Salinger (1964). You will meet Holden Caulfield, a very real, very smart, and very funny, albeit confused, young man with whom nearly every teenager who has ever read the book can identify. You will also meet Holden's history teacher, "old Spencer," with whom he visits just before leaving, or rather flunking out of, Pency Prep. Old Spencer doesn't resemble Mr. Chips, but his personality and conversation with Holden can also reveal some useful glimpses into the nature of teacher behavior and roles.

Find a copy of the book and read pages 10 through 16. This segment permits you to observe both the kind of guy this Holden Caulfield is and the kind of teacher old Spencer represents; some might say he comes from "the old school." He says what he thinks, not at all like Caulfield's former headmaster, Mr. Haas, "the phoniest bastard I ever met in my life" (pp. 13–14). Holden doesn't like phonies.

It is Mr. Spencer's straightforward behavior that you should consider as you read these pages. In his role as teacher and evaluator, old Spencer does not spare Holden's feelings. There are some teachers who, when they evaluate a student, are careful about phrasing their criticism in such a way that they will not injure the student's self-esteem. Certainly there is a multitude of teacher education texts that provide several ways for teachers to convey their judgments of a student's work while leaving the student's dignity intact.

Perhaps you could read pages 10–16 aloud in class and then together address these questions:

a. How would you describe this dialogue between student and teacher?

b. How honest should a teacher be? Is it necessary to couch assessments in euphemistic terms? (Think back to your own experiences, in this case, your memories of teachers whose style of criticism you accepted as well as those whose styles were hurtful. Note the characteristics of both styles.)

c. Considering that Holden thinks Spencer's words are "crap" and that he "was beginning to sort of hate him" (p. 11), even though he went out of his way to visit him, do you think that it is ever possible for students and teachers to communicate fully with each other, especially if there are wide age differences between them? Can the traditional student–teacher hierarchy be overcome? Discuss these questions with your peers and refer also to your own experiences. Try to recall the nature of the communication you had with certain teachers.

d. Consult teacher education texts in which verbal evaluation and assessment techniques are described. Talk with teachers about their views on directness and its effects on students, and, finally, talk to students about their preferences regarding how a teacher talks to them about the quality of their work. Observe the ways in which teachers interact with students during discussions, particularly the ways in which teachers deal with students' work when it is wrong, and they are clearly able to do better.

Conclude your discussion of *The Catcher in the Rye* by deciding whom you would rather emulate, old Spencer or Mr. Chips, and why.

1.3 *Good Morning, Miss Dove* (1954)

Frances Gray Patton

Like *Goodbye, Mr. Chips* in the preceding excerpt, Frances Gray Patton's novel, *Good Morning, Miss Dove,* brings to life a memorable, traditional teacher who is beloved by students because of her distinct, eccentric teaching style and personality underneath, which shows a sincere love for her students.

Unlike Chips, Miss Dove taught elementary geography in a small public school in a small American town. She did not undergo any transformations, and the author, Patton, lets us know this through the use of subtle humor, a characteristic of both her work and Hilton's (1963) in *Goodbye, Mr. Chips*. For example, she writes that as the children came into the classroom, they "gauged the various moods of the various teachers" (Patton, 1954, p. 8), then notes, "Miss Dove had no moods. Miss Dove was a certainty" (p. 8), but this consistency is portrayed in a positive light. While there are educators who would applaud this kind of predictability, there are others who would argue for some departure from that behavior to avoid the "creeping dry rot of pedagogy" referred to in *Goodbye, Mr. Chips*.

Miss Dove's style, clearly described here, may or may not impress you, but one thing is for sure, Patton would have us believe that Miss Dove's students learned, and learned well, and that they respected and, yes, loved her too. What is your view of her teaching and managing style? Is there still a place for this kind of teacher or are the Miss Doves of this world doomed to fail with the students of the 21st century? Consider these questions as you read this excerpt.

Single file they would enter her room. Each child would pause on the threshold as its mother and father had paused, more than likely, and would say—just as the policeman had said—in distinct, formal accents: "Good morning, Miss Dove." And Miss Dove would look directly at each of them, fixing her eyes directly upon theirs, and reply: "Good morning, Jessamine," or "Margaret," or "Samuel." (Never "Sam," never "Peggy," never "Jess." She eschewed familiarity as she wished others to eschew it.) They would go to their appointed desks. Miss Dove would ascend to hers. The lesson would begin.

There was no need to waste time in preliminary admonitions. Miss Dove's rules were as fixed as the signs of the zodiac. And they were known. Miss Dove rehearsed them at the beginning of each school year, stating them as calmly and dispassionately as if she were describing the atmospheric effects of the Gulf Stream. The penalties for infractions of the rules were also known. If a child introduced a foreign object— a pencil, let us say, or a wad of paper, or a lock of hair—into his mouth, he was required to wash out his mouth with the yellow laundry soap that lay on the drain-board of the sink in the corner by the sand table. If his posture was incorrect he had to go and sit for a while upon a stool without a back-rest. If a page in his notebook was untidy, he had to copy it over. If he emitted an uncovered cough, he was expected to rise immediately and fling open a window, no matter how cold the weather, so that a blast of fresh air could protect his fellows from the contamination of his germs. And if he felt obliged to disturb the class routine by leaving the room for a drink of water (Miss Dove loftily ignored any other

necessity) he did so to an accompaniment of dead silence. Miss Dove would look at him— that was all—following his departure and greeting his return with her perfectly expressionless gaze and the whole class would sit idle and motionless, until he was back in the fold again. It was easier—even if one had eaten salt fish for breakfast—to remain and suffer.

Of course, there were flagrant offenses that were dealt with in private. Sometimes profanity sullied the air of the geography room. Sometimes, though rarely, open rebellion was displayed. In those instances, the delinquent was detained, minus the comfort of his comrades, in awful seclusion with Miss Dove. What happened between them was never fully known. (Did she threaten him with legal prosecution? Did she beat him with her long map-pointer?) . . .

Occasionally a group of progressive mothers would contemplate organized revolt. "She's been teaching too long," they would cry. "Her pedagogy hasn't changed since we were in Cedar Grove. She rules the children through fear!" They would turn to the boldest one among themselves. "*You* go," they would say. "You go talk to her!"

The bold one would go, but somehow she never did much talking. . . . Without firing a shot in the cause of freedom she would retreat ingloriously from the field of battle.

And on that unassaulted field—in that room where no leeway was given to the personality, where a thing was black or white, right or wrong, polite or rude, simply because Miss Dove said it was, there was a curiously soothing quality. The children left it refreshed and restored, ready for fray or frolic. For within its walls they enjoyed what was allowed them nowhere else—a complete suspension of will.

On this particular Wednesday the first-graders, to whom Miss Dove gave a survey course in the flora and fauna of the Earth, drew pictures of robins. They drew them in crayon on eight-by-eleven sheets of manila paper. They did not draw them from memory. They copied the bird Miss Dove had drawn for them on the blackboard. (She knew exacly how a robin looked and saw no sense in permitting her pupils to rely upon their own random observations.) They left an inch-wide margin, measuring it with a ruler, around each picture. (Miss Dove believed in margins—except for error!) All the first-grade's robins would look alike. Which was as it should be. Which was true of robins everywhere. Miss Dove was concerned with facts, not with artistic impressions.

She divided the second-grade into activity groups. One group cut scenic photographs from old magazines and pasted them in a scrapbook. Another modeled clay caribou for the sand table. Still another drew a colored mural on the rear blackboard. The groups did not talk among themselves, asking questions and pooling advice. They had no need to. Miss Dove had told them what to do.

The third grade recited the states of the Union. It was Miss Dove's experience that the eight-year-old mind learned best by rote.

At a quarter past eleven the fourth grade filed in. This grade was studying economic geography—the natural resources of different regions and their manifold uses in civilized life—and on Monday was to take a proficiency test prepared by the state Board of Education. Each year in April all grammar-grade students—students in the fourth, fifth and sixth grades—were so examined. Regarding these tests, Miss Dove's sentiments were mixed. She resented them as an intrusion upon her privacy and as an implication that her efficiency was open to question. But she recognized in them, grudgingly, a certain practice-value to the children.

Questions for Discussion and Debate

1. Although this piece may at first seem dated, there are still teachers similar to Miss Dove in classrooms today. Maybe you even had such a teacher. Describe Miss Dove's style. Are there any aspects of her style that you like and/or would consider developing? Why? Why not? Discuss and debate.

2. Did you ever have a teacher like Miss Dove? If so, did you like being in her or his class? Why? Why not?

3. List some of the typical infractions committed by Miss Dove's students and, next to each, the penalties she assigned. Would you have assigned different consequences for these infractions? Discuss the typical infrac-tions *you* have seen in classes and the kinds of penalties assigned to them. Are the punishments fitting? How similar or different are the "crimes" students committed then versus now? Discuss and debate responses to these questions.

4. Debate the pros and cons of the predictable, consistent teacher versus the less predictable, more spontaneous approach. Make distinctions between such variability in terms of discipline policy and instructional techniques.

5. Have you had the experience—as have many of Miss Dove's students—of having a teacher that your parent(s) or sibling(s) have

had? What is the nature of this experience in terms of:

a. Their labeling or stereotyping you before they knew you.

b. Your labeling or stereotyping *them* before you knew them firsthand.

c. The advantages as well as the disadvantages of this situation.

6. Which is the more effective style: familiarity or formality with students? Divide into two groups, one arguing for familiarity (not Miss Dove's choice); the other, against it.

Activities and Projects

1. Consult a number of classroom management texts that contain disciplinary models and suggestions. Choose one or more aspects of several of them that you like and share them with the class.

2. Interview teachers about their classroom management policies or observe them to discover:

   • Their rules (and how they were established).

   • The consequences for breaking the rules.

   • Their degree of rigidity and consistency in relation to these rules and consequences.

   Share your findings. Then create a classroom management policy that you believe in, one that fits your beliefs and style. What do you think will be the most effective part of your plan?

3. In Miss Dove's class, students had no doubt about the rules and the consequences and thus could feel liberated, in a sense, from the need to "test out"; they "enjoyed . . . a complete suspension of will" (Patton, 1954, p. 12). This suspension of will existed as a result of external discipline, not self-discipline. Find out through research how teachers help students to develop self-discipline.

4. In the last part of the excerpt, there are a number of issues raised that are related to pedagogy and curriculum.

   • Teaching facts versus allowing for interpretation of facts

   • Group work *without* student collaboration versus cooperative learning

   • Learning facts by rote versus learning using diverse methods

   • Standardized tests versus more authentic classroom-based assessment

   Clearly we know where Miss Dove stands on all of these issues, which continue to be hotly debated by teachers, educational philosophers, and the public. Where do you stand on each one? Divide the class into four groups, each one taking one of the above issues to explore through research and observation. Return to the class with panel presentations on the topic that your group explored.

1.4   *What Lisa Knew* (1990)

Joyce Johnson

Children are abused daily behind closed doors at the hands of people who are supposed to be providing them with a safe and loving environment. Teachers can play an important role in stopping such abuse and are, in fact, required by law to report any signs of abuse. Though the Child Abuse Prevention and Treatment Act of 1974 (P.L. 100–294) establishes teachers as mandated reporters, the law was not able to protect Lisa Steinberg from her father's wrath. Hedda Nussbaum, Steinberg's lover, who was also arrested for the murder of their 6-year-old adopted daughter, testified at the trial not only about the blows that killed Lisa but also about the abuse she herself had suffered for years at the hands of this apparently well-educated middle-class lawyer. These facts reminded the public that child abuse transcends all socioeconomic levels. Millions of people read Nussbaum's testimony or watched her tell her story on television in "a halting voice that mesmerized the jury . . . [and] ended with the image of a helpless and innocent child, lying comatose on a bathroom floor while her parents ignored her and freebased cocaine" ("The Steinberg Case," 1988, p. 58).

In her book, *What Lisa Knew: The Truth and Lies of the Steinberg Case*, Joyce Johnson not only reports the facts of the case but raises several questions in order to come to terms with what went wrong so that other children will not have to suffer the abuse that Lisa experienced. Why didn't more teachers notice Lisa's bruises and disheveled appearance and do something about it? Why hadn't agencies that had been notified of possible abuse pursue the case? In other words, why had the system failed?

One of the answers to these questions has to do with the fear teachers and others have that they may be sued by a family if their suspicions turn out to be wrong. On the other hand, under the 1974 law, teachers who do *not* report instances of suspected child abuse can face similar lawsuits brought by the legal authorities, or they may be fined from $500 to $1,000, given a prison sentence of up to a year, or penalized by their school system (McCarthy & Cambron-McCabe, 1992). Many professionals walk a fine line between "protecting a family's right to privacy and upholding their legal responsibility to report cases of suspected abuse" ("The Steinberg Case," 1988, p. 59). It is a dilemma you may be confronted with, especially considering such statistics as an estimated 2.6 million abuse cases reported every year (U.S. General Accounting Office, 1992), with no recent evidence of any dramatic decrease.

Johnson tells us what Lisa's teacher and student teacher did—and did not—do. Notice the reasons why the teacher chose not to pursue any course of action that might have led to a formal abuse report. Do you think different behavior on Mrs. Haron's part might have led to Lisa's survival? What would you have done if you were the student teacher whose suspicions were voiced but ignored? These are, indeed, difficult questions but questions you will need to begin thinking about because you could be faced with a similar situation. Finally, do you agree with Johnson's implicit message that everyone must rid themselves of the apathy that she believes is the indirect accomplice in crimes against children?

What were the secrets of Lisa Steinberg's life by the age of six, the things that no one ever really saw? The bruises that began appearing that August carried no fingerprints. They showed up, then faded, because a child heals very quickly. The neighbors who considered themselves watchful never saw them at all. Those who saw them or thought they saw them were reluctant to probe into their origin. If Joel Steinberg threw his daughter a sandwich, he might have been just roughhousing with her; although to an outsider it may have seemed that he was treating her the way you'd treat a dog. Sal Friscia, a man who lived on Tenth Street but never really knew the Steinbergs, remembers seeing Hedda walking down the street wheeling Mitchell and yelling at Lisa, who was in tears. But who hasn't seen such scenes on the streets, mothers provoked to the point where they're out of control, dragging along a shamed, sobbing child? And then perhaps there were things that didn't show, that left no visible marks. Law-enforcement experts, however, will tell you that in households like the Steinbergs', the sexual abuse of children is almost a given.

Lisa must have wondered that summer what it was that she was doing wrong. What was it about her, now that she was six, that made Joel act as if he didn't love her anymore, even though he said he did. She seemed to be losing her specialness in her father's eyes, the favor she'd always been able to count on that protected her from the awful wrath that descended on Hedda. Perhaps it was very confusing that everyone else still thought she was special, the waiters and waitresses in Knickerbocker's, the friends of Daddy's she met who always bought her little presents. She'd cuddle up to her daddy's friends and say to them, "Aren't I your little girl, too?"

School began on September 14. Lisa was very late that day and the student teacher, Stacey Weiss, was surprised when she arrived escorted by her father. Usually the mothers brought the children. She saw Lisa's father for only a moment.

Perhaps the sense that there was something irregular in Lisa Steinberg's situation prompted her to take a good look at the child the following morning during story hour. Sylvia Haron, the homeroom teacher, was reading and the children were seated in a semicircle on the floor. Lisa was directly in front of Stacey Weiss, wearing a very short skirt and shirt that she had obviously outgrown. The shirt crept up on her when she sat down and Stacey Weiss saw a large purple bruise on her lower back; there were many other bruises of various colors on her bare thighs and calves.

Stacey Weiss was in her senior year at Yeshiva University, and this was the first classroom she had worked in. She didn't quite know what to do about Lisa. She consulted her student-teacher adviser that afternoon, and the next day had a word with Mrs. Haron.

From the start, there was friction in Stacey Weiss's relationship with Sylvia Haron. Mrs. Haron, a woman with a rather childlike manner but an excellent reputation, had been teaching for twenty years. She had problems in delegating responsibility, and Stacey Weiss's eagerness to handle more and more by herself seemed to offend her; perhaps she felt a little threatened by the earnest and enthusiastic young woman. Weiss's report to her about Lisa may have smacked of overzealousness. In the past, Haron herself had taken immediate action in instances where she had suspected child abuse. Lisa Steinberg just did not worry her, although after a while, "I watched her, I watched her." As Haron testified in a Board of Education hearing, Lisa's behavior indicated only that she was going to be an outstanding student. "She wanted to be monitor, wanted to read her stories, wanted to write, she was really just the kind of kid you wanted to have in your class."

Oddly enough, Mrs. Haron later could not recall Stacey Weiss's ever saying anything to her about those bruises she had seen on the second day of school. In one early October talk about Lisa, she did find Weiss's observations "helpful," but their topic of conversation was merely Lisa's interactions with other students—the kind of exchange they'd have about any other kid. By then however, Mrs. Haron herself had seen some yellowish gray marks on Lisa's back when Lisa "stretched from her desk to the little boy's desk across from her and her shirt went up in back . . . I asked her what happened? How did you get those? And absolutely true-faced, eye to eye, without a moment's hesitation, the reply was, as well as I can recollect, 'My brother did that.' " Later in the hearing, Mrs. Haron added, "I really thought at the time her brother just took something, a toy or whatever and just like . . . "

"No, there was nothing, there was nothing," she insisted after the UFT attorney asked her whether Lisa had seemed at all hesitant or defensive. "It was open-faced, it was given to me full-faced. It was given to me clear-eyed, there was no hesitation, there was no withdrawal. . . . There was no shame." During the brief conversation she had with Lisa, Mrs. Haron did not think to ask her how old her brother was.

As the weeks of the fall term went by, Lisa Steinberg kept arriving late or missing school. (There were forty schooldays between September 14 and November 2; she was there for only twenty-two of them.) This was something measurable and it did not escape Mrs. Haron's notice, though again, it did not inspire alarm—even coupled with the child's consistently unkempt appearance and those marks on her body.

Finally, in mid-October, Mrs. Haron asked Lisa why she had been absent so frequently, and "her reply was that they woke up too late to come to school." "You come here even if you're late," Mrs. Haron told Lisa, and imparted the same message to Joel when he arrived at three to pick her up. "He kind of scolded her like it was her fault, that was the message that came across to me." About a week later, Hedda Nussbaum sent Mrs. Haron a note, explaining that for the past few weeks they had been rearranging their schedule. That was enough to satisfy the teacher. She saw no need to bring the matter up with the school aide, who might then have talked to the guidance counselor.

Questions for Discussion and Debate

1. Find the reasons given throughout the excerpt that explain why Mrs. Haron, Lisa's teacher, chose not to recognize the signs of abuse or to report them. You might quote those reasons during your discussion. What is your reaction to her decisions?

2. Teachers seem to face a catch-22 dilemma. If they report suspected abuse and there is none, they can get sued by parents. If they don't report suspected abuse and there *is* abuse, they can be sued by law under the Child Abuse Prevention and Treatment Act

of 1974. Which of these suits would you be more willing to risk? Why?

3. Debate the merits of this statement: The student teacher should have gone over and above her cooperating teacher's head with her suspicions of abuse.

4. If you have had any experiences directly or indirectly with child abuse situations or have read about such cases, share those experiences with your peers by using a questioning format (i.e., "As a teacher, what if you faced the following situation:").

Activities and Projects

1. Divide into small groups, with each group pursuing one of the following research topics. Then come together and have panel presentations to share your findings.
   - Signs of and types of abuse
   - Causes of abuse
   - Effects of abuse
   - Ways of preventing abuse
   - Teachers' stories about their mandated reporter role

2. Invite to class an authority on child abuse, perhaps someone from the Department of Social Services.

3. Interview a school social worker about the nature of his or her job. Also, ask the following questions:
   - What are the extent and nature of the abuse cases you are dealing with in this school system?
   - What is the step-by-step procedure that occurs from the time a teacher reports suspected abuse to the principal to the final point in the procedure? What are some of the possible outcomes of the process?

1.5 *Small Victories* (1990)

Samuel G. Freedman

The teachers who work at Seward Park High School on the Lower East Side of New York City care about helping "children of poverty" (Freedman, 1990, p. 164). But according to some of these teachers, the conditions of the job don't make that task easy. Samuel G. Freedman's book, *Small Victories: The Real World of a Teacher, Her Students, and Their High School,* portrays the realities of having to contend with five classes a day and over 150 students, overseeing a homeroom, assisting with various other duties, and often doing without adequate resources. At the same time, however, he tells of the small victories that many of these teachers and students experience on a daily basis.

Freedman shares the motivations that led many of these teachers into the classroom, and we learn about what their lives were like before coming to Seward Park, what they're like while teaching there, and where some of them choose to go afterward. He takes the reader into the halls, the offices, and several of the classrooms to "observe" curricula and methods as well as the lively and sometimes funny, sometimes frustrating interchanges between students and teachers, between teachers and teachers, and between administrators and teachers. It is easy to identify with one or more of these mostly hardworking public servants.

Jessica Siegel initially struggles with her decision to become a high-school history teacher, but once she gains experience and confidence, she becomes the model and mentor for one new teacher after another. This excerpt traces Jessica's journey from novice to veteran. As you read about her transformation consider this question: Are teachers born or are they made? And if they're made, what variables went into making Jessica a teacher? Try to put yourself in her place. Decide if you would have responded as she did to both the obstacles and the support she encountered. Is there anything in this excerpt that is familiar to you, that reflects *your* own feelings or experiences?

Lunch was important. The Seward Park faculty cafeteria was more than a collection of long formica tables; it was a collection of world views. There was a table for talk of investments and there was a table for whispers of discos and there were lots of tables for bitching and moaning. Lanni Tama sat at a table for teachers who cared about teaching—not Pollyannas, to be sure, but realists who believed in possibility. Teaching is a solitary task, and so lunch was the one time of the day when the believers could share ideas, trade theories, and reinforce in one another the very ethos of believing.

The woman at the table who impressed Jessica most was Hannah Hess, an English teacher of stocky build and owlish eyes. She was a German Jew whose family had escaped the Nazi regime in 1939 and reached the expatriate colony in Manhattan's Washington Heights district by way of Ecuador. As a girl of six, unable to speak a word of English, Hannah had entered the New York public schools, and as a woman of twenty-three, she had become a teacher in the same system. She had lived the

legend of immigrants and schools and success, but she had lived long enough to question it. For when Hannah left teaching in 1962 to raise her three children, she began to learn precisely how resistant a public school could be to dismissing incompetents and accepting innovation. Her awakening reached its peak during the 1968 teachers' strikes, when she joined a group of parents in keeping open their neighborhood elementary school. To the United Federation of Teachers, that act branded Hannah a traitor, and even when she resumed teaching after a twelve-year hiatus, she faced a spiritual blacklist. The union could not deny Hannah a job, but some of its supporters could conspire to make her job miserable. During Hannah's first year at Seward Park, various colleagues ignored her in conversation, slammed doors in her face, and refused to lend her change for a pay telephone. When her car was ticketed by mistake in a school parking zone, an administrator declined to verify for the Traffic Court that she indeed taught at Seward Park. Hannah outlasted the petty harassment, but she never forgot it, and the experience gave her a special empathy for the outsider.

Hannah invited Jessica to watch her teach. In the English office afterward, she talked to Jessica about the children in the class. When Passover arrived, Hannah welcomed Jessica to her family's seder. Their conversations over the months gradually moved from the purely educational to the political and the personal, and for the first time at Seward Park, Jessica trusted someone enough to confide her radical past, a past she had feared might cost her her job. Hannah was, if anything, relieved. She knew the lonely lot of the freethinker, and she appreciated the company out on Seward Park's left wing.

To Hannah and Lanni and the rest of the lunch table, it was obvious that Jessica should become a teacher. Jessica had the mind and she had the soul and she had a frightening capacity for labor, for "working herself to a frazzle and thinking she should be working herself to two frazzles," as Hannah put it. The campaign required a lot of tuna and yogurt and coffee and cajoling, but eventually Jessica agreed to try. She refused to begin immediately with a temporary license, but she consented to taking the English licensing exam and to entering Teachers College while remaining a paraprofessional. There was so much Jessica needed to know, and Teachers College, with its international reputation, seemed the place to learn it. Hannah knew better. The only classes she had cut as an undergraduate at Hunter College were in education, and her graduate studies at Fordham University had taught her "zip." There were only two ways anyone really learned how to teach, by teaching and by watching others teach. Learning how to teach was not an academic process as much as a tribal rite, a secret passed from elder to child, atavistic as charting the stars or planting the maize.

But Jessica had her plan: She would go to Teachers College and learn to teach reading. Reading classes were small, reading instruction

was individual. A reading class was a theater built for a thespian with stage fright. If only Jessica had been able to stay awake during her reading-education classes at Teachers College. So little in her courses struck her as practical. The professors could not be bothered with subjects as pedestrian as writing a lesson plan. The students marched toward graduation blithely unaware of anything as fundamental as New York City's licensing system.

Jessica doubled her course load to graduate in time for the reading-license exam in fall 1980. In her final, frantic semester, she took the single memorable class of graduate school, "Arts and American Education," from Professor Maxine Greene. Greene was a presence, a self-deprecating wit whose craggy voice and constant cigarette reminded Jessica of Lillian Hellman. Whereas her colleagues rode the rut of narrow theory, Greene uncoiled skeins of ideas, spanning education, painting, fiction, and politics. "What's going on?" Jessica could hear some of the younger students mutter during the reveries. "This is too fast." But Jessica thrilled to the pace. She learned from Maxine Greene the texts she someday would teach her own students—*The Great Gatsby* and "Bartleby the Scrivener"—but what was more important, she learned the way she would teach them, by "showing the connections between things."

Her master's degree completed, Jessica entered her third full year at Seward Park as an overeducated paraprofessional. It was then, in September 1980, that events overtook her cautious design. One of the teachers of Spanish bilingual social studies died of a heart attack only a few weeks into the term. As a search was mounted for a successor, his classes were placed in the receivership of a substitute, whose pedagogy consisted of perusing *The New York Times* while his flock ran wild. Jessica heard the whooping from an adjacent classroom, and when she peered in the door she saw the anarchy. She hurried to the social studies office and described the scene to Stan Carter, the department chairman.

They were Seward Park's odd couple, Stan a combat Marine veteran still strapping in his fifties, and Jessica, a bundle of self-doubt and bright colors. "The sixties are over," he would tease her, and she would laugh, because she sensed the affection behind the barb. Like Hannah Hess and Lanni Tama, Stan judged Jessica to be teacher material, and now she would have her chance. He told her to assign homework to the chaotic class. How could you give homework, Jessica asked, without teaching a lesson? And how could you teach a lesson to a class of recent immigrants from a textbook written at twelfth grade level? The only solution, as Jessica saw it, was to create and teach a lesson of her own. So she did.

Then she taught a second and a third. An aide could not officially lead a class alone, so Stan hired another substitute to sit in the room. A few weeks later, he located a fully licensed Spanish bilingual history teacher, and relieved Jessica, but the new man proved so poor that Stan fired him and restored Jessica to the lectern. By now, she had received her temporary license, so she took over the deceased teacher's entire load—four sections of bilingual social studies and one section of World History II.

She felt herself sinking in quicksand. She did not speak Spanish. She had never taught. She had never even studied much history. What caused World War I? She would find out the night before informing her classes. Stan lent Jessica some of his lesson plans, as did a teacher named Maureen Lonergan, but working from another's outline was like wearing a stranger's shoes. The classes, sensing Jessica's inexperience, burst into blizzards of spitballs and invective. Jessica asked Hannah for advice on discipline, and Hannah said, "Just give them the beady eye." The beady eye worked better for a veteran than a beginner, and soon Jessica was back to the same

plaints: "Turn around! Stop tickling her! No, you can't go to the bathroom. Sit down! Leave the window alone! Where's your homework?"

Stan scheduled his first formal observation, and of all Jessica's classes, he chose to watch World History II, her worst. The room brimmed with thirty-four brigands, "repeaters" who had failed the course from one to three times already. They had bedeviled Jessica daily with fake passes, profane answers, and sundry roughhousing, and they had delighted in their demonism. Jessica was terrified to smile; she marshaled all her strength just to dam her tears until the end of the day. But the November morning Stan Carter swaggered through the door, a redwood on legs, her tormentors fell silent. It was not fear of Stan that had hushed them, it was the fear he had come to fire Ms. Siegel. Jessica taught a lesson on Renaissance artists, and to her amazement, hands rose and inquiries filled the air. Grace was all. Stan left the room with five minutes remaining in the period, and the second the door closed behind him, a voice shouted, "Now we can get back to normal." As paper balls cross-hatched the air before her, Jessica ventured her first laugh of the term.

Not long after, Jessica received word she had passed the English licensing exam she dimly recalled having taken two years earlier; the Board of Examiners was operating at its customary crawl. She reported to the English Department chairman. Lew Saperstein, a man she distrusted utterly. When Jessica had been Lanni Tama's aide, Saperstein had tried to commandeer her as his personal file clerk. She resisted, and he bullied: "You can follow my orders, or I can get you fired." While Saperstein had relented, his threat still rung in Jessica's ears, for now, as a new teacher, she was most vulnerable to caprice.

Saperstein first offered Jessica several sections of English 8. The course, world literature for second-semester seniors, was usually awarded as a plum to a skilled veteran. Jessica, fearing its scope beyond her abilities, wavered.

"OK," Saperstein said. "English Four. The annex."

Jessica sobbed. English 4 was a course in oral communication for first-semester sophomores. Public speaking mortified her, and the annex was the annex, a dismal old academy far from Hannah and Stan, Jessica's mainstays.

"But no one will bother you," Saperstein said.

Suddenly Jessica realized Saperstein had been trying to mend fences. He would send her to the Outback, and she would be left alone. She could falter in sublime isolation. Saperstein had designed his own office so that a phalanx of filing cabinets guarded him from all petitioners, and he had appropriated a diminutive paraprofessional as his factotum. As far as Jessica could tell, not being bothered was, to Saperstein, the highest plane of existence.

"But I *want* to be bothered," Jessica pleaded.

The spring term of 1981 was her worst ever. Now that she finally had a career, she was failing at it. She asked Hannah what she should teach, and Hannah said, "Anything you want." She asked Hannah what to choose as an aim for a lesson, and Hannah said, "Anything you find interesting." What Hannah was saying was, "Trust yourself," but what Jessica heard was, "You're on your own, kid." As for Saperstein, after observing Jessica teaching a typically disastrous class, he assured her, "I won't write it up." Ignoring her faults, Jessica realized, was his idea of helping.

"Jessica was overwhelmed," Hannah Hess recalls. "She probably spent seven hours on every paper she read. Would go home with a humongous stack of paper every night. Would plan a lesson and if it didn't work would be beside herself. And she was always convinced everyone else was doing something better than her. She'd say, 'X is a better teacher than I am,' and I'd say, 'Have you ever seen X teach?' and Jessica would say, 'No.' I'd say, 'So how do you know X is better?' and Jessica would say, 'X said so.'"

As much as Hannah knew Jessica was foundering, as deeply as she sensed Jessica was suffering, as many times as she watched Jessica slink home for her nightly cry, she had no doubts about her protégée. "I knew Jessica wouldn't quit because Jessica's not a quitter," Hannah says. "Jessica couldn't walk away from something she felt she'd failed. She could only walk away from a success."

One day late in the spring term, Jessica was summoned to the main building. There, she and the rest of the English teachers were introduced to Ben Dachs, a hulking man with a full brown beard who would become their chairman in the fall. Lew Saperstein had been nudged toward a transfer; he would leave Seward Park for—it was only appropriate—the Board of Examiners. Neither Ben nor Jessica knew much about the other. Canadian born and American educated, Ben was coming from Edward R. Murrow High School, a magnet school in Brooklyn, where he had taught English, advised the yearbook, directed plays, and coordinated a writing program. Jessica was less than a year out of the paraprofessional ranks, and Ben assumed she had gained her teaching position less by merit than by patronage. Here, he thought, was a case of a corrupt system taking care of its own.

Early in September 1981, he began to change his mind. Jessica warmed to Ben for returning her to the main building, and for rearranging the office furniture so he faced teachers instead of hiding from them, as had his predecessor. Ben installed a work table and a magazine rack and a chair beside his desk for personal chats.

Jessica planted herself in that chair at the first opportunity and poured out all the frustration of the previous year.

"I'm really glad you're here," she said. "I need someone like you. I'm overwhelmed and underconfident. I never got any help from

Saperstein. I want to learn how to be a good teacher. I need to know so many things. I want to learn from you."

Then she exploded into tears.

Ben could not have wished for more. He was an accomplished educator tiring of the classroom. Oh, he still enjoyed teaching well enough, but he had gotten too good at it. Ben played poker and bet the horses because he loved risk and challenge: effortless triumph held no satisfaction. He had sought a chairmanship because he believed that in teaching teachers, he could find that spark, that serendipity he called "the 'Aha' effect." And now, in Jessica, he had the consummate pupil, intellect in search of form and insecurity in search of fealty.

Over the weeks, Ben advised Jessica on constructing lessons, framing questions, and planning curriculum, but he never intended that counsel alone would suffice. Midway through the term, he taught his English 8 class a series of lessons on *Hamlet*. He typed a schedule of dates and topics and issued the faculty an invitation with only one caveat: whoever saw him teach had to provide him with a critique of the lesson. The school buzzed. There was substantial debate in Seward Park about whether inner-city kids could understand *Hamlet*, much less enjoy it, and here was an untenured chairman teaching Shakespeare as nakedly as a stripper. Even before Jessica made it to Ben's classroom, word was racing through school: The new guy took some old newspapers, whirled the sheets into a hat and a sword, leapt onto the desktop, and started teaching from there. Jessica sat in on nothing quite so dramatic, but she was dazzled by Ben's personal alchemy of entertainment and education. He orated. He inquired. He told shaggy-dog stories. He physically shaped students into armies and courts.

Jessica trod through a story or poem line by line, following elaborately scripted lesson plans that dragged on for days. The idea of fibbing a little to invigorate a class seemed as illicit as perjury. She was a public servant; she was a bore; she was a raisin and Ben was a great juicy grape. Yet Jessica had a restless mind, and she had a motherly warmth, and Ben considered that combination all too rare. The first time he observed her, he noted that thirty-one of her thirty-four pupils had turned out for a first-period class on a bitter, blustery December Friday. They were voting with their feet. And when Ben inspected several students' notebooks, he saw they were comprehending. He cushioned his criticism of Jessica's stiff style with plenty of praise. "You are your own toughest critic," Ben wrote after that class. "Lighten up on yourself and you will see that this was a fine lesson that needed only some finer tuning."

The more Jessica trusted Ben, the safer she felt loosening the standard lesson. Teaching under his stewardship, she would later say, "was like flying with a net." If she recognized that she could never be a stemwinder, a classroom natural, then she realized she could infuse literature with her humor and her values. "You want kids to love literature," Ben often told her, "not just the piece you're teaching." Outside class, he encouraged her to chaperone field trips and to advise *Seward World.* He lobbied for approval of the Lower East Side course she had designed with Bruce Baskind.

Ben was not the only one to notice Jessica's metamorphosis. One day in spring 1986, he said to her, "That was *some* letter." She asked, "What letter?" Ben withdrew it from his desk:

Mr. Robert Mastruzzi, Superintendent
Manhattan High Schools
Martin Luther King, Jr. High School
122 Amsterdam Avenue
New York, New York 10023

Dear Mr. Mastruzzi:

My nominee for Teacher of the Year for 1985–86 is Jessica Siegel. Ms. Siegel, it should be noted, began her career in education as an educational assistant and now has become an excellent role model for colleagues and students.

Jessica Siegel is a teacher of English, but this describes her as well as daVinci might be described were we to call him a medical illustrator. She serves as advisor to our newspaper, *Seward World,* and has overseen expansion of this publication to four issues annually. In addition, recent recognition by the Robert F. Kennedy Foundation and the Columbia Press Association gives testimony to the effectiveness of her guidance and leadership. Further, together with a superb colleague, Bruce Baskind, she has created a humanities course which focuses on the Lower East Side and its history of immigration, which has earned the plaudits of New York University in the form of financial backing for her research and curriculum development, in addition to their enthusiastic encomiums.

Ms. Siegel is a creative self-starter who commits herself wholeheartedly to professional activities. She attends evening and weekend functions which we sponsor, strives constantly to improve her classroom performance, and involves herself in a myriad of activities which contribute to a viable school environment. I nominate her for your consideration.

Sincerely,
Noel N. Kriftcher
Principal

Jessica did not win the boroughwide award, and she wondered why she had to learn of her nomination secondhand. But she carried home a plaque as a distinguished also-ran, and she dined at a four-star restaurant as Bruce Baskind's guest. By now, Hannah Hess had left Seward Park to become chairwoman of the English Department at Chelsea Vocational High School. Ben, feeling his familiar craving for new terrain, was quietly surveying the city for a principal's position. Jessica was the veteran. At the start of the 1986–87 school year, Ben's last at Seward Park, he appointed her the "buddy teacher" for a newcomer named Steve Anderson. Steve called Jessica every single night for months, with desperate pleas for aid in writing lessons and tips on buying grade books, and each time Jessica answered she indulged in a private pleasure: She knew something; she had something to share.

When Ben departed Seward Park in September 1987 to become principal of Beach Channel High School, he could view Jessica as perhaps his greatest single success. He had always maintained that a teacher did not have to be born, that a teacher could be trained. His sole regret was that he had trained Jessica rather too well. Her skills were high, with standards to match. She held *Seward World* to a professional benchmark. Never did she deny a student in need. He saw in her pride and assurance, and he saw in her exhaustion and heartbreak. And he, more than most, had helped engineer this benign Frankenstein, nourishing to students and colleagues, damaging only to herself.

Questions for Discussion and Debate

1. Learning to teach is a cumulative experience made up of both direct and indirect influences, some not necessarily so obvious. Noting all of the information contained in this excerpt, make a list of those influences and the pages on which they appear, perhaps entitling the list "The Education of Jessica." Then compare your list with those of your peers. Discuss which variables seemed to be most significant in preparing Jessica in the

art and science of teaching. Compare these variables to the influences that have shaped you as a teacher.

2. Do you agree with Ben Dachs that "a teacher did not have to be born, that a teacher could be trained"? (Freedman, 1990, p. 186). Debate this supposition.

3. What do you learn about administrative styles from this excerpt? With your peers, describe your idea of the perfect administrator from a new teacher's perspective.

4. What are some of the frustrations as well as the rewards of teaching according to this excerpt?

5. What is your overall reaction to this excerpt? What did you learn from it? What did you like about it? Compare your views with peers.

6. The chapter from which this excerpt is taken is entitled "Raccoon Badge," which is explained as follows:

> That they [the teachers] are tired is a given. The proof is in their eyes. . . . On the flesh beneath them, dark lines fan toward the cheeks. . . : the

raccoon badge of honor . . . the medal of the devoted teacher, the teacher up late reading essays, the teacher up early decorating a classroom, the teacher still in school as Friday's firmament darkens. (Freedman, 1990, pp. 186–187)

Visualize this metaphor. What other metaphors might characterize the dedicated teacher? Find another metaphor in the excerpt itself.

7. Freedman makes references to Jessica's courses at Columbia Teachers College, a respected teacher education school. But not all of her courses met her needs or seemed to be relevant to the roles she needed to play at Seward Park. Describe her feelings about those courses. Then evaluate with your peers the teacher education program in which you are enrolled. What aspects are serving your objectives—assuming that you have explicitly formulated objectives for yourself—and what changes would you suggest, if any, for improving the program in terms of preparing student teachers for the many roles they'll need to play?

Activities and Projects

1. This excerpt portrays the growth of Jessica Siegel from an aide to a veteran teacher and, as such, may be worthy of dramatic presentation. With peers, write a screenplay with several scenes and appropriate roles. Then rehearse the play and videotape it. Discuss the purposes the video might serve both within other education courses and within in-service workshops in the schools.

2. Interview your cooperating teacher or another teacher about his or her evolution from beginning teacher to experienced teacher. Particularly, try to find out what

people, policies, training, and education affected him or her. In class compare Jessica's experience with that of the teacher you interviewed.

3. Jessica became a teacher when she was about 30 years old, as opposed to when she was the more typical age of the beginning teacher—although more and more men and women are, indeed, switching careers at the ages of 30 to 50. Find out what studies show about the differences between the two groups. If little material can be found, consider devising a questionnaire that you

could administer to a sample of first- or second-year teachers from both age groups.

4. Reread the part about the faculty lunchroom at the beginning of the excerpt. Faculty lunchrooms can offer a look at the cross section of teachers in the school and their *real* interests and personalities. After everyone in your class investigates the activities and conversations in at least one lunchroom, reconvene and discuss what you observed and whether or not the data you collected differ from the observations you have made of those teachers *outside* of the lunchroom. What did you learn from your lunchroom research? (Please keep one thing in mind as you collect the lunchroom data: Teachers often say things quite openly during this presumably relaxing time, and some might resent having their conversations quoted. To uphold good public relations, you might not want to use the teachers' names or any other information that might threaten the relationships the education department at your school has with the faculties in the public schools.)

1.6   *A Tree Grows in Brooklyn* (1943)

Betty Smith

When Francie Nolan, the lead character in Betty Smith's classic novel, *A Tree Grows in Brooklyn,* returns to her street as a young woman she sees a beloved tree she thought had died. But the tree hadn't died. "A new tree had grown from the stump and its trunk had grown along the ground until it reached a place where there were no wash lines above it. Then it started to grow towards the sky again. . . . It lived! And nothing could destroy it" (Smith, 1943, p. 420). So reads the metaphor that Betty Smith invokes at the end of her novel to convey the way in which Francie herself had risen above the poverty and prejudice that threatened to chop her down.

Smith's novel is set during the first two decades of the 20th century, when the Williamsburg section of Brooklyn was a sea of immigrants and throbbing with daily life. (It still is in many respects.) In fact, the novel reveals several aspects of living and learning in a diverse society (chapter 6) as well as a number of scenes from America's educational history (chapter 2). Smith wanted to write about Brooklyn as she knew and loved it, although, she notes, not one of the episodes is exact truth. Another of her motives was wanting "to protest in some way against intolerance." Through her portrayal of both the good folk and the bad—teachers included—Smith does, indeed, convey such lessons with details rich in universal experience.

Francie's mother, Katie Nolan, recognizes that her daughter's only ticket out of a life of poverty is education. "Education would pull them out of grime and dirt" (Smith, 1943, p. 175). And to make sure that she gets the best education, Francie's parents allow her to switch to a better school. This excerpt, however, portrays teachers in Francie's first school, which was bearable only because of the two teachers you will meet here, both specialists, one in music and the other in art. The implication here is that there were other teachers in this school who discriminated against the poorer children in the class, made them feel inferior, and used them as scapegoats (pp. 128–131). Contrast the behavior of these kinds of teachers with that of Mr. Morton and Miss Bernstone and think about the statement made in the introduction to this chapter, that teachers' behavior, like that of other groups in society, cannot be stereotyped as good or bad. They come in all shapes, sizes, and personalities, like it or not. However, as you read the excerpt, you might try to figure out how teacher education can help to ensure that most teachers will be healthy individuals, happy with themselves, their students, and their jobs.

Francie liked school in spite of all the meanness, cruelty, and unhappiness. The regimented routine of many children, all doing the same thing at once, gave her a feeling of safety. She felt that she was a definite part of something, part of a community gathered under a leader for the one purpose. The Nolans were individualists. They conformed to nothing except what was essential to their being able to live in their world. They followed their own standards of living. They were part of no set social group. This was fine for the making of individualists but sometimes bewildering to a small child. So Francie felt a certain safety and security in school. Although it was a cruel and ugly routine, it had a purpose and a progression.

School was not all unrelieved grimness. There was a great golden glory lasting a half hour each week when Mr. Morton came to Francie's room to teach music. He was a specialized teacher who went around to all of the schools in that area. It was holiday time when he appeared. He wore a swallow-tailed coat and a puffed-up tie. He was so vibrant, gay and jolly—so intoxicated with living—that he was like a god come from the clouds. He was homely in a gallant vital way. He understood and loved children and they worshiped him. The teachers adored him. There was a carnival

spirit in the room on the day of his visit. Teacher wore her best dress and wasn't quite so mean. Sometimes she curled her hair and wore perfume. That's what Mr. Morton did to those ladies.

He arrived like a tornado. The door burst open and he flew in with his coattails streaming behind him. He leaped to the platform and looked around smiling and saying, "well-well," in a happy voice. The children sat there and laughed and laughed out of happiness and Teacher smiled and smiled.

He drew notes on the blackboard; he drew little legs on them to make them look as though they were running out of the scale. He'd make a flat note look like humpty-dumpty. A sharp note would rate a thin beat-like nose zooming off it. All the while he'd burst into singing just as spontaneously as a bird. Sometimes his happiness was so overflowing that he couldn't hold it and he'd cut a dance caper to spill some of it out.

He taught them good music without letting them know it was good. He set his own words to the great classics and gave them simple names like "Lullaby" and "Serenade" and "Street Song" and "Song for a Sunshiny Day." Their baby voices shrilled out in Handel's "Largo" and they knew it merely by the title of "Hymn." Little boys whistled part of Dvorak's

New World Symphony as they played marbles. When asked the name of the song, they'd reply "Oh, 'Going Home.'" They played potsy, humming "The Soldiers' Chorus" from *Faust* which they called "Glory."

Not as well loved as Mr. Morton, but as much admired, was Miss Bernstone, the special drawing teacher who also came once a week. Ah, she was from another world, a world of beautiful dresses of muted greens and garnets. Her face was sweet and tender, and, like Mr. Morton, she loved the vast hordes of unwashed and unwanted children more than she loved the cared-for ones. The teachers did not like *her*. Yes, they fawned on her when she spoke to them and glowered at her when her back was turned. They were jealous of her charm, her sweetness and her lovely appeal to men. She was warm and glowing and richly feminine. They knew that she didn't sleep alone nights as they were forced to do.

She spoke softly in a clear singing voice. Her hands were beautiful and quick with a bit of chalk or a stick of charcoal. There was magic in the way her wrist turned when she held a crayon. One wrist twist and there was an apple. Two more twists and there was a child's sweet hand holding the apple. On a rainy day, she wouldn't give a lesson. She'd take a block of paper and a stick of charcoal and sketch the poorest, meanest kid in the room. And when the picture was finished, you didn't see the dirt or the meanness; you saw the glory of innocence and the poignancy of a baby growing up too soon. Oh, Miss Bernstone was grand.

These two visiting teachers were the gold and silver sunsplash in the great muddy river of school days, days made up of dreary hours in which Teacher made her pupils sit rigid with their hands folded behind their back while she read a novel hidden in her lap. If all the teachers had been like Miss Bernstone and Mr. Morton, Francie would have known plain what heaven was. But it was just as well. There had to be the dark and muddy waters so that the sun could have something to background its flashing glory.

Questions for Discussion and Debate

1. What made Mr. Morton, the music teacher, and Miss Bernstone, the art teacher, so special?

   a. Identify some of the specific teaching techniques they used to make the children love them and their lessons.

   b. Consider how you might apply some of those techniques to your subject matter and lessons. Share your ideas with your peers.

   c. Contrast Miss Bernstone and Mr. Morton with the other teachers and with Teacher, in particular.

2. Share with the class your own experiences in school with the "dark and muddy waters" and the sun in "its flashing glory." In other words, describe the qualities of a teacher who had a positive influence on you and of one who did not. Explain the effects each of these teachers had on who you are today. Then, together with your peers, make up a list of all of those qualities of your favorite teachers. Try to reach a consensus on which three qualities are the most important. Analyze yourself in relation to those qualities.

3. Discuss and debate strategies and curriculum that teacher education programs should

include to assure that their preservice teachers will develop the qualities your class identified in question 2.

4. Both Mr. Morton and Miss Bernstone are specialists. Discuss the role of the specialists in your school. How are they scheduled in? What are the students' attitudes toward them and other teachers' attitudes toward having them?

5. Mr. Morton's behavior as a teacher perfectly reflects how to integrate all of the formal teaching domains into a lesson. For example, he demonstrates how he uses his head (knowledge, or the cognitive domain), heart (attitudes or affective domain), and hands (skills or psychomotor domain) in his teaching of music. With your class analyze a lesson plan of yours/theirs to see if all three domains are reflected in the objectives. Discuss observations you have made of teachers who weave these domains throughout their lessons.

Activities and Projects

1. One of the reasons the students loved Mr. Morton and Miss Bernstone was because it was clear to them that these teachers loved their subject and their students. Students generally become excited about a subject when they see their teacher's excitement. One way of bringing that passion to your teaching is by integrating an interest, hobby, or talent of yours into some of your lessons. What is your personal passion? Cooking? Skiing? Poetry? Folk music?

   a. Design a lesson in which you integrate your interest or talent with the subject matter you are expected to teach.

   b. Then become a STAR (Student Teacher as Researcher) and see if you can devise an experiment whereby you teach a similar lesson to two similar groups, one lesson integrating your personal interest and the other one without it. Observe the differences in the learning of the subject matter between the two groups. Did the use of your personal passion make a difference?

   This kind of original experiment—and there are thousands you could develop and do in the classroom—makes use of the *scientific method* that John Dewey, philosopher of education (chapter 3), believed was important for teachers to carry out in order to establish effective practices. Following are the steps of the scientific method, also listed in chapter 3. Use these steps to carry out experiment 1b with your lesson plans, or substitute the library for the classroom and see if there are studies that confirm the hypothesis that teachers who use their personal talents and interests in their lessons meet with success in terms of student learning.

Steps of the Scientific Method

1. Begin with your question (i.e., Will integrating my personal interest make a difference in learning among my students?).

2. Optional: Do some informal initial research or experimentation.

3. Develop a hypothesis.

4. Do research (that is, actively carry out steps of your experiment or consult similar experiments described in journals in order to test your hypothesis).

5. Observe results. Weigh evidence. (Ask questions during this process, such as, What variables could have influenced the outcome? Did I keep everything constant except the experimental variable, i.e., my personal passion? In the case of library research, what are the possible flaws or biases in this person's study?)

6. If evidence supports the hypothesis, form a conclusion. (Continue to test to see if the hypothesis is reliably, consistently supported. If it is, then you might be able to formulate a theory!) If evidence does not support the hypothesis, create a new one and test it.

2. This excerpt portrays some teachers as jealous of other teachers who appear to be more creative, self-reliant, and confident than they are. Have you seen such behavior among teachers? If so, how does this jealous attitude affect the school environment? Talk to teachers, both beginning and veteran, about this phenomenon, why they think jealousy exists, and, also, what, if anything, can be done about it.

3. Writes Smith (1943), "The cruelest teachers were those who had come from homes similar to those of the poor children. It seemed that in their bitterness towards those . . .

little ones, they were somehow exorcizing their own fearful background" (p. 130).

Talk to a psychologist or mental-health expert about the validity of this possibility. Do research on the mental illnesses or common personality disorders that are found among teachers.

4. Often art and music specialists are let go when school finances are tight. Discuss this situation with your peers. Focus on the role that art and music do and should play in education. Consider developing a questionnaire in which you survey attitudes of teachers, students, parents, school committees, and the general public regarding these specialists. In addition, do research on what policies exist in school systems and state education departments regarding art and music within the curriculum. After doing your research, draw up a position statement in which you express your personal perspective on the role that art, music, and other specialties should play within a school.

5. Often it is difficult to remove incompetent, unethical, and bigoted teachers from the profession because of tenure, although tenure can be defended as well as criticized. Do research on this issue and hold a formal debate on tenure: yes or no? Present the debate in front of other teacher education classes.

1.7　*The Chocolate War* (1974)

Robert Cormier

Evil exists in the world and some of that evil resides in teachers. So Robert Cormier would have us believe in *The Chocolate War,* a chilling novel about the misuse of power at Trinity, a New England boarding school for boys. Brother Leon is portrayed as a cool, sadistic, ambitious, and scheming Machiavellian, that is, someone who will use any means to accomplish his goal. In this case, the goal is to sell 20,000 boxes of chocolates, or rather, to get the boys to sell them, as a means of raising funds for the school. Leon must pull in funds this particular year because he has abused his power of attorney while acting as interim headmaster and spent money on the stock of chocolates, money that the school didn't have in the first place. If the sale is not successful, his overextension of the school's finances will be discovered (Cormier, 1974, p. 119).

Jerry Renault, the hero of this novel and a student at the school, is at this time pondering his identity. A poster in his locker reads, "Do I dare disturb the universe?" a phrase from T. S. Eliot that had "moved him mysteriously" (Cormier, 1974, p. 97). He decides not to sell the chocolates, thus defying tradition and, worse, Brother Leon. When the sale appears to be flagging, Brother Leon intimidates Archie Costello, leader of the Vigils, a secret school society, into having the Vigils spearhead the sale. Archie, himself a master of intimidation, then puts pressure on Jerry, threatening to punish him if he doesn't conform and accept the chocolates.

At first Jerry becomes a hero for refusing to sell the chocolates, but his defiance is a threat to Archie, the Vigils, and Brother Leon, and eventually there is a showdown.

This excerpt reveals one of the many incidents in which Brother Leon's sadistic behavior and lack of ethics reduce a student, in this case, David Caroni, to a quaking mass. Leon implies, not too subtly, that he will give Caroni an undeserved failing grade if he doesn't give him information about Renault's behavior. He blackmails Caroni into telling him about Jerry's behavior, although it turns out that even Caroni doesn't know the whole story.

Do Brother Leon's intimidating threats and probing surprise you? Have you ever observed—or been on the receiving end of—such teacher behavior? Do you believe that teachers ever get away with such behavior? Ponder these questions as you read this excerpt. Think also about what ethical standards should guide teacher behavior.

"Such a terrible mark, Caroni."

"I know, I know."

"And you are usually such a spléndid scholar."

"Thank you, Brother Leon."

"How are your other marks?"

"Fine, Brother, fine. In fact, I thought . . . I mean, I was aiming for high honors this term. But now, this *F* . . ."

"I know," the teacher said, shaking his head sorrowfully, in commiseration.

Caroni was confused. He had never received an *F* before in his life. In fact, he had seldom received a mark lower than an *A*. In the seventh and eighth grades at St. Jude's, he had received straight *A*'s for two years except for a *B*-plus one term. He had scored so high on the Trinity entrance exam that he had been awarded one of the rare Trinity scholarships— one hundred dollars contributed toward his tuition, and his picture in the paper. And then this terrible *F*, a routine test turning into a nightmare.

"The *F* surprised me as well," Brother Leon said. "Because you are such an excellent student, David."

Caroni looked up in sudden wonder and hope. Brother Leon seldom called a student by his first name. He always kept a distance between himself and his pupils. "There is an invisible line between teacher and student," he always said, "and it must not be crossed." But, now, hearing him pronounce "David" in such friendly fashion and with such gentleness and understanding, Caroni allowed himself to hope—but for what? Had the *F* been a mistake, after all?

"This was a difficult test for several reasons," the teacher went on. "One of those exams where the wrong, subtle interpretation of the facts made the difference between pass and fail. In fact, that was it exactly—a pass-fail test. And when I read your answer, David, for a moment I thought it was possible that you had passed. In many respects you were correct in your assertions. But, on the other hand . . ." His voice trailed away, he seemed deep in thought, troubled.

Caroni waited. A horn blew outside—the school bus lumbering away. He thought of his father and mother and what they would do when they learned of the *F.* It would drag down his average—it was almost impossible to overcome an *F* no matter how many other *A*'s he managed to make.

"One thing students don't always realize, David," Brother Leon went on, speaking softly, intimately, as if there were no one in the world except them, as if he had never talked to anyone in the world the way he was talking to David at this moment, "one thing they don't grasp is that teachers are human too. Human like other people." Brother Leon smiled as if he had made a joke. Caroni allowed himself a small smile, unsure of himself, not wanting to do the wrong thing. The classroom was suddenly warm, it seemed crowded although there were just the two of them there. "Yes, yes, we are all too human. We have our good days and our bad days. We get tired. Our judgment sometimes becomes impaired. We sometimes—as the boys say—goof. It's possible even for us to make mistakes correcting papers, especially when the answers are not cut and dried, not one thing or another, not all black nor all white . . ."

Caroni was all ears now, alert—what was Brother Leon driving at? He looked sharply at Brother Leon. The teacher looked as he always did—the moist eyes that reminded Caroni of boiled onions, the pale damp skin, and the cool talk, always under control. He held a piece of white chalk in his hand like a cigarette. Or maybe like a miniature pointer.

"Did you ever hear a teacher admit that it's possible for him to make a mistake, David? Ever hear that before?" Brother Leon asked, laughing.

"Like an umpire saying he made the wrong call," Caroni said, joining in the teacher's little joke. But why the joke? Why all this talk of mistakes?

"Yes, yes," Leon agreed. "No one is without error. And it's understandable. We all have our duties and we must discharge them. The Headmaster is still in the hospital and I take it as a privilege to act in his behalf. Besides this, there are the extra-curricular activities. The chocolate sale, for instance . . ."

Brother Leon's grip was tight on the piece of chalk. Caroni noticed how his knuckles were almost as white as the chalk itself. He waited for the teacher to continue. But there was only silence. Caroni watched the chalk in Brother Leon's hands, the way the teacher pressed it, rolled it, his fingers like the legs of pale spiders with a victim in their clutch.

"But it's all rewarding," Leon went on. How was it that his voice was so cool when the hand holding the chalk was so tense, the veins sticking out, as if threatening to burst through the flesh?

"Rewarding?" Caroni had lost the thread of Brother Leon's thought.

"The chocolate sale," Leon said.

And the chalk split in his hand.

"For instance," Leon said, dropping the pieces and opening the ledger that was so familiar to everyone at Trinity, the ledger in which the daily sales were recorded. "Let me see—you have done fine in the sale, David. Eighteen boxes sold. Fine. Fine. Not only are you an excellent scholar but you possess school spirit."

Caroni blushed with pleasure—it was impossible for him to resist a compliment, even when he was all mixed up as he certainly was at the moment. All this talk of exams and teachers getting tired and making mistakes and now the chocolate sale . . . and the two pieces of broken chalk abandoned on the desk, like white bones, dead men's bones.

"If everyone did his part like you, David, the sale would be an instant success. Of course, not everyone has your spirit, David . . ."

Caroni wasn't sure what tipped him off. Maybe the way Brother Leon paused at this point. Maybe the entire conversation, all of it off-key somehow. Or maybe the chalk in Brother Leon's hands, the way he had snapped it in two while his voice remained cool and easy—which was the phony thing: the hand holding the chalk, all tense and nervous, or the cool, easy voice?

"Take Renault, for instance," Brother Leon continued. "Funny thing about him, isn't it?"

And Caroni knew. He found himself staring into the moist watchful eyes of the teacher and in a blinding flash he knew what this was all about, what was happening, what Brother Leon was doing, the reason for this little conversation after school. A headache began to assert itself above his right eye, the pain digging into his flesh—migraine. His stomach lurched sickeningly. Were teachers like everyone else, then? Were teachers as corrupt as the villains you read about in books or saw in movies and televison? He'd always worshiped his teachers, had thought of becoming a teacher himself someday if he could overcome his shyness. But now—this. The pain grew in intensity, throbbing in his forehead.

"Actually, I feel badly for Renault," Brother Leon was saying. "He must be a very troubled boy to act this way."

"I guess so," Caroni said, stalling, uncertain of himself and yet knowing really what Brother Leon wanted. He had seen Brother Leon every day in the classroom calling out the names and had watched him recoil as if from a blow when Jerry Renault continued to refuse the chocolates. It had become a kind of joke among the fellows. Actually, Caroni had felt badly for Jerry Renault. He knew that no kid was a match for Brother Leon. But now he realized that Brother Leon had been the victim. He must have been climbing the walls all this time, David thought.

"Well, David."

And the echo of his name here in the classroom startled him. He wondered if he still had aspirins left in his locker. Forget the aspirins, forget the headache. He knew now what the score was, what Leon was waiting to hear. Yet, could he be sure?

"Speaking of Jerry Renault . . ." Caroni said—a safe beginning, a statement he could draw back from, depending on Brother Leon's reaction.

"Yes?"

The hand had picked up one of the pieces of chalk again, and that "Yes?" had been too quick, too sudden to allow any doubt. Caroni found himself hung up between choices and the headache didn't help matters. Could he erase that *F* by telling Brother Leon simply what he wanted to hear? What was so terrible about that? On the other hand, an *F* could ruin him. And how about all the other *F*'s it was possible that Leon could give him in the future?

"Funny thing about Jerry Renault," Caroni heard himself saying. And then instinct caused him to add, "But I'm sure you know what it's all about, Brother Leon. The Vigils. The assignment . . ."

"Of course, of course," Leon said, sitting back, letting the chalk fall gently from his hand.

"It's a Vigil stunt. He's supposed to refuse to sell chocolates for ten days—ten school days—and then accept them. Boy, those Vigils, they're really something, aren't they?" His head was killing him and his stomach was a sea of nausea.

"Boys will be boys," Leon was saying, nodding his head, his voice a whisper—it was hard to tell whether he was surprised or relieved. "Knowing Trinity's spirit, it was obvious, of course. Poor Renault. You remember, Caroni, that I said he must be troubled. Terrible, to force a boy into that kind of situation, against his will. But it's all over then, isn't it? The ten days—why they're up, let's see, tomorrow." He was smiling now, gayly, and talking as if the words themselves didn't matter but that it was important to talk, as if the words were safety valves. And then Caroni realized that Brother Leon had used his name but this time he hadn't said *David* . . .

"Well, I guess that's it then," Brother Leon said, rising, "I've detained you too long, Caroni."

"Brother Leon," Caroni said. He couldn't be dismissed at this point. "You said you wanted to discuss my mark . . . "

"Oh, yes, yes, that's right, my boy. That *F* of yours."

Caroni felt doom pressing upon him. But went on anyway. "You said teachers make mistakes, they get tired . . . "

Brother Leon was standing now. "Tell you what, Caroni. At the end of the term, when the marks close, I'll review that particular test. Perhaps I'll be fresher then. Perhaps I'll see merit that wasn't apparent before . . . "

Now it was Caroni's turn to feel relief from the tension, although his headache still pounded and his stomach was still upset. Worse than that, however, he had allowed Brother Leon to blackmail him. If teachers did this kind of thing, what kind of world could it be?

"On the other hand, Caroni, perhaps the *F* will stand," Brother Leon said. "It depends . . . "

"I see, Brother Leon," Caroni said.

And he did see—that life was rotten, that there were no heroes, really, and that you couldn't trust anybody, not even yourself.

He had to get out of there as fast as possible, before he vomited all over Brother Leon's desk.

Questions for Discussion and Debate

1. Summarize the encounter between David Caroni and Brother Leon. Specify the nature of the blackmailing episode.

2. Because Cormier is an effective writer he is able to put words in Brother Leon's mouth that, on the face of it, sound reasonable and just, yet convey without question the sarcasm and sadism beneath. Identify examples of these pretenses.

3. Have you ever encountered a teacher whose veneer was caring but whose feelings were, in fact, quite the opposite? How could you tell?

(" . . . the hand holding the chalk, all tense and nervous" while his voice remained cool and easy [Cormier, 1974, p. 85]). What was the circumstance and how did you feel about the situation?

4. Teachers are role models for students whether they like it or not. Being a role model, however, is not always so easy. Should teachers pretend to be one kind of person in school while they may act differently at home? Debate this statement: Teachers' personal lives should be a reflection of the professional role they are expected to fulfill.

Also, how honest should teachers be with students about their position on controversial issues involving standards of morality? For example, take a position on this question: Should a teacher who believes in a woman's right to choose abortion state this *personal* view forthrightly if a student asks him or her about the morality of abortion?

Activities and Projects

1. Clearly Brother Leon not only acted unethically toward David by trying to blackmail him, but also broke school law by abusing his power of attorney and ·overextending school funds. What is your definition of an ethical person? The NEA's (1975) "Code of Ethics of the Education Profession" is perhaps the best guiding statement for teachers and administrators. Among its provisions are these two: "The educator . . . shall not intentionally expose the student to embarrassment or disparagement . . . [and] . . . shall not use professional relationships with students for private advantage."

   Clearly Brother Leon abused these ethical standards.

   Find out what clout the NEA's "Code of Ethics" would have had if Brother Leon had been employed by a public school. Talk to a teachers' union president, an administrator, a school committee member, and a lawyer about what recourse a school system has when faced with a teacher's unethical behavior. What consequences do *you* think are appropriate in responding to behavior such as Brother Leon's?

   Try to locate an example of a real case with which a school system had to deal.

2. Make a list of ethical standards to which you believe teachers should be held accountable. Then locate or send for the NEA's (1975) "Code of Ethics" or your own state's educa-

tion code and see what else it contains. Compare your list of standards with these codes.

3. Take the following scenario and do an improvisation integrating your perspective on how a school committee or principal should deal with this unethical situation:

   Evidence indicates that a guidance counselor has purposely lowered the grades of two students while he was transferring them from their teachers' grade sheets to the students' transcripts. These two students' averages *and* the counselor's son's average put them all in line for selection as valedictorian. The evidence of his grade tampering comes to light. What do the principal and school committee do?

4. Brother Leon might be a perfect person for a psychologist to analyze in terms of his dysfunctional personality. Sadly, there are such teachers. On the other hand, there are more teachers with healthy personalities.

   Abraham Maslow (1908–1970) developed humanist psychology, which involves the study of characteristics of healthy people. Maslow claimed that if their basic needs are met, people can live happy, productive lives. He developed a hierarchy of those needs, the ultimate one being the need for self-actualization, or the self-fulfillment and realization of one's potential. The healthiest of all personalities belongs to the self-actualized individual. Maslow (1968) studied the lives of a number of successful people and tried to identify the common qualities that accounted for their success, or self-actualization. He also believed that the most successful teachers, *his* best teachers, had achieved self-actualization. Following are a few of the characteristics of such people. Which qualities do you believe you exhibit? Think of your favorite teacher. Was he or she self-actualized?

- Perceive reality better than most individuals.

- Accept themselves, others, and the natural world without worrying about what they cannot control.

- Are spontaneous in their thought and behavior but seldom do bizarre or unusual things.

- Identify with the rest of humanity in a positive way.

- Maintain deep emotional relationships with a limited number of people.

- Are democratic in their values and attitudes and free of prejudice.

- Enjoy the process of reaching a goal as much as the achievement itself.

- Are capable of great creativity, often in a number of different fields (Green & Sanford, 1983).

1.8 "Professional Standards for Teachers" (2001)

Massachusetts Department of Education

The "Professional Standards for Teachers" are part of the document, *Regulations for Educator Licensure and Preparation Program Approval,* prepared by the Massachusetts Department of Education. These standards define the "pedagogical and other professional knowledge and skills required of all teachers" and are "used by teacher preparation programs in preparing their candidates. . . . " Each state education department issues such standards for its prospective teachers, and while there are some differences among these documents, they have a lot in common in terms of defining pedagogical behavior. The Massachusetts standards are divided into five major categories: (a) Plans Curriculum and Instruction, (b) Delivers Effective Instruction, (c) Manages Classroom Climate and Operation, (d) Promotes Equity, and (e) Meets Professional Responsibilities.

Approach these standards with a critical eye since such lists are open to revision on a frequent basis. Perhaps before reading through the list of standards, you might try making a list of standards that you think would be appropriate under each of the five categories. Then compare your list to the following standards.

STANDARDS FOR ALL TEACHERS EXCEPT LIBRARY TEACHERS

(a) Plans Curriculum and Instruction

1. Draws on content of the relevant curriculum frameworks to plan activities addressing standards that will advance students' level of content knowledge.

a. Identifies prerequisite skills, concepts, and vocabulary that students need to know in order to be successful in a learning activity.

    b. Identifies reading and writing needs that must be addressed for successful learning.

2. Plans sequential units of study that make learning cumulative and that are based on the learning standards in the frameworks.

3. Draws on results of formal and informal assessments as well as knowledge of human development to plan learning activities appropriate for the full range of students within a classroom.

4. Plans lessons with clear objectives and relevant measurable outcomes.

5. Plans the pedagogy appropriate to the specific discipline and to the age and cognitive level of the students in the classroom.

6. Seeks resources from colleagues, families, and the community to enhance learning.

7. Incorporates appropriate technology and media in lesson planning.

8. Uses information in Individualized Education Programs (IEPs) to plan strategies for integrating students with disabilities into general education classrooms.

(b) Delivers Effective Instruction

1. Communicates high standards and expectations when beginning the lesson:

    a. Makes learning objectives clear to students.

    b. Communicates clearly in writing and speaking.

    c. Finds engaging ways to begin a new unit of study or lesson.

    d. Builds on students' prior knowledge and experience.

2. Communicates high standards and expectations when carrying out the lesson:

    a. Uses a balanced approach to teaching skills and concepts of elementary reading and writing.

    b. Employs a variety of teaching techniques from more teacher-directed strategies such as direct instruction, practice, and Socratic dialogue, to less teacher-directed approaches such as discussion, problem solving, cooperative learning, and research projects (among others) as they apply to the content area being taught.

    c. Employs a variety of reading and writing strategies for addressing learning objectives.

    d. Uses questioning to stimulate thinking and encourages all students to respond.

    e. Uses instructional technology appropriately.

3. Communicates high standards and expectations when extending and completing the lesson:

    a. Assigns homework or practice that furthers student learning and checks it.

    b. Provides regular and frequent feedback to students on their progress.

    c. Provides many and varied opportunities for students to achieve competence.

4. Communicates high standards and expectations when evaluating student learning:

    a. Accurately measures student achievement of, and progress toward, the learning objectives with a variety of formal and informal assessments, and uses results to plan further instruction.

b. Translates evaluations of student work into records that accurately convey the level of student achievement to students, parents or guardians, and school personnel.

(c) Manages Classroom Climate and Operation

1. Creates an environment that is conducive to learning.

2. Creates a physical environment appropriate to a range of learning activities.

3. Maintains appropriate standards of behavior, mutual respect, and safety.

4. Manages classroom routines and procedures without loss of significant instructional time.

(d) Promotes Equity

1. Encourages all students to believe that effort is a key to achievement.

2. Works to promote achievement by all students without exception.

3. Assesses the significance of student differences in home experiences, background knowledge, learning skills, learning pace, and proficiency in the English language for learning the curriculum at hand and uses professional judgment to determine if instructional adjustments are necessary.

4. Helps all students to understand American civic culture, its underlying ideals, founding political principles, and political institutions, and to see themselves as members of a local, state, national, and international civic community.

(e) Meets Professional Responsibilities

1. Understands his or her legal and moral responsibilities.

2. Conveys knowledge of and enthusiasm for his/her academic discipline to students.

3. Maintains interest in current theory, research, and developments in the academic discipline and exercises judgment in accepting implications or findings as valid for application in classroom practice.

4. Participates in building a professional community by collaborating with colleagues to continuously improve instruction, assessment, and student achievement.

5. Works actively to involve parents in their child's academic activities and performance, and communicates clearly with them.

6. Reflects critically upon his or her teaching experience, identifies areas for further professional development as part of a professional development plan that is linked to grade level, school, and district goals, and is receptive to suggestions for growth.

7. Understands legal and ethical issues as they apply to responsible and acceptable use of the Internet and other resources.

Questions for Discussion and Debate

1. Critically assess this list of standards for teachers by identifying in writing:

   a. Any standards that you think are inappropriate.

   b. Any omissions (that is, are there certain standards or categories that should be added?).

c. Where wording might be changed to increase clarity.

d. Whether or not the standards are realistic and attainable.

2. These standards are the criteria upon which teacher education candidates in Massachusetts are judged before they are granted their initial license. Supervisors and cooperating teachers observe the candidates while they do their student teaching to see if they are fulfilling the standards. With this fact in mind, carry on a debate of the following resolution, with one side arguing the affirmative and the other the negative position: Resolved, that it is fair and appropriate to expect student teachers—by the end of their practica—to demonstrate *all* of the standards listed in the "Professional Standards for Teachers." (See "Debate Format," Appendix A, for instructions on how to carry on a formal debate, or discuss the resolution informally.)

3. In small groups, reach a consensus on what you consider to be the single most important standard listed under *each* of the five categories, a–e. Provide reasons for your choices. Then compare your group's five standards to those chosen by the other groups in the class.

Activities and Projects

1. Locate sets of professional teaching standards from at least two other states, your own included, and compare them to the standards in the Massachusetts document. After determining the similarities and differences, share that information with the class and together decide on the strengths and weaknesses of each set. (Most state education departments publish their standards on the Internet.)

2. Read (or reread, as the case may be) the selections that appear in this chapter. Then, using the list of standards like a chart, write down next to each standard the page number on which appears a teacher who has either implemented *or* disregarded a standard. Share some of these examples with the class.

3. Visit one or more classrooms and observe the teacher for at least 1 hour. Note which of the behaviors or standards the teacher exhibits and in what ways he or she demonstrates certain ones. Hold a discussion with the teacher afterward in which you ask how he or she carries out some of the other standards you did not get to observe. If you are now in a practicum, ask someone to observe *you* in terms of the standards and then prepare a self-evaluation. Use this assessment as *you* work toward demonstrating all of the standards.

4. In Appendix C is a sample lesson plan format. (It is only one of *many* ways to arrange a lesson plan.) Study the plan and then prepare a lesson using that format. (The content of the lesson will depend on whether you are going to teach this lesson to your peers or to students in your practicum, should you be doing one at this time.) See how many of the professional standards you can satisfy as you fill in the sections of the lesson plan and present it to your peers or your students.

5. In his memoir, *'Tis,* former high-school English teacher and Pulitzer Prize-winning author Frank McCourt (1999) writes about

his teaching experiences. In his first teaching job, at a vocational high school, the Academic Chairman tells him what is expected. Included among his school's "standards" are the following:

- Make sure students keep notebooks clean and neat and their textbooks covered.

- Check to see that windows are open six inches from the top.

- Never ask a question requiring a yes or no answer.

- Insist on boys removing their hats (McCourt, 1999, p. 231).

Day-to-day rules or standards like these imparted by principals and other administrators, at best, are helpful in keeping order and safety in the classroom and, at worst, exemplify how professionally prepared teachers are treated like imbeciles.

Invite a cross section of K–12 teachers and administrators to your class and moderate a forum, "Where Do State Teaching Standards Intersect with Local Standards? Is There Need for Reform?" Consider inviting members of the school committee and others to participate. If appropriate, invite the press to report on the forum.

Short of carrying out the above suggestion, consider reading McCourt's book. His tales will provide endless springboards for discussion about what constitutes appropriate professional behavior.

6. There are no behaviors prescribed in these lists of professional standards for *how* teachers should adjust their curriculum to meet the academic and emotional needs of their students during a national crisis such as that brought on by the terrorist attacks of September 11, 2001, and the threats to the nation's security that followed. Teachers must look elsewhere to answer such questions as:

a. What are the best methods for helping students grasp the realities of a crisis?

b. How can they help students cope with and, ultimately, respond to tragedy?

c. To what extent are increased patriotic expressions appropriate, and at what point do these expressions cross the line of constitutional behavior? (For example, the debate was renewed on whether or not states should require students to say the Pledge of Allegiance on a daily basis. Twenty-four states have laws requiring the recitation of the Pledge even though a 1943 ruling by the Supreme Court, *West Virginia State Board of Education* v. *Barnette*, prohibits mandatory recitation.)

d. How can we respond to terrorists while protecting the civil liberties Americans have treasured? (For example, during World War II, over 100,000 Japanese Americans were deprived of their right to due process of law when the government ordered them from their homes into relocation camps. Subsequently, the government acknowledged that this was a mistake and paid reparations to the internees. With this history in mind, many teachers and others expressed concern about the acts of some citizens who, angered by the September 11 attacks, lashed out against innocent Arab and Muslim Americans.)

e. To what extent should teachers interrupt their regular curriculum schedule to address tragic events and related issues? (Some teachers are reluctant to address current events since such material will not be on the standardized tests for which they must prepare their students. Granted, there is some comfort and reassurance when teachers *do* proceed with their normal routines and curriculum.)

f. What can be done to expand students' knowledge of other cultures, world geography, world religions, modern warfare, and their own culture?

g. Why has America become a target of terrorists?

h. How can art, music, and literature be utilized in the classroom to clarify the crisis and help students heal? (For example, several of Norman Rockwell's paintings, including *The Golden Rule,* in chapter 6, remind students about the importance of tolerance and freedom.)

i. What activities can teachers develop to empower students at a time when they may feel powerless? (Several students responded to the September 11 tragedy by raising money to assist the children of police officers and firefighters who died trying to save lives; others created works of art locally to express their feelings.)

A variety of educational publications had the previous questions in mind as they tried to meet the needs of teachers following the September 11 attacks (Borja, 2001; Chartock, 2001; Sandham, 2001; "Teaching about Tragedy," 2001; Wyatt, 2001).

Interview a cross section of teachers about how *they* responded to the events of September 11, 2001. In addition to asking them some of the questions listed here, create some of your own. Share the results of your interviews. Consider submitting your findings in the form of an article to an educational journal or a local newspaper. You will find that it is never too early to begin doing original research and contributing to the educational literature.

1.9 ▌ *Among Schoolchildren* (1989)

Tracy Kidder

Chris Zajac, a fifth-grade teacher in Holyoke, Massachusetts, was shadowed by Tracy Kidder for a year, and the result is the book *Among Schoolchildren*. Kidder's reportorial style is so sensitive to detail that you feel you are witnessing firsthand the daily routines—the ups and downs–of teaching in an inner-city school, from the frustrations that come with students' misbehavior to the rewards that come with making an emotional or intellectual connection with a child. Mrs. Zajac is a teacher who makes a difference in children's lives. The book should be required reading for those who continue to believe that teaching is a cushy job that ends at 3:30 p.m. each day and offers a carefree summer.

Mrs. Zajac is a teacher who brings her job home with her, and that homework includes her concern for the development of Pam Hunt, a student interning in her classroom. This excerpt focuses on Mrs. Zajac in her roles as cooperating teacher and classroom manager, or, more precisely, disciplinarian. She shares with Pam the wisdom she gained about discipline from several years in the trenches. You might even feel a little jittery as you read this excerpt, so clear are the descriptions of the students' antics, both verbal and physical, that Pam has to contend with while left on her own in the class. This excerpt can serve as a minitext on classroom management, an area over which many student teachers agonize.

As you read this excerpt, put yourself in Pam's place and decide what you would have done in each instance. Would you have responded the same way that Pam did to the "Clarences" and "Roberts" in the class? To what extent do you think Pam's responses were spur-of-the-moment, as opposed to being the result of previous reflection and planning ahead for such misbehavior? Evaluate Mrs. Zajac in her cooperating teacher role. In the end, after meeting some of the most difficult children, see if you feel, as Mrs. Zajac does, that even the most troubled children have qualities about them that endear them to you forever.

Now when Chris drove down to the Flats, the canals steamed in frigid air. She started wearing her green cloth winter coat, which would answer for all the seasons and all the fashion she needed from now until after St. Patrick's Day. For her week of recess duty in November, she brought wool socks to slip over her stockings before going outside. The first snowstorm struck just before Thanksgiving. At home that evening Chris kept peering out windows; Billy told their son, "Mom's on blizzard alert," the way he always did; and Chris spent the next day at home, rejoicing about snow days until nightfall, when she got out her homework and reminded herself that this day would still be served, tacked on to June. A few small epidemics passed through the class, and children with puffy eyes and reddened noses, walking Petri dishes, were driven home by the outreach workers, leaving temporary holes in the room.

In October, fire had gutted the tenement where Lisette lived with her mother and her mother's boyfriend. The girl moved away in November. Chris had set out, as her first goal for Lisette, to get the girl to smile, and though Chris had succeeded only a few times, she had begun to see flickers of aptitude, if not of great interest, in the girl. Lisette had written compositions about several boyfriends, and of "rapping" with them, sometimes with two on the same day. Unfortunately, Chris, who always had to play catch-up with the latest student lingo, did not know until long after Lisette had left that "rapping" had acquired new meanings, which ranged from kissing to intercourse. Chris mourned Lisette's departure: "I thought I was making some progress with her. And now where is she?" As for the children, only Clarence, as usual noting any change in the room, mentioned the fact of Lisette's empty desk.

The potted plant on the corner of Chris's desk died from lack of water. A teacher friend had sent it to Chris on the first day of school. It was the only plant in the room. Chris hummed the funeral dirge—"Dum dum dum, dum da-dum da-dum da-dum"—and dumped the withered remnant in the wastebasket, saying, "I don't have time to water plants."

Massachusetts law didn't require that schoolchildren say the Pledge of Allegiance. The Jehovah's Witnesses, of whom Chris had several, weren't allowed to say it. She led the class through the Pledge only once that fall. The exercise turned up the fact that Clarence wasn't quite sure which hand was his right, which suggested that there might be better things, arguably more patriotic, for Chris to do with those few hurried minutes before math.

That fall, Chris ran the class and Pam practiced on them for a while every day. For the first several weeks Chris sat in on Pam's lessons, and afterward gave her advice. Pam tried to cover too much ground; Chris showed her how to plan against the clock. Pam spoke too softly. "We need to give you a mean, horrid voice like mine," Chris told her. All in all, Chris felt pleased about Pam's teaching. She liked the way Pam enfolded her lessons in games for the children. She could tell that Pam labored over her lesson plans. Pam came from Westfield State, which was Chris's alma mater. Chris imagined her planning at night in her dormitory room, just as Chris had done in her own practice-teaching days. One time Chris told Pam, "Jimmy loves you," and Pam replied, "I think I'd rather have him hate me and do his work." Chris felt pleased. Pam had the right instincts, Chris thought.

Above all, Chris approved of the emotion that Pam brought to the job. In Chris's philosophy, a brand new teacher needed to feel strong affection for her first students in order to sustain her. The first days of school, when Pam merely sat as an observer in the back of the room, Chris spied on her, including Pam in the searchlight sweeps she made of the room. She saw Pam gazing fondly at the children. Some, especially Clarence and Felipe, kept turning around at their desks to smile at Pam. Pam hunched her shoulders and smiled back, a smile she might have used to entertain a baby in a crib. Pam was falling in love with these children, Chris thought, and the gentle spectacle took her back to her own first class, to a time when she had felt that there never were more fetching children than the ones placed in her care, and she had indulged herself by crying a little at night, in her room at her parents' house, over her first deeply troubled student—the boy

who had stolen the class's goldfish. That boy had possessed so little sense of right and wrong that when the fish had been extracted, gasping, from his pockets, he had declared indignantly, "I didn't hurt 'em. They're still breathin'."

Chris felt confident that Pam had all the equipment to become a good teacher. She needed only to learn how to control a classroom. "The discipline part," Chris thought. "She's got all the rest of it."

At the end of her sixteen weeks of practice, Pam would have to teach the class for three entire days without Chris in the room. After the third week of school, to start breaking Pam in, Chris left her alone for a half hour to teach spelling. The first couple of times, Pam's spelling went well. On a Friday, however, Clarence struck.

Pam was trying to administer the weekly spelling test. Robert, Felipe, Arnie, and Clarence kept telling each other to shut up. As Mrs. Zajac had advised, Pam gave them all warnings, and then she wrote the next offender's name on the board: Robert. That meant he was in for recess. Robert shrugged. Then Pam wrote Clarence's name on the board, explaining that he was not to disturb the rest of the class anymore.

"So?" said Clarence, glaring.

"If you don't care, then go out and stand in the hall," said Pam. Mrs. Zajac had said to put him out there if he was disturbing the class and wouldn't stop.

"No," said Clarence.

"Yes," said Pam. But she didn't make him go. She wasn't sure how to do so. If she laid hands on the boy, he'd make a fuss, Pam thought. So, instead, she told him, "You're not impressing anyone by having that attitude. Clarence, get up and go sit at this front desk. Clarence, right now."

He obeyed, but he banged chairs as he went.

"I feel bad for the people who want to take the test and do a good job."

"So?" said Clarence angrily.

"Don't answer me back!"

She turned her back on him and read the next spelling word. Behind her, Clarence muttered, making faces at her. She wheeled around. "Clarence, get up and go stand in the hall!"

She lowered her voice. "Please."

She stood over him and said softly, "Please move your body into the hallway."

Clarence jumped up. He made a small cry. In the doorway, he turned back and said to Pam, "I'll punch you out! I'll punch you in the face!"

"All right!" Her voice hit her upper register. "You can say that to Mr. Laudato!"

Mrs. Zajac had said that you need to know your ultimate threat, which at Kelly was usually Mr. Laudato, but that you should never go to it right away. And as Pam explained later, "The reason I get wishy-washy, part of me wants to yell at him, and another part wants to wait until he's cooled down a little and I can talk to him." Now she obeyed the second impulse. She didn't take Clarence to Mr. Laudato.

Behind her, Robert was chortling. "He said he'd punch her!" Robert squirmed in his seat. Julio and Jimmy grinned at each other.

Pam returned to stand in front of the class. Behind her, Clarence edged himself around the doorjamb. He peeked in. Several children giggled. Pam turned. Clarence vanished. "Clarence, I don't want to see your face!" Pam turned back to the class to read the next spelling word. Clarence's face came back around the doorjamb, mouthing silently at her back, "Fuckin' bitch. Gonna get you." The class giggled. Clarence began to grin.

Pam went to the door. Clarence's face disappeared. She closed the door and said to the class, "I hope you'll just ignore him." But in that contest of personalities, hers as a teacher still unformed and divided, she was bound to lose.

The door was closed, but Clarence's face now appeared in the small, rectangular, gun-slit window in the door, his nose and lips distended as he pressed them against the glass. Even Judith ducked her head and shook with the giggles. Others laughed openly. "I'd appreciate it if you'd ignore him and not laugh. You're making things worse," said Pam. But how could they help it? School days were long and this was something new.

Clarence was making faces in the window, bobbing up and down in it. The sound of his drumming on the door—*bang, bang, bang,*—accompanied Miss Hunt's reading of the words for the remainder of the test.

The dénouement was predictable by then. Pam tried to talk to Clarence in the hall, and he wouldn't look at her. So she held his chin in her hand, to make him, and a few minutes later he got even with her by sneaking up behind Felipe—in the hallway, on the way to reading. Quickly thrusting both arms between Felipe's legs, Clarence lifted his friend up and dumped him, face down, on the hallway carpet. Felipe arose weeping. Clarence got suspended. Pam spent the afternoon worrying about his mother punishing him.

Chris stayed after school with Pam that day. They sat at the front table. Pam told Chris the whole story. Chris said, "You've got to remember there are twenty other kids, and you *are* getting to them. Clarence may be beyond us. We'll do our best, but don't let him ruin your time here. It's not your fault. He walked in like this. You've got to take your little advances and try to forget things like this."

Pam nodded and smiled. She had a confession to make. "The thing is, I almost cried, and then he'd know he'd gotten to me, and I'm thinking, 'He's only ten years old. I can't let him make me cry.'"

Chris went home worried. She told Billy the story. When she got to the end, she said, "Oh, God. If she had cried . . ."

Chris didn't want to preside over the destruction of a promising career. She worried that Pam would lose her enthusiasm if being alone with this class turned into torture. Chris wanted Pam to taste success, so from time to time Chris continued to sit in on some of her lessons. The children always behaved on those occasions. It was obvious why. They kept glancing at Mrs. Zajac. "If I stay in the room, she won't learn how to discipline," Chris thought. Within months Pam would become a certified teacher. Next year, probably, she would have her own class. Then there'd be no Mrs. Zajac to intervene and help out. Pam had to learn how to control a class now. So for the most part, when it was Pam's turn to teach, Chris gathered up her books and went out to the hall, and told herself as she left, "You have to sink a few times before you learn."

Chris did her own practice teaching in the old West Street School, where, war stories had it, the staff wore mittens indoors in the winter and often got bruised when breaking up fights on the playground. Chris's supervising teacher eventually left Chris alone, to teach her lessons in a dank, decrepit basement room—one day the blackboard fell off the wall. Chris found herself with a class of thirty-four children, many of whom didn't speak much English. Chris remembered coming into that room one day and finding the class bully perched on a chair with one chair leg planted on the stomach of a writhing classmate. She didn't do much real teaching, she thought, but in truth she always could manage, almost from the start, to get a class under control. Chris's skills had grown. Now she could make discipline into a game, as on the day this fall when, apparently looking elsewhere, she noticed some girls passing a piece of paper down the back row during reading. "I'm not even going to ask you for that note," Chris said ten minutes later. The girls' mouths fell open in astonishment. Chris smiled

at them. "Teachers have eyes *all around* their heads," she said. She leaned down to get her face close to the girls' faces and drew her fingers all the way around her head, as if encircling it with a scarf. "That's why I don't cut my hair shorter. I *hide* them."

Chris knew that confidence is the first prerequisite for discipline. Children obeyed her, she knew, because she expected that they would. But that kind of confidence can't be invented. Pam would have to find it herself. Chris tried to help. For an hour on Wednesday afternoons, during art and music, Chris and Pam would sit down on the brown vinyl sofa in the balcony corridor between Room 205 and the boys' lavatory. Then, and also after school, the two women would sit facing each other, both dressed in clothes fit for church, the elder looking old only in comparison to the neophyte, the rookie teacher eyeing the veteran respectfully. Pam compressed her lips and nodded as Chris gave her tips:

— No college course prepares you for the Clarences and Roberts, so don't think that you should have known how to handle them when you got here. You are doing a good job, at least as good a one as the other practice teachers in the building.

— Don't let yourself imagine that you are a cause of a troubled student's misbehavior. If you do, you become entangled in the child's problems. You must cultivate some detachment. You have to feel for troubled children, but you can't feel too much, or else you may end up hating children who don't improve.

— When teaching a lesson, don't only call on the ones with their hands up.

— While you teach, scan the room with your eyes for signs of incipient trouble.

— Don't put a child in a situation where he, for the sake of his pride, has to defy you.

— If a child starts getting "hoopy," call on him at once. Stand beside his desk while you teach the class.

— If he acts up anyway, send him to the hall. You must not allow one child to deprive the others of their lessons.

— Before you even start a lesson, wait until all the children have taken their seats. Don't try to teach until all of them have stopped talking.

That was easy for Mrs. Zajac to say. Before starting a lesson, she would simply fold her arms and, leaning a shoulder against the front chalkboard, stare at the class. The children would scurry to their desks. They'd stop talking at once. But what if Pam did that and some of them just went on talking and wandering around the room? What should she do then?

Pam wanted the class to do some work at their desks, quietly. She was trying to get Clarence to sit down first. He was walking around the room backwards. She touched his arm. He threw her hand aside and proceeded, walking backwards. She turned to Robert, who was making choking, chuffing sounds. "Robert!"

"My motor ran out of gas," Robert explained.

She turned again, and there were Felipe and Arnie wrestling on the carpet. She ordered them to stop, but while she was doing that, Courtney had gotten up from her desk and had gone over to Kimberly's to gossip.

"Courtney, go back to your desk."

"Wait a minute," said Courtney, who had never talked back before.

"No, I'm not waiting!"

Robert was babbling. "That cold. Cheat. Cheat. Cheat. Five-dollar food stamps." He stood up as Pam approached, and did a shimmy in front of her, his big belly jiggling. He was protesting that he couldn't get to work. "I don't have no book," he said.

Mrs. Zajac walked in. The sentries had failed.

"Then you go over there and get one!" thundered Mrs. Zajac.

Robert froze. His face turned pink.

Pam was trying to show a film strip about colonial days, but Clarence kept putting his hand in the beam. Then Robert put his hand in the beam. Then the usually well-behaved Julio tried it, too. Then Clarence put his hand on the rump of the colonial maid on the screen. Felipe leaned way back in his chair, laughing and laughing.

Pam stopped the film strip. She put the names Clarence, Robert, and Felipe on the board, which meant they couldn't go outside after lunch. As the class arose for lunch, Clarence said, right in front of Pam but as though she weren't there, "Lunch! I'm goin' outside."

"*I'm* goin' outside," said Robert.

As for Felipe, he refused to get up and go to lunch at all. He had his arms folded. He pouted.

"Felipe, you are going to lunch," said Pam.

"No, I ain't!"

"Yes, you are!"

"Read my lips!" said Felipe. "I'm stayin' here!"

"Tsk, tsk, tsk," said Robert.

"Because we were laughin', then she had to put my name down. I hate her! I'm sick of her!" yelled Felipe as Pam, twisting her mouth, decided to leave him there and get help.

One day, when sent to the hall, Clarence stood in the doorway, pointed a finger at Pam, and declared, "I ain't stayin' after school either." Then he watched Pam wrangle with Robert. He cheered Robert on, saying, "Crunch her, crunch her."

Pam said, "Okay, Robert, would you get up and go down the hall to the office?"

"No, please. I wanta stay," said Robert, smirking up at her.

"Robert, get up," she said. "Robert, get up."

"I wanta stay here."

"If you're going to stay here, you have to be good."

"See dat?" said Clarence from the doorway. "She doesn't make Robert go. She prejudice, too. See, she didn't get Robert."

"Shut up, Clarence," said Robert.

"Robert, go to the office," said Pam.

"No," said Robert, smirking.

Another time, Pam said to Clarence, "Shut your mouth!"

Clarence replied, "No. It's *my* mouth."

Pam said to Robert, "You can work on your story now."

"No, I can't," said Robert. "I don't know what to write."

"Use your brain," said Pam.

"My brain gooshed out," said Robert. Then he looked up at her and began beating on his cheeks, a popping sound. Then he gnawed on his hand. Then he slapped his own wrist.

"I don't want any more foolish comments!" she thundered. "Do you under-*stand*?"

Clarence watched. "She not human," he said.

Pam turned to Clarence. "You don't disturb twenty other people."

"There aren't twenty people," said Clarence. "There's . . ." He started counting.

"He knows how to count," said Robert.

Chris returned to find Pam sitting at the teacher's desk, staring out the window, with her jaw misaligned.

It wasn't as if Pam did no teaching. The children would sidle up to her table throughout the day, bringing her pictures they'd drawn and asking for help. She tutored many individually. Some of the lessons she taught without Chris in the room went smoothly. Once in a while when Miss Hunt was teaching, Judith or Alice or Arabella spoke up and told Clarence and Robert to be quiet and stop making trouble. But usually that just egged the boys on, especially Clarence. Some of those boys' responses to Pam's efforts to tame them seemed surprisingly sophisticated, as if they themselves had read handbooks on classroom management. Once, for instance, Pam turned her back on Robert, and Robert called to her, "That's right. Just ignore me."

As for Clarence, he often wrote his name and Judith's on the board, as if to claim her, but that didn't give Judith any special power over him. He told her once that she needed someone "to pop her cherry." One time, after he had been especially nasty to Pam, Judith told him, "You have the brain of a caterpillar."

Without hesitation—the lines seemed to have been already planted—Clarence replied, "I'll take yours out and put it in your hand and make you eat it." Clarence made his slow, threatening nod at Judith.

Judith looked skyward. She said to Alice, "How did God make such a mistake? He had no choice but to put Clarence on earth. He didn't want him up *there*."

On one of those bad days that fall, on the way to lunch, Judith said softly to Pam, "Are you reconsidering your decision to become a teacher?"

"No, Judith," said Pam, and she smiled. *"You* make it all worthwhile."

Judith herself had begun reconsidering her embryonic plans for becoming a teacher. She wondered why Pam kept coming back, and didn't even take a sick day. Judith believed that Pam had to be a very strong and admirable person, but even as the days of Pam's travails wore on and Clarence's antics lost their novelty, Judith still couldn't help laughing when Clarence, banished to the hall, did a soft-shoe routine for the class in the doorway. As Robert indignantly pointed out—"Hey, the teacher's laughin', you're not sposed to laugh"—even Pam couldn't always hide her amusement. For example, the day when she told the class that primates have tails, and Clarence stood up, poked out his rear end, patted it, and said, "Check out mines."

Questions for Discussion and Debate

1. This excerpt portrays a role some teachers opt to take upon themselves, that of mentor to a student teacher. Discuss what Mrs. Zajac's cooperating teacher role requires of her according to the excerpt. Then evaluate how effective Mrs. Zajac appears to be in that role. Is Mrs. Zajac someone with whom you would want to work? Why, or why not?

2. Have you had the guidance of a cooperating teacher? If so, compare her or him to Mrs. Zajac.

3. Review Chris Zajac's assessment of Pam's teaching. Why does Chris believe that Pam will be a good teacher? Cite her specific thoughts and comments.

   With which of Pam's strengths and weaknesses do you identify, if any? What do you believe are *your* greatest strengths at this point and the areas in which you need to improve?

4. Describe the disciplinary strategies Pam employs under Mrs. Zajac's guidance. Do you approve of them? Discuss alternative approaches for dealing with the "Clarences" in your classes. What approaches does Mrs. Zajac mention as being effective in her experience as a teacher?

5. Evaluate the teaching tips Chris gives to Pam. Which ones really speak to you? Why? Add your special tips to the list and share them with the class.

6. Compare your student-teaching or prepracticum experiences with Pam's. How are they the same or different?

7. At one point Pam turns her back to Clarence and returns to giving the spelling test. Some teacher educators warn student teachers, "Never turn your back to the class, never, even when you are writing on the board." Debate the wisdom and necessity of this advice, with half the class supporting this advice and the other half arguing against it.

Activities and Projects

1. "Children obeyed her, she knew, because she expected they would" (Kidder, 1989, p. 123). Teacher expectations play a significant role in the success of a class in terms of learning and behavior. Find studies that have been done on the role of teacher expectations—and there have been several. Bring your findings to the class.

2. Classroom management strategies vary from those that involve the lowest degree of teacher involvement and the least distraction from the teaching to those that are very teacher-directed and controlling. Find a number of texts dealing with classroom management models. What models do you like, and why? How does one determine the appropriateness of each model? Keep notes on the models that span the continuum from least to most teacher control. What are some examples of each? (Note: Just as teachers need a repertoire of diverse teaching strategies, so, too, must they have a repertoire of management strategies.)

3. Interview a sample of teachers about the management strategies they favor.

4. Observe several teachers and record how they deal with misbehavior. Analyze the effectiveness of their techniques and keep a record of those strategies that seemed most and least effective.

5. With your peers, draw up a formal list of "Principles of Classroom Management," integrating some of those noted in this excerpt. Post these principles on the bulletin board or the walls of the education department.

6. This excerpt makes all too clear the stresses involved in student teaching. Some of these causes of stress apply also to veteran teachers and reflect the reasons why thousands of teachers—disabled by stress-related illnesses—leave teaching. Besides the frustrations of classroom management, there are many other causes of stress: large classes, homework, parental and societal expectations or apathy, extra duties over and above teaching, not being able to reach every student, and more. How do *you* manage stress? Do research on the subject of teacher stress (and student stress) and, if possible, find out what programs exist for dealing with it. With your peers, create a list of suggestions for reducing stress that could be helpful to both beginning and experienced teachers.

7. Have you been keeping a journal of your student-teaching experiences? The fact is that writing about the frustrations you feel helps to relieve stress. Writing is a safety valve, a healthy outlet, *and* a journal can also become a useful vehicle for reflecting on your teaching and learning.

A first-year teacher, Jonas C., wrote the following in his journal. Compare his attitudes and experiences to your own and to Pam Hunt's, the student teacher in this excerpt. How are they the same or different? Discuss this question with your peers.

October 22, 1997

. . . I got flipped off by one of the kids today on the playground. Talk about being angry with the world . . . geesh. Patience hasn't always been my strong point and . . . I can't help but lose it sometimes, but I try to control myself and keep calm. It is tough though.

. . . I feel, on the one hand like I'm not doing as much as I could, and on the other like I have no idea how to successfully do more. It is hard to explain, really.

. . . It is soooooo frustrating just how much time is taken away from actual teaching time by the administration and other school sh__. This totally unexpected phenomenon makes it nearly impossible for me (and my kids) to get into any kind of groove. Grrrr.

Well, I'm beat and must go now to watch television and read teachers' editions!

1.10 "Attention, Class!!! 16 Ways to Be a Smarter Teacher" (2001)

Chuck Salter

FC, Fast Company, is a magazine whose target audience is made up of CEOs of corporations that range from universities, including Yale, to car manufacturers such as General Motors. In the December 2001 issue of *FC,* Chuck Salter, a *Fast Company* senior writer, offers this advice: A good leader must first be a good teacher; knowledge of teaching skills is a priority for top staff within a corporation if it is to be successful. He then lists 16 behaviors of great teachers based on his consultation with those who know the most about teaching: teachers themselves. He spoke with and observed all sorts: some who teach formally in classrooms; some who teach informally—in their offices, during dinner, or on the fly—as they're running companies. His experts have taught senior executives, software developers, sales reps, and MBA students, as well as middle-school students, musicians, surgeons, and other teachers.

Writes Salter, "Good teaching, it turns out, is universal. Whether the topic is a new product launch, social studies, or a triple bypass, the same principles—and many of the same techniques—apply" (p. 114). Read the following list of principles and see if you agree with him. Then reread Selection 1.8, "Professional Standards for Teachers," and decide if, together, the two lists compose a kind of handbook for first-year teachers. Can you add anything to Salter's list?

Good teaching, it turns out, is universal. Whether the topic is a new-product launch, social studies, or a triple bypass, the same principles—and many of the same techniques—apply. Are you ready to learn? Grab a desk, and open your notebooks.

1. It's not about you; it's about them. Some teachers see themselves as the designated expert whose role is to impart their knowledge to students who are empty vessels. That's the wrong metaphor, says William Rando, who has been training college-level teachers for 15 years. The best instructors see themselves as guides. They share what they know, but they understand that they are not the focus. Their students are.

"It's hard for some teachers to understand that teaching is really not about them," says Rando, who runs the Office of Teaching Fellow Preparation and Development at Yale University. "There's something counterintuitive about that. But it doesn't mean that you don't matter. It means that instead of asking, 'What am I going to do today?' you ask, 'What are my students going to do today?'"

2. Study your students. It's not enough to know your material. You need to know the people you're teaching—their talents, prior experience, and needs. Otherwise, how can you know for certain what they already know and what they need to learn? "I tell my teachers to imagine that someone called and said, 'I'm trying to get to Yale,'" says Rando. "The first question you have to ask is, 'Where are you?' You have to know where the person is starting from before you can help him reach the destination. It may sound obvious, but as teachers, we sometimes begin the journey and forget to ask our students, 'Where are you? Where are you starting from?'"

Yoheved Kaplinsky, chair of the piano department at the Juilliard School, pays attention to her students' self-awareness. (See "The Keys to Good Teaching," page 124.) "I want to see my students evaluate their own playing," she says. "That gives me an idea of how astute or delusional they are. You can listen between the lines and get a sense of their personality."

3. Students take risks when teachers create a safe environment. Learning requires vulnerability, says Michele Forman, who teaches social studies at Middlebury Union High School in Middlebury, Vermont. Students have to acknowledge what they don't know, take risks, and rethink what they thought they knew. That can be an uncomfortable—even scary—situation for anyone. A little warmth goes a long way, says Forman, the 2001 National Teacher of the Year. Like having a couch and floor pillows in one corner of the classroom. Or decorating the walls with her students' work, because "it's their space." The result is a learning environment that is emotionally, intellectually, and psychologically safe.

"If they aren't feeling well, I make them a cup of peppermint tea. If they're hungry, I feed them," says Forman. "It can be the simplest thing, but it sends an important message." Students need to know that they can trust the instructor. Hence, another Forman rule: No sarcasm in the classroom. "It creates the fear that you're going to make them look bad," she says.

4. **Great teachers exude passion as well as purpose.** The difference between a good teacher and a great one isn't expertise. It comes down to passion. Passion for the material. Passion for teaching. The desire is infectious, says H. Muir, global marketing training manager at SC Johnson, in Racine, Wisconsin. If the teacher has it, the students will most likely catch it.

"Both of my parents were high-school teachers," Muir says. "My mother taught behaviorally disabled students, and my father taught history and government. The most important thing I learned from them is that you need to have passion, and it has to be genuine. It isn't something you can fake. Students can tell whether you care or not."

5. **Students learn when teachers show them how much they need to learn.** Teaching adults has given Tom McCarty, director of consulting services at Motorola University, an appreciation for the old adage, "When the student is ready, the teacher will appear." Some

of the people who show up for the Six Sigma continuous-improvement workshop aren't ready, because they don't think they need to improve. They don't see the gap between where they are and where they need to be. Making them aware of that gap is one of McCarty's first objectives.

"Is your team aligned around customer expectations?" he'll ask. "Of course we are," one of the team leaders will reply. McCarty will then ask each team member to write down the top-four customer priorities and post them on the wall so that everyone can read them. "If there are 15 team members, you'll get 60 different priorities," he says. "Once they see that for themselves, they'll turn to me and ask, 'Can you help us here?'"

6. **Keep it clear even if you can't keep it simple.** One of the chief attributes of a great teacher is the ability to break down complex ideas and make them understandable. These days, the same can be said for business leaders, says Gary Grates, executive director of internal communications for General Motors. In fact, he says that the essence of teaching—and learning—is communication. "The biggest issue that leaders face is whether people understand them," says Grates. "Whether you're talking about Wall Street, partners, customers, or employees, people must understand the organization's story—where it's headed, why you are making these changes, how you work, and how you think. Otherwise, you're going to lose valuation, sales, new opportunities, or employees. That's why teaching is important."

7. **Practice vulnerability without sacrificing credibility.** To some people, being a teacher—or a leader—means appearing as though you have all the answers. Any sign of vulnerability or ignorance is seen as a sign of weakness. Those people can make the worst teachers, says Parker Palmer, a longtime

instructor and author of *The Courage to Teach: Exploring the Inner Landscape of a Teacher's Life* (Jossey–Bass, 1997).

Sometimes the best answer a teacher can give is, "I don't know." Instead of losing credibility, she gains students' trust, and that trust is the basis of a productive relationship. "We all know that perfection is a mask," says Palmer. "So we don't trust the people behind know-it-all masks. They're not being honest with us. The people with whom we have the deepest connection are those who acknowledge their struggles to us."

Acknowledging what you don't know shows that you're still learning, that the teacher is, in fact, still a student. For the leader of an organization, this is a delicate balancing act, says Mike Leven, former president of Holiday Inn Worldwide and now chairman and CEO of U.S. Franchise Systems Inc. "While it's okay not to know a lot of things, people do depend on you to know the answers to certain questions. You don't want people asking, 'Why is he running the company?'"

8. **Teach from the heart.** The best teaching isn't formulaic; it's personal. Different people teach Shakespeare in different ways because of who they are and how they see the world. Or, as Palmer says, "We teach who we are." The act of teaching requires the courage to explore one's sense of identity. If you don't fully know yourself, Palmer says, you can't fully know your students, and therefore, you can't connect with them. People compensate by using clever technique until they figure this out. Maybe, he says, the jazz musician Charlie Parker put it best: "If you don't live it, it won't come out of your horn."

9. **Repeat the important points.** If you want your employees to remember that new mission statement or market strategy, you need to give it to them more than once. "The first time you say something, it's heard," says William H. Rastetter, who taught at MIT and Harvard before becoming CEO of Idec Pharmaceuticals Corp. "The second time, it's recognized, and the third time, it's learned."

The challenge, then, is to be consistent without becoming predictable or boring. The best teachers keep it fresh by finding new ways to express the same points. For Craig E. Weatherup, chairman and CEO of the Pepsi Bottling Group, the message that he is constantly pushing is that bottled water—not cola—represents the biggest future growth potential for the company. (See "The Business of Teaching," page 122.) The 25-member operating council has heard him expound on this strategy repeatedly—but he hasn't repeated himself too much. "You have to cheat a little bit and disguise the themes so that people think, 'I haven't heard this before,'" he says. "I always try to find a new slant on the water category, but the underlying message doesn't change: It's important to the success of this company."

10. **Good teachers ask good questions.** Effective teachers understand that learning is about exploring the unknown and that such exploration begins with questions. Not questions that are simply lectures in disguise. Not yes-or-no questions that don't spark lively discussion. But questions that open a door to deeper understanding, such as, "How does that work?" and "What does that mean?" And GM's Grates's personal favorite, "Why?" "If you want to get to the heart of something, ask why five times," he says.

David Garvin, who teaches at Harvard Business School, interviewed a number of teaching executives for his book *Learning in Action: A Guide to Putting the Learning Organization to Work* (Harvard Business School Press, 2000). He found that one way they teach sound decision making is by playing devil's advocate. Teaching

Teacher Behavior, Teacher Roles / **57**

executives ask colleagues, "What if we did the opposite of what you're suggesting?" The idea is not to undermine a decision but to bolster it through a thorough examination of the options—even the outlandish ones. "Although you get promoted by having the right answer," he says, "it's more important to ask the right questions as you climb higher."

11. You're not passing out information. You're teaching people how to think. The last thing you want to do is stand up and tell people what to do. Or give them the answers that you want to hear. The best instructors are less interested in the answers than in the thinking behind them. What leaders have to offer is a "teachable point of view," says Noel Tichy, a professor at the University of Michigan Business School and author of *The Leadership Engine: How Winning Companies Build Leaders at Every Level* (HarperBusiness, 1997). It's how they look at the world, interpret information, and think through problems. The best teaching leaders help people learn how to think on their own rather than telling them what to think.

"You want a forceful group of people who know what you want but at the same time feel free enough to make the day-to-day judgments themselves," says Gene Roberts, a longtime editor at the *Philadelphia Inquirer* and the *New York Times* who now teaches journalism at the University of Maryland at College Park. (During his 18 years at the *Inquirer*, the paper won 17 Pulitzer Prizes.) "You have to know when to let go so that people don't become dependent on you. In the newspaper business, speed is everything, and if you have people waiting to hear what you have to say before they will react, you'll get beat."

12. Stop talking—and start listening. When it comes to teaching, what you do is nearly as important as what you say. After all, your students are watching you. One way to show that you care about them and that you're interested in them is by listening. Effective learning is a two-way street: It's a dialogue, not a monologue. After asking a question, bad teachers fill in the silence rather than wait for a response. Instead, says Muir, the training manager at SC Johnson, try this: Wait 10 seconds. "If you want to be a good teacher, you need to get comfortable with silence," he says. It's in those quiet, perhaps awkward, moments that some of the most productive thinking occurs. Don't interrupt it.

13. Learn what to listen for. Levi Watkins teaches heart surgery at Johns Hopkins Hospital in Baltimore, where the residents learn by working side by side with attending and faculty surgeons. (See "Teacher With Heart," page 126.) Before surgery, Watkins asks a resident to walk him through the diagnosis and procedure, as if the tables were turned and he were assisting the trainee. "I'm listening for how the resident assembles all of this information, how well she organizes her thoughts," says Watkins. "Choosing to operate on someone's heart is a very complex decision. You may have a difference of opinion among doctors, but the buck stops there. We're the ones who decide which vessels are worthy or not worthy of a bypass procedure."

When Pepsi's Weatherup visits general managers at one of the company's 300 sites, he pays particular attention to the language he hears. In a manager's analysis of the local market, for example, Weatherup listens for references to the company's overall mission statement or to a new strategy that he has laid out. He's not interested in mimicry. He wants a sense that the manager is thinking about her piece of the business in the right framework. "If I hear the language of the company coming back to me, I know that I'm reaching people," Weatherup says.

He was forced to become a good listener while working in Japan, his first assignment with Pepsi. Because English was a second language to his colleagues, he became sensitive to the emotion behind people's words. He still listens for it today. "I'm interested in people's feelings, not just the latest volume and pricing numbers. I want to know what frustrates them and what they feel good about."

14. **Let your students teach each other.** You're not the only one your students learn from. They also learn on their own and from their peers. "That's how the triangle of learning works," says Marilyn Whirry, who teaches 12th-grade AP English at Mira Costa High School in Manhattan Beach, California. She's a big believer in small groups. She'll give the groups a question that is based on the book the students are reading, and they have to respond to the previous comment before making a new point. "They listen to each other," says Whirry, the 2000 National Teacher of the Year. "Maybe their friend has an insight that they hadn't thought of. Maybe it's something that they can build on. It's exciting to watch."

Yale's Rando has taken the idea one step further. He has designated small groups to become experts on different topics and then intermingled students in new groups so that they have to teach another person what they've learned. "This method replicates how problems occur in life," he says. "Everybody has a piece of relevant information, making everyone a teacher and a learner."

15. **Avoid using the same approach for everyone.** Good teachers believe that every student can learn, but they understand that students learn differently. Some are visual. Some grasp the abstract. Some learn best by reading. So the instructor might adopt a multidimensional approach, something along these lines: Lecture for 20 minutes, then pose a multiple-choice question to the class, which is displayed on the board or on a slide. Next, ask everyone to write down an answer to the question, and then have people take turns explaining it to someone else in class. After several minutes, poll the class to find out who chose which answer. Then ask someone from each of those groups to explain their answer. Rando calls this "active lecturing."

16. **Never stop teaching.** Effective teaching is about the quality of the relationship between the teacher and the student. It doesn't end when the class or the workday is over. "I try to stay away from a 9-to-5 attitude, which means that for the hour you're here, I care about you, but don't bother me afterwards," says Kaplinsky, the Juilliard professor. "One of the most important ingredients of teaching is loving it. I come from Israel, where we have a saying: 'More than the calf wants to suck its mother's milk, the mother wants to impart the milk to the calf.'"

That concludes our lesson on teaching. Any questions? *Anyone?* All right then. Class dismissed.

Questions for Discussion and Debate

1. List each of the 16 one-line principles in your notebook, leaving some space under each one. In those spaces record an actual experience or observation in which you saw this principle in action. Share your notes in a small or large group discussion.
2. Are there any points in the article that you find debatable? Cite them and explain why.

3. Can you add any principles of smart teaching to Salter's list? If so, share your thoughts with the class.

4. In what ways is this list of principles different from and similar to the "Professional Standards for Teachers" (Selection 1.8)? List some similarities and differences. Then decide whether or not the two lists complement each other.

5. Salter states that good teaching is universal and that the same principles apply whether you're teaching social studies or how to perform a triple bypass. Debate this assumption with your peers.

Activities and Projects

1. Enter these principles on a chart. Next to the briefly stated principles draw several columns, each one representing the behavior of one of several (minimum, three) classroom teachers you will observe. In each column enter a Y (yes) or an N (no) indicating whether or not that teacher exhibited each principle during your observation of his or her teaching. When the chart is complete, draw some conclusions about teacher behavior based on your data. Share them with colleagues who will be able to contribute their own observations based on charted—as well as uncharted—data.

2. Take the 16 one-line principles of smarter teaching and express them in song or verse. Or if your talents lie in the visual arts, try drawing on a poster 16 scenes in which you portray the principles being applied. Consider including locations or sites such as a traditional classroom as well as some of the sites to which Salter refers, such as an office or hospital. Label each scene and place the poster on a bulletin board where others can benefit from this information.

3. Create a lesson plan in which you try to incorporate all 16 principles. If possible, teach the lesson in a student-teaching context or in front of your peers. Have someone sit with the list and observe you. Then have a meeting in which you receive feedback from your observer, or have your lesson videotaped and evaluate your lesson in terms of your implementation of the principles. (Note: Don't worry if you don't apply all 16 principles in a single lesson. The objective is to recognize both the value of the principle and when it is appropriate to use one or more.)

4. Watch at least one of the films listed in the Activities and Projects section at the end of Selection 1.2. With the list of 16 principles beside you, study the behavior of the teacher in the film. Write down the way in which he or she applies them or does the opposite in his or her interactions with students. Evaluate this teacher in a presentation to the class. What can be learned about good teaching from observations of this type as well as on-site visits to classrooms?

Chapter References

Alexander, K., & Alexander, M. D. (1992). *American public school law.* St. Paul, MN: West.

Ayers, W. (1993). *To teach. The journey of a teacher.* New York: Teachers College, Columbia University.

Borja, R. R. (2001). Student poll asks how schools talked about terrorist attacks. *Education Week, 21*(6), 14–15.

Chartock, R. (2001, December). Lessons of Norman Rockwell. *Educational Leadership, 59,* 70–73.

Cormier, R. (1974). *The chocolate war.* New York: Dell.

Einstein, A. (1954). *Ideas and opinions.* New York: Bonanza Books.

Feldman, S. (2001, November). Survival lessons. *On Campus, 21*(3), 5.

Fischer, J., & Kiefer, A. (1994). Constructing and discovering images of your teaching. In P. Joseph & G. Burnaford (Eds.), *Images of school teachers in twentieth-century America* (pp. 29–53). New York: St. Martin's Press.

Freedman, S. G. (1990). *Small victories: The real world of a teacher, her students, and their high school.* New York: Harper.

Green, C. R., & Sanford, W. R. (1983). *Psychology, a way to grow.* New York: Amsco School.

Hilton, J. (1963). *Goodbye, Mr. Chips.* New York: Bantam.

Hunter, M., & Russell, D. (1981). Planning for effective instruction: Lesson design. In M. Hunter & D. Russell (Eds.), *Increasing your teaching effectiveness.* Palo Alto, CA: The Learning Institute.

Johnson, D. W., & Johnson, R. T. (1991). Classroom instruction and cooperative learning. In H. C. Waxman & H. J. Walberg (Eds.), *Effective teaching: Current research* (pp. 277–293). Berkely, CA: McCutchan.

Johnson, J. (1990). *What Lisa knew: The truth and lies of the Steinberg case.* New York: Kensington.

Joseph, P., & Burnaford, G. (Eds.). (1994). *Images of school teachers in twentieth-century America.* New York: St. Martin's Press.

Kantor, K. (1994). In P. Joseph & G. Burnaford (Eds.), *Images of school teachers in twentieth-century America* (pp. 175–189). New York: St. Martin's Press.

Kidder, T. (1990). *Among schoolchildren.* New York: Avon.

Lifton, B. J. (1989). *The king of children: Janusz Korczak.* London: Pan Books.

Lortie, D. (1975). *School teacher: A sociological study.* Chicago: University of Chicago Press.

Mann, H. (1891). *Annual reports.* Boston: Lee and Shepard.

Maslow, A. (1968). *Toward a psychology of being* (2nd ed). New York: Van Nostrand Reinhold.

Massachusetts Department of Education. (2001, October). Professional standards for teachers. In *Regulations for educator licensure and preparation program approval* [Document]. Boston: Author (massdoe.com).

McCarthy, M., & Cambron-McCabe, N. (1992). *Public school law: Teachers' and students' rights.* Boston: Allyn & Bacon.

McCourt, F. (1999). *'Tis.* New York: Touchstone.

National Education Association. (1975). *Code of ethics of the education profession* [Document]. Washington, DC: Author.

National Education Association. (1997). *Status of the American public school teacher, 1995–1996.* Washington, DC: Author.

The Norman Rockwell album. (1961). Garden City, NY: Doubleday.

Patton, F. G. (1954). *Good morning, Miss Dove.* New York: Dodd, Mead.

Perrone, V. (1991). *A letter to teachers: Reflections on schooling and the art of teaching*. San Francisco: Jossey–Bass.

Rockwell, P. (1990). My father's paintings about painting. In J. Goffman et al. (Eds.), *Norman Rockwell*. Milano, Italy: Electa.

Salinger, J. D. (1964). *Catcher in the rye*. New York: Bantam.

Salter, C. (2001, December). Attention, class!!! 16 ways to be a smarter teacher. *Fast Company, 53*, 114–126. (Electronic version: www.fastcompany.com)

Sandham, J. L. (2001). On disaster's doorstep, schools strain to cope. *Education Week, 21*(3), 1, 22–23.

Shulman, L. (1987). Knowledge and teaching: Foundations and the new reform. *Harvard Educational Review, 3*, 1–22.

Smith, B. (1943). *A tree grows in Brooklyn*. New York: Harper and Bros.

Teaching about tragedy. (2001, October). *Social Education, 65*(6), 336–340, 383–384.

The Steinberg case. (1988, December 12). *Newsweek*, 58–59.

Trousdale, A. M. (1994). Teacher as gatekeeper, schoolteachers in picture books for young children. In P. Joseph & G. Burnaford (Eds.), *Images of school teachers in twentieth-century America* (pp. 195–214). New York: St. Martin's Press.

U.S. General Accounting Office. 1992. *Child abuse: Prevention programs need greater emphasis*. Washington, DC: Author.

Wyatt, E. (2001). Board votes to require recitation of pledge at public schools [Electronic version]. *The New York Times*.

Additional Readings

Albom, M. (1997). *Tuesdays with Morrie*. New York: Doubleday.

Borich, G. (1995). *Becoming a teacher*. Bristol, PA: Falmer Press.

Burnaford, G. E., et al. (2001). *Teachers doing research. The power of action through inquiry*. Mahwah, NJ: Lawrence Erlbaum Associates.

Feistritzer, C. E. (1996). *Profile of teachers in the U.S.* Washington, DC: National Center for Education Information.

Flake, C. L., Kuhs, T., Donnelly, A., & Ebert, C. (1995). Reinventing the role of teachers: Teacher as researcher. *Phi Delta Kappan, 76*(5), 405–407.

Girdano, D. A., Everly, G. S., & Dusek, D. E. (1990). *Controlling stress and tension*. Upper Saddle River, NJ: Prentice Hall.

Knowles, J. G., Cole, A. L., & Presswood, C. S. (1994). *Through preservice teachers' eyes: Exploring field experiences through narrative and inquiry*. Upper Saddle River, NJ: Merrill/Prentice Hall.

Kohl, H. (1999). *The discipline of hope. Learning from a lifetime of teaching*. New York: Simon & Schuster.

Loughran, J., & Northfield, J. (1996). *Opening the classroom door*. Bristol, PA: Falmer Press.

Moller, G., & Katzenmeyer, M. (Eds.). (1996). *Every teacher as a leader. Realizing the potential of teacher leadership*. San Francisco: Jossey–Bass.

Nussbaum, J. F. (1992). Effective teacher behaviors. *Communication Education, 41*(2), 167–180.

Smith, L. G., & Smith, J. K. (2002). *Lives in education. A narrative of people and ideas*. Mahwah, NJ: Lawrence Erlbaum Associates.

Weber, S., & Mitchell, C. (1995). *That's funny you don't look like a teacher. Interrogating images, identity, and popular culture.* Bristol, PA: Falmer Press.

Zehm, S. J., & Kottler, J. A. (1993). *On being a teacher: The human dimension.* Newbury Park, CA: Corwin Press.

Web Sites

National Council for the Social Studies: http://www.ncss.org
National Council for Teachers of English: http://www.ncte.org
National Council for Teachers of Mathematics: http://www.nctm.org

For lessons, articles, and resources related to terrorism, grief, tolerance, and other issues, go to:

a. The New York Times Learning Network
   www.nytimes.com/learning/teachers

b. Association for Supervision and Curriculum Development
   www.ascd.org

c. National Council for the Social Studies
   www.socialstudies.org/resources/moments

d. Southern Poverty Law Center
   www.tolerance.org

e. U.S. Department of Education
   www.ed.gov/inits/september11/index.html

f. American Federation of Teachers
   www.aft.org

Chapter 2

Historical Perspectives

In this chapter key concepts including the historic roots of American education, the growth of public education, and the influence of religion on education are brought to life through a wide variety of primary sources and literature.

"Those who forget the past are doomed to repeat it," is the familiar warning of philosopher George Santayana. One of the basic premises of this anthology is that, indeed, you can learn how to avoid some of the mistakes in education's history by learning that history. Such knowledge can also provide you with a rich array of educational ideas and practices that had their origins in decades, often centuries, past.

Too often the origins of certain ideas are forgotten. In fact, the credit for much of the wisdom generated by historic men and women frequently goes to contemporary researchers who repackage the wisdom and superimpose new jargon. The fact is, there's not that much that is new under the (educational) sun.

Brief Background

The roots of America's system of public education extend as far back as ancient Greece and Rome and post-Renaissance Europe. A brief look at just a few of the international and historic contributors to the present system can be illuminating.

Greek philosopher, Plato (427–347 B.C.E.), the pupil of Socrates (470–399 B.C.E.) and the teacher of Aristotle (384–322 B.C.E.), wrote *The Republic*, the earliest-known account of a Utopian society. In this society the philosophers, or the thinkers, are praised as society's real truth-seekers; for Plato, to seek the truth was the highest goal of education *and* of life. (An excerpt from *The Republic*, "The Allegory of the Cave," appears in chapter 3). As for Socrates, so profound and effective was his use of contemplation and the tutorial approach for seeking truth that they continue to be practiced today. Characterized by a dialogue or an exchange of questions and answers between teacher and students, this tutorial approach or Socratic method nurtures critical thinking and the use of reasoning skills. And while posterity honors him, little was done, according to public education advocate Horace Mann, by any of the ancient nations to promote Socrates or his colleagues. Indeed, "Socrates was put to death for his excellences" (Mann, 1969, p. 223).

History records others, including Pythagoras, Galileo, and Copernicus, whose teachings brought hostile public reactions because they challenged the prevailing notions or powers of their time. Even Aristotle was accused by politicians of disrespect. Indeed, has anyone ever demonstrated innovative thinking without disturbing the establishment?

Aristotle's philosophy is most closely associated with the Hellenistic fondness for the aesthetic of balance in all things and for the Golden Mean, the idea that virtue lies somewhere between two extremes. In line with that belief he considered as equally real and important the tangible world and the intangible—although he leaned more toward the world of the senses. For that reason he has been called the "father of philosophical realism." With his wisdom expressed in the form of pithy sayings such as "Everything in moderation" and "Know thyself," Aristotle is perhaps the most quoted of the trio that includes Socrates and Plato. In terms of his more specific contribution to education, he is credited with being the first to teach about the importance of categorizing or conceptualizing things; in fact, he categorized subject matter into a number of disciplines, including logic, biology, mathematics, and astronomy, among others. And educators would do well to remember the wisdom of balance when considering climbing onto the latest bandwagon.

Quintilian (35–95 C.E.) was another challenger of the status quo. This Roman believed that education should be relevant and have practical application. Long before Johnson and Johnson (1989) did their studies on cooperative learning, Quintilian had demonstrated the value of an approach whereby students could learn with and from one another. And he may have been the first and only one among the ancients who condemned whipping in school.

The work of John Amos Comenius (1592–1670), a Moravian bishop and teacher, deserves attention for his advocacy of universal education more than two centuries before Horace Mann's efforts. Philosopher John Dewey (1859–1952) likely knew of Comenius's promotion of experiential learning and his consideration of a child's developmental readiness. Comenius's work reads like a modern-day text for teachers, which is why he is referred to as "the father of modern pedagogy" (Bowen, 1966, p. 182).

And add to these movers and shakers the following historic and global assortment: from Germany, Friedrich Froebel (1782–1852) and Johann Friedrich Herbart (1776–1841); from Switzerland, Johann Heinrich Pestalozzi (1746–1827) and Jean Piaget (1896–1980); from France, Jean Jacques Rousseau (1712–1778); from Italy, Maria Montessori (1870–1952); from England, John Locke (1632–1704); and so many more who cumulatively and indirectly helped to shape what is now the largest system of universal public education in the world.

The preceding evidence seems to illustrate that most of today's educational practices and ideas have historic and global roots, that often what appears to be new and exciting in education is not really a major change of any kind but actually a reappearance of an historically expanded concept. There has, on the other hand, been a great deal of change in terms of American education's growth and expansion from colonial times to the present.

First, the system of American education expanded from one in which only well-to-do white males were educated into one that is tax-supported, with access for all. With the common-school (public-school) movement led by Horace Mann in the mid-19th century, the system gradually democratized to include the poor, women, African Americans, Native Americans, and other minorities.

Second, the size and location of schools expanded. Initially there were small one-room schoolhouses interspersed around an agrarian countryside. By the 19th century smaller schools were merging into larger ones and school districts were formed. The urbanization of America that came with industrialization and immigration also required more and larger schools to accommodate the growing population of the cities (Spring, 1986).

Third, in the 19th century the system expanded from one in which free compulsory education was provided up through the middle grades to one that included public funding of education through Grade 12. (The Kalamazoo Case, 1874, resulted in a ruling that the state legislature had the right to pass laws levying taxes for the support of *both* elementary and secondary schools.) Around this time schools began to expand their curricula as well as adding practical and applied arts to formal subjects.

And fourth, the reason for going to school expanded well beyond its original nonsecular (religious) purpose. The necessity for learning to read had been linked with the need to read the Bible and be saved from the influences of Satan. In fact, the Old Deluder Satan Act was passed in the Massachusetts Bay Colony in 1642 for just that purpose. But in *The Abington School District* v. *Schempp*, 374 U.S. 203 case (1963), the Supreme Court ruled that the Jeffersonian "wall of separation" between church and state would prevail, and the decision upheld the prohibition of reading the Bible or reciting the Lord's Prayer in school, although the court ruled that students could read the Bible as literature or as an historical document. Jefferson and the Founding Fathers had argued for the shift from educating for religious purposes to educating for an informed citizenry able to participate in the new democracy. However, there are Americans today, some of whom are referred to as the Christian Right, who believe that the curriculum should return to its historically religious grounding. They object to courses that appear to be contrary to their religious values. The controversy over church and state issues continues unabated to this day.

And so, too, does the debate over expansionism and its challenges. For example, how do teachers deal with the pressures placed upon them to expand the curriculum? How do they integrate technology education, character education, and more? How do schools cope with the need to expand programs to meet the needs of diverse populations? What problems arise with other kinds of growth? What are the limits of expansion?

By adopting the role of the historian, you can begin to discover how others have addressed such issues in the past. For, indeed, one thing is certain: Many educational issues revisit society again and again. Problems and ideas that seem new are rarely new at all. The readings in this section demonstrate the swing of the educational pendulum from past to present and back again. Focus now on how historical perspectives on education can inform the present.

Selections

The figure of Ichabod Crane as portrayed by Norman Rockwell captures several characteristics of the rural schoolteacher of the early 19th century. And the excerpts in this chapter include two accounts of the public schools in rural America during the 18th and 19th centuries, the first from a children's book by Laura Ingalls Wilder and the second from a book by Charles Taylor (*History of Great Barrington*). A time line of influential people and events in the history of American education provides a useful overview of the field.

A selection (*Emerson on Education*) by the outstanding man of letters, Ralph Waldo Emerson, reminds readers about the timeless pedagogical principle of recognizing the individual needs and interests of every student. Then, in her essay from *Aesthetic Papers*, Elizabeth Palmer Peabody, the 19th-century historian and teacher, credits the Dorians of Ancient Greece with making important contributions to American educational thought and practice.

Two groups, African Americans and women, historically were not provided with the kind of education that both Emerson and Peabody advocate. In his autobiographical *Narrative*, Frederick Douglass describes the conditions of slavery under which he was denied the right to an education. And in his biography of Thomas Jefferson, Albert Jay Nock (*Jefferson*) describes the president's bias concerning education for females, which reflects the common opinion of his time.

The principle of separation of church and state, strongly supported by Jefferson, was a source of controversy that began brewing in the early years of public education and remains in the forefront today. Although a century apart, both public education advocate Horace Mann ("Twelfth Report, for 1848"), and playwrights Jerome Lawrence and Robert E. Lee (*Inherit the Wind*) convey similar attitudes about this issue, which had its roots as far back as the 17th century in New England, where the Puritans developed a system of education in which religion was central. In the 19th century when W. H. McGuffey created his reading series, he perpetuated the Puritan legacy by including prose such as the example provided here, by William Ellery Channing (1879), who, in stark contrast to his contemporary, Horace Mann, advocates religion as the basis of society.

In an excerpt from Sydney Taylor's *All-of-a-Kind Family*, there is a glimpse of how urban immigrants were educated indirectly on their way into the mainstream; and finally, there are the timeless and universal educational ideas of Friedrich Froebel as conveyed by Baroness B. von Marenholz-Bülow in her *Reminiscences* and Johann Heinrich Pestalozzi (*How Gertrude Teaches Her Children*), both prominent pioneers in the field of early childhood education. (In chapter 5, "School Environments," you will find an excerpt from the novel *Christy* that sheds light on the nature of teaching in a rural environment during the early years of the 20th century. Other excerpts throughout the text also have historical significance.)

The cliché that "history repeats itself" certainly applies to educational history. As you read these selections, note some of the common themes and ideas that seem to recur consistently throughout America's educational history, from its ancient—and global—origins to the present. Notice also the inconsistencies. Observe how these excerpts mirror the growing pains and the progress that accompanied the expansion of American education and, with this knowledge, try to predict what issues Americans will be facing in the 21st century.

2.1   Work of Art: *Ichabod Crane* (1937)

Norman Rockwell

The painting of Ichabod Crane by Norman Rockwell portrays the fictional schoolteacher in Washington Irving's (1783–1859) story, "The Legend of Sleepy Hollow," which is historically accurate in many ways in terms of local superstitions, life in Dutch upstate New York, and the lives of rural schoolteachers in the early 19th century.

Irving put it this way: " . . . He [Ichabod] was, according to country customs in those parts [upstate New York], boarded and lodged at the houses of the farmers, whose children he instructed. With these he lived successively a week at a time; thus going the rounds of the neighborhood, with all his worldly effects tied up in a cotton handkerchief" (Neider, 1975, p. 34). Charles Taylor's description of the way in which teachers in early rural Massachusetts were provided for corroborates this passage. Read his nonfictional account in this chapter (Selection 2.4).

After studying the painting, answer the questions that follow and notice the connections among art, education, and history.

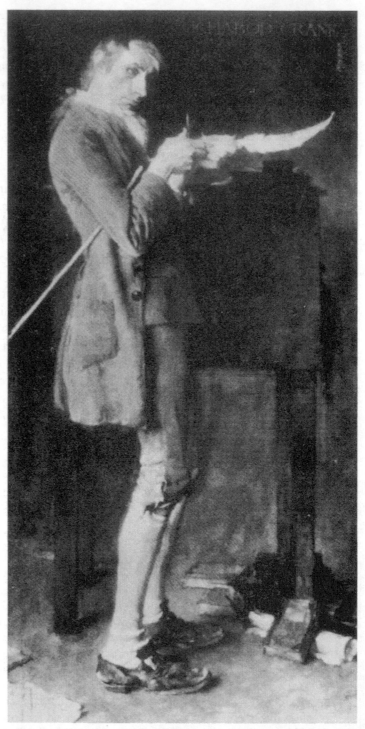

Printed by permission of the Norman Rockwell Family Trust. Copyright © 1996, the Norman Rockwell Family Trust. Photo courtesy of the Norman Rockwell Museum at Stockbridge, Massachusetts.

======== **Questions for Discussion and Debate** ========

1. What image of a teacher does this painting convey?

2. Is there anything in the painting that is historically accurate? (Read Washington Irving's tale after you have answered these questions and see if the story reinforces or contradicts your initial assessment of Ichabod and the historical accuracy of the painting.)

3. From an artistic perspective, Rockwell's portrayal of Ichabod Crane is much more impressionistic than his usual illustrations, leaving more to the imagination. He painted this work in the 1930s, at the peak of his artistic prowess. He used a painterly manner in which everything is less defined by line and more defined by color and texture. According to Linda Pero, curator of The Norman Rockwell Museum in Stockbridge, Massachusetts, Rockwell was influenced in this painting by European Old Master painters such as Rembrandt and Reubens in terms of his use of mostly dark, warm, earthy colors, accompanied by the extreme contrast of light, seen here in Crane's collar, cheek, and quill pen. The use of such contrast of light and dark in a painting is referred to as *chiaroscuro*. As you examine the paintings by Rockwell in other chapters in this book, look for characteristics of his different styles, that is, his use of a more impressionistic approach and his more illustrative style in which lines are more pronounced. Which approach to painting do you prefer, and why?

======== **Activities and Projects** ========

1. Often when you observe a scene or person with an eye toward sketching them, you scrutinize them more carefully. As you observe various classroom environments and teachers, study them with such an eye; sketch them or photograph them. Examine your sketches and/or photographs and see what they tell you about the nature of that teacher's pedagogy and/or the nature of the school and classroom environment. Compare and contrast your sketches and photographs. How are they the same or different? Which ones reflect a "picture" of *your* approach or your ideal environment? Which ones, if any, portray a valid historical picture of today's teacher and classroom? Explain. Share your work and views with your peers.

2. Look at the photographs of teachers and situations that are contained in your education-related texts. What do they tell an observer about education, teaching, and schools today? Which photos from these education texts do you feel are most accurate? Which ones, if any, are misleading? Prepare a display of these photographs along with a critique of them.

2.2 Time Line: Influential People and Events in the History of American Education

A time line is an invaluable resource for the student of education because it provides an historical perspective of the field. While there might be some debate about why a few of the people and events were chosen for inclusion, suffice it to say that most of them have made a difference in the general directions, philosophical as well as political, that public education has traveled, is traveling now, and will travel: For indeed, a time line can be a useful tool for making predictions about future educational trends and tribulations.

Read through this chronological history of people and events and see what patterns emerge in terms of the six major themes of this anthology: teacher behavior and roles, history, philosophy, politics, school environments, and sociology (diversity). Can you formulate any generalizations about American public education as a result of this time line? Such generalizations will serve you well as you continue to use this text.

470–399 B.C.E. *Socrates:* Known for his method of teaching. Plato memorializes his famous teacher Socrates's ideas in his dialogues or conversations, in which Socrates talks with his students using inquiry, questioning, and discussion to reveal truths. When he was convicted of corrupting the young, Socrates died after drinking hemlock. Father of idealism.

427–347 B.C.E. *Plato:* Pupil of Socrates and teacher of Aristotle; wrote *The Republic,* the earliest-known account of a Utopian society, in which he promotes the philosopher as king and chief educator of society.

384–322 B.C.E. *Aristotle:* Father of realism; concerned with knowing objects through direct contact *and* through contemplation; developed idea of classifying ideas into categories.

35–95 C.E. *Quintilian:* Roman educator who believed that education should be relevant and have practical application.

1225–1274 *St. Thomas Aquinas:* Believed that both faith *and* reason are sources of the truth.

1466–1536 *Erasmus:* Believed in humanistic education in the liberal arts and advocated the systematic training of teachers.

1561–1626 *Francis Bacon:* Englishman who popularized scientific inquiry and the use of reason in understanding the universe.

1592–1670 *John Amos Comenius:* A Moravian bishop and teacher who advocated universal public education and believed that there is a general body of knowledge (*paideia*) that all should possess.

1632–1704 *John Locke:* Englishman who believed that people enter the world with a clean slate (*tabula rasa*) and, through education, develop reason and morality.

1635 *Boston Latin Grammar School,* Boston, Massachusetts, is established to prepare young men for college.

1636 *Harvard College,* the first college in America, is established.

1642 The *Massachusetts Compulsory School Law* is passed; places responsibility for enforcement of schooling on local authorities.

1647 The *Old Deluder Satan Act* requires every town of 50 or more families to hire teachers of reading and writing to be paid by community or parents; establishes public responsibility for education. The name derives from a rationale for education as a protection against Satan's influence.

The *Massachusetts Act* requires Latin grammar schools.

1712–1778 *Jean Jacques Rousseau:* Frenchman who advocated recognizing the individuality and goodness of each child as well as the development of natural abilities.

1743–1826 *Thomas Jefferson:* Proponent of free and universal elementary education and, to a lesser extent, state provision of secondary and higher education. Founds the University of Virginia (1825).

1746–1827 *Johann Heinrich Pestalozzi:* Swiss educator who believed in child-centered education and recognition of individual differences among children.

1751 *Benjamin Franklin* (1706–1790): Founder of Academy in Philadelphia. Although a private school, it promoted movement toward public secondary schools. He also proposed the first state school system.

1776–1841 *Johann Friedrich Herbart:* Believed that education should be motivating and should stimulate students' interests; education should develop moral character and should be studied scientifically.

1782–1852 *Friedrich Froebel:* German educator who established the first kindergartens and promoted activity-based early-childhood education.

1785 The *Northwest Ordinance:* The first federal education law that called for support of schools within newly established townships. Led to federal land grants to the states for public schools and colleges.

1789 The *U.S. Constitution* is ratified, but with no provisions for education. It is at this stage that the power to establish schools becomes the responsibility of the states.

1798 *Monitorial schools* are started by Joseph Lancaster (1753–1838). In 1806, the first such school is established in New York City. A master teacher would teach monitors, or talented students, who would then go out and teach classrooms of children. In this way one teacher, in effect, was essentially teaching hundreds of students through these monitors. Considered a cost-effective way to educate poor children in urban areas.

1817 *Thomas Gallaudet* establishes a school for the deaf in Boston, Massachusetts.

1821 *Emma Willard* (1787–1870) establishes the Troy Female Seminary, the first institution of higher education for women, to educate women in many subject areas including pedagogy. Her seminary leads to public normal schools (1839) to train women to be teachers.

The *Boston English Classical School*, the first public high school, is opened in Boston, Massachusetts.

1824 The *Bureau of Indian Affairs* is established by the federal government. However, most education for Native Americans was still provided by missionaries. Throughout the 19th century little was done by the government to establish education for Native Americans.

1825 *Noah Webster* issues *The American Dictionary*, which helps to standardize spelling.

1827 Massachusetts is the first state to mandate that every town with 500 or more families establish a public high school.

1836 *McGuffey's Readers* are published, to be used as texts throughout America's schools.

Oberlin College is established in Ohio and is America's first college for both men *and* women.

1837 *Mary Lyon* (1797–1849) founds Mt. Holyoke, the first women's college in the United States.

Horace Mann is appointed Secretary of the Massachusetts State Board of Education. He calls for universal free education in common schools or public schools. He is often referred to as "father of the common school."

1839 The first public *normal school,* or school for teaching teachers about "normal" subjects and pedagogical routines, is opened in Lexington, Massachusetts.

1803–1882 *Ralph Waldo Emerson:* Transcendentalist, poet, essayist, and writer on education.

1852 *Massachusetts* establishes the first *state compulsory school attendance law.*

1854 The first *college for free African Americans,* Lincoln University, is established in Pennsylvania.

1855 The *American Journal of Education,* the first education journal in the United States, is established by Henry Barnard.

The first *private kindergarten* (German-speaking) in the United States is established by Margaretta Schurz in Wisconsin. She had been a former pupil of Friedrich Froebel.

1857 The *National Education Association* (NEA) is founded as the first professional organization for teachers.

1860 *Elizabeth Palmer Peabody* opens the first private English-speaking kindergarten, in Boston.

1867 The *National Department of Education* is established as part of the federal government.

1873 *Kindergartens* become part of public schools with the assistance of William T. Morris, superintendent of schools in St. Louis, Missouri, and Susan E. Blow, who carried on Elizabeth Peabody's work.

1874 The *Kalamazoo Case* establishes the use of taxes to fund secondary schools.

1879 A *Native American school* is established with government funds in Carlisle, Pennsylvania.

1881 *Tuskegee Normal School* is founded by Booker T. Washington (1858–1915), a major spokesperson for education for African Americans, especially in vocational areas.

1882 The *Morrill Land-Grant College Act* begins the land-grant college movement, by which the government provides funding for the establishment of public colleges.

1890 *Universities* begin to include the formal study of education.

Alfred Binet (1857–1911) and *Theophile Simon* from France develop intelligence tests. In the early part of the next century, these tests are revised at Stanford University in California and become the standardized tests for measuring IQ.

1892 The *Committee of Ten Report* recommends that public high schools focus on college preparation and standardize their curricula.

1896 *Plessy* v. *Ferguson,* the "separate but equal" decision by the Supreme Court, allows for segregated public schools as well as segregation in other public places.

1811–1900 *Henry Barnard:* Leader of the common or public school movement and the first U.S. Commissioner of Education

(1867–1870); advocated public high schools and education for women.

1870–1952 *Maria Montessori:* Italian physician who developed preschool methods that acknowledged students' individual readiness to learn certain skills. Her methods enabled children to manipulate objects in order to discover concepts about matter and space. Montessori opened her first school in Rome in 1907.

1859–1952 *John Dewey:* Humanistic philosopher and "father of progressive education." He was a prolific writer who believed that the scientific method should be applied to education. In 1916 he published *Democracy and Education.* And in 1919 the Progressive Education Association is formed.

1875–1955 *Mary McLeod Bethune:* African-American educator who, in 1923, founded Bethune–Cookman College in Florida, which began as a normal school or teacher's college for black women in 1904. She becomes an influential advisor to President Franklin D. Roosevelt by 1936.

1868–1963 *W. E. B. DuBois:* Black civil rights pioneer who helped to found the NAACP (National Association for the Advancement of Colored People, 1909) and who advocated academic education for Blacks and equal opportunities in education, unlike Booker T. Washington, who believed that Blacks should try to advance primarily through vocational education.

1896–1980 *Jean Piaget:* Swiss educator who believed that learning can be organized into meaningful patterns that can be adapted to the stages of the child's cognitive development that are determined by age and experience. Usually the child moves from concrete to abstract modes of learning.

1890–1920 *Immigration increases* and schools must expand to meet the needs of students from many areas of Europe, particularly eastern Europe.

1909 The first *junior high schools* are established in Berkeley, California, and Columbus, Ohio.

1910 The first *junior college* is established in Fresno, California. High schools continue to grow.

The *Intercollegiate Athletic Association,* formed in 1905 to draft new rules for the game of football, changes its name to the National Collegiate Athletic Association, or NCAA.

1912 The first *Montessori school* in the United States is opened in Tarrytown, New York.

1916 The *American Federation of Teachers* (AFT) is formed as a union for public school teachers. It is affiliated with the American Federation of Labor–Congress of Industrial Organizations (AFL-CIO), labor unions that advocate more militant action than docs the National Education Association.

1917 The *Smith-Hughes Act* encourages vocational schools in public high schools.

1918 *Cardinal Principles of Secondary Education* is published by the Commission on The Reorganization of Secondary Education.

The Curriculum, by Franklin Bobbitt, is the first publication marking the emergence of curriculum as a formal field of study.

All states have passed some kind of *compulsory school attendance* legislation.

1919 The first *Waldorf school* is established by Rudolf Steiner (1861–1925) in Stuttgart, Germany, for the children of factory workers at the Waldorf cigarette factory. Waldorf schools emphasize learning through the senses, creative play, and spirituality.

1923 *Curriculum Construction,* by W. W. Charters, continues to bring curriculum into the arena for formal study, including both curriculum content and the methods for deciding that content.

1925 The *Scopes Trial* ("Monkey Trial"). High-school biology teacher, John Scopes, is accused and convicted of teaching students about evolution, against the law in Tennessee, where the Biblical story of creation was considered more appropriate for the classroom.

1926 The *College Entrance Examination Board,* created in 1900 to supply standardized entrance exams to its member colleges, administers the first Scholastic Aptitude Test (SAT).

1930 The *Dick and Jane books,* a series of reading primers, is published by Scott, Foresman & Company and dominates the textbook market for decades.

1932 President Franklin Delano Roosevelt's *New Deal,* his response to the Depression, provides funding for school construction and various forms of education for the unemployed.

1943 June 14. The United States Supreme Court rules that students cannot be compelled to *pledge allegiance* to the flag if the ceremony conflicts with their personal or religious beliefs (*West Virginia State Board of Education* v. *Barnette*).

1944 June 22. President Franklin D. Roosevelt signs the Servicemen's Readjustment Act, known as the *G.I. Bill,* which enables veterans to pursue higher education.

1947 October 20. The *United Nations International School* (UNIS) is founded in New York City.

1949 *Ralph Tyler* publishes his *Basic Principles of Curriculum and Instruction,* a classic text on how to develop and teach curriculum units of instruction.

1950 The *National Science Foundation* is established.

1954 *Brown* v. *The Board of Education of Topeka, Kansas,* Supreme Court decision desegregates the schools and overturns the Plessy decision of "separate but equal."

1955 Rudolf Flesch publishes *"Why Johnny Can't Read,"* which advocates teaching reading by the sounds of letters, or phonics, rather than by whole words.

1957 President Dwight D. Eisenhower enforces the Supreme Court's *Brown* v. *Board of Education* ruling to integrate schools by sending the National Guard to Little Rock, Arkansas.

1958 The *National Defense Education Act* is passed, in part as a reaction to the Soviet Union's launching of Sputnik I, the first artificial satellite. This legislation is a major step taken by the federal government to strengthen the nation by improving the teaching of mathematics, science, and foreign language. The act also provides additional guidance programs and low-interest loans for college students. The Kennedy and Johnson administrations continued these programs.

1963 The *School District of Abington Township* v. *Schempp* decision by the Supreme Court upholds the separation of church and state in public schools by making prayer and Bible reading unconstitutional.

1964 The *Economic Opportunity Act,* part of President Lyndon Johnson's war on poverty, establishes the Head Start Program to encourage education for preschool-age children from low-income families and to involve parents in their children's education.

The *Civil Rights Act* reinforces the movement to desegregate the schools.

1965 The *Elementary and Secondary Education Act* establishes funds for K–12 programs for children from low-income families.

November 8. The *Higher Education Act* becomes law and establishes financial aid to college students in the form of Pell Grants (1980) and Guaranteed Student Loans (Stafford Loans, 1988), both named for the senators who served on the Senate education subcommittee.

1966 The *Adult Education Act* establishes funding for states to provide educational programs for adults.

Cognitive psychologist *Jerome Bruner* publishes *Toward a Theory of Instruction,* in which he describes his interdisciplinary unit of instruction, "M:ACOS, Man: A Course of Study," which utilizes his theories about discovery learning, concept formation, and curriculum development.

1967 *Death at an Early Age,* by Jonathan Kozol, reveals the deplorable conditions of inner-city schools and the unequal education that exists for African American children and the poor. Kozol goes on to publish other books on related subjects (*Savage Inequalities,* 1991, and *Amazing Grace,* 1995).

1968 The *Bilingual Education Act* is passed, calling for instruction in two languages for students for whom English is a second language. Most programs serve Hispanic populations; by 1998 California rejects the policy.

1970 *Pedagogy of the Oppressed,* by Paulo Freire, is published. The text spreads the concept of critical literacy, which refers to the idea that, with education, the poor will become aware of the power they have to control and better their lives.

May 4. *Ohio National Guardsmen* shoot four students at Kent State University during an antiwar rally protesting the expansion of the Vietnam War into Cambodia.

1971 Benjamin Bloom's *Taxonomy of Educational Objectives* is published. The cognitive (knowledge), affective (attitudes), and psychomotor (skills) objectives delineate hierarchical sets of behaviors that students should try to satisfy as they learn a subject.

April 20. The Supreme Court rules that busing is permissible as a means to further integration in public schools. Protests and racial tensions in Boston and other areas are among the responses.

1972 The *Title IX Education Amendment* prohibits sex discrimination in educational institutions receiving federal funds.

1975 *Public Law 94-142* (Education for All Handicapped Children Act) is passed to provide equal educational opportunities to students in the form of an individualized education plan (IEP) that would meet students' individual needs in the least restrictive environment. The act implies that students should be mainstreamed into regular classes. (In 1990, the act was amended to change the term *handicapped* to *with disabilities* and expanded the age range from students 5–17 to those aged 2–21, regardless of the nature of their disability.)

The *Indian Self-Determination and Educational Assistance Act* is passed by Congress.

1977 The *U.S. Supreme Court* rules that the Constitution does not prohibit the use of corporal punishment in schools, thus allowing states to determine its use (*Ingraham* v. *Wright*).

1978 In the *Bakke* decision the Supreme Court decides against affirmative action while, at the same time, stating that minority status *may be used* as a factor in admitting students to, in this case, public medical schools.

June. *Hanna Holborn Gray* becomes president of the University of Chicago, the first woman to head a major American research university.

1979 The *Department of Education* is established, with cabinet status.

1982 June 15. The Supreme Court rules that the *children of illegal aliens* have the right to a free public-school education.

1983 *A Nation at Risk* is published, along with other reports and books advocating national reforms, among them raising standards in education (*Tomorrow's Teachers* [The Holmes Group, 1986], *A Nation Prepared: Teachers for the 21st Century* [Carnegie Forum on Education and the Economy, 1986], and *Visions of Reform: Implications for the Education Profession* [Association of Teacher Educators, 1980] among others).

1984 *Theodore Sizer* of Brown University publishes *Horace's Compromise: The Dilemma of the American High School,* a plea for reforms to be implemented through the network of the Coalition for Essential Schools, the organization he helped to form in 1984.

1985 *The Harvey Milk School* opens in New York City, the first high school in the United States for gay and lesbian students. Controversy ensues over whether to educate diverse groups in integrated settings or separately. (Harvey Milk was the gay San Francisco supervisor murdered in 1978.)

1986 The *Drug-Free Schools and Committees Act* establishes funding for drug abuse and prevention programs to be integrated with ongoing community efforts. The federal government continues to establish related legislation (1988, 1991).

January 28. *Christa McAuliffe* is killed along with seven astronauts when the space shuttle *Challenger* explodes after liftoff from Cape Canaveral. The New Hampshire school teacher was to have broadcast two lessons from space to millions of students around the country.

1987 The *National Board for Professional Teaching Standards* (NBPTS) is established.

In *Edwards* v. *Aguillard,* the Supreme Court rules that Darwin's evolution theory is more appropriate to teach in science classrooms than creationism, the biblical theory.

The *E. D. Hirsch* book, *Cultural Literacy: What Every American Needs to Know,* outlines the knowledge he believes all citizens should share in order to be considered literate. He is criticized for including knowledge related mostly to Western civilization.

1904–1987 *Theodore Brameld* leads the social reconstructionist movement, which goes beyond the progressivism of John Dewey to espouse the belief that schools should play a major part in bringing about social change and equality.

1904–1990 *B. F. Skinner:* A psychologist who was a major proponent of behaviorism, the idea that behavior is determined primarily by environmental factors rather than by heredity or free will. Operant conditioning, he said, shapes behavior, thus emphasizing the power of external stimuli.

1989 March 21. The *National Council of Teachers of Mathematics* issues guidelines for a new approach to teaching math. Referred to as "whole math," it stresses creative problem-solving as opposed to memorization.

September 27. At the National Education Summit in Virginia, President George Bush calls for *national curriculum standards* in public schools.

1990   *Teach for America* (TFA) is created by Wendy Kopp as a result of her senior thesis at Princeton University. This teacher corps places some of the brightest college graduates in inner-city and rural schools for 2 years. Most of these teachers come to the experience without formal training but receive training on the job and in graduate programs.

The *National Board for Professional Teaching Standards* is established.

March 5. *Christopher Whittle,* a media mogul, produces Channel One, a 12-minute newscast with 2 minutes of commercials. It begins in 400 high schools, with some criticism from teachers.

September 4. *State vouchers* covering tuition enable 400 low-income children in Milwaukee, Wisconsin, to attend private schools.

1991   The first *charter school* legislation is passed in Minnesota. Charter schools, which are public schools supported by state funds, operate independently of the standard policies that govern other public schools. The expectation is that such schools may generate innovative ideas that can be emulated as well as providing the kind of education advocated by their creators.

May 16. Christopher Whittle announces the *Edison Project,* which evolves into a for-profit business that operates individual public schools. The first four schools operated by Edison opened in 1995, and there are now over 25.

1992   *Bill Clinton* is elected president and declares that education is a major priority of his administration. In his second inaugural address (1996), Clinton states that by third grade every child should be able to read, by eighth grade every child should be computer literate, and by the end of high school every student should be able to attend college.

1993   March 1. President Bill Clinton outlines his plan for a national service corps, *Americorps,* which enables students to earn tuition for college by performing community service jobs.

1994   *School-to-Work Opportunities Act* is passed. Establishes programs to educate students about the world of work through courses, internships, and other exposures to careers that may result in a job or higher education.

Goals 2000: Educate America Act integrates the original six education goals formulated in 1989 during the Bush presidency with two additional goals and provides funding of state and local programs to carry out these goals.

1995   The *Children's Media Protection Act* establishes legislation related to the following provisions: a television violence rating code, parental ability to block programs, restrictions on violent programming, and appropriate programming for children.

1995–2005   The United Nations Decade for Human Rights Education.

1996   The *Education Summit* is held in Palisades, New York, with President Clinton and government and corporate leaders.

October 5. *World Teacher's Day* is launched by UNESCO.

1997   April 5. A *Harvard University report* indicates that the United States has, since

1991, experienced the "largest backward movement toward *segregation* since the Supreme Court's 1954 decision to desegregate schools."

1998 The motion to merge the two national teacher unions/associations, the NEA and AFT, is defeated at the NEA national convention.

2001 July. Leaders of the two teachers' unions, the NEA and the AFT, approve a new "NEAFT Partnership" that will permit joint projects at the local, state, and national levels, ranging from education conferences to political and legal campaigns.

2002 January 8. The first major revision of the 1965 *Elementary and Secondary Education Act* (ESEA) is signed by President George W. Bush. The legislation, dubbed the "No Child Left Behind Act," is considered a major component in the education reform movement and includes provisions for annual testing in reading and mathematics for Grades 3 through 8 and for federal assistance for low-income families. The numerous mandates mark an increase in the federal government's role in education.

February. More than a dozen years after dropping phonics for a more imaginative approach to teaching known as "whole language," the California Board of Education adopts new reading programs that rely on *phonetic skills* such as the sounding of vowels and consonants.

June 27. The U.S. Supreme Court rules, in a 5–4 decision (*Zelman* v. *Simmons-Harris,* Case No. 00-1751), that vouchers do not violate the U.S. Constitution's prohibition against a government establishment of religion. The decision upholds the Cleveland, Ohio, voucher program, in which public funds in the form of vouchers are provided to those parents who choose to send their children to private or parochial schools. The school choice debate continues.

Trustees of the College Board vote to overhaul the SAT I by dropping two sections, the quantitative comparisons and verbal analogies, and adding a 20- to 30-minute written essay, multiple-choice grammar questions, and a section devoted to higher-level mathematics. The revised test will begin in 2005.

Questions for Discussion and Debate

1. Reread the time line. What concepts or generalizations seem to emerge naturally from this history? Formulate a generalization related to each of the themes in this text. Share your theme with your peers. Then at the end of the semester, after you have completed this text, take out your list of generalizations to see if they reflect the major ideas contained in the book.

2. Are there any people or events you believe should have been included in this time line? Discuss with the class any additional entries. Debate the merit of including some of the entries already there.

3. How would you explain the absence of any entries on the time line between 95 C.E. and 1225?

Activities and Projects

1. Ask a number of teachers who and what they believe are among the most important people and events in the history of American public education. Record the data and then see if their views are reflected in the time line. Bring these data to class for discussion.

2. How could you display this time line in a way that would enable you and your peers to integrate its contents more easily? (a) You might split the time line up by centuries and have four committees illustrate key items, (b) you could make transparencies of the time line and hold discussions while projecting them on a screen, or (c) you could take your six major generalizations and demonstrate them dramatically. The possibilities are up to you.

3. Pick out five (or more) names from the time line whom you consider to be major movers and shakers in education. Read more about each one and then compose a poem or song in which you describe their contributions. (For an example, see the song about Horace Mann in the Activities and Projects section following Selection 2.9.)

2.3 *These Happy Golden Years* (1943)

Laura Ingalls Wilder

Laura Ingalls Wilder portrayed life on the American prairie in the 19th century in her series of "Little House" books, the most famous one of which is entitled *The Little House on the Prairie.* A television series of the same name further popularized her work, and there are few young readers today who have not encountered at least one of her books, some of which were published in over 40 languages. She died in 1957 at the age of 90. In a recent biography, John Miller (1998) indicates that while many of the books appeared to be based on some of Wilder's actual experiences in Missouri, she intended that the books be novels, and she wrote them that way. She spent most of her adult life on a farm and wrote for local newspapers. Interestingly, Miller attributes much of the credit for the quality of Wilder's books to her daughter, Rose Wilder Lane, who was also a journalist and author.

This chapter from *These Happy Golden Years* is about Laura's "First Day of School" as a teacher. As you read it, keep in mind that Laura is younger than two of her students, a most unusual and improbable situation in public schools today unless one is a teacher of adult education. And try to imagine what it must have been like not

only to have to teach each child but also to keep them warm. According to Eric Sloane (1972), whose sketches of one-room schoolhouses bring them to life, heating the classroom was always a major problem. "The students' parents were responsible for heating the old-time classroom. . . . As late as 1825 in Hartford, Connecticut, the 'out country' schools voted that: 'Each scholar shall furnish ten feet of seasoned hardwood . . . to be delivered at commencement time, or a penalty of forty cents in money shall thereby be subjected" (Sloane, 1972). Heating the classroom is likely *not* one of the challenges you will be facing. On the other hand, notice similarities between the challenges Laura faced and the ones you *will* face. Does this excerpt make you eager to take the reins? Is Laura's display of perseverance a lesson in itself?

Laura heard a stove lid rattle. For one instant she was in bed with Mary, and Pa was building the morning fire. Then she saw the calico curtain and she knew where she was, and that today she must begin to teach school.

She heard Mr. Brewster take down the milk pail, and the door slammed behind him. On the other side of the curtain Mrs. Brewster got out of bed. Johnny whimpered, and was still. Laura did not move; she felt that if she lay still enough, she might keep the day from coming.

Mr. Brewster came in with the milk, and she heard him say, "I'm going to start a fire in the schoolhouse. I'll be back by the time breakfast's ready." The door slammed behind him again.

All at once, Laura threw back the covers. The air was biting cold. Her teeth chattered and her fingers were so stiff that she could not button her shoes.

The kitchen was not so cold. Mrs. Brewster had broken the ice in the water pail and was filling the teakettle, and she replied pleasantly to Laura's "Good morning." Laura filled the wash basin and washed her hands and face at the bench by the door. The icy water made her cheeks tingle, and her whole face was rosy and glowing in the looking glass above the bench while she combed her hair before it.

Slices of salt pork were frying, and Mrs. Brewster was slicing cold boiled potatoes into another frying pan on the stove. Johnny fussed in the bedroom, and Laura quickly pinned her braids, tied on her apron, and said, "Let me fix the potatoes while you dress him."

So while Mrs. Brewster brought Johnny to the stove and made him ready for breakfast, Laura finished slicing the potatoes, and salted and peppered and covered them. Then she turned the slices of meat and set the table neatly.

"I'm glad Ma told me to bring this big apron," she said. "I like a real big apron that covers your whole dress, don't you?"

Mrs. Brewster did not answer. The stove was red now and the whole room was warm, but it seemed bleak. Nothing but short, necessary words were said at the breakfast table.

It was a relief to Laura to put on her wraps, take her books and her tin dinner pail, and leave that house. She set out on the half-mile walk through the snow to the schoolhouse. The way was unbroken, except for Mr. Brewster's footsteps, which were so far apart that Laura could not walk in them.

As she floundered on, plunging into the deep snow, she suddenly laughed aloud. "Well!" she thought. "Here I am. I dread to go on, and I would not go back. Teaching school can not possibly be as bad as staying in that house with Mrs. Brewster. Anyway, it cannot be worse."

Then she was so frightened that she said aloud, "I've *got* to go on." Black soft-coal smoke rose against the morning sky from the old claim-shanty's stovepipe. Two more lines of footprints came to its door, and Laura heard voices inside it. For a moment she gathered her courage, then she opened the door and went in.

The board walls were not battened. Streaks of sunshine streamed through the cracks upon a row of six homemade seats and desks that marched down the middle of the room. Beyond them on the studding of the opposite wall, a square of boards had been nailed and painted black, to make a blackboard.

In front of the seats stood a big heating stove. Its round sides and top were cherry-red from the heat of the fire, and standing around it were the scholars that Laura must teach. They all looked at Laura. There were five of them, and two boys and one girl were taller than she was.

"Good morning," she managed to say.

They all answered, still looking at her. A small window by the door let in a block of sunshine. Beyond it, in the corner by the stove, stood a small table and a chair. "That is the teacher's table," Laura thought, and then, "Oh my; I am the teacher."

Her steps sounded loud. All the eyes followed her. She put her books and dinner pail on the table, and took off her coat and hood. She hung them on a nail in the wall by the chair. On the table was a small clock; its hands stood at five minutes to nine.

Somehow she had to get through five minutes, before the time to begin school.

Slowly she took off her mittens and put them in the pocket of her coat. Then she faced all the eyes, and stepped to the stove. She held her hands to it as if to warm them. All the pupils made way for her, still looking at her. She must say something. She must.

"It is cold this morning, isn't it?" she heard herself say; then without waiting for an answer, "Do you think you can keep warm in the seats away from the stove?"

One of the tall boys said quickly, "I'll sit in the back seat; it's the coldest."

The tall girl said, "Charles and I have to sit together, we have to study from the same books."

"That's good; then you can all sit nearer the stove," Laura said. To her joyful surprise, the five minutes were gone! She said, "You may take your seats. School will begin."

The little girl took the front seat; behind her sat the little boy, then the tall girl and Charles, and behind them the other tall boy. Laura rapped her pencil on the table. "School will come to order. I will now take your names and ages."

The little girl was Ruby Brewster; she was nine years old. She had brown hair and sparkling brown eyes, and she was as soft and still as a mouse. Laura knew she would be sweet and good. She had finished the First Reader, and in arithmetic she was learning subtraction.

The little boy was her brother Tommy Brewster. He was eleven, and had finished the Second Reader, and reached short division.

The two sitting together were Charles and Martha Harrison. Charles was seventeen; he was thin and pale and slow of speech. Martha was sixteen; she was quicker, and spoke for them both.

The last boy was Clarence Brewster. He, too, was older than Laura. His brown eyes were even brighter and livelier than his little sister Ruby's, his dark hair was thick and unruly, and he was quick in speaking and moving. He had a way of speaking that was almost saucy.

Clarence, Charles and Martha were all in the Fourth Reader. They had passed the middle of the spelling book, and in arithmetic they were working fractions. In geography they had studied the New England states, and they answered questions so well that Laura set them to learn the Middle Atlantic states. None of them had studied grammar or history, but

Martha had brought her mother's grammar and Clarence had a history book.

"Very well," Laura said. "You may all begin at the beginning in grammar and history, and exchange the books, to learn your lessons."

When Laura had learned all this, and assigned their lessons, it was time for recess. They all put on their wraps and went out to play in the snow, and Laura breathed a sigh of relief. The first quarter of the first day was over.

Then she began to plan; she would have reading, arithmetic, and grammar lessons in the forenoon, and, in the afternoon, reading again, history, writing, and spelling. There were three classes in spelling, for Ruby and Tommy were far apart in the spelling book.

After fifteen minutes, she rapped on the window to call the pupils in. Then until noon she heard and patiently corrected their reading aloud.

The noon hour dragged slowly. Alone at her table, Laura ate her bread and butter, while the others gathered around the stove, talking and joking while they ate from their dinner pails. Then the boys ran races in the snow outdoors, while Martha and Ruby watched them from the window and Laura still sat at her table. She was a teacher now, and must act like one.

At last the hour was gone, and again she rapped on the window. The boys came briskly in, breathing out clouds of frosty breath and shaking cold air from their coats and mufflers as they hung them up. They were glowing from cold and exercise.

Laura said, "The fire is low. Would you put more coal on, please, Charles?"

Willing, but slowly, Charles lifted the heavy hod of coal and dumped most of it into the stove.

"I'll do that next time!" Clarence said. Perhaps he did not mean to be impertinent. If he did mean to be, what could Laura do? He was a tough, hardy boy, bigger than she was, and older. His brown eyes twinkled at her. She stood as tall as possible and rapped her pencil on the table.

"School will come to order," she said.

Though the school was small, she thought best to follow the routine of the town school, and have each class come forward to answer. Ruby was alone in her class, so she must know every answer perfectly, for there was no one to help her by answering some of the questions. Laura let her spell slowly, and if she made a mistake, she might try again. She spelled every word in her lesson. Tommy was slower, but Laura gave him time to think and try, and he did as well.

Then Martha and Charles and Clarence did their spelling. Martha made no mistakes, but Charles missed five words and Clarence missed three. For the first time, Laura must punish them.

"You may take your seat, Martha," she said. "Charles and Clarence, go to the blackboard, and write the words you missed, three times each."

Charles slowly went, and began to write his words. Clarence glanced back at Laura with a saucy look. Rapidly he wrote large and sprawling letters that covered his half of the blackboard with only six words. Then turning toward Laura, and not even raising his hand for permission to speak, he said, "Teacher! The board's too small."

He was making a joke of punishment for failing in his lesson. He was defying Laura.

For a long, dreadful moment he stood laughing at her, and she looked straight at him.

Then she said, "Yes, the board is small, Clarence. I am sorry, but you should erase what you have written and write the words again more carefully. Make them smaller, and there will be room enough."

He had to obey her, for she did not know what she could do if he did not.

Still grinning, good-naturedly he turned to the blackboard and wiped out the scrawls. He wrote the three words three times each, and below them he signed his name with a flourish.

With relief, Laura saw that it was four o'clock.

"You may put away your books," she said. When every book was neat on the shelves beneath the desk tops, she said, "School is dismissed."

Clarence grabbed his coat and cap and muffler from their nail and with a shout he was first through the doorway. Tommy was at his heels, but they waited outside while Laura helped Ruby into her coat and tied her hood. More soberly, Charles and Martha wrapped themselves well against the cold before they set out. They had a mile to walk.

Laura stood by the window and watched them go. She could see Mr. Brewster's brother's claim shanty, only half a mile away. Smoke blew from its stovepipe and its west window glinted back the light from the sinking sun. Clarence and Tommy scuffled in the snow, and Ruby's red hood bobbed along behind them. So far as Laura could see from the eastern window, the sky was clear.

The school shanty had no window from which she could see the northwest. If a blizzard came up, she could not know that it was coming until it struck.

She cleaned the blackboard, and with the broom she swept the floor. A dustpan was not needed, the cracks between the floorboards were so wide. She shut the stove's draughts, put on her wraps, took her books and dinner pail, and shutting the door carefully behind her, she set out on her morning path toward Mrs. Brewster's house.

Her first day as a teacher was over. She was thankful for that.

Questions for Discussion and Debate

1. All things considered, would you say Laura's first day of teaching was a success? Why, or why not?

2. Notice how she handles certain sticky situations. Would you have handled them in similar ways?

3. If you have already had an opportunity to try your hand at teaching solo, where did you identify with Laura? Did you have any other reactions to this excerpt?

4. What might be some of the problems/pleasures of having students of widely varying ages in your class? Debate the pros and cons of an ungraded classroom.

5. Write down as many examples as you can of how the typical classroom of today differs both physically and educationally from Laura's classroom. Do you have any interest in turning the clock back?

Activities and Projects

1. Wilder presents a vivid verbal picture of Laura's first day of teaching. Literally draw the scenario as you see it.

2. In groups create a first-day scenario—*any* first-day scenario you imagine—and present it to the larger class. At least one group

should act out Wilder's particular version of the first-day. Following each scenario, discuss teacher behaviors and their effectiveness. Compare and contrast the presentations.

3. Interview several teachers about their history, specifically their first day of teaching in their own classroom. Record their descriptions and assess them. Then offer some advice to your peers on the "do's and don'ts" of their first day of teaching.

2.4　*History of Great Barrington, Massachusetts* (1882)

Charles J. Taylor

In this excerpt, Charles J. Taylor implies that historians such as himself often face great difficulty when trying to uncover the history of American public education. We can infer from his description of the negotiations and expenditures made on behalf of establishing Great Barrington, Massachusetts, schools that many local records could not be found. As a result, he had to do a great deal of hypothesizing. There are two advantages to reading about Taylor's struggle to determine the accuracy of his information about these schools. First, you can discover the basis on which he draws his conclusions; and, second, you can confront the fact that much of what gets passed on as authentic history is very often *not* accurate. Taylor's piece can perhaps act as a reminder that, before believing what you read about the history of American education—or anything else, for that matter—it is wise to take the stance of a healthy skeptic and read other sources of information on the same subject.

As you read this excerpt about how some of the earliest local schools came to be established, identify some of the obstacles to growth that public education had to deal with over 250 years ago. Is there any similarity between the problems of colonial Great Barrington schools and the problems some school districts face today, say, around the time for voting on the annual school budget?

In 1740, Sheffield provided for a school to be kept in the upper part of the town; and in 1743 having raised the sum of £35 Old Tenor for schools, voted that the "Inhabitants of the town of Sheffield dwelling north of the Indian Land or Beech Tree, (1) shall have the benefit of drawing the money they are assest, *provided* they put it to the use of schooling."* This provision seems to convey a gentle insinuation that the people living north of the "Beech Tree" took no great interest in the matter of education. From 1743 forward, the North Parish shared equally

_____

(1.) The Beech tree—a boundary in the south line of the parish.

_____

From Charles J. Taylor, *History of Great Barrington, (Berkshire County,) Massachusetts.* Great Barrington, MA: Clark W. Bryan and Co., 1882, pp. 147–149, 349–353.

with other sections of the town of Sheffield, in all appropriations made by the town for the support of schools, and the inhabitants of the parish were treated with as much liberality as were those of other parts of the town. But these appropriations were small, made at irregular intervals, and the schools were consequently irregularly kept. The sparse population was scattered over so large an area that the children could not be conveniently assembled at any one place for instruction; school-houses had not been built in different parts of the parish, and the appropriations made for schooling were inadequate to the employment of a number of teachers. The custom then prevailed—which was continued in later years—of gathering the children of a certain section at some dwelling house, or other place conveniently located for the purpose, where they were taught for a stated length of time; at the expiration of this period the teacher removed to another part of the parish, where the children from that part were assembled and instructed; by this method the children enjoyed nearly equal advantages; the teacher itinerated, and one "master, mistress or dame" sufficed for nearly the whole of the parish. . . .

The earliest school-house, of which we have positive information, seems to have been built in 1748. No vote authorizing its erection is found; but that it was built, and at the expense of the parish, appears from the following from the parish records, December 22d 1748:

> "Voted to give fifteen shillings Old Tenor, to those men that built the school house; fifteen shillings per day each man, and withal to pay for the Glass, Nails and Plates, and Beams, and Posts, Boards, Hooks, Hinges at a reasonable rate."

> March 28, 1749. "Voted to John Pixley one pound old Tenor for making School-House Hearth."

Oct. 27, 1749. "Vot. to Sergeant Henry Borghghardt for four boards for the School House teen shillings old tenor," also "to Josiah Phelps, Lime, Boards and work to the school twenty two shillings old tenor. . . . "

. . . In 1761, the town of Great Barrington, then recently incorporated passed a vote "that the school for the present be kept *in the school-house now built,*" from which we infer that there was *one* and *but one* school-house then standing, and that this was the house which was built in 1748. We may therefore conclude that the house sold in 1757 was in existence previous to the incorporation of the parish. It is to be presumed that it was built under the auspices of the town of Sheffield, and that its location was south of the Great Bridge,—probably in the south part of the present village. . . .

The statutes in force in the early years of our parish and town organization, required that every town of fifty or more families "should be constantly provided of a schoolmaster, to teach children and youth to read and write," and towns of one hundred families were required to maintain a grammar school and employ "some discreet person of good conversation, well instructed in the tongues, to keep such school." Under this last requirement, Sheffield, in 1752, made provision for a grammar school to be kept four months in the Upper parish, five months in the middle part, and three months at the south end of the town; and in the next year a similar school was provided for in the North parish. . . .

. . . In 1771, the town refused to raise money for schools, and the school was apparently unkept. In consequence of this, the town was summoned to answer before the Court of Sessions—February, 1772—"for being unprovided with a school," and through its agent, David Ingersoll, Junior, Esq., made virtual confession, in the plea, "Will not contend with the King," whereupon it was fined £3, 6s., 8d., and costs. In 1776 the inhabitants voted not to raise money for schooling; and during the war the subject of appropriations for this object was seldom acted upon. Still, schools were to some extent maintained by private enterprise. . . .

. . . The early schools of the town were not of a high order; reading, writing, spelling, and arithmetic—the rudiments only, were taught. The town had not attained to the dignity of a grammar school; and in 1769 a proposition to hire a grammar school master was negatived. But there is some evidence that Mr. Gideon Bostwick, before 1770, and previous to his settlement as a missionary, was engaged here in teaching a school above the ordinary grade. The schools are supposed to have been kept at the dwellings of the inhabitants in separate neighborhoods, as the different sections of the town were not supplied with school-houses. . . .

. . . The old center school-house of the Center District was erected by an association of villagers, formed December, 15th, 1794. The gentlemen engaged in this enterprise entered into an agreement for purchasing of Captain Walter Pynchon one-half acre of land for a building site—the same on which the Center school house now stands—with a pass-way of twenty four feet in width from the highway to the premises, and to erect theron a building 44 by 25 feet on the ground, nine feet between floors, to contain rooms respectively 22 by 24 feet, 12 by 14 feet, and 9 by 10 feet, with a fire place in each; the land and house to be held in twenty-four shares, for the purposes of schooling only. The shares were fixed at £5 each, and the proprietors were permitted to pay two-thirds of their subscriptions in material and labor. Moses Hopkins, Samuel Whiting, and Stephen Sibley were appointed a building committee, and Thomas Ives treasurer. An annual meeting of the proprietors was provided for, at which committees were to be chosen for employing instructors, furnishing firewood, and making repairs; and for a fund for repairs, it

was agreed that a charge of nine pence per quarter should be made for each scholar. . . .

. . . The land was, soon after, purchased at a cost of £13, and the building erected in 1795, though its internal arrangement varied somewhat from the plan proposed. This eventually became the property of the Center District, and the building continued in use until 1850, when it was destroyed by fire. The present Center school-house was erected nearly upon the site of the old one, in 1851.

No other school-houses are *known* to have been built in town prior to the year 1800, though it is not improbable that others may have been erected in localities remote from the village; and of those mentioned, two only—the Center and Southern—were then in use. In 1782 and '83 the town refused to raise money for schooling, but in 1785 the sum of £100 was raised and a committee appointed "to divide the town into districts for the purpose of schools." A vote was also passed giving to the inhabitants of each district, the sums which they might be assessed in raising the above sum. The committee above mentioned, divided the inhabitants into five, so called, districts. Similar divisions were made in 1788, '94 and '97. But these were simply classifications of the inhabitants into neighborhoods, made for the purpose of equitably expending the money granted, and did not constitute school districts. In 1791 the inhabitants, perhaps with a tinge of irony to the proprietors of the school-house by the bridge, voted to raise *forty shillings* for schools, and that the same "be expended in the school-house near the Great Bridge." In 1792, and again in 1794, the town was indicted "for not keeping schools according to law," and perhaps with good effect.

From 1794 to 1800 an increased interest was manifested in schools, and in that period the annual appropriations for their support varied from $300 to $500.

Questions for Discussion and Debate

1. Describe the nature of the school(s) that were established in colonial and postcolonial Great Barrington. (Great Barrington was referred to as the North Parish before 1761. After 1761 the North Parish of Sheffield was incorporated as Great Barrington.) For example, how many schools were there per number of families? What were the *number* and *nature* of the teacher(s)? Describe the physical characteristics of the school.

2. Read the excerpt by Horace Mann in this chapter (Selection 2.9). What would his reaction be to the problems Great Barring-ton seemed to have generating support for public education? (Notice that in the 1800s Mann promoted common schooling as a way to alleviate social ills and eradicate ignorance. Did attitudes about public education change from the 1750s to the 1850s?)

3. As in many American towns today, the people of this New England town voted on school monetary allotments. School taxes "were assessed upon them," and a school committee was established for decision-making purposes. What are some of the differences between then and now? Identify as many as you can.

Activities and Projects

1. Clearly this excerpt conveys the fact that control of the schools was primarily local in nature. What limitations were placed on this local control? Do such limitations still exist? For example, what controls do the state and federal authorities have over local schools? Make a chart with three columns, labeled "Local," "State," and "Federal." After researching the powers at each level vis-à-vis local schools, list those powers in the appropriate columns.

2. Delve into the early records that document the establishment of the first schools in *your* town or one that interests you. Compare their origins to those of the first schools in Great Barrington. Present your findings in diagram format.

3. Using the information contained in the excerpt about the actual physical measurements of the school built in 1794, take a measuring tape and block it out so you can actually *see* it. Then discuss how many desks would fit into the three rooms? How might the rooms have been arranged? How many students would comfortably fit in this space?

4. In small groups, go out into the community and do field research related to why some people take "no great interest in the matter of education" or vote "not to raise money for schooling." Interview people from a cross section of a town or city on the issues surrounding funding for public education and why they do or do not support it—or to what extent they do support it. Before you do your interviews, research the possible sources for funding schools. How do those interviewed believe schools *should* be funded? Property taxes? Lottery? Other? Prepare to share your group's findings.

2.5   *Emerson on Education* (1966)

Ralph Waldo Emerson

Ralph Waldo Emerson (1803–1882) looms large in the history of American literature and philosophy. But despite this fame, Emerson "has been consistently ignored by historians of American education" (Jones, 1966, p. vii). According to editor Howard Mumford Jones, in his introduction to *Emerson on Education: Selections,* this oversight may be based on the fact that such historians have focused mainly on the growth of America's public schools and those associated with that development. They may have ignored Emerson, "assuming that his profound anti-institutional bias minimized his contribution . . . " (1966, p. vii).

Indeed, the following excerpt contains evidence of Emerson's anti-institutional bias, but is his bias without foundation? He is critical of teaching when it is delivered in schools where education is streamlined, reduced to "safe uniformity," and made to be efficient. Such systematization, he says, affects us with "a certain yawning of the jaws" (Jones, 1966, p. 210). And he notes that the cost to the student and teacher is great: the inability of teachers to address the individual needs and interests of their students, who are of an infinite variety.

While he does not have the solution for this dilemma, Emerson wisely reminds teachers of the pedagogue's primary objective: to reach each and every student.

We teach boys to be such men as we are. We do not teach them to aspire to be all they can. We do not give them a training as if we believed in their noble nature. We scarce educate their bodies. We do not train the eye and the hand. We exercise their understandings to the apprehension and comparison of some facts, to a skill in numbers, in words; we aim to make accountants, attorneys, engineers; but not to make able, earnest, great-hearted men. The great object of Education should be commensurate with the object of life. It should be a moral one; to teach self-trust: to inspire the youthful man with an interest in himself; with a curiosity touching his own nature; to acquaint him with the resources of his mind, and to teach him that there is all his strength, and to inflame him with a piety towards the Grand Mind in which he lives. Thus would education conspire with the Divine Providence. A man is a little thing whilst he works by and for himself, but, when he gives voice to the rules of love and justice, is godlike, his word is current in all countries; and all men, though his enemies, are made his friends and obey it as their own.

In affirming that the moral nature of man is the predominant element and should therefore be mainly consulted in the arrangements of a school, I am very far from wishing that it should swallow up all the other instincts and faculties of man. It should be enthroned in his mind, but if it monopolize the man he is not yet sound, he does not yet know his wealth. He is in danger of becoming merely devout, and wearisome through the monotony of his thought. It is not less necessary that the intellectual and the active faculties should be nourished and matured.

. . . I call our system a system of despair, and I find all the correction, all the revolution that is needed and that the best spirits of this age promise, in one word, in Hope. Nature, when she sends a new mind into the world, fills it beforehand with a desire for that which she wishes it to know and do. Let us wait and see what is this new creation, of what new organ the great Spirit had need when it incarnated this new Will. A new Adam in the garden, he is to name all the beasts in the field, all the gods in the sky. And jealous provision seems to have been made in his constitution that you shall not invade and contaminate him with the worn weeds of your language and opinions. The charm of life is this variety of genius, these contrasts and flavors by which Heaven has modulated the identity of truth, and there is a perpetual hankering to violate this individuality, to warp his ways of thinking and behavior to resemble or reflect your thinking and behavior. A low self-love in the parent desires that his child should repeat his character and fortune; an expectation which the child, if justice is done him, will nobly disappoint. By working on the theory that this resemblence exists, we shall do what in us lies to defeat his proper promise and produce the ordinary and mediocre. I suffer whenever I see that common sight of a parent or senior imposing his opinion and way of thinking and being on a young soul to which they are totally unfit. Cannot we let people be themselves, and enjoy life in their own way? You are trying to make that man another *you*. One's enough.

Or we sacrifice the genius of the pupil, the unknown possibilities of his nature, to a neat and safe uniformity, as the Turks whitewash the costly mosaics of ancient art which the Greeks left on their temple walls. Rather let us have men whose manhood is only the continuation of their boyhood, natural characters still; such are able and fertile for heroic action; and not that sad spectacle with which we are too familiar, educated eyes in uneducated bodies. . . .

. . . So to regard the young child, the young man, requires, no doubt, rare patience: a patience that nothing but faith in the remedial forces of the soul can give. You see his sensualism; you see his want of those tastes and perceptions which make the power and safety of your character. Very likely. But he has something else. If he has his own vice, he has its correlative virtue. Every mind should be allowed to make its own statement in action, and its balance will appear. In these judgments one needs that foresight which was attributed to an eminent reformer, of whom it was said "his patience could see in the bud of the aloe the blossom at the end of a hundred years." Alas for the cripple Practice when it seeks to come up with the bird Theory, which flies before it. Try your design on the best school. The scholars are of all ages and temperaments and capacities. It is difficult to class them, some are too young, some are slow, some perverse. Each requires so much consideration, that the morning hope of the teacher, of a day of love and progress, is often closed at evening by despair. Each single case, the more it is considered, shows more to be done; and the strict conditions of the hours, on one side, and the number of tasks, on the other. Whatever becomes of our method, the conditions stand fast,—six hours, and thirty, fifty, or a hundred and fifty pupils. Something must be done, and done speedily, and in this distress the wisest are tempted to adopt violent means, to proclaim martial law, corporal punishment, mechanical arrangement, bribes, spies, wrath, main strength and ignorance, in lieu of that wise genial providential influence they had hoped, and yet hope at some future day to adopt. Of course the devotion to details reacts injuriously on the teacher. He cannot indulge his genius, he cannot delight in personal relations with young friends, when his eye is always on the clock, and twenty classes are to be dealt with before the day is done. Besides, how can he please himself with genius, and foster modest virtue? A sure proportion of rogue and dunce finds its way into every school and requires a cruel share of time, and the gentle teacher, who wished to be a Providence to youth, is grown a martinet, sore with suspicions; knows as much vice as the judge of a police court, and his love of learning is lost in the routine of grammars and books of elements.

A rule is so easy that it does not need a man to apply it; an automaton, a machine, can be made to keep a school so. It facilitates labor and thought so much that there is always the temptation in large schools to omit the endless task of meeting the wants of each single mind, and to govern by steam. But it is at frightful cost. Our modes of Education aim to expedite, to save labor; to do for masses what cannot be done for masses, what must be done reverently, one by one: say rather, the whole world is needed for the tuition of each pupil. The advantages of this system of emulation and display are so prompt and obvious, it is such a time-saver, it is so energetic on slow and on bad natures, and is of so easy application, needing no sage or poet, but any tutor or schoolmaster in his first term can apply it,—that it is not strange that this calomel of culture should be a popular medicine. On the other hand, total abstinence from this drug, and the adoption of simple discipline and the following of nature, involves at once immense claims on the time, the thoughts, on the life of the teacher. It requires time, use, insight, event, all the great lessons and assistances of God; and only to think of using it implies character and profoundness; to enter on this course of discipline is to be good

and great. It is precisely analogous to the difference between the use of corporal punishment and the methods of love. It is so easy to bestow on a bad boy a blow, overpower him, and get obedience without words, that in this world of hurry and distraction, who can wait for the returns of reason and the conquest of self; in the uncertainty too whether that will ever come? And yet the familiar observation of the universal compensations might suggest the fear that so summary a stop of a bad humor was more jeopardous than its continuance.

Now the correction of this quack practice is to import into Education the wisdom of life. Leave this military hurry and adopt the pace of Nature. Her secret is patience. Do you know how the naturalist learns all the secrets of the forest, of plants, of birds, of beasts, of reptiles, of fishes, of the rivers and the sea? When he goes into the woods the birds fly before him and he finds none; when he goes to the river-bank, the fish and the reptile swim away and leave him alone. His secret is patience; he sits down, and sits still; he is a statue; he is a log. These creatures have no value for their time, and he must put as low a rate on his. By dint of obstinate sitting still, reptile, fish, bird and beast, which all wish to return to their haunts, begin to return. He sits still; if they approach, he remains passive as the stone he sits upon. They lose their fear. They have curiosity too about him. By and by the curiosity masters the fear, and they come swimming, creeping and flying towards him; and as he is still immovable, they not only resume their haunts and their ordinary labors and manners, show themselves to him in their work-day trim, but also volunteer some degree of advances towards fellowship and good understanding with a biped who behaves so civilly and well. Can you not baffle the impatience and passion of the child by your tranquillity? Can you not wait for him, as Nature and Providence do? Can you not keep for his mind and ways, for his secret, the same curiosity you give to the squirrel, snake, rabbit, and the sheldrake and the deer? He has a secret; wonderful methods in him; he is,— every child,—a new style of man; give him time and opportunity. Talk of Columbus and Newton! I tell you the child just born in yonder hovel is the beginning of a revolution as great as theirs. But you must have the believing and prophetic eye. Have the self-command you wish to inspire. Your teaching and discipline must have the reserve and taciturnity of Nature. Teach them to hold their tongues by holding your own. Say little; do not snarl; do not chide; but govern by the eye. See what they need, and that the right thing is done.

I confess myself utterly at a loss in suggesting particular reforms in our ways of teaching. No discretion that can be lodged with a school-committee, with the overseers or visitors of an academy, of a college, can at all avail to reach these difficulties and perplexities, but they solve themselves when we leave institutions and address individuals. The will, the male power, organizes, imposes its own thought and wish on others, and makes that military eye which controls boys as it controls men; admirable in its results, a fortune to him who has it, and only dangerous when it leads the workman to overvalue and overuse it and precludes him from finer means. Sympathy, the female force,— which they must use who have not the first,— deficient in instant control and the breaking down of resistance, is more subtle and lasting and creative. I advise teachers to cherish mother-wit. I assume that you will keep the grammar, reading, writing and arithmetic in order; 't is easy and of course you will. But smuggle in a little contraband wit, fancy, imagination, thought. If you have a taste which you have suppressed because it is not shared by those about you, tell them that. Set this law up, whatever becomes of the rules of the school: they must not whisper,

much less talk; but if one of the young people says a wise thing, greet it, and let all the children clap their hands. They shall have no book but schoolbooks in the room; but if one has brought in a Plutarch or Shakspeare or Don Quixote or Goldsmith or any other good book, and understands what he reads, put him at once at the head of the class. Nobody shall be disorderly, or leave his desk without permission, but if a boy runs from his bench, or a girl, because the fire falls, or to check some injury that a little dastard is inflicting behind his desk on some helpless sufferer, take away the medal from the head of the class and give it on the instant to the brave rescuer. If a child happens to show that he knows any fact about astronomy, or plants, or birds, or rocks, or history, that interests him and you, hush all the classes and encourage him to tell it so that all may hear. Then you have made your schoolroom like the world. Of course you will insist on modesty in the children, and respect to their teachers, but if the boy stops you in your speech, cries out that you are wrong and sets you right, hug him!

To whatsoever upright mind, to whatsoever beating heart I speak, to you it is committed to educate men. By simple living, by an illimitable soul, you inspire, you correct, you instruct, you raise, you embellish all. By your own act you teach the beholder how to do the practicable. According to the depth from which you draw your life, such is the depth not only of your strenuous effort, but of your manners and presence.

The beautiful nature of the world has here blended your happiness with your power. Work straight on in absolute duty, and you lend an arm and an encouragement to all the youth of the universe. Consent yourself to be an organ of your highest thought, and lo! suddenly you put all men in your debt, and are the fountain of an energy that goes pulsing on with waves of benefit to the borders of society, to the circumference of things.

Questions for Discussion and Debate

1. Which of Emerson's words of wisdom in this excerpt would *you* be most apt to *quote* and want to remember? Why?

2. In your own words explain Emerson's analogy between the way a naturalist approaches nature and the way a teacher should approach his or her students. Then, using Emerson's words, list the different kinds of advice he offers teachers through this analogy.

3. In the last segment of the excerpt, Emerson, by way of further advice, tells you how to make "your school-room like the world."

List some of those ways. Do you agree with him? Why, or why not?

4. Have you seen teachers who operate according to Emerson's prescriptions? Explain. How is his advice timeless and universal? Do you see any connections between Emerson's ideas and any of the views in other excerpts in this chapter or in other chapters? Note, for example, Peabody on the Dorians (Selection 2.6) and the historical figures mentioned in the Brief Background to this chapter.

Activities and Projects

1. Emerson was a transcendentalist, a believer in a philosophy based on the value of the spiritual world, the beauties of nature, and self-reliance. Find out more about transcendentalism and prepare a brief report on this philosophy. Include your perception of how these values can play a role in your teaching.

2. Emerson implies a belief in the value of spontaneity in the classroom. If possible, observe some classes in local schools and record any instances in which spontaneity, that is, activity that appears to be unplanned, is utilized by the teacher as a teachable moment. If you are unable to observe any classes, consider watching one of the many films that contain stories of teachers or classroom scenes in which spontaneity may play a role. Among such movies are *Conrack, Stand and Deliver, Dead Poets' Society,* and *To Sir, with Love.* (A longer

list of films is given in chapter 1, Selection 1.2, Activities and Projects, No. 2.)

3. In this excerpt and his other writings, Emerson explains his belief in individualism and nonconformity. In the Brief Background to this chapter, the editor points out the fact that most of the movers and shakers in the history of education were nonconformists, risk-takers, and challengers to the status quo. Is that image of teachers still true today? Share your views on this question with colleagues. Then debate these resolutions: that teachers should play the role of transmitters of culture and maintain the status quo; that teachers should teach a fixed body of knowledge and discourage student-initiated topics; and that teachers should view themselves as risk-takers rather than as preservers of the status quo.

2.6 ‖‖‖‖ *Aesthetic Papers* (1849)

Elizabeth Palmer Peabody

Elizabeth Palmer Peabody (1804–1894) was an extraordinary woman with a multitude of achievements, though few, if anyone—even educators—could tell you much about her. Although best known among early-childhood educators for her establishment of the first English-speaking private kindergarten (*children's garden*) in the United States in Boston in 1860, Peabody was also an historian with over 40 books to her credit. In addition, she was an editor, a teacher, a teacher educator, and the owner of a bookstore that served as a salon for transcendentalists including Emerson, Thoreau, and Hawthorne. Their work, in fact, appears alongside her essay (excerpted here), "The Dorian Measure, with a Modern Application," in the journal *Aesthetic Papers*, which she also edited.

In this essay, Peabody writes from her frame of reference as both teacher *and* historian. She makes the claim that the Dorians, one of the ancient Greek tribes, have a great deal to teach us about education. She notes, for example, their high degree of toleration, their ability "to express the beauty of the most beautiful," and their practice of moderation and balance in all things. She admires their cultivation of conversations between youths and elders ("inspirers"), a pedagogical technique that Peabody wrote about and attempted to spread among teachers. She herself was inspired by the fact that the Dorians' "recreation was music." In fact, the Dorians referred to education as *learning music*. They did not confine this to learning harmony of sounds; it was a study of the "harmonies of man within himself, with the state, and with nature." In the Doric state, education was a subject of greater importance than government, and its constitution promoted education for people of all ages.

As you read in more detail about the education of Dorian youths, both male and female, think about the role that music and dance play in the schools today. Do you agree with the arguments for these activities that Peabody makes at the end of her essay? And, most important, can the Dorians of old teach us anything "new"?

That to which we sequestrate the name of *music* stands in the forefront of Dorian education. The musical ear is that region which connects the bodily and spiritual life, and it occupies a large portion of the consciousness in the favored organizations of the people of the South of Europe. Its *due* proportion denotes physical perfection, and is one of the most obvious indications of the capacity of an individual or of a people for a high culture.

Since this is so, in the character of the music must be the deepest secret of the education of a people; and that the Dorians thought this, is evident from the rigidity and solemnity of all their regulations about music, and that the penalty of death was threatened against any one

---

From Elizabeth P. Peabody (Ed.), *Aesthetic Papers.* New York: G. P. Putnam, 1849, pp. 89–93, 103–104, 109–110.

who violated the sanctity of the ancient music by new measures, or even new strings to the lyre.

The true Dorian music was that which entirely expressed the idea of the Dorian character. It was *the sound of Apollo* in the soul. The movement was just that which waked up the intellect to the perception of all law, and checked the passions from falling into deliquescence; making the whole human being a calm, clear-sighted, creative power. That they believed this music was in the universe, objective to the soul, is expressed by the Pythagorean symbol of the music of the spheres, apprehensible through the *silence* which was but another name for the perfect act of intellection. There was therefore ideal propriety in the Dorians making music their central activity. Not only did all bodily exercise thus become more or less of a dance, and an intellectual impress was made upon passion, but, what is more important, thus they formed, in the consciousness of each individual, a standard by which all their activity was measured.

The dances of the Dorians were intellectual in their character,—sometimes representative of historical events,—sometimes of foreign customs,—sometimes they were allegorical; in all instances, even when comic, they expressed thought, and stimulated intellectual activity; while the dances of other nations expressed the softer passions merely, and tended to immorality.

The dancing in chorus of young men, of virgins, and of old men, were parts of the public worship. The motions of the young men, says Müller, were vigorous, and often of a military character; those of the virgins were in measured steps, with feminine gestures; and the whole was solemn and grave for the participation of age.

It is impossible here to go into the history of Dorian music and dancing; but its early purity, as well as its subsequent corruption, its action upon the ceremonies of other worships than that of Apollo, and the re-action of other worships upon it,—all testify to the wisdom of the Dorians in making the music and dance an affair of legislation.

The power of music and the dance is exemplified especially in the fact, that with the Dorians they entered even into war, and elevated the exercise of destructiveness into an elegant art. It may be thought that this has been of no advantage to humanity, in the long run (a point of which we may not judge, perhaps, as the end is not yet); but there can be no doubt that, if war does exist, the subjection of it to the Dorian measure of music and motion has robbed it, as Burke would say, of half its ferociousness, by taking away all its brutality.

Song was the accompanying, or immediately consequent, step to the mimetic and allegoric dance; and perhaps here we may discover the origin of the multitude of measures in Greek poetry. Lyric poetry prevailed over every other among the Dorians, and was cultivated by both sexes. It originated with the Dorians, as epic poetry has originated in almost all the other tribes, and is to be referred to the predominance of religion. The ode is the natural address of the cultivated mind to the god whose very nature is proportion, and whose own sound is music. The later history of the drama is well known. The earlier history of comedy, as well as tragedy, leads us immediately to the Dorians, whose intellectual sharpness and power originated humorous expression, if not wit itself, to a remarkable degree. Humor is impossible with the intellectually effeminate. Bucolics were the accompaniment of rustic dances, and elegies of those dances which celebrated astronomical changes; and this opens out a new vista of thought as to the derivation of the very idea of dancing from the motions of the heavenly bodies. The poems of Homer were recited at first by Ionian rhapsodists; but Terpander the Dorian is said to have first set them to a regular tune. He is also said to have first mixed Greek and Asiatic music. Another consequence of the Dorian music and dance was the sculpture of Greece, which took its ideal character from the Dorians, who had Apollo for model, and the unveiled human form, beheld with a chaste delight in the gymnasium, for their school of art. Their love for proportion, harmony, and regularity, rather than for luxuriance of ornament and glitter, is also exemplified in their architecture, which betrays a certain relation to the sculpture of the nation and era. Thus the Dorian measure came to characterize their artistic eye, as well as ear and limb, and the body received its highest education; almost reminding one of the sublime image of Milton, who speaks of the time when, by the natural ascension of matter,——

——"bodies shall at last all turn to spirit,
Improved by tract of time, and, wing'd, ascend Ethereal."

But the *music* of the Dorians comprehended their moral and intellectual culture, which was very much the same in both sexes. We may infer a natural education of the affections, and that discipline which precludes selfishness in its grossest form, from the fact, that the family spirit was free and genial. The Dorian called his wife, mistress; and it was no unmeaning title; for women enjoyed a real influence in the management of their families, and as mothers. "Aristotle speaks," says Müller, "of their influence on the government, in the time of the ascendency of Sparta: it increased," he says, "still more when a large part of the landed property fell into the hands of women." He adds, that, "little as the Athenians esteemed their own women, they involuntarily revered the heroines of Sparta; and this feeling is sometimes apparent even in the coarse jests of Aristophanes." Again, "In general, it may be remarked, that, while among the Ionians women were merely considered in an inferior and sensual light, and though the Æolians

allowed their feelings a more elevated tone, as is proved by the amatory poetesses of Lesbos,—the Dorians, as well at Sparta as in the South of Italy, were almost the only nation who esteemed the higher attributes of the female mind as capable of cultivation."

. . . Though music is made a part of almost all Christian worship, and though its great masters have proved by their compositions, that it expresses the highest ideas, and even the most varied thoughts, as well as sentiments, of humanity more adequately than words can do; yet it does not take its place in American education, even upon a par with reading. Somewhat of the practice of music in choral singing, it is true, begins to enter into our common-school education. But this hardly goes beyond the metropolis; and the theory of music is not taught in any school or college in our country, with the exception of the asylums for the blind, and a few private schools. There are multitudes of the fathers of our country who, as school-committee men, direct its education, who never have thought of music but as an amusement of the senses; who never have dreamed of its moral, far less of its intellectual, influences. . . .

But it is time that the importance of music, taught thoroughly, especially in its theory, should be recognized in education. . . .

One objection that is made to the introduction of music into common education is the time that it would occupy which, it is said, should be taken up with more useful exercises. But, waiving the circumstance, that this objection entirely begs the question respecting the comparative importance of music in education, we reply, that, were music and dancing a regular part of school exercises every day, as they should be, it would be no hardship to children to remain more hours at school. These exercises could profitably be so arranged that they would break the monotony of book-studies, and supersede the boisterous, and too often mischievous play-hours, which make the neighborhood of a school a thing to be eschewed by all decent society. The advantages to health of mind and body are no less to be esteemed than the elegance of carriage and general gracefulness which would inevitably take the place of the uncouth, romping manner, or awkward, stiff want of manner, not only of our country people, but even of the inhabitants of our cities. . . .

. . . There is no reason why we should not instantly begin to work on this plan. Our country is full of means. Europe is pouring out upon us her artists and scholars. We are rich, and can tax ourselves for conservative as well as for destructive purposes. Why not employ these artists and scholars to make a new revival of learning, which shall be, to times to come, what that, produced by the dislodged Greeks of the captured Eastern Empire, was to Europe in the fourteenth century? Why should not our merchants become, like the merchant-princes of Italy, the patrons of science and art, and give their children as well as their money to these pursuits? . . .

It is plain, that, if we can spend a hundred millions of dollars in a year for so questionable a purpose as the late war of Mexico, we have resources on which we might draw for public education. And, were education organized and set to music, as the art of destruction is, and that which it is to gain made as definite an object to the imagination, can it be doubted that it could raise its corps of volunteers, ready to spend and be spent for the truth, beauty, and power over nature, which are offered as rewards to the striving?

Questions for Discussion and Debate

1. List some of the Dorians' criteria for how to live. What do you like about the Dorian measure or standard for how to live? Would you suggest that aspects of the Dorian way be applied in education and/or society today? (Note also the information presented about the Dorians in the introduction to the excerpt.)

2. What role did music and dance play in *your* formal education? What role do they play in society today? What are the differences between Dorian education and American education? Are there any similarities?

3. Referring to specific phrases from the excerpt, explain how the study of music was a meaningful political, moral, and intellectual activity for the Dorians.

4. Peabody clearly has a bias in favor of the Dorian measure. What does *she* say that educators can learn from the Dorians?

Activities and Projects

1. Several current education scholars, including Elliot Eisner (1985, 1991), have written about the value of adopting an artistic or aesthetic sensibility across the curriculum. Find out what they mean by this perspective.

2. Locate a piece of music that you believe has influenced American political, moral, or intellectual life or that reflects one of these aspects. Share it with the class, explaining its influence, or write a brief essay about its influence.

3. Peabody admired the concept of balance advocated by the Dorians. Make a chart with two columns, one labeled "Too Much" and the other "Too Little," and brainstorm with your peers about the nature of today's schools: Of what do they have too much, and of what do they have too little?

4. Go beyond "The Dorian Measure" and dig more deeply into Dorian culture. See what research reveals that either confirms or sheds some doubt on the Dorians' potential for improving education in America. Play the devil's advocate and list aspects of the Dorians' practices that might *not* be so popular, practical, or admirable today.

5. As indicated in the introduction to this excerpt, Peabody opened the first English-speaking private kindergarten in America in Boston in 1860. In Wisconsin, however, Margaretta Schurz, who was German-speaking, opened the *first* kindergarten in 1855. She had studied in Germany with Friedrich Froebel, who created the concept of kindergartens there and whose work is also excerpted in this chapter. Peabody herself had traveled to Germany in the 1850s and brought back many of Froebel's ideas.

By 1873, kindergartens were beginning to be incorporated into public school systems. Do some research on the development of early childhood education in this country and the roles played by Schurz, Peabody, and others in the latter part of the 19th century.

2.7 | *Narrative of the Life of Frederick Douglass: An American Slave* (1968)

Frederick Douglass

Slavery is perhaps the ugliest period in the history of American education because it legally deprived thousands of children of even the minimum of education.

This narrative was written in 1845 by an ex-slave who became a famous orator, U.S. minister to Haiti, and leader of his people. It not only is a most eloquent indictment of slavery but also helps to explain why public education has not yet been able to recover from one of the greatest injustices of its past.

Frederick Douglass (1818–1895), the son of an African American woman and a White slaveholder, was sold repeatedly in the slave markets of the South. Despite daily humiliations and laws that made learning to read and write a crime punishable by death, Douglass taught himself those skills, then fled from his owners in Maryland. He was befriended by Northern abolitionists and went on both to write and to speak about his life.

His narrative was initially published by the Boston Anti-Slavery Society with a preface written by William Lloyd Garrison, abolitionist and editor of the newsletter, *The*

From Frederick Douglass, *Narrative of the Life of Frederick Douglass: An American Slave.* New York: New American Library, 1968, pp. 52–58.

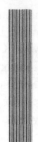

Liberator. Wrote Garrison of Douglass, "As a public speaker, he excels in pathos, wit, comparison, imitation, strength of reasoning, and fluency of language. There is in him that union of head and heart, which is indispensable to an enlightenment of the heads and a winning of the hearts of others" (Douglass, 1968, p. viii).

In Chapter VII of his *Narrative* Douglass describes how he persevered in his desire to become educated despite risks and obstacles. While there are, of course, no longer laws prohibiting anyone from receiving an education, think about obstacles that still prevent certain children from receiving equal educational opportunities (Kozol, 1995b). What are the historical roots of these obstacles?

I lived in Master Hugh's family about seven years. During this time, I succeeded in learning to read and write. In accomplishing this, I was compelled to resort to various stratagems. I had no regular teacher. My mistress, who had kindly commenced to instruct me, had, in compliance with the advice and direction of her husband, not only ceased to instruct, but had set her face against my being instructed by any one else. It is due, however, to my mistress to say of her, that she did not adopt this course of treatment immediately. She at first lacked the depravity indispensable to shutting me up in mental darkness. It was at least necessary for her to have some training in the exercise of irresponsible power, to make her equal to the task of treating me as though I were a brute.

My mistress was, as I have said, a kind and tender-hearted woman; and in the simplicity of her soul she commenced, when I first went to live with her, to treat me as she supposed one human being ought to treat another. In entering upon the duties of a slaveholder, she did not seem to perceive that I sustained to her the relation of a mere chattel, and that for her to treat me as a human being was not only wrong, but dangerously so. Slavery proved as injurious to her as it did to me. When I went there, she was a pious, warm, and tender-hearted woman. There was no sorrow or suffering for which she had not a tear. She had bread for the hungry, clothes for the naked, and comfort for every mourner that came within her reach. Slavery

soon proved its ability to divest her of these heavenly qualities. Under its influence, the tender heart became stone, and the lamblike disposition gave way to one of tiger-like fierceness. The first step in her downward course was in her ceasing to instruct me. She now commenced to practise her husband's precepts. She finally became even more violent in her opposition than her husband himself. She was not satisfied with simply doing as well as he had commanded; she seemed anxious to do better. Nothing seemed to make her more angry than to see me with a newspaper. She seemed to think that here lay the danger. I have had her rush at me with a face made all up of fury, and snatch from me a newspaper, in a manner that fully revealed her apprehension. She was an apt woman; and a little experience soon demonstrated, to her satisfaction, that education and slavery were incompatible with each other.

From this time I was most narrowly watched. If I was in a separate room any considerable leangth of time, I was sure to be suspected of having a book, and was at once called to give an account of myself. All this, however, was too late. The first step had been taken. Mistress, in teaching me the alphabet, had given me the *inch,* and no precaution could prevent me from taking the *ell.*

The plan which I adopted, and the one by which I was most successful, was that of making friends of all the little white boys whom I met in the street. As many of these as I could, I converted into teachers. With their kindly aid, obtained at different times and in different places, I finally succeeded in learning to read. When I was sent on errands, I always took my book with me, and by doing one part of my errand quickly, I found time to get a lesson before my return. I used also to carry bread with me, enough of which was always in the house, and to which I was always welcome; for I was much better off in this regard than many of the poor white children in our neighborhood. This bread I used to bestow upon the hungry little urchins, who, in return, would give me that more valuable bread of knowledge. I am strongly tempted to give the names of two or three of those little boys, as a testimonial of the gratitude and affection I bear them; but prudence forbids;—not that it would injure me, but it might embarrass them; for it is almost an unpardonable offence to teach slaves to read in this Christian country. It is enough to say of the dear little fellows, that they lived on Philpot Street, very near Durgin and Bailey's ship-yard. I used to talk this matter of slavery over with them. I would sometimes say to them, I wished I could be as free as they would be when they got to be men. "You will be free as soon as you are twenty-one, *but I am a slave for life!* Have not I as good a right to be free as you have?" These words used to trouble them; they would express for me the liveliest sympathy, and console me with the hope that something would occur by which I might be free.

I was now about twelve years old, and the thought of being *a slave for life* began to bear heavily upon my heart. Just about this time, I got hold of a book entitled "The Columbian Orator." Every opportunity I got, I used to read this book. Among much of other interesting matter, I found in it a dialogue between a master and his slave. The slave was represented as having run away from his master three times. The dialogue represented the conversation

which took place between them, when the slave was retaken the third time. In this dialogue, the whole argument in behalf of slavery was brought forward by the master, all of which was disposed of by the slave. The slave was made to say some very smart as well as impressive things in reply to his master—things which had the desired though unexpected effect; for the conversation resulted in the voluntary emancipation of the slave on the part of the master.

In the same book, I met with one of Sheridan's mighty speeches on and in behalf of Catholic emancipation. These were choice documents to me. I read them over and over again with unabated interest. They gave tongue to interesting thoughts of my own soul, which had frequently flashed through my mind, and died away for want of utterance. The moral which I gained from the dialogue was the power of truth over the conscience of even a slaveholder. What I got from Sheridan was a bold denunciation of slavery, and a powerful vindication of human rights. The reading of these documents enabled me to utter my thoughts, and to meet the arguments brought forward to sustain slavery; but while they relieved me of one difficulty, they brought on another even more painful than the one of which I was relieved. The more I read, the more I was led to abhor and detest my enslavers. I could regard them in no other light than a band of successful robbers, who had left their homes, and gone to Africa, and stolen us from our homes, and in a strange land reduced us to slavery. I loathed them as being the meanest as well as the most wicked of men. As I read and contemplated the subject, behold! that very discontentment which Master Hugh had predicted would follow my learning to read had already come, to torment and sting my soul to unutterable anguish. As I writhed under it, I would at times feel that learning to read had been a curse rather than a blessing. It had given me a view of my wretched condition, without the remedy. It opened my eyes to the horrible pit, but to no ladder upon which to get out. In moments of agony, I envied my fellow-slaves for their stupidity. I have often wished myself a beast. I preferred the condition of the meanest reptile to my own. Any thing, no matter what, to get rid of thinking! It was this everlasting thinking of my condition that tormented me. There was no getting rid of it. It was pressed upon me by every object within sight or hearing, animate or inanimate. The silver trump of freedom had roused my soul to eternal wakefulness. Freedom now appeared, to disappear no more forever. It was heard in every sound, and seen in every thing. It was ever present to torment me with a sense of my wretched condition. I saw nothing without seeing it, I heard nothing without hearing it, and felt nothing without feeling it. It looked from every star, it smiled in every calm, breathed in every wind, and moved in every storm.

I often found myself regretting my own existence, and wishing myself dead; and but for the hope of being free, I have no doubt but that I should have killed myself, or done something for which I should have been killed. While in this state of mind, I was eager to hear any one speak of slavery. I was a ready listener. Every little while, I could hear something about the abolitionists. It was some time before I found what the word meant. It was always used in such connections as to make it an interesting word to me. If a slave ran away and succeeded in getting clear, or if a slave killed his master, set fire to a barn, or did any thing very wrong in the mind of a slaveholder, it was spoken of as the fruit of *abolition*. Hearing the word in this connection very often, I set about learning what it meant. The dictionary afforded me little or no help. I found it was "the act of abolishing;" but then I did not know what was to be abolished. Here I was perplexed. I did not dare to ask any one about its meaning, for I was satisfied that it was

something they wanted me to know very little about. After a patient waiting, I got one of our city papers, containing an account of the number of petitions from the north, praying for the abolition of slavery in the District of Columbia, and of the slave trade between the States. From this time I understood the words *abolition* and *abolitionist*, and always drew near when that word was spoken, expecting to hear something of importance to myself and fellow-slaves. The light broke in upon me by degrees. I went one day down on the wharf of Mr. Waters; and seeing two Irishmen unloading a scow of stone, I went, unasked, and helped them. When we had finished, one of them came to me and asked me if I were a slave. I told him I was. He asked, "Are ye a slave for life?" I told him that I was. The good Irishman seemed to be deeply affected by the statement. He said to the other that it was a pity so fine a little fellow as myself should be a slave for life. He said it was a shame to hold me. They both advised me to run away to the north; that I should find friends there, and that I should be free. I pretended not to be interested in what they said, and treated them as if I did not understand them; for I feared they might be treacherous. White men have been known to encourage slaves to escape, and then, to get the reward, catch them and return them to their masters. I was afraid that these seemingly good men might use me so; but I nevertheless remembered their advice, and from that time I resolved to run away. I looked forward to a time at which it would be safe for me to escape. I was too young to think of doing so immediately; besides, I wished to learn how to write, as I might have occasion to write my own pass. I consoled myself with the hope that I should one day find a good chance. Meanwhile, I would learn to write.

The idea as to how I might learn to write was suggested to me by being in Durgin and Bailey's ship-yard, and frequently seeing the ship carpenters, after hewing, and getting a piece of timber ready for use, write on the timber the name of that part of the ship for which it was intended. When a piece of timber was intended for the larboard side, it would be marked thus—"L." When a piece was for the starboard side, it would be marked thus—"S." A piece for the larboard side forward would be marked thus—"L. F." When a piece was for starboard side forward, it would be marked thus—"S. F." For larboard aft, it would be marked thus—"L. A." For starboard aft, it would be marked thus—"S. A." I soon learned the names of these letters, and for what they were intended when placed upon a piece of timber in the ship-yard. I immediately commenced copying them, and in a short time was able to make the four letters named. After that, when I met with any boy who I knew could write, I would tell him I could write as well as he. The next word would be, "I don't believe you. Let me see you try it." I would then make the letters which I had been so fortunate as to learn, and ask him to beat that. In this way I got a good many lessons in writing, which it is quite possible I should never have gotten in any other way. During this time, my copy-book was the board fence, brick wall, and pavement; my pen and ink was a lump of chalk. With these, I learned mainly how to write. I then commenced and continued copying the Italics in Webster's Spelling Book, until I could make them all without looking on the book. By this time, my little Master Thomas had gone to school, and learned how to write, and had written over a number of copy-books. These had been brought home, and shown to some of our near neighbors, and then laid aside. My mistress used to go to class meeting at the Wilk Street meetinghouse every Monday afternoon, and leave me to take care of the house. When left thus, I used to spend the time in writing in the spaces left in Master Thomas's copy-book, copying what he had written. I continued to do this until I could write a hand very similar to that of Master Thomas. Thus, after a long, tedious effort for years, I finally succeeded in learning how to write.

Questions for Discussion and Debate

1. What evidence does Douglass provide to support his point that slavery is as injurious to the *slave holder* as it is to the slave?

2. Take each of these related questions one at a time: Why were slaves prohibited from learning to read and write? What kinds of knowledge, for example, did Douglass gain from being able to read? What did this knowledge enable him to do? Does one's ability to read and write still hold such awesome claims?

3. Who were Douglass's teachers, and in what circumstances?

4. List the techniques by which Douglass taught himself reading and writing. Are these techniques in any way related to the way *you* learned to read and write? Explain.

5. Noting his master's wife's initial inclination to teach Douglass and then her later change in behavior, debate the pros and cons of this question: Women of the house had the power to change the course of events in the slaveholding South. (This question might also be debated with additional research.)

Activities and Projects

1. Locate copies of *The Liberator,* William Lloyd Garrison's antislavery newsletter, and read aloud some of his historic abolitionist arguments.

2. Read aloud from this excerpt of Douglass's *Narrative* so you can hear the eloquence that Garrison attributes to him.

3. Hold a mock conversation between Douglass and the mistress of the house in which he was enslaved. Perhaps "Douglass" could inquire as to the mistress's change of heart as well as make a number of other related inquiries.

4. Research the issue of laws prohibiting slaves from gaining an education and try to find examples of men and women who committed acts of nonviolent civil disobedience by secretly helping slaves learn to read and write. Civil disobedience, that is, the nonviolent disobeying of laws that one considers unjust, is a strategy that Martin Luther King, Jr., used successfully on behalf of African Americans in the 1950s and 1960s. Compare historic 19th-century civil disobedience related to educating slaves with the groundbreaking acts that led to the integration of schools some 100 years later (*Brown v. The Board of Education of Topeka, Kansas, 1954*).

5. Although nonwhites have access to education today, school can still be a hostile place for many of them. Locate in the news media any evidence indicating that schools are becoming *less* hostile environments for non-White students.

2.8   *Jefferson* (1963)

Albert Jay Nock

Albert Jay Nock, the late English essayist, captures Thomas Jefferson, the farmer, in his biographical essay, and he reveals aspects of this enigmatic author of the Declaration of Independence that few will ever read about in textbooks.

     Most sources give Jefferson credit for being ahead of his time in a number of ways. For example, he was very much a Renaissance man. His architectural genius and devotion to higher education led to his founding the University of Virginia. His Bill for Establishing Religious Freedom in the Virginia Assembly (1779) led to the constitutional principle of separation of church and state; in his spare time he embraced poetry and music and played the violin. And at a time when few people considered the possibility of a system of public education, Jefferson reminded Americans of the role education could play in building an informed citizenry who would participate in and strengthen this budding democracy.

And he promoted another progressive policy. In his draft of the Declaration of Independence, based on the ideas of John Locke and Jean Jacques Rousseau (see chapter 3) and the natural rights of man, Jefferson included a statement about ending the slave trade. However, it was omitted because of Southern resistance. Ironically, despite his rhetoric about education *and* slavery, Jefferson, in fact, never freed his own slaves, though many of his contemporaries did so. And he did not seek for his female offspring the kind of education he spoke about publicly. Jefferson believed that education was necessary for a participatory democracy, and, since women did not have the right to vote, he saw no need to educate them.

In this excerpt from *Jefferson,* Albert Jay Nock brings to light Jefferson's limited concern about education for women as well as the limited purpose to which he believed women should put whatever education they did receive. As you read, keep in mind that his views were not particularly unusual for his time and his class and may, in fact, be consistent with the beliefs of certain groups in America today. Do you, for example, know of any parents or religious groups that consider the education of their sons a priority over the education of their daughters? Do you know of any countries where women are still deprived of an equal education?

Woman's duty being so incomplex, and the grasp of it needing so little brains, the education of women was correspondingly simple; so simple, indeed, that one would not think much about it. Mr. Jefferson bent his mind to the theory and practice of education for nearly fifty years; yet at the age of seventy, he says that "a plan of female education has never been a subject of systematic contemplation with me. It has occupied my attention so far only as the education of my own daughters occasionally required." Seeing that his girls were likely to live in a sparsely settled agricultural country, he thought that for vocational reasons they ought to have a solid education "which might enable them, when become mothers, to educate their own daughters, and even to direct the course for sons, should their fathers be lost or incapable or inattentive." Such few general thoughts as ever took rise from this experience are put down in a letter to a neighbor in Virginia. He finds that a great obstacle to good education for women is their inordinate passion for novels. In those who seek this release for the pent desire for romance, "the result is a bloated imagination, sickly judgment and disgust towards all the real businesses of life." Some novels of a historical type, however, are well enough. "For a like reason, much poetry should not be indulged. Some is useful for forming taste and style"; Dryden and Pope, for example, and Thomson! French is indispensable. Music is "invaluable where a person has an ear." Drawing is an innocent and engaging amusement, often useful, and "a qualification not to be neglected in one who is to become a mother and an instructor." Dancing is a healthy and elegant exercise, a specific against social awkwardness, but an accomplishment of short use, "for the French rule is wise, that no lady dances after marriage . . . gestation and nursing leaving little time to a married lady when this exercise can be either safe or innocent." Women must be taught to dress neatly at all hours, for vocational reasons. "A lady who has been seen as a sloven or slut in the morning," he tells Martha, "will never efface the impression she has made, with all the dress and pageantry she can afterwards involve herself in. . . . I hope therefore, the moment you rise from bed, your first work will be to dress yourself in such style as that you may be seen by any gentleman without his being able to discover a pin amiss." Finally, always for vocational reasons, women must be taught to wash themselves; it is the acme of impracticality for them to go dirty, since "nothing is so disgusting to our sex as a want of cleanliness and delicacy in yours."

Mr. Jefferson did his best by his daughters. He put Patsy in a convent school in Paris, where he bombarded her with letters in which the expression of a larvated love was, as usual, inhibited into a diffident formalism by the combination of natural reticence and a more or less puzzled sense of responsibility. "I rest the happiness of my life in seeing you beloved by all the world, which you will be sure to be if to a good heart you join those accomplishments so peculiarly pleasing in your sex." That is about the best he can do, except by way of suggesting occupations for her leisure hours, and in this his fertility is endless. To be sure, her leisure hours were not many; they never had been many, even when she was at home. The year before she went abroad, her father had laid out the following schedule of her time:

From 8 to 10, practice music.

From 10 to 1, dance one day, and draw another.

From 1 to 2, draw on the day you dance, and write a letter the next day.

From 3 to 4, read French.

From 4 to 5, exercise yourself in music.

From 5 till bed-time, read English, write, etc.

In Paris he is continually anxious about her not having enough to do and about a certain listlessness toward her duties, a kind of boredom. He has a harpsichord sent her from London; he tries to get her interested in the note of the nightingale, so that when she returns to Virginia she may compare it with that of the mockingbird; he informs her all about the literary and historical associations of certain places in Italy and the South of France; he redoubles his solicitations toward the industrious life, urging her to remember that "a mind always employed is always happy. This is the true secret, the grand recipe, for felicity. The idle are the only wretched." How could one doubt it? He himself had never been idle for an aggregate of twelve hours in his whole life, and in the large sense, he had always been happy; when Satan had approached him with the proverbial wares of mischief, they found a closed market. But while Martha did her best to realize upon her prescribed pursuits, they seemed for some reason to pass their dividends. She was interested in her father's stories of the fountain of Vaucluse, the tomb of Laura and the château of Petrarch, but her interest was sentimental rather than antiquarian; they seemed to generate, if not "a sickly judgment and disgust towards all the real businesses of life," at least a disturbing halfheartedness and irresolution about facing them. She tried to do everything in reason for the nightingales, but here again she did not find her father's exhortations as animating as they should be. Presently, after looking over the prospects which the future seemed to hold in store for an amiable dreamy wench in her teens, Patsy decided that she would probably do well to dedicate the rest of her life to the service of God. She accordingly wrote her father for permission to enter the holy sisterhood. Two days afterward, he appeared at the convent and took her away, with no intimation either by word or manner that she had expressed any such wish; and as long as he lived he never once alluded to her request, nor did she. Thenceforth he kept her with him, mothering her younger sister, Maria; both returned to America with him; both fulfilled their destiny as their father's daughters by becoming dutiful and assiduous wives, mothers, housekeepers; and they continued in the joy of these occupations as long as their strength held out.

▰▰▰▰▰▰▰▰ Questions for Discussion and Debate ▰▰▰▰▰▰▰▰

1. What elements of education does Jefferson consider the appropriate or "solid" curriculum for his daughters?

2. What is Jefferson's rationale for this kind of education? That is, for what purpose did he believe his daughters needed a solid education?

3. What is your reaction to the prescribed curriculum? Does it fit your definition of a "solid" education? What do you like or not like about the "schedule of her time"?

▰▰▰▰▰▰▰▰ Activities and Projects ▰▰▰▰▰▰▰▰

1. Do research on the status of women in developing countries. For example, in some parts of the world girls still do not go to school. The reasons may have to do with poverty and lack of access or they may have to do with certain religious or social beliefs that view education as being unnecessary for girls. Bring the research back "home" and see if there are areas in America where similar attitudes about education for women still prevail.

2. Prepare a report on the *origins* of education for women in this country. What, for example, were some of the first women's schools, and when were women first admitted into colleges? (See time line, Selection 2.2.) What were the responses to such revolutionary changes?

3. Imagine that Jefferson could see what women in America have accomplished, that is, as executives, politicians, astronauts, and so on. What do you think he would have to say? Do some improvisations in which Jefferson encounters some of these women or in which his daughters rebel against his prescriptions for them.

2.9 ▐▌ "Twelfth Report, for 1848"

Horace Mann

Because of his contribution to the growth of free public schools for all, Horace Mann has been called "the father of American education." It was his influence that led to the first compulsory education law (1852) and to the establishment of teacher training schools (normal schools). He is also remembered for his role as the first president (1852) of Antioch College in Ohio. Under his administration, it became the first college to admit African Americans.

From Horace Mann, Annual Reports of the Secretary of the Board of Education of Massachusetts for the Years 1845–1848. In *Life and Works of Horace Mann*, Vol. 14. Boston: Lee and Shepard Publishers, 1891, pp. 334–337.

After practicing law himself and serving in the state legislature, Mann became the first secretary of the Massachusetts Board of Education (1837–1849) and, as such, presented annual reports to the board in which he outlined his educational philosophy and reported on the status of the schools in Massachusetts.

In his "Twelfth Report," excerpted here, Mann reveals still another of his roles, that of scholar. In part, he discusses what he believes should be the curriculum components of the state's free public schools, also known as common schools. For the most part, however, he addresses the religious character of these schools and presents a lengthy defense against the accusations lodged against him by Christians who believed that these new public schools were too secular, un-Christian, and antireligious. Conservative Calvinist Protestants wanted a stronger religious component and a more sectarian approach. Convert-to-Catholicism proponent Orestes Brownson agreed but argued that Protestants, in general, and Mann, in particular, were, in effect, turning the public schools into Protestant parochial schools.

In his lengthy response to these attacks, Mann asserts his belief that religious instruction does not belong in the public schools. Because religion was, for the most part, not meant to be a formal part of instruction, many of his critics called the schools anti-Christian. Mann (1891) questions why such attacks were made when teachers were, in fact, definitely encouraged to affirm such principles as "piety, justice, . . . a sacred regard to truth, love to their country, humanity, and universal benevolence, sobriety, industry, and frugality, chastity, moderation, and temperance and those other virtues which are the ornament of human society and the basis upon which a republican constitution is founded" (pp. 318–319).

His most eloquent defense of his nonsectarian position appears here in his references to the bloody historical episodes that resulted when governments established religion and "secured faith by force" (Mann, 1891, p. 301). For example, at one point he recalls the Massacre of St. Bartholomew's Day (August 24, 1572) in France, when 30,000 Protestant men, women, and children—labeled as heretics or nonbelievers by the Catholics—were butchered, and "all true believers . . . rejoice[d] together at so glorious an event" (p. 301).

Mann wrote that in all such oppressions committed in the name of religion, each side upheld its faith to be the true faith. Each claimed the same external revelations from God. In the following excerpt, Mann concludes his "Twelfth Report" by repeating why he believes that there are real dangers in store if religion pervades the public sphere. Religious instruction, he says, is best determined by parents.

As you read this excerpt, "listen" to Mann's language, his dramatic phrasing, and use of metaphor and try to think of anyone else who has spoken out for public education in similar ways. Think also about whether there are groups in society today who would still *oppose* Mann's position. And, while separation of church and state is the constitutional policy, can you identify any examples of religious observance in the public schools today—or in connection with government in any form?

Incidentally, primary source documents such as Mann's "Twelfth Report" are one of the most authentic ways of discovering the history of education because they bring you firsthand the ideas and words of the movers and shakers in education. Such sources, it is said, are "from the horse's mouth." No one else has filtered these words through his or her own lenses or interpreted them for you. So as you read the excerpt, pretend that you are sitting there among the board members listening to Mann read from his report.

If, then, a government would recognize and protect the rights of religious freedom, it must abstain from subjugating the capacities of its children to any legal standard of religious faith with as great fidelity as it abstains from controlling the opinions of men. It must meet the unquestionable fact, that the old spirit of religious domination is adopting new measures to accomplish its work,—measures which, if successful, will be as fatal to the liberties of mankind as those which were practised in by-gone days of violence and terror. These new measures are aimed at children instead of men. They propose to supersede the necessity of subduing free thought *in the mind of the adult*, by forestalling the development of any capacity of free thought *in the mind of the child*. They expect to find it easier to subdue the free agency of children by binding them in fetters of bigotry than to subdue the free agency of men by binding them in fetters of iron. For this purpose, some are attempting to deprive children of their right to labor, and, of course, of their daily bread, unless they will attend a government school, and receive its sectarian instruction. Some are attempting to withhold all means even of secular education from the poor, and thus punish them with ignorance, unless, with the secular knowledge which they desire, they will accept theological knowledge which they condemn. Others still are striving to break down all free public-school systems where they exist, and to prevent their establishment where they do not exist, in the hope, that, on the downfall of these, their system will succeed. The sovereign antidote against these machinations is free schools for all, and the right of every parent to determine the religious education of his children.

This topic invites far more extended exposition; but this must suffice. In bidding an official farewell to a system with which I have been so long connected, to which I have devoted my means, my strength, my health, twelve years of time, and, doubtless, twice that number of years from what might otherwise have been my term of life, I have felt bound to submit these brief views in its defence. In justice to my own name and memory; in justice to the Board of which I was originally a member, and from which I have always sought counsel and guidance; and in justice to thousands of the most wise, upright, and religious-minded men in Massachusetts, who have been my fellow-laborers in advancing the great cause of popular education, under the auspices of this system,—I have felt bound to vindicate it from the aspersions cast upon it, and to show its consonance with the eternal principles of equity and justice. I have felt bound to show, that so far from its being an irreligious, an anti-Christian, or an un-Christian system, it is a system which recognizes religious obligations in their fullest extent; that it is a system which invokes a religious spirit, and can never be fitly administered without such a spirit; that it inculcates the great commands upon which hang all the law and the prophets; that it welcomes the Bible, and therefore welcomes all the doctrines which the Bible really contains; and that it listens to these doctrines so reverently, that, for the time being, it will not suffer any rash mortal to thrust in his interpolations of their meaning, or overlay the text with any of the "many inventions" which the heart of man has sought out. It is a system, however, which leaves open all other means of instruction,—the pulpits, the Sunday schools, the Bible classes, the catechisms, of all denominations,—to be employed according to the preferences of individual parents. It is a system which restrains itself from teaching that what it does teach is all that needs to be taught, or that should be taught; but leaves this to be decided by each man for himself, according to the light of his reason and conscience, and on his responsibility to that Great Being, who, in holding him to an account for the things done in the body, will hold him to the strictest account for the manner in which he has "trained up" his children.

Such, then, in a religious point of view, is the Massachusetts system of common schools. Reverently it recognizes and affirms the sovereign rights of the Creator, sedulously and sacredly it guards the religious rights of the creature; while it seeks to remove all hinderances, and to supply all furtherances, to a filial and paternal communion between man and his Maker. In a social and political sense, it is a *free* school-system. It knows no distinction of rich and poor, of bond and free, or between those, who, in the imperfect light of this world, are seeking, through different avenues, to reach the gate of heaven. Without money and without price, it throws open its doors, and spreads the table of its bounty, for all the children of the State. Like the sun, it shines not only upon the good, but upon the evil, that they may become good; and, like the rain, its blessings descend not only upon the just, but upon the unjust, that their injustice may depart from them, and be known no more.

To the great founders of this system we look back with filial reverence and love. Amid the barrenness of the land, and in utter destitution of wealth, they coined the rude comforts, and even the necessaries, of life, into means for its generous support. Though, as laborers by day, they subdued the wilderness, and, as sentinels by night, they guarded the camp, yet they found time for the vigilant administration and oversight of the schools in the day of their infancy and weakness. But for this single institution, into which they transfused so much of their means and of their strength, and of which they have made us the inheritors, how different would our lot and our life have been! Upon us its accumulated blessings have descended. It has saved us from innumerable pains and perils that would otherwise have been our fate,—from the physical wretchedness that is impotent to work out its own relief, from the darkness of the intellect whose wanderings after light so often plunge it into deeper gloom, and from the moral debasement whose pleasures are vices and crimes. It has surrounded us with a profusion of comforts and blessings of which the most poetic imagination would never otherwise have conceived. It has found, not mythologic goddesses, but gigantic and tireless laborers, in every stream; not evil and vindictive spirits, but beneficent and helping ones, in all the elements; and, by a profounder alchemy than the schoolmen ever dreamed of, it transmutes quarries and ice-fields into gold. It has given cunning to the hand of the mechanic, keenness to the artisan's eye, and made a sterile soil grow grateful beneath the skill of the husbandman. Hence the absence of poverty among our native population; hence a competency for the whole people, the means for mental and moral improvement, and for giving embellishment and dignity to life, such as the world has never known before, and such as nowhere else can be found upon the face of the earth.

Questions for Discussion and Debate

1. Identify the sentence or sentences that best express the reasoning behind Mann's belief that public schools should remain free from any religious affiliation. Explain why you believe these sentences are effective in explaining his position.
2. Mann was a very eloquent speaker and proficient in his use of persuasive techniques—

not so different from those who produce commercials today. He knew how to appeal to the emotions and values of his audience. In which paragraph do you see his most persuasive technique at work? (Remember that his audience is the Massachusetts Board of Education and, more broadly, the citizens of the state, whom Mann had charged with *not* cherishing the cause of public education enough!) (Mann, 1969, p. 220)

3. For whom are these "free" schools being established? Quote Mann's description of the kinds of children who would benefit from this system.

4. What is the difference between religious instruction and teaching *about* religion? Do you think that Mann would support teaching *about* religion? Why, or why not?

5. In your view, what role should religion play in the public schools?

Activities and Projects

1. Set up a simulation of the meeting of the Massachusetts Board of Education at which Mann presented his "Twelfth Report." The person representing Mann not only should read his words as Mann might have spoken them, but also should respond to hypothetical questions from "members" of the board.

2. Arrange for half of the class to research other reports prepared by Mann during his position as secretary of the board, as well as his speeches, his lectures, and any available biographies. The other half could research the inaugural speeches and/or State of the Union addresses of a sample of U.S. presidents in which they have outlined their plans for improving American education.

   Make lists of the views and policies of a sample of these presidents. Then compare Mann's beliefs to those of the presidents. Conclude the project by assessing with which president Mann would have most liked to work. (Which president governed during Mann's tenure as board secretary? And what were *his* views on education?)

3. Prepare a speech in which you articulate arguments that run counter to Mann's position. Research the position, for example, of his contemporary, Orestes Brownson, or simply find sources that contain the words of the current spokespersons for the Christian organizations that promote religion in the public schools. Hold a one-on-one debate between Mann and his opposition; or assign one half of the class to represent Mann's view and the other half his opposition's.

4. Find the Supreme Court decisions that define the Court's current interpretation of the First Amendment freedom of religion provision. For example, gather information on the Court's decision regarding school prayer. (Such decisions can be found in texts on school law and in traditional foundations texts.)

5. Historic and mythical figures such as engineer Casey Jones and steel-drivin' man, John Henry, have had songs praising their bravery or perseverance, but there has yet to be a song about an outstanding—and brave—promoter of public education . . . until now!

   On page 110 is a song praising Horace Mann's struggle. Sing it to the tune of "Oh, Susanna." Then create another verse noting the contributions of an historical or current educational mover and shaker.

Oh, Man, Horace Mann

(1) Oh, he came from Boston, Mass., and
    was a lawmaker of note
Who cared 'bout common folk so common schools
    he did promote.
He argued loud for public schools and access
    for the poor.
Said democracy means *all* of you
    should pass through learning's door.

Chorus:

Oh, man, Horace,
Oh don't you cry for me,
'Cause I'm where you helped to get me
Stud-y-ing ped-a-go-gy.

(2) "Well, it's fine to see these public schools
    but they're not quite enough.
What we need are Grade A teachers
    with some standards that are tough."
So he pushed for normal schools, then for the
    liberal arts as well.
'Til by 1890 tons of schools were ringing
    out the bell.

Chorus

2.10 *Inherit the Wind* (1955)

Jerome Lawrence and Robert E. Lee

The issue of separation of church and state reappears again and again in the history of American public education, usually with sparks flying. Fact versus faith, science versus religion, teaching *about* religion versus teaching religion: such are the competing interests constantly vying for dominance in public schools. And there has been no more dramatic an example of this clash than the Scopes Trial, which took place in Dayton, Tennessee, in 1925 and upon which Jerome Lawrence and Robert E. Lee based their play.

John Scopes, a biology teacher, was charged with breaking a Tennessee law that prohibited teaching about Darwin's theory of evolution, which indirectly supports the idea that humans evolved from apes and lower species of living things. The nature of this theory led to the media's reference to the proceedings as the "Monkey Trial."

Although Scopes, referred to in the play as Bertram Cates, was defended by the American Civil Liberties Union, his chief defender was the noted and eloquent lawyer, Clarence Darrow, referred to as Henry Drummond in the play. He battled with William Jennings Bryan, Matthew Harrison Brady in the play, the well-known orator of the populist movement and outspoken opponent of evolution, which he called *evil-ution*.

The trial was characterized by a clear delineation of two points of view: The first, espoused by Darrow, was based on scientific, humanistic perspectives of the theory of evolution; the other view, Bryan's, was based on the Judeo-Christian biblical interpretations of creation. Passions ran high, and H. L. Mencken, a well-known journalist (E. K. Hornbeck in the play), captured much of the rhetoric and spitfire in his newspaper columns.

The outcome of the trial reflected the local nature of the jury; that is, Scopes was found guilty. However, because the judge likely weighed the evidence more objectively, he fined Scopes a mere $100.

The Scopes Trial became a battlefield on which religion clashed with science, and from the perspective of public education, science—or, according to Darrow, truth—prevailed. The Supreme Court, in the 1987 *Edwards* v. *Aguillard* (197 S.Ct. 2573) decision, ruled that evolution theory was more provable and that creationism, the biblical theory, did not belong in the science classroom, although it was a legitimate topic for a social studies discussion of religious perspectives. The court based its decision on the first amendment to the Constitution, which—among other provisions—contains these two clauses: "Congress shall make no law respecting an establishment of religion, or prohibiting the free exercise thereof. . . . " It is the first clause, known as the "establishment clause," that prevailed and prevents teachers of science from teaching Judeo-Christian beliefs as scientific fact. Nevertheless, many who espouse creationism, including the citizens of Dayton, still argue for its reinstatement in the science curriculum.

This excerpt from the play captures both Darrow's and Bryan's beliefs. Each questions Howard, a student in Scopes's class, and, through him, challenges the other's assumptions about evolution. As you read his testimony, imagine that you are Howard. How might you have answered the large questions put to you by these formidable men?

SCENE II

The courtroom, two days later. It is bright midday, and the trial is in full swing. The JUDGE *is on the bench; the jury, lawyers, officials and spectators crowd the courtroom.* HOWARD, *the thirteen-year-old boy, is on the witness stand. He is wretched in a starched collar and Sunday suit. The weather is as relentlessly hot as before.* BRADY *is examining the boy, who is a witness for the prosecution.*

BRADY Go on, Howard. Tell them what else Mr. Cates told you in the classroom.

HOWARD Well, he said at first the earth was too hot for any life. Then it cooled off a mite, and cells and things begun to live.

BRADY Cells?

HOWARD Little bugs like, in the water. After that, the little bugs get to be bigger bugs, and sprouted legs and crawled up on the land.

BRADY How long did this take, according to Mr. Cates?

HOWARD Couple million years. Maybe longer. Then comes the fishes and the reptiles and the mammals. Man's a mammal.

BRADY Along with the dogs and the cattle in the field: did he say that?

HOWARD Yes, sir.

>   (DRUMMOND *is about to protest against prompting the witness; then he decides it isn't worth the trouble.*)

BRADY Now, Howard, how did *man* come out of this slimy mess of bugs and serpents, according to your—"Professor"?

HOWARD Man was sort of evoluted. From the "Old World Monkeys."

>   (BRADY *slaps his thigh.*)

BRADY Did you hear that, my friends? "Old World Monkeys"! According to Mr. Cates, you and I aren't even descended from good American monkeys! (*There is laughter*) Howard, listen carefully. In all this talk of bugs and "Evil-ution," of slime and ooze, did Mr. Cates ever make any reference to God?

HOWARD Not as I remember.

BRADY Or the miracle He achieved in seven days as described in the beautiful Book of Genesis?

HOWARD No, sir.

>   (BRADY *stretches out his arms in an all-embracing gesture.*)

BRADY Ladies and gentlemen—

DRUMMOND Objection! I ask that the court remind the learned counsel that this is not a Chautauqua tent. He is supposed to be submitting evidence to a jury. There are no ladies on the jury.

BRADY Your Honor, I have no intention of making a speech. There is no need. I am sure that everyone on the jury, everyone within the sound of this boy's voice, is moved by his tragic confusion. He has been taught that he wriggled up like an animal from the filth and the muck below! (*Continuing fervently, the spirit is upon him*) I say that these Bible-haters, these "*Evil*-utionists," are brewers of poison. And the legislature of this sovereign state has had the wisdom to demand that the peddlers of poison—in bottles or in books—clearly label the products they attempt to sell! (*There is applause.* HOWARD *gulps.* BRADY *points at the boy*) I tell you, if this law is not upheld, this boy will become one of a generation, shorn of its faith by the teachings of Godless science! But if the full penalty of the law is meted out to Bertram Cates, the faithful the whole world over, who are watching us here, and listening to our every word, will call this courtroom blessed!

>   (*Applause. Dramatically,* BRADY *moves to his chair. Condescendingly, he waves to* DRUMMOND.)

BRADY Your witness, sir.

>   (BRADY *sits.* DRUMMOND *rises, slouches toward the witness stand.*)

DRUMMOND Well, I sure am glad Colonel Brady didn't make a speech!

>   (*Nobody laughs. The courtroom seems to resent* DRUMMOND'S *gentle ridicule of the orator. To many, there is an effrontery in*

DRUMMOND'S *very voice—folksy and relaxed. It's rather like a harmonica following a symphony concert*) Howard, I heard you say that the world used to be pretty hot.

HOWARD That's what Mr. Cates said.

DRUMMOND You figure it was any hotter then than it is right now?

HOWARD Guess it musta been. Mr. Cates read it to us from a book.

DRUMMOND Do you know what book?

HOWARD I guess that Mr. Darwin thought it up.

DRUMMOND (*Leaning on the arm of the boy's chair*) You figure anything's wrong about that, Howard?

HOWARD Well, I dunno—

DAVENPORT (*Leaping up, crisply*) Objection, Your Honor. The defense is asking that a thirteen-year-old boy hand down an opinion on a question of morality!

DRUMMOND (*To the* JUDGE) I am trying to establish, Your Honor, that Howard—or Colonel Brady—or Charles Darwin—or anyone in this courtroom—or *you*, sir—has the right to *think*!

JUDGE Colonel Drummond, the right to think is not on trial here.

DRUMMOND (*Energetically*) With all respect to the bench, I hold that the right to think is very much on trial! It is fearfully in danger in the proceedings of this court!

BRADY (*Rises*) A *man* is on trial!

DRUMMOND A thinking man! And he is threatened with fine and imprisonment because he chooses to speak what he thinks.

JUDGE Colonel Drummond, would you please rephrase your question.

DRUMMOND (*To* HOWARD) Let's put it this way, Howard. All this fuss and feathers about Evolution, do you think it hurt you any?

HOWARD Sir?

DRUMMOND Did it do you any harm? You still feel reasonably fit? What Mr. Cates told you, did it hurt your baseball game any? Affect your pitching arm?
   (*He punches* HOWARD'S *right arm playfully*)

HOWARD No, sir. I'm a leftie.

DRUMMOND A southpaw, eh? Still honor your father and mother?

HOWARD Sure.

DRUMMOND Haven't murdered anybody since breakfast?

DAVENPORT Objection.

JUDGE Objection sustained.
   (DRUMMOND *shrugs.*)

BRADY Ask him if his Holy Faith in the scriptures has been shattered—

DRUMMOND When I need your *valuable* help, Colonel, you may rest assured I shall humbly ask for it. (*Turning*) Howard, do you believe everything Mr. Cates told you?

HOWARD (*Frowning*) I'm not sure. I gotta think it over.

DRUMMOND Good for you. Your pa's a farmer, isn't he?

HOWARD Yes, sir.

DRUMMOND Got a tractor?

HOWARD Brand new one.

DRUMMOND You figure a tractor's sinful, because it isn't mentioned in the Bible?

HOWARD (*Thinking*) Don't know.

DRUMMOND Moses never made a phone call. Suppose that makes the telephone an instrument of the Devil?

HOWARD I never thought of it that way.

BRADY (*Rising, booming*) Neither did anybody else! Your Honor, the defense makes the same old error of all Godless men! They confuse material things with the great spiritual realities of the Revealed Word! (*Turning to* DRUMMOND) Why do you bewilder this child? Does Right have no meaning to you, sir?

> (BRADY'S *hands are outstretched, palms upward, pleading.* DRUMMOND *stares at* BRADY *long and thoughtfully.*)

DRUMMOND (*In a low voice*) Realizing that I may prejudice the case of my client, I must say that "Right" has no meaning to me whatsoever! (*There is a buzz of reaction in the courtroom*) Truth has meaning—as a direction. But one of the peculiar imbecilities of our time is the grid of morality we have placed on human behavior: so that every act of man must be measured against an arbitrary latitude of right and longitude of wrong—in exact, minutes, seconds, and degrees! (*He turns to* HOWARD) Do you have any idea what I'm talking about, Howard?

HOWARD No, sir.

DRUMMOND Well, maybe you will. Someday. Thank you, son. That's all.

Questions for Discussion and Debate

1. Identify the sentence spoken by Drummond (Darrow) and the sentence delivered by Brady (Bryan) that best capture their respective points of view at this trial.
2. With whom do you agree, and why?
3. Sarcasm is used by both lawyers in their attempts to diminish the other in the eyes of the jury. Locate at least two examples of sarcasm in the excerpt. Is sarcasm an effective debating tool? Why, or why not? Does sarcasm have a role in the classroom? Explain your view.
4. Read Howard's testimony again. Did his answers hurt or help Scopes (Cates)?

Activities and Projects

1. Act out the excerpt as realistically as possible. Following the dramatization discuss the first three questions.
2. Watch the outstanding film, *Inherit the Wind*, that was based on Lawrence and Lee's play, with Spencer Tracy playing the

role of Darrow. In particular, find the scene in which Howard is on the stand. After watching the film, discuss what scene you were most affected by and why.

3. Do research on one of the following:

a. Whatever became of Scopes following the trial?

b. The 1950s, when the play was written and performed, was a decade in which the McCarthy Era wreaked havoc on the lives of many Americans. Find out who Joseph McCarthy was and what he did, and find out if the playwrights, Lawrence and Lee, had any thoughts about McCarthy's behavior when they wrote the play.

c. There are likely as many stories of creation as there are religions. Find out what some of these stories say and compare them to the Judeo-Christian story. Is it possible both to believe in one's religion and its stories and to believe in evolution? Discuss.

d. What position do professional teacher organizations take on the questions of separation of church and state that this trial calls to mind? Where do these organizations stand on the issue of teaching religion versus teaching *about* religion? You might want to write to the National Science Teachers Association and the National Council for the Social Studies, among others.

4. What is the meaning of the concept of academic freedom? What have the courts decided in cases involving academic freedom? Do research on this issue, defining it and its limits. What connection, if any, is there between the limits on Scopes's academic freedom and the limits of local school boards in deciding curriculum? Do you agree with the court's decisions on academic freedom?

2.11 │││ *All-of-a-Kind Family* (1951)

Sydney Taylor

Sydney Taylor's *All-of-a-Kind Family* series of children's books was beloved by many, girls in particular, growing up in the 1950s and 1960s. Taylor captures the daily joys and frustrations of an immigrant family with five sisters from their arrival in the early part of the 20th century, when immigration was at its peak, up through the Depression years. The family's life on the Lower East Side of New York City comes alive with pushcarts, holidays, relatives, and settlement houses where many such families from Eastern Europe were helped literally to settle into this country and become part of its mainstream.

While this excerpt is not directly related to education, it nevertheless reveals another way in which immigrant children came to learn about American values and rituals: through the celebration of American holidays, in this case the Fourth of July. The excerpt may not seem so remote if you consider that during the latter part of the 20th century there has been a resurgence of immigration, and you may even have immigrants attending the schools in which you are teaching or will be teaching. And the current outcry against immigration, as well as its celebration, is also reminiscent of the responses of earlier days.

Assimilation was the goal of many of these immigrants: to fit in, to learn English, to become American. And this family, too, wanted to participate in "American" rituals but, at the same time, maintain connections to their native culture, as seen in Mama's preparation of an old recipe brought with her to America. This practice of assimilating into the larger culture while still maintaining some of the uniqueness of one's native culture is what is meant by *pluralism*: America as a "tossed salad" as opposed to a "melting pot." America has always been a nation of immigrants, and schools, in particular, have struggled to find appropriate ways to reflect that precious balance between societal and individual identity, which is what pluralism is all about.

This struggle to find the pluralistic balance is currently mirrored in the ongoing debates about bilingual education programs, multicultural education, and the legitimacy of Black English or Ebonics. What do you think this family would have to say about these contemporary issues? What do *you* think about them? Discuss these issues after reading about the *All-of-a-Kind Family*.

"Such a nice flag," said Gertie, as she put her hand out gingerly to touch the red-white-and-blue bunting which lay rolled up on the kitchen couch.

Henny picked it up and began to unroll it.

"Put it down," ordered Papa. "I don't want the American flag on the floor."

Henny was glad to obey; the flagpole Papa had made was heavy. "Bet you don't know what day this is," she said to Gertie.

It was true. Gertie didn't know. Usually Papa left for his shop before the children awoke. But here he was in the kitchen with them. It wasn't the Sabbath. Well then, it must be a holiday. "I do, too," she told Henny triumphantly, "It's a holiday."

"Everybody knows it's a holiday," Henny said. "But what holiday? Don't you remember from last year?"

"Let her alone," Mama said. "She's too little to remember last year." Turning to Gertie, she explained. "It's the Fourth of July."

"Fourth of July?" Gertie repeated questioningly.

"Independence Day," Ella answered. "It's a holiday all over the country."

Papa carried the flag carefully into the front room so it could be displayed from a window overlooking the street. Gertie and Charlotte looked out the window and noticed that almost all the neighbors, up and down the street, had hung out flags also.

Ella was grating potatoes for potato kugel. After a while her right arm was beginning to ache. "Mama," she asked, "how many kugels are you making?"

"One, but it's got to be a big one. Charlie's staying for supper and you know how he loves potato kugel."

Since it was for Charlie, Ella didn't care how much her arm ached. I'll have to hurry if I want to do my hair again before he gets here, she decided, and fell to grating busily.

As soon as the task was done, she ran into the bedroom. She unbraided her thick black hair and brushed it till it lay shiny and silken against her small head. She tied the front ends back with a wide pink bow to match her dress, then studied herself in the mirror. Yes, this made her look much more grown-up.

It wasn't any too soon, for there was a knock on the kitchen door and in walked Charlie with a large box in his hand. The children gathered around him. They knew the package must be for them because he kept pulling it out of their reach and holding it high above their heads, teasingly. Only Ella stood apart. She felt she was getting too big for such childish romping, and besides, her hair might get mussed.

"Take these young scamps off me, Mama," he begged. "They're tearing me apart." But all the while he was laughing as if he didn't really want them to leave him alone. Finally he thrust the box into Ella's hands. "Here you are!" The children left Charlie and surrounded Ella instead.

Charlie sat down on the couch. He took off his straw hat and wiped the inside band with his pocket handkerchief. "Phew!" he exclaimed, rubbing his hand over the red ring on his forehead the tight hatband had made.

Meanwhile the children were shouting, "Let's see, Ella. What's in it?" and trying to poke their heads into the box all at the same time.

"Wait a minute!" Ella said. "You're tearing the box." She put it down on the kitchen table and took off the cover. Inside was an assortment of small red tubes with little wicks attached.

"Red candles!" cried Gertie.

"Firecrackers!" her sisters all yelled. "Ooh—let's shoot them off right away!"

"Let's get the matches!" Henny flew to the shelf above the kitchen stove where they were kept.

"Hold on there!" Charlie called out warningly. "I'll take those." And his long legs strode across the kitchen floor to rescue the matches. "We can't shoot off firecrackers in the house. Get the box, Ella, and I'll see you all downstairs." He was out the kitchen door like a shot,

and the children tumbled over each other in their haste to catch up with him.

The streets were full of excitement. Everybody was expressing their joy in freedom today. From tenement house windows and from store fronts flew American flags of all sizes. The air was filled with the clang of cowbells and the blasts of horns. Youngsters in small groups yelled and hopped up and down as they waited with bated breath for their firecrackers to explode. At times the noise was deafening! And now Mama's children were to add their share to the general hubbub.

"Firecrackers are a lot of fun, but they can be dangerous," cautioned Charlie. "So we will have to be careful. I was careless once when I was a little boy and I burnt my hands badly."

"Tell us about it, Charlie," said Ella eagerly.

"Well, it was a long time ago. I must have been about Charlotte's age. You should have seen me then. I was dressed in white pants and white blouse with a blue-striped sailor collar."

"I bet you looked cute," Henny said.

"I suppose so," Charlie smiled at the memory. "We had just moved to a summer cottage at the seashore. It was a pleasant place, with tall trees shading the front lawn. There were lots of flowers, too. And there was always a fresh, clean breeze from the ocean." Charlie's voice faded away for a moment. He half closed his eyes as if trying to recall the scene.

"Father and I were shooting off firecrackers and Mother watched us from the front porch. Father warned me to be careful but I paid no attention. I held the lighted firecracker in my hand and watched the bright flame. The next second, it exploded in my hands.

"Father rushed me to the kitchen and put oil on my burnt fingers. I ran to Mother and she took me in her arms. I cried, and cried . . ."

Charlie seemed to have forgotten the children. He stopped talking and looked off into the distance.

Ella watched Charlie, trying to imagine him as a small boy. But her sisters were tugging at his elbow. "Charlie," they shouted. He shook himself as if to get free of his memory. He was back on the East Side now—back to the narrow, smelly streets, teeming with people.

"Charlie, did it hurt?" Gertie asked.

"Did what hurt?"

"When you burnt your hand."

Charlie smiled down at Gertie so full of concern for him. "Uh—yes, it hurt, but not too much. Come on—let's shoot off the first one."

Charlie lit the firecrackers and threw them away from the little group. The girls stood fascinated, holding their hands to their ears and jumping when the firecrackers exploded.

When the firecrackers were all gone, Mama called them up for supper.

What a wonderful meal it was! Five pairs of eyes shone both from the excitement of the firecrackers and the pleasure of having Charlie there for supper.

"Charlie," said Mama as she served the meat course, "I've made one of your favorite dishes today."

"Oh boy! Potato pudding, I bet!"

Mama took the kugel out of the oven and bore it triumphantly to the table. It looked very festive in all its crusty, brown deliciousness on Mama's best company platter. She set it down right before Charlie. "All for me?" Charlie looked at the children. "Too bad, kids, there won't be any for you."

"Well," Mama laughed, "if you have a mind to be generous, you might give us each a small portion. . . ."

Questions for Discussion and Debate

1. What are the Fourth of July traditions that the family observes with pride and joy? Which of the family's holiday traditions becomes connected to this American celebration?

   Can you think of any American celebrations that you and your family have integrated with cultural traditions that characterize *your* heritage?

2. Is it possible both to assimilate into the mainstream *and* to maintain one's original cultural ties? Debate this question, and consider as well the following questions:

   - Why might immigrants not want to maintain any identification with their native culture once they arrive in America?

   - What does it mean to be American?

   - Should English be declared the official language of America?

   - Are bilingual education programs necessary?

   - Should Black English (Ebonics) be considered a language?

   - Should schools increase emphasis on multicultural education?

Activities and Projects

1. Do research on the nature of the curriculum that was taught in schools in New York City and other cities at the time of the greatest influx of immigrants, 1890–1920. Did the curriculum reflect the multiculturalism of the students already in these schools? (Keep in mind, of course, that even if curricula at that time did not reflect a multicultural focus, it is

likely that many teachers devised their own ways of including cultural diversity.)

2. Locate American history texts and/or interview teachers of American history at many grade levels. Find out what these books contain on such subjects as immigration, pluralism, and multiculturalism. Find out how a sample of teachers view these subjects and how they teach about them.

3. Imagine that you are currently a superintendent of schools or a curriculum coordinator in a large city school system in which hundreds of newly arrived Vietnamese and Hispanic children are enrolled. What curricular provisions would you make? How would you expect your teachers and staff to meet the needs of these children and their families?

4. The members of the *All-of-a-Kind Family* likely benefited from the educational programs provided by the settlement houses on the Lower East Side of New York City. These settlement houses were established by people—in many cases, women—who wanted to help poor urban immigrants to adjust to their new country and new language.

One of the pioneers in this social and education movement was Jane Addams (1860–1935), who opened Hull House with Ellen Gates Starr in Chicago in 1889. Her broad curriculum went beyond that of the schools and touched the lives of thousands of immigrants of all ages from many countries. She was honored with the Nobel Peace Prize in 1931.

Do research on the settlement-house movement and on Jane Addams. Try to discover what impact they had on the lives of the immigrants, the role played by women in their establishment, and whether or not there are similar types of institutions today in areas where large numbers of immigrants are settling.

If possible, locate one of the many books Jane Addams wrote and bring what you learned to class as the prelude to a discussion of her work in social welfare, education, and politics. Her most famous work, *Twenty Years at Hull House* (1910), has become a classic in the field of social work and American history in general.

2.12 ▌▌ *How Gertrude Teaches Her Children* (1915)

Johann Heinrich Pestalozzi

Johann Heinrich Pestalozzi (1746–1827) laid the foundation for a science of education (Pestalozzi, 1915, p. xxvii). And in his book, *How Gertrude Teaches Her Children,* he explains that science. In a series of 14 letters to a friend and colleague that make up the book, Pestalozzi explains how he developed his conception of popular education, the conditions under which he worked, the experiments he made, their failure or success, and the teaching method he learned through the direct study of nature (p. xxvi). He states his theories, gives details of his teaching, and shows how his principles grew

From Johann Heinrich Pestalozzi, *How Gertrude Teaches Her Children: An Attempt to Help Mothers to Teach Their Own Children and an Account of the Method*, 5th ed. Translated by Lucy E. Holland and Francis C. Turner. London: George Allen & Unwin Ltd., 1915, pp. 25–28, 194.

and how we, the readers, may follow him in spirit. His intended readers were to be teachers and parents, especially mothers, whom he considered to be the chief teachers, symbolized by Gertrude. It is thought that his conception of Gertrude was based on his warm memories of the devoted servant who helped raise him after his father died (p. xviii). Pestalozzi's method of teaching begins in the natural relation that exists between infants and their mothers and rests on the idea that education through the senses can build upon this natural connection (p. 191). He notes that educators can learn about the elements of good teaching by closely scrutinizing a mother's interaction with her baby. That maternal behavior is what constitutes Pestalozzi's "method," and its chief ingredient is *Anschauung,* or sense impressions, the idea that the teacher must enable children to bring all of their senses into the learning process. What seems so simple a formula has for decades provided the foundation upon which the modern science of education has been built.

How Gertrude Teaches Her Children was first published in 1801, the same year that Pestalozzi opened his Institute for Training Teachers. While the Institute lasted only 3.5 years, it nevertheless made him famous, helped to spread his educational principles far and wide, and gained him many disciples.

Pestalozzi himself had been a disciple of Jean Jacques Rousseau (1712–1778), considered by many historians to be the educational philosopher who bridged the transition from the traditional to the modern child-centered period of education. In 1762, when Pestalozzi had been in Zurich, Switzerland, for 2 years, he was deeply impressed by the words of Rousseau, one of the most powerful influences of the pre-French Revolutionary period. '"Do the opposite of what is usually done, and you will be right," is Rousseau's maxim in education. "All is artificial; we must return to nature. Man is bad by institutions, not by nature'" (Pestalozzi, 1915, p. xvi) These views were consistent with the emergence in the 18th century of the Age of Enlightenment or the Age of Reason, a period characterized by an emphasis on the abilities of science and human reason to explain the workings of the universe. The old religious system had insisted on blind faith, authority, and tradition. "The [French] Revolution demanded free investigation of facts, free thought, and free speech, a culture of reason and intelligence, and the natural claims of all to justice and education" (p. xvi). Rousseau had included such ideas in *Emile* and *The Social Contract,* which were considered treasonous by the pre-Revolutionary government of Geneva and the Paris Parliament, which condemned his works in 1762. On the other hand, Pestalozzi called these works "visionary." He was stirred by Rousseau's ideas that children should be educated in harmony with nature, unrestricted by the shackles of society. Through observation and experiment, seeing and doing, Pestalozzi attempted to put Rousseau's ideas into practice. The methods that evolved were based in part on the idea that children mature through natural stages; educators thus need to develop child-centered methods to fit those stages, and the child must perfect learning at each stage before going on to the next set of tasks. Like Rousseau and many others, Pestalozzi considered his faith in God to be compatible with his more modern ideas of *Anschauung* and his application of psychology to educational method.

As you read the following excerpt, think about when and where you have learned about or seen in action some of Pestalozzi's ideas. Think about your own educational views and on what points you and Pestalozzi agree.

So, without knowing the principles on which I was working, I began to dwell upon the nearness with which the objects I explained to the children were wont to touch their senses, and so, as I followed out the teaching from its beginning to its utmost end, I tried to investigate the early history of the child who is to be taught, back to its very beginning, and was soon convinced that the first hour of its teaching is the hour of its birth. From the moment in which his mind can receive impressions from Nature, Nature teaches him. The new life itself is nothing but the just-awakened readiness to receive these impressions; it is only the awakening of the perfect physical buds that now aspire with all their power and all their impulses towards the development of their individuality. It is only the awakening of the now perfect animal; that will and must become a man.

All instruction of man is then only the Art[1] of helping Nature to develop in her own way; and this Art rests essentially on the relation and harmony between the impressions received by the child and the exact degree of his developed powers. It is also necessary, in the impressions that are brought to the child by instruction, that there should be a sequence, so that beginning and progress should keep pace with the beginning and progress of the powers to be developed in the child. . . .

This was clear to me. The child must be brought to a high degree of knowledge, both of things seen and words, before it is reasonable to teach him to spell or read. I was quite convinced, that at their earliest age, children need psychological training in gaining intelligent sense-impressions of all things. But since such training, without the help of art, is not to be thought of or expected of men, as they are, the need of picture-books struck me perforce.

These should precede the A B C books, in order to make those ideas, that men express by words, clear to the children [by means of well-chosen real objects, that either in reality, or in the form of well-made models and drawings, can be brought before their minds.] . . .

. . . We leave children, up to their fifth year, in the full enjoyment of nature; we let every impression of nature work upon them; they feel their power; they already know full well the joy of unrestrained liberty and all its charms. The free natural bent which the sensuous happy wild thing takes in his development, has in them already taken its most decided direction. And after they have enjoyed this happiness of sensuous life for five whole years, we make all nature round them vanish from before their eyes; tyrannically stop the delightful course of their unrestrained freedom, pen them up like sheep, whole flocks huddled together, in stinking rooms; pitilessly chain them for hours, days, weeks, months, years, to the contemplation of unattractive and monotonous letters (and, contrasted with their former condition), to a maddening course of life.

I cease describing; else I shall come to the picture of the greater number of schoolmasters, thousands of whom in our days, merely on account of their unfitness for any means of finding a respectable livelihood, have subjected themselves to the toilsomeness of this position, which they, in accordance with their unfitness for anything better, look upon as a way that leads little further than to keep them from starvation. How infinitely must the children suffer under these circumstances, or, at least, be spoiled! . . .

. . . Friend! It is not possible to join the bonds of the feelings on which true reverence for God rests, more tightly than it is done by the whole spirit of my method. By it I have preserved the mother for the child, and procured

---

[1]The art of instruction or education.

permanence for the influence of her heart. By it I have united God's worship with human nature, and secured their preservation by stimulating those emotions, from which the impulse of faith is germinated in our hearts. Mother and Creator, mother and Preserver, become through it, one and the same emotion for the child.

Questions for Discussion and Debate

1. According to Pestalozzi, what are the *purposes* of education that he refers to as the Art. (You may list them using his words.) Then list the methods he prescribes for accomplishing each purpose.

2. Pestalozzi paints a rather frightening picture of the traditional classrooms of his time and the schoolmasters who ran them. While you might want to do some research to discover how much truth there is to his description, you can—even without doing the research—think about the reasons for his use of such vehement, melodramatic language. Would he have had a reason for using such language? Could his book have been political in the sense that he wrote it as propaganda to "sell" his methods to the public? Discuss this aspect of the book and expand the discussion to include an exploration of the reasons why anyone might write such a book about education.

3. What is Nature's role in educating the child? At what point does formal education take over? And how does Pestalozzi explain how the two can be connected? (Begin by identifying or listing the five senses.)

4. What is Pestalozzi's conception of God? What does Pestalozzi imply about God's role in education? Do you agree? Disagree? Why?

5. Pestalozzi's ideas may not sound revolutionary to you, but they were considered radical during his time. Discuss with the class any of your ideas or ideas that you have read about or seen in action that might be considered radical in today's world.

Activities and Projects

1. Pestalozzi's ideas not only reflected Rousseau's but also were similar to those of Johann Amos Comenius (1592–1670), who lived a century before Pestalozzi. And Johann Friedrich Herbart (1776–1841), the German educator, philosopher, and theorist, echoed the ideas of these three thinkers when he developed methods that emphasized both the individuality of the child and the gearing of instruction to the child's particular needs and interests. His methods were adopted by teacher educators beginning in the 19th century. Do research on the beliefs and methods of both Pestalozzi's predecessors and his successors. After documenting the similarities and differences among them, reach your own conclusions about the value of their respective contributions to modern education.

2. Design a scenario in which the characters you create portray two classroom situations, one based on the modern ideas of Rousseau and Pestalozzi and the other based on the more traditional classrooms that Pestalozzi decries in most melodramatic terms in the excerpt. Present these scenes dramatically. Then discuss with your peers how the scenes compare with the classrooms you have been observing recently or have experienced in the past.

3. Write your own version of *Gertrude*. In other words, in three to five pages explain *your* theory or philosophy of education, your conception of the purposes of education, and how best to accomplish those purposes.

4. Observe a baby and his or her mother interacting. If possible, observe more than one baby and mother for a minimum of 30 minutes. Record what you see "Gertrude" do and what the baby does. Perhaps take photographs from time to time throughout the process. Analyze the sense interactions and relate what you saw to the views Pestalozzi expresses in the first part of the excerpt. What are the educational implications of these mother and baby interactions?

2.13 *Reminiscences of Friedrich Froebel* (1889)

Baroness B. von Marenholz-Bülow

Friedrich Froebel (1782–1852) is the father of the kindergarten or "children's garden," and his work laid the foundation for early-childhood education. Froebel viewed children as flowers, all with their own unique personalities, who, with proper nurturing, would grow and blossom into healthy adults.

Baroness B. von Marenholz-Bülow studied with Froebel, became a teacher of kindergartners (a term referring to teachers of kindergarten), and started the first such school in Berlin, Germany, in the middle of the 19th century. (Interestingly, Elizabeth Palmer Peabody, author of the essay on "The Dorian Measure" in this chapter [Section 2.6], went to Germany, studied Froebel's methods, and started the first English-speaking American kindergarten in Boston in 1860.)

This excerpt is an appropriate one for this chapter on "Historical Perspectives," because Froebel honors the role that history plays in education and urges us to recognize the interconnectedness between the past and the present. He challenges us with this all-encompassing question: "What use shall we now make of this fact of an inseparable connection of all things and all times for the education of our children?"

Note how *he* answers the question. Then try to answer it yourself after reading this excerpt and reviewing the entire chapter. Can you include in your answer some details from each of the selections?

From Baroness B. von Marenholz-Bülow, *Reminiscences of Friedrich Froebel.* Translated by Mrs. Horace Mann. Boston: Lee and Shepard Publishers, 1889, pp. 149–152.

. . . With great courtesy he [Dr. R. Benfey, a promoter of Froebel] yielded to our request to illustrate in short discourses historical epochs and personalities, by which occasion was afforded almost always to compare Froebel's views with those of others, and particularly with the pedagogic views of Greek antiquity, especially with the ideas of Plato on the education of children, which in manifold ways concurred with Froebel's.

On a social walk to Altenstein, where I had invited the company to sup at the little inn at that place, some remarks of Dr. Benfey's upon the Greek manner of viewing things were fully discussed in a lively manner by Froebel.

Upon my saying how history, particularly the history of culture, demonstrated the uninterrupted connection between the past and present, the consideration of which Froebel always pointed out to us as one of the most important principles of education, Froebel said: "In human development, unity and connection show themselves everywhere; the past, present, and future form a chain whose links are joined inseparably. Human history shows the same uninterrupted development as the universe, and all development in the spiritual, as in the material world, proceeds according to the same law. The height of culture in the Greek world could not possibly have been reached without the preceding stages of development of that and other nations. Beauty of body, suppleness of limb, power of muscle, and gracefulness of movement in the Greek were the result of the physical exertions and exercises of their forefathers, and the inheritance of a culture measured by centuries. But the higher development always has the task of influencing and elevating the steps of culture below it.

"Thus the Greek, afterward the Roman culture and civilization have acted upon other uncultivated races and made them capable of higher cultivation. Indeed, even at the present time that cultivating influence is indirectly at work on ourselves, as well as directly through the classical literature of the time.

"As the life of the human race moves on through all epochs, in living connection, like a single life, so the life and development of every individual proceeds in uninterrupted connection.

"The peculiar character whose germ even the nursling shows to him who contemplates the child's nature understandingly is found again in the older child, still further on in the youth, again in the adult, and at last in the graybeard. No one stage of life can be separated from the others. So each generation of men is connected with the preceding, and at the same time determines the character of the following.

"What use shall we now make of this fact of an inseparable connection of all things and all times for the education of our children?

"This use: that we look upon them and treat them as individual spiritual beings, and then that we teach them to perceive things in this connection."

One of the company present interrupted Froebel with the question: "How is this practicable in the first years of life? The child may be treated in this manner by the grown-up educators, but how to effect the object of making the child perceive things in their connection is inconceivable to me."

Froebel replied: "Every child brings with him into the world the natural disposition to see correctly what is before him, or, in other words, the truth. If things are shown to him in their connection, his soul perceives them thus, as a conception. But if, as often happens, things are brought before his mind singly, or piecemeal and in fragments, then the natural disposition to see correctly is perverted to the opposite, and the healthy mind is perplexed.

"How one shall begin practically to make for the child the first representation of things in their constant connection, in a correct and clear manner, I have shown plainly in my 'Mother and Cosset Songs,' and still further in my play-gifts.

"Look upon these last; how they proceed from the ball as a symbol of unity, and then pass over from this in a consecutive manner to the manifoldness of form in the cube; how the cube is then divided according to the law of the connection of opposites; how each succeeding form (in the play) goes forth from the preceding, and how not only the connection according to a law of all the parts of the play-material exhibits clearly the union into one whole, but the child perceives through his own action that he only obtains his building (or other figures) when he

unites into a whole, in a regular and lawful manner, the parts which he is handling. In such ways he is to perceive that all connection implies opposites which can be joined together, and again that no opposites are to be seen in the properties of things which cannot be connected.

"The linking together that is everywhere found, and which holds the universe in its wholeness and unity, the eye receives, and thereby receives the representation, but *without understanding it,* except as an impression and an image; but these first impressions are the root fibres for the understanding that is developed later. The correct perception is a preparation for correct knowing and thinking.

Questions for Discussion and Debate

1. Answer the question Froebel poses in the excerpt: "What use shall we now make of this fact of an inseparable connection of all things and all times for the education of our children?" Integrate ideas from several excerpts in this chapter *and* from others in the text.

2. Compare and contrast Froebel's references to the Greek legacy in education and E. P. Peabody's references to the same legacy. Note also information contained in the Brief Background to this chapter.

3. What is the value for teachers of knowing educational history?

Activities and Projects

1. Write a paper in which you respond *personally* to Froebel's question. The contents of your paper will likely reflect your own philosophy of education and the role that your personal educational history has played in the formation of your educational beliefs. What are the connections between your educational past and your educational present?

2. Find out about Froebel's life and his contribution to early–childhood education and

interdisciplinary approaches to education. Prepare a biographical sketch to share with others.

3. Do research on the movers and shakers in early–childhood education. Then draw a tree with Froebel as the trunk. Place branches extending upward and roots below. Label the roots (i.e., relating to Greek and other influences on Froebel), and label the branches with the names of those individuals who became his disciples and spread his

philosophy. Besides E. P. Peabody, who else would be on a branch?

4. Take a current teaching or curriculum trend, say, the whole-language approach to teaching reading, and try to find out—in this case by doing research on the history of teaching reading—whether or not whole language, *or any other innovative idea*, is, in fact, not new at all but simply the reappearance of an earlier idea with a new name.

5. Specific practices developed by Froebel can be observed in many schools today, although some of the practitioners of his philosophy may not be aware of the origins of their techniques. For example, in some schools, you can observe Froebel's belief in designing the curriculum around the student's interests and needs; in Rudolf Steiner, or Waldorf, schools, you can observe Froebel's belief in the integration of music and art across the curriculum; and in Montessori schools, you can observe his belief in children learning concepts by discovery and through manipulation of objects. Find out if there are any Montessori or Steiner schools in your area. Call and ask if you can observe there and talk to the teachers about their views regarding Froebel. Watch for their application of Froebel's ideas. Share your experience with the class.

2.14 "Religion the Only Basis of Society" (1879)

William Ellery Channing

"In most traditional cultures, parents, older peers, and religious institutions act as educational agents. In secular societies [like the United States] schools take over many pedagogical functions . . . " (Gardner, 1999, p. 101). What the Puritans did when they first settled in the New World was to merge religion with schooling and to fashion a curriculum that consisted of the 4 R's: religion, reading, writing, and arithmetic. Using the *New England Primer* that they developed as early as 1690, the Puritans wove throughout each lesson several values that specified "right behavior," the fifth R. And today, despite a multicultural society that has not uniformly bought into those values, they nonetheless persist in influencing what teachers teach and publishers publish throughout the country.

No doubt the New England Puritans, followers of John Calvin's strict Protestant creed, brought their primers across the ocean with them (Freeman, 1960, pp. 7–8). Originally the "primer" was a book of private devotions that contained the Lord's Prayer, the Ten Commandments, a few psalms, and some simple instructions in Christian knowledge. *McGuffey's Fifth Eclectic Reader,* from which the following excerpt is taken, strays only slightly from the primers that began in the Massachusetts Bay Colony and were picked up by other parts of New England.

From William Holmes McGuffey (Ed.), *McGuffey's Fifth Eclectic Reader*, Revised Edition. Cincinnati and New York: Van Antwerp, Bragg & Co., 1879, pp. 284–286.

McGuffey's Reader, like the *New England Primer,* contained the alphabet and simple to complex words, divided into syllables, with keys to pronunciation. The rest of the *Reader* was made up of religious and moral verses and prose gathered from many sources including the works of such noted writers as Charles Dickens, Henry David Thoreau, and Shakespeare.

William Holmes McGuffey (1879) developed his series of reading materials in 1836 in order to "present the best specimens of style, insure interest in the subjects, impart valuable information, and exert a decided and healthful moral influence" (p. iii). His graded readers sold well over 100 million copies before being replaced by more scientifically constructed, secularized texts. While his books were decidedly Christian in content and tone, he did not go so far as to include the more extreme examples of Puritan tenets such as this verse from the *New England Primer* of 1690:

In Adam's Fall
We Sinne'd all
. . . Thy Life to Mend
This Book Attend
. . . The Idle Fool
Is Whipt at School.
(Pulliam & Van Patten, 1995, p. 31)

While McGuffey may not have chosen to include such verses, we do know that many schools even today have adopted the controversial practice of corporal punishment that the verse advocates. In fact, various elements of the Puritan legacy, like this one, not only are controversial but also can be viewed as blatantly undemocratic. For example, racism and intolerance are also part of that legacy. Readers are likely familiar with the 17th-century Salem witch trials, promulgated by the fact that Puritan leaders did not tolerate religious freedom in the Massachusetts Bay Colony. There is no question that examples of both the positive and the negative aspects of the Puritan legacy can be seen everywhere and continue to play a role in ongoing conflicts central to education, including the debates about vouchers, school prayer, and affirmative action, among others. To understand these conflicts, it is important for educators to recognize their links to the early settlers of New England.

The following essay, "Religion the Only Basis of Society," was written by William Ellery Channing (1780–1842) and appeared in the 1879 Revised Edition of *McGuffey's Fifth Eclectic Reader.* Channing, Harvard-educated and pastor of the Federal Street Church in Boston, wrote extensively on theology and was considered one of the founding fathers of Unitarianism, a more liberal version of Protestantism. Though he rejected the restrictive Calvinist doctrines of the early settlers, Channing's essay leaves little doubt that Puritan theology provided the basis for his beliefs and, indeed, for the beliefs of many people today who advocate narrowing the divisions between church and state.

1. Religion is a social concern; for it operates powerfully on society, contributing in various ways to its stability and prosperity. Religion is not merely a private affair; the community is deeply interested in its diffusion; for it is the best support of the virtues and principles, on

which the social order rests. Pure and undefiled religion is, to do good; and it follows, very plainly, that if God be the Author and Friend of society, then, the recognition of him must enforce all social duty, and enlightened piety must give its whole strength to public order.

2. Few men suspect, perhaps no man comprehends, the extent of the support given by religion to every virtue. No man, perhaps, is aware, how much our moral and social sentiments are fed from this fountain; how powerless conscience would become without the belief of a God; how palsied would be human benevolence, were there not the sense of a higher benevolence to quicken and sustain it; how suddenly the whole social fabric would quake, and with what a fearful crash it would sink into hopeless ruin, were the ideas of a Supreme Being, of accountableness and of a future life to be utterly erased from every mind.

3. And, let men thoroughly believe that they are the work and sport of chance; that no superior intelligence concerns itself with human affairs; that all their improvements perish forever at death; that the weak have no guardian, and the injured no avenger; that there is no recompense for sacrifices to uprightness and the public good; that an oath is unheard in heaven; that secret crimes have no witness but the perpetrator; that human existence has no purpose, and human virtue no unfailing friend; that this brief life is every thing to us, and death

is total, everlasting extinction; once let them *thoroughly* abandon religion, and who can conceive or describe the extent of the desolation which would follow?

4. We hope, perhaps, that human laws and natural sympathy would hold society together. As reasonably might we believe, that were the sun quenched in the heavens, *our* torches would illuminate, and *our* fires quicken and fertilize the creation. What is there in human nature to awaken respect and tenderness, if man is the unprotected insect of a day? And what is he more, if atheism be true?

5. Erase all thought and fear of God from a community, and selfishness and sensuality would absorb the whole man. Appetite, knowing no restraint, and suffering, having no solace or hope, would trample in scorn on the restraints of human laws. Virtue, duty, principle, would be mocked and spurned as unmeaning sounds. A sordid self-interest would supplant every feeling; and man would become, in fact, what the theory in atheism declares him to be,—*a companion for brutes.*

DEFINITIONS.—1. Com-mū´ni-ty, *society at large, the public.* Dĭf-fū´ṣion, *extension, spread.* En-līght´ened, *elevated by knowledge and religion.* 2. Făb´ric, *any system composed of connected parts.* E-rāsed´, *blotted out.* 3. Pẽr´pe-trā-tor, *one who commits a crime.* Ex-tĭnc´tion, *a putting an end to.* 4. Fẽr´ti-līze, *to make fruitful.* A´the-ĭ̯sm, *disbelief in God.* Sĕn-sū-ăl´i-ty, *indulgence in animal pleasure.*

▰▰▰▰▰▰▰ Questions for Discussion and Debate ▰▰▰▰▰▰▰

1. In your own words express the main idea in Channing's essay. Then discuss with the class the extent to which you think Americans still agree with that idea. In which of Channing's ideas do you think most

Americans still believe, and which are dated? Provide evidence for your conclusions.

2. Identify one sentence in the essay that reflects *your* own view and one sentence that

contains a view with which you disagree. Share your choices and explain why you made them.

3. Channing's essay reflects the views of the Puritans that came before him, including a strong aversion to atheism. To what extent is there tolerance in this country for nonbelievers or atheists? And on what do you base your response to this question? (For example, do you think an atheist could ever be elected president?)

4. No real consensus exists among parents regarding the teacher role specified in this verse found in a Boston primer of 1791. (Note the *f* for *s*, which was carried over from Middle English.)

The School-Mam, fee, whofe only care
    Is to inftruct her tender youth,
How they may vice's ways beware,
    And tread the fteps of peace and truth
                (Freeman, 1960, p. 13)

Express the idea in the poem in your own words. Then debate the following resolution with your peers: *Resolved, that a teacher's role should include teaching of certain values.* Before the debate, prepare your views and your reasoning in writing. Consult other chapters in this anthology (i.e., chapter 3, for philosophical perspectives relevant to teaching values). See also the list of values in item 3 on page 130.

Activities and Projects

1. There are currently educational programs that specify methods for teaching certain values, albeit devoid of religious connections. Often referred to as "character education" (Lickona, 1993) and "moral education" (Gardner, 1999), these programs are mired in controversy. Unlike the value-laden teachings of the Puritans, which received the unquestioning support of the colonial government and community, these secular programs disturb some parents who either believe that teaching values is best done in the home and religious institution or believe, as the fundamentalist religious groups do, that the Puritan ethos should be reinstated. Do research on the subject of character education and moral education. Describe three or four examples of such programs. If possible, find evaluations of their effectiveness. Share your findings with your peers.

2. Find out if there are any teachers in your community who are using one of the published character education programs in their classes. Describe one of the programs, its rationale, and the teacher's assessment of the program's effects.

3. Read the following list of values derived from the Puritans (Pulliam & Van Patten, 1995, p. 36). Then locate at least three elementary texts used to teach reading in the classroom today. Do an analysis of the stories, poetry, and prose in those texts to determine which, if any, of these values are still—after hundreds of years—being transmitted through *today's* readers. Share your analysis with the class.

a. Respect for authority
b. Postponing immediate gratification
c. Neatness
d. Punctuality
e. Responsibility for one's own work
f. Honesty

g. Patriotism and loyalty

h. Striving for personal achievement

i. Competition

j. Repression of aggression and overt sexual expression

k. Respect for rights and property of others

l. Obeying rules and regulations

4. We are reminded of the Puritan legacy not only when we consider the familiar values listed in item 3, but also when, in the media, we read items such as the following:

> Conservative Christian church leaders protest that Harry Potter [the title character in the novels by J. K. Rowling about the adventures of a boy wizard and his pals at Hogwart's School of Witchcraft and Wizardry] dabbles in the occult and thus undermines Biblical values. Taking the fantasy literally, they claim the books and the movie teach children to be immoral and to worship Satan. . . . (Means, 2001)

In fact, some church leaders and parents have attempted to have the books removed from school libraries.

(a) As you peruse current newspapers and the Internet, look for other examples of Puritan attitudes. Record them and share them with your peers. (b) Check out how well the Harry Potter books are doing in the schools. For example, some teachers testify that the Harry Potter books have been prime motivators in getting children to read, children who have never before been interested in reading. Ask teachers what they think children are learning from these books besides reading skills.

5. Some of the values derived from the Puritans' teaching (see item 3) may be incompatible with the cultural backgrounds of some students, and imposing such values on them can lead to failure. If possible, visit classrooms characterized by diversity and interview the teachers about this issue. Try to gather information from other sources that might provide evidence of this problem.

6. Cotton Mather and John Cotton were among the most orthodox of the Puritan ministers who, like their predecessor, John Calvin, supported punishment, even death—as in the witch trials—for any disobedience. Read some of their primary source materials and bring samples of their work to class. Read parts of them aloud to experience their full power. Then hold a discussion about how such views influenced educational practice, and how they still do.

Chapter References

Addams, J. (1910). *Twenty years at Hull House.* New York: Macmillan.

Association of Teacher Educators (ATE). (1980). *Visions of reform: Implications for the education profession.* Reston, VA: ATE.

Bowen, H. C. (1966). *Froebel and education by self-activity.* In *The Great Educators Series.* New York: Cedric Chivers, Ltd./August M. Kelley. (Original work published 1898)

Bruner, J. (1975). *Toward a theory of instruction.* Cambridge, MA: Harvard University Press.

Carnegie Forum on Education and the Economy. (1986). *A nation prepared: Teachers for the 21st century. Report of the Carnegie Task Force on Teaching as a Profession.* Washington, DC: Author.

Douglass, F. (1968). *Narrative of the life of Frederick Douglass: An American slave*. New York: New American Library.

Eisner, E. W. (1985). *The educational imagination* (2nd ed.) New York: Macmillan.

Eisner, E. W. (1991). *The enlightened eye. Qualitative inquiry and the enhancement of educational practice*. New York: Macmillan.

Freeman, R. S. (1960). *Yesterday's school books, a looking glass for teachers of today*. Watkins Glen, NY: Century House.

Gardner, H. (1999). *The disciplined mind. What all students should understand*. New York: Simon & Schuster.

Hirsch, E. D., Jr. (1987). *Cultural literacy: What every American needs to know*. Boston: Houghton Mifflin.

The Holmes Group. (1986). *Tomorrow's teachers: A report of the Holmes Group*. East Lansing, MI: Author.

Johnson, D. W., & Johnson, R. T. (1989). *Cooperation and competition: Theory and research*. Edina, MN: Interaction Book.

Jones, H. M. (Ed.). (1966). *Emerson on education. Selections:* In *Classics in Education Series*, No. 26. New York: Teachers College Press, Columbia University.

Kozol, J. (1991). *Savage inequalities: Children in America's schools*. New York: Crown.

Kozol, J. (1995). *Amazing grace*. New York: Crown.

Lawrence, J., & Lee, R. E. (1955). *Inherit the wind*. New York: Bantam.

Lickona, T. (1993, November). The return of character education. *Educational Leadership, 51* (3), 6–11.

Mann, H. (1891). Annual reports of the Secretary of the Board of Education of Massachusetts for the years 1845–1848. In *Life and works of Horace Mann* (Vol. IV). Boston: Lee and Shepard.

McGuffey, W. H. (1879). *McGuffey's fifth eclectic reader* (Rev. ed.). New York: Van Antwerp, Bragg.

Means, M. (2002, November 25). Hooray for Harry! *The Berkshire Eagle*, p. A8.

Miller, J. E. (1998). *Becoming Laura Ingalls Wilder: The woman behind the legend*. Columbia: University of Missouri.

Neider, C. (Ed.). (1975). *The complete tales of Washington Irving*. New York: Doubleday.

Nock, A. J. (1963). *Jefferson*. New York: Hill and Wang.

The Norman Rockwell Album. (1961). Garden City, NY: Doubleday.

Peabody, E. P. (1849). *Aesthetic papers*. New York: G. P. Putnam.

Pestalozzi, J. H. (1915). *How Gertrude teaches her children: An attempt to help mothers to teach their own children and an account of the method* (L. E. Holland & F. C. Turner, Trans.). London: George Allen & Unwin.

Plato. (1892). *The republic* (B. Jowett, Trans.). In *The dialogues of Plato* (Vol. III, 3rd ed.). London: Oxford University Press.

Pulliam, J. D., & Van Patten, J. (1995). *History of education in America*. Upper Saddle River, NJ: Merrill/Prentice Hall.

Rousseau, J. J. (1933). *Emile; Or, education* (B. Foxley, Trans.). New York: E. P. Dutton.

Sloane, E. (1972). *The little red schoolhouse. Sketchbook of early American education*. Garden City, NY: Doubleday.

Spring, J. (1986). *The American school, 1642–1985. Varieties of historical interpretations of the foundations and development of American education*. White Plains, NY: Longman.

Taylor, C. J. (1882). *History of Great Barrington, (Berkshire County,) Massachusetts*. Great Barrington, MA: Clark W. Bryan.

Taylor, S. (1980). *All-of-a-kind family*. New York: Dell.

von Marenholz-Bülow, Baroness B. (1889). *Reminiscences of Friedrich Froebel* (Mrs. H. Mann, Trans.). Boston: Lee and Shepard.

Wilder, L. I. (1963). *These happy golden years*. London: Butterworth.

Additional Readings

Button, H. W. & Provenzo, E. E., Jr. (1989). *History of education and culture in America.* Englewood Cliffs, NJ: Prentice Hall.

Butts, R. F., & Cremin, L. A. (1953). *A history of education in American culture.* New York: Holt, Rinehart and Winston.

Cohen, R. M., & Scheer, S. (Eds.) (1997). *The work of teachers in America. A social history through stories.* Mahwah, NJ: Lawrence Erlbaum Associates.

Cordasco, F. (1976). *A brief history of education.* Totowa, NJ: Littlefield, Adam.

Gatto, J. T. (2000–2001). *The underground history of American education: A schoolteacher's intimate investigation into the problem of modern schooling.* Oxford, NY: Oxford Village Press.

Gutek, G. L. (2001). *Education in the United States: An historical perspective.* (3rd ed.) Upper Saddle River, NJ: Merrill/Prentice Hall.

Lemisch, L. J. (Ed.). (1961). *Benjamin Franklin. The autobiography and other writings.* New York: New American Library.

Rippa, S. A. (1992). *Education in a free society: An American history* (7th ed.). White Plains, NY: Longman.

Warren, D. (Ed.). (1989). *American teachers: Histories of a profession at work.* New York: Macmillan.

Chapter 3

Philosophical Foundations

Approaches to Curriculum Development

What is truth?
What has value?
What rules govern correct thinking?

What is worth teaching?
How do we come to know?
How should we teach?

Answers to these and other lofty philosophical questions vary greatly depending on the point of view of the educational philosophers formally addressing them. Have you ever wondered about such things? If so, *your* responses might serve as the beginning of *your* educational philosophy, and your beliefs may, in fact, resemble those of established philosophers. Their theories may be no more valid than yours, especially if you, too, base your responses on long-term observations of human behavior, particularly in the contexts of teaching and learning. So what value is there in studying traditional and modern philosophies if it's possible to develop your own set of beliefs as a result of personal experience? Well, first, studying these systems of thought can be useful in providing you and teachers, in general, a rationale, a framework, and a language with which to explain your own beliefs and actions related to curriculum and teaching. Second, the formal philosophies are useful when comparing and contrasting different theories. And third, there may be systems of thought that differ from the ones guiding your current practice; by consulting the spectrum of beliefs, you may learn about other approaches you can test. In the end, what and how we choose to teach are based on our beliefs about what constitutes the truth about good teaching, the purpose of education, and the nature of the student–teacher relationship. All of these factors determine the curriculum approach we choose and are tied to our underlying attitudes about human nature and human potential.

Unfortunately, for newcomers about to embark on a study of these formal philosophies for the first time, the task does not come without certain obstacles. For example, there's the inconsistency among texts in referring to one or another of these thought systems as a theory or as a philosophy. In some texts, for example, perennialism is referred to as a philosophy (Pulliam & Van Patten, 1995, pp. 244–246), while in others it is referred to as a theory (Farris, 1996, pp. 6–15). The distinctions between the two terms is not as important as recognizing that both a philosophy *and* a theory are hypothetical in nature; they are assumptions that describe what *could or should* be, as opposed to what actually is.

In addition to facing the challenge of distinguishing between a philosophy and a theory, you will frequently encounter *different* descriptions for the same philosophy from text to text. In some cases you will also be required to wade through thick and abstract jargon. Further, the gap between the definitions of the theories and their practical applications may be so wide as to make them unbridgeable. And, finally, some of the thinkers within the same school of thought don't always see eye to eye. Suffice it to say, then, that philosophical waters can get pretty muddy.

Perhaps because of this muddiness, many teachers either never consult these theories after leaving college or latch on to one that appears plausible and stay with it no matter what. Then there are teachers who become "true believers," who see only one way of thinking as the "right way," forgetting that all educational ideas are philosophical in nature and thus open to scrutiny and improvement. Although it may be quite natural for teachers or administrators to lean toward one philosophy or approach more than another, one-sided thinking can rarely serve the needs of all children.

A story that illustrates this point comes from a new teacher in California who reported to this editor that the principal of her elementary school prohibited teachers from using phonics to teach reading. Whole language, the holistic approach, was to be the only method, and teachers were scolded if they "resorted to" phonics. She and her colleagues felt like subversives whenever they encouraged a child to sound out a word. Perhaps familiarity with the whole spectrum of educational thought, together with a sense of balance (Aristotelian wisdom), can keep such administrative or other extremism to a minimum. (And, not surprisingly, more than a dozen years after the state of California dropped phonics for what it felt was the more imaginative approach to reading known as whole language, it is returning to basic phonics in a big way [Schemo, 2002].) The late educational psychologist, Madeline Hunter, put it this way: "There are no supposed-to's in education," no set principles or practices that are inherently "right" or "better than" all the rest all of the time. As a result of her work at UCLA, however, Hunter did conclude that while it may look different, "a good music teacher is doing what a good calculus teacher is doing" (cited in Gursky, 1991, p. 30), one example of such behavior being the use of a "hook" or motivational device to get the students' attention. She agreed with philosopher John Dewey that both of their fields were experimental *and* scientific because both "start with the facts of experience and have . . . a knowledge . . . of the nature and meaning of experience" (Rockefeller, 1991, p. 94). Dewey, in fact, argued in favor of completely identifying philosophy with psychology because both deal with questions about human nature and rely to some degree on the scientific method. The point here is that both fields can broaden your perspectives on what constitutes good teaching.

Brief Background

Periodically in American history there have been movements back and forth across the philosophical spectrum just as there have been pendulum swings in terms of the several educational trends referred to in chapter 2. Conceptions of curriculum (what to teach and how), like historical issues, tend to appear, disappear, and then reappear again. Certain philosophies of education, for example, will take on importance as a result of changing political, social, or economic conditions. A case in point: During the 1950s, there was a philosophical shift toward essentialism and more traditional approaches emphasizing the basics or essentials in all subjects, especially the sciences. This shift is thought to have come about because of the competition between the United States and the Soviet Union for predominance in space after the Soviets launched the first satellite, Sputnik. America was also waging a Cold War with the Soviets, pitting the capitalist and democratic system against the Communist and totalitarian one. With an emphasis on the basics, the government believed that American schools could produce the kinds of minds capable of matching those of the Soviets. Now, however, with the end of the Cold War and the downfall of Communism, and a more cooperative relationship with Russia, the philosophical shift has been toward more progressive, experiential, interdisciplinary approaches—such as technology education—which combine the teaching of several disciplines in relation to one another and their application to real issues. The National Science Foundation, in conjunction with several educational organizations, is funding these approaches. While this shift may have occurred for other reasons as well, there is little doubt that a relationship exists between what's "in" in terms of educational beliefs and what is going on in other circles—political, social, and others—at a particular time in history. Thus it is helpful to look at philosophies of education within the context of history, which accounts for the proximity of this chapter to chapter 2, "Historical Perspectives."

The purpose of this chapter is to introduce to you several educational philosophies, and it is, indeed, only an introduction. For a more complete understanding of this complex subject, you will need to branch out into the library and onto the bookshelves of your education department. There you will discover texts providing details about the teacher's role, the student's role, and the preferred curriculum content and method espoused by several traditional as well as modern educational philosophies. The point of this chapter is simply to start you on the journey by helping you recognize, first, that very diverse ideas about education exist; second, that these ideas can be and have been categorized (see next section); and, third, that these systems of thought continue to influence teachers, departments of education, and school boards whenever they need a rationale for their educational decisions or need to shift gears. You will soon discover, if you haven't already done so, that arguing educational philosophies is like arguing about religion or politics. For every belief there is likely to be an equal and opposite belief and data to support both. That's why the field of education is never dull.

Philosophies of Education and Some Proponents

Existentialism: There is no set content or method in the curriculum, but rather the focus is on the personal choices, attitudes, and perceptions of the individual teacher and student. *Proponents:* Søren Kierkegaard, Jean-Paul Sartre, A. S. Neill, Carl Rogers

Idealism: Ideas and reason are central to the content of education. This intangible world of ideas also encompasses the spiritual world and values. *Proponents:* Plato, Immanuel Kant, Georg Wilhelm Friedrich Hegel, Ralph Waldo Emerson

Pragmatism: Student-centered perspectives in terms of active, integrated, firsthand learning experiences are the most effective. This philosophy is also somewhat subject-centered in terms of teaching knowledge, attitudes, and skills that students will need to function in the world. *Proponents:* John Dewey, Charles Pierce, William James

Postmodernism: This philosophy emphasizes the idea that there are many paths to knowledge but that critical theory and pedagogy are central; that is, the central goals are to challenge all aspects of the status quo *and* empower the powerless through education. *Proponents:* William Stanley, C. A. Bowers, Henry Giroux, Peter McLaren, Cleo Cherryholmes, Paulo Freire

Realism: The physical, observable world is central to educational study. The scientific method, personal experience, and the senses are relevant. *Proponents:* Aristotle, John Amos Comenius, Johann Heinrich Pestalozzi, Alfred North Whitehead, John Locke

Behaviorism (usually classified as a psychological theory): These beliefs support the idea that behavior is shaped by a carefully planned environment and by external forces. What's important is behavior or learning that is observable and measurable. *Proponents:* Thomas Hobbes, Ivan Pavlov, John Watson, B. F. Skinner

Theories of Education and Some Proponents

Essentialism: The liberal arts are emphasized along with basic academic skills. Testing is approved for determining mastery of these subjects along with support for vigorous national standards. *Proponents:* Arthur Bestor, William Chandler Bagley

Experimentalism: Experimenting or testing curricular ideas is essential. The process of learning is stressed over product, and proponents advocate a student-centered approach, active learning, and relevant subject matter. *Proponents:* John Dewey, George Herbert Meade, William James

Perennialism: This theory seeks truth and the development of students' intellect by means of the classics of Western civilization that appear to have stood the test of time. *Proponents:* St. Thomas Aquinas, Robert Maynard Hutchins, Mortimer Adler

Progressivism: Students' needs and interests are central. Students actively help direct the projects and the problem-solving in which they engage. **Constructivism** is a related and more recent term describing progressive behaviors. *Proponents:* Jean-Jacques Rousseau, William Heard Kirkpatrick, Francis Parker, John Dewey, Jean Piaget, Helen Parkhurst, Lev Semenovich Vygotsky

Social Reconstructionism: The primary purpose of curriculum and method is to find ways to solve global problems and make the world a more just and fair place in which to live. *Proponents:* George Counts, Harold Rugg, John Holt, Ivan Illich, John Dewey

All of the above educational philosophies and theories are essentially curriculum theories or conceptions of curriculum, for there is an organic relationship between one's educational beliefs (philosophy) and the content and method (curriculum) one chooses to apply in the classroom.

The most common conceptions of curriculum are as follows.

- Student-centered
- Subject-centered (structure of the disciplines)
- Teacher-centered (traditional)
- Society-centered (related to society's needs)
- Broad fields (interdisciplinary)
- Technology-based (behavioral, measurable)

Try to match these concepts of curriculum with one or more of the philosophies or theories. For example, the theory of perennialism, based on the use of the classics, can be linked to a subject-centered curriculum conception.

Finally, it should be noted that there is a certain narrowness of perspective presented here in that all of these theories or philosophies are Western in origin;

that is, they have been constructed and documented by European and American thinkers. At a time when multiculturalism and non-Western studies are increasing across the disciplines, many educators say that it is perhaps time for students to recognize the role that Eastern systems of thought such as Hinduism, Islam, and Buddhism can play in curriculum content and method. Few foundational texts, however, address their role. Nevertheless, Eastern philosophies, with their emphasis on the intangible inner life, human intuition, and the attainment of harmony among mind, body, and nature, can serve to expand thinking about curriculum development in contrast to Western approaches to educational thought and practice (Reagan, 1996). Often when we examine theories that stem from different cultural origins, we are better able to understand those that govern more familiar approaches. In addition, by critically assessing the familiar, we might find ways to integrate the less familiar and, in so doing, improve education for all students and, even better, improve our own lives.

Selections

Norman Rockwell's painting, *The Connoisseur,* provides an excellent springboard for a discussion of the contrasts that exist among educational philosophies. The readings in this chapter include excerpts from the works of philosophers John Dewey and Rudolf Steiner, doctor and teacher Maria Montessori, and mathematician and philosopher Alfred North Whitehead. Plato's work appears here ("Allegory of the Cave") in the form of one of his most famous dialogues, in which he explains the connection between politics and education. Another allegorical piece from *Saber-Tooth Curriculum* satirizes the way in which curriculum develops and becomes entrenched. Two autobiographical perspectives, one by John Holt (*How Children Fail*) and the other by Mark Salzman (*Iron and Silk*), reveal the experiences and thinking of two teachers, one a veteran education writer, the other a young novelist who taught for several months in China. Walt Whitman's poem No. 9 from *Leaves of Grass* and a poem by José Calderon capture the essence of effective curriculum: making connections and meaning. Tom Paxton's "What Did You Learn in School Today?" raises a number of philosophical questions in a simple but provocative song. And Diane Ravitch, in *Left Back,* answers some of those questions, as do several other educators (e.g., Randal C. Archibold, in "What Kind of Education Is Adequate?") who are concerned with the purpose and meaning of education.

As you read each of the selections, try to identify the beliefs about teaching and the curriculum implicit in the words and/or actions of these writers or the characters they have met or created. You may find that you agree with some of the ideas in these selections. Others will cause you to rethink the philosophical perspectives you have already developed as a result of personal experience both in and outside of the classroom.

Fill in the following chart (after reproducing it in your notebook). Refer to the list of philosophies and theories. Then read the excerpts in this chapter and consult outside sources related to philosophies of education. Come back to the chart and make changes and additions.

Chart of Philosophies and Theories of Education				
Philosophy/Theory	Essential Idea	Role of Teacher	Role of Student	Your Thoughts, i.e., Pros and Cons
Existentialism				
Idealism				
Pragmatism				
Postmodernism				
Realism				
Behaviorism				
Essentialism				
Experimentalism				
Perennialism				
Progressivism				
Social Reconstructionism				

3.1 Work of Art: *The Connoisseur* (1962)

Norman Rockwell

Confronting educational philosophies can be a little like coming face-to-face with an abstract painting, in other words, perplexing. On the other hand, the experience might be enlightening. Since we can't see the expression on the face of the rather urbane, conservatively dressed gentleman in Norman Rockwell's painting, *The Connoisseur,* as he contemplates the Jackson Pollock-like painting, we don't know what his response is to the colorful paint splotches and drippings. What we can see is that his highly polished shoes and perfectly fitting suit reveal him to be a perfectionist, depicted in classic Rockwellian style and antithetical to Pollock's random, rather chaotic forms that Rockwell has imitated here.

In *The Connoisseur,* a *Saturday Evening Post* cover in January 1962, Rockwell rather convincingly replicates Pollock's famous drip painting, "a non-representational style completely at odds with Rockwell's own meticulous realism" (Hennessey & Knutson, 1999, p. 82). Is his gentleman bewildered or delighted? Rockwell isn't saying.

These two contrasting painting styles can be compared to two extremes within the spectrum of educational philosophies, realism, on the one hand, and postmodernism, on the other, with postmodernism clearly akin to the abstract expression of painters such as Pollock and realism comparable to the figurative style of Rockwell. Postmodernists in education and abstract painters in art challenged the status quo during the latter half of the 20th century by tossing out all of the long-standing rules and assumptions within their respective fields. They seemed to be saying, "Now start building your own meaning from scratch."

Their more conservative counterparts include, in education, the realists and, in art, painters like Norman Rockwell, whose representational illustrations correspond with some of the ideas of educational realists, such as Pestalozzi. Both base their orientation on the physical, observable world, personal experience, and the senses.

Unlike abstract paintings, which are wide open for interpretation, a clear and simple story seems to emerge from many of Rockwell's paintings. But this apparent simplicity can be deceptive, since Rockwell often incorporates details and techniques that, once recognized, show his work to be far more complex. For example, in *The Connoisseur* notice the diamond-patterned floor beneath the gentleman's feet. The ordered and tidy world of this man, as shown by his attire and stance, is thus reinforced by the earthbound repetitive pattern of the floor, and both of these contrast with the chaos and disorderliness of the mock Pollock painting. According to Wanda M. Corn, Professor of Art History at Stanford University, Rockwell's work conveys all sorts of meanings. In this one she points out that you, the viewer, might choose to see *The Connoisseur* as portraying any number of contrasts: imagination versus rationality, feminine versus masculine, or left brain versus right. According to her, "Rockwell [has] vested this illustration . . . with some of the grandest and most elementary conflicts in the universe" (Hennessey & Knutson, 1999, p. 87).

The term **connoisseur** is defined as "an expert, one who is knowledgeable enough about art to be a critical judge." Was Rockwell satirizing the very concept of connoisseurship, the idea that one must be an expert in art to be a critic (or an expert in philosophy to be able to construct one)? After all, art is really a matter of taste, so aren't we all connoisseurs? Or was Rockwell poking fun at an art world made up of snobs (postmodernists?) who called him old-fashioned and out-of-touch because his work reached the hearts of common people? Or was he just trying to show them that—if he wanted to—he could paint like Pollock? The answers are unclear.

Whatever his motivation may have been, Rockwell still maintained a sense of humor, and he even expressed interest in abstract expressionism. Soon after painting *The Connoisseur,* he said, "If I were young now I might paint that way myself. Recently I attended some classes in modern art technique. I learned a lot and loved it" (Hennessey & Knutson, 1999, p. 188).

Could this painting serve as a metaphor for contrasting educational philosophies? Note the parallels that exist between art and philosophy. Ask yourself what lessons can be learned from these parallels and how you might apply them in a classroom.

Questions for Discussion and Debate

1. List the two philosophies of education mentioned in the introduction to the painting and define each one. Then, next to each definition, sketch or describe the aspect of the painting that illustrates each of the philosophies.

2. Some called Pollock's work "art" and others called it "junk." Different critics applied similar labels to Rockwell's work. Whose style do you prefer, and why? Similarly, why might contrasting philosophies such as postmodernism and realism be praised or refuted?

3. Whether or not a philosophy or painting asks more questions than it answers, the beholder must still bring to each one his or her own experiences and questions. Share any personal experiences or questions you may have in relation to this Rockwell painting and the canvas he painted within it.

4. Are we all connoisseurs? Or must a person have extensive knowledge of art before his or her opinion of a painting is taken seriously? Similarly, must one have extensive knowledge of philosophy to evaluate particular philosophies? Debate these questions and provide reasons for your position.

Activities and Projects

1. Carry out research on postmodernism and realism *and* on abstract expressionism and representational art. Discover the views of their proponents *and* critics. Then share your findings with the class. Lead a discussion related to your research.

2. Ironically, the postmodernism currently in vogue in the *art* world has led critics to a whole new way of looking at Rockwell's work. Postmodernists believe in challenging the status quo. The status quo among art critics with regard to Rockwell's work held that Rockwell was old-fashioned, not a real artist, merely an illustrator, albeit technically skilled. But with the postmodernist trend in the art world, these same critics are now applauding his talents and embracing Rockwell's art as a venerable cultural institution and Rockwell as a great American artist. Do research on what factors changed the minds of the art critics about Rockwell's place in the art world.

3. Find copies of paintings that reflect the two educational philosophies discussed in the introduction to this selection and present them to the class for analysis.

4. Form research teams to explore the political, economic, and social conditions in the country during the last quarter of the 20th century that might account for the eclecticism that developed within the art *and* education worlds. Find out if similar developments occurred in other fields.

3.2   *Dewey on Education: Selections* (1959)

John Dewey

John Dewey's (1859–1952) philosophical works have challenged many a reader, but the wisdom contained in such volumes as *Experience and Education* (1939), *Reconstruction in Philosophy* (1920), and *Democracy and Education* (1916) are worth the struggle. The following excerpts from "My Pedagogic Creed" (in Dworkin, 1959) are examples of Dewey's clearer, more succinct statements that can perhaps pave the way to his more difficult works.

His "Creed" is among hundreds of his published works. Prolific describes Dewey's output of writing on religion, democracy, and education, much of which he completed during his tenures in the philosophy departments of the University of Michigan (1884–1894), the University of Chicago (1894–1904), and, finally, Columbia University (1904–1939).

Dewey wrote with the conviction that the world could become a fairer and more democratic place for all peoples, and as a result, he became "the philosophical voice of the Progressive Era" (1890–1920) (Rockefeller, 1991, p. 3). With others, including Charles Sanders Pierce and William James, he led the revolutionary American philosophical movement known as pragmatism, which would be the vehicle for achieving that fairness. This philosophy, or theory, which had it roots in the European thought of John Locke, Rousseau, and others, is grounded in the belief that the scientific method can serve humanity and education by transforming the interactions of human beings with their world (p. 225).

When he applied pragmatism to education, Dewey concluded that children learn best by actively engaging in experiences. **Pragmatism** comes from the Greek word *work* and, thus, stands for the belief that the best methods in education are those that appear to work most effectively after being tested in the teaching and learning process. Because he believed that intelligence must become the *instrument* for guiding these experiments, Dewey's philosophy has also been referred to as instrumentalism. And because he so effectively challenged traditional approaches that conceived of the child as a spectator and listener, not a doer, he has been called the "father of progressive education." However, Dewey believed that this label should have been applied not to him but rather to Francis Wayland Parker. An American educator, Parker adopted Pestalozzi's modern methods, which were based on child psychology, an awareness of child development, and respect and love for children. Toward the end of his life, Parker worked with Dewey at the University of Chicago School of Education, and as a result of this affiliation, Dewey called Parker the "father of progressive education." He had admired Parker's work as superintendent of schools in Quincy, Massachusetts, where he implemented what is known as the Quincy System of education, which involved learning by doing, learning with meaning, and a curriculum that encouraged the unique talents and interests of each teacher.

Reprinted by permission of the publisher from Dworkin, M. D. (Ed.), DEWEY ON EDUCATION: SELECTIONS (New York: Teachers College Press, © 1959 by Teachers College, Columbia University. All rights reserved.), pp. 22–31.

With an international following, Dewey shared these and his own ideas in lectures in Japan, Mexico, Russia, South Africa, and Turkey, as well as in China, where he lived for 2 years (Rockefeller, 1991, p. 3).

"My Pedagogic Creed" contains five articles, and the following excerpts are from Articles II–V, which define Dewey's beliefs about "What the School Is," "The Subject-Matter of Education," "The Nature of Method," and "The School and Social Progress," respectively.

Above all, Dewey cared about making education meaningful to the learner. Contemporary theorists, among them Harvard's Howard Gardner, are keeping that part of Dewey's credo alive. As you read "My Pedagogic Creed," or Dewey's beliefs about teaching, think about which of his beliefs you would want to include in *your* pedagogic creed.

ARTICLE II—WHAT THE SCHOOL IS

I believe that the school is primarily a social institution. Education being a social process, the school is simply that form of community life in which all those agencies are concentrated that will be most effective in bringing the child to share in the inherited resources of the race, and to use his own powers for social ends.

I believe that education, therefore, is a process of living and not a preparation for future living.

I believe that the school must represent present life—life as real and vital to the child as that which he carries on in the home, in the neighborhood, or on the playground.

I believe that education which does not occur through forms of life, or that are worth living for their own sake, is always a poor substitute for the genuine reality and tends to cramp and to deaden.

I believe that the school, as an institution, should simplify existing social life; should reduce it, as it were, to an embryonic form. Existing life is so complex that the child cannot be brought into contact with it without either confusion or distraction; he is either overwhelmed by the multiplicity of activities which are going on, so that he loses his own power of

orderly reaction, or he is so stimulated by these various activities that his powers are prematurely called into play and he becomes either unduly specialized or else disintegrated. . . .

I believe that much of present education fails because it neglects this fundamental principle of the school as a form of community life. It conceives the school as a place where certain information is to be given, where certain lessons are to be learned, or where certain habits are to be formed. The value of these is conceived as lying largely in the remote future; the child must do these things for the sake of something else he is to do; they are mere preparation. As a result they do not become a part of the life experience of the child and so are not truly educative. . . .

I believe that under existing conditions far too much of the stimulus and control proceeds from the teacher, because of neglect of the idea of the school as a form of social life.

I believe that the teacher's place and work in the school is to be interpreted from this same basis. The teacher is not in the school to impose certain ideas or to form certain habits in the child, but is there as a member of the community to select the influences which shall affect the child and to assist him in properly responding to these influences.

I believe that the discipline of the school should proceed from the life of the school as a whole and not directly from the teacher.

I believe that the teacher's business is simply to determine on the basis of larger experience and riper wisdom, how the discipline of life shall come to the child.

I believe that all questions of the grading of the child and his promotion should be determined by reference to the same standard. Examinations are of use only so far as they test the child's fitness for social life and reveal the place in which he can be of the most service and where he can receive the most help.

ARTICLE III—THE SUBJECT-MATTER OF EDUCATION

I believe that the social life of the child is the basis of concentration, or correlation, in all his training or growth. The social life gives the unconscious unity and the background of all his efforts and of all his attainments. . . .

I believe that we violate the child's nature and render difficult the best ethical results, by introducing the child too abruptly to a number of special studies, of reading, writing, geography, etc., out of relation to this social life.

I believe, therefore, that the true center of correlation on the school subjects is not science, nor literature, nor history, nor geography, but the child's own social activities.

I believe that education cannot be unified in the study of science, or so called nature study, because apart from human activity, nature itself is not a unity; nature in itself is a number of diverse objects in space and time, and to attempt to make it the center of work by itself, is to introduce a principle of radiation rather than one of concentration.

I believe that literature is the reflex expression and interpretation of social experience; that hence it must follow upon and not precede such experience. It, therefore, cannot be made the basis, although it may be made the summary of unification.

I believe once more that history is of educative value in so far as it presents phases of social life and growth. It must be controlled by reference to social life. When taken simply as history it is thrown into the distant past and becomes dead and inert. Taken as the record of man's social life and progress it becomes full of meaning. I believe, however, that it cannot be so taken excepting as the child is also introduced directly into social life.

I believe accordingly that the primary basis of education is in the child's powers at work along the same general constructive lines as those which have brought civilization into being.

I believe that the only way to make the child conscious of his social heritage is to enable him to perform those fundamental types of activity which make civilization what it is.

I believe, therefore, in the so-called expressive or constructive activities as the center of correlation . . . and that it is possible and desirable that the child's introduction into the more formal subjects of the curriculum be through the medium of these activities. . . .

I believe finally, that education must be conceived as a continuing reconstruction of experience; that the process and the goal of education are one and the same thing.

I believe that to set up any end outside of education, as furnishing its goal and standard, is to deprive the educational process of much of its meaning and tends to make us rely upon false and external stimuli in dealing with the child.

ARTICLE IV—THE NATURE OF METHOD

I believe that the question of method is ultimately reducible to the question of the order of development of the child's powers and interests.

The law for presenting and treating material is the law implicit within the child's own nature. Because this is so I believe the following statements are of supreme importance as determining the spirit in which education is carried on:

1. I believe that the active side precedes the passive in the development of the child nature; that expression comes before conscious impression; that the muscular development precedes the sensory; that movements come before conscious sensations; I believe that consciousness is essentially motor or impulsive; that conscious states tend to project themselves in action.

    I believe that the neglect of this principle is the cause of a large part of the waste of time and strength in school work. The child is thrown into a passive, receptive, or absorbing attitude. The conditions are such that he is not permitted to follow the law of his nature; the result is friction and waste.

    I believe that ideas (intellectual and rational processes) also result from action and devolve for the sake of the better control of action. What we term reason is primarily the law of orderly or effective action. To attempt to develop the reasoning powers, the powers of judgment, without reference to the selection and arrangement of means in action, is the fundamental fallacy in our present methods of dealing with this matter. As a result we present the child with arbitrary symbols. Symbols are a necessity in mental development, but they have their place as tools for economizing effort; presented by themselves they are a mass of meaningless and arbitrary ideas imposed from without.

2. I believe that the image is the great instrument of instruction. What a child gets out of any subject presented to him is simply the images which he himself forms with regard to it.

    I believe that if nine tenths of the energy at present directed towards making the child learn certain things, were spent in seeing to it that the child was forming proper images, the work of instruction would be indefinitely facilitated. . . .

3. I believe that interests are the signs and symptoms of growing power. I believe that they represent dawning capacities. Accordingly the constant and careful observation of interests is of the utmost importance for the educator.

    I believe that these interests are to be observed as showing the state of development which the child has reached.

    I believe that they prophesy the stage upon which he is about to enter.

    I believe that only through the continual and sympathetic observation of childhood's interests can the adult enter into the child's life and see what it is ready for, and upon what material it could work most readily and fruitfully. . . .

4. I believe that the emotions are the reflex of actions.

    I believe that to endeavor to stimulate or arouse the emotions apart from their corresponding activities, is to introduce an unhealthy and morbid state of mind.

    I believe that if we can only secure right habits of action and thought, with reference to the good, the true, and the beautiful, the emotions will for the most part take care of themselves.

    I believe that next to deadness and dullness, formalism and routine, our education is threatened with no greater evil than sentimentalism.

I believe that this sentimentalism is the necessary result of the attempt to divorce feeling from action.

ARTICLE V—THE SCHOOL AND SOCIAL PROGRESS

I believe that education is the fundamental method of social progress and reform.

I believe that all reforms which rest simply upon the enactment of law, or the threatening of certain penalties, or upon changes in mechanical or outward arrangements, are transitory and futile.

I believe that education is a regulation of the process of coming to share in the social consciousness; and that the adjustment of individual activity on the basis of this social consciousness is the only sure method of social reconstruction.

I believe that this conception has due regard for both the individualistic and socialistic ideals. . . .

I believe that in the ideal school we have the reconciliation of the individualistic and the institutional ideals.

I believe that the community's duty to education is, therefore, its paramount moral duty.

By law and punishment, by social agitation and discussion, society can regulate and form itself in a more or less haphazard and chance way. But through education society can formulate its own purposes, can organize its own means and resources, and thus shape itself with definiteness and economy in the direction in which it wishes to move.

I believe that when society once recognizes the possibilities in this direction, and the obligations which these possibilities impose, it is impossible to conceive of the resources of time, attention, and money which will be put at the disposal of the educator.

I believe that it is the business of every one interested in education to insist upon the school as the primary and most effective interest of social progress and reform in order that society may be awakened to realize what the school stands for, and aroused to the necessity of endowing the educator with sufficient equipment properly to perform his task.

I believe that education thus conceived marks the most perfect and intimate union of science and art conceivable in human experience.

Questions for Discussion and Debate

1. List three beliefs in Dewey's creed that you most strongly favor. Discuss your choices with your peers and provide reasons for your choices. Were there any beliefs that you opposed?

2. Identify something Dewey said that you don't fully comprehend. Bring those questions to the group for discussion.

3. Dewey believed that psychology and philosophy are closely linked since both are concerned with human behavior and phenomena based on direct experience. Locate phrases in the creed that reflect the psychological basis of his philosophy.

4. As a student in several classrooms, you have experienced a number of philosophies via the content and methods of your teachers. Do you recall one whose teaching reflected the progressive or Deweyan credo? If so, discuss your memories of that teacher.

Activities and Projects

1. Dewey believed the scientific method to be the most potent force in the modern world. The scientific method, when simplistically stated, is all about learning what is "good" or "bad," "true" or "untrue," through trial and error, testing hypotheses and observing the results. As you read the steps listed here, try to think of a situation or question that you confronted by following similar steps.

   Then become a STAR! (Student Teacher as Researcher) and try to solve a problem you are having in your teaching *now* by implementing the scientific method. Carefully document all the steps. Then share your experiment and its outcome with your peers.

   The steps of the scientific method are as follows.

   a. Pose a question.

   b. Research the question briefly through either reading or activity.

   c. Construct a tentative answer to your question. (Form a hypothesis.)

   d. Test the hypothesis (through more research and/or experimentation).

   e. Observe the results or data and then weigh the quality of the results (i.e., ask additional questions, reassess the sources of information, look at all variables that could have influenced the results).

   f. If the hypothesis is proven to be true, form a conclusion; if not, create a new hypothesis and repeat the same steps.

2. Observe a teacher for at least 1 hour. Watch for that teacher's informal use of the scientific method and describe the situation in which he or she used it. (Teachers experiment on a daily basis every time they make a decision on content, method, and management.)

3. Dewey's philosophy, of course, integrated many of the modern educational ideas of European educators such as Friedrich Froebel, Johann Heinrich Pestalozzi, and Jean Jacques Rousseau. Pestalozzi's (1746–1827) books, including *How Gertrude Teaches Her Children* (1801) (see Selection 2.12), influenced Dewey's beliefs. Pestalozzi emphasized the equal relevance of three elements to the learning process; the head, the heart, and the hand. The head refers to intelligence or cognitive development, the hand indicates learning by doing through experience and physical development, and the heart or spirit plays a role in developing positive attitudes and values. Do additional research on the roots of Dewey's philosophy. Prepare a chart in which you indicate those individuals in educational history who most affected Dewey's perspectives. Briefly explain where in his ideas the different roots can be identified.

4. While it may be easier to study educational philosophies according to their *differences* and identify yourself as being allied with one in particular, there are aspects of each philosophy that you may find useful and meaningful in that multifaceted position, teacher. The likelihood is that you will be choosing great ideas from philosophies that are, indeed, on opposite ends of the spectrum. While Dewey is identified as a progressive, he admired the work of the perennialists whom he came to know at the University of Chicago, whose president, Robert Maynard Hutchins (1899–1977), was a leader among them. Hutchins believed that knowledge consists of universal and unchanging truths. He, along with Mortimer Adler, created the Great Books Program, which involved teaching from a set of books that they professed were

able to convey timeless and universal truths and reveal the nature of human nature. Find out what books are on the Great Books list. Bring the list to class. Together discuss classics that appear on the lists for both elementary and high-school students.

a. What books on the list have you read, and what do they have in common?

b. Should new books be added to the list, and if so, what criteria should be used to

determine that decision? (You might try to locate the list of the 100 most important books of the 20th century issued by the New York Public Library in 1998 to see if there are any candidates there for the Great Books list.)

c. How long must a book be around before it can prove itself to be a classic?

d. Is the Great Books Program a good way to teach? Why, or why not?

3.3 | *Saber-Tooth Curriculum* (1939)

J. Abner Peddiwell

The authors of *Saber-Tooth Curriculum . . . Including Other Lectures in the History of Paleolithic Education. . . .* (Yup, paleolithic!) are J. Abner Peddiwell, Ph.D., and several Tequila Daisies as told to Raymond Wayne. So together, the title of this work *and* the author's name prepare you for this satirical and allegorical look at the caveman's development of a "curriculum." Clearly the author—whoever he or she may be—is bothered by the nature of curriculum development in more modern times, and this satire serves as a humorous critique of several academic and philosophical practices.

In addition, this story indirectly and sarcastically lambasts certain philosophies of education listed in the Brief Background to this chapter. As you read the excerpt, see if you can identify the philosophies with which Peddiwell is unhappy. Also, decide which group in this excerpt represents your point of view. Do you agree with the "radicals" or the "wise old men?"

The first great educational theorist and practitioner of whom my imagination has any record (began Dr. Peddiwell in his best professorial tone) was a man of Chellean times whose full name was *New-Fist-Hammer-Maker* but whom, for convenience, I shall hereafter call *New-Fist*.

New-Fist was a doer, in spite of the fact that there was little in his environment with which to do anything very complex. You have undoubtedly heard of the pear-shaped, chipped-stone tool which archeologists call the *coup-de-poing* or fist hammer. New-Fist gained his name and a considerable local prestige by producing one of these artifacts in a less rough and more useful form than any previously known to his tribe. His hunting clubs were generally superior weapons, moreover, and his fire-using techniques were patterns of simplicity and precision. He knew how to do things his community needed to have done, and he had the energy and will to go ahead and do them. By virtue of these characteristics he was an educated man.

New-Fist was also a thinker. Then, as now, there were few lengths to which men would not go to avoid the labor and pain of thought. More readily than his fellows, New-Fist pushed himself beyond those lengths to the point where cerebration was inevitable. The same quality of intelligence which led him into the socially approved activity of producing a superior artifact also led him to engage in the socially disapproved practice of thinking. When other men gorged themselves on the proceeds of a successful hunt and vegetated in dull stupor for many hours thereafter, New-Fist ate a little less heartily, slept a little less stupidly, and arose a little earlier than his comrades to sit by the fire and think. He would stare moodily at the flickering flames and wonder about various parts of his environment until he finally got to the point where he became strongly dissatisfied with the accustomed ways of his tribe. He began to catch glimpses of ways in which life might be made better for himself, his family, and his group. By virtue of this development, he became a dangerous man.

This was the background that made this doer and thinker hit upon the concept of a conscious, systematic education. The immediate stimulus which put him directly into the practice of education came from watching his children at play. He saw these children at the cave entrance before the fire engaged in activity with bones and sticks and brightly colored pebbles. He noted that they seemed to have no purpose in their play beyond immediate pleasure in the activity itself. He compared their activity with that of the grown-up members of the tribe. The children played for fun; the adults worked for security and enrichment of their lives. The children dealt with bones, sticks, and pebbles; the adults dealt with food, shelter, and clothing. The children protected themselves from boredom; the adults protected themselves from danger.

"If I could only get these children to do the things that will give more and better food, shelter, clothing, and security," thought New-Fist, "I would be helping this tribe to have a better life. When the children became grown, they would have more meat to eat, more skins to keep them warm, better caves in which to sleep, and less danger from the striped death with the curving teeth that walks these trails by night."

Having set up an educational goal, New-Fist proceeded to construct a curriculum for reaching that goal. "What things must we tribesmen know how to do in order to live with full bellies, warm backs, and minds free from fear?" he asked himself.

To answer this question, he ran various activities over in his mind. "We have to catch fish with our bare hands in the pool far up the creek beyond that big bend," he said to himself. "We have to catch fish with our bare hands in the pool right at the bend. We have to catch them in the same way in the pool just this side of the bend. And so we catch them in the next pool and the next and the next. Always we catch them with our bare hands."

Thus New-Fist discovered the first subject of the first curriculum—fish-grabbing-with-the-bare-hands.

"Also we club the little woolly horses," he continued with his analysis. "We club them along the bank of the creek where they come down to drink. We club them in the thickets where they lie down to sleep. We club them in the upland meadow where they graze. Wherever we find them we club them."

So woolly-horse-clubbing was seen to be the second main subject in the curriculum.

"And finally, we drive away the saber-tooth tigers with fire," New-Fist went on in his thinking. "We drive them from the mouth of our caves with fire. We drive them from our trail with burning branches. We wave firebrands to drive them from our drinking hole. Always we have to drive them away, and always we drive them with fire."

Thus was discovered the third subject—saber-tooth-tiger-scaring-with-fire. . . .

For a long time, however, there were certain more conservative members of the tribe who resisted the new, formal educational system on religious grounds. "The Great Mystery who speaks in thunder and moves in lightning," they announced impressively, "the Great Mystery who gives men life and takes it from them as he wills—if that Great Mystery had wanted children to practice fish-grabbing, horse-clubbing, and tiger-scaring before they were grown up, he would have taught them these activities himself by implanting in their natures instincts for fish-grabbing, horse-clubbing, and tiger-scaring. New-Fist is not only impious to attempt something the Great Mystery never intended to have done; he is also a damned fool for trying to change human nature."

Whereupon approximately half of these critics took up the solemn chant, "If you oppose the will of the Great Mystery, you must die," and the remainder sang derisively in unison, "You can't change human nature."

Being an educational statesman as well as an educational administrator and theorist, New-Fist replied politely to both arguments. To the more theologically minded, he said that, as a matter of fact, the Great Mystery had ordered this new work done, that he even did the work himself by causing children to want to learn, that children could not learn by themselves without divine aid, that they could not learn at all except through the power of the Great Mystery, and that nobody could really understand the will of the Great Mystery concerning fish, horses, and saber-tooth tigers unless he had been well grounded in the three fundamental subjects of the New-Fist school. To the human-nature-cannot-be-changed shouters, New-Fist pointed out the fact that paleolithic culture had attained its high level by changes in human nature and that it seemed almost unpatriotic to deny the very process which had made the community great. . . .

It is to be supposed that all would have gone well forever with this good educational system if conditions of life in that community had remained forever the same. But conditions changed, and life which had once been so safe and happy in the cave-realm valley became insecure and disturbing.

A new ice age was approaching in that part of the world. A great glacier came down from the neighboring mountain range to the north. Year after year it crept closer and closer to the headwaters of the creek which ran through the tribe's valley, until at length it reached the stream and began to melt into the water. Dirt and gravel which the glacier had collected on its long journey were dropped into the creek. The water grew muddy. What had once been a crystal-clear stream in which one could see easily to the bottom was now a milky stream into which one could not see at all.

At once the life of the community was changed in one very important respect. It was no longer possible to catch fish with the bare hands. The fish could not be seen in the muddy water. For some years, moreover, the fish in this creek had been getting more timid, agile, and intelligent. The stupid, clumsy, brave fish, of which originally there had been a great many, had been caught with the bare hands for fish generation after fish generation, until only fish of superior intelligence and agility were left. These smart fish, hiding in the muddy water under the newly deposited glacial boulders, eluded the hands of the most expertly trained fish-grabbers. Those tribesmen who had studied advanced fish-grabbing in the secondary school could do no better than their less well-educated fellows who had taken only an elementary course in the subject, and even the university graduates with majors in ichthyology were baffled by the problem. No matter how good a man's fish-grabbing education had been, he could not grab fish when he could not find fish to grab. . . .

The community was now in a very difficult situation. There was no fish or meat for food, no hides for clothing, and no security from the hairy death that walked the trails day and night. Adjustment to this difficulty had to be made at once if the tribe was not to become extinct.

Fortunately for the tribe, however, there were men in it of the old New-Fist breed, men who had the ability to do and the daring to think. One of them stood by the muddy stream, his stomach contracting with hunger pains, longing for some way to get a fish to eat. Again and again he had tried the old fish-grabbing technique that day, hoping desperately that at last it might work, but now in black despair he finally rejected all that he had learned in the schools and looked about him for some new way to get fish from that stream. There were stout but slender vines hanging from trees along the bank. He pulled them down and began to fasten them together more or less aimlessly. As he worked, the vision of what he might do to satisfy his hunger and that of his crying children back in the cave grew clearer. His black despair lightened a little. He worked more rapidly and intelligently. At last he had it—a net, a crude

seine. He called a companion and explained the device. The two men took the net into the water, into pool after pool, and in one hour they caught more fish—intelligent fish in muddy water—than the whole tribe could have caught in a day under the best fish-grabbing conditions.

Another intelligent member of the tribe wandered hungrily through the woods where once the stupid little horses had abounded but where now only the elusive antelope could be seen. He had tried the horse-clubbing technique on the antelope until he was fully convinced of its futility. He knew that one would starve who relied on school learning to get him meat in those woods. Thus it was that he too, like the fish-net inventor, was finally impelled by hunger to new ways. He bent a strong, springy young tree over an antelope trail, hung a noosed vine therefrom, and fastened the whole device in so ingenious a fashion that the passing animal would release a trigger and be snared neatly when the tree jerked upright. By setting a line of these snares, he was able in one night to secure more meat and skins than a dozen horse-clubbers in the old days had secured in a week. . . .

As the knowledge of these new inventions spread, all the members of the tribe were engaged in familiarizing themselves with the new ways of living. Men worked hard at making fish nets, setting antelope snares, and digging bear pits. The tribe was busy and prosperous.

There were a few thoughtful men who asked questions as they worked. Some of them even criticized the schools.

"These new activities of net-making and operating, snare-setting, and pit-digging are indispensable to modern existence," they said. "Why can't they be taught in school?"

The safe and sober majority had a quick reply to this naïve question. "School!" they snorted derisively. "You aren't in school now. You are out here in the dirt working to preserve the life and happiness of the tribe. What have these practical activities got to do with schools? You're not saying lessons now. You'd better forget your lessons and your academic ideals of fish-grabbing, horse-clubbing, and tiger-scaring if you want to eat, keep warm, and have some measure of security from sudden death."

The radicals persisted a little in their questioning. "Fishnet-making and using, antelope-snare construction and operation, and bear-catching and killing," they pointed out, "require intelligence and skills—things we claim to develop in schools. They are also activities we need to know. Why can't the schools teach them?"

But most of the tribe, and particularly the wise old men who controlled the school, smiled indulgently at this suggestion. "That wouldn't be *education*," they said gently.

"But why wouldn't it be?" asked the radicals.

"Because it would be mere training," explained the old men patiently. "With all the intricate details of fish-grabbing, horse-clubbing, and tiger-scaring—the standard cultural subjects—the school curriculum is too crowded now. We can't add these fads and frills of net-making, antelope-snaring, and—of all things—bear-killing. Why, at the very thought, the body of the great New-Fist, founder of our pale-olithic educational system, would turn over in its burial cairn. What we need to do is to give our young people a more thorough grounding in the fundamentals. Even the graduates of the secondary schools don't know the art of fish-grabbing in any complete sense nowadays, they swing their horse clubs awkwardly too, and as for the old science of tiger-scaring—well, even the teachers seem to lack the real flair for the subject which we oldsters got in our teens and never forgot."

"But, damn it," exploded one of the radicals, "how can any person with good sense be interested in such useless activities? What is the point of trying to catch fish with the bare hands when it just can't be done any more. How can a boy learn to club horses when there are no horses left to club? And why in hell should children try to scare tigers with fire when the tigers are dead and gone?"

"Don't be foolish," said the wise old men, smiling most kindly smiles. "We don't teach fish-grabbing to grab fish; we teach it to develop a generalized agility which can never be developed by mere training. We don't teach horse-clubbing to club horses; we teach it to develop a generalized strength in the learner which he can never get from so prosaic and specialized a thing as antelope-snare-setting. We don't teach tiger-scaring to scare tigers; we teach it for the purpose of giving that noble courage which carries over into all the affairs of life and which can never come from so base an activity as bear-killing."

All the radicals were silenced by this statement, all except the one who was most radical of all. He felt abashed, it is true, but he was so radical that he made one last protest.

"But—but anyway," he suggested, "you will have to admit that times have changed. Couldn't you please *try* these other more up-to-date activities? Maybe they have *some* educational value after all?"

Even the man's fellow radicals felt that this was going a little too far.

The wise old men were indignant. Their kindly smiles faded. "If you had any education yourself," they said severely, "you would know that the essence of true education is timelessness. It is something that endures through changing conditions like a solid rock standing squarely and firmly in the middle of a raging torrent. You must know that there are some eternal verities, and the saber-tooth curriculum is one of them!"

Questions for Discussion and Debate

1. What are the basic beliefs about curriculum of
   a. New-Fist
   b. The radicals
   c. The wise old men
      - With which of the philosophies or theories listed in the Brief Background to this chapter can you match the radicals? The wise old men?
      - With whom do you agree, and why?
      - Debate the pros and cons of the two major positions, perhaps one group in class taking the position of the radicals and another that of the wise old men.

2. Review again the ideas in the previous excerpt, from John Dewey's "My Pedagogic Creed" (Selection 3.2). Would the author of *Saber-Tooth Curriculum* agree with Dewey? Defend your conclusion by referring to specific sections of both works.

3. With your peers, cite the author's use of sarcasm. Is this device effective as a tool for critiquing education? Why, or why not?

Activities and Projects

1. Identify an aspect of educational practice that you think is either absurd, irrational, or in need of some rethinking, perhaps something you personally suffered with as a student. Then create a simple story in which you use as your vehicle for critique either sarcasm or a satirical allegory similar to *Saber-Tooth Curriculum* or another medium that grabs the reader's attention, possibly an editorial cartoon. Share your critique with your peers and possibly with others who may benefit from your perspective.

2. Read the comics section of the newspaper every day for at least a week. Likely you will find comic strips in which the cartoonist has satirized some aspect of education. Share your findings and interpret and discuss them with your peers. Why do you think the cartoonists chose to raise certain issues?

3. With such different perspectives on curriculum as portrayed by the radicals and the wise old men, how is it possible that teachers ever reach an agreement on what and how to teach? Interview teachers at your school or a school in the area about how they reach decisions on curriculum.

3.4 ▦ # "A Break of Consciousness" (1997)

José Calderon

The Internet has revolutionized communication and provided instant access to resources one might never encounter otherwise. Such is the case with this poem by José Calderon. As a participant in the Diversity Web Information Providers, sponsored by the American Association of Colleges and Universities (AAC&U), this editor visited the Diversity Web site (http://www.inform.umd.edu/diversityweb) and discovered some original and useful information including this poem, available in the Diversity Works Leader's Guide. The poem clearly conveys José Calderon's philosophy of education, one that bears some resemblance to some of the philosophies listed in this chapter's Brief Background. Calderon is Associate Professor of Sociology and Chicano Studies at Pitzer College in California and is on the board of the AAC&U.

Read the poem silently, then out loud. What do you see and what do you learn from this poem and its imagery? What does it mean to you? Are there other poems you know of that convey a perspective on what is worth learning and on how learning can be achieved?

There comes a moment
When there is the connection
Between what is academic
And what is exhilarating experience

The moment of light
Between the silence of expression
And the bursting of critical consciousness

A glimpse of institutionalization
Without the loss of values
A foundation of a movement
Still fighting Goliath

The rain pattering on foreheads
Turning into a raging river
Taking everything in its way

The sounds of shovels on concrete
Of saws on fallen trees
And branches

Reaching everywhere

Reprinted with permission of José Calderon.

From the grave site
Of Cesar Chavez
To the streets of Delano
To the air waves

To Claremont
And Connection
Alongside the tired hands
But living spirit of Abayani
With Brother Pete
And rose cuttings
Planted like ideas
To grow, To grow

Alongside Magdaleno, Maria Elena,
Arturo, Paul, Abe, Rebecca, Socorro,
Helen, and so many others
Whose lives
Became a living piece
Of what was read
As history, as legend,
As a moment in time

Delano-La Paz

Clouds on hilltops
Blanketed by green
With blue sky
Breaking through

An idea of De Colores
Made a reality
With circles of song
And chains of hands,
Hearts, Minds

Never to be broken

The wisdom of leaders
Men and Women
Of Generations
From the fields
Shared with young
Open minds
Absorbing like the ground
To raindrops

Little streams
Can make a sea
To the streets of Delano
A train passing by
Making the ground shake
Giving warning
To those up ahead

The sun hides behind the clouds
But reappears—

It is always there
If one seeks to find it

The moment, I mean—
The connection, I mean—
When what is academic
Becomes the lived experience
Outside the shadows of the classroom
To that moment of light
Between the silence of expression
And the bursting of critical consciousness.

Questions for Discussion and Debate

1. In your own words, what do you think Calderon is saying? What does he believe?
2. Find the lines that are repeated. Interpret them with your peers, then discuss which philosophy or theory of education is reflected in those lines.
3. One of Calderon's implied beliefs about curriculum is that it must in some way reveal to the student aspects of his or her heritage. Find the lines in which he establishes that position. Why do you think he believes it is important for curriculum to provide a connection between students and their cultural heritage?

Activities and Projects

1. José Calderon makes references to real people and places, for example, Cesar Chavez and the streets of Delano. Who is Chavez? Where is Delano? Try to find out through discussion or research. Then discuss why Calderon refers to them in the context of his poem.

2. Try by yourself or with a partner to add another stanza to this poem that is in keeping with Calderon's references and philosophy.

3. As noted in question 3 above, Calderon implies that he believes that a curriculum

should provide a connection between students and their cultural heritage. A noted educator, Eliot Wigginton (1985), created Foxfire, a curriculum constructed with precisely that belief in mind. This interdisciplinary curriculum became very famous as a result of the *Foxfire* magazine, which his students researched, wrote, edited, laid out, and published. At this point there are more than 10 hardbound compilations of these magazines, which are based on interviews and field research done by Wigginton's English students at Rabun Gap (Georgia) High School in their own community and related to their local culture. Though Wigginton, a recipient of the McArthur Foundation Award (The Genius Award), was, after many years, found to have sexually abused several of his students, a crime for which he served time in prison, his legacy remains intact. He inspired hundreds of teachers in many disadvantaged areas of America and abroad to create similar curricula related to their students' heritage and geographical location. Do research on the Foxfire approach to curriculum and then, with others, design a curriculum related to the area in which *you* are now teaching or student teaching.

3.5 | *Rudolf Steiner in the Waldorf School* (1996)

Rudolf Steiner

Rudolf Steiner (1861–1928) was an Austrian philosopher and spiritual scientist whose influence on education spread during the 1980s and 1990s both in America and internationally. There are more than 120 private Waldorf schools in the United States, and a public Waldorf-inspired magnet school opened recently in the Sacramento (California) Unified School District, financed by a federal grant. Nevertheless, many Americans have never heard of Steiner.

"The Pedagogical Basis of the Waldorf School" can serve as a brief introduction to Steiner education. The essay is part of a collection of lectures and addresses that Steiner gave between 1919 and 1924 at the first Waldorf School, in Stuttgart, Germany. The name, Waldorf School, came about because it was at the Waldorf-Astoria cigarette factory that owner Emil Molt (1876–1936) founded the school that he created initially "for the children of the blue- and white-collar workers of his factory. He asked Rudolf Steiner to take on the organization and leadership of the school" (Steiner, 1996, p. 1).

While there is some value placed on religion and on Christ as the archetype of humanity, the real value of *anthroposophy* (the name of Steiner's philosophy) as applied to pedagogy is in its support for a holistic approach, whereby the curriculum is

From Rudolf Steiner in the Waldorf School: Lectures and Addresses to Children, Parents, and Teachers, 1919–1924. Translated by Catherine E. Creeger. Hudson, NY: Anthroposophic Press, 1996. Copyright © 1996, Anthroposophic Press. Reprinted by permission of the publisher.

intended to nurture the body, mind, *and* spirit of the student. In practice, Steiner curriculum is interdisciplinary. Traditional subject matter, including heavy doses of art, music, and literature, is constructed around a theme, such as Hero and Heroine, thus placing the content within a recognizable context. In this way, Steiner shared Dewey's concerns for making education meaningful. The two men also shared a belief in experiential learning, a concern for rebuilding and reforming society and taking note of both the psychological and the physical development of the child when molding the curriculum.

In particular, Steiner philosophy takes heed of what scientists have always known to some extent: the interconnectedness of things. Poet Francis Thompson (1859–1907) captured that Newtonian conception in his poem, "The Mistress of Vision," when he wrote,

All things by immortal power
　Near or far
　Hiddenly
To each other linked are,
That thou canst not stir a flower
Without troubling of a star.
　　　(in Hardin, 1977, p. 43)

As you read this excerpt from Steiner's 1919 essay, see if you can find examples of this interconnectedness in his concept of the curriculum, the child, and society.

. . . This school is associated with an industrial enterprise, and the way in which modern industry has taken its place in the evolution of human life and society has left its stamp on the practices of the contemporary social movement. The parents entrusting their children to this school can only hope and expect that these children will be educated to become competent in life in a sense that takes this social movement fully into account. This makes it necessary for us in founding this school to take our start from pedagogical principles that are rooted in what life in the present demands of us. Our children are to be educated to become people who are prepared for a life that corresponds to these demands, which are ones that anyone can support, regardless of what social class he or she comes from. What real present-day life demands of people must be reflected in the organization of this school. The spirit that is to govern this life must

be stimulated in the children through how they are taught.

It would be disastrous if a spirit foreign to life were to prevail in the basic pedagogical views on which the Waldorf School is to be founded. Such a spirit appears all too easily nowadays wherever we develop a feeling for the part that our immersion in a materialistic attitude and way of life in recent decades has played in the breakdown of our civilization. This feeling leads to the desire to introduce an idealistic attitude into our administration of public affairs, and anyone who has been paying attention to the development of our educational system will want to see this attitude realized there more than anywhere else. Naturally, we must acknowledge the great deal of good will that is expressed in this way of looking at things. If it becomes active in the right way, it will be of great service in rallying human forces for a social undertaking for which new prerequisites must be created. And yet, in just such a case it is necessary to point out that even the best will must fail if it sets out to turn intentions into realities without fully taking into account the prerequisites that are based on insight into the matter.

This characterizes one of the challenges that must be taken into consideration nowadays in founding institutions such as the Waldorf School is intended to be. Idealism must be at work within the spirit of its pedagogy and methods, but this must be an idealism that has the power to awaken in growing human beings those forces and abilities that they will need for the rest of their lives in order to work competently for their community of contemporaries and to have a livelihood that will sustain them.

Educational theory and methodology will be able to meet this challenge only if they possess a real understanding of the growing human being. Nowadays people of insight are demanding an education that aims not at one-sided knowledge, but at the ability to do things, not at merely cultivating intellectual gifts but at training the will. This idea is undoubtedly correct. However, it is not possible to educate the will and the healthy soul that underlies it unless we develop insights that awaken energetic impulses in the soul and will. A frequent mistake nowadays in this regard consists not in presenting the growing human being with an excess of insight, but in cultivating insights that lack impact as far as life is concerned. Anyone who believes that it is possible to educate the will without cultivating the insight that enlivens it is succumbing to illusion. Clear-sightedness on this point is a task for present-day pedagogy, but it can come only from a life-filled understanding of the whole human being.

As it is imagined for the time being, the Waldorf School will be a primary school that teaches its students through basing its educational goals and curriculum on insight into the nature of the total human being, an insight that must be alive in each teacher to the extent that this is already possible under current circumstances. Naturally, the children in each grade must be brought to the point where they can meet demands that are made in accordance with contemporary ways of looking at things. Within this framework, however, the shape that all instructional goals and curricula take must result from the above-characterized understanding of the human being and of life. . . .

When what we introduce into the children's world of ideas and feelings is in line with the direction of the developmental forces of a given stage of life, we strengthen the entire developing person in a way that remains a source of strength throughout that person's life. If we work counter to the direction of development at any given stage, however, we weaken the person.

The basis for developing an appropriate curriculum lies in recognizing the specific challenges of different stages of life. This also forms the basis for how subject matter is treated in successive stages. By the end of the children's ninth year, we will need to have brought them to a certain level in everything that has streamed into human life through the evolution of culture. Therefore, we are right in spending the first few school years in teaching writing and reading, but we must arrange this instruction in a way that does justice to the nature of child development in this stage of life. If our teaching one-sidedly takes advantage of the children's intellect and abstractly acquired abilities, their willing and feeling nature will be stunted. In contrast, if the children learn in a way that allows the whole human being to take part in the activity, they will develop in a well-rounded way. When children draw or do rudimentary painting, the whole human being develops an interest in what is being done. This is why we should allow writing to develop from drawing. We should derive the forms of the letters from shapes that allow the child's naive artistic sense to make itself felt. We should develop writing, which guides us toward the element of meaning and intellect, out of an activity that is artistic and attracts the interest of the whole human being. Reading, which draws our attention very strongly into the intellectual realm, should be allowed to develop only as a result of writing.

Once we realize how much can be gained intellectually from a naive artistic education, we will tend to grant art its fair place in early elementary education. We will incorporate the musical and graphic arts appropriately into the classroom and link physical education to the artistic element as well. We will turn gymnastics and movement games into expressions of emotions that are stimulated by music or recitation. Meaningful eurythmic movement will replace movement that depends only on anatomical and physiological aspects of the body. We will find that a very strong force shapes the will and the feelings when we compose our classroom instruction artistically. However, only teachers whose keen understanding of the human being permits them to see the connection between their methods and the developmental forces that reveal themselves at a specific stage of life will be able to teach really fruitfully in the way described here. The true teachers and educators are not those who have learned pedagogy as the science of dealing with children, but those in whom pedagogy has awakened through understanding the human being.

For the emotional development of children under the age of nine, it is important that they develop their relationship to the world as people tend to do when they conceive of it imaginatively. If teachers themselves are not idle dreamers, they will not turn the children into dreamers simply by allowing the world of plants, animals, air, and stars to live in the hearts and minds of the children in the form of a fairy-tale or fable.

Visual instruction is certainly justified within certain limits. However, if our materialistic viewpoint makes us want to extend it to virtually everything, we fail to take into account the fact that the human being must also develop forces that cannot be imparted solely through the ability to visualize. For example, learning certain things purely through memory is related to the developmental forces that are present between the sixth or seventh year and the fourteenth year of life. This quality of human nature is what mathematical instruction should be based on. It can even be used to cultivate the power of memory. If we do not take this into account, we may emphasize the visual over the memory-strengthening element in our math lessons in an unpedagogical way. . . .

If we pay attention in the way that has been described to the educational principles that result from the inner development of the human being, we need not fear that students will leave primary school with constitutions of body and soul that are foreign to outer life. Our life itself takes shape out of individuals' inner development, and the best possible way of entering it is for people to develop their potentials and link them to what their predecessors incorporated into civilization as it developed as a result of similar individual potentials. Of course, in order for the students' development and the outer development of civilization to coincide, we need a faculty whose interest is not limited to specialized educational practices. Rather, this faculty must be fully involved in the broader aspects of life. A faculty of this sort will find it possible to awaken in people who are growing up, not only a sense for life's spiritual and intellectual substance, but also an understanding of its practical organization. When taught in this way, fourteen or fifteen-year-olds will not lack understanding of the essential aspects of agriculture, industry and commerce that serve the overall life of humankind. The insights and capabilities that they have acquired will enable them to feel oriented in the life that embraces them.

If the Waldorf School is to achieve the goals that its founders have in mind, it will have to build upon the educational theory and methods that have been described here. They will enable it to provide an education that allows the bodies of the students to develop healthily and in accordance with their needs because the souls of which these bodies are expressions are unfolding in line with their developmental forces. . . .

Questions for Discussion and Debate

1. Locate examples of Steiner's idea of the interconnectedness that exists among the curriculum, the child, and the real world. Cite line and page and share your discoveries in a class discussion. What other examples of the connection among things does he identify or imply?

2. Offer a critique of this essay. What do you consider to be its strengths and weaknesses in terms of sound educational thinking? Support your views by referring to the essay and to your own experiences, observations, and/or research on curriculum, teaching, and child development.

3. What value, if any, does Steiner's philosophy have for public education? Debate this question: Can Steiner's philosophy have a positive influence on public education?

Activities and Projects

1. Find out if there is a Steiner school in your area. If so, visit classes and talk to the teachers. Compile data for a short presentation on Steiner's philosophy as interpreted by the educators you interviewed. Are there aspects of the curriculum about which you have further questions?

2. Do research on Steiner himself to discover what and who were the major influences on *his* life and thinking. Share your findings.

3. Steiner was a contemporary of John Dewey's (and also of the poet Francis Thompson, referred to in the introduction to this excerpt). See if you can locate in their respective biographies evidence of their knowing one another. If you are unable to find such evidence, then try to explain through historical research what may account for the similarities as well as the differences between Steiner and Dewey. Identify some of those similarities.

4. Russian author Leo Tolstoy's name is synonymous with his epic novels *War and Peace* and *Anna Karenina*. Few people, however, are aware of Tolstoy (1828–1910) the teacher and educational philosopher, who helped to found an experimental school for peasant children (1862) at Yásnaya Polyána, his family's estate near Tula in Russia. Do research on the school and on Tolstoy's theories of education, which he published in a journal with the same name as his school.

Compare his theories to those of Rudolf Steiner and determine the similarities between them.

5. The idea of the interconnectedness of all life manifested in Steiner's philosophy is found in many Eastern philosophies and religions within sects that can be described as mystical, or believing in a person's intuitive ability to discover truths *beyond* human understanding and reason. The mystic Islamic Persian poet, Jelaluddin Rumi (1207–1273), expressed this idea of interconnectedness in one of his poems, which his translator Coleman Barks refers to as **birdsong** because of its lyrical playfulness and spontaneity.

Every forest branch moves differently
in the breeze, but as they sway
they connect at the roots.

(Rumi, 1993, p. 27)

Interestingly, Steiner's educational emphasis on the spiritual life of the child had its roots in his interest in mystical Christianity, and he, too, alludes to birdsong. Writes Barks in his introduction to Rumi's (1993, p. 10) poetry, "One of the loveliest scientific ideas that I know of is Rudolf Steiner's understanding of how plants are part of sonic systems, responding subtly to swallow wingbeats, pre-dawn warbling, and the flamboyant swamp-chorus of the peepers. Certain sounds waken cellular functions. . . . The birds are helping the plants." (Recent studies also report that the music of composers such as Mozart and Bach can stimulate human cells in a way that increases students' ability to learn.)

a. Explore the mystical sects within several Eastern religions and decide what, if anything, they say that could enhance your educational thinking.

b. Research the recent studies indicating that classical music can improve thinking and reasoning skills. Bring your findings back to class.

3.6 *The Discovery of the Child* (1967)

Maria Montessori

"The task of the child," said Dr. Maria Montessori (1870–1952), "is to construct a man [or woman] orientated to his environment, adapted to his time, place and culture" (1967, p. xiv). The Montessori Method of education is thus based on her belief in the powers of all children, particularly from age 3 to age 6, to adapt to their environment through guided as well as spontaneous activity. Contrary to traditional approaches whereby the teacher is viewed as the power behind learning, Montessori believed that all children are endowed with an absorbent mind that can integrate all that constitutes their culture. The real power lies in the child's mind.

From Maria Montessori, *The Discovery of the Child*. Translated by M. Joseph Costelloe. Notre Dame, IN: Fides Publications, 1967 (pp. 159–160, 162, 163).

In her book, *The Discovery of the Child,* Montessori describes the principles and methods underlying a central purpose of her system—the training of the senses. Montessori's method involves training the child's senses through manipulation of three-dimensional objects as well as letters of the alphabet. In this way, children can discover lasting insights on their own, and this discovery of their own powers will then lead to a continued curiosity and love of learning.

Initially, Montessori's scientific education of children received recognition because of the intellectual and spiritual transformations in the poor children who came to her Children's House, a kind of school within a house, which she ran in her native Italy during the early part of the 20th century. Those inspired by what they saw opened other Children's Houses after receiving Montessori training, and soon there were Montessori schools all over the world. Today, there are hundreds of these schools throughout the United States, and Montessori, the medical doctor, is now best known for her pedagogical philosophy.

Writer Dorothy Canfield Fisher was one of the many people inspired by Montessori, and in her book, *A Montessori Mother,* Fisher (1914) expressed the central idea underlying the Montessori system: "a full recognition of the fact that no human being can be educated by anyone else. He must do it himself or it is never done. And this is as true at the age of three as at the age of thirty" (p. 49).

Do you agree?

As you read the excerpt from Montessori's book, try to recall your early-childhood education. Were you aware of the underlying rationale behind the activities you engaged in then?

I believe that up until now we have not been very practical in our approaches to concrete problems. We start with theories and then go on to carry them out in practice. Education, for example, has always attempted to teach through an intellectual approach and then gone on to action. As a rule when we teach we talk about objects that interest us and try to induce a pupil to carry out some task connected with them. But frequently a student, even after he has understood something, finds it enormously difficult to execute a task he is expected to perform, since his education lacks a factor of prime importance—the perfecting of his sensations.

A few examples can bring this out. We tell a cook to buy some fresh fish. She understands the command and sets about executing it. But if she does not have her nose and eyes trained to recognize freshness in fish she will not be able to carry out the order received.

The same can be said of manual labor and, in general, of all the arts and crafts. Everyone must acquire skills through repeated exercises. And learning of this sort includes a training of the senses. . . . For example, spinners have to learn how to use their sense of touch to distinguish threads; weavers and embroiderers have to acquire a notable keenness of vision in order to be able to distinguish details in their work, especially differences in colors. . . .

Aesthetic and moral education are also closely connected with the training of the senses. By multiplying sense experiences and developing the ability to evaluate the smallest differences in various stimuli, one's sensibilities are refined and one's pleasures increased. Beauty is found in harmony, not in discord; and harmony implies affinities, but these require a refinement of the senses if they are to be perceived. . . .

Questions for Discussion and Debate

1. What reasons does Montessori (1967) give to support her assertion that "the training of the senses is a matter of the greatest importance in education" (p. 157).

2. In this excerpt, Montessori essentially makes an argument for the inductive approach to learning, as opposed to the deductive. Explore the meaning of these approaches with your peers, then find the sentence(s) in which Montessori expresses or implies her belief in an inductive or child-centered approach to learning. Share your selection(s) with the class.

3. Reread the definitions of the philosophies and theories of education presented in the Brief Background to this chapter. Which one(s) would encompass Montessori's method and system of thought? Why?

Activities and Projects

1. Visit a Montessori classroom or school. Observe, in particular, how the children operate in terms of utilizing "both hand and senses" to discover insights. Put your observations in writing and then return to the excerpt. Are Montessori's words more meaningful to you now that you have observed children in her type of structured environment? If so, in what way? If not, why not?

   Interview the Montessori teacher about the additional training he or she received in order to use this method.

2. Read all or a part of a biography of Montessori and then prepare a presentation on one of the following topics or a topic of your own choosing: (a) Montessori's own education, (b) the influence of social conditions in Italy on Montessori's thinking, or

(c) Montessori's travels to other countries and the effects of her lectures around the world.

3. Try to locate adults who attended a Montessori school as children. Interview them about influences they believe this education had—or did not have—on them.

4. Write down all that you remember about your own kindergarten and first-grade experiences. Which activities would be suitable according to Montessori? Do you recall feeling any sense of power over your own learning? Compare your answers to these questions with those of your peers.

5. Investigate how Montessori's method might be applied in higher grade levels and subjects, say, middle- and secondary-school curricula. What would a Montessori approach look like at these levels?

3.7   *Leaves of Grass,* Poem No. 9 (1860)

Walt Whitman

A poem is a rhythmical arrangement of words expressing experiences, ideas, and emotions in a style more imaginative, concentrated, and powerful than that of ordinary speech or prose (*Webster's New World Dictionary,* 1982, p. 1099). Though not a very poetic definition of a poem, this definition perfectly describes the poetry of Walt Whitman (1819–1892).

One of Whitman's most "imaginative" and "powerful" collections of poems, *Leaves of Grass* (1855–1882) is considered to be one of the world's major literary works. In the more popular poems in this volume, Whitman sings the praises of democracy and America, but in the lesser known poem No. 9, Whitman speaks of a child and how he comes to know his world. In this most concentrated of formats, Whitman is able to say what takes some philosophers many pages: that we are essentially products of our environment, for better or worse.

Read the poem aloud several times. You will notice that this strategy can help to make the poem a part of you in the same way that everything the child encountered "became a part of him."

1. There was a child went forth every day,
    And the first object he looked upon and received with wonder, pity, love, or dread, that object he became,
    And that object became part of him for the day, or a certain part of the day, or for many years, or stretching cycles of years.

2. The early lilacs became part of this child,
    And grass, and white and red morning-glories, and white and red clover, and the song of the phoebebird,
    And the Third Month lambs, and the sow's pink-faint litter, and the mare's foal, and the cow's calf,
    And the noisy brood of the barn-yard, or by the mire of the pond-side,
    And the fish suspending themselves so curiously below there—and the beautiful curious liquid,

    And the water-plants with their graceful flat heads—all became part of him.

3. The field-sprouts of Fourth Month and Fifth Month became part of him,
    Winter-grain sprouts, and those of the light-yellow corn, and the esculent roots of the garden,
    And the apple-trees covered with blossoms, and the fruit afterward, and wood-berries, and the commonest weeds by the road;
    And the old drunkard staggering home from the outhouse of the tavern, whence he had lately risen,
    And the school-mistress that passed on her way to the school,
    And the friendly boys that passed—and the quarrelsome boys,
    And the tidy and fresh-cheeked girls—and the barefoot negro boy and girl,

---

From Walt Whitman, *Leaves of Grass.* Boston: Thayer and Eldridge, 1860, pp. 221–223.

And all the changes of city and country, wherever he went.

4. His own parents,
   He that had fathered him, and she that conceived him in her womb, and birthed him,
   They gave this child more of themselves than that,
   They gave him afterward every day—they and of them became part of him.

5. The mother at home, quietly placing the dishes on the supper-table,
   The mother with mild words—clean her cap and gown, a wholesome odor falling off her person and clothes as she walks by;
   The father, strong, self-sufficient, manly, mean, angered, unjust,
   The blow, the quick loud word, the tight bargain, the crafty lure,
   The family usages, the language, the company, the furniture—the yearning and swelling heart,
   Affection that will not be gainsayed—the sense of what is real—the thought if, after all, it should prove unreal,
   The doubts of day-time and the doubts of night-time—the curious whether and how,
   Whether that which appears so is so, or is it all flashes and specks?

Men and women crowding fast in the streets—if they are not flashes and speaks, what are they?
The streets themselves, and the façades of houses, and goods in the windows,
Vehicles, teams, the heavy-planked wharves—the huge crossing at the ferries,
The village on the highland, seen from afar at sunset—the river between,
Shadows, aureola and mist, light falling on roofs and gables of white or brown, three miles off,
The schooner near by, sleepily dropping down the tide—the little boat slack-towed astern,
The hurrying tumbling waves, quick-broken crests, slapping,
The strata of colored clouds, the long bar of maroontint, away solitary by itself—the spread of purity it lies motionless in,
The horizon's edge, the flying sea-crow, the fragrance of salt-marsh and shore-mud;
These became part of that child who went forth every day, and who now goes, and will always go forth every day,
And these become part of him or her that peruses them here.

Questions for Discussion and Debate

1. Identify the theme of this poem. Compare the theme you identified with those suggested by your peers. Support your point of view. Refer to the poem itself in reaching a conclusion on the theme.

2. Go through each verse, five in all, and label it, thus informing the reader about the subthemes in this poem. Debate the most appropriate labels with your peers.

3. Poetry is usually characterized by the use of symbolism, imagery, and a rhythmical pattern of words. This particular poem lacks the use of the first device but incorporates the latter two. The rhythm of the lines is especially apparent when you read the poem aloud. What accounts for the rhythm? How does Whitman develop it?

As for imagery, this poem is packed with it. Notice the imagery that Whitman uses to portray nature, people, and objects. Write down or sketch the images that are most vivid for you or to which you relate.

4. Which of the formal philosophies or theories of education is reflected in this poem? Debate your view with your peers.

5. Do you like this poem? Why? Why not?

6. Is there any language in the poem that dates it? Are there other images that Whitman might have used if he had written the poem today? Discuss these other images.

Activities and Projects

1. Locate *Leaves of Grass* in the library, on the Internet, or elsewhere and treat yourself to the other poems. Thematically, how does poem No. 9 fit into the context of *Leaves of Grass?*

2. Create a sixth segment for this poem continuing the theme and supplying another subtheme in line with the others. Share your creation.

3. Illustrate one or more sections of the poem. Afterward, analyze the effect your visual art has on the way you and others perceive the poem. Is there a difference between your perception and theirs? Why? Why not?

4. It may not surprise you—based on the content of this poem—that Whitman was, among his other occupations, a schoolteacher in New York City. Locate a biography of Whitman and read about his experience as a teacher. Prepare a brief report on Whitman as teacher and how that position might have influenced his poetry.

5. Now that you have observed the power of a poem to express succinctly significant and useful ideas—in this case related to informal education—discuss with your peers your personal experiences with poetry. Did you ever have a teacher who helped you to discover—or have you discovered on your own—that poetry can offer wisdom *and* pleasure on many levels? Do research to find out about teachers who have created successful units of instruction on poetry. Share your findings with your peers.

Are there ways you can integrate poetry into your teaching? Before embarking on this research, amass several collections, including *Leaves of Grass,* and start reading. You may find the habit hard to break.

3.8 | *The Aims of Education* (1949)

Alfred North Whitehead

Alfred North Whitehead (1861–1947) was an English mathematician and philosopher who taught at Harvard University after coming to the United States in 1924. His book, *The Aims of Education,* is comprised of 10 essays, most of which were originally addresses he delivered at educational and scientific conferences between 1912 and 1917. The second chapter in the book, from which the excerpt below is taken, is an example of the kind of wisdom that, like Dewey's and Montessori's, remains relevant and meaningful far beyond the time period in which it was written. For example, Whitehead, Montessori, and Dewey, who were all contemporaries, believed that education should connect with the students' experience in some way so that they can make new ideas their own and apply them to their lives.

Most of the essays in the book reflect Whitehead's criticisms of the educational practices of his day, many of which *still* exist. First, he objected to the "curse of departmentalization," in particular. The late Supreme Court Justice Felix Frankfurter wrote, in the introduction to the Mentor edition of Whitehead's (1949) book, "Among students, as well as among teachers, there has been a tendency to regard [academic] courses as something which exist in nature, instead of artificial simplifications for the mastery of . . . nature, or reason, or society. Professor Whitehead exerted powerful influence to break down this separation in the various departments of the university" (p. vii). Because of his belief in the interdependence of ideas, it is difficult to categorize Whitehead as either a realist or an idealist, since he himself did not completely separate objective reality and the world of ideas. There is still some question about the extent to which educators recognize the interdependence that exists among the various disciplines, which, in most cases, have remained separate and somewhat territorial.

Second, Whitehead (1949) intended that his book serve as a "protest against dead knowledge, that is to say, inert ideas" (p. v) that are "merely received into the mind without being utilized, or tested, or thrown into fresh combinations" (p. 1). He called for living ideas that connected to the learners' experiences and could be useful to them.

Third, Whitehead (1949) criticized the practice of teaching little pieces of a large number of subjects, which, he said, resulted in "the passive reception of disconnected ideas" (p. 2). What could be more relevant today than his two commandments: "Do not teach too many subjects" and "What you do teach, teach thoroughly" (p. 2)? His is a "less-is-more" philosophy that is echoed by many contemporary theorists, from Sizer (1985) to Wiggington (1985) to Bruner (1975).

There is no question, for instance, that Jerome Bruner's work especially reflects Whitehead's philosophy. Bruner, a cognitive psychologist who also taught at Harvard,

---

believes, as did Whitehead, that if complex ideas are expressed in an appropriate format, a child of any age can learn them. He constructed his complex and controversial fifth-grade curriculum, "Man: A Course of Study" (M:ACOS) based on this belief (Bruner, 1975). Whitehead had written earlier, as shown in the excerpt, that there was no sense to assuming that children had to learn simple concepts before they could learn difficult ones.

Further, Whitehead (1949) wrote, "From the very beginning of his education, the child should experience the joy of discovery" of how general ideas can bring understanding to events (p. 2). So, too, in his writing about curriculum and instruction, Bruner has consistently championed the discovery method, concept formation, and the idea of students constructing new knowledge by bringing their past experiences to new learning and building upon them, a process now referred to as constructivism.

Much of Whitehead's work, like Steiner's in an earlier excerpt (Selection 3.5), was based on his underlying search for patterns and unity both in the universe and in education. One of his most vivid expressions of such a pattern can be found in the following excerpt from "The Rhythm of Education." For Whitehead, learning, like life, was a cyclical process. In the case of learning, he saw a threefold cycle made up of stages that interact and repeat themselves: the first stage being Romance, the second Precision, and the third Generalization. Every lesson should be an example of this cycle in action, because it is the cycle's three elements that make curriculum meaningful to students. In addition, every unit, which is a series of lessons connected by a common theme, should also be cyclical, but on a larger scale. (Units are curriculum structures that, linked together, comprise an academic course.)

As you read this excerpt, think about the way in which Whitehead defines the three stages of the learning cycle. How have the lessons you have constructed or observed integrated each of the stages? Can a lesson be considered complete and meaningful if one of the stages of the cycle is missing? And, finally, think about how Whitehead's philosophy compares to those of other authors in this chapter.

By the Rhythm of Education I denote a certain principle which in its practical application is well known to everyone with educational experience. Accordingly, when I remember that I am speaking to an audience of some of the leading educationalists in England, I have no expectation that I shall be saying anything that is new to you. I do think, however, that the principle has not been subjected to an adequate discussion taking account of all the factors which should guide its application.

I first seek for the baldest statement of what I mean by the Rhythm of Education, a statement so bald as to exhibit the point of this address in its utter obviousness. The principle is merely this—that different subjects and modes of study should be undertaken by pupils at fitting times when they have reached the proper stage of mental development. You will agree with me that this is a truism, never doubted and known to all. I am really anxious to emphasise the obvious character of the foundational idea of my address; for one reason, because this audience will certainly find it out for itself. But the other reason, the reason why I choose this subject for discourse, is that I do not think that this obvious truth has been handled in educational practice with due attention to the psychology of the pupils.

The Tasks of Infancy

I commence by challenging the adequacy of some principles by which the subjects for study are often classified in order. By this I mean that these principles can only be accepted as correct if they are so explained as to be explained away. Consider first the criterion of difficulty. It is not true that the easier subjects should precede the harder. On the contrary, some of the hardest must come first because nature so dictates, and because they are essential to life. The first intellectual task which confronts an infant is the acquirement of spoken language. What an appalling task, the correlation of meanings with sounds! It requires an anlysis of ideas and an analysis of sounds. We all know that the infant does it, and that the miracle of his achievement is explicable. But so are all miracles, and yet to the wise they remain miracles. All I ask is that with this example staring us in the face we should cease talking nonsense about postponing the harder subjects.

What is the next subject in the education of the infant minds? The acquirement of written language; that is to say, the correlation of sounds with shapes. Great heavens! Have our educationists gone mad? They are setting babbling mites of six years old to tasks which might daunt a sage after lifelong toil. Again, the hardest task in mathematics is the study of the elements of algebra, and yet this stage must precede the comparative simplicity of the differential calculus.

I will not elaborate my point further; I merely restate it in the form, that the postponement of difficulty is no safe clue for the maze of educational practice.

The alternative principle of order among subjects is that of necessary antecedence. There we are obviously on firmer ground. It is impossible to read *Hamlet* until you can read; and the study of integers must precede the study of fractions. And yet even this firm principle dissolves under scrutiny. It is certainly true, but it is only true if you give an artificial limitation to the concept of a subject for study. The danger of the principle is that it is accepted in one sense, for which it is almost a necessary truth, and that it is applied in another sense for which it is false. You cannot read Homer before you can read; but many a child, and in ages past many a man, has sailed with Odysseus over the seas of Romance by the help of the spoken word of a mother, or of some wandering bard. The uncritical application of the principle of the necessary antecedence of some subjects to others has, in the hands of dull people with a turn for organisation, produced in education the dryness of the Sahara.

Stages of Mental Growth

The reason for the title which I have chosen for this address, the Rhythm of Education, is derived from yet another criticism of current ideas. The pupil's progress is often conceived as a uniform steady advance undifferentiated by change of type or alteration in pace; for example, a boy may be conceived as starting Latin at ten years of age and by a uniform progression steadily developing into a classical scholar at the age of eighteen or twenty. I hold that this conception of education is based upon a false psychology of the process of mental development which has gravely hindered the effectiveness of our methods. Life is essentially periodic. It comprises daily periods, with their alternations of work and play, of activity and of sleep, and seasonal periods, which dictate our terms and our holidays; and also it is composed of well-marked yearly periods. These are the gross obvious periods which no one can overlook. There are also subtler periods of mental growth, with their cyclic recurrences, yet always different as we pass from cycle to cycle, though the subordinate stages are reproduced in each cycle. That is why I have chosen the term "rhythmic," as meaning essentially the conveyance of difference within a framework of repetition. Lack of attention to the rhythm and character of mental growth is a main source of wooden futility in education. I think that Hegel was right when he analysed progress into three stages, which he called Thesis, Antithesis, and Synthesis; though for the purpose of the application of his idea to educational theory I do not think that the names he gave are very happily suggestive. In relation to intellectual progress I would term them, the stage of romance, the stage of precision, and the stage of generalisation.

The Stage of Romance

The stage of romance is the stage of first apprehension. The subject-matter has the vividness of novelty; it holds within itself unexplored connexions with possibilities half-disclosed by glimpses and half-concealed by the wealth of material. In this stage knowledge is not dominated by systematic procedure. Such system as there must be is created piecemeal *ad hoc*. We are in the presence of immediate cognisance of fact, only intermittently subjecting fact to systematic dissection. Romantic emotion is essentially the excitement consequent on the transition from the bare facts to the first realisations of the import of their unexplored relationships. For example, Crusoe was a mere man, the sand was mere sand, the footprint was a mere footprint, and the island a mere island, and Europe was the busy world of men. But the sudden perception of the half-disclosed and half-hidden possibilities relating Crusoe and the sand and the footprint and the lonely island secluded from Europe constitutes romance. I have had to take an extreme case for illustration in order to make my meaning perfectly plain. But construe it as

an allegory representing the first stage in a cycle of progress. Education must essentially be a setting in order of a ferment already stirring in the mind: you cannot educate mind in *vacuo*. In our conception of education we tend to confine it to the second stage of the cycle; namely, to the stage of precision. But we cannot so limit our task without misconceiving the whole problem. We are concerned alike with the ferment, with the acquirement of precision, and with the subsequent fruition.

The Stage of Precision

The stage of precision also represents an addition to knowledge. In this stage, width of relationship is subordinated to exactness of formulation. It is the stage of grammar, the grammar of language and the grammar of science. It proceeds by forcing on the students' acceptance a given way of analysing the facts, bit by bit. New facts are added, but they are the facts which fit into the analysis.

It is evident that a stage of precision is barren without a previous stage of romance: unless there are facts which have already been vaguely apprehended in their broad generality, the previous analysis is an analysis of nothing. It is simply a series of meaningless statements about bare facts, produced artificially and without any further relevance. I repeat that in this stage we do not merely remain within the circle of the facts elicited in the romantic epoch. The facts of romance have disclosed ideas with possibilities of wide significance, and in the stage of precise progress we acquire other facts in a systematic order, which thereby form both a disclosure and an analysis of the general subject-matter of the romance.

The Stage of Generalisation

The final stage of generalisation is Hegel's synthesis. It is a return to romanticism with added advantage of classified ideas and relevant technique. It is the fruition which has been the goal of the precise training. It is the final success. I am afraid that I have had to give a dry analysis of somewhat obvious ideas. It has been necessary to do so because my subsequent remarks presuppose that we have clearly in our minds the essential character of this threefold cycle.

The Cyclic Processes

Education should consist in a continual repetition of such cycles. Each lesson in its minor way should form an eddy cycle issuing in its own subordinate process. Longer periods should issue in definite attainments, which then form the starting-grounds for fresh cycles. We should banish the idea of a mythical, far-off end of education. The pupils must be continually enjoying some fruition and starting afresh—if the teacher is stimulating in exact proportion to his success in satisfying the rhythmic cravings of his pupils.

An infant's first romance is its awakening to the apprehension of objects and to the appreciation of their connexions. Its growth in mentality takes the exterior form of occupying itself in the coordination of its perceptions with its bodily activities. Its first stage of precision is mastering spoken language as an instrument for classifying its contemplation of objects and for strengthening its apprehension of emotional relations with other beings. Its first stage of generalisation is the use of language for a classified and enlarged enjoyment of objects.

This first cycle of intellectual progress from the achievement of perception to the acquirement of language, and from the acquirement of language to classified thought and keener perception, will bear more careful study. It is the only cycle of progress which we can observe in its purely natural state. The later cycles are necessarily tinged by the procedure of the current mode of education. There is a characteristic of it which is often sadly lacking in subsequent education; I mean, that it achieves complete success. At the end of it the child *can* speak, its ideas *are* classified, and its perceptions *are* sharpened. The cycle achieves its object. This is a great deal more than can be said for most systems of education as applied to most pupils. But why should this be so? Certainly, a new-born baby looks a most unpromising subject for intellectual progress when we remember the difficulty of the task before it. I suppose it is because nature, in the form of surrounding circumstances, sets it a task for which the normal development of its brain is exactly fitted. I do not think that there is any particular mystery about the fact of a child learning to speak and in consequence thinking all the better; but it does offer food for reflection.

In the subsequent education we have not sought for cyclic processes which in a finite time run their course and within their own limited sphere achieve a complete success. This completion is one outstanding character in the natural cycle for infants. Later on we start a child on some subject, say Latin, at the age of ten, and hope by a uniform system of formal training to achieve success at the age of twenty. The natural result is failure, both in interest and in acquirement. When I speak of failure, I am comparing our results with the brilliant success of the first natural cycle. I do not think that it is because our tasks are intrinsically too hard, when I remember that the infant's cycle is the hardest of all. It is because our tasks are set in an unnatural way, without rhythm and without the stimulus of intermediate successes and without concentration.

I have not yet spoken of this character of concentration which so conspicuously attaches to the infant's progress. The whole being of the infant is absorbed in the practice of its cycle.

It has nothing else to divert its mental development. In this respect there is a striking difference between this natural cycle and the subsequent history of the student's development. It is perfectly obvious that life is very various and that the mind and brain naturally develop so as to adapt themselves to the many-hued world in which their lot is cast. Still, after making allowance for this consideration, we will be wise to preserve some measure of concentration for each of the subsequent cycles. In particular, we should avoid a competition of diverse subjects in the same stage of their cycles. The fault of the older education was unrhythmic concentration on a single undifferentiated subject. Our modern system, with its insistence on a preliminary general education, and with its easy toleration of the analysis of knowledge into distinct subjects, is an equally unrhythmic collection of distracting scraps. I am pleading that we shall endeavour to weave in the learner's mind a harmony of patterns, by co-ordinating the various elements of instruction into subordinate cycles each of intrinsic worth for the immediate apprehension of the pupil. We must garner our crops each in its due season.

Questions for Discussion and Debate

1. How does Whitehead define the three stages of the learning or lesson cycle (Romance, Precision, and Generalization)? Locate the phrases in the excerpt that best define the three concepts.

2. There continues to be debate about the best approach to curriculum construction. There are two approaches that appear to be antithetical. The "structure of the disciplines" refers to the traditional approach, whereby subject matter is constructed according to the concepts within a particular discipline. The "broad fields," or interdisciplinary, approach refers to designing curriculum that integrates concepts from a variety of disciplines around a theme. Debate the advantages and disadvantages of these two approaches. (You may first want to consult the work of some of the philosophers referred to in the Brief Background to this chapter as well as additional essays by Whitehead.)

3. Discuss your *own* experience with curriculum development. What are the curriculum components you use in preparing lessons and units? Do you include the cycle of elements described by Whitehead? If not, discuss ways you might begin to integrate them.

4. Debate the advantages and disadvantages of constructing a course by units. Then share courses you have had or are now taking that are constructed in this way.

Activities and Projects

1. Jerome Bruner's social studies curriculum, M:ACOS, referred to in the introduction to Whitehead's excerpt, has been called both "one of the most elegant, scholarly and ingenious curricula" and "one of most disastrous attempts . . . in curriculum development" (Posner, 1992, p. 23). The content was a source of controversy, for example, man's evolution from other animals, as was the method; that is, some teachers were uncomfortable

with an inductive, or discovery, approach. The concerns surrounding the development and implementation of his unit mirror the kinds of philosophical questions that can arise whenever curriculum is created, the three biggest issues being, What should we teach? How should we teach it? and, Who should construct the curriculum? (Classroom teachers had had no role in developing M:ACOS.)

Do research on Bruner's controversial curriculum and, with the class, decide what lessons can be learned about curriculum development from the limited success of Bruner's model unit. Find out about Bruner's other curriculum theories, which are among the most respected in the educational field.

2. Interview a number of teachers about curriculum development. Consider these questions for starters.

   a. Is it possible to teach a *published* curriculum effectively without first making it *yours* in some way? How do you make such a curriculum, that is, one you did not create, into your own?

   b. Does your school have a curriculum committee? If so, what is its role? If not, why isn't there one? (If there is one, you may ask to sit in on one of its meetings.)

3. Find out if there is a curriculum committee at your college. If so, interview the chair of the committee about its function and philosophy. Share the information with your peers. Who has input into curriculum development and approval at your school?

4. Whitehead refers to the philosopher Hegel and his analysis of progress as a three-stage process (thesis, antithesis, and synthesis). After reading more about Hegelian thought, compare his three stages to Whitehead's threefold cycle. Also, consider these questions: (a) Is it possible to apply Hegel's three stages to education? and (b) Are there other aspects of Hegel's philosophy that can be applied to educational thinking?

5. An educational project that reflects Whitehead's philosophy is currently ongoing. An innovative group of parents, teachers, and scholars in Reggio Emilia, Italy, has developed an internationally acclaimed early-childhood program (New, 1991). Using a constructivist approach to early education, this program emphasizes children's symbolic languages, including drawing, sculpture, drama, and writing, within the context of a project-oriented curriculum. The approach also solicits *multiple* points of view regarding children's needs and interests. Find out more about the Reggio Emilia approach and share your findings. Which philosophy of education or conception of curriculum does this approach resemble? What are some of the ways in which the Reggio Emilia approach could be adapted for elementary-, middle-, and high-school levels?

3.9   *Left Back: A Century of Failed School Reforms* (2000)

Diane Ravitch

"School reform is in America's bloodstream and that's not necessarily a sign of good health" ("Schools, Dazed," 2001, p. 9). That quote comes from a reviewer of Diane Ravitch's book, *Left Back: A Century of Failed School Reform,* from which the following excerpt is taken. The book is a detailed account of what has been done in America's schools over the past century in the name of reform, and, according to Ravitch, what's been done has mostly not worked. Referring to the "failed reforms" of the progressive movement, she advises, "Avoid all 'movements' in education. They throw reason to the winds" ("Schools, Dazed," 2001, p. 9), a view, by the way, with which this editor concurs.

In response to her arguments against progressive reformers of the 20th century, Ravitch has been attacked by members of that camp. In a review of her book, William G. Wraga (2001) of the University of Georgia faults Ravitch not simply because she villainizes progressive education compared to the academic curriculum, but especially because she devotes little attention to the shortcomings of the latter. For this reason he labels her a traditionalist. But does the label fit someone who believes—as she does—that schools should educate kids, *all* kids? And that all teachers should be well educated in the subjects they teach? The fact is that while the labels "traditionalist" and "progressive" still serve a purpose, say, in generally discussing the two sides of the standardized testing debate, such labels may reduce the quality of current discussions on how best to improve the nation's schools. To resolve ongoing problems, it may be helpful to keep an open mind and resist any labeling that might prevent us from hearing diverse points of view, especially those with which we may not, at first, agree. Perhaps there are kernels of truth—maybe more—emanating from all philosophical camps that can contribute to the health of American education and the various ways of thinking about the purpose of education and school reform.

Historian Ravitch served as Assistant Secretary in Charge of Research of the U.S. Department of Education from 1991 to 1993 and is now a senior research scholar at New York University, with affiliations with a number of think tanks. The following excerpt is a plea for the philosophical orientations often referred to as "structure of the disciplines," "subject-centered," and "traditional," which she believes well-meaning progressives lost sight of in their quest for social reform. Her argument for teaching the disciplines is a response to the progressive notions that, first, assume that large numbers of children are not capable of learning a great deal of what the schools have traditionally taught and, thus, offer students different options to meet their needs and, second, assume that it is more important to engage students in activities and experiences than in learning bodies of knowledge. She writes, "The century-long effort to diminish the intellectual purposes of the schools had harmful consequences, especially for children from disadvantaged backgrounds. . . . While youngsters from poor and modest circumstances had greatest need for the intellectual stimulation that schools were supposed to provide, they were the targets of such 'reforms' as curricular differentiation and industrial education, which purposely limited their prospects for intellectual development . . . and undermined the democratic promise of public education" (Ravitch, 2000, pp. 459–460).

On the other hand, Ravitch admits that there exists within progressivism a positive tradition that respects intellectual development, and as examples, she refers to some private schools and to some of her progressive contemporaries, Theodore Sizer, Deborah Meier, and Howard Gardner. She calls them "intellectual progressives" and sees some meaningful connections between them and the "liberal (egalitarian) traditionalists," the most prominent one being E. D. Hirsch, Jr. (Ravitch, 2000, pp. 462–464). (See also Selection 4.8.)

Before reading Ravitch's plea for the teaching of the disciplines, consider (re-)reading Selection 3.2, Dewey's creed, a counterview, and Selection 4.8, in which E. D. Hirsch, Jr., echoes Ravitch. Then ask yourself the question, Must educational reform be addressed with an either/or approach?

In the debates about standards, the concept of knowledge was constantly under attack. Efforts to define which knowledge should be taught and tested opened up schisms among academics, who made their reputations (and living) by arguing whether knowledge was real, valid, particular, universal, relevant, or the privileged property of some elite group. Schools and the writers of state standards avoided such battles by focusing only on skills and bypassing any definition of what knowledge was important for students to master. In the early decades of the century, progressives had derided the knowledge taught in school as useless or aristocratic; late-twentieth-century critics called it arbitrary or trivial. The counter-argument, however, remains valid: Knowledge is power, and those who have it control the debate and ultimately control the levers of power in society. A democratic system of education, as Lester Frank Ward wrote a century earlier, disseminates knowledge as broadly as possible throughout society. . . .

. . . The society that allows large numbers of its citizens to remain uneducated, ignorant, or semiliterate squanders its greatest asset, the intelligence of its people.

The disciplines taught in school are uniquely valuable, both for individuals and for society. A society that does not teach science to the general public fosters the proliferation of irrational claims and antiscientific belief systems. A society that turns its back on the teaching of history encourages mass amnesia, leaving the public ignorant of the important events and ideas of the human past and eroding the civic intelligence needed for the future. A democratic society that fails to teach the younger generation its principles of self-government puts these principles at risk. A society that does not teach youngsters to appreciate great works of literature and art permits a coarsening and degradation of its popular culture. A society that is racially and ethnically diverse requires, more than other societies, a conscious effort to build shared values and ideals among its citizenry. A society that tolerates anti-intellectualism in its schools can expect to have a dumbed-down culture that honors celebrity and sensation rather than knowledge and wisdom.

Schools will not be rendered obsolete by new technologies because their role as learning institutions has become even more important than in the past. Technology can supplement schooling but not replace it; even the most advanced electronic technologies are incapable of turning their worlds of information into mature knowledge, a form of intellectual magic that requires skilled and educated teachers.

To be effective, schools must concentrate on their fundamental mission of teaching and learning. And they must do it for all children. That must be the overarching goal of schools in the twenty-first century.

Questions for Discussion and Debate

1. Write a one-paragraph summary of this excerpt in which you express Ravitch's main ideas. Compare your summary of key ideas with those of your peers. On which points do you agree with Ravitch?

2. Ravitch attacks the postmodernists with this line from the excerpt: "Efforts to define which knowledge should be taught and tested opened up schisms among academics, who made their reputations (and living) by arguing whether knowledge was real, valid, particular, universal, relevant, or the property of some elite group" (p. 451). Divide the class into two groups, "postmodernists," who *oppose* the idea that it is possible to define what knowledge is important for students to master, and "traditionalists," like Ravitch, who believe that it is not only possible but vital to construct such a definition. Engage in an informal debate. (Because both sides may not have the opportunity to do background research, students should consult the Brief Background to this chapter before engaging in the debate.)

3. Note the comments in the introduction to this excerpt that question the use of labels in discussing the various philosophies of education. Hold a discussion in which the class establishes *both* the advantages and the disadvantages of applying labels such as "traditional" and "progressive" to the participants in discussions on school reform. (See also the political spectrum in chapter 4, following Selection 4.5.)

Activities and Projects

1. Write a letter to Diane Ravitch (perhaps in care of her publisher: Simon & Schuster, Rockefeller Center, 1230 Avenue of the Americas, New York, NY 10020). Express your perceptions of her ideas. Ask her a number of questions that the excerpt raises for you. If you receive an answer (you might include a stamped, self-addressed envelope), share it with the class.

2. Locate a copy of Ravitch's book, *Left Back,* from which this excerpt was taken. Read the first chapter, "The Educational Ladder," in which she traces the roots of public education during the 19th century and the attempts that reformers made to establish standards and common schools for all children. Summarize the chapter and report on its contents. (Or choose another chapter to

report on, such as chapter 11, "In Search of Standards.")

3. Write a position paper in which you express your beliefs about school reform and the directions in which those reforms should take public education. Consider not only Ravitch's views but also the views of others included in this chapter and in chapter 4, "Politics of Education." After reading your finished position paper, can you place yourself within a particular philosophical or political camp?

4. Study the reform issues facing the school system in the community in which you live. Attend a school committee meeting. Study one of the more controversial issues facing that system and decide where you stand on it. Then write a letter to the editor of the local newspaper expressing your view and the reasons for your position.

5. Some educational theories are so contradictory that practitioners trying to understand them are left immobilized and at a loss about which ones to heed. Indeed, for every educational study that espouses a theory, there seems to be an equal and opposite study decrying it. Imagine that you are talking to someone about to take the plunge into these waters. What criteria would you suggest they use (a) for understanding each philosophy and (b) for evaluating each one?

6. Mortimer J. Adler (1902–2001) is the educational philosopher who is quoted by *both* conservatives and liberals when they debate education reform, in much the same way that the Republicans and Democrats both lay claim to Abraham Lincoln. Adler dedicated his book *The Paideia Proposal* (1982) to Horace Mann, John Dewey, and Robert Hutchins, and two of the books' greatest proponents today are E. D. Hirsch, Jr., in many ways Adler's disciple, and Diane Ravitch. Hirsch's belief in balancing intellectual rigor with equal access comes straight from Adler. Do research on the life and work of Mortimer Adler and reach your own conclusions about whether his reputation as an elitist is justified. Prepare a speech for the class in which you share the educational manifesto contained in *The Paideia* (py-dee-a) *Proposal*. (Paideia essentially refers to the general learning that all human beings should possess. The term originated with Plato in *The Republic*. See Selection 3.10.) Include in your presentation reasons why both perennialists (conservatives) and progressives (liberals) might claim Adler as theirs.

7. Ravitch uses the label "intellectual progressivist" in referring to people such as Ted Sizer, of whose form of progressivism she approves. As for labeling herself and E. D. Hirsch, Jr., she implies comfort with being a "liberal traditionalist." There are distinctions between the two labels, but also similarities. For example, both positions believe in the compatibility of academic rigor and social justice. Read Hirsch's piece (Selection 4.8), Sizer's piece (Selection 5.10), and Ravitch's piece again. Write a brief paper describing where the two philosophies diverge as well as intersect.

3.10 ▌ "Allegory of the Cave" (Trans. 1956)

Plato

Plato's (427–347 B.C.E.) "Allegory of the Cave" could just as appropriately have been placed in the chapter on "Historical Perspectives" or the one on "Politics of Education," since Plato is among the Greek thinkers who have significantly shaped Western culture's ideas about education and the political role it plays in our society. However, this excerpt has been placed in this "Philosophical Foundations" chapter because the allegory expresses Plato's—and his teacher Socrates's—political and social philosophy related to the connections they see between politics and education.

Socrates was known as an independent thinker who questioned authority and the accepted ways of thinking of his time. The desire to challenge tradition, which he passed on to his students, was viewed by the ruling establishment as a threat and resulted in his being convicted of treason and sentenced to death. He accepted the sentence but maintained his beliefs, and he died after drinking poison made from the hemlock plant.

Much of what we know about Socrates's philosophy comes from the writings of Plato, because Plato made his mentor a major character in his famous dialogues. The following excerpt from the "Allegory of the Cave" is taken from Book VII of *The Republic,* Plato's most famous dialogues, which portray his vision of a perfect society. The excerpt illustrates the format of a dialogue or a conversation in which Socrates is shown using his well-known method of questioning someone, in this case, Glaucon, a fellow philosopher. Two things are accomplished through the use of his (Socratic) method: The questioner guides the other person into rethinking his or her beliefs, and at the same time, the questioner is able to convey his or her own ideas. Together they bring the conversation closer to a discovery of truths. (As you think about Plato's allegory, keep in mind that the ideas he is recording are those of Socrates, his teacher.)

Plato reveals in this allegory the essence of education, or what he calls *paidea.* Plato compares the human condition to an underground cave populated by "prisoners" or ordinary people not yet touched by philosophical education. They are tied down and can see only straight ahead. An artificial light in the cave casts shadows on the wall of objects being carried by unseen "bearers." The prisoners' concept of reality is extremely limited, for they see only the images of objects. Moreover, they don't recognize these limitations and may resent anyone who tries to point them out. Here Plato may be thinking of those individuals who resisted Socrates's challenge to established thinking and who then punished him for his behavior.

On the other hand, there are prisoners who see the shadows and are aware that they are merely images. These prisoners represent the people who, in a less than ideal society, would be governing. However, in an ideal society there would exist a philosopher-king who has been educated to ascend from the realm of shadows into the world of sunlight, Plato's symbol for the world of ideas, knowledge, and education, or "the Good," the most real of worlds. This philosopher-king is able to make distinctions among shadows, images, actual objects, and ideas, or the mental conceptions of things, that allow people to make use of the objects and "to shine." The point is that the real world must be understood according to ideas, that is, the Good to which Plato refers. And with education one is able, finally, to perceive that Good in the form of very real eternal and absolute ideas such as truth, beauty, and justice.

Continuing with the allegory, Plato indicates that leaving the cave is painful at first, but he tries to show that ultimately the life of ideas can bring happiness to both the individual and the state. He then concludes that the philosopher-king must eventually return to the cave—that is, participate in the practical politics of everyday life—so he can help others attain wisdom, that is, escape from the realm of images or ignorance. By ruling the society wisely, the philosopher-king can bring about justice for all, in addition to stimulating an intellectual curiosity among his people.

Put simply, then, according to Plato, in the stage of life before education and the ability to reason, human beings are essentially prisoners in caves, enslaved by their senses and by their ignorance (Ozman & Craver, 1999, pp. 1–5). It is because of Plato's conviction that ideas are *more* real than material objects that he has been referred to as the "father of idealism."

Interestingly, Plato's views are not entirely democratic. For example, he believes that only the intelligent and educated should govern. What constitutes a good government, he says, is not the consent of the governed, because the governed would rather remain imprisoned than give up what they have been used to believing as real, that is, the images. According to Plato, if citizens fail to understand what is good for them, then it is the task of political leaders, philosopher-kings, to educate them. Such education should consist of guiding people to discover their innate powers to learn, to turn from images to realities (in today's terms, from television to ideas?), from the world of the senses to the world of the intellect. Society needs men and women who see things as they are, says Plato. However, the number of philosophers will be small, as there are only a few who are capable of grasping the great ideas and gaining the intellect and ability to reason and, thus, to rule: an elitist perspective, perhaps, yet one that advocates education for all.

Coincidentally, the questions following the "Allegory of the Cave" will have you doing precisely what Plato and Socrates believe that education should lead you to do: Think about important ideas, question your own conception of things, and see new truths.

An allegory is a story in which people, things, and events have a hidden or symbolic meaning, and it is usually used to teach a lesson. What lessons do you learn in this allegory? With which of them do you agree? Where do Plato and Socrates challenge your existing beliefs?

BOOK VII

"Next, then," I said, "take the following parable of education and ignorance as a picture of the condition of our nature. Imagine mankind as dwelling in an underground cave with a long entrance open to the light across the whole width of the cave; in this they have been from childhood, with necks and legs fettered, so they have to stay where they are. They cannot move their heads round because of the fetters, and they can only look forward, but light comes to them from fire burning behind them higher up at a distance. Between the fire and the prisoners is a road above their level, and along it imagine a low wall has been built, as puppet showmen have screens in front of their people over which they work their puppets."

"I see," he said.

"See, then, bearers carrying along this wall all sorts of articles which they hold projecting above the wall, statues of men and other living things,[1] made of stone or wood and all kinds of stuff, some of the bearers speaking and some silent, as you might expect."

"What a remarkable image," he said, "and what remarkable prisoners!"

"Just like ourselves," I said. "For, first of all, tell me this: What do you think such people would have seen of themselves and each other except their shadows, which the fire cast on the opposite wall of the cave?"

"I don't see how they could see anything else," said he, "if they were compelled to keep their heads unmoving all their lives!"

"Very well, what of the things being carried along? Would not this be the same?"

"Of course it would."

"Suppose the prisoners were able to talk together, don't you think that when they named the shadows which they saw passing they would believe they were naming things?"[2]

"Necessarily."

"Then if their prison had an echo from the opposite wall, whenever one of the passing bearers uttered a sound, would they not suppose that the passing shadow must be making the sound? Don't you think so?"

"Indeed I do," he said.

"If so," said I, "such persons would certainly believe that there were no realities except those shadows of handmade things."[3]

"So it must be," said he.

"Now consider," said I, "what their release would be like, and their cure from these fetters and their folly; let us imagine whether it might naturally be something like this. One might be released, and compelled suddenly to stand up and turn his neck round, and to walk and look towards the firelight; all this would hurt him, and he would be too much dazzled to see distinctly those things whose shadows he had seen before. What do you think he would say, if someone told him that what he saw before was foolery, but now he saw more rightly, being a bit nearer reality and turned towards what was a little more real? What if he were shown each of the passing things, and compelled by questions to answer what each one was? Don't you think he would be puzzled, and believe what he saw before was more true than what was shown to him now?"

"Far more," he said.

"Then suppose he were compelled to look towards the real light, it would hurt his eyes, and he would escape by turning them away to the things which he was able to look at, and these he would believe to be clearer than what was being shown to him."

"Just so," said he.

"Suppose, now," said I, "that someone should drag him thence by force, up the rough ascent, the steep way up, and never stop until he could drag him out into the light of the sun, would he not be distressed and furious at being dragged; and when he came into the light, the brilliance would fill his eyes and he would not

---

[1]Including models of trees, etc.
[2]Which they had never seen. They would say "tree" when it was only a shadow of the model of a tree.

---

[3]Shadows of artificial things, not even the shadow of a growing tree: another stage from reality.

be able to see even one of the things now called real?"[4]

"That he would not," said he, "all of a sudden."

"He would have to get used to it, surely, I think, if he is to see the things above. First he would most easily look at shadows, after that images of mankind and the rest in water, lastly the things themselves. After this he would find it easier to survey by night the heavens themselves and all that is in them, gazing at the light of the stars and moon, rather than by day the sun and the sun's light."

"Of course."

"Last of all, I suppose, the sun; he could look on the sun itself by itself in its own place, and see what it is like, not reflections of it in water or as it appears in some alien setting."

"Necessarily," said he.

"And only after all this he might reason about it, how this is he who provides seasons and years, and is set over all there is in the visible region, and he is in a manner the cause of all things which they saw."

"Yes, it is clear," said he, "that after all that, he would come to this last."

"Very good. Let him be reminded of his first habitation, and what was wisdom in that place, and of his fellow-prisoners there; don't you think he would bless himself for the change, and pity them?"

"Yes, indeed."

"And if there were honours and praises among them and prizes for the one who saw the passing things most sharply and remembered best which of them used to come before and which after and which together, and from these was best able to prophesy accordingly what was going to come—do you believe he would set his desire on that, and envy those who were honoured men or potentates among them? Would he not feel as Homer says,[5] and heartily desire rather to be serf of some landless man on earth and to endure anything in the world, rather than to opine as they did and to live in that way?"

"Yes indeed," said he, "he would rather accept anything than live like that."

"Then again," I said, "just consider; if such a one should go down again and sit on his old seat, would he not get his eyes full of darkness coming in suddenly out of the sun?"

"Very much so," said he.

"And if he should have to compete with those who had been always prisoners, by laying down the law about those shadows while he was blinking before his eyes were settled down—and it would take a good long time to get used to things—wouldn't they all laugh at him and say he had spoiled his eyesight by going up there, and it was not worth-while so much as to try to go up? And would they not kill anyone who tried to release them and take them up, if they could somehow lay hands on him and kill him?"[6]

"That they would!" said he.

"Then we must apply this image, my dear Glaucon," said I, "to all we have been saying. The world of our sight is like the habitation in prison, the firelight there to the sunlight here, the ascent and the view of the upper world is the rising of the soul into the world of mind; put it so and you will not be far from my own surmise, since that is what you want to hear; but God knows if it is really true. At least, what appears to me is, that in the world of the known, last of all,[7] is the idea of the good, and

---

[4] To the next stage of knowledge: the real thing, not the artificial puppet.

[5] *Odyssey* xi. 489.

[6] Plato probably alludes to the death of Socrates. See *Apology*, p. 444.

[7] The end of our search.

with what toil to be seen! And seen, this must be inferred to be the cause of all right and beautiful things for all, which gives birth to light and the king of light in the world of sight, and, in the world of mind, herself the queen produces truth and reason; and she must be seen by one who is to act with reason publicly or privately."

"I believe as you do," he said, "in so far as I am able."

"Then believe also, as I do," said I, "and do not be surprised, that those who come thither are not willing to have part in the affairs of men, but their souls ever strive to remain above; for that surely may be expected if our parable fits the case."

"Quite so," he said.

"Well then," said I, "do you think it surprising if one leaving divine contemplations and passing to the evils of men is awkward and appears to be a great fool, while he is still blinking—not yet accustomed to the darkness around him, but compelled to struggle in law courts or elsewhere about shadows of justice, or the images which make the shadows, and to quarrel about notions of justice in those who have never seen justice itself?"

"Not surprising at all," said he.

"But any man of sense," I said, "would remember that the eyes are doubly confused from two different causes, both in passing from light to darkness and from darkness to light; and believing that the same things happen with regard to the soul also, whenever he sees a soul confused and unable to discern anything he would not just laugh carelessly; he would examine whether it had come out of a more brilliant life, and if it were darkened by the strangeness; or whether it had come out of greater ignorance into a more brilliant light, and if it were dazzled with the brighter illumination. Then only would he congratulate the one soul upon its happy experience and way of life, and pity the other; but if he must laugh, his laugh would be a less downright laugh than his laughter at the soul which came out of the light above."

"That is fairly put," said he.

"Then if this is true," I said, "our belief about these matters must be this, that the nature of education is not really such as some of its professors say it is; as you know, they say that there is not understanding in the soul, but they put it in, as if they were putting sight into blind eyes."

"They do say so," said he.

"But our reasoning indicates," I said, "that this power is already in the soul of each, and is the instrument by which each learns; thus if the eye could not see without being turned with the whole body from the dark towards the light, so this instrument must be turned round with the whole soul away from the world of becoming until it is able to endure the sight of being and the most brilliant light of being: and this we say is the good, don't we?"

"Yes."

"Then this instrument," said I, "must have its own art, for the circumturning or conversion, to show how the turn can be most easily and successfully made; not an art of putting sight into an eye, which we say has it already, but since the instrument has not been turned aright and does not look where it ought to look—that's what must be managed."

"So it seems," he said.

"Now most of the virtues which are said to belong to the soul are really something near to those of the body; for in fact they are not already there, but they are put later into it by habits and practices; but the virtue of understanding everything really belongs to something certainly more divine, as it seems, for it never loses its power, but becomes useful and helpful or, again, useless and harmful, by the direction in which it is turned. Have you not noticed men who are called worthless but clever, and how keen and sharp is the sight of their petty soul, and how it sees through the things towards which it is turned? Its sight is clear enough, but it is compelled to be the servant of vice, so that the clearer it sees the more evil it does."

"Certainly," said he.

"Yet if this part of such a nature," said I, "had been hammered at from childhood, and all those leaden weights of the world of becoming knocked off—the weights, I mean, which grow into the soul from gorging and gluttony and such pleasures, and twist the soul's eye downwards—if, I say, it had shaken these off and been turned round towards what is real and true, that same instrument of those same men would have seen those higher things most clearly, just as now it sees those towards which it is turned."

"Quite likely," said he.

"Very well," said I, "isn't it equally likely, indeed, necessary, after what has been said, that men uneducated and without experience of truth could never properly supervise a city, nor can those who are allowed to spend all their lives in education right to the end? The first have no single object in life, which they must always aim at in doing everything they do, public or private; the second will never do anything if they can help it, believing they have already found mansions abroad in the Islands of the Blest."[8]

"True," said he.

"Then it is the task of us founders," I said, "to compel the best natures to attain that learning which we said was the greatest, both to see the good, and to ascend that ascent; and when they have ascended and properly seen, we must never allow them, what is allowed now."

"What is that, pray?" he asked.

"To stay there," I said, "and not be willing to descend again to those prisoners, and to share their troubles and their honours, whether they are worth having or not."

"What!" said he, "are we to wrong them and make them live badly, when they might live better?"

"You have forgotten again, my friend," said I, "that the law is not concerned how any one class in a city is to prosper above the rest; it tries to contrive prosperity in the city as a whole, fitting the citizens into a pattern by persuasion and compulsion, making them give of their help to one another wherever each class is able to help the community. The law itself creates men like this in the city, not in order to allow each one to turn by any way he likes, but in order to use them itself to the full for binding the city together."

"True," said he, "I did forget."

"Notice then, Glaucon," I said, "we shall not wrong the philosophers who grow up among us, but we shall treat them fairly when we compel them to add to their duties the care and guardianship of the other people. We shall tell them that those who grow up philosophers in other cities have reason in taking no part in public labours there; for they grow up there of themselves, though none of the city governments wants them; a wild growth has its rights, it owes nurture to no one, and need not trouble to pay anyone for its food. But you we have engendered, like king bees[9] in hives, as leaders and kings over yourselves and the rest of the city; you have been better and more perfectly educated than the others, and are better able to share in both ways of life. Down you must go then, in turn, to the habitation of the others, and accustom yourselves to their darkness; for

---

[8]Cf. *Banquet*, p. 77, n. 3.

[9]Both the Greeks and Romans spoke always of "king," not "queen," of a hive.

when you have grown accustomed you will see a thousand times better than those who live there, and you will know what the images are and what they are images of, because you have seen the realities behind just and beautiful and good things. And so our city will be managed wide awake for us and for you, not in a dream, as most are now, by people fighting together for shadows, and quarrelling to be rulers, as if that were a great good. But the truth is more or less that the city where those who are to rule are least anxious to be rulers is of necessity best managed and has least faction in it; while the city which gets rulers who want it most is worst managed."

"Certainly," said he.

"Then will our fosterlings disobey us when they hear this? Will they refuse to help, each group in its turn, in the labours of the city, and want to spend most of their time dwelling in the pure air?"

"Impossible," said he, "for we shall only be laying just commands on just men. No, but undoubtedly each man of them will go to the ruler's place as to a grim necessity, exactly the opposite of those who now rule in cities."

"For the truth is, my friend," I said, "that only if you can find for your future rulers a way of life better than ruling, is it possible for you to have a well-managed city; since in that city alone those will rule who are truly rich, not rich in gold, but in that which is necessary for a happy man, the riches of a good and wise life: but if beggared and hungry, for want of goods of their own, they hasten to public affairs, thinking that they must snatch goods for themselves from there, it is not possible. Then rule becomes a thing to be fought for; and a war of such a kind, being between citizens and within them, destroys both them and the rest of the city also."

"Most true," said he.

"Well, then," said I, "have you any other life despising political office except the life of true philosophy?"

"No, by heaven," said he.

"But again," said I, "they must not go awooing office like so many lovers! If they do, their rival lovers will fight them."

"Of course they will!"

"Then what persons will you compel to accept guardianship of the city other than those who are wisest in the things which enable a city to be best managed, who also have honours of another kind and a life better than the political life?"

"No others," he answered. . . .

Questions for Discussion and Debate

1. Summarize in your own words the "Allegory of the Cave." (See the introduction to the excerpt for assistance.)

2. Try to visualize the cave after reading the excerpt several times. Then sketch the cave and the scene that Socrates describes within and outside of it. Compare your conception with those of others in the class. Discuss the meaning of each of Plato's and Socrates's symbols. Quote from the allegory to back up your interpretations. (Remember that while Plato is the writer of the dialogues, he is recording the ideas of his teacher, Socrates.)

3. According to Plato, what is the connection between education and politics or government? Refer to the allegory in explaining the connection.

4. Do you agree that in some ways we are all prisoners? If so, what must we do to escape our "caves," according to Plato?

5. Do you agree with Plato's notion that only a limited number of people are capable of achieving higher education and greater intellect? Why, or why not?

6. Debate Plato's idea that only the highly educated and highly intelligent philosopher-kings should be allowed to govern. Do you agree with him? Why, or why not?

Activities and Projects

1. Invite a philosophy professor to explain his or her interpretation of the allegory and, in a seminar, discuss the allegory from the various frames of reference of the class.

2. Create an allegory or symbolic story in which you convey *your* ideas about (a) the meaning and purpose of education and (b) the relationship between education and politics or government. (The ancient Greeks also believed in a relationship between education and leisure. They conceived of schooling [*scholē*] as "leisure and discussion." Wrote the scholar Edith Hamilton in *The Greek Way*, 1930: "Reasoned the Greek, given leisure, a man will employ it in thinking and finding out about things. Leisure and the pursuit of knowledge, the connection was inevitable to a Greek." Your story might deal with *your* conception of *leisure*.)

3. Look at the leaders that now govern the country. Do they appear to be "philosopher-kings"? Men and women of ideas? Are they in any way carrying out the role Plato prescribes for those who govern in a society? Record your responses to these questions.

4. Some of the interpretations and analyses of Plato's allegory are more daunting and obscure than the allegory itself. What makes this excerpt so special is the beauty and accessibility of his language. Nevertheless, (a) seek out some of the interpretations of the "Allegory of the Cave" to discover the depths of its symbolism, and (b) read a portion of the allegory *aloud* to see if its meaning is enhanced.

5. In the poem, "The Blind Men and the Elephant," by John Godfrey Saxe (1936) there are six blind men, each of whom touches only one part of an elephant and believes he knows what an elephant is. For example, the blind man who touches the elephant's tail believes that the elephant is much like a rope! The poem ends with the lines, "So oft in theologic wars/The disputants, I ween/Rail on in utter ignorance/Of what each other mean/And prate about an elephant/Not one of them has seen!"

   Compare and contrast the idea in this poem to the ideas contained in Plato's "Allegory of the Cave." How can both the poem and the allegory be of service in "educational wars," which are ongoing?

3.11 "What Kind of Education Is Adequate? It Depends"(2001)

Randal C. Archibold

The question expressed in the title of this excerpt, "What Kind of Education Is Adequate?" is at the very heart of discussions centering around educational philosophy. Just such a discussion took place in January 2001, soon after Justice of the State Supreme Court in Manhattan, Leland De Grasse, ruled that New York State's formula for public-school financing was unconstitutional and deprived students in New York City of the constitutional right to an adequate education. The participants in the discussion offered different answers to the question but agreed with the judge's conclusion that, if one used as the criterion of an adequate education a citizen's ability to vote and serve on a jury, then too few students were being equipped with *that* kind of basic education.

The judge agreed with the plaintiff, The Campaign for Fiscal Equity, on the usefulness of the jury service criterion. He noted, ". . . Jurors may be called on to decide complex matters that require the verbal, reasoning, math, science and socialization skills that should be imparted in public schools. Jurors today must [also] determine questions of fact concerning DNA evidence, statistical analyses and convoluted financial fraud, to name only three topics" (Archibold, 2001, p. 26). Justice De Grasse's ruling in the school financing case may not be the final word, as New York State must decide whether to appeal, and the state legislature will examine other financing models. And there is no question that the debate over what constitutes an adequate education will continue as well.

Before reading this cross section of opinions about what constitutes an "adequate education," refer back to the beginning of this chapter and the chart on philosophy that you completed (under Selections). Then write down your view on what kind of education is adequate. Whose ideas quoted in this excerpt are in line with yours? Which comments influence your thinking?

Are you the product of a sound, basic education?

In the eyes of the president of Bard College, Leon Botstein, "a good education teaches you how to ask a question."

"It's knowing what you don't know," Dr. Botstein said, "the skills of critical thought."

The president of the New York Public Library, Paul LeClerc, has a somewhat different take. "Ideally, one should know who Shakespeare was and why Shakespeare was important to us," Mr. LeClerc said, "At the same time, one should know who Toni Morrison is and why her voice and take on America is important to us."

And what might enable you to pass muster with Michael Goldstein, the founder of a charter school in Boston?

"Write and e-mail a persuasive, three-paragraph letter to the editor about voting improprieties in your local district; research online and analyze the statistical differences between Pat Buchanan's vote totals during the '96 and '00 elections; read and comprehend the 'No Cell Phone' sign at restaurants."

Of course, there is no one meter to measure whether you have received a sound, basic education, as required by the constitutions of New York and many other states.

But there is a general view that besides practical skills like making change or reading a map, such an education should include critical reasoning and the ability to form judgments and opinions independently and, as Robert Silvers, an editor of The New York Review of Books, said, "to acquire some intellectual curiosity about learning more and exploring the possibilities of science and the understanding you get from literature and the arts."

For all the differing views of what a sound, basic education comprises, there is also seemingly overwhelming agreement that many people are not getting one. . . .

As information and its sources grow more complex, the ability to evaluate information becomes ever more important, said Dr. Botstein, of Bard. "Computers can create the appearance of a good statistical argument when it is not an argument at all," he said. "The capacity to analyze argument is ever more important. Knowing how to distinguish good information from bad information."

And those whose job is to teach such skills say the challenge is more than daunting. "This is a generation that watches a sitcom and gets a problem solved in 20 minutes," said Phyllis C. Williams, the principal of Eleanor Roosevelt Intermediate School in Washington Heights, Manhattan. She said she hoped that the future good citizens at her school would graduate with respect for others and for themselves.

She said that one way in which she steers her students toward that goal is by arranging for them to volunteer at nursing homes and day care centers and by attracting business professionals and artists to visit the school.

"The child has to feel they can achieve," she said.

Likewise Mr. Goldstein, who is the executive director of the Media and Technology Charter High School in Boston, also known as Match, suggested that graduating with a diploma should not be the final measure of a student's success at that age.

"The statistic is that two-thirds of kids who start college don't finish—even fewer from the inner city," Mr. Goldstein said. "So in the long run, the Match School defines by outcome: an educated high school grad must read, compute, persevere, organize and problem-solve well enough not just to attend college, but to graduate from college."

An education professor at the University of Illinois at Chicago, Gerald Graff, said . . . the larger debate over what constitutes a sound education stemmed from the movement to raise school standards, and the inevitable back-and-forth over whether they are too high or too low.

A combination of basic factual knowledge along with some ability to think critically is emerging as a compromise of sorts among traditional educators and those who want to experiment with new ideas.

"We still have a long way to go to get across to people in the schools and citizens that the kinds of testing we are doing and the standards we are applying emphasize the ability to think and argue rather than cramming minds with a lot of facts," Dr. Graff said.

The Rev. Joseph Parkes, a Jesuit priest who is the president of Fordham Preparatory School in the Bronx, holds up the study of the classics as a route to a sound and relevant education.

"The whole point of a liberal education is freedom," Father Parkes said. "People say, 'Why do students at Fordham Prep study Latin and Greek? It's useless.' And I say it frees the mind and the heart. Jesuits still emphasize the classics, language, expression."

In the end, he said, graduates should go forth with "confidence, compassion and commitment so they can compete in a lot of areas. We want them committed to country, faith and family first, and committed to the world."

Those nurtured on books push them as tools critical to a basic education.

"When I was young, I was one of those people who read everything from 'Huck Finn' to 'The Red and the Black,' to novels like Sinclair Lewis's 'Arrowsmith' and Sherlock Holmes," said Mr. Silvers of The New York Review of Books. "I feel that an enormous part of growing up is to have the appetite for omnivorous reading, trying one book after another."

The goal, Mr. LeClerc of the New York Public Library agreed, should be to instill "a love of lifelong learning."

"The single greatest contribution an educator can make is turning her or him onto more education, more learning," he said. "The first 16 or 20 years is a prelude. We don't stay in the same job all our lives, or the same careers. So you have to have an ability to adapt to rapidly evolving change. . . ."

Questions for Discussion and Debate

1. List all of the *speakers* in the article, their affiliation, and their point of view. Decide whose opinions you most agree with and place an "A" next to their names, then decide whose views you least agree with and place a "D" next to their names. Bring your list to class and compare and contrast your responses with those of your peers. Support your opinions by referring to some of the other readings in this chapter or, if appropriate, in other chapters. Referring to the list of philosophies at the beginning of the chapter (under Brief Background), label each of the speakers.

2. What is *your* answer to the question, "What Kind of Education Is Adequate?"

3. Have *you* received an adequate education based on the jury service criterion specified in the introduction to this excerpt? Evaluate yourself. What part(s) of the criterion could you satisfy? Discuss the results of your self-evaluation with the class.

Activities and Projects

1. Interview a cross section of faculty from different grade levels and ask them the question, "What Kind of Education Is Adequate?" Collate their answers and determine on what points they agree. (Consider videotaping your interviews—make them brief—and then show the "program" to your peers. Use the program as a springboard for further discussion of the question.)

2. As a result of the challenge in the courts by the New York City schools, New York State

was required to come up with a more equitable means of funding education. Do some research to find out what has happened with this case since Judge De Grasse's decision in January 2001. Try to find out about existing models of equitable funding for education.

3. This article about a conversation that took place among contemporary educators can become the basis for a simulation in which either of the following two scenarios is developed.

   a. Students in the class take the roles of the educators in the article and hold a forum on the question, "What Kind of Education Is Adequate?" The "players" should go beyond the quotes provided and ad lib appropriately.

   b. Students in the class take on the roles of the philosophers whose names are associated with the philosophies and theories listed at the beginning of the chapter (see Brief Background). Each participant should do research on his or her role or philosopher so as to contribute to the discussion of the question appropriately.

4. Create a graphic organizer in which you place the variables and criteria of a sound, basic education for all students. Elaborate wherever you can without losing the simplicity and power of your design and message.

3.12 *Iron and Silk* (1986)

Mark Salzman

Mark Salzman graduated from Yale in 1982 with a degree in Chinese language and literature. After graduating he moved to China for 2 years, where he studied martial arts and taught English at Hunan Medical College. The book *Iron and Silk* is an extraordinary collection of anecdotes and episodes based on those 2 years; one of these episodes is recounted here. In 1989, Salzman completed the filming of a movie based on the book, in which he plays the lead role, performing some amazingly difficult Chinese martial arts maneuvers.

In this excerpt, Salzman writes about how cultural differences—and perhaps political differences as well—can account for different attitudes about education. (China has been a totalitarian Communist country since 1949, though today one can observe some concessions to capitalism and Western ways.) While the philosophical belief that for instruction to be effective there must be mutual respect between the learner and the teacher may transcend cultures, the way in which that respect is practiced may differ from culture to culture, as exemplified here by Salzman's use of humor.

Note also some of the creative teaching methods Salzman employs to get his students to practice their English, methods quite different from those to which the students are accustomed. As you read about Salzman's cross-cultural experience, try to imagine yourself in a similar situation.

Most of my teaching hours the second year were spent with a group known as the 1983 English Medical Class. This group of first-year medical students, ranging in age from seventeen to twenty, were chosen from among hundreds of talented freshmen for their superior performance on a series of English tests. They were to spend their entire first year studying English, then the remainder of their medical education was to be taught in English by doctors and teachers in our college who could speak it. Although medical schools all over China were offering rudimentary English classes to their students, our college was one of the few to set up a comprehensive English-language medical course. Controversy surrounded this program; on the one hand, the current "Open Door" policy promoted learning from the West, but on the other hand, conducting science classes in English implied that China could not really modernize on its own, with only cosmetic assistance from Western technology. Furthermore, most members of the faculty and administration of our college with the foresight to support this program had had that foresight before official policy supported it, and had been criticized or punished for it. Understandably, the program created all sorts of pressures for those involved with it.

These pressures inevitably fell on the shoulders of the thirty students of each English Medical Class—my group was the third. For days before their classes actually began, they had to endure marathon lectures by political cadres who warned them that ". . . the college, the Party, and the whole country" depended on them to succeed. Success in this case meant that they were to become fluent in English, get higher marks in their regular medical exams than other students to prove that they were not slacking off, excel in their political study to show that they did not lose sight of the Socialist Spirit, and above all, display model personal behavior at all times to show that their contact with Westerners had not "corrupted" them.

The first time I saw them I had to sit in front of the class while one of the Chinese teachers gave them a long speech about behaving well, entitled "The Twelve Be's, the Twelve Don't Be's, the Eight Do's and the Eight Don't Do's." After forty-five minutes of this he at last introduced Jan, my co-teacher for the year, and me. Jan and I stood up and said hello, but there was no response. We faced a mass of trembling paralysis.

Miraculously, though, some of them loosened up after a few weeks. Once they got over the shock and fear of being called on individually rather that reciting together as a group, classes became more interesting. Personalities began to emerge and some of the students even dared to experiment with imagination and humor. Naturally, this led to trouble. One day Teacher Wu brought Terry Lautz, the Yale-China Field Staff Director visiting that week from Hong Kong, to observe our class. The students became nervous right away, so I called on the most confident boy, whom I had given the English name Lenny, hoping that he would get things going. True to form, when I asked him what he would like to do today, he stood up, smiled and answered, "Today I would like to eat your heart and drink your blood." Everyone got excited after that, and we ended up having an energetic lesson. When the bell rang, I walked over to Teacher Wu and Terry and asked, "Aren't they a good group?" Terry, who well understood how dreary English classes in China can be, said he'd had a delightful time and complimented Teacher Wu on the quality of the students' English. Teacher Wu, looking distinctly pale, said "Mm," and called me into her office.

"What did that boy say?" she asked, horrified. "You mean Lenny? Oh, he said he wanted to eat my heart and drink my blood! Isn't he something?" Her face turned dark. "That's what I thought he said. He must be punished severely! The Field Staff Director must be furious! Think of the report he will give to your Leaders! What a horrible thing to say! You can't speak like that to a teacher! And the other students laughed! They must all be severely criticized!" I tried to convince Teacher Wu that Lenny's comment and the other students' laughter did not reflect disrespect at all, but demonstrated how perceptive they all were. "And how do you figure that?" she asked. "Because, Teacher Wu, in a very short time they have noticed that American teachers have different expectations from Chinese teachers. We like some humor and laughter in our classes, and we enjoy it if the students can occasionally joke with the teacher. The students have never insulted us. If they spoke that way to their Chinese teachers, perhaps you might criticize them, but I don't think they do. How can you criticize them for acting the way Jan and I encourage them to?" "Mm. This is terrible. If they ever spoke like that to a Chinese teacher, can you imagine what would happen to all of us? They must be criticized—this is China, and they are Chinese students." Classes were noticeably quieter for a few days after that, but in time the incident blew over and laughter returned to our classroom.

One of the greatest challenges of teaching English in China was breaking students of

their compulsion to learn everything by rote and getting them to learn English by using it, instead. My favorite method was to divide them into small groups, each of which had to prepare or improvise short skits based on a given situation. At first this went very slowly. "Julian, you are a policeman. Sinbad, you are a criminal and Julian has just caught you. Have a conversation on the way to the police station." Silence. "Come on, don't be nervous. You can think of something—Julian, you start."

JULIAN: "You are a criminal."

SINBAD: "I'm sorry."

Silence. "Sinbad, why don't you try to bribe Julian?"

SINBAD: "Do you want some money?"

JULIAN: "No, thank you."

With practice, however, they became quite good at this. One assignment was to interview a Martian who had just landed on Earth and to ask him about his first impressions and so on. A pair of boys had the Martian flee to Earth to seek political asylum. He was a Communist and had been condemned to death by the ruling Fascist Bourgeois Oppressors on Mars. He hoped that the Earthlings would help him by setting him up with a human girl—if he got married he would be safe, for on Mars, he explained, there is a strict law against making widows.

Another assignment was to come up with a convincing advertisement for a product, then perform it as a television commercial. Three girls walked to the front of the classroom, all with their heads hung low. One said "I'm unhappy. I'm very fat." The second shook her head and said, "I'm unhappy, too. I'm too skinny." The third blushed, giggled, faced the blackboard and said, "I'm unhappy, too. I can't find a husband." Suddenly Juliet—she had chosen her English name after hearing my Romeo and Juliet lecture—marched to the front of the classroom with a basket filled with rolled up pieces of paper. (The students, of course, all knew that in China it is customary at weddings for the bride and groom to distribute "Happiness Candy"— any candy, preferably with the character known as "Double Happiness" printed on the wrapping—to all of their relatives and friends.) Adopting a television announcer's huge smile and enthusiastic voice, she said, "Ladies and Gentlemen! I am pleased to tell you about a wonderful thing! It is called Juliet's Happiness Candy, and it is the most wonderful thing in the world! You must have it—you must buy it today. Let me tell you about it, please. This candy makes wishes come true. If you are too fat and you eat it, you will become skinny. If you are too skinny and you eat it, you will become fat. If you are lonely, it will help you get married. Truly it solves all of your problems. Guaranteed—no sad, no cry." The three sad-looking girls ran to the desk and asked if Juliet's Happiness Candy could solve their problems. "Of course it can," Juliet assured them, "but you must buy it first."

Questions for Discussion and Debate

1. What is your view of the role of humor in the classroom?

    What did Lenny say to Mark at the beginning of class? And what were two philosophical perspectives regarding Lenny's remark (Mark's and Teacher Wu's)?

2. The two traditional Chinese teaching methods that Mark rejects are rote-learning and group response. Explain these two methods and then cite the methods that Mark employs instead. Debate the pros and cons of the two traditional methods. Can they ever be effective pedagogical approaches?

3. Discuss the possible rewards as well as difficulties that might accompany teaching in a country quite different historically and culturally from your own. Do the rewards outweigh the difficulties, or the other way around?

Activities and Projects

1. Watch *Iron and Silk,* the film, likely available at a video store. What do you think about Salzman, his talents and his experiences?

2. Imagine yourself to be a teacher in another country. Write a story in which you find yourself teaching in a place culturally different from your home. In fact, you may find yourself in just that situation in *your own* country since the United States, being a mosaic, is made up of many neighborhoods and regions where immigrants or members of different racial, ethnic, or religious groups live and maintain practices and attitudes quite different from those of the mainstream. So set your story either in such a location or in a different country. Share your story with others. (You might refer to the episodes and anecdotes that Salzman included in his excerpt to help you get started.)

3. Find someone who has taught in another country, perhaps as a member of the Peace Corps, and interview him or her about the

experience, particularly about the philosophical differences, if any, among the native teachers and students.

4. Research all of the possible opportunities that exist for teaching abroad. Share them with your peers. Also, explore organizations such as Teach for America and Americorps, that provide opportunities for teaching in the inner cities and rural areas of this country.

5. Comparative education, or the study of education in other countries compared with our system, can be rewarding for two reasons. First, you can learn about methods, policies, and philosophies that might be worth considering for use in this country. And, second, looking at our system alongside systems that differ from ours can enable you to examine ours more closely and critically than you could by studying it in isolation.

Look around your campus and community and find individuals who were educated in other countries. Ask them to participate in a panel discussion in which they will share the major differences between education in their native country and that in America. Be prepared to ask them questions.

3.13　*How Children Fail* (1976)

John Holt

In the foreword to his book, *How Children Fail,* the late education writer John Holt writes that children fail "because they are afraid, bored, and confused . . . afraid of failing . . . the many anxious adults around them . . . bored because the things they are given and told to do in school are so trivial, so dull . . . [and] confused because most of the torrent of words that pour over them in school makes little or no sense . . . and hardly ever has any relation to what they really know" (p. 16). In this book and several of his others, Holt struggles to find out why the schools are not meeting the needs and interests of so many students.

Although he bases his discussion on observations he made in a number of private schools, clearly a very small and perhaps not very representative sample of educational institutions, Holt raises some important and relevant questions for educators and parents to ponder no matter where they are educating their children. For example, in this excerpt Holt questions the philosophy of essentialism and, in so doing, forces us to grapple with that most difficult of philosophical questions—one that permeates this chapter—How do we decide what is worth knowing? Can we, in fact, tailor a curriculum to fit all of the needs and personal interests of every child? And can educators really allow every child to express himself or herself as he or she chooses without creating chaos?

The question you may ask as you read this excerpt is, Has Holt proven that his radical departure from essentialism can produce educated, proud, and self-aware children? Perhaps the answer doesn't really matter if, indeed, he has stirred up our consciousness about how to improve the curriculum. And there is no question that Holt was here to raise questions, not to offer us answers about curriculum, and that may be his greatest service to teachers. Certainly complacency is a characteristic he abhors in teachers, along with dishonesty and rigidity. As you read Holt's arguments, think about whether or not you are disturbed by the same issues that he is. Do you agree with him that "one piece of learning is as good as another" (Holt, 1976, p. 219)? How would you defend *your* position?

Behind much of what we do in school lie some ideas, that could be expressed roughly as follows: (1) Of the vast body of human knowledge, there are certain bits and pieces that can be called essential, that everyone should know; (2) the extent to which a person can be considered educated, qualified to live intelligently in today's world and be a useful member of society, depends on the amount of this essential knowledge that he carries about with him; (3) it is the duty of schools, therefore, to get as much of this essential knowledge as possible into the minds of children. Thus we find ourselves trying to poke certain facts, recipes, and ideas down the gullets of every child in school, whether the morsel interests him or not, even if it frightens him or sickens him, and even if there are other things that he is much more interested in learning.

These ideas are absurd and harmful nonsense. We will not begin to have true education or real learning in our schools until we sweep this nonsense out of the way. Schools should be a place where children learn what they most want to know, instead of what we think they ought to know. The child who wants to know something remembers it and uses it once he has it; the child who learns something to please or appease someone else forgets it when the need for pleasing or the danger of not appeasing is past. This is why children quickly forget all but a small part of what they learn in school. It is of

no use or interest to them; they do not want, or expect, or even intend to remember it. The only difference between bad and good students in this respect is that the bad students forget right away, while the good students are careful to wait until after the exam. If for no other reason, we could well afford to throw out most of what we teach in school because the children throw out almost all of it anyway.

The notion of a curriculum, an essential body of knowledge, would be absurd even if children remembered everything we "taught" them. We don't and can't agree on what knowledge is essential. The man who has trained himself in some special field of knowledge or competence thinks, naturally, that his specialty should be in the curriculum. The classical scholars want Greek and Latin taught; the historians shout for more history; the mathematicians urge more math and the scientists more science; the modern language experts want all children taught French, or Spanish, or Russian; and so on. Everyone wants to get his specialty into the act, knowing that as the demand for his special knowledge rises, so will the price that he can charge for it. Who wins this struggle and who loses depends not on the real needs of children or even of society, but on who is most skillful in public relations, who has the best educational lobbyists, who best can capitalize on events that have nothing to do with education, like the appearance of Sputnik in the night skies.

The idea of the curriculum would not be valid even if we could agree what ought to be in it. For knowledge itself changes. Much of what a child learns in school will be found, or thought, before many years, to be untrue. I studied physics at school from a fairly up-to-date text that proclaimed that the fundamental law of physics was the law of conservation of matter—matter is not created or destroyed. I had to scratch that out before I left school. In economics at college I was taught many things that were not true of our economy then, and many more that are not true now. Not for many years after I left college did I learn that the Greeks, far from being a detached and judicious people surrounded by chaste white temples, were hot-tempered, noisy, quarrelsome, and liked to cover their temples with gold leaf and bright paint; or that most of the citizens of Imperial Rome, far from living in houses in which the rooms surrounded an atrium, or central court, lived in multi-story tenements, one of which was perhaps the largest building in the ancient world. The child who really remembered everything he heard in school would live his life believing many things that were not so.

Moreover, we cannot possibly judge what knowledge will be most needed forty, or twenty, or even ten years from now. At school, I studied Latin and French. Few of the teachers who claimed then that Latin was essential would make as strong a case for it now; and the French might better have been Spanish, or better yet, Russian. Today the schools are busy teaching Russian; but perhaps they should be teaching Chinese, or Hindi, or who-knows-what? Besides physics, I studied chemistry, then perhaps the most popular of all science courses; but I would probably have done better to study biology, or ecology, if such a course had been offered (it wasn't). We always find out, too late, that we don't have the experts we need, that in the past we studied the wrong things; but this is bound to remain so. Since we can't know what knowledge will be most needed in the future, it is senseless to try to teach it in advance. Instead, we should try to turn out people who love learning so much and learn so well that they will be able to learn whatever needs to be learned.

How can we say, in any case, that one piece of knowledge is more important than another, or indeed, what we really say, that some knowledge is essential and the rest, as far as school is concerned, worthless? A child who wants to learn something that the school can't and doesn't want to teach him will be told not to waste his time. But how can we say that what he wants to know is less important than what we want him to know? We must ask how much of the sum of human knowledge anyone can know at the end of his schooling. Perhaps a millionth. Are we then to believe that one of these millionths is so much more important than another? Or that our social and national problems will be solved if we can just figure out a way to turn children out of schools knowing two millionths of the total, instead of one? Our problems don't arise from the fact that we lack experts enough to tell us what needs to be done, but out of the fact that we do not and will not do what we know needs to be done now.

Learning is not everything, and certainly one piece of learning is as good as another. One of my brightest and boldest fifth graders was deeply interested in snakes. He knew more about snakes than anyone I've ever known. The school did not offer herpetology; snakes were not in the curriculum; but as far as I was concerned, any time he spent learning about snakes was better spent than in ways I could think of to spend it; not least of all because, in the process of learning about snakes, he learned a great deal more about many other things than I was able to "teach" those unfortunates in my class who were not interested in anything at all. In another fifth-grade class, studying Romans in Britain, I saw a boy trying to read a science book behind the cover of his desk. He was spotted, and made to put the book away, and listen to the teacher; with a heavy sigh he did so. What was gained here? She traded a chance for an hour's real learning about science for, at best, an hour's temporary learning about history—much more probably no learning at all, just an hour's worth of daydreaming and resentful thoughts about school.

Questions for Discussion and Debate

1. Debate these controversial questions with your peers: Should children in school learn only that which *they* choose to learn? That is, should school be "a great smörgåsbord of intellectual, artistic, creative, and athletic activities from which each child could take whatever he wanted, and as much as he wanted, or as little" (Holt, 1976, p. 222)? (There are, incidentally, some private schools where the only curriculum is that created from the declared interests of the students. One example of a school with this radical student-centered philosophy is Sudbury Valley School in Framingham, Massachusetts.) Or are there certain essential knowledge, attitudes, and skills that *all* children should possess? Is "one piece of learning as good as another"?

2. Locate your favorite and your least favorite sentences in this excerpt. Explain your selections.

3. Debate this question related to the source of Holt's data: Do Holt's perceptions and attacks on schools have value for us even though most of his observations were made in private schools?

4. Which philosophy or theory listed in the Brief Background to this chapter most closely resembles Holt's views?

Activities and Projects

1. Locate other works by John Holt and see what valuable insights you can gather from them. Share your findings with the class.

2. Hold a mock debate in which someone becomes Holt and goes up against, say, E. D. Hirsch, Jr. (Selection 4.8), author of, among other books, *Cultural Literacy* (1987). Hirsch became known for defining a core curriculum, that is, the essential knowledge that *all* educated students should possess. He doesn't believe that it is possible or even desirable to shape a curriculum to the individual needs and interests of each student. Rather, he thinks that the curriculum should be shaped by the assessment of what knowledge is reflective of Western civilization and tradition. Both roles, Holt and Hirsch, should be played with conviction!

3. Read the book from which this excerpt is taken. Then write a critique of Holt for an educational journal. Interview teachers and students regarding his beliefs; read others' critiques of his work.

4. Holt would likely argue that, to satisfy the needs and interests of their students, teachers should involve themselves in professional development activities, that is, continue their

own education in the area of curricular content and methods. Explore the professional development activities available to teachers in your area. What courses are offered at local colleges, or what professional conferences and in-service workshops are available? Talk with teachers about the activities they have engaged in and the usefulness of these educational activities in terms of their teaching. What kinds of professional development do they find to be of most value?

3.14 "What Did You Learn in School Today?" (1962)

Tom Paxton

Tom Paxton, folk songwriter and singer, has used his talents not only to entertain children and adults but to satirize some key people and policies in America during the latter part of the 20th century. Many of his songs are humorous but also sharply critical, and some could be labeled protest songs.

"What Did You Learn in School Today?" might be considered a protest against certain kinds of teachers and the way in which they approach curriculum. This song raises many philosophical questions about curriculum, including: To what extent should teachers be totally honest about certain topics such as our nation's past and present? At what age is it appropriate to tell children historical truths? To what extent should a teacher share his or her own personal views and values regarding American history and policy? To what extent, if any, should a teacher be allowed to criticize the government and other authorities? Is holding back certain information from students a form of lying? All of these hefty questions are raised by Paxton's little song. What other philosophical questions does the song suggest to you? Add these questions to the list.

What did you learn in school today
Dear little child of mine? (repeat)
    I learned that Washington never told a lie
    I learned that soldiers seldom die
    I learned that everybody's free
    And that's what the teacher said to me
That's what I learned in school today
That's what I learned in school

What . . . ? / I learned that policeman are my friends
I learned that justice never ends
I learned that murderers die for their crimes
Even if we make a mistake sometimes / **That's . . .**

. . . I learned our government must be strong
It's always right & never wrong
Our leaders are the finest men
And we elect them again & again . . .

. . . I learned that war is not so bad
I learned about the great ones we have had
We fought in Germany & in France
And someday I might get my chance . . .

Questions for Discussion and Debate

1. What is the implied philosophical perspective of the teacher in this song who taught the child that "Washington never told a lie"? To what extent do you identify with or agree with this teacher? (In your discussion try to address *all* of the questions presented in the introduction to the song.)

2. What other philosophical questions does this song raise about curriculum content and method?

3. Paxton would likely be a fan of John Holt. Debate the validity of the following quote from Holt's (1976) book, *How Children Fail*; "School tends to be a dishonest as well as a nervous place. We adults are not often honest with children, least of all in school. We tell them, not what we think, but what we feel they ought to think" (p. 211).

4. Discuss with your peers the nature of the historical education *you* received. Did your teachers teach you the truth, that is, give you the chance to learn both sides of an issue? Explain.

5. Debate this statement: Teachers should never share with students their own values about particular controversial issues, for example, the merits or rightness of a particular war.

Activities and Projects

1. Collect a number of history books at the elementary-, middle-, and high-school levels. Choose a particular topic, say, the Civil War or slavery, and read the chapters on this subject in a cross section of texts. Note how coverage differs or is the same. Note which texts seem to reveal a full picture of the issue or a less-than-full perspective. Then make some generalizations regarding the value of these texts in giving students a more complete perspective of the past. Decide as a result of your research whether you agree with John Holt's (1976) statement that "even in the most noncontroversial areas, our teaching, the books, and the textbooks we give children present a dishonest and

distorted picture of the world" (p. 211). Share your research with the class and discuss ways to deal with this problem, if, indeed, it is a problem.

2. Are there any current songs or songwriters that, like this one, protest the way in which schools and teachers operate? If so, bring them to the attention of your peers and, together, analyze them and discuss their accuracy.

3. Write another verse to the song in which you include subject matter about which you believe you were misled or misinformed. Or add a verse in which you criticize Paxton's

thesis that students are not addressed honestly by their teachers.

4. Interview a number of teachers about the questions this song addresses, that is, Should teachers present all sides of an issue, including their own, in class, no matter what the issue? and Should their answers be the same for children of all ages? See the other questions in the introduction to the song and include them in your interviews as well. Share the responses you gather.

Chapter References

Adler, M. J. (1982). *The paideia proposal.* New York: Macmillan.

Archibold, R. C. (2001, January 14). What kind of education is adequate? It depends. *The New York Times,* pp. 25–26.

Bruner, J. (1975). *Toward a theory of instruction.* Cambridge, MA: Harvard University Press.

Calderon, J. (1997). A Break of Consciousness. In *Diversity works leader's guide.* http://www.inform.umd.edu/diversityweb.

Dworkin, M. S. (Ed.). (1959). *Dewey on education: Selections.* Classics in Education series, No. 3. New York: Bureau of Publications, Columbia University.

Farris, P. J. (1996). *Teaching, bearing the torch.* Dubuque, IA: Brown and Benchmark.

Fisher, D. C. (1914). *A Montessori mother.* New York: Henry Holt.

Gursky, D. (1991, October). Madeline! (Madeline Hunter). *Teacher Magazine,* 30.

Hamilton, E. (1930). *The Greek way.* New York: New American Library.

Hardin, G. (1977). *Exploring new ethics for survival, the voyage of the spaceship Beagle.* New York: Penguin.

Hennessey, M. H., & Knutson, A. (1999). *Norman Rockwell: Pictures for the American people.* New York: Harry N. Abrams.

Hirsch, E. D., Jr. (1987). *Cultural literacy.* Boston: Houghton Mifflin.

Holt, J. (1976). *How children fail.* New York: Dell.

Marler, C. P. (1975). *Philosophy and schooling.* Boston: Allyn & Bacon.

Montessori, M. (1967). *The discovery of the child.* (M. J. Costelloe, Trans.). Notre Dame, IN: Fides.

New, R. (1991). Early childhood teacher education in Italy: Reggio Emilio's master plan for master teachers. *Journal of Early Childhood Teacher Education, 12,* 3.

Ozman, H., & Craver, S. (1999). *Philosophical foundations of education* (6th ed.). Upper Saddle River, NJ: Merrill/Prentice Hall.

Paxton, T. (1992). What did you learn in school today? In P. Blood & A. Patterson (Eds.), *Rise up singing. The group-singing song book* (p. 6). Bethlehem, PA: Sing Out.

Peddiwell, J. A. [pseudonym]. (1939). *Sabertooth curriculum.* New York: McGraw–Hill.

Posner, G. J. (1992). *Analyzing the curriculum.* New York: McGraw–Hill.

Pulliam, J. D., & Van Patten, J. (1995). *History of education in America.* Upper Saddle River, NJ: Prentice Hall.

Ravitch, D. (2000). *Left back. A century of failed school reforms.* New York: Simon & Schuster.

Reagan, T. (1996). *Non-Western educational traditions.* Mahwah, NJ: Lawrence Erlbaum.

Rockefeller, S. C. (1991). *John Dewey, religious faith and democratic humanism.* New York: Columbia University Press.

Rumi, J. (1993). *Birdsong, fifty-three short poems* (C. Barks, Trans.). Athens, GA: MAYPOP.

Salzman, M. (1990). *Iron and silk.* New York: Vintage.

Saxe, J. G. (1936). The blind men and the elephant. In *The best loved poems of the American people, selected by Hazel Felleman.* (pp. 521–522). New York: Garden City Books.

Schemo, D. J. (2002, February 9). California leads chorus of sounded-out syllables. *The New York Times.*

Schools, dazed. (2001). *The Wilson Quarterly,* Winter, 9.

Steiner, R. (1996). *Rudolf Steiner in the Waldorf School. Lectures and addresses to children, parents and teachers.* Hudson, NY: Anthroposophic Press.

Weiner, L. (Trans.). (1967). *Tolstoy on education.* Chicago: University of Chicago Press.

Whitehead, A. N. (1949). *The aims of education.* New York: New American Library.

Whitman, W. (1860). *Leaves of grass.* Boston: Thayer and Eldridge.

Wigginton, E. (1985). *Sometimes a shining moment.* New York: Doubleday.

Wraga, W. G. (2001, October). Left out: The villainization of progressive education in the United States. *Educational Researcher,* pp. 34–39.

Additional Readings

Adler, M. J. (1988). *Reforming education: The opening of the American mind.* New York: Macmillan.

Angus, D. L., & Mirel, J. E. (1999). *The failed promise of the American high school.* New York: Teachers College Press.

Apple, M. (2000). Can critical pedagogies interrupt rightist policies? *Educational Theory, 50*(2), 229–254.

Beck, C. (1974). *Educational philosophy and theory: An introduction.* Boston: Little, Brown.

Beyer, L. E., & Liston, D. P. (1996). *Curriculum in conflict. Social visions, educational agendas, and progressive school reform.* New York: Teachers College Press, Columbia University.

Corbin, H. (1993). *History of Islamic philosophy.* London: Kegan Paul International.

Dewey, J. (1899). *School and society.* Chicago: University of Chicago Press.

Dewey, J. (1909). *Moral principles in education.* Boston: Houghton Mifflin.

Dewey, J. (1916). *Democracy and education.* New York: Macmillan.

Dewey, J. (1938). *Experience and education.* New York: Macmillan.

Fosnot, C. T. (Ed.). (1996). *Constructivism, theory, perspectives, and practice.* New York: Teachers College Press, Columbia University.

Goodman, P. (1960). *Growing up absurd.* New York: Vintage Books.

Gutek, G. L. 1988. *Philosophical and ideological perspectives on education.* Needham Heights, MA: Allyn & Bacon.

Hiatt, D. B. (1994, October). No limit to the possibilities: An interview with Ralph Tyler. *Phi Delta Kappan,* 786–787.

Ikeda, D. (2001). *Soka education. A Buddhist vision for teachers, students and parents.* Santa Monica, CA: Middleway Press.

Lipman, M. (1996). *Natasha, Vygotskian dialogues.* New York: Teachers College Press, Columbia University.

Miller, R. (1990). *What are schools for? Holistic education in American culture.* Brandon, VT: Holistic Education Press.

Nakagawa, Y. (2000). *Education for awakening: An Eastern approach to holistic education.* Brandon, VT: Foundation for Educational Renewal.

Nash, R. J. (1997). *Answering the "virtuecrats." A moral conversation on character education.* New York: Teachers College Press, Columbia University.

Rambachan, A. (1992). *The Hindu vision.* Delhi: Motilal Banarsidass.

Semel, S. F., & Sadovnik, A. R. (1999). *"Schools of tomorrow, schools of today": What happened to progressive education?* New York: Peter Lang.

Snelling, J. (1987). *The Buddhist handbook: A complete guide to Buddhist teaching and practice.* London: Century.

Warmington, E. H., & Rouse, P. (Eds.). (1956). *Great dialogues of Plato* (W. H. D. Rouse, Trans.). New York: New American Library.

Wittgenstein, L. (1961). *Philosophical investigations* (D. F. Pears & B. F. McGuinness, Trans.). New York: Humanities Press.

Wolf, R. M. (1998). National standards: Do we need them? *Educational Researcher, 27*(4), 22–25.

Web Site

John Dewey:
http://www.siu.edu/-deweyctr/index2.html

Chapter 4

The Politics of Education

*School Governance, School Funding,
and Legal Issues*

If you attempt to exert your influence on educational decision-making, then you are involved in the politics of education. Essentially, the term "politics" refers to the methods and tactics used by government *or* other parties to gain power or influence.

The fiction and nonfiction selections in this chapter feature teachers and others who either tried to influence educational policy or were affected by such policies. There are literally thousands of groups and individuals whose elected or appointed status means that they have a designated role to play in governing education. For this reason, the politics of education is one of the most complex and data-filled areas of study within educational foundations. This chapter is designed to help you conceptualize some of the key issues related to school governance, as opposed to exposing you to the endless and formidable data. A study of educational politics is incomplete without a look at legal issues and the financing of education. Therefore, you will find scattered among the excerpts, their introductions, and the follow-up questions several references to these important topics. Essentially, the purpose of these readings, viewed as a whole, is to make clearer the role politics plays on a multitude of levels, from an individual teacher's classroom, to the local community, to the nation as a whole.

Some people consider politics a dirty word, perhaps because of the shady dealings of some of the people who seek power of one kind or another. And such behavior certainly occurs. Others refer to politics as a game in which the ends justify the means, that is, a game in which the teams use any methods at their disposal to win their goal. Yes, politics can be dirty, but it can also be honorable and ethical. It was, after all, politics that led to the establishment of universal public education in this country. In the end, the nature of educational politics depends on the nature of the people who hold positions of authority, whether they be school committee members, governors, or school superintendents. The degree of their ethical behavior also depends on how informed and involved the people in their constituency are, that is, the parents, students, and taxpayers. There is one thing for certain, however: The political arena is like the sports arena—a place where people take sides. And sometimes sparks fly! But while some of the "players" may come out winners and others losers, there is also the possibility that the art of compromise will resolve differences. Indeed, all around this country, on a daily basis, teachers, as master politicians, utilize that artful solution.

Brief Background

The U.S. Constitution does not mention education. Thus the Tenth Amendment, which delegates to the states those powers not delegated to the federal government by the Constitution, makes education the responsibility of the states. However, the Preamble contains a clause requiring that the U.S. government "promote the general welfare," thus implying a federal role in education. Likewise, the 14th Amendment notes that "no state shall make . . . any law which shall abridge the privileges . . . of citizens of the United States . . . nor deny to any person within its jurisdiction the equal protection of the laws." It was under this provision, in fact, that Presidents Eisenhower and Kennedy ordered the National Guard to go to Arkansas and Mississippi, respectively, to enforce the integration of schools. They saw to it that federal power prevailed when state laws were in defiance of the 1954 U.S. Supreme Court decision, *Brown* v. *The Board of Education of Topeka, Kansas*. What's more, federal legislation related to education is extensive and supercedes any state or local policies. Such legislative mandates as Public Law 94-142 (1975), related to the education of disabled students, and Title IX (Educational Amendments Act of 1972), which prohibits discrimination based on sex, are among the far-reaching examples of the role of the federal government in education. There is little doubt about the tremendous financial implications that such mandates have for the budgets of local school systems.

While the federal government clearly plays many roles in educational policymaking, local control has, historically, been preferred from colonial times to the 20th century. For the last few decades, however, the role of the state in making educational policy has increased, particularly in the area of funding schools and establishing standards that control curriculum, personnel, teacher certification, and scheduling. But the *actual* power of the state government over schools is open to question. For while the state and federal governments may, in fact, issue key legislation, the local powers, such as school boards, often have a great deal of freedom to interpret and implement that legislation. (Some school boards, for example, interpret students' free speech rights more broadly or narrowly than do other boards.) But there is no question about the fact that every level and branch of government possesses some power over school standards and policy.

In the area of school financing, all three levels of government contribute to the funding of education, with the state (47%) and local governments (47%) providing all but about 6% (National Center for Education Statistics, 1994, p. 49). There is also some input from industry, educational foundations, and, in rare cases, generous individuals.

The federal government's 6% involves funding breakfast and lunch programs, vocational education, programs for disadvantaged and exceptional youth, and literally hundreds of other programs, some of which were established as a result of the extensive body of federal legislation related to education.

Total government spending for education, inclusive of elementary, secondary, and public higher education and other needs, comes to over $480 billion annually (National Center for Education Statistics, 1994). Yet even with all three levels of government playing a vital role in governing and financing education, none of them has yet developed a policy that will ensure the fair funding of all public schools. Despite attempts by some states to subsidize systems where property taxes are low, such inequities as referred to by Kozol, Conroy, and Stuart in this chapter still continue to deprive students of materials and resources they need for a quality education. To a greater or lesser extent, all of the excerpts in this text touch on school funding issues. Try to perceive how each one is indirectly or directly connected to that all-important political component: the dollar!

All right, now you have an idea about what roles the three levels of government play in school politics. But where is the teacher in all of this? Teachers are political by the very fact that they are public servants in public institutions that depend on the taxpayer for their support. Teachers' voices can be heard on all levels, from national to local. Many speak through associations or unions that lobby or put pressure on federal, state, and local legislatures to support education and the teaching profession. Most notable among these organizations on the national level are the National Education Association (NEA) and the American Federation of Teachers (AFT). There is usually a state teachers' association, often affiliated with one of the national groups, and on the local level, teachers may express themselves through the teacher's association at their school and possibly the Parent–Teacher Association (PTA). These organizations are among the many pressure groups, or interest groups, that try to influence educational policy and governance. As a constituency, educators tend to vote for liberal politicians who support public education. Thus teachers, voting as a bloc, can wield considerable power.

In some school systems where there is movement toward site-based management, teachers are seeing their political power expand locally. Such management empowers a school's teachers and administrators to make decisions that affect their school, as opposed to acting on decisions handed down from the top (Odden and Wohlstetter, 1995, pp. 32–36).

So, like it or not, *you* are a political creature and need to know how to utilize your voice for education.

Selections

The painting in this chapter is Norman Rockwell's *The Problem We All Live With,* which portrays an African American girl, Ruby Bridges, walking to school—a school that was undergoing integration as a result of the landmark decision of the U.S. Supreme Court in 1954, *Brown* v. *The Board of Education*. The Rockwell painting reminds us that, while this country has continued to grow in the direction of equality of opportunity, we still have not reached that goal.

The excerpts will assist you in learning about the players in the arena of educational politics. They may also help you decide how to plan *your* strategies for participation. The excerpts include an editorial cartoon by Jeff Danziger in which he illustrates his concept of the forces at work when a school committee "considers an increase to the budget." Two fictional accounts, one by Jesse Stuart (*The Thread That Runs So True*), the other by Pat Conroy (*The Water Is Wide*), and a nonfictional account from Jonathan Kozol's *Death at an Early Age* are all based on the authors' real-life experiences as teachers whose livelihoods were greatly affected by political forces. There are also excerpts from a federal law involving school-to-work programs and a Supreme Court decision on affirmative action (the Bakke decision). (In chapter 1, you will find an excerpt, *What Lisa Knew* [Selection 1.4], that provides some insight into other legal issues about which teachers need to be informed.) Selections by two educators on opposite ends of the political (and philosophical) spectrum, Paulo Freire (*The Politics of Education*) and E. D. Hirsch, Jr. ("Test Evasion"), reveal just why sparks fly when political issues related to education are raised. Finally, a newspaper account outlines a young teacher's encounter with the politics of education when her "Lesson on Intolerance Fails."

Dissecting issues related to the politics of education is not a simple task, but the readings and the activities that follow will help you analyze the forces at work in educational decision-making.

As you read the selections, try to put yourself in the place of the key figures and decide if you would have acted in the same ways that they did. If you find yourself disagreeing with their behavior, what would you have done differently? And keep in mind that *you* might find yourself in similar situations once you start teaching.

4.1　Work of Art: *The Problem We All Live With* (1964)

Norman Rockwell

This powerful painting by the artist and illustrator Norman Rockwell depicts Ruby Bridges walking to a newly desegregated school where she may be the only African American student. She is accompanied by U.S. marshals, there to protect her from angry Southern Whites who are protesting integration. (See also the discussion accompanying Selection 4.5, in which the U.S. Supreme Court decision *Brown v. The Board of Education* (1954) is mentioned. After that decision ordered an end to segregation, scenes like this occurred for many years in countless schools and colleges across America.)

Following his 47 years with *The Saturday Evening Post*, Norman Rockwell began working for *Look* magazine in 1963. His illustrations then focused on the social issues of the time, such as the emergence of the Peace Corps, the Civil Rights movement, and school desegregation.

In this painting, which appeared in *Look* in 1964, Rockwell shows how one young African American child was both a symbol of the Civil Rights movement *and* a target in the struggle to overcome the discrimination that gave rise to the movement. Look closely at the clues Rockwell puts in this scene to indicate social attitudes. What is Ruby holding, and what do these things tell you about her?

"Rockwell used many artistic elements to catch your eye, including contrast, line, and rhythm" (Melinda Georgeson and staff, The Norman Rockwell Museum at Stockbridge, Massachusetts; notes accompanying exhibit, Spring 1997). Rockwell clearly wants you to notice the girl immediately, because he painted her dress, sneakers, and socks white to *contrast* with the dark brown of her skin. On the other hand, note the lack of contrast between the marshals and the wall.

He also uses *line* to draw our attention to the girl. If you follow the sidewalk cracks, they point right to her. "*Rhythms* of repeated shapes tie the painting together." The shape of a loose fist is repeated throughout the painting, and there is a rhythm in the position of the legs. What else produces rhythm?

Study this powerful painting and then consider the questions and activities that follow.

Printed by permission of the Norman Rockwell Family Trust. Copyright © 1996, the Normal Rockwell Family Trust. Photo courtesy of The Norman Rockwell Museum at Stockbridge, Massachusetts.

Questions for Discussion and Debate

1. List *everything* you see in the painting, including the shades of colors and placement of objects and people—faces, hands, legs, and graffiti. What do these details tell you about the situation of Ruby Bridges? The marshals? The unseen crowd? Why do you think Rockwell did not show the heads of the U.S. deputy marshals?

2. What is the meaning of the painting's title? What was Rockwell trying to "say"?

3. What can a painting achieve that prose or the written word cannot?

4. As you view this scene, what questions would you ask the little girl? How do you think she would answer? What questions would you ask the federal marshals? How would they answer?

====== **Activities and Projects** ======

1. Connect the words *race, politics,* and *education* in a format—artistic or other—that reveals the way(s) in which they are all related. Share your synthesis with your peers.

2. Do research on the 1960s in terms of the ways in which *artists besides* Rockwell responded to integration, civil rights, and other political and education movements of that decade. Prepare an exhibit of some of the examples you find; that is, mount prints of some of the artwork or, if possible, show slides you have prepared or borrowed.

3. Review all of the selections in this chapter and then draw or paint an illustration of one or more of them in which you convey your view or perspective on that excerpt.

4. African American freedom songs and some of the songs of Bob Dylan, Pete Seeger, and Civil Rights movement participants reflect aspects of this painting and Rockwell's implied purpose. Locate at least one of these songs and share it with your peers. Have *them* explain the connections they see between the song and Rockwell's painting.

4.2　Editorial Cartoon

Jeff Danziger

In his editorial cartoon bearing the title, "Your Local School Board Considers an Increase to the Budget," Jeff Danziger has expressed his point of view about the *nature* of the folks who choose to run for positions on their local school board. The issue the board members are addressing here is an increase to the budget, bringing to the forefront one of the most controversial areas of school politics: funding for education and how to provide revenues so that all children, no matter where in this country they live, can receive an equal education. The issue is not a new one. Horace Mann, whom you met in chapter 2, remarked on the manner in which school moneys should be apportioned among the districts. In his "Ninth Report" to the Massachusetts Board of Education (1845), he lays down the sound principle of "equality of school privileges for all the children of the town, whether they belong to a poor district or a rich one, a large district or a small one" (in Hinsdale, 1898, p. 175).

Property values are usually the primary measure of the wealth of a community, so school boards in poorer communities obviously have more difficulty providing the kind of quality education that wealthier communities can provide. In many states where there is a discrepancy in the wealth among communities, lawsuits have been brought by districts in which property taxes are low. Suggestions on how to rectify such inequities include regional tax pooling, under which "revenues are redistributed to a region's neediest jurisdictions" (Smith, 1996, p. 108). Does that suggestion make sense to you? What do you think *these* board members would say about that idea?

Danziger's cartoon is clearly a form of satire, a humorous form of criticism or protest. After studying the cartoon—both the words and the picture—try to determine what this cartoonist is criticizing and *why* you think he feels that way. Do you think this form of personal expression and protest can be effective in getting others to notice a problem and, possibly, to do something to change the situation?

YOUR LOCAL SCHOOL BOARD CONSIDERS AN INCREASE TO THE BUDGET

Henry "Hank" Grobel, owner of Grobel Hardware, thinks kids today should be trained more in retail merchandising. He favors the start of a new "hardware arts" program for students from seventh to twelfth grade. Is against any budget increase.

Arthur "Art" Windwort, CPA, elected on promise to get the district's books in order. Favors cutting sports and arts as frills. Recent quote, "You can't put music in the bank." Is against any budget increase.

Margaret "Margaret" Bloptz, former mother of three, favors a "back to basics" approach. Opposes teachers' request for new books until they account for all the old ones. Opposes teachers' request for more salary until they account for the salary they already got. Is against any budget increase.

George "Mr." Smith, former local English teacher, was elected because of his experience as an educator. However, Mr. Smith has quit teaching to open his own video store. He now opposes any increase in property taxes and therefore is against any budget increase.

Elizabeth Ann Boot, insurance agent, favors a well-insured school and a very well-insured fleet of buses, preferably insured by the Boot Insurance Agency. Otherwise she is willing to go along with the majority, which makes her against any budget increase.

Robert "Bob" Roberts favors a lot more spending for sports, the sciences, higher salaries for teachers, hot lunches, field trips, Head Start programs, a lot more spending on arts, dance and music, favors summer "fun" camp. "Bob" favors spending more on anything you name. Favors a hefty budget increase. Unfortunately, "Bob" couldn't be here tonight. He's at a strategy meeting of the "Bob" Roberts for Congress committee.

DANZIGER
The Christian Science Monitor

Questions for Discussion and Debate

1. Look up the definition of *satire* and then explain how Danziger's editorial cartoon is an example.

2. What issue is Danziger addressing here? What is his position on this issue? Do you agree with him? Why, or why not? Do you believe that Danziger's message is effectively delivered?

3. What techniques does he use to deliver his message?

4. Do you believe that most people enter politics for personal gain or for public service? This question could become the focus of a debate for your class to engage in after gathering evidence from a variety of sources, including newspapers and observation.

5. Make a chart with two columns, labeled "Typical Reasons for Voting *for* a Budget Increase" and "Typical Reasons for Voting *Against* an Increase." Refer to the cartoon and gather additional reasons on both sides.

Debate the pros and cons of budget increases in general.

6. Would you ever consider running for school committee? Why? Why not?

Activities and Projects

1. Find out when your local school committee meets and attend one or more of the meetings. What issues are they discussing? Listen to the comments of the school committee members. Do any of them remind you of Hank, Art, Margaret, George, Elizabeth, . . . or Bob? Write a brief report describing your observation of the meeting and its relationship to the cartoon. Share the report with your class.

2. Interview at least three fourths of the members of a school committee about their *reasons* for running for school committee. Show them the cartoon and record their responses to it. In a brief report, describe these interviews and responses and then share the report with the class.

3. Invite a panel of school committee members to the class and—by questioning them—try to gather the kinds of information noted in items 1 and 2. Ask other questions related to their political office.

4. The issue of funding education presents unlimited opportunities for debate and discussion. Try engaging in a debate about one or more of the following.

   a. Some of the funding sources for *local* schools are as follows.

      • Local property taxes (at present the major sources of funding for local schools)

      • Regressive taxes (taxes on items that are paid for at the time of purchase,

      including sales tax on furniture, appliances, and other items and tobacco and gasoline taxes)

      • Inheritance taxes

      • Progressive taxes (such as income tax)

      • Fees collected for items such as licenses and lotteries

      Debate the advantages and disadvantages of each of these funding sources. Which socioeconomic groups might support or oppose an increase in each one in order to support education?

   b. Respond to this question: Should the states take over *all* of the funding of local schools so as to make funding equitable and based on needs? If so, what formula should the states design? There are many possible formulas for state funding; they could fill an entire text by themselves! The decisions surrounding these funding formulas are highly political and not easily agreed upon (Kowalski, 1995).

   c. Respond to this question: Should the courts play a role in school funding decisions? Why, or why not? (The Supreme Court added its voice to the funding issue when, in a 1994 decision, it ruled that the funding of schools in the state of New Jersey using property taxes was unconstitutional. New Jersey, it said, had to provide equally to all school districts.)

d. The issue of funding schools equitably in order to provide equal education for all students was raised in the case *Serrano* v. *Priest*, 487 p. 2d 1241, in the California Supreme Court. Find out as much as you can about this case and the decision the court reached. Do you agree with its decision?

e. One of the most controversial issues related to school funding is the question of *school choice*. Parents in many states now have the right to send their children to the *public* school of their choice. However, more questionable is the voucher system advocated by many political conservatives—and some minority parents—which involves grants or vouchers of public moneys for parents who choose to send their children to private or parochial schools. The U.S. Supreme Court's landmark ruling in June 2002 upholding the Cleveland, Ohio, voucher program "reinvigorated the debate over how best to improve the education of all the nation's schoolchildren" (Walsh, 2002, p. 1). The Court decided that vouchers do not violate the U.S. Constitution's prohibition against a government establishment of religion. Do research on the voucher system and then debate the issue.

4.3   *The Water Is Wide* (1972)

Pat Conroy

Conroy is the author of several works, including *The Water Is Wide, The Prince of Tides,* and *The Great Santini,* all of which were made into films and are based on the author's own life. *The Water Is Wide* became a motion picture entitled *Conrack,* starring Jon Voight and conveying the story of a white male teacher who, to avoid going to Vietnam in the late 1960s, ends up teaching on a small island off the coast of South Carolina where several poor African American families live, whose children have been receiving a less-than-satisfactory education. Conroy, whom the children come to call Conrack, a name they find easier to pronounce, appears to be a naturally gifted teacher who demonstrates qualities many teacher education programs hold in esteem. He uses interdisciplinary approaches, humor, and entertaining forms of drill; he also connects all of the learning to the needs and interests of the students and recognizes their individuality.

However, in bringing innovation and excitement to the children on Yamacraw Island, he upsets the status quo, challenges the notions of race of both the Black and the White establishment, and, in the end, is called insubordinate and dismissed for his behavior by the forceful and prevailing school superintendent, Henry Piedmont.

In this excerpt from the book, Conroy describes his attempts to get reinstated after his dismissal and the responses of the school board to those attempts. What is your view of the strategies Conroy uses to retrieve his job? Consider what steps you would have taken if you were in Conroy's place.

I called a meeting at the community house on Wednesday afternoon. I sent word that I wanted to talk to all of the people about my dismissal. Richie Matta, my singing friend, offered his boat and we went to the island for the meeting. Edna Graves met us at the dock in her ox cart, looking far younger than her seventy years. Her eyes were afire when she saw us. As I walked up the dock, she shouted, "We gonna strike the school. We gonna strike the school."

It was an odd meeting that day. The Yamacraw people were not a political people. They tended to be passive during crises and concurred with the unwritten law that the bad times would pass after a while. Throughout their history, they had found it easier and safe to ride the waves no matter how savage or dangerous it became to do so. The white man made the decisions and enforced the rules; the black man paid lip service to these rules then lived according to his own tradition. The purpose of the meeting was to let the islanders know what exactly happened and why it happened. I wanted them to know that white men sometimes played dirty with white men, too.

About fifty people had assembled in the community house. All my students were there looking puzzled and disquieted by the recent chain of events. I began talking rapidly and angrily. It was not a speech I gave that day, but a harangue. Conrack discovered that afternoon, much to his dismay, that he had a bit of demagogue in him. I told them exactly what I thought about the administration, the island school, and the education their children were receiving. In the middle of my delivery, one lady shouted, "Let's get a petition."

"Petitions were fine this summer, but they ain't worth a damn now," I answered. "The time for petitions is over."

Then Edna the Beautiful said majestically, "Only one thing to do. We gonna strike the school. Ain't no chillun gonna go to that schoolhouse door."

Then all the mothers were shouting, "We gonna strike the school. Strike it startin' tomorrow."

I issued a warning about the danger of a boycott. "If you strike the school, you are going to have men coming out here threatening to put you in jail. Bennington's [school deputy superintendent] gonna come to your doors with a carful of white men and say you've gotta get your kids back in school. The sheriff will come out here and say it's against the law. It is gonna take more guts to strike the school than anything you've ever done."

"Man, that ol' empty school bus gonna look so sweet ridin' by my house with no chillun in it," said Cindy Lou's grandmother.

"Anybody send their chillun to school, they git beat up bad by the other parents," Edna said.

"Beat' em with sticks," cried another voice.

I turned to my students right before they left the room. Richard and Saul were crying. The other kids still looked puzzled.

"I will try like hell to get back to teaching you," I said. "I promise I will try like hell." And it was ironic to note that one of my most voluble supporters at the meeting was Iris Glover, the alleged root doctor and mistress of darkness whom I once had identified as the greatest threat to my survival on the island. It seemed like a good omen.

The next morning the yellow school bus drove the long dirt road that ran the length of the island without a single child in it. The Yamacraw Island boycott had begun.

But the people and I knew nothing of power and how it works. We were to have several swift and unforgettable lessons. The day after the boycott began a man appeared on the island and went from door to door delivering a stern message. If the children were not in school by Monday, the parents would face a thirty-day jail sentence and a fine of fifty dollars per day, in violation of the compulsory-attendance law. This plunged the island into a mild panic and many of the mothers feared that the man was the harbinger of the law. On Monday four children were back in school. It was interesting to note that the children who broke the boycott had parents who worked in the school and whose only income was derived from the school being open. A rumor spread that these two mothers had been threatened with the loss of their jobs. When I heard about this intimidation, I returned to the island to tell the people that the compulsory-attendance law had never been enforced in the state of South Carolina. Edna Graves was one of the first people I talked to that day.

"Did a man come to see you, Edna?" I asked.

"Yeh, he come to say some stuff."

"What did he say?"

"He tell Edna that she go to jail if she don't send no chillun back to that school. He tell me that I owe fifty dollar for ev'ry day my chillun not in no schoolhouse. I tell him to get his ass out my yard. I tell him he can put Edna under the jail for ninety-nine years. Her chillun ain't goin' to no schoolhouse."

A group of mothers had gathered in Edna's yard. I told them that they were going to have to play it tough from now on. They nodded their heads in solemn agreement. Lois, Ethel's mother, said that another man had come to her house and said that her welfare checks would be cut off if she didn't send her children back to school. I tried to calm her down and explain that some white people would say anything to get them to return their children to school. Then I asked the six mothers why they had all gathered together at Edna's house. This was the largest congregation of mothers I had ever seen at a private home.

"We waitin'," one of the ladies said.

"Waitin' for what?" I asked.

"Waitin' for Lizzie," the lady replied. Lizzie was Mary's mother.

"Why?"

"We gonna beat her up," was the answer.

"Why are you gonna beat her up?"

"She break the strike. We say we beat up anyone who break the strike. She break it. So we beat her good."

"Oh, that's great. That is just great. Man, you cannot just go around beating up people who don't agree with the strike. If Lizzie doesn't want to keep her children out of school, then that's her business."

"We jes' gonna hurt' er a little bit."

"No, I don't want that to happen. Lizzie is probably worried she's gonna lose her job. Don't hold that against her."

"You keep her girl, Mary, in your house, don't you?" Edna said.

"Yes, Edna, you know I do."

"The whites don't like those colored chillun stayin' wit' you, do they? That's why they tell you to leave Yamacraw. You got colored chillun in your house. They don't want nobody who helps the colored. Nobody, I tell you. If I were you, I'd go home and t'row Mary into the street. If her mama cain't keep her chillun out a no school, I wouldn't keep her gull in my house in Beaufort."

"Lizzie is just afraid, Edna. She isn't doing this because she is against us. She is just afraid."

"Edna ain't afraid of nuttin'."

"I know that, Edna. But you can't beat up another person because they are." Lizzie was not cudgeled that afternoon, though someone must have exerted a certain amount of pressure on her. For on the next day the boycott was total again. The next day was significant for another reason, for it marked the very first time that Henry Piedmont felt the compulsion to set foot on Yamacraw Island.

He came with Bennington and the truant officer. It was to be the classic show of force, the moving of the big guns into strategic position. They called for a meeting at the schoolhouse to begin at one o'clock. No one showed up. Bennington then went around the island, rounding people up, and telling them they were required to attend the meeting with the superintendent of schools. I watched the action around the school from the edge of the woods. Sidney and Samuel had led me from Edna's house through the swamp and across the pond to a spot that gave us a commanding view of the entire scene. Six people eventually arrived for the meeting. Edna was one of them. I could hear her shouting for the rest of the afternoon.

Piedmont told the parents some interesting things. He told them I had not paid my rent when I lived on the island. He told them I had not paid my electric bills. He told them that many times I had left the landing at Bluffton and had never arrived on Yamacraw. It had also been reported that I spent a large amount of my time in the nightclub on Yamacraw. This Conrack was not an honorable lad. He was not worth following. Piedmont reiterated the threat of jail and fines, then left. I never found out how he liked his first trip to the island.

A reporter for a local Beaufort paper had come with me to the island. He was not allowed inside but listened at the door. By the time the meeting was over, he was ready to break the story to Beaufort. I had said nothing to the press prior to this day since I wanted to give Piedmont, the board, and the politicians time to reconsider their decision. After this, I was going to sing like a canary to anyone who would listen. But when I got home that day I heard that the draft board was reclassifying me 1-A. I was being outflanked again.

On Friday I called off the boycott completely. Too many of the women were frightened by the economic and legal threats against them. When I talked to them, some of them would almost weep out of fear. The threats, spoken and unspoken, about reprisals against those who supported me increased each day. I finally decided that the boycott was more of a prop for my deflated ego than something that was doing the island and my students any good. It was not worth the suffering etched in the faces of these parents who were trying so hard and succeeding at being brave. Edna, however, would not send her grandchildren back to school. I pleaded with her and she shook her head firmly. Nor would Cindy Lou's mother send her children back. Their personal boycott lasted a week longer than anyone else's. Curiously enough, Edna did not receive her Social Security check for five months after the boycott.

The next act in the circus was my appeal before the board of education. I had enlisted the help of George Trask, a young Beaufort lawyer, to present my case before the board. George was astonished at the ferocity of the charges levied against me by Piedmont. He also told me that the law gave great powers to school boards and that all they needed to impale me was "good and sufficient cause." In the parlance of lawyers, I could urinate on the wrong part of a commode and if the board of education decided that this was "good and sufficient" reason for dismissal, then the courts would automatically side with them. It looked rather bleak, but I had decided to fight it anyway.

When I walked into the board room on a tension-filled Tuesday night, I knew instantly that I would lose this phase of the appeal. The board members wore immovable, intransigent expressions, the unblinking faces of soldiers in a Greek tragedy. The dentist on the board sneered when he saw me. The doctor felt much too self-righteous to sneer. The entire board had all the more cheerful characteristics of a lynch mob. My friends had assembled again, a far more somber, truculent group than before. They had come to watch an execution and they saw no way to prevent it. The members of the board had already closed their minds to arguments on my behalf and all the laws of the world could not prevent them from rendering a decision against me. Yet the meeting brought out some emotional responses from the administrators that I will always treasure. Piedmont responded to a question from George Trask at the beginning of the meeting by saying, "I run the most democratic school system in the country. If a teacher doesn't like something his principal does, then he can come to me with his complaint. If I do not give him a satisfactory answer, he can appeal to the board of education. Pat should know this better than anybody. He's the only teacher I know of that has followed this chain to the top. Of course, Pat feels that teachers are afraid of me. I told him that no one should be afraid of me." Nor did he sense the irony in his words as he addressed the assembled crowd. And Bennington later answered a question from a board member by saying, "Mr. Conroy does not communicate well with his elders. Communication is his major problem."

After it had been proven that Mrs. Brown left the island for ten days without telling anyone, George Trask said to the board, "You've got a principal at your school who doesn't inform anybody when she is absent on school days and doesn't make any provisions for substitutes. You don't do anything to her. You've got a teacher at your school who sends the authorized substitute with lesson plans and you fire him. As I say, the whole thing is absurd."

My stomach crawled throughout the entire meeting; it felt ulcerous and dangerously acidic. The people who rose to defend me did so out of desperation. All of us knew what the final result would be. The talking was simply a showy preliminary to the final banishment. Eventually, however, George motioned for me to rise and give my farewell address.

The speech was not exactly my forte. I would have preferred to tell the board members to kiss my baby-pink behind. But the only chance I had was to crawl before the nine judges who stared at me. I traced my teaching career in the county. I told them how I had been offered the job of assistant principal at the high school but turned it down because I wanted to remain in the classroom. Then I told them that when I found out that school was a place of timeclocks and rules, of teachers more concerned with attendance reports than with students, and students praying for the day of graduation when their reprieve from the stale grip of public education would be granted, I tried to make my classes a stimulating experience for my students . . . life experiences, creative experiences. I tried to get them to drop prejudices and conditioned responses from their thinking. In essence, I tried to teach them to embrace life openly, to reflect upon its mysteries, rejoice in its surprises, and to reject its cruelties. Like other teachers, I failed. Teaching is a record of failures. But the glory of teaching is in the attempt. I dislike poor teachers. They are criminals to me. I've seen so much cruelty toward children. I've seen so many children not given the opportunity to live up to their potential as human beings. Before you fire me, ask yourselves these questions that I feel are most critical and essential in the analysis of any teacher who comes before you. Did he love his kids? Did he love the act of teaching? Did his kids love him? If you answer negatively to any of these questions, I deserve to be fired.

After this saccharine presentation, the doctor glared at me and asked, "Why are you trying to intimidate us?" George finally ended my defense by suggesting that the members of the board read a book that seemed to apply to the case, *Catch-22*.

The board voted to sustain my dismissal. But because they were exemplary men, they offered me the chance to resign with honor and without a blot on my record, if I did not take the case to court.

Two months later Judge Street ambled heavily into his courtroom. Everyone rose according to custom. Dr. Piedmont rose, as did Bennington, Mrs. Brown, Ted Stone, and several board members summoned to testify against me. All the major protagonists of the year stood reverently as Judge Street cleared his throat, shuffled a few papers, then brought the court to order. It would be convenient to report that Judge Street was a gum-chewing illiterate ex-Klansman elevated to the judgeship by decadent politicians who wished to preserve the status quo. On the contrary, he was a magnificent man with a stentorian voice and a gray, leonine head who gave the appearance that justice was a frail maiden whom he served with unswerving fidelity. He treated all the witnesses with paramount consideration, though I thought he treated all the lawyers in the court with a visible contempt.

The trial was interesting. Most of my witnesses were from the island. The O.E.O. boat was making a special trip at seven o'clock in the morning to bring the seven parents who were testifying in my behalf. When the captain tried to start the engine, he discovered that the ignition system, which had worked perfectly the night before, did not even turn the engine over. At precisely the same time, the people saw Ted

Stone's boat pass their stranded boat on the way to the trial. The people later told me that a part was missing from the engine. I did not have any witnesses from the island, but I learned still another lesson in the exercise of power.

The trial was a necessary, but masochistic, ritual. People from my past paraded to the witness stand to prove that I was really Jack Armstrong and not Godzilla. The administration paraded witnesses to the stand to show that I was a lousy teacher, a liar, an impudent troublemaker, and a discredit to the hallowed profession of teaching. I also had tried to politicize my students by letting them draw black power posters on the bulletin board. During the trial Piedmont did discover that Bennington and Sedgwick had authorized the use of the gas. His arguments that I did not follow the chain of command were a bit tepid after that. The judge discovered that the only punishment that existed in Piedmont's democratic kingdom was instant dismissal.

"Doctor Piedmont, what other punishment could you have levied against this young man besides firing him?"

"We have no other punishment, Your Honor."

"You have no lesser punishment than dismissal? You mean if he is late to school a couple of times, you have no punishment like docking his pay or reducing his leave time?"

"Our teachers all obey the rules. We never have to discipline them."

"You have certainly disciplined this young man, Doctor Piedmont. You fired him. That is a form of discipline, isn't it?"

Dr. Piedmont came down from the witness stand nervous and shaking. He was the final witness in the two-day trial. I walked up and shook his hand, and told him that I hoped the ordeal had not been too painful. He responded by saying that I must always do what I thought was right, no matter what the consequences might be. After all the crap, Piedmont and I still grudgingly liked each other. Of course, I have to admit of a momentary desire to milk his rat[1] as we stood there talking.

The lawyers, my friends, and I thought we had won the trial. The rest of that week was a celebration; the smoke had finally cleared and the villains had been exposed. Naturally we lost. When the judge delivered his opinion, he stated that the board of education was invested with the power to fire any teacher it considered undesirable. That was the law. It was very, very simple.

Questions for Discussion and Debate

1. Trace, from the beginning of the excerpt to the end, the political methods of protest that Conroy and the citizens of Yamacraw used in trying to influence the school board to reinstate him as a teacher.

   a. What was the response to each method?

   b. What are your conclusions about the power of school boards as a result of reading this excerpt?

   c. Would your conclusions also serve as the "unforgettable lessons" Conroy refers to at the beginning of the excerpt?

2. What means did the law and the school officials have at their disposal for putting down the protests of the parents? What could the parents—and Conroy—have done to bring about a different outcome?

3. Why did all of the people who spoke up for Conroy do so even though they "knew what the final result would be"?

4. In what way could Conroy's speech before the board be considered intimidating, if at all?

Activities and Projects

(See also items 1 and 3, dealing with school committees [school boards], in the Activities and Projects following the editorial cartoon, Selection 4.2).

1. Do research on the following question: How representative of a community is its school board? You could start by asking the chairperson of the local school board about where to find answers to this question and other questions related to the politics of school boards. Check also with a librarian about sources that cover school board politics.

2. Hold a mock school board meeting. Assign roles that reflect the different people in this excerpt (i.e., school board, citizens, lawyers), but in your role-playing situation, do not feel restricted to reaching the same decision! Also, consider role-playing a board meeting at which another issue is being addressed, an issue that typically confronts school boards or perhaps one that interests you.

   Consider this diagram when allocating roles to be played:

---

[1]Milk the rat: a form of torture that involves pressing the fingernail of a victim with one's thumb and more.

The 7 P's of Educational Decision-Making

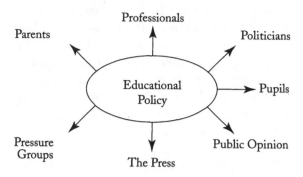

Have one or two members of the class represent the press during the mock meeting. Have them write up articles describing the meeting as it is going on. Compare their articles to the actual meeting. Discuss how the press can influence public opinion by the way in which it chooses to cover a meeting.

3. What if Conroy had called on more of the people and groups who comprise the local educational apparatus to support him in his efforts to get reinstated? Look in texts for charts that indicate the hierarchy or power structure of your school's system, from top to bottom. Is there any part of this apparatus that Conroy could have tapped for more effective support in dealing with Bennington, Piedmont, and the principal, Mrs. Brown? Why, or why not?

4. Find out about some of the pressure groups who use their influence to get certain educational policies passed into law. Consider, for example, the AAUW (American Association of University Women) or the NAACP (National Association for the Advancement of Colored People).

4.4   *The Thread That Runs So True* (1949)

Jesse Stuart

Jesse Stuart has written realistically and poignantly about his many positions in the rural schools of Kentucky and, for a brief time, Ohio during the early and middle part of the 20th century. Many of the best writers we have on the subject of teaching are former teachers who, like Stuart, loved the profession but left it to pursue writing. As you read this selection—and Jonathan Kozol's (Selection 4.5)—think about the choices both authors made. Are people like Stuart and Kozol, as critics of the system, more effective in bringing about changes in education in their roles as writers, or should they have remained teachers? After reading the excerpt, weigh the significance of the two roles, teacher and writer, and compare their characteristics.

There had been a time when Kentucky teachers had to take what they could get. If they followed their profession in Kentucky, in the rural schools, they had to take sixty-five dollars a month for seven months per year. And in Greenwood County many teachers had fears of losing this, which was part of their livelihood. Now something was taking place. Something

Reprinted with the permission of Scribner, a Division of Simon & Schuster, Inc., from THE THREAD THAT RUNS SO TRUE by Jesse Stuart. Copyright © 1949 by Jesse Stuart; copyright renewed © 1977 by Jesse Stuart.

big was in the wind. They would not have to teach in the rural schools of Greenwood County. They could throw overboard the side-lines that supplemented their little salaries.

There were calls for help in the industries of Ohio, Michigan, Maryland, Pennsylvania. New industries were beginning to arise. Europe had burst into flames. Aggressive armies were on the march. Industry in America was beginning to boom. Rural teachers marched away with skilled and unskilled laborers. They went to Willow Run. They went to Dayton, Akron, Youngstown. They went to Pittsburgh and Baltimore. There was a great exodus North. Many went North to teach school. Positions for teachers were opening in the North as never before. Qualifications were not as rigid as they had been. The northern teachers, too, were going into industrial work. James married Betsy Sutton, whose hair he used to pull in Landsburgh High School. They went to Michigan to teach. Don Conway, Guy Hawkins, Olive Binion, Lucinda Sprouse, Ann Bush, and Budge Waters went North. Thalia and Charles Meyers went to West Virginia. Kentuckians were moving in all directions. Teachers left until the schools were almost depleted of their first-rate teachers.

The teachers I had worked with when I first started teaching were all gone. I had held out longer than any of them, for I had held better positions and had received better pay. The youth I had taught, including the seventy-one rural teachers in Greenwood County, moved to better-paying teaching positions in the North, or they went to work in factories. I saw a gener-ation of young, vigorous, excellent teachers that I had helped to make, disappear like ripe au-tumn leaves with a strong November wind.

And at a later date, these teachers were re-placed by poorer-qualified teachers to whom emergency certificates were granted. The salaries were too low to hold the teachers with emergency certificates. In one year Greenwood County had four rural schools that never even started. Sixteen more rural schools had to close shortly after they had started, because the teachers quit and they could not find replace-ments among emergency certificate holders. Kentucky youth were without any schooling whatsoever! Kentucky youth were forced to grow up like uncultivated plants.

. . . O hypocritical, shortsighted, ignorant politicians, living in the middle of this twentieth century, allowing schools to remain closed for lack of financial appropriations, perpetuators of continued ignorance and future crime, I at least shall go on record to rebuke you! Tax us. Tax us to death to pay our teachers. Let them work upon immortal minds to brighten them to all eternity. We educate our people or we perish. . . .

I had not let Naomi Deane know what I had done. But on this Sunday evening I would tell her. While teachers were leaving their posi-tions in Greenwood County for better pay in factories and mills in the North and East, I re-turned to the land they were leaving. I returned to my father's house in W-Hollow. My salary at Dartmouth High School had been the best I had received since I had been a member of the teaching profession. I had made $200 per month. But school salaries didn't matter now. I had other ideas.

I dressed in a dark, summer suit for it was better to wear dark on this June night when there was a bright moon in the sky. Because I had returned to my homeland and the land of my enemies. I put my derringer in my coat pocket and my .38 Special Smith and Wesson in the holster on my hip. My father, brother, and I never went any place unless we were armed. We didn't know where or when one of us would be attacked. My fight had been their fight; my quarrels had been their quarrels, and they would stick by me to the last.

There were four paths that led from my father's house to Landsburgh. I always went one path and returned on another. This evening I walked the Seaton Ridge and looked at the deep valley in the head of Tanyard Hollow. I'd never seen the country more beautiful. Little clouds of mist ascended from the valley toward the bright moon. The whippoorwills called to each other from the jutted hilltops. Twice, before I reached Academy Branch, I heard nightingales singing. The air was cool, fresh, and good to breathe. The land was filled with the freshness of spring. It was filled with insects' and night birds' singing. It was a night of music in a land that was poetry. Maybe this was because I was more in love than I had ever been in my life. This was the time to live. It was great to be in love with the girl whose books I had carried down the street to school when she was in the seventh grade and I was in the ninth. I knew that I was going to marry her if I could. No money in my pocket but I had love in my heart. I had possessions too. I couldn't wait to tell Naomi Deane.

When I walked to the end of the ridge, I walked down a steep path that zigzagged back and forth down into the valley of rising mists. I hurried down Academy Branch and down the back road west of Landsburgh. This way I didn't meet too many people. On this evening I never met a person. Not even when I walked through a back alley to the railroad tracks. I crossed the railroad tracks and was soon on Main Street, where I hurried to the Norris' residence. I walked upon the porch and rang the doorbell.

"You've made it all right?" Naomi Deane said.

"Never met a person on my way here," I said, as I took the derringer from my pocket and unfastened the holster and gave her my .38.

"How lucky," she said. She took my pistols to put in a safe place so her young brother wouldn't get hold of one. Once he did get them

and ran through the house among other members of the Norris family, screaming and pulling on the triggers. It was fortunate for everybody in the house the safety was locked on each pistol. This incident did cause some excitement among the members of this quiet-living and highly respected family.

"Plenty has happened in the last few days, Naomi Deane," I said. "I've got a lot to tell you."

"What is it, Jesse? Come sit down and tell me."

"I've come home to stay," I said, as I sat down beside her on the divan.

"But you will go back to Dartmouth High School to teach next September, won't you?" she asked. "You'll just be home for the summer?"

"I will not be back at Dartmouth next September," I answered. "My special work of teaching Remedial English is over. No more Remedial English in Dartmouth High School. Not any other positions open there. Not that I know of. I just didn't reapply!"

"But, Jesse, what will you do now?"

"I'm going to raise sheep."

She was stunned when I told her this.

"I've bought three hundred acres of rough land," I said. "I've bought two hundred of the prettiest ewes you ever saw."

"How did you do it?" she asked. "I thought you were in debt."

"I was just about out of debt," I said. "But I've borrowed thirty-eight hundred dollars more."

"Oh, Jesse, you've never raised sheep before!" she said. "I wonder if you know what you're doing? You can teach school. You've been educated for that profession. But what if you fail raising sheep? Then what? You'll have a big debt to pay back, teaching school. It will take you at least four years to pay it back. That is," she continued, "if you get as good pay as you did at Dartmouth High School. We may not make much teaching school, but it is sure pay."

"Naomi Deane, why haven't we married before now?" I asked. "It's not because I haven't asked you to marry me. It's not because we don't love each other. How long have we known each other?"

Naomi Deane didn't answer. She looked at me but didn't speak.

"Six years ago I asked you to marry me," I said. "That was when I was Superintendent of Greenwood County Schools. You know the reason you didn't. Four years I was Principal of the second-largest high school in this county. One year I was in Europe on a Guggenheim Fellowship with my expenses paid. While this past year I did special teaching in one of the best high schools in Ohio. Yet we can't get enough ahead to get married. Isn't it time I try something else?"

"Maybe you're right," she said thoughtfully, "but you're taking a big chance when you leave the profession you know."

"You said once that we were intelligent people, and we had to face the facts," I reminded her. "That was on the evening I brought the poems here for you to read. That was six years ago. Now I have some facts."

Naomi Deane sat in silence watching me as I took an envelope from my inside coat pocket.

"In the nine years I've been employed in my profession," I said, "I've made an approximate total of ten thousand, eight hundred and thirty-two dollars. This makes an annual wage of a thousand, two hundred, three dollars and fifty-five cents. On a twelve months' basis, I have averaged one hundred dollars and thirty cents a month. Yet," I continued, as I turned from the paper to Naomi Deane, "I have an A.B. degree and I've done approximately two years of graduate work. I've spent approximately six years of my life preparing myself for my profession. I've been Principal of two large high schools and Superintendent of a large county school system in Kentucky. I've held one of the better-paying teaching positions in one of Ohio's highest-rating high schools. Yet you and I have not been able to get married, because we both could not live from my salary. Isn't that the truth?"

"That's the truth," she admitted.

"Then how intelligent are we?" I asked. "Teaching is not charitable work. It is a profession. It is the greatest profession under the sun. I don't know of any profession that is more important to the people upon this earth. I've loved it. I still love it. But I'm leaving it because it's left me. I'm goin' to raise sheep and farm and write a novel! Then," I added in a softer tone of voice, "I want to marry you. You're a city girl but I want you to come soon as you can to see my farm and sheep."

Questions for Discussion and Debate

1. In what ways could you say that writers like Stuart (and Kozol), though not politicians themselves, are actually involved in the politics of education?

2. Have you or has anyone you know ever lobbied (put pressure on) a school board or the state legislature to get a policy changed or passed? Explain.

3. What problems of rural schools does Stuart identify? What could be done to solve some of those problems? Who does Stuart hold responsible for the fact that many of the excellent teachers in Kentucky go North and East to teach? Do you agree with him? Why, or why not?

4. What is Stuart's final decision? Do you agree with his decision? Explain.

Activities and Projects

1. Research the topic of rural schools and prepare a brief report on their unique problems. How have these problems been handled during the last 20 years? Are the problems still the same as those identified by Stuart?

2. In small research groups, investigate teacher salaries around the country. Each group should report back to the class with its findings on the following.

   • Differences in salaries between rural and urban areas and among various regions of the country (and what accounts for the differences).

   • Who sets teachers' salaries?

   • Areas of the country where the greatest numbers of teachers are leaving the profession, and why. (Foundations of education textbooks will often contain this kind of information. Check with your instructor.)

3. Do research on the decision-making role of the students and teachers in the school where you are or will be student teaching. Has the student government and/or the teacher's association there ever lobbied the *state legislature* or *school board*? Bring the results of your investigation back to the class. (Look in local newspapers to keep track of activities of the student government and teacher's association regarding educational policy.)

4.5 *Death at an Early Age* (1967)

Jonathan Kozol

In the following selection from Jonathan Kozol's classic exposé, problems of an urban school system are presented through the eyes of a white teacher at a Boston school attended by African-American children. (Kozol uses the term *Negro,* which was still common in the 1960s. However, at that time—the decade of the Civil Rights movement and the growth of racial pride—the term *black* began to emerge and replace *Negro*.)

Kozol clearly feels uncomfortable both with the way his teaching colleagues, Black and White, are responding to the civil rights protests going on down South and with their response, or lack of response, to the unequal education Boston's African American children are receiving in its segregated schools.

These schools were, of course, not segregated by law (de jure segregation) as had been the case in parts of the South. Instead, many northern schools were segregated because of where people lived (de facto segregation). With the U.S. Supreme Court decision of 1954, *Brown* v. *The Board of Education of Topeka, Kansas,* schools in every state, North and South, were expected to integrate, either by busing students or by other

Jonathan Kozol, *Death at an Early Age*. New York: Bantam, 1968, pp. 123–125. Copyright © 1967 by Jonathan Kozol. Reprinted by permission of the author.

means. The judiciary of the United States had decided that separate schools based on race could not be and, indeed, were not equal.

The Boston schools were among the most segregated and faced the biggest challenge in terms of how to respond to the court's decision.

According to Kozol in a subsequent book, *Savage Inequalities* (1994), there hasn't been much change in terms of either segregation or the allocation of educational resources for urban minority school children. In this earlier work, however, Kozol implies that there is some hope for these children if parents and teachers make the political moves necessary to bring about change.

As you read this excerpt, think about the other readings in this chapter. What similarities do you see among them?

Much of the news that held the attention of the Boston papers during February and March in 1965 had to do with civil rights. Stories of murder from the South competed for space on the front page with news about the behavior of the Boston School Committee, all of this being given an occasional flourish on the editorial page in a letter to the paper from School Committee member Joseph Lee. The one event which dominated all others, however, was the death in Selma, Alabama, of Reverend Reeb. The reaction to his death, on the part of thousands of Bostonians, was angry and anguished and articulate. A crowd of 30,000 people gathered on a Sunday afternoon in Boston Common to mourn and eulogize this minister, while two hundred young civil rights workers chose to demonstrate their feelings in another way by organizing a massive sit-in at the U.S. Federal Building. Several of the people who rose to speak before the crowd in Boston Common did not hesitate to draw a line of similarity between the events that were then taking place in Alabama and the less bloody but, in the long run, no less destructive processes of injustice that were being carried out within the Boston Public Schools. Possibly I found this connection the more reasonable and more believable because the death of Reverend Reeb coincided almost to the day and week with one of the very

deepest periods of withdrawal in Stephen's[1] private life, as well as with one of the most serious periods of difficulty in his life at school. It was also at the same time, as I have described already, that the Reading Teacher confided in me, with warm energy and glowing complacence, that at least it was wonderful that we could come to school and forget about what was happening down in Alabama.

That weekend I was having dinner with friends in Cambridge and I was trying to describe to them some of the conditions that we faced at school. I also described to them the struggle I was having to bring myself up to the point of being truthful and the hesitation I felt about braving the certain hostility of other teachers at my school if I should be more forthright. I said, what was the truth, that I felt compromised by my compliance and in particular that I felt disturbed by the degree to which I had permitted myself to be appropriated by the Reading Teacher and the Art Teacher, so that I was continually being stifled and suppressed precisely at those moments when I knew it was most imperative that I speak out.

From talking about my own school, the conversation drifted gradually to the problem in

---

[1]Stephen was one of Kozol's students and a ward of the state.

general and inevitably, to the protest at the Federal building that was taking place at that hour. Young people whom I admired greatly had spent close to thirty hours unfed and unwashed and sleepless on the floors of that government building and had refused to allow police to drive them away. This was the only way that they could think of to protest our Federal Government's timidity in defending the lives of whites and Negroes in the South. A respectable and ambitious Harvard Law student offered us the information that he considered it all "very young and immature," and there was not any doubt in my mind at all that he would indeed have to have found it young and immature since to approve of it and not find it immature might well make him feel that he should be a part of it and to be a part of it might prejudice his offered job at a leading New York firm. I said that to him and I also said that I thought the greatest risk those demonstrators were undergoing was not physical harm or physical arrest but rather the sophisticated and supercilious ridicule of people exactly like him. I said that even if they were mostly young and scruffy and beatnik-looking they seemed to me to be the only people in Boston that night who were in visible touch with American reality because they were actually sitting down on the floor of a building that represented federal power. Everybody else was at dinner tables like ourselves discussing the government's inaction. Millions disapproved of the President's hesitation, yet they confined themselves to talk. Only those young SNCC[2] and CORE[3] workers had had the courage to act on what they thought.

Now at night at this comfortable dinner party, after I had said what I did, the law student suddenly questioned me: "If you mean what you said and you really admire them for doing what they have done, then why aren't you right down there with them on the floor instead of sitting here talking about it and enjoying yourself just like the rest of us?" I felt a moment of panic at being put on the spot. And then I got up and said that he was right and I would have to go there. It seems a slight enough thing but it is not always so easy to do that in your own home town if you have grown up caring a great deal about pleasing adult people and when some of the people your family has been closest to are the people who command a large portion of respect. Two other people at the dinner table announced that they were coming with me. In the next three hours the three of us sat, sang, joined arms with dozens of others, were dragged, hauled, thrown into wagons, and I discovered all at once that I had been arrested for civil disobedience for the first time in my life.

Thirty-seven others were arrested with us. The demonstration had been organized by SNCC. So far as I could see, no one had participated in the sit-in without full knowledge of what was at stake and nobody had joined in without understanding the legal danger. No violence had occurred and there was no roughness from the demonstrators. The only roughness came from the police. Young college students were dragged into a police station and a number were thrown down on the hard concrete so that their heads cracked audibly against the floor. All were allowed bail but court hearing was for Monday. This meant I would have to miss a day of school. I did not like missing school but I hadn't a doubt in my mind but that one day out of school to confirm to myself that I could do something in which I believed would make me a better, not worse, teacher, so the only things I regretted were the lost lessons of that one day. The judge on Monday, confronted by a battery of lawyers who had come forward

---

[2]Student Non-Violent Coordinating Committee.
[3]Congress on Racial Equality.

to defend us without pay, decided at length to throw out the case, only not before recommending to the young people involved in the sit-in that they would do better to go out and picket an employment agency. I would like to have had a chance to answer him.

Next day at school I was not surprised to find some repercussions. The Principal called me in and said that the Deputy Superintendent, Miss Sullivan, had noticed my name in the paper among those hauled into court and had wondered whether I felt I was fulfilling my obligation to the children by spending a day outside of school. I said I had not expected to be arrested but that I knew I would be penalized by the loss of a day's pay and that I did not expect to be arrested again that year. What I didn't add was that I felt I had fulfilled my obligation to these children very well by doing what I did and much better than she. A boy in the schoolyard whom I had taught the summer before and whose mother was the maid of the Reading Teacher took me aside and asked me confidentially if it was true that I had been arrested. He said he had heard I was, but that the Reading Teacher had told his mother "it was nothing." I didn't like her covering up for me that way and so I told him she was wrong. "It was not nothing. It was something. It was something I cared about and something you'll care about too later on." The Reading Teacher only told me that she regretted "the whole thing."

What I regretted most was that Stephen had gotten into trouble the day I was out and he had been punished more roughly than he had ever been punished while I was at school. What happened was that in my absence, one of the other male teachers had come up to cover for me. While he was there Stephen said "God damn you!" to him. He said, "What did you say?" and the little boy said the same thing, "God damn you!" only a little louder than before. The teacher who had to handle this was a good-natured

casual person and he told me later that he understood perfectly why Stephen was confused by the rearrangement and that he was not personally bothered and could not have cared less. But the Reading Teacher overheard it and she took Stephen to the Principal's office. The Principal suspended him from the building for five days.

Next morning, when I was back, Stephen suddenly appeared in the doorway of the auditorium, not having the courage to come in, holding his little lunch bag in his hand and looking up out of his pleading hopeful eyes. When he saw me at the blackboard he caught my eye and smiled. He was, however, instantly driven out of the forbidden classroom once again by the Reading Teacher and, a little while later, out of the school building as well. People thought it was extraordinary, funny, unexpected, that such a rotten kid would want so much to come back to school after he had been kicked out. It *was* extraordinary, too, although it was not funny, because he got so little here and the school had done him so much harm. And still he wanted to come in, not knowing what else to do and having perhaps no other place to go. After that morning, and in fact for the duration of five days, the Reading Teacher would pop in on me at nine o'clock and, if Stephen had not yet appeared, she would smile and she would say, "Let's cross our fingers." Then, when he showed up finally, down-regarding and timid, she would say to me glumly: "Do you see what I see standing in the door?"

On a day soon after that I wrote myself a note about Stephen. The note says he did not do his homework for the Math Teacher and was consequently not allowed to receive help in arithmetic from me. It also says that he pleaded with me privately to come over to his house after school to help him with division so that he would have a chance to catch up with the rest of the class. I remember that I felt my willingness rise, and then fall, and then I told him I could not.

In the basement the same day there was a conversation about the Fourth Graders.

"Just a bad group," said one of the teachers. "No one would have stayed."

Another teacher told me: "They got what they deserved. They had those nice older women for teachers and they talked back to them and wouldn't listen to them and so it's their own damn fault they didn't learn."

When we came out of that room there was a Negro mother talking to one of the other teachers by the door. The teacher I had just been talking to muttered to me nervously that he hoped she hadn't heard us. . . .

At a teachers' meeting around that time, the Principal gave us some advice that seemed keyed to the same point and that recognized, by implication, some of the unrest and some of the controversy which had been taking place around us. "Please," she said, "be extremely careful in what you say and realize that anything you say may be overheard. People also may repeat your words. I know that none of you would have to be ashamed of anything you say but just remember that anything you say can be twisted and misunderstood." Her use of the word "misunderstood" seemed backwards: I felt she meant the opposite. I received the same impression on another occasion when she came in to talk to me about something else and noticed a little black and white equal pin that I was wearing.

"It's a nice pin," she said to me instantly, "but don't wear it here."

I said to her: "All it means is equal."

She answered immediately, always confident, never without authority: "I know it. And that's fine. But you never know when it could be misunderstood."

I thought that astonishing. "How could it be misunderstood? Look at it. All it is is an equal sign. Who could misunderstand it?"

She answered me: "You never can tell."

I asked her if she meant my supervisor from the School Department. Was he the one who might not understand? I said: "Do you think he's going to think it's for a fund drive?"

She laughed at that and told me: "Oh come now! We're not as unsophisticated as that!"

I did not answer her but I felt that she was very unsophisticated to think that I could have believed what she had told me.

Other changes came into our school during that period—some of them due to the arrival of a new Negro teacher. There already were a small number of Negro teachers in the school, but in this case there was a great difference because the new teacher was from a different background and had had a different kind of education than any of the others. He was a great deal more sophisticated than almost all of the other Negro teachers, yet he was not for that reason any more willing to go along with gestures of white tokenism but was, on the contrary, far more shrewd and bitter and percipient and cool. I remember the day on which he came into the school because it was on the same morning that two of the first American astronauts were shot up into space. It was not long after James Reeb's death in Selma. Nobody at school had thought of a school program to discuss Alabama and its significance for us, but the decision had been made to bring everyone up into the auditorium to look at the space flight on television. Two giant sets were propped up on the stage and the pupils were prepared for the program by the Assistant Principal. Then, with some fascination and some boredom, they watched and listened to all the curious language about everything being "Go" and all systems being "A-okay" and the flight being a real honey and so forth, the whole rest of the Buck Rogers-Jack Armstrong lingo that surrounds the public relations aspect of a serious event. While all this was happening, the new teacher stood a few feet from me and, when I said to him, "What do you think of it?" he said: "I think it's boring." And then he added: "I think that the whole business is absurd." I didn't think it was absurd, not scientifically anyway, and I am sure that, if he had been questioned, he would have admitted also that the space-shot must have technical importance. But what he meant became clear right after that when he said: "There are more important things going on in this room and in this country and not one hundred miles above the surface of the earth."

Afterward I told the Reading Teacher that I thought he was going to create some differences in the school, and that proved to be correct. He was appointed, I believe, a provisional teacher, like myself, only instead of having a class to teach upstairs he had been put in the basement to work as an assistant to an older teacher. The man to whom he was assigned was not well qualified. He was, I thought, one of the least competent teachers in the school. His attitude toward the children varied between dislike and apathy—with apathy, of a sleepy, sluggish, heavy-footed nature, being the overriding feeling. When I had asked him once about the curriculum he was teaching, he answered me, pleasantly: "I figure I give them the same curriculum that they'd be getting any place else. If I put in a little less meat, I figure that they get the same number of potatoes." He talked a lot about killing crabgrass on his lawn and about the change in the neighborhood we taught in and he kept his class of forty pupils well in line by a hefty use of the rattan. I used to think that, within a dreary school and in an awful cellar room with such an overload of pupils, for a man of very few qualifications he probably did a reasonably good job. But the arrival of the new Negro teacher suddenly changed things.

The change was brought about because, by all obvious credentials, the new Negro teacher was so many miles out of the older teacher's league. Educated at Michigan State, cultivated,

thoroughly resourceful, the new teacher literally could not open his mouth without shattering the regular teacher with insecurity. The other thing, of course, which was most important, was that the boys in the room, kept down all year by the old potato-teacher, responded promptly to the obvious differences between the two men who were now in front of them each morning and got a rapid-fire education, and what must have appeared to them as a carefully planned indoctrination, in the natural advantages of being black. Almost everything the regular teacher could do, it seemed, the new teacher could do better. The only serious problem, as the new teacher quickly told me, was that he was getting almost no opportunity to teach. Sometimes he got to do a little history, sometimes a little bit of something else. If the carpentry shop was not occupied, he could take a group of boys in there for remedial work in math or reading. They would have to sit between drills and jigsaws or whatever other equipment might be around them or else on top of sawdust-covered planks, but at least it did give him a little chance to teach. When that room was occupied, he would take the boys up into our auditorium but, perhaps because he had a higher sense of his own dignity than other teachers had—or else perhaps a higher sense of dignity of the Negro boys—he refused finally to work there, saying flatly that to work with his pupils in such a crossfire of voice was futile. The futility of which he spoke was the futility amidst which I had been working, without much objection, all that year.

His open clean objections were uncluttered by the fear that tied down certain other Negro teachers, of losing their jobs or losing the chance for the small good they could get done with their one class, because he was looking toward a much larger goal and had, it seemed, a much less provincial and much less parochial past. He also had very few of the white inhibitions that had rendered me for so long rather ineffective, for the very uncomplicated reason that his skin was black. Yet many of our ideas, independently arrived at, proved to be the same and we soon grew to be friends.

I went over to his house one Saturday and met his wife and daughter and talked with him about what was happening in the school and in the neighborhood and we developed the idea of joining in a meeting with local parents and offering them some information about what was going on. Although I felt a knot of instantaneous fear in my stomach at the thought of what I was doing, I knew I couldn't back out and I knew while we were talking that I was going to be obliged to do it. The other teacher, whom I will call Carl, contacted some of the parents and the result of his telephoning, which followed a few days later, was perhaps one of the first real parents' and teachers' meetings ever held in a Negro neighborhood of Boston because it was not under the supervision of the school administration and it was therefore honest and untrammeled by any false supplications to the power of the school. The meeting was held at a church near the school building. It was not large but it brought about half a dozen teachers from various Boston schools and about fifteen or twenty parents from our school. The new teacher spoke first and then I did and then we answered questions and we told the parents, in answer to their inquiries, about the classes in the cellar, those in the auditorium, the outdated curriculum, the dilapidated materials and outdated textbooks and the overall worthlessness of the compensatory program as a viable means of making up for the deficiencies of a segregated school. A mother of Fifth Grade children was surprised to be told of a practice by which an entire class would be rattanned for the misbehavior of one pupil. A Fourth Grade mother was embittered to learn for the first time that one of the Fourth Grades had been stuck all year with a teacher who could

not control children and who had already had similar difficulties within another school. Other parents had not been advised by the Principal that reading levels were far behind the national average at our school and that the reading levels seemed to be growing worse with every year the children spent in school.

The outcome of this meeting was a decision on the part of the parents to make a complaint to the school in the form of stated demands and also to join in a picket at School Committee Headquarters which had been begun by a Boston minister and then had been joined and supported by members of various parent organizations. As soon as possible after that meeting, both Carl and I went in and told the Principal about it. We did not want to leave the chance that she might view it as something secret or something of which we were ashamed. It is true that, when I went in to talk to her, my hands were shaking and my voice was trembling badly. At a distance from the school I had joined in protests without reluctance but here it seemed different and it created a great deal of anxiety in me when the confrontation of opposites came so close. I did not tell her about our meeting truculently, but quietly. I said it was something I believed in and that nothing said at the meeting would have been news to her, but I added that I knew very well it was still the kind of meeting of which she would have to strongly disapprove.

And that was so. She said it had been a mistake. She told me also that she did not know if a person accepting the pay of the Boston School Committee had the right to join in a picket against his own employer, adding that she felt it was an improper way to do things and that in time many problems with which she and I were both concerned would undoubtedly begin to be corrected, although not due to pressure from people who were misinformed. I just said quietly that I felt she was wrong, that I was not misinformed, nor were the parents any longer. So I went out of her office feeling more free and more at peace with myself than I had felt the whole year long, and taught, I imagine, more effectively for it too, although the Reading Teacher told me later that, since I had gone in to talk to her, the Principal had been in a very unpleasant state of mind.

Carl, as it happened, left our school almost as suddenly as he had come there. Four or five weeks of it was about all that he could stand and then one day he just walked out. The teacher who had worked with him downstairs said of him, "He couldn't take it," meaning, I guess, that the children were too rough for him, but this was not the case. And upstairs the Reading Teacher told me: "It just doesn't look good for them. Even if he did feel it was degrading to him here. He had no right to walk out on his own people. The other Negro teachers are embarrassed." But I thought that Carl had a clearer sense of what was happening in this building than some of the more traditional Negro teachers had. And so, even though I would not have said it to them since I had no wish to act as a judge of them and of what they had to endure, still in one way, not as a teacher but just as a person, I admired him more than I admired any of the rest: because he had the courage not only of his convictions but also of his race. Selfishly, for the sake of having a friend I could talk to openly, I found I wished that he had stayed.

Questions for Discussion and Debate

1. Find evidence in this selection that can explain the title of the book from which it is taken, that is, *Death at an Early Age: The Destruction of the Minds and Hearts of Negro Children in the Boston Public Schools*.

2. The idea of a "hidden curriculum" refers to what schools *indirectly* teach students by the actions they take outside of the classroom or indirectly in the classroom. Cite examples of the hidden curriculum in this section.

3. Describe the attitudes of the Reading Teacher and the Math Teacher. Are they typical? Untypical? How could you go about reaching some conclusions on this question?

4. What was the new teacher, Carl, able to achieve in his short stay? What were his methods? What evidence, if any, is there that his attempt to raise the political consciousness of the parents and teachers will result in change?

5. Debate the pros and cons of busing to achieve integration. There have been *many* articles written on this subject.

6. Divide the class into two groups and assign one to argue in favor of and the other against Kozol's decision to spend a day outside of school participating in acts of civil disobedience in the form of demonstrations at the Federal Building in Boston, where hundreds were protesting the government's lack of defense of the lives of Black and White civil rights workers in the South.

7. *A Political Spectrum for Education*. Following is a rather simplistic and approximate diagram of liberal and conservative political views related to education.

    a. Assuming that it has validity, place yourself on the spectrum. Where do you stand, and why?

    b. Place Kozol on the spectrum. Explain your choice.

Liberal	Moderate	Conservative
a. More money for public schools. Limit school choice to *public* school choice.		a. Less money for public education. (Favor cutting taxes.) Open to the use of public money for attending private and parochial school (vouchers); in favor of *unlimited* school choice.
b. More government involvement in bringing about equality of education.		b. Less government involvement in bringing about equality of education.
c. Separation of church and state (no prayers in school).		c. School prayer is acceptable.
d. Allow for controversial issues in the curriculum.		d. Prefer no controversial content.

Activities and Projects

1. The following topics are excellent issues on which to do research because, while they have been historically significant, they are *still* being debated inside educational and political circles today.

   - Busing to achieve integration (The views of both Blacks and Whites are not necessarily what you might predict. The issue of the value of the neighborhood school versus integrated schools comes up here.)

   - Laws mandating that the funding of public schools be based on property taxes (Taxes, of course, are based on the income and value of the property in particular districts, poorer areas obviously taking in less revenue for their schools.)

   - *Brown* v. *The Board of Education* (1954) and how that decision came about; also, the response, or lack of response, to the mandate to integrate schools.

   - Innovations of the 1990s and early 21st century taking place in urban schools, for example, takeovers by universities and businesses.

   - Civil disobedience as a form of political protest: Many of the greatest figures in history, from Jefferson to Thoreau to Gandhi and Martin Luther King, Jr., have utilized this form of protest. Investigate its meaning, methods, and historic effectiveness in bringing about change.

   - The Goals 2000 Act (1994), developed to better to integrate efforts of the local, state, and federal governments toward improving education: The debate continues as to how well we are doing in this effort. According to Albert Shanker (1997, p. 5), the late leader of the American Federation of Teachers, and "Building a Nation of Learners, 1996" (National Education Goals Report, 1997), there has not been much progress. Find out the provisions of the act so that you can join in the debate. Then check out how successful your school system has been in meeting Goals 2000.

2. Compare and contrast Kozol's experiences with the educational politics experienced by Stuart and Conroy. Prepare a brief report on the similarities and differences among them.

4.6 ▌ School-to-Work Opportunities Act of 1994

103rd Congress of the United States

The School-to-Work Opportunities Act of 1994 is an example of legislation that originated on the federal level but is being implemented by state and local authorities, a process that brings with it certain difficulties. One of those difficulties, for example, has to do with the ability of the federal government to oversee all of the state and local agencies responsible for the law's implementation: Will all of them work at the same pace? Spend equal amounts of time on the effort? Designate comparable personnel? Design equally effective projects? Allocate the funding received in similar ways? These and many more difficulties make the implementation of this worthwhile and detailed legislation a mighty big task.

The School-to-Work Opportunities Act is the product of the federal legislative political process and promotes programs that educate students about careers and the working world. Excerpted here is Section 2 of the law, "Findings," a list of reasons why Congress decided that there was a need for this legislation. Together these 10 reasons provide the rationale for the act. Also included is Section 3, "Purposes and Congressional Intent," which delineates the 14 purposes of this act, as well as the overall intent of Congress in establishing it.

Frankly, not all congressional acts are as clearly and simply expressed as this one is. Fortunately, you will find the language of the act direct and to the point. *Before* you read it, however, take a sheet of paper and a pen and see if you can predict some of the items in the two sections included in this excerpt. For example, what are some of the possible *reasons* for needing a school-to-work policy? What do you think are some of its *purposes*? After you write down a few answers, read the excerpt and see if any of your responses appear there.

Public Law 103-239   H.R. 2884
108 Stat 568
May 4, 1994

Begun and held at the City of Washington on Tuesday, the twenty-fifth day of January, one thousand nine hundred and ninety-four

AN ACT

To establish a national framework for the development of School-to-Work Opportunities systems in all States, and for other purposes.

Be it enacted by the Senate and House of Representatives of the United States of America in Congress assembled . . .

SECTION 2. FINDINGS.

Congress finds that—

(1) three-fourths of high school students in the United States enter the workforce without baccalaureate degrees, and many do not possess the academic and entry-level occupational skills necessary to succeed in the changing United States workplace;

(2) a substantial number of youths in the United States, especially disadvantaged students, students of diverse racial, ethnic, and cultural backgrounds, and students with disabilities, do not complete high school;

(3) unemployment among youths in the United States is intolerably high, and earnings of high school graduates have been falling relative to earnings of individuals with more education;

(4) the workplace in the United States is changing in response to heightened international competition and new technologies, and such forces, which are ultimately beneficial to the Nation, are shrinking the demand for and undermining the earning power of unskilled labor;

(5) the United States lacks a comprehensive and coherent system to help its youths acquire the knowledge, skills, abilities, and information about and access to the labor market necessary to make an effective transition from school to career-oriented work or to further education and training;

(6) students in the United States can achieve high academic and occupational standards, and many learn better and retain more when the students learn in context, rather than in the abstract;

(7) while many students in the United States have part-time jobs, there is infrequent linkage between—

(A) such jobs; and

(B) the career planning or exploration, or the school-based learning, of such students;

(8) the work-based learning approach, which is modeled after the time-honored apprenticeship concept integrates theoretical instruction with structured on-the-job training, and this approach, combined with school-based learning, can be very effective in engaging student interest, enhancing skill acquisition, developing positive work attitudes, and preparing youths for high-skill, high-wage careers;

(9) Federal resources currently fund a series of categorical, work-related education and training programs, many of which serve disadvantaged youths, that are not administered as a coherent whole; and

(10) in 1992 approximately 3,400,000 individuals in the United States age 16 through 24 had not completed high school and were not currently enrolled in school, a number representing approximately 11 percent of all individuals in this age group, which indicates that these young persons are particularly unprepared for the demands of a 21st century workforce.

SECTION 3. PURPOSES AND CONGRESSIONAL INTENT.

(a) **Purposes.** The purposes of this Act are—

(1) to establish a national framework within which all States can create statewide School-to-Work Opportunities systems that—

(A) are a part of comprehensive education reform;

(B) are integrated with the systems developed under the Goals 2000: Educate America Act and the National Skill Standards Act of 1994; and

(C) offer opportunities for all students to participate in a performance-based education and training program that will—

(i) enable the students to earn portable credentials;

(ii) prepare the students for first jobs in high-skill, high-wage careers; and

(iii) increase their opportunities for further education, including education in a 4-year college or university;

(2) to facilitate the creation of a universal, high-quality school-to-work transition system that enables youths in the United States to identify and navigate paths to productive and progressively more rewarding roles in the workplace;

(3) to utilize workplaces as active learning environments in the educational process by making employers joint partners with educators in providing opportunities for all students to participate in high-quality, work-based learning experiences;

(4) to use Federal funds under this Act as venture capital, to underwrite the initial costs of planning and establishing statewide School-to-Work Opportunities systems that will be maintained with other Federal, State, and local resources;

(5) to promote the formation of local partnerships that are dedicated to linking the worlds of school and work among secondary schools and postsecondary educational institutions, private and public employers, labor organizations, government, community-based organizations, parents, students, State educational agencies, local educational agencies, and training and human service agencies;

(6) to promote the formation of local partnerships between elementary schools and secondary schools (including middle schools) and local businesses as an investment in future workplace productivity and competitiveness;

(7) to help all students attain high academic and occupational standards;

(8) to build on and advance a range of promising school-to-work activities, such as tech-prep education, career academies, school-to-apprenticeship programs, cooperative education, youth apprenticeship, school-sponsored enterprises, business-education compacts, and promising strategies that assist school dropouts, that can be developed into programs funded under this Act;

(9) to improve the knowledge and skills of youths by integrating academic and occupational learning, integrating school-based and work-based learning, and building effective linkages between secondary and postsecondary education;

(10) to encourage the development and implementation of programs that will require paid high-quality, work-based learning experiences;

(11) to motivate all youths, including low-achieving youths, school dropouts, and youths with disabilities, to stay in or return to school or a classroom setting and strive to succeed, by providing enriched learning experiences and assistance in obtaining good jobs and continuing their education in postsecondary educational institutions;

(12) to expose students to a broad array of career opportunities, and facilitate the selection of career majors, based on individual interests, goals, strengths, and abilities;

(13) to increase opportunities for minorities, women, and individuals with disabilities, by enabling individuals to prepare for careers that are not traditional for their race, gender, or disability; and

(14) to further the National Education Goals set forth in title I of the Goals 2000: Educate America Act.

(b) **Congressional Intent.** It is the intent of Congress that the Secretary of Labor and the Secretary of Education jointly administer this Act in a flexible manner that—

(1) promotes State and local discretion in establishing and implementing statewide School-to-Work Opportunities systems and School-to-Work Opportunities programs; and

(2) contributes to reinventing government by—

(A) building on State and local capacity;

(B) eliminating duplication in education and training programs for youths by integrating such programs into one comprehensive system;

(C) maximizing the effective use of resources;

(D) supporting locally established initiatives;

(E) requiring measurable goals for performance; and

(F) offering flexibility in meeting such goals.

Questions for Discussion and Debate

1. Reread the list of reasons for enacting this policy as stated in Section 2, "Findings." Which three reasons do you think comprise the strongest rationale for this legislation? Explain why. Then debate *your* conclusions with those reached by your peers.

2. Do the same thing for Section 3, "Purposes and Congressional Intent," that you did for Section 2; that is, identify the three most significant purposes in your opinion. Hold a similar session comparing and contrasting your responses with those of the rest of the class.

3. What did you learn from this excerpt that you did not know before?

4. If you have been exposed to—or actually participated in—any of the programs that came about as a result of this act, share that information with the class.

5. Do you favor this act? Why, or why not?

Activities and Projects

1. Interview the person responsible for overseeing the school-to-work legislation in the school system closest to you. Among the questions you might ask him or her are, What are the difficulties of implementing this act? and What input is there from the federal government at this point?

2. Since this legislation covers Grades K–12, the kinds of programs teachers are designing to fulfill the prescribed goals are likely to be very diverse. Before doing research on what elementary versus high-school teachers are doing with their classes, brainstorm with your peers and come up with a few creative curricular activities on both levels that *you* think would satisfy the objectives of the act. Then go out into the field or use library sources to find out what is actually happening as a result of the School-to-Work Act.

You might want to try your hand at utilizing several of the research sources that contain educational studies and literature. Three of the most valuable references are ERIC (Educational Resources Information Center), RIE (Resources in Education), and CIJE (Current Index to Journals in Education). Do any of them sound familiar? Perhaps you have used them before. They all provide access to information related to teaching and education, and many are now on the Internet. The National Center for Education Statistics (NCES), for example, issues Research and Development Reports and other publications that are also available on the Internet, at http://www.ed.gov/NCES.

And, of course, you may find relevant information on school-to-work programs in other foundations of education texts.

3. All three levels of government—federal, state, and local—are actively involved in some way in this congressional act, either in its passage or in its execution. Look at the following chart. This editor has inserted the law in a box on the chart, indicating that the law was a product of the legislative branch of Congress, at the federal level. Across the top of the chart are listed the branches of government, and in the left-hand column, from top to bottom, are the levels. Fill in the chart with the following information.

a. The title of the person *or* group responsible for making educational decisions on that level and in that branch (both the elected politician[s] *and* the school or education personnel).

b. The name of a policy or law passed by that group and/or administered by that group or person.

Level of Government	Branch of Government		
	Legislative	Executive	Judicial
Federal	Congress ------------- School-to-Work Act	------------	-------------
State	-------------	------------	-------------
Local	-------------	------------	-------------

You will find all of the educational sources mentioned in item 2 above useful in locating items to insert in this chart. The Time Line (Selection 2.2) is a useful source as well. Good luck! Compare your findings with those of the rest of the class or complete the chart in pairs or trios.

4. The Department of Education (DOE), during the Clinton administration, was supportive of the school-to-work legislation.

However, there is some question as to the future of the DOE, which is a cabinet-level department established in 1979. Before it existed, there was the Department of Health, Education, and Welfare. Liberal administrations support the existence of a separate department, while conservatives have called for its demise in an effort to conserve money.

(There are also Departments of Education on the state level, which have many functions, including certifying teachers and overseeing educational policy in general.)

Do research on the U.S. DOE. Then decide if *you* think it is a necessary agency of government and needs to stand separately.

4.7 *The Politics of Education* (1985)

Paulo Freire

Critical theory, Paulo Freire's (1922–1987) postmodernist perspective, goes beyond the belief that the poor should be taught to read and write. He believes that education must be connected to the act of transforming society so that the learner—through critical reflection—recognizes that, in addition to having the right to be literate, he or she also has the right to a political voice (Freire, 1985, p. 50). Freire coined the word "conscientization" as the label for the process by which human beings participate in such acts of transformation, which, according to Freire, empower the learner to improve his or her life and change the real world in a revolutionary manner (pp. 106–107). Freire's theory is about education for liberation. There can be no conscientization without the oppressed class's struggling to liberate itself. Education that empowers and liberates is, indeed, political education, "just as political as the education that claims to be neutral, while actually serving the power elite" (p. 125). An important step in the conscientization process involves the learners' gaining an awareness of reality and their own social status in order to change both.

To appreciate Freire's theory, it is useful to know the context out of which it grew. Freire worked with Brazilian peasants in literacy campaigns in the country's northeast. There he developed a dialogue with his students, using everyday terms, implying that he could learn from them as well. He believed that dialogue between learner and teacher was necessary to avoid what he called "the banking conception" of teaching, in which the teacher deposits knowledge into the student's brain. According to Freire, *that* conception is part of the ideology of oppression. The banking conception of teaching is satirized in Tom Paxton's song, "What Did You Learn in School Today?" (Selection 3.14) and is often seen in more traditional, teacher-centered models.

Freire's radical theory—neo-Marxist in its revolutionary nature—proposed eliminating the ideology of repression. Because of his theory, Freire was feared by some in his country as a subversive and jailed in 1964. He was then exiled for 15 years but continued to publish and lecture widely. In 1980, Freire returned to Brazil under a political amnesty, and throughout the 1980s his pedagogy of liberation was embraced in the United States by many African American, Hispanic, and feminist organizations.

From THE POLITICS OF EDUCATION. CULTURE, POWER, AND LIBERATION by Paulo Freire (Translated by Donaldo Macedo). South Hadley, Massachusetts: Bergin & Garvey, 1985, pp. 104, 170.

Reading Freire's writing can be challenging to someone not used to his way of expressing ideas, but you will likely understand the excerpt below, in which he explains his belief in the political nature of education. Essentially Freire believes that education is never neutral. It is a political act. Do you agree with him?

. . . If we don't transcend the idea of education as pure transference of a knowledge that merely describes reality, we will prevent critical consciousness from emerging and thus reinforce political illiteracy. . . .

. . . Whether this is done ingenuously or astutely, separating education from politics is not only artificial but dangerous. To think of education independent from the power that constitutes it, divorced from the concrete world where it is forged, leads us either to reducing it to a world of abstract values and ideals (which the pedagogue constructs inside his consciousness without even understanding the conditioning that makes him think this way), or to converting it to a repertoire of behavioral techniques, or to perceiving it as a springboard for changing reality.

In fact, it is not education that molds society to certain standards, but society that forms itself by its own standards and molds education to conform with those values that sustain it. Since this is not a mechanical process, a society that structures education to benefit those in power invariably has within it the fundamental elements for its self-preservation. . . . This is the reason any radical and profound transformation of an educational system can only take place (and even then, not automatically or mechanically) when society is also radically transformed.

This does not mean, however, that those educators who want and, even more so, are committed to the radical or revolutionary transformation of their society can do nothing. They have a lot to do, and without resorting to prescriptive formulas, they should determine their goals and learn how to reach them according to the concrete historical conditions under which they live.

Questions for Discussion and Debate

1. Explain the basis for Freire's belief that education and politics are connected by referring to portions of this excerpt.

2. Do you agree with Freire that education is a political act? Why, or why not? Discuss your views with the rest of the class.

3. Based on the knowledge you now have about Freire's ideas, what do you think he would say about tracking, the tradition in many high schools of separating students based on ability? What do *you* think about this practice? Debate the pros and cons of tracking with your peers.

4. Have you observed any practices in schools that foster interaction among *all* groups? If so, describe them.

5. Politically disenfranchised adults were likely once politically disenfranchised students. Discuss the question of whether or not the kind of conscientization Freire espouses can be effective with students, who, unlike the adults with whom Freire worked, might not yet bring life experience to their literacy lessons.

Activities and Projects

1. Read excerpts from the works of critical theorists, proponents of Freire, such as Henry A. Giroux (1985) and Stanley Aronowitz (Aronowitz & Giroux, 1985). Share their ideas with the class and lead a critical discussion assessing their views. Consider playing the devil's advocate if more conservative perspectives are not forthcoming from the class.

2. Freire's ideas are popular with groups who seek a political voice in their society. On the other hand, his revolutionary ideas are very controversial among conservative groups, in Freire's words, "the ruling social classes" or the "dominant class," who prefer the status quo. (See the political spectrum in this chapter, Selection 4.5, question 7.) Work with a colleague to set up a dialogue in which you become Freire and your colleague takes the role of one of the top conservative theorists, such as E. D. Hirsch, Jr. After doing research on your respective personas, carry on the dialogue in front of the class. Focus on two or three ideas about which the two disagree.

3. Find out more about Freire's work with peasants in his native Brazil. Then read the excerpt by Sylvia Ashton-Warner (Selection 6.2) in which she describes her work with Maori students in New Zealand. Share your findings with the class or write a short paper in which you compare and contrast their experiences in their respective countries working with, in Freire's words, "oppressed peoples."

4. One of the methods used by African Americans to call attention to, in Jonathan Kozol's words, the "savage inequalities" existing in parts of the United States, was nonviolent civil disobedience. This method included such acts as sitting in the front of a bus in the South in the 1950s and 1960s, when to do so was against the law, and marching peacefully for voter registration and against the poll tax. Find out about Freire's ideas and behaviors related to civil disobedience.

5. Protest songs such as "Oh, Freedom" and "We Shall Overcome" express people's desire for freedom, liberation, and an equal voice in their society. Locate several of these freedom songs and research their role in the 1950s/1960s U.S. Civil Rights movement. Play recordings of the songs in class. You might also transcribe the words so the class can analyze the messages in the songs. Compare these messages with the ideas of Paulo Freire.

6. Howard Gardner, in his book, *The Disciplined Mind, What All Students Should Understand* (1999), writes, "Education is politicized everywhere, but rarely as much as in the United States. In most other democratic (and even some nondemocratic) countries, a relatively non-politicized ministry or civil service endures despite changes in government. In the United States, however, education at every level, federal, state, and local, is suffused with political considerations. Newly appointed heads of bureaucracies . . . routinely overthrow the policies of their predecessors" (p. 223). To what extent is Gardner's view valid? Choose *one* level of government for the purposes of research and gather data supporting or refuting the quote.

7. In his book, *The Schools We Need and Why We Don't Have Them* (1996), E. D. Hirsch, Jr. (Selection 4.8), attacks progressive educational programs using arguments similar to those contained in Diane

Ravitch's (2000) book (Selection, 3.9); he attacks, in particular, Freire's idea that politics and education are connected. Hirsch (1966) believes in what he calls political progressivism, that is, social justice, but believes that it can be achieved only through *educational conservatism*, the acquisition by the oppressed classes of *traditional* knowledge in order to understand the worlds of nature and culture surrounding them (p. 7). Writes Hirsch, ". . . Nations (including our own) that have stuck to the principles of Freire have failed to change the social and economic status quo" (p. 7).

Is this statement true? Do research on the *results* of Freire's work in Brazil and in other parts of the world—including America—where his followers have applied his principles. Who is right: Hirsch or Freire?

8. While current critical theories such as those of Freire appear to be radical and innovative in their response to the needs of the masses, the fact is that Leo Tolstoy, the noted Russian author, expressed those same ideas in his educational journal over 100 years ago: "For the educating class to know what is good and what is bad, the classes which receive the education must have the full power to express their dissatisfaction, or, at least, to swerve from the education which instinctively does not satisfy them . . . [for] the criterion of pedagogies is only liberty" (Weiner, 1967, p. 29).

Such remarks place Tolstoy among today's most progressive thinkers on education and support the idea expressed in chapter 2 that there is nothing really new under the educational sun. Do research on some of the 19th-century theorists on education from various parts of the world and see if you can discover other precursors of Freire's critical theory besides Tolstoy.

4.8 "Test Evasion" (1996)

E. D. Hirsch, Jr.

E. D. Hirsch, Jr., has been on the battlefield in a lot of "wars"; first, there were the so-called culture wars (chapter 6) and, more recently, education's *testing* wars. Like the earlier battles, the current one pits liberals against conservatives, or progressives against traditionalists. While all sides believe that it is necessary to hold teachers and students accountable for their respective roles in the educational process, they differ as to how best to achieve that accountability. At present there are no standards in American public education, that is, no officially recognized, mandated, agreed-upon expectations of what students should know at each level of schooling. So another battle in the ongoing testing wars involves the issue of whether or not there *should* be such official standards. Indeed, it is difficult to advocate standardized testing without first having a clear delineation of what curriculum standards those tests should be measuring. And it is, indeed, unfair to test students without devoting the resources necessary to helping them meet those standards (Mosle, 1996, pp. 46, 68). Hirsch addresses many of these concerns in the book from which this excerpt is taken, *The Schools We Need and Why We Don't Have Them* (1996).

He identifies himself as a political liberal who believes that the only means for achieving social justice is through traditional methods including high-stakes testing. Unlike Freire (Selection 4.7), Hirsch does not see any contradiction between being a political liberal (for social justice) and being an educational conservative (for high-stakes testing).

Just as with the culture wars of the 1980s and 1990s, the ongoing debates have resulted in a proliferation of articles and treatises for and against testing (Caputo-Pearl, 2001; Ehrenfeld, 2001; Gehring, 2001; Hirsch, 1996; Hoff, 2001; Merrow, 2001; Popham, 2001; Ravitch, 2000; Sacks, 2000; Suchak, 2001; Winerip, 2001).

Based on the increasing number of state legislatures that are passing so-called reform acts that mandate testing students on a regular basis, and on Congress's 2001 version of the ESEA (Elementary and Secondary Education Act), which requires, among other things, that states frequently test students in reading and mathematics, it appears that the educational conservatives are winning. The success of the *pro*-testers may be due in part to the kinds of arguments Hirsch makes here for testing.

While Hirsch admits that standardized tests may sometimes be poorly constructed and misused—problems, he argues, that should be exposed and corrected—he goes on to say that these tests are, nevertheless, the most accurate and fair instruments available. He refutes the argument by liberals that standardized tests, for example, aren't capable of testing real-world reading activities. Writes Hirsch (1996), " . . . More 'authentic' types of reading tests are not only uncontrolled, hence unfair, but also unable to replicate real-world reading, and no "performance" (mocking the liberals' support for performance testing) that takes place in school reproduces performance in the real world" (p. 194).

Unlike his book *Cultural Literacy* (1987), which was greeted with hostility because of the heavily pro-Western list of ideas he believed every educated person should know, Hirsch's more recent book, from which this excerpt is taken, has drawn favorable reviews from the ranks of liberal organizations such as the American Federation of Teachers, who were impressed with the results of his Core Knowledge curriculum. This reform movement embodies a proposal to introduce grade-by-grade content standards. More than 900 schools have become Core Knowledge schools, but unlike the schools that have aligned themselves with Ted Sizer's Coalition for Essential Schools (see Selection 5.10), which model progressive assessment techniques, the Core Knowledge schools advocate more traditional instruments for testing students' grasp of Hirsch's core curriculum. As you read Hirsch's arguments for traditional testing and his blunt dismissal of the liberal perspective, decide where you stand on this controversial issue. Reflect also on your personal experiences with testing.

Using reliable tests to gauge the achievement of well-defined and reachable educational goals, while at the same time ensuring that teachers and parents are provided with the tools to meet them, illustrates a proper use of high-stakes standardized tests. If there is to be responsible accountability, there is at the same time a moral imperative to provide sufficient advice and guidance. Not to provide the means for accomplishing the teaching goals on the one hand, and not to hold parents, teachers, and students accountable for achieving them on the other, are equal abandonments of adult responsibility to children. Testing without guidance is as irresponsible as guidance without testing. Neither side of the equation should be neglected.

. . . Some of the complaints concern the unfairness of standardized tests: that, being standardized, they are culturally and racially biased, insensitive to individual differences, and conducive to social inequality. Other objections concern their impact on the quality of education: that standardized tests measure only lower-order skills, encourage passivity and superficiality in learning, and convey a hidden message that there is a simple right answer to every problem, no matter how complex and ambiguous. . . .

The effect of such criticism is to suggest that those who oppose standardized tests are the true advocates of greater social equity, more demanding education, higher real-world competencies, and greater independent-mindedness. By contrast, those who favor standardized tests are depicted as supposing that human worth can be rated on a linear scale, as wrongly assuming that the language of test accountability is the language of genuine education, and as entertaining the misguided belief that the world can be purged of its complexity, diversity, and ambiguity. . . . It is true that some of the existing multiple-choice tests do encourage superficiality and passivity. But it is also true that some do not. The wholesale indictment of standardized tests

is facile and inaccurate. And since the proposed alternatives (i.e., performance tests) are not by themselves reliable or fair, a successful campaign to abolish standardized tests would result in our schools becoming even less equitable and our students less competent than they now are. . . .

The final irony of the antitesting movement is that in the name of social fairness it opposes using high-stakes tests as gatekeepers, monitors, and incentives—functions that are essential to social fairness. Without effective monitoring and high incentives, including high-stakes testing programs, no educational system has achieved or could achieve excellence and equity. Good tests are necessary to instruct, to monitor, and to motivate. John Bishop has shown in great detail the importance of high-stakes tests in motivating students to work hard.[1] The Romantic idea that learning is natural, and that the motivation for academic achievement comes from within, is an illusion that forms one of the greatest barriers to social justice imaginable, since poor and disadvantaged students must be motivated to work even harder than advantaged students in order to achieve equality of educational opportunity. It was Antonio Gramsci, that wise spokesman for the disadvantaged and disenfranchised, who wrote that the gravest disservice to social justice entailed by Romantic theories of education is the delusion that educational achievement comes as naturally as leaves to a tree, without extrinsic motivation, discipline, toil, or sweat. . . .

Education schools currently do not convey to our teachers the results of . . . firmly established research showing the superior effectiveness of clear focus, definite standards, diligent practice, and continual monitoring through tests and other means. Instead, American

---

[1]Bishop, J. (1992, March). Why U.S. students need incentives to learn. *Educational Leadership*, 15–18.

education schools derogate such traditional practices in favor of the progressive program of individual pacing, discovery learning, thematic teaching, nonobjective testing, and so on. Their captive audiences, consisting of millions of teachers, are offered no intellectual alternatives to these constantly repeated mistakes, which are, indeed, presented as fruits of the most recent research. The resulting pandemic of mistaken ideas may be the gravest barrier to America's educational improvement. If this disabling indoctrination continues unabated, then something quite revolutionary will have to be done about our system of training and certifying teachers. A beginning can be made by insisting upon more intellectual diversity within education schools. The tenacity and unanimity with which they adhere to the progressive doctrine may be owing to that doctrine's inability to withstand empirical and intellectual challenge in a free and open encounter. If such is the case, as I believe, then perhaps a rather small cadre of maverick professors in every education school might soon make the whole Wizard of Oz apparatus collapse like a punctured balloon.

Questions for Discussion and Debate

1. Hirsch notes two arguments against multiple-choice testing—that some of them encourage superficiality *and* passivity—arguments he believes are weak.

   a. List other arguments *against* multiple-choice testing.

   b. Below each of the arguments against this type of testing, list some arguments *for* multiple-choice testing.

   c. Look at both viewpoints, then write down *your* position in a one-page paper. Share it with the rest of the class or in a small group.

2. Is there a way to maintain standardized state testing, which many people, like Hirsch, believe is necessary as an objective measure of student performance, and still keep teachers lively and the curriculum current and relevant? Debate this question.

3. What is the nature of Hirsch's critique of education schools? Summarize his opinion in your own words, then critique his critique. To what extent is he accurate? Provide evidence to support your perspective.

4. Write down what you consider to be the most accurate, logical sentence in this excerpt and explain why it makes so much sense to you. Share your view with others.

5. Teacher and author, Frank McCourt, wrote in his memoir *'Tis* (1999) about his experiences teaching English and his frustrations with all of the mandated curricula: "There are teaching guides so detailed and comprehensive I need never think for myself. They are packed with enough quizzes, tests, examinations to keep my students in a constant state of nervous tension" (p. 335). To keep from leaving the profession altogether, McCourt decides to begin enjoying the act of teaching and teach what he loved, and "to hell with the curriculum" (p. 340). Debate his decision. Consider the benefits as well as the consequences of his decision for his students (and himself). Might his decision actually be a better approach to preparing students to take major tests?

6. Some of the sentiments expressed by singer and songwriter Billy Joel in his classic song,

"Pressure" (Joel Songs [BMI], 1981), apply to the testing situation, in which some students experience a disabling kind of pressure and feelings of isolation and frustration. You can almost hear a student saying these words to himself or herself:

You have to pace yourself
Pressure
You're just like everybody else
Pressure
You've only had to run so far
So good
But you will come to a place
Where the only thing you feel
Are loaded guns in your face
And you'll have to deal with
Pressure

Joel's metaphors are meaningful in the context of testing. For some students, and not just those with learning disabilities, tests are "loaded guns in [their] face," and try as they might, they are immobilized and frozen by them. Few of us have escaped such pressure at one time or another, perhaps caused not by a test but by another frightening situation that makes our hearts race and our temples pulsate beyond the comfort level.

Assuming that tests are always going to be a part of a child's life in school, what are some ways that teachers can help students deal with these pressures? (Perhaps your suggestions are worth putting together in a brochure and disseminating to school faculty.)

7. Richard K. Atkinson, President of the University of California, Santa Barbara, has proposed that his system stop requiring the main SAT exam (SAT 1), which he considers an inappropriate and unfair measure of high-school students (Steinberg, 2001). He is supported by many of the nation's public university professors and administrators who identify the exam's shortcomings as follows: It is a distraction to too many high-school students and further handicaps disadvantaged students, particularly minority students. Argue the other side. What do you think the lobbyists from the College Board, the SAT establishment, and the test-coaching industry might say, as well as the proponents of the exam from among the Ivy League? (Note of interest: In an effort to make the SAT 1 show more accurately what students learn in high school and how prepared they are for college, the Trustees of the College Board *agreed* to overhaul the test. Beginning in 2005, the SAT 1 will drop two of its most challenging—and for many students, dread-inducing—sections: quantitative comparisons and verbal analogies. The revised exam will feature a 20- to 30-minute written essay, multiple-choice grammar questions, and a section devoted to higher-level mathematics [Cavanagh, 2002, pp. 1, 28].)

Activities and Projects

1. Hand in hand with the controversy over high-stakes testing is the debate over whether or not to establish national standards, that is, a curriculum set in Washington, DC, and monitored in every town and city through testing, much like the systems that exist in most European countries and elsewhere in the world. "Resistance to standards [however] comes from both liberal and conservative quarters. Progressive educators worry

that a national curriculum would lead to more rote-learning and a greater reliance on standardized tests. [Some] conservatives, who you might think would cozy up to standards, are deeply suspicious of any sort of outside meddling in their neighborhood schools" (Mosle, 1996, p. 47).

Yet there are strong arguments (equality of education, higher achievement) in favor of standards coming from both sides (Hirsch, 1996; Mosle, 1996; Ravitch, 2000). Even the late Albert Shanker, the noted liberal leader of the AFT, believed that standards with accompanying assessments were a priority before any other type of reform. While some states such as Massachusetts have devised Curriculum Frameworks, a set of mandated *national* standards does not yet exist. Should there be one? Here is a chance for you to do some research in comparative education. With a partner, do research on countries such as France, Sweden, India, and Russia to determine the pros and cons of a national curriculum. Then present a debate, one of you taking the affirmative position and the other the negative. Following the debate invite the rest of the class to voice their opinions.

2. Consider the fact that the nation will need 2 million qualified teachers over the next decade, people who will be responsible for raising test scores and meeting standards. Do research on (a) why the problem of finding teachers exists; (b) the ways in which some states are tackling this problem; (Note also which school systems are not facing teacher shortages and why they are not) (c) what role money is playing in this quest; and (d) the alternative routes, or shortcuts, into the teaching profession that exist.

3. The Texas Assessment of Academic Standards (TAAS), dubbed by some the "Texas Miracle," is perhaps the crowning glory of President George W. Bush's years as governor of Texas. Upheld by business and political leaders from both sides as an unequivocal success, the "miracle" has been attacked in a series of in-depth studies by educators as nothing more than a myth. Research both sides of this miracle and come to your own conclusions. Present all viewpoints, including your own, to the class along with ample documentation.

4. Some critics of the current testing craze might call Richard Mills "Dr. Jekyll and Mr. Hyde." As Education Commissioner of Vermont, he was "Mr. Portfolio," advocating the use of portfolios, considered to be a progressive and authentic means of assessment. More recently, however, in his role as New York State's Education Commissioner, he became more of a "scorekeeper," coming down on the side of traditional periodic testing. Find out more about Mills's perspectives and those of others who appear to have switched sides. If possible, interview teachers and others about these two types of assessments. Then prepare a chart or rubric in which you include the pros and cons of both the traditional and the more progressive, authentic methods of assessing students.

5. In the reauthorized version of the ESEA (Elementary and Secondary Education Act) passed by Congress in 2001, dubbed "No Child Left Behind" by the Bush administration, the provisions for testing require the following.

   • All states develop and administer annual proficiency tests in reading (with an emphasis on phonics) and math for all students in Grades 3 through 8 by the 2005–2006 school year. (Congress will provide $400 million to help states develop and administer these tests.) The tests must align with each state's current academic content standards.

• Test data are used to measure the performance of each school. The data are broken down and reported by race, gender, income, and other criteria to measure and compare the performance of groups.

• A sample of fourth and eighth graders in each state participates in the National Assessment of Educational Progress (NAEP) in reading and math every year to verify the state's results on its own tests.

• States provide parents with annual report cards detailing the school's performance and their child's progress in the key subject areas.

The revised legislation (http://www.nochildleftbehind.gov) also contains provisions on accountability and academic improvement, teacher quality, reading, bilingual education, and flexibility. Find out about the entire act, including the degree of funding for poor children and those with special needs. Then evaluate the legislation and the testing and accountability measures, in particular. Find out about the implementation of the act and the results thus far. Does the 2001 ESEA live up to its name "No Child Left Behind"?

6. The journal *Educational Leadership* explored the use of standards to improve teaching and learning (September 2001) and received letters from many teachers in response (December 2001/January 2002), all of whom explained how standards made their professional lives better for a number of reasons. In addition to researching the use of standards—one of the main components of Hirsch's Core Knowledge program—interview a cross section of teachers about how they have utilized standards in their instructional program.

7. Locate the movie *Stand and Deliver* in a video store and watch the behavior of the mathematics teacher (Jaime Escalante, in real life) who prepares his mostly Hispanic students for the Advanced Placement exams in calculus. The story centers around the students' impressive success and the subsequent challenge from authorities regarding the validity of their scores. Summarize the film for the class and prepare a list of discussion questions so the class can explore with you the implications this film has for the status of standardized tests.

4.9   "Bakke Syllabus": *Regents of the University of California* v. *Bakke* (1978)

Supreme Court of the United States

Bakke, a White medical-school applicant, was refused admission to medical school while minority applicants with lower scores on the admissions exam were admitted based on the policy of affirmative action. The notion of affirmative action designates that opportunities should be made available—that is, affirmative action should be taken—to make up for past discrimination. Such discrimination had prevented minorities from attaining an equal education, and as a result, they were at a disadvantage when applying to institutions such as medical schools.

Bakke brought his case to the Supreme Court, charging that his rights had been violated; in other words, he charged the university with reverse discrimination.

While there are parts of the actual court decision in this selection, much of what follows is known as the "Bakke Syllabus" and was prepared by the Reporter of Decisions for the convenience of the reader.

Currently, affirmative action is being debated around the country and those against the policy appear to be gaining more followers, as shown by some universities, among them the University of California, eliminating their affirmative action policies. While the Court in this case took an active stand against reverse discrimination, its decision was just murky enough to allow universities to consider race among their admissions criteria.

Courts have played a major role in education since the 1954 *Brown* v. *The Board of Education* decision mandating desegregation of the public schools. Nearly all of what is considered appropriate behavior for teachers and students is defined by laws and/or court decisions, as are the rights of these two groups. In addition, laws and court decisions govern everything from your teaching contract to your retirement policy. Legal and judicial issues thus comprise a large part of the educational political process and rate as one of the most fascinating areas of study for teachers. Such issues appear not only in this chapter, and in this particular selection, but elsewhere in this text. As you study other excerpts, read between the lines for the possible legal and judicial implications involved therein.

NOTE: Where it is feasible, a syllabus (head-note) will be released, as is being done in connection with this case, at the time the opinion is issued. The syllabus constitutes no part of the opinion of the Court but has been prepared by the Reporter of Decisions for the convenience of the reader. See *United States* v. *Detroit Lumber Co.*, 200 U.S. 321, 337.

The Medical School of the University of California at Davis (hereinafter Davis) had two admissions programs for the entering class of 100 students—the regular admissions program and the special admissions program. Under the regular procedure, candidates whose overall undergraduate grade point averages fell below 2.5 on a scale of 4.0 were summarily rejected. About one out of six applicants was then given an interview, following which he was rated on a scale of 1 to 100 by each of the committee members (five in 1973 and six in 1974), his rating being based on the interviewers' summaries, his overall grade point average, his science courses grade point average, and his Medical College Admissions Test (MCAT) scores, letters of recommendation, extracurricular activities, and other biographical data, all of which resulted in a total "benchmark score." The full admissions committee then made offers of admission on the basis of their review of the applicant's file and his score, considering and acting upon applications as they were received. The committee chairman was responsible for placing names on the waiting list and had discretion to include persons with "special skills." A separate committee, a majority of whom were members of minority groups, operated the special admissions program. The 1973 and 1974 application forms, respectively, asked candidates whether they wished to be considered as "economically and/or educationally disadvantaged" applicants and members of a "minority group" (blacks, Chicanos, Asians, American Indians). If an applicant of a minority group was found to be "disadvantaged," he would be rated in a manner similar to the one employed by the general admissions committee. Special candidates, however, did not have to meet the 2.5 grade point cut-off and were not ranked against candidates in the general admissions process. About one-fifth of the special applicants were invited for interviews in 1973 and 1974, following which they were given benchmark scores, and the top choices were then given to the general admissions committee, which could reject special candidates for failure to meet course requirements or other specific deficiencies. The special committee continued to recommend candidates until 16 special admission selections had been made. During a four-year period 63 minority students were admitted to Davis under the special program and 44 under the general program. No disadvantaged whites were admitted under the special program, though many applied. Respondent, a white male, applied to Davis in 1973 and 1974, in both years being considered only under the general admissions program. Though he had a 468 out of 500 score in 1973, he was rejected since no general applicants with scores less than 470 were being accepted after respondent's application, which was filed late in the year, had been processed and completed. At that time four special admission slots were still unfilled. In 1974 respondent applied early, and though he had a total score of 549 out of 600, he was again rejected. In neither year was his name placed on the discretionary waiting list. In both years special applicants were admitted with significantly lower scores than respondent's. After his second rejection, respondent filed this action

in state court for mandatory injunctive and declaratory relief to compel his admission to Davis, alleging that the special admissions program operated to exclude him on the basis of his race in violation of the Equal Protection Clause of the Fourteenth Amendment, a provision of the California Constitution, and § 601 of Title VI of the Civil Rights Act of 1964, which provides, *inter alia,* that no person shall on the ground of race or color be excluded from participating in any program receiving federal financial assistance. Petitioner cross-claimed for a declaration that its special admissions program was lawful. The trial court found that the special program operated as a racial quota, because minority applicants in that program were rated only against one another, and 16 places in the class of 100 were reserved for them. Declaring that petitioner could not take race into account in making admissions decisions, the program was held to violate the Federal and State Constitutions and Title VI. Respondent's admission was not ordered, however, for lack of proof that he would have been admitted but for the special program. The California Supreme Court, applying a strict-scrutiny standard, concluded that the special admissions program was not the least intrusive means of achieving the goals of the admittedly compelling state interests of integrating the medical profession and increasing the number of doctors willing to serve minority patients. Without passing on the state constitutional or federal statutory grounds the court held that petitioner's special admissions program violated the Equal Protection Clause. Since petitioner could not satisfy its burden of demonstrating that respondent, absent the special program, would not have been admitted, the court ordered his admission to Davis.

[Majority Decision] *Held:* The judgment below is affirmed insofar as it orders respondent's admission to Davis and invalidates petitioner's special admissions program, but is reversed insofar as it prohibits petitioner from taking race into account as a factor in its future admissions decisions.

18 Cal. 3d 34, 553 P. 2d 1152, affirmed in part and reversed in part.

MR. JUSTICE POWELL concluded:

1. Title VI proscribes only those racial classifications that would violate the Equal Protection Clause if employed by a State or its agencies. Pp. 12–18.

2. Racial and ethnic classifications of any sort are inherently suspect and call for the most exacting judicial scrutiny. While the goal of achieving a diverse student body is sufficiently compelling to justify consideration of race in admissions decisions under some circumstances, petitioner's special admissions program, which forecloses consideration to persons like respondent, is unnecessary to the achievement of this compelling goal and therefore invalid under the Equal Protection Clause. Pp. 18–49.

3. Since petitioner could not satisfy its burden of proving that respondent would not have been admitted even if there had been no special admissions program, he must be admitted. P. 49.

MR. JUSTICE BRENNAN, MR. JUSTICE WHITE, MR. JUSTICE MARSHALL, and MR. JUSTICE BLACKMUN concluded:

1. Title VI proscribes only those racial classifications that would violate the Equal Protection Clause if employed by a State or its agencies. Pp. 4–31.

2. Racial classifications call for strict judicial scrutiny. Nonetheless the purpose of overcoming substantial, chronic minority underrepresentation in the medical profession is sufficiently important to justify petitioner's remedial use of race. Thus, the judgment below must be reversed in that it prohibits race from being used as a factor in university admissions. Pp. 31–55.

[Minority Decision] MR. JUSTICE STEVENS, joined by THE CHIEF JUSTICE, MR. JUSTICE STEWART, and MR. JUSTICE REHNQUIST, being of the view that whether race can ever be a factor in an admissions policy is not an issue here that Title VI applies; and that respondent was excluded from Davis in violation of Title VI, concurs in the Court's judgment insofar as it affirms the judgment of the court below ordering respondent admitted to Davis. Pp. 1–14.

POWELL, J., announced the Court's judgment and filed an opinion expressing his views of the case, in Parts I, III–A, and V–C of which WHITE, J., joined; and in Parts I and V–C of which BRENNAN, MARSHALL and BLACKMUN, JJ., joined. BRENNAN, WHITE, MARSHALL, and BLACKMUN, JJ., filed an opinion concurring in the judgment in part and dissenting in part. WHITE, MARSHALL, and BLACKMUN, JJ., filed separate opinions. STEVENS, J., filed an opinion concurring in the judgment in part and dissenting-in part, in which BURGER, C. J., and STEWART and REHNQUIST, JJ., joined.

Questions for Discussion and Debate

1. Did Bakke win? Can race be taken into account as a factor in future admissions decisions? Locate in the document the precise phrases and sentences that identify the Supreme Court's majority decision *and* the reasoning behind it. Then explain the decision in your own words.

2. Do you agree with the decision? Why? Why not?

3. Are the universities that have recently withdrawn their affirmative action policies violating the intent of the Supreme Court in the Bakke decision? Defend your conclusion.

4. Debate the issue of affirmative action. Whichever side you take, be sure to support your position using philosophical, sociological, historical, and political perspectives—as does the Court in reaching *its* decisions.

(See item 2 below and consider combining it with this debate.)

5. In what way is the Supreme Court playing a political role in making such decisions? Or *is* it a political role?

Note: Thurgood Marshall, the first African American man to sit on the Supreme Court, was one of the judges deciding the Bakke case. In 1954, he had been the NAACP lawyer who argued the *Brown* v. *The Board of Education* case in front of the Supreme Court—and won.

Activities and Projects

1. Prepare a survey, then sample a random selection of voters to assess their opinions on affirmative action. Report back to the class.

2. Do a study of affirmative action and its effects over the last 20 years. Then reach a conclusion on this question: Is affirmative action *necessary* to prevent discrimination in education and employment? Perhaps the whole class could become involved in this rather hefty research project.

3. Translate your perspective on the issue of affirmative action into literature or drama. In small groups, write short stories or prepare a skit in which you include characters similar to those referred to in this syllabus, that is, a White male, a member of a minority group, medical-school officials, and possibly Supreme Court judges. Read the stories or present the skits.

4. Locate at least three other Supreme Court cases that define the constitutionality or legality of certain teacher or student behaviors about which *you* personally have a question. Find out the following for each case:

a. The name and date of the case.

b. The issue or law involved.

c. The plaintiff's *and* the defendant's position.

d. The Court's decision.

e. The rationale for the decision.

f. Your sources.

Share your information and your view about the Court's decision in each case with the class. Encourage class members to offer their views about the cases you located.

5. Since the fragmented Supreme Court ruling in the Bakke case, the Court has issued three constitutional rulings rejecting affirmative action plans and two constitutional rulings upholding affirmative action plans (Imber and van Geel, 2000, p. 207). Do research on the nature of these cases and the bases for the Court's decision in each case. Then write a position paper in which you share your findings, defend your position on affirmative action, *and* predict the direction you believe the Court will take in future cases.

4.10 "Teacher's Lesson on Intolerance Fails" (1995)

Nancy Roberts Trott

Back to the boards again! School boards, that is. Penny Culliton was fired as an English teacher by a New Hampshire school board. Why she was fired is one of the issues discussed in this newspaper article about Culliton's use of literature to counter homophobia, or intolerance against gays and lesbians. Her struggle to incorporate controversial literature brings home the point that curriculum is political. Curriculum, no matter how objective it appears to be, has been written by people with particular frames of reference or points of view. And texts are chosen—or omitted—by teachers and politicians with definite values in mind. Choosing curriculum is a political act!

As you read the article, try to put yourself in Culliton's place. What would you have done if faced with the same dilemma: Stop distributing books that you believe are educationally sound but that the school board has prohibited *or* distribute them and risk insubordination charges for disobeying your superiors—and getting fired?

Teachers who have taken risks by being innovative, by dealing with controversial issues in class, or by challenging school authorities in other ways are sometimes successful in carrying through their innovations and even in influencing their peers to do likewise. However, Culliton's story is not uncommon in the history of education, for risk-takers often suffer abuse and/or loss of their jobs, or they make the decision on their own to leave a system where they feel they must make compromises with which they are not comfortable. (Carl, in the Kozol piece, [Selection 4.5], is an example of someone who did just that.) In Culliton's case, she was politically correct in terms of the current meaning of that phrase (on the side of tolerance) but apparently politically *incorrect* according to the regional standards of the school system.

Again, what would you have done?

WILTON, N.H.—Penny Culliton thumbs through the thin E.M. Forster paperback, its black cover weathered by months of handling, and shakes her head.

She had hoped Forster's "Maurice" and two other books with homosexual characters could teach her students about intolerance. Instead, it led to her own saga on the subject.

Culliton, 34, was fired last week from Mascenic Regional High School in rural New Ipswich because she disobeyed the school board last May and distributed books portraying homosexuals.

TWO POINTS OF VIEW

Although the official reason was insubordination, her supporters—including many students and parents—doubt the school board's explanation.

"This school board doesn't admit it, but I think it was the homosexual issue. I don't believe it was an insubordination issue," said Sharon DeFranza, whose daughter was in Culliton's English class.

Culliton selected "Maurice," "The Education of Harriet Hatfield" by May Sarton and "The Drowning of Stephan Jones" by Bette Greene to show students that homosexuals, such as those portrayed in the books, were "normal folks."

"There was nothing in the book," said student Gretchen Dussault, who was halfway through "Maurice" when she was ordered to return it to the school. "It was a guy and his life. It wasn't like saying homosexuality is good. He went to school. He made friends. It was nothing graphic at all."

Culliton said she wanted the books to counter negative homosexual stereotypes in society and in some literature, such as classics like "Catcher in the Rye" and "The Chocolate War."

A QUESTION OF BALANCE

"I would never take these books away, but you need a balance," she said. "It's not to say every gay person is wonderful and heroic, but it is to say every gay person is not a child molester."

Although not gay, Culliton empathizes with kids who are. She has organized a youth group to help teen-age homosexuals. As evidence of the need for education, she cited a student's admission to her that he would consider suicide if he were gay at Mascenic.

But for school board member Charles Saari, that argument doesn't wash. Before Saari was elected in March, he publicly opposed Culliton's organizing a faculty workshop on homophobia in 1993.

"It was basically a promotional workshop for the gay lifestyle. It really was," Saari said, pointing to literature distributed at the workshop "that says 'Is homosexuality sin?' and having all these theologians explaining why it isn't sin."

"In my opinion it is," Saari said. "I love the homosexual. I just don't love the sin. I don't promote it as OK."

The workshop was paid for by the same grant that was meant to pay for the books. The school board accepted the grant in June 1993, eight months before Saari and new members were elected. The money later was returned.

Saari refused to remove himself from the board vote to dismiss Culliton, insisting he could be impartial.

"The reason we fired her was for insubordination," he said of the board's unanimous vote.

He said Culliton was a good teacher, but "to me, if an employee cannot follow directives, then she has to pay the consequences."

Culliton and the National Education Association are appealing the board's decision. Todd DeMitchell, assistant professor of education administration at the University of New Hampshire, said they could have a tough fight.

"No individual has the right to control the curriculum or reject decisions made by a school board," he said. "As educators, we do not hold a trump card when it comes to curricular matters."

Culliton, who stands barely 5 feet, does not shy away from controversy. She has taken on the school board in nearby Merrimack, protesting a new policy that prevents any mention in the schools of homosexuality "in a positive light."

"I am the scarlet woman, and I'm sure that's not going to stop," Culliton said, folding her delicate hands.

Nora Tuthill, who put up the money for the grant, said by firing Culliton, the school board facilitates the kind of homosexual bigotry her gay son grew up with.

HERO IN SOME EYES

"Penny is a hero. She has put her values on the line, and her values are to teach children the factual information and teach them how to think," Tuthill, of Kensington, said.

School Board Chairman Steven Lizotte denied the board encourages discrimination against homosexuals.

"There are books that are used right now with homosexual authors," he said. "To claim that is homophobic is ludicrous."

Culliton's students did not take the school board's decisions lightly. They confronted members after Culliton was suspended in May. When she was fired, about 80 protested during class on school grounds. Forty were suspended.

Jennifer Bedet, 18, was one of the students who initially confronted the school board.

"I felt awful. These were prominent members of the community; and they were snickering and rolling their eyes at these general concerns. Those books were taken out of our hands, and I think we deserved an explanation," she said.

But Bedet, a freshman at Roanoke College in Virginia, learned a bigger lesson. She recently completed an English assignment to write about someone whose insolence made her a better person. She wrote about Culliton.

"Martin Luther King said 'One has not only a legal but a moral responsibility to obey just laws. Conversely, one has a moral responsibility to disobey unjust laws.' If Ms. Culliton was disobedient, it was out of moral duty. That to me is far more admirable," Bedet said.

Bedet said Culliton is one of the best teachers she ever had, inspiring her eventually to become a teacher.

For Culliton, it is students like Bedet who encourage her to fight.

"I know I can teach well," Culliton said. "I spend much more of my time with students. I've gotten their trust, so I would never walk away."

Questions for Discussion and Debate

1. Summarize in writing Culliton's dilemma and the outcome of her situation. Take an initial position on the question, Did she make the right decision?

   Hold a discussion in which the class informally debates the pros and cons of Culliton's decision to use the "questionable" books.

2. Make a chart in which you list all of the factions and individuals mentioned in the article. Arrange them in this way: in the left column, all the people and groups supporting Culliton; in the right column, those against her. Then, looking at this graphic portrayal of the two sides, decide if you still agree with *your* initial position on Culliton's

   actions. (Note the political role played by the high-school students.)

3. This article reveals that as the members of a school board change, so, too, may the policies and curriculum the teachers are allowed to carry out. What are the political implications of this fact? (The school board members' votes hold a lot of weight, but then so do the votes of the community members who put them there!) Discuss these implications.

4. What is the National Education Association (NEA), and what political role does it play? Do you predict that the NEA *or* the school board will win on the appeal? Why?

Activities and Projects

1. Prepare a role-playing scenario reflecting the issues or people described in the article.

2. Design a mock propaganda campaign in which you try to persuade the public that Culliton should be reinstated. Create slogans, artistic devices, and maybe even a song. Share your "campaign."

3. The NEA joined Culliton in appealing the board's decision. Find out if they were successful. Then research the political role played by teachers' associations and unions historically—and in the present. What have they accomplished? Where are they on the political spectrum (see Selection 4.5, question 7)? What are the advantages and disadvantages of joining a local, state, and/or national association or union?

4. The history of unions in this country is filled with emotion and controversy. Locate songs that union organizers sang that contain reasons why workers should join unions. The chorus here from one of those songs, "Solidarity Forever," can be sung to the tune of the "Battle Hymn of the Republic." The chorus sums up the major belief:

   Solidarity forever,
   Solidarity forever,
   Solidarity forever,
   For the union makes us strong.

   Share the songs you find with the class. Then elicit from the class their views concerning:

   - The use of the term *union* versus the term *association*
   - The degree to which teachers are *workers* versus *professionals*
   - The appropriateness of militant behavior, that is, going out on strike, on the part of teachers

5. Draw a Venn diagram on a large poster and then compare and contrast *two* of the selections in this chapter. Share your poster with the class.

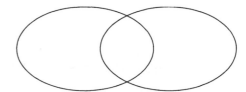

Chapter References

Aronowitz, S., & Giroux, H. A. (1995). *Education under siege.* South Hadley, MA: Bergin & Garvey.

Caputo-Pearl, A. (2001). Challenging high stakes standardized testing. . . . *Taboo, 5*(1), 87–121.

Cavanagh, S. (2002, July 10). Overhauled SAT could shake up curricula. *Education Week, 11*(42), 1, 28.

Conroy, P. (1994). *The Water Is Wide.* New York: Bantam.

Ehrenfeld, J. (2001, October 24). The trouble with testing. *Education Week, XXI*(8), 43.

Freire, P. (1985). *The politics of education. Culture, power and liberation.* South Hadley, MA: Bergin & Garvey.

Gardner, H. (1999). *The disciplined mind, what all students should understand.* New York: Simon & Schuster.

Gehring, J. (2001, October 24). Massachusetts school policies praised as test scores rise. *Education Week, XXI*(8), 26, 29.

Giroux, H. A. (1985). *Theory and resistance in education.* South Hadley, MA: Bergin & Garvey.

Hinsdale, B. A. (1898). *Horace Mann and the common school revival in the U.S.* New York: Somerset. (Reprinted ed. 39)

Hirsch, E. D., Jr. (1996). *The schools we need and why we don't have them.* New York: Doubleday.

Hoff, D. J. (2001, October 13). Teaching, standards, tests found not aligned. *Education Week, XXI*(9), 6.

Imber, M., & van Geel, T. (2000). *Education law.* Mahwah, NJ: Lawrence Erlbaum Associates.

Kowalski, T. (1995, June). Chasing the wolves from the schoolhouse door. *Phi Delta Kappan, 76,* 486–489.

Kozol, J. (1968). *Death at an early age.* New York: Bantam.

Kozol, J. (1994). *Savage Inequalities.* New York: Crown.

McCourt, F. (1999). *'Tis. A memoir.* New York: Simon & Schuster.

Merrow, J. (2001, October 17). That sinking feeling. Assessment comes to Atlantis. *Education Week, XXI*(7), 32, 35.

Mosle, S. (1996, October 27). The answer is national standards. *The New York Times Magazine,* pp. 45–47, 56, 68.

National Center for Education Statistics (NCES). (1994). *Digest of education statistics.* COERI Publication No. 94-115. Washington, DC: Government Printing Office.

National Education Goals Report. (1997). *Executive summary: Commonly asked questions about standards and assessments.* PA: DIANE.

Odden, E. R., & Wohlstetter, P. (1995, May). Making school-based management work. *Educational Leadership, 52,* 32–36.

Ozman, H., & Craver, S. (1995). *Philosophical foundations of education.* Upper Saddle River, NJ: Prentice Hall.

Popham, W. J. (2001). *The truth about testing.* Alexandria, VA: Association for Supervision and Curriculum Development.

Ravitch, D. (2000). *Left back. A century of failed school reforms.* New York: Simon & Schuster.

Sacks, P. (2000). *Standardized minds: The high price of America's Testing culture and what we can do to change it.* New York: Perseus.

Shanker, A. (1997, February). Marking time. In *On Campus.* Washington, DC: American Federation of Teachers, p. 5.

Smith, S. (1996). Saving our cities from the experts. In W. Ayers & P. Ford (Eds.), *City kids, city teachers* (pp. 91–109). New York: New Press.

Steinberg, J. (2001, November 19). Challenge revives SAT test debate. *The New York Times* [Electronic version].

Stuart, J. (1949). *The thread that runs so true.* New York: Charles Scribners' Sons.

Suchak, B. (2001). Standardized testing: High stakes for students and for corporate bottom lines. *Journal for Living, 23,* 36–41.

Supreme Court of the United States. (1978). *Bakke syllabus.*

Trott, N. R. (1995, October 2). Teacher's lesson on intolerance fails. *The Berkshire Eagle.*

Walsh, M. (2002, July 10). Charting the new landscape of school choice. *Education Week, 11*(42), 1, 18–22.

Weiner, L. (1967). *Tolstoy on education.* Chicago: University of Chicago Press.

Winerip, M. (2001, November 18). Never mind the inventive curriculum. One test fits all. *The New York Times,* p. A27.

Web Sites

Coalition for Authentic Reform in Education (CARE):
www.caremass.org

Student Coalition for Alternatives to MCAS (SCAM):
www.scam_mcas.org

Additional Readings

Augenblick, J. (1991). *School finance: A primer.* Denver: Commission of the States.

Freire, P. (1970). *Pedagogy of the oppressed.* New York: Seabury Press.

Gabbard, D. A. (2000). *Knowledge and power in the global economy. Politics and the rhetoric of school reform.* Mahwah, NJ: Lawrence Erlbaum Associates.

Good, T. L., & Braden, J. S. (2001). *The great school debate. Choice, vouchers, and charters.* Mahwah, NJ: Lawrence Erlbaum Associates.

Hermann, R., et al. (1999). *An educator's guide to school reform.* Washington, DC: American Institutes for Research (www.aasa.org).

Horn, R. A., Jr., & Kincheloe, J. L. (Eds.) (2001). *American standards. Quality education in a complex world. The Texas case.* New York: Peter Lang.

National Association of State Boards of Education. (1996, January). *State education governance at-a-glance.* Alexandria, VA: NASBE.

Nelson, F. H. (1991). *International comparisons of public spending on education.* Washington, DC: American Federation of Teachers.

Parrish, T. B., Matsumoto, C. S., & Fowler, W., Jr. (1995). *Disparities in public school district spending: 1989–90.* Washington, DC: U.S. Department of Education, National Center for Education Statistics (NCES Research and Development Report No. 95–300).

Pigford, A. B., & Tonnsen, S. (1993). *Women in school leadership.* Lancaster, PA: Technomic.

Reed, D. S. (2001). *On equal terms. The constitutional politics of educational opportunity.* Princeton, NJ: Princeton University Press.

Richardson, J. (1992, May). Who benefits? School/business partnerships. *Education Reporter,* 1, 2, 7.

The Secretary's Commission on Achieving Necessary Skills. (1992). *What work requires of schools: A SCANS report for America 2000.* Washington, DC: U.S. Department of Labor.

Sergiovanni, T. J., Burlingame, M., Coombs, F. S., & Thurston, P. W. (1992). *Educational governance and administration.* Boston: Allyn & Bacon.

Spring, J. H. (1988). *Conflict of interests: The politics of American education.* New York: Longman.

Spring, J. H. (1997). *Political agendas for education: From the Christian Coalition to the Green Party.* Mahwah, NJ: Lawrence Erlbaum Associates.

Stotsky, S. (Ed.). (2001). *What's at stake in the K–12 standards wars. A primer for educational policy makers.* New York: Peter Lang.

Swirski, S. (1999). *Politics and education in Israel, Comparisons with the United States.* New York: Falmer Press.

Underwood, J. K., & Verstegen, D. A., (Eds.). (1990). *The impacts of litigation and legislation on public school finance: Adequacy, equity, and excellence.* New York: Harper and Row.

Witte, J. F. (2001). *The market approach to education. An analysis of America's first voucher program.* Princeton, NJ: Princeton University Press (www.pup.princeton.edu).

Web Sites

American Federation of Teachers:
http://www.aft.org

Core Knowledge:
http://www.coreknowledge.org

Education-related topics:
http://www.education-world.com

National Education Association:
http://www.nea.org

School boards' political role:
http://www.nsbf.org

U.S. Department of Education:
http://www.ed.gov/index.jsp

Chapter 5

School Environments

Webster's New World Dictionary (1984) defines environment as "all the conditions, circumstances and influences surrounding and affecting the development of an organism or a group of organisms" (p. 468). There is little or no doubt that the school environment influences the nature and quality of education a student receives. The debate among educators, however, stems from the question of which aspects of the environment most affect learning. Is it the excellence of the teachers and curriculum that really matters; or the physical characteristics and resources of the schools; or the geographical setting; or the socioeconomic class, race, ethnicity, and aptitudes of the school population? Certainly all of these factors and more play a role in learning, and in so doing, they challenge educational evaluators, who are in the business of monitoring and measuring the relationship of these factors to effective education.

The selections in this chapter will enable you to view a wide variety of school environments in different time periods in which several of these variables play a direct or indirect role.

Brief Background

Elements within the internal environment of a school, other than the curriculum that is formally taught, are part of what is often referred to as the *hidden curriculum*. This term refers not only to the ideas conveyed in informal ways, but also to the very fabric of a school and its day-to-day operation, all of which can influence students' attitudes and thinking in ways that are difficult to determine fully (Apple, 1979, 1988).

External factors related to the environment from which a student comes will also influence how that student responds to the schools' environment because "students don't park their problems at the front door of the school . . . [or] separate the reality outside the classroom walls from the reality inside" (Ayers & Ford, 1996, p. 270). When you consider these environmental influences along with the geographical setting of the school (rural, urban, or suburban), its physical characteristics and condition, and the attitudes and values of its teachers, you are faced with a hidden curriculum vastly more pervasive than the formal one. And, again, while all of these variables related to school environment are difficult, perhaps impossible, to measure in terms of their effects, one thing is certain: Environment, including the hidden curriculum, matters.

While the school's physical environment constitutes a more tangible part of the hidden curriculum, attitudes, particularly those of the teachers, comprise a less tangible and perhaps more significant part. Anyone who has benefited from the caring attitude of a passionate teacher knows this. On the other hand, when attitudes are biased or cynical, student learning, no matter how effective the formal curriculum may be, is negatively affected. It is really not so surprising that there are teachers with prejudices who stereotype and label students; teachers are, after all, living in a society in which prejudices clearly exist. The real danger occurs when those attitudes are unleashed and allowed to cause an unhealthy learning environment and, worse, psychological harm. Teachers need to be conscious of their own attitudes as well as other aspects of the hidden curriculum and their potential for affecting the formal curriculum in either positive or negative ways.

In addition to looking more carefully at their own attitudes and values, teachers might ponder this question: What can we learn from teachers operating in different environments that will help us improve *our* learning environment? To what extent is it beneficial to bring an urban perspective or structure to rural schools or, conversely, to bring the lessons of the countryside to the city? Actually, this question has been answered to some extent. During the last 30 years, a common scenario in small-town and rural areas has been the *merging* or consolidation of smaller school systems into regional school districts (Campbell, Cunningham, Nystrand, & Usdan, 1985). The benefits of regionalization are many: Students encounter a larger and more diverse student body. A wider array of academics and cocurricular activities can be offered. And for the taxpayers, the costs are lower than if they had to provide such variety locally. In these situations, bigger seems to be better in terms of educational services (Conant, 1959), although the effects of consolidation still need further study (Sher & Tompkins, 1976).

As for the downside, ask any locals who have ever opposed such a merger and they may say that they mourn the loss of intimacy, sense of community, and smallness that comes with centralization. They may voice their fear of the encroachment of an impersonal and intimidating environment characterized by monotonous, strict, and often irrational routines. But must the positive qualities of the earlier and smaller incarnations be sacrificed when more institutional urban proportions are established? There is some evidence that they need not be. Deborah Meier, one of the founders of Central Park East Secondary School (CPESS) in New York City, reported how she and others created a high school that was essentially like a good kindergarten. She insisted that "big buildings need not be our enemy" (Takanishi, 1994) and described how her school of a thousand operates in a decentralized and humanistic fashion. CPESS is a living example of how educators in one type of environment recognized the positive qualities of another type of environment and adapted them. And in this example set by Meier and others lies one of the reasons for looking at different school environments.

Selections

The work of art in this chapter is Norman Rockwell's *New Television Antenna* (1949), which hints at a fairly recent technological environment that is competing for children's attention. The excerpts in this chapter include several autobiographical or semiautobiographical accounts set in a cross section of school environments: Claude Brown's experiences in a school for delinquent boys and his "education" on the streets of Harlem (*Manchild in the Promised Land*); Countee Cullen's poem about an "Incident" in the city of Baltimore; a report on homeschooling by Nancy Friedland; Catherine Marshall's depiction of a rural school in the Great Smoky Mountains (*Christy*); LouAnne Johnson's attempt to transform lives at an alternative school in inner-city Los Angeles (*The Girls in the Back of the Class*); and Bel Kaufman's account of urban teaching (*Up the Down Staircase*). The fictional work of Dorothy Canfield (*Seasoned Timber*) offers a contrast between urban and rural settings, while the excerpt from William Gibson's play, *The Miracle Worker*, is less a look at the power and influence of a particular school environment and more a demonstration of the power and influence of a single teacher in a unique environment. And, finally, Theodore Sizer (*Horace's Compromise*)—with no particular school in mind, or perhaps all schools—lays out what he considers to be the necessary criteria for an effective educational environment.

As you read each selection, note the unique educational features of each of the school environments depicted. Then identify characteristics that transcend their differences. Which environments would benefit from adopting some of the qualities of the other settings? Could "street smarts" then be taught in a rural school, or a naturalist's perspective be developed in an urban one? You, of course, have come out of one or more school environments and are functioning in still another one now. How have the aspects of the hidden curriculum affected *your* learning? Compare and contrast your various school environments with the ones described in these excerpts. What lessons can you learn about effective teaching from these diverse settings? The complexities of environmental factors make this subject a most challenging one to explore. See what helpful information you can discover as you travel from one environment to another.

5.1 Work of Art: *New Television Antenna* (1949)

Norman Rockwell

The television environment is competing for children's attention with the school environment, and statistics show that the television environment is winning. Neil Postman (1979), who devotes a portion of his book *Education as a Conserving Activity* to comparisons between the TV and the school environments, states that television is a total learning environment with a curriculum that constitutes the "major educational enterprise now being undertaken in the United States" (p. 50). That is why he calls TV the "first curriculum," and school the second. And, says Postman, not only is television the first curriculum in terms of the time students devote to it, but also it is "first in their hearts" (pp. 50–51).

"A typical American child will be in the presence of a school curriculum 2,340 days, which comes to about 11,500 hours," reports Postman (1979, p. 50). But he notes that, after sleeping, the next major activity of children is watching television. "A fair estimate is that from age five to eighteen, an American child watches TV approximately 15,000 hours" (p. 50), which is 30% more time than he or she is engaged at school. Add to these hours the time children now spend sitting in front of a computer screen viewing and listening to CD-ROMs or other media that, like TV, are noninteractive, and the amount of time spent in the electronic information environment surely doubles, widening even further the gap between the electronic and the school environments. (Interactive software does not fall into the same category as TV.)

Artist Norman Rockwell marked the advent—or, perhaps more appropriately, the onslaught—of television and its potential effects with a number of paintings depicting the then new and miraculous machine that had its first major public debut at the New York World's Fair in 1939. One of his illustrations, "Enchanted Lands . . . Right in Your Own Home," was an advertisement for a TV manufacturer and included two children and their dog sitting in front of the family's new television set with their backs turned to the pile of new toys they had just received for Christmas (Moffatt, 1986, p. 362). Rockwell, who died in 1978, lived to see his prediction come true, as thousands of American children, while not forsaking their toys entirely, continue to express their obsession with television. The painting shown here, *New Televison Antenna* (also referred to as *The New TV Set*), was a *Saturday Evening Post* cover published in 1949, the peak year of the television bonanza, when "100,000 sets were sold in a single hectic week" (Marling, 1997, p. 81). The wood-encased box that glowed and brought sound and picture into people's living rooms was another infallible mark of postwar prosperity (p. 81).

The painting itself exemplifies the way in which artists use geometrical shapes to position a scene and draw the viewer's attention to the most important objects. "In

Printed by permission of the Norman Rockwell Family Trust. Copyright © 1996, the Norman Rockwell Family Trust. Photo courtesy of The Norman Rockwell Museum at Stockbridge, Massachusetts.

this cover, the architectural setting is the whole story" (Marling, 1997, p. 81). The central object is a triangular-shaped roof that holds the new TV antenna. Above it is a workman installing the antenna, and below it the gleeful owner of the house, who points to a lit TV screen behind him. Look at the picture. Can you tell how Rockwell feels about the potential effects of TV? The central positioning of the antenna and TV may imply Rockwell's view that TV is becoming the center of people's lives, displacing the church, whose empty steeple can be seen to the right and is also triangular in shape. Karal Ann Marling (1997), who has analyzed this Rockwell painting and many others, writes that the message is clear: "The modern American worships at a new church now" (p. 81). TV takes the owner's attention away from his hobbies (note the potted plant not yet imbedded in the window box) and away from his household tasks (note the can of paint sitting there yet unused for freshening up the scalloped siding of this Victorian house in need of repair).

What can be done about the dominance of television in the home? Are you as concerned as skeptics like educator Postman and artist Rockwell? Do you agree with Postman that one of the many negative effects of TV is students' being rendered into passive, almost-vegetative states? Do you agree with him that the subject of education must be devoted to, among other things, "the development of school environments which supply a balance to such effects . . . that are clearly one-sided and which without opposition and mitigation are likely to be disabling to our youth" (Postman, 1979, p. 47)? Or do you see another kind of impact such as that cited in a study by University of Massachusetts Professor Michael Morgan, who found that for youngsters with a low IQ, TV serves as a major source of stimulation? Morgan maintains that television has a leveling effect, pulling the brightest down but the less bright up (cited in Sanoff et al., 1987, p. 92).

What is your view on the television environment? How much TV do you watch on average? Do you agree with Postman that the school environment is losing the battle for students' hearts and minds? If so, what should or can be done? And, finally, is Rockwell's 1949 painting still relevant and accurate?

Questions for Discussion and Debate

1. Study *New Television Antenna*. Look for the characteristics described in the introduction to the painting. Do you notice any other features related to the use of geometry or other elements? Share your observations with your peers.

2. What is your view of the television environment? Share with the class your personal history with this particular environment and its effects on you. (If you are working with students, ask them about their TV-watching habits and the nature of the competition in their lives between the school and the TV environments. Compare their experiences with your own at their age. Then share these comparisons with your peers. How have things changed or remained the same?)

3. Using the results of your discussion with students and/or the results of some initial research on the effects of television, hold a debate around this resolution: The negative effects of television outweigh the positive effects.

4. Is this painting still relevant and accurate in terms of Rockwell's symbolism and meaning? Support your point of view with evidence.

5. House Resolution HR 1390, the Children's Media Protection Act of 1995, establishes, among other provisions, that new televisions be constructed so as to enable individuals—parents, in particular—to block certain programming or time slots. Postman (1979) also argues for the "sane management of the information life of children" (p. 46). Do you think that parents should control the amount of TV their children watch? Why, or why not? Would it not be better to try and help children to develop self-control by discussing with them the reasons for limiting TV watching? Discuss these questions in class.

6. Many computer-related activities do not share all of the traits of TV about which Postman warns. For example, surfing the Internet is an interactive adventure in which the student is not passively sitting and staring. Nevertheless, this relatively new technology is at the center of a debate similar to the one related to television:

   a. Is the computer replacing the television as the center of the home? Would you be concerned if it did? Why, or why not?

   b. List the ways the Internet has changed, and will change, the nature of education. (Think about local as well as global results.)

7. *Infotainment* is a newly coined word referring to the fact that even news and information are being delivered in ways that are intended to entertain. What is your view of infotainment? What do you think Postman would say about this new phenomenon?

Activities and Projects

1. Restricting the time spent watching television correlates with higher achievement as measured by the 1990 National Assessment of Educational Progress. Find studies in educational journals or on the Internet in which researchers have reached such conclusions or in which they have disproved this correlation. Bring your findings to class and discuss them.

2. Find out about Christopher Whittle's Channel One, which, in conjunction with Capital Cities/ABC, Inc., broadcasts current events accompanied by commercials daily in over 10,000 schools that have opted to use it. Then debate the pros and cons of this kind of TV programming in the schools.

3. Make a chart on the board with two columns, one labeled, "TV Curriculum"; the other, "School Curriculum." With your class, brainstorm all of their contrasting characteristics. Then respond to Postman's question: How can the biases of the school environment counteract the consequences of an "unchallenged television education"?

4. Viewing a work of art is a very subjective experience. Often what a person sees in a painting tells more about him or her than it does about the painting or the artist. A person brings to a work of art his or her own experiences, desires, fears, and biases. Put another way, one person may view a glass as half-empty; another, as half-full. Compare and contrast your response to *New Television Antenna* (or another work of art) with those of your peers. How are the responses the same or different? What do you think accounts for the differences or similarities?

5. If everyone in the class illustrates the *same* excerpt from this book, you will be able to compare and contrast your various interpretations of that excerpt. Try it. Then ask the class to study your work and tell you what they think your point of view of the excerpt is based on the nature of your illustration.

5.2 | *Manchild in the Promised Land* (1965)

Claude Brown

"As with many of our kids today, the scars of distrust and poor preparation are plainly visible, but so are the strengths of knowledge and experience concerning survival on some complex and sometimes mean streets" (Ayers & Ford, 1996, p. 216).

Claude Brown (1937–2002) was one of those kids who learned about surviving life on mean streets, plagued by drug-dealing, gangs, and violence. His parents had been southern sharecroppers, among the poorest people in the South, who migrated to New York City after the Depression thinking that it held unlimited opportunities for them, that they would be living in the "Promised Land," not a slum. "There was a tremendous difference in the way life was lived up North. There were too many people full of hate and bitterness crowded into a dirty, stinky, uncared-for closet-size section of a great city" (Brown, 1965, p. viii). The children of these sharecroppers saw little hope of escaping this life. But Brown was lucky.

In his autobiography, he describes his beginnings in Harlem, his delinquency, and being sent away to Wiltwyck School for Boys, an interracial institution for delinquent boys aged 8 to 12. Brown returned to the streets, then was sent away three times to a more secure juvenile detention center, the New York State Training School for Boys, in Warwick. His encounters with the wife of the superintendent of Warwick School, noted in this excerpt, seemed to be a turning point for Brown. Mrs. Cohen planted seeds in Claude's mind that no one else ever had. He returned to Harlem and realized—after a few detours back into hustling and selling dope—that its streets would lure him into the web of crime again and again. So he decided to move to the Lower East Side, get a job, which was required of all parolees, and go to school. Brown eventually graduated from Howard University at age 28 and became a lawyer and a writer active in the Civil Rights movement.

The question is, What if Claude had never met Mrs. Cohen? Would he have been able to break out of the cycle of poverty and crime into which he and his friends found themselves swept by their environment (as do many students today)? Consider these questions as you read this excerpt and reflect on the kind of strength and insight it takes to break out of a familiar environment. Reflect also on the power of one person's caring spirit and ability to plant the seeds of self-esteem.

One night in December of 1952, I was sitting at home at about seven o'clock in the evening, when I heard a knock on the door. It sounded just like the police knock, and I knew that knock pretty well by now. So I stopped with the cards and just listened.

I heard a white voice ask, "Is Claude Brown here?" I just went in my room and got my coat. I knew I hadn't done anything, and I figured I'd just have to go down to the police station and see about something and I'd be right back. But I'd forgotten about what had happened the day before. Alley Bush and Bucky and another cat from downtown had broken into somebody's house and stolen some silverware and furs. They brought it uptown for me to off it to a fence for them. I did it and forgot about it.

Mama said, "Yeah, he's here," and I came to the door with my coat on.

One of the white detectives asked me if I knew Alley Bush and Bucky, and I said, "Yeah, I know 'em."

He said, "You want to come with us?"

I just walked out of the door, and Mama kept asking, "What's he done; what's he done?"

They just said, "Well, we don't know yet." And they told her where they were taking me.

I went to the police station and found out what had happened. Then I knew I wasn't going to be coming home that night, and I knew I wasn't going to be there for Christmas. It seemed that one of the furs was a cheap piece that wasn't any good; but Alley Bush, who was kind of stupid and did a lot of stupid things, went around in the same neighborhood trying to sell this piece of junk. I had told him to throw it away. Instead of throwing it away, he tried to sell it, and he got busted—and he mouthed on everybody he knew. He didn't know the fence or he would have mouthed on him too.

The police told me I could get off if I would tell them who the fence was and if they

could get the stuff back. I told them that I didn't know, that it was the first time I'd ever seen the guy. They never found out who it was. And a few days before Christmas, I was on my way back up to Warwick, for the third and last time. I was fifteen, and that was the only thing that saved me. Alley Bush was sent to Elmira, but Bucky, the luckiest cat I ever knew, got out of it somehow or other. A couple of weeks later, Tito got busted with a gun, and he was sent to Woodburn. Just about everybody was gone off the streets.

About a week after Christmas, I was sitting in the cottage that they'd put me in, C3. Al Cohen came in. Mr. Cohen was the superintendent of Warwick, and I had known him before, but only slightly, just to say hello to. I didn't think he really knew me. He used to call me Smiley, since I was always smiling. This time he said, "Hi, Smiley, what are you doin' here?" He looked sort of surprised, because he knew I had gone home.

I just looked up and said, "Hello, Mr. Cohen. Like, I just didn't make it, you know? I had some trouble."

He didn't say anything else. He just left.

I still had my rep at Warwick. Before I left the second time, I was running B1 cottage; I had become the "main man." The cottage parents and the area men thought I was real nice. I knew how to operate up there. I had an extortion game going, but it was a thing that the cats went along with because I didn't allow anybody to bully anybody and that sort of thing. Since I didn't get many visitors from home, I made other guys pay protection fees to me when they received visits or packages from home. I just ran the place, and I kept it quiet. I didn't have to bully anybody—cats knew that I knew how to hit a guy and knock out a tooth or something like that, so I seldom had to hit a cat. My reputation for hurting cats was indisputable. I could run any cottage that I'd been in with an iron hand.

After a few weeks, they told me that my work assignment would be Mr. Cohen's house. One of the nice things about that was that I got to know Mrs. Cohen. She was the nicest lady I'd ever met. She was a real person. I didn't get to know Mr. Cohen too well. I'd see the cat, and he'd talk. I'd see him in the morning when I first came in, before he left, and I'd see him in the afternoon if he came home for lunch. But I didn't really know him. I only got to know Mrs. Cohen, the cook, and the chauffeur.

Mrs. Cohen was always telling me that I could be somebody, that I could go to school and do anything I wanted to, because I had a good head on my shoulders. I thought she was a nice person, but I didn't think she was really seeing me as I was. She'd go on and on, and I'd say, "Yeah, uh-huh, yeah, Mrs. Cohen." I didn't believe it. She would get real excited about it and would start telling me about the great future that lay ahead for me. She tried to get me interested in it, but I couldn't tell her how I really felt about it. Even though I was in the third term, I knew I wasn't going to finish high school. I didn't even know anybody who had finished high school. Cats around my way just didn't do that. It wasn't for me; it was for some other people, that high-school business.

She said that I could even go to college if I wanted to. She was nice, but she didn't know what was happening. I couldn't tell her that all cats like me ever did was smoke reefers and steal and fight and maybe eventually get killed. I couldn't tell her that I wasn't going anyplace but to jail or someplace like it. She'd say all these nice things, and I'd try to treat her nice and pretend I believed what she was saying. I couldn't have made her understand that this stuff was impossible for me. Cats who went to college, these were the boys who were in school and playing ball and reading and stuff like that

when cats like me were smoking pot and having gang fights and running around with little funky girls. Those other cats were the kind who went to school. Cats like me, they didn't do anything but go to jail.

One time she got Mr. Cohen to talk to me about staying at Warwick, going to high school in the town there until I finished, and then going back to New York after I had gotten my high-school diploma. He just suggested it. He tried to show me that it wasn't being forced on me. I said, "Yeah, Mr. Cohen; like, that's nice," but I think he understood that I wasn't interested in this stuff. He wasn't really going to try too hard, because if I wasn't interested, there was nothing he could do.

All I wanted to do was get back to Harlem. I wanted to get back to Jackie and pot and the streets and stealing. This was my way of life. I couldn't take it for too long when I was there, but this was all I knew. There was nothing else. I wouldn't have known how to stay at Warwick and go to school. I didn't tell him that. When he asked me about staying and going to school, I just said, "Yeah, that would be nice." He saw that I wasn't what you could call excited about it.

One day, Mrs. Cohen gave me a book. It was an autobiography of some woman by the name of Mary McLeod Bethune. When she gave it to me, she said, "Here's something you might like to read." Before that, I had just read pocketbooks. I'd stopped reading comic books, but I was reading the trashy pocketbooks, stuff like *Duke, The Golden Spike*, that kind of nonsense.

I just took it and said, "Yeah, uh-huh." I saw the title on it, but I didn't know who the woman was. I just took it because Mrs. Cohen had given it to me. I said, "Yeah, I'll read it," and I read it because I figured she might ask about it, and I'd have to know something. It wasn't too bad. I felt that I knew something; I knew who Mary McLeod Bethune was, and I figured I probably knew as much about her as anybody else who knew anything about her, after reading a book about her whole life. Anyway, I felt a little smart afterward.

Then Mrs. Cohen gave me other books, usually about people, outstanding people. She gave me a book on Jackie Robinson and on Sugar Ray Robinson. She gave me a book on Einstein and a book on Albert Schweitzer. I read all these books, and I liked them. After a while, I started asking her for books, and I started reading more and more and liking it more and more.

After reading about a lot of these people, I started getting ideas about life. I couldn't talk to the cats in the cottage about the people in the books I was reading. I could talk to them about Jackie Robinson and Sugar Ray Robinson, but everybody knew about them, and there was nothing new to say. But this Einstein was a cat who really seemed to know how to live. He didn't seem to care what people thought about him. Nobody could come up to him and say, "Look, man, like, you're jive," or "You're not down," or any stuff like that. He seemed to be living all by himself; he'd found a way to do what he wanted to in life and just make everybody accept it. He reminded me a lot of Papanek, somebody who seemed to have a lot of control over life and knew what he was going to do and what he wasn't going to do. The cat seemed to really know how to handle these things.

Then I read a book by Albert Schweitzer. He was another fascinating cat. The man knew so much. I really started wanting to know things. I wanted to know things, and I wanted to do things. It made me start thinking about what might happen if I got out of Warwick and didn't go back to Harlem. But I couldn't really see myself not going back to Harlem. I couldn't see myself going anyplace else, because if I didn't go to Harlem, where would I have gone? That was the only place I ever knew.

I kept reading, and I kept enjoying it. Most of the time, I used to just sit around in the cottage reading. I didn't bother with people, and nobody bothered me. This was a way to be in Warwick and not to be there at the same time. I could get lost in a book. Cats would come up and say, "Brown, what you readin'?" and I'd just say, "Man, git the fuck on away from me, and don't bother me."

July 12, 1953, I went home for good. There was hardly anybody else out. Just about all the people I used to swing with were in jail. They were in Coxsackie, Woodburn, Elmira, those places. The only ones who were left on the street were Bucky and Turk. Tito was in Woodburn, Alley Bush was in Elmira, Dunny was in Woodburn, and Mac was in Coxsackie.

I felt a little bad after I left, because I knew that the Cohens would find out sooner or later that I wasn't the angel that they thought I was. Actually, I would have had to be like a faggot or something to be the nice boy that Mrs. Cohen thought I was. I think Mr. Cohen knew all the time that although I acted nice in the house and did my work, I still had to raise a little bit of hell down at that cottage and keep my reputation or I wouldn't have been able to stay there as his houseboy. Those cats would have had me stealing cigarettes for them and all kinds of shit like that. I just had to be good with my hands, and I had to let some people know it sometimes.

I guess Mrs. Cohen learned to live with it if she found out. It didn't matter too much, because I was back on the Harlem scene now. I was sixteen years old, and I knew that I'd never be going back to Warwick. The next stop was Coxsackie, Woodburn, or Elmira. I came back on the street and got ready for it. I started dealing pot. I had all kinds of contacts from Warwick.

Butch, Danny, and Kid were all strung out. They were junkies all the way. They had long habits. Kid had just come out of the Army. Danny had been out all the time. Butch had gone into the Army to try to get away from his habit, but they had found the needle marks and had thrown him out. Now they were all out there, and they were just junkies. I used to feel sorry for them, especially Danny, because he had tried so hard to keep me off the stuff.

I was hanging out with just Turk from the old crowd. A guy I hadn't known before but had heard about was on the scene. This was Reno, another of Bucky and Mac's brothers. Reno was slick. He was about twenty-one, and he'd just come out of Woodburn when I came out of Warwick for the last time.

He used to kid me about being a better hustler than I was and said he would show me how to make twice the money. He'd heard about me, and we were sort of friends already when we first met. He told me, "If you gon be a hustler, you gon have to learn all the hustlin' tricks." I agreed with him.

When I first came out, I had to get a job in the garment district, because I was on parole, and I had to keep that job for a while to show my parole officer that I was doing good. I kept the job, and I kept dealing pot. I had the best pot in town. Word got around; after a while, I was making a lot of money. I used to always have about two hundred dollars on me. I started buying hundred-dollar suits and thirty-five-dollar shoes and five-dollar ties and dressing real good. . . .

Questions for Discussion and Debate

1. What had Claude done that resulted in his being sent to Warwick again?

2. Summarize the nature of Claude's relationship with Mrs. Cohen. List the specific ways in which she planted seeds of self-esteem and awareness that enabled Claude to see a world beyond the streets.

3. Nature versus nurture: The debate continues among educators about what influences human development more, the biological and natural endowments with which a person is born or the quality of the environment in which a person grows up and receives nurturing. While this excerpt from Claude Brown's life story may be too brief to provide a conclusive answer, nevertheless, try to decide which factor you believe has more influence on a person's life, nature or nurture, and base your answer, in part, on what you learn from this excerpt.

4. Discuss the possible answers to this question: Why do certain students coming out of terrible family or environmental situations survive and flourish? And, conversely, why do some children coming from seemingly ideal circumstances fail to grow up and function healthily?

Activities and Projects

1. "Hungry children can't learn; hurt children can't learn" (Ayers & Ford, 1996, p. 212). Poverty and violent surroundings affect the body, mind, and spirit. After doing research on the nature of the effects of poverty and violence on children, prepare a report on

these effects for preservice and in-service urban and rural teachers that would assist them in becoming more aware and sensitive to the needs of such affected students.

2. Draw up a list of principles of good teaching that you believe can mitigate the effects of living in environments characterized by crime, drugs, violence, and gangs. Is it unrealistic to believe that good teaching can counteract the effects of a damaging environment? Tackle that important question. Then discuss the alternatives that exist for dealing with students who, no matter what attempts are made to help, continue to act in ways that are destructive.

3. Read at least one other nonfiction work that can add to your knowledge of the experiences of youth living in poor, multiracial, urban neighborhoods. Consider these classics: *Down These Mean Streets,* by Piri Thomas, who survived the difficulties of living in Spanish Harlem; and the autobiography by Nathan McCall, *Makes Me Wanna Holler* (1994). *Slums and Suburbs* (1959), a report by James B. Conant, clarifies the differences that exist between public schools serving non-White slums and those in White suburbia. More current books, such as *Savage Inequalities* (1994) and *Amazing Grace* (1996), by Jonathan Kozol and his earlier work, *Death at an Early Age* (1968) (excerpted in Selection 4.5), are also possibilities here. Share the story you read and compare it with aspects of Claude Brown's story.

4. Claude Brown notes in his autobiography how he came out of Warwick having learned many new ways to commit crimes and having met new teenage criminals. With these facts in mind, look into the nature of reform institutions that exist today. Visit one if possible. Find out if this "education in crime" still persists in such schools and what kind of treatment and curriculum exist to rehabilitate the youthful residents. Has the situation changed?

5. In a visit to 117th Street in Harlem, Charles Kurault, the late television journalist and host of the *On the Road with Charles Kurault* series, exposes a rich fabric of life in Harlem that Brown's saga does not reveal: children in starched white dresses jumping rope; old men on the stoops of their brownstone tenements playing jazz and the blues; kids playing stoop ball; young men raising pigeons on the rooftops of their buildings, where they also go to be alone with a book (*Sunday Morning,* July 6, 1997). Most depictions of a place or a group of people that derive from just one source show only one side of the story, often the side that is problematic, albeit prevalent. Do research on life in Harlem and/or other urban enclaves and, like Charles Kurault, try to uncover specific activities and people that make life in that environment rich and hopeful. Bring your findings back to class.

5.3 "Incident" (1925)

Countee Cullen

African American poet and novelist, Countee Cullen (1903–1946), taught in the New York City public schools after receiving a master's degree from Harvard and spending 2 years in Paris on a Guggenheim Fellowship. While the New York City environment experienced by Cullen was vastly kinder than the one described by Claude Brown in the preceding excerpt, both men learned a similar lesson on the streets about how it feels to be Black, to be a visible minority in a White society. Cullen conveys in his poem what he learned on the streets of Baltimore during a visit there. Is a nurturing home and school environment—as in Cullen's case—powerful enough to insulate and protect non-White children from the humiliation and pain that come from living within a larger environment of racism?

Once riding in old Baltimore,
    Heart-filled, head-filled with glee,
I saw a Baltimorean
    Keep looking straight at me.

Now I was eight and very small,
    And he was no whit bigger,
And so I smiled, but he poked out
    His tongue, and called me, "Nigger."

I saw the whole of Baltimore
    From May until December;
Of all the things that happened there
    That's all that I remember.

Questions for Discussion and Debate

1. What lesson did Cullen learn on the streets of Baltimore? If integrated into the curriculum of a school, what role do you think this kind of poem could play in changing prejudiced attitudes held by students?

2. The laws and documents of the United States reflect respect for the law, for tolerance, and for democracy. Thus the racism and intolerance that permeate our society could perhaps be said to be a part of the society's hidden curriculum, the concept defined in the Brief Background to this chapter. Debate the validity of this claim. What are some other values and ideas of this country's hidden curriculum?

Activities and Projects

1. Countee Cullen was one of the leading poets of the Harlem Renaissance, a period in the 1920s and 1930s during which African Americans representing all of the arts created a body of work that continues to inspire and move people of all ages and identities. Do research on the Harlem Renaissance. Identify some of the works from that time that you could use in your classroom to demonstrate the effects of environment on the artists' lives. The works of Zora Neale Hurston and Langston Hughes are but two examples. Share samples of their work and others' with your peers and discuss how you would use them in a lesson.

2. Go out into the community where you are teaching or studying and talk to a cross section of the people, read the local papers, and talk to clergy and social-service professionals as well as teachers to find out what they consider to be the hidden curriculum of the students' community.

3. School–community relations is a major area of study within the education field. Find out what the literature on school–community relations can teach you about how the two environments can become mutually supportive to improve education. What does this literature have to say about the role of parents? Religious institutions? Businesses? Others?

4. Hold a discussion in which you and your peers share your perceptions of your former schools, your communities, and your families. Which aspects of these environments have had the most profound effects on you?

5. Write a poem in which you capture the environmental factor that you believe has affected *you* the most. You might want to follow the poetic rhythm of Cullen's poem.

5.4 "Unschooling" (1995)

Nancy Friedland

Meet Nancy Friedland, who is "unschooling" her children at home. Her approach to home education is based on the work of the late education theorist, John Holt (1997), who recommended "unschooling." (An excerpt from Holt's work appears in Chapter 3, Selection 3.13.) He believed that child-led, interest-based learning minus the emphasis on testing and ranking would enable kids to learn freely and allow education to become a natural part of daily family life.

Hundreds of thousands of parents now teach their kids at home: "Brian Ray, president of the National Home Education Research Institute in Salem, Oregon, estimates that 700,000 to 1.15 million kids learn at home; other sources put the numbers as high as 2.5 million" (Roorbach, 1997, p. 32). Besides those who hold the more secular orientation of Holt and Friedland, there are advocates of homeschooling who follow a more conservative approach in which Christian or other religious values are at the core, and there is greater emphasis on parental leadership and skills. What they all seem to have in common, however, is a concern "about the method and quality of their children's education" (p. 32).

The very mention of the term *homeschooling* evokes sharp differences of opinion as well as many misconceptions. Proponents point to the many college acceptances of homeschooled students, lower problem behavior, higher self-esteem, and more student-centered, less fragmented curriculum. On the other hand, skeptics cite the isolation of homeschooled children, the lack of interaction with peers, the loss of the democratic education that comes with learning together with a cross section of students in public, hierarchical institutions. Although these settings may not always be pain-free, say the skeptics, they teach lessons for life.

Are you a skeptic or a proponent of home education? As you read this selection, think about what aspects of Nancy Friedland's approach are worthwhile. Perhaps you will note some techniques that differ from those you have observed in public and private schools, but then again, you may encounter ideas you have already observed in child-centered classrooms. Are there ways that schoolteachers and parent teachers can assist one another in improving learning in both environments?

When we hear about homeschooling for the first time, or decide to try homeschooling, the model many of us first think of and emulate is a school model. One of the lessons we learned at school was that school is where learning takes place, and that school methods are the right way to educate people. We get a similar message from the media—even from homeschooling media—that the way to homeschool should be school-at-home. Homeschoolers are stereotypically portrayed as a well-groomed family sitting around workbooks on the kitchen table with the American flag and chalkboard in the background. The adult decides what subject matter should be learned (in conjunction with what the state has decided should be learned), the methods to teach it and the materials to use. If we are of an alternative education mindset we might allow a great deal of flexibility within these areas, but still we "know" which subject matter is indispensable and required (math and reading being paramount).

With this model in mind, our homeschooling tasks are well defined. We shop for a curriculum. We look at the official lists of what our kids are "supposed" to be learning. We plan out lessons or units of study. We prepare ourselves to spend many hours teaching our children. We invest large amounts of money on math manipulatives, educational games, workbooks, reference materials, and other educational paraphernalia that we previously did not need. We might hire a tutor for subject matter in which we are unsure. We look into all the available classes, and frequently sign up for too many. Often when people look into the possibility of homeschooling they look at all of these "necessary" things to do, become overwhelmed, and quit before they have begun. Or, we survive a year or two of this highly organized, expensive, time-intensive education and then send the kids back to school feeling like failures because we cannot keep up with it all. Even though I feel very comfortable with our unstructured, unschooling approach, as I read articles about recommended units of study and creative uses of materials, I get the impression that I should be doing more teaching, more interacting, and more decision making as to how and what my kids should be learning.

It is rare to see descriptions of a more relaxed unschooling approach.

The unstructured model that has guided our family's approach to homeschooling offers a different philosophy of education and an alternative way of learning than the linear, structured school model. But part of the reason this approach is so little discussed is that it is difficult to give an adequate description of unschooling that captures the details as well as the true spirit of the learner-led approach. Since it is not defined by its outward structure, how can we talk about and explain it in a way that shows unschooling as a viable alternative? The people who have school-at-home can explain their education through the structure, which provides an outline, a definition, and concrete examples of learning taking place. For instance, a finished workbook, report, or unit of study can be held up as a finished product, or a measurable skill. But unschooling has no such external structure with which to explain.

Unschoolers often end up responding to direct questions about what we do with avoidance, contrivances and veiled references. I find myself, or other homeschoolers, saying things like, "learning through play", "learning all the time", "life long learning", "we're taking this week off", couching our play in "educationese", or making sure I bring up an example of concrete learning in math or science. I feel dishonest and dissembling when I do this. This sidestepping does not further anyone's understanding about how we learn what we learn. It perpetuates the stereotypic image people have about home-schooling being school-at-home.

The more we talk about the unschooling approach, and present it as another acceptable model for homeschooling, the less we have to rely on that school model that was imprinted on us unrelentingly for so many years.

And, a loosely structured model may convince more people that they are capable of homeschooling.

Instead of describing our homeschooling approach in terms of a structure or an outcome, I try to explain it in terms of intensity, depth, relevance to daily life, independence, self sufficiency and self confidence. I can talk about how our approach embraces discovery learning, exploration, experimentation, research, and immersion at the child's initiation.

Though this does not easily translate into curriculum ideas or "educationese", focusing on these features can convey a sense of the expectations and goals of our family in our actual day-to-day experiences.

To be more specific I can describe a sample day in our life, some of the various activities we might do on any given day.

Upon waking, Marina immediately gets a book—fiction, historical fiction and biographies are her favorite, but often she will peruse the non-fiction shelf of our home library and pick out a science or social studies type book—and spends the next few hours reading. Ethan might head for the computer and choose from a variety of programs that cover just about every subject area, and mostly subjects combined. (A non-math program elicits the comment that his score this time is 36 more than the last time.) Or, he will take out the Rise Up Singing songbook and spend an hour going through the index to find songs he knows, and proceed to read and sing every verse. They get themselves fed with varying amounts of help. Marina might rediscover her ongoing project of making postcards out of favorite photos. Ethan sits down with his Legos and is intensely engaged in hours of intense building and fantasy play. This includes creating characters, a story line, a climax and a conclusion, a process that has been going on for months. We fit in some chores somewhere in there. Marina will get an idea and work on a story she is writing, Ethan will make up a new club to start and make a sign. They take out the set of stencils and design fantasy machines, each building on the last, each feeding off each other's ideas and again, something they have been working on over a few weeks. They make doll clothes and develop an in-depth ongoing "game" around it. We read aloud, we do some gardening, they have time with friends, or go to the beach, or to a class, or visit grandparents. In "educationese" I could find a great deal of language arts, math, science and social studies in what they do. To them these are just interesting things to do toward small goals they want to achieve.

The result of having a lot of unstructured time to develop ideas, visions, games, theories and rhythms is a great deal of depth. For example, there is one particular ongoing activity that my children do with a specific group of friends that we see frequently. These children have evolved a dress up/fantasy game that they refer to as "The Usual", as in, "Let's play The Usual!". There are some fixed points of reference that always enter into the game. There is the basic concept of extended family relationships (parents, children, grandparents, aunts and uncles), a situation (a fatal illness, a physical handicap, an orphaned child), a climax (a kidnapping, a murder, a robbery), and a resolution (a reunion, a miraculous recovery, an escape). Every time they play this game there are tremendous changes. They choose a different character, adventure, interaction, and resolution. As they mature, as they experience or hear about or read about something new, these events show up in the fantasy.

This produces waves of change in the way every other child acts out his own role. The amount of new information, new ways to look at issues, new ways to interact, new ways to resolve concerns, is ever changing, growing, evolving. The mixture of ages (five to ten) allows some cross pollination of ideas and approaches equally influencing each other's position in the play. The learning here may not be a linear, fact oriented kind of education. But with this kind of approach to any problems they come up with there will be limitless ways to find answers, work out solutions and approach difficult situations with enthusiasm and confidence.

Learning at home without a structured schedule allows us to engage in ongoing projects in a way that may be non-linear and inconsistent, yet allows intense and thorough learning. A friend asked the kids whether they played some games she saw on the shelf. To my surprise they responded that no, they do not use them. After thinking about it I understood their answer, which to me was not completely accurate. When they played the Monopoly game a few months before, they set up an ongoing, non-stop series of games. They completely immersed themselves in the tasks of buying and selling and trading properties and houses, mortgaging, paying percentages on income tax and multiplying on the dice to pay rent on the utilities. And then have not touched it since. They learned all they needed to at this stage in their development, and then went on to be immersed in other things.

When child-led learning is allowed, when there is a need to know something in order to get along in the world, the learning is automatic, the challenge is enjoyable, there is no test at the end, no pressure to be right, and correction comes from the task itself. They learn a concept because it is important to them to know it, and they enjoy the exercise.

When I tell people that my children learned to read magically, it is because I never sat down and taught them alphabet sounds, rules of syntax, phonics, sounding out words, and so on. They learned because they enjoyed what they heard read to them and were desperate when I would not read that next exciting chapter. They had to struggle through it themselves to find out what happens. And every time it got easier. No one made them read aloud if they did not want to. No one made them work laboriously over an unknown word unless they wanted to for their own satisfaction—they either skipped it or asked for help. Other children will have other motivators; needing the instructions for a model, a sign in a store, or a computer manual. The satisfaction is integral with the learning and knowledge. It is all one and does not easily break down into parts without destroying the activity.

Rather than a description of specific learning outcomes, I keep coming back to the intensity, the depth, the connectedness, the continuity, the persistence, the enthusiasm, the self assuredness, the independence, the sense of self that is a part of everything the children do. I cannot always say specifically what they are learning through this kind of freedom, nor can I always explain the deeper levels of enrichment and discovery that occur for them almost all the time. We cannot know everything inside our children, or every step towards understanding and knowledge. The process they go through to get from A to Z is a part of their whole personality, something that cannot be separated from their body of knowledge. How then do we know they are doing OK—learning, developing, moving successfully toward adulthood? How do we know that this works, that we are not just dooming our children to living the guinea pig's life of experimentation and trial and error? How can we be sure that they will be able adapt to a life in the real world of work, commitment, structure, deadlines, diversity and adversity as well as, or better, than education otherwise? I depend on a multitude of answers and assurances.

By being together a great deal of the day—though we may not be interacting all of that time—parents are the recipient of flying ideas, wisdom in passing, facts at a glance. It is those things thrown our way that keep us aware that our children are indeed full of knowledge, curiosity, opinions, and creativity. It keeps the worry, if not invisible, at least at bay. I am there when at the end of a novel my daughter crows about the great plot, the character development, the hated ending, and how she would do it better. I am there when she tells a friend about the book and hear her synopsis and know she has comprehended her reading. This gives me a great deal of faith in our approach.

I often get feedback from people who, upon meeting my children, are complimentary and supportive, even when they do not agree with what we do.

The children in our homeschooling group come across as articulate, well informed and enthusiastic learners. Without depending on the compliments to substantiate what we do, we nevertheless feel assured, validated and encouraged to continue with what is working so well. This is really the best way to spread the word about unschooling, because the bottom line is always, "How are the kids doing?" As more people change their ideas about how people learn, and think about education in new ways, the more accepted unschooling becomes and the more accessible it is to everyone.

Another element that keeps me going is learning from the experience of others before us. We are no longer the front runners, trying something that has never been done. There are over a hundred issues of *Growing Without Schooling* magazine, which includes thousands of testaments to the process of patient waiting and trusting children. We have books that describe the individual struggles and achievements of unschoolers, such as the Colfax's "Homeschooling for Excellence", and Agnes Leistico's

"I Learn Better By Teaching Myself", among others.

We can also learn from our homeschooling peers as we watch them struggle through the same doubts and challenges. We see them overcome those fainthearted moments, we see their children thrive, grow into admirable young people, strong in traits important to us: inquisitiveness, concentration, a thirst for knowledge, creative, enthusiastic, quick-witted, articulate, willing, kind.

But most of the answer as to whether we are doing OK has to come from a sense of trust. As time passes we weather the doubts. My worries for my daughter at age seven: wondering at the wisdom of allowing and encouraging invented spelling, worry that I should insist on proper handwriting technique, worry about the postponement of bike riding, about the refusal to learn math facts by rote. Now at age ten these are non-issues. I have a child who insists on being an excellent speller, has beautiful handwriting, has a good grasp of basic math, and though she still is not an avid bike rider, has not fallen off in years! So as new challenges arise I call up these successes, and alleviate the worries with a solid sense of trust in their approach, wonder at their creativity, and satisfaction in their contentment.

I remind myself continually that in spite of any doubts or mistrust, this experiment is working. I am confident that it will continue to work as long as I retain that trust and positive attitude. And when a current doubt passes into a non-concern, I learn the lesson anew and am strengthened for when the doubts revisit. The accomplishments of my children remind me over and over of the possibilities and the promise that exist for a child who is free to make choices, who is allowed control over the way she learns, who coexists with adults doing real work in the community and at home, who sees all around him people learning, overcoming hardships and challenges.

Questions for Discussion and Debate

1. Pick out the characteristics of "unschooling" in the article that you think could be adapted in public schools and explain why you would favor their integration. Are some of these approaches already being used to some extent in some classrooms you have observed or read about?

2. What approaches that Friedland describes do you especially like? Why?

3. What aspects of unschooling trouble you, if any? Why?

4. Summarize Friedland's description of a "sample day," in your own words.

5. There are many ways for parents to establish home education. Discuss the advantages and disadvantages of both the structured approach and the more organic approach described by Friedland. Divide the class in half, with one side arguing the affirmative and the other the negative on this resolution: The more organic approach of weaving instruction into everyday life will deprive children of the skills and knowledge they would acquire if they learned in a more institutional and structured home setting. You might also debate this resolution: Homeschooling, no matter what the format, is not as effective as learning in a more public, multiethnic environment.

6. What evidence does Friedland provide that lends strength to her argument that homeschooling in general is effective schooling?

Activities and Projects

1. "The very mention of homeschooling excites distrust: What about the kids' socialization? Are parents competent to teach? Does the home environment work?" (Roorbach, 1997, p. 32). With these questions in mind, consult articles and studies on homeschooling in education journals. After doing your research, answer the preceding questions, documenting your conclusions. (Form hypotheses in response to the questions *before* you proceed.) Are your findings in line with your initial hypotheses? Explain.

2. Research the rules and regulations that govern homeschooling in your community. If possible, get a copy of the official policy from the superintendent and discuss it in class. Are there any provisions that you and your peers believe are inappropriate? Are there any additions you would make to the policy?

3. Construct a questionnaire that will enable you to survey attitudes and knowledge that exist regarding homeschooling in the community in which you live. Consult with someone who has devised such questionnaires and find out how to collect and report on your data. Share your findings with the class.

4. Devise a set of questions with which to interview parents who are homeschooling their children. Report on their responses. Perhaps you could interest a local newspaper in publishing an article you write based on these interviews.

5. Homeschooling is still another version of "school choice," the movement to give parents the right—and sometimes the money, in the form of vouchers—to place their children in the learning environment of their choice. Do research on school choice and vouchers and decide where you stand on this controversial subject. (School choice, broadly defined, goes beyond simply choosing the public school you prefer to choosing a private or parochial school and receiving financial support from the government.)

6. One of the most radical arguments in favor of "unschooling" can be found in Ivan Illich's book, *Deschooling Society* (1971). Illich concludes that mass education has had disastrous effects on poor children and that for most people the "right to learn is curtailed by the obligation to attend school" (p. vii). While it is not likely that his recommendation will ever be followed, his rationale for "deschooling" might begin the important process of questioning and reforming public educational institutions and the social and economic forces that affect them. After doing research on Illich's philosophy, hold a seminar in which his views are used in drawing up a list of recommendations for reforming schools to provide success and quality education for all, regardless of social class.

7. There is no question that, with our access to nearly every corner of the earth via computers and the Internet, we can engage in learning about all kinds of subjects from the seat of the chair that faces our computer screen. Technology has developed to the point where distance learning is becoming more and more common, and it is particularly useful in areas where students do not have physical access to schools and colleges. Distance learning—the ability of students to interact with their teachers and others over great distances—is a topic worthy of research. Find out about different parts of the world where this type of learning is being utilized and how effective it has been. With your peers, try to predict the future of cyberspace as a major learning environment.

5.5 | *Christy* (1967)

Catherine Marshall

It's around 1910 and Christy Huddleston is on her way to teach in a one-room schoolhouse in Cutter Gap, in the Appalachian Mountains of East Tennessee, an environment dramatically different from the one in which she was raised and educated. This excerpt reveals the origins of her decision to take risks and go where few had gone before. Like so many teachers before and after her, Christy was inspired by someone whose words and actions made her decision seem an inevitable one. As you read this excerpt, think about the mentors and models *you* have had and how they have influenced—or are influencing—your decision about where you will teach or are teaching. Were there other factors that played a role in your decision?

Christy entered a different world and time when she went to live in Cutter Gap. It was a world where people spoke English sprinkled with Anglo-Saxon and Gaelic words, where they still sang ballads and told haunt stories from the 17th and 18th centuries, where people still held onto superstitions and outdated religious beliefs—death over life and fatalism—and where men and women often felt defenseless in the face of a harsh environment. She met a proud people, self-reliant and brave, with a love of liberty, but who often went shoeless, lived in homes without plumbing or electricity, and were illiterate. She adapted to this environment, and not only loved these families but learned a great deal about living from them.

Oddly, despite the stark differences between poor urban and poor rural environments, their inhabitants share many common problems, problems that seem to arise naturally as a result of their poverty. Look for these common problems as you read this excerpt and look also for the values Christy might have come to learn from the people of Cutter Gap.

Catherine Marshall's *Christy* was adapted as a television series during the 1980s, and if you have seen any reruns, you will appreciate this encounter with the book on which they were based.

"Ticket, please. You're Christy Huddleston, aren't you?" I nodded, hoping that if I managed the proper dignified expression he would notice that I was simply another adult passenger. After all, this was not my first train trip, not by any means. The past year and a half at Flora College in Red Springs I had taken the train both ways, a trip of three hours, and once I had taken the sleeper to my aunt's home in Charleston on the coast. But this worldly experience seemed lost on the conductor.

"I'm Javis MacDonald," he went on. "I've known your father a long time." He punched my ticket, handed it back. "So you're bound for El Pano, young lady. Your father said you were going to teach school. In El Pano?"

"No—in a new school—seven miles or so behind El Pano, back in Cutter Gap."

Mr. MacDonald rubbed his chin whiskers reflectively. His eyes took on a wary look. He seemed about to speak, thought better of it, but then finally said impulsively, "That Cutter Gap is right rough country. Only last week followin' a turkey shootin' match, one man got tired of shootin' turkeys and shot another man in the back. Well—probably I oughten to be tellin' you, but you'll be hearin' the likes soon enough."

Then Conductor MacDonald went on gathering tickets, and I was grateful to be left to my own thoughts. I was glad that I had not been forced to explain the reason for my trip. The old man would have thought me sentimental and girlishly impressionable to be basing my whole future on a talk given by a total stranger the past summer.

The scene floated before my eyes . . . the church conference grounds at Montreat where the Huddlestons had spent a part of every summer as far back as I could remember. The big semicircular auditorium with its rustic benches. The men and women in their light-colored summer clothes. The ladies in voile or lawn or crepe de Chine, some with long strands of carved ivory beads or jade brooches they had bought at the missionary's shop on the hill. So many palm fans moving, and the cardboard ones that had been stuck in the hymnbook racks with their advertisements of religious publishing houses or HUMP hairpins or pulpit furniture. In the stillness before the service had begun, there had been the pleasant hum of whispering voices and, in between, the gurgle of the mountain stream that sang its way through laurel thickets and ferns to the left of the auditorium.

But then an elderly man with a neatly clipped white goatee and a resonant voice—such a big voice for a small man!—had risen and begun to speak. He explained that he was a medical doctor, and that he was therefore not going to preach a sermon, just tell his own story. He told the facts simply, almost starkly—how during the War Between the States he had ridden horseback through the Cumberland Mountains on his way to join the Confederate Army. Of course there were few inns in that area, so people in the mountain cabins had taken him in. He had been impressed with how poor the people were, yet how intelligent. Years later when he was a successful doctor in Arkansas, he had become desperately ill with scarlet fever. At a crisis point in his illness, he had made a solemn vow that if he lived, he would go back to the Appalachians and help those people. He had sacrificed his fine medical practice to start mission work in Arkansas and Kentucky, and finally in the Great Smokies.

There he had met someone with as much passion as he to help the mountain people: Miss Alice Henderson, a Quaker of Ardmore, Pennsylvania, a new breed of woman, he said, who had braved hardship and danger to serve where she saw need.

My heart beneath my frilled lace jabot beat faster. I would like to know that woman. On her own, he went on to say, Miss Henderson had established three schools: Big Lick Spring, Cataleechie, and the Cutter Gap school, the latter only a couple of years before.

Dr. Ferrand explained that a year ago Miss Alice Henderson had placed her three schools under the auspices of his American Inland Mission, believing that this unifying of forces would strengthen the work.

"How I wish this vital woman could be here today," the little doctor said, "to stand beside me on this platform so that all of you could catch her enthusiasm. It isn't for want of traveling that she isn't here," he chuckled, "she rides horseback all over the Great Smokies from school to school—rather because she would not leave her work."

Then Dr. Ferrand was painting vivid word pictures of individual "highlanders" as he called them: of Minna Bess who had gotten married at fifteen; of Branner Bill, who had been the feuding terror of Cataleechie Cove until he had heard the gospel story for the first time and had suddenly become a changed man; of Uncle Jason whose sole income was gathering and selling galax leaves at twenty cents a thousand; of Rob Allen who wanted book learning so much that he came to school barefooted through six-foot snows.

I could still hear Dr. Ferrand's voice describing how such deserving people had inspired him to found the American Inland Mission with only one other worker and three hundred and sixty dollars. And then he talked about needing something more important than money: recruits. "Beyond the great mountains, outstretched hands and beseeching voices cry, 'Come over and help us.' These highlanders are your countrymen, your neighbors. Will you hear and help, or will you leave them to their distress and ignorance?" And with that, the little doctor had sat down.

It was a new experience for me to hear someone speak who had a Cause, a mission in which he believed with every tissue and cell of his heart and mind. There in the auditorium I glanced down at my little pointed buttoned white kid shoes with the black patent tops, the ones that I had bought the week before, and I thought about the contrast between my well-shod feet and those of the boy who had gone barefooted in freezing weather. Of course I had always heard about need in places like China and Africa, but I'd had no idea that such awful conditions existed within a day's train ride of Asheville, right in our mountains. Why had not father or mother told me about things like that? Perhaps they did not know either.

As we sang the closing hymn, "Just As I Am," a feeling of exhilaration grew so strong inside me that I could scarcely sing the words.

After the benediction, I made my way slowly down the long inclined aisle. Dr. Ferrand gripped my hand warmly, looked directly into my eyes.

My voice shook a little. "You asked for volunteers," I told him. "You are looking at one."

The little man's goatee had bobbed up and down. "And for what do you volunteer, my child?"

"For the highlanders—I could teach, anywhere you want to use me."

There was a long silence. The man's eyes were penetrating. "Are you sure, child?"

"Quite sure."

So it was done. Then I had gone back up the hill to the Alba Hotel to break the news to father and mother and begin the long task of persuading them. And I had never wavered since—through all their weeks of pleas and arguments. After all, up there in the mountains were boys and girls who ought to have the chance at least of learning to read. I was not the best educated girl in the world, but I could teach children to read. Of course I could. . . .

▤ Questions for Discussion and Debate ▤

1. Locate phrases within this excerpt that reveal the nature of the poverty and problems of living in Cutter Gap. What other problems not mentioned here do you think exist in this area? Compare the problems of this rural area to those of the inner city revealed in Claude Brown's *Manchild in the Promised Land* (Selection 5.2). How is rural poverty the same as or different from urban poverty?

2. What motivated Dr. Ferrand to want to devote his life to helping the "highlanders"? Quote phrases that indicate the basis for his mission.

3. What seems to have motivated Christy to want to teach in an environment very different from the one in which she was raised and educated? What clues does she weave into her description?

4. Compare the socioeconomic environment of Cutter Gap with the one in which you were raised. What factors do you think account for the differences between them?

5. What aspects of the rural environment do you think you would like most? Least?

Activities and Projects

1. Dr. Ferrand and Miss Henderson are clearly models of individuals who seek to help those in need, with little concern for their own personal financial gain. Christy seems to be inspired by their example. However, if recruits are to be attracted to rural teaching today, monetary compensation will likely be an issue. Find out what salaries are like in the Appalachians, for example. Are they adequate, in your opinion? What are the U.S. government and the Department of Education doing to improve educational services in rural areas? After gathering this information, assess it and draw up a list of recommendations you believe would attract quality teachers to these areas.

2. Programs are already in place that enable college graduates to teach in the inner cities and rural areas of the United States as well as in developing countries for 1 or 2 years. Prepare a report on one of the following: AmeriCorps, Teach for America, or the Peace Corps. What other programs exist? Describe them briefly. Find out what percentage of the people who participate in these programs remain in teaching after their initial commitment has been completed. Would you be interested in any of these programs? Why, or why not?

3. Using your *imagination* and some of the information about Cutter Gap and the non-denominational mission school to which Christy is traveling, pretend to be Christy or a male equivalent and write a letter home describing your first encounters with the highlanders, the parents as well as the children, and the school and its surroundings. Remember to use your imagination.

4. Draw or paint the environment of Cutter Gap as you imagine it to be. Looking at your rendition, what kind of curriculum (knowledge, attitudes, and skills) could you develop that would enable students to use their natural surroundings in an educational manner and, also, in a manner that could lead to raising the economic levels of the people? (You might first want to look into Eliot Wigginton's Foxfire approach to curriculum development [Foxfire Fund, 1990], in which students do field research in their local environment and publish their findings in a magazine. Over 10 Foxfire volumes of students' work exist and are available in bookstores and libraries.) Share your curriculum ideas with the class.

5. Sam Smith (in Ayers & Ford, 1996, p. 108) writes that "the existence of enormous differences in property tax revenue . . . is at the

heart of many . . . fiscal inequities." Until that type of discrimination is remedied, there may not be a way to change the school environments of poor districts in rural areas and cities. Find out what some states are doing now to equalize the revenue apportioned to underfinanced schools.

5.6   *The Girls in the Back of the Class* (1995)

LouAnne Johnson

LouAnne Johnson followed up her best-selling book, *My Posse Don't Do Homework* (1992), with *The Girls in the Back of the Class,* both based on her teaching experiences in the inner city. The former book was made into a movie, *Dangerous Minds,* starring Michelle Pfeiffer, but in this editor's opinion, Johnson's books far surpass the film in terms of representing both the realities of teaching in an urban, multicultural, and disadvantaged environment and the reactions of a young woman struggling to meet, and sometimes succeeding in meeting, the needs of her students.

In this excerpt, those struggles come to life through the voices of Raul and Gusmaro, two Hispanic students in Johnson's class in a "school within a school, an academy for at-risk students who had the intelligence to succeed in school, but lacked the motivation or means to do so" (p. ix). Raul and Gusmaro want to accept Johnson's offer to help them better themselves, but the reality of their entering a strange and intimidating environment pushes them away from their chance to grab onto a future they could "be proud of" (p. 121).

Many good teachers, like Johnson, are left frustrated as a result of such attempts to help their students. Perhaps they would be spared the frustration if they understood how to prepare the students for handling the environments they are encouraging them to enter. As you read the excerpt, think about what content could be integrated into the school curriculum that would address this need and, in so doing, would diminish the frustrations of both student and teacher.

"*Señores,*" I said, placing one hand on each of their shoulders. "Please step into my office. I have good news."

"Is it short news?" Raul asked, as they followed me into my office. "I gotta get some lunch so my stomach don't make noise all day and everybody thinks I'm farting or something."

"Short and sweet," I promised. "You both have interviews at Sun Microsystems tomorrow afternoon, three P.M. sharp." Neither boy moved, except to shift his eyes sideways to check the other's reaction.

"What's the problem?" I asked. "Need a ride? No problem. I'll drive you."

Raul stuck the tip of his tongue between his front teeth and inhaled slowly. Gusmaro rubbed his chin, a habit he had recently acquired, along with a feathery mustache and a few tentative whiskers. Gusmaro shrugged. "How much does that job pay?"

"Five fifty an hour to start," I said.

"We make five seventy-five now," Gusmaro said and turned to leave.

"But you'll get a raise, I'm sure."

"Yeah. but we woulda probably had a bigger raise at Wilbur Hall before then," Gusmaro argued. Raul nodded.

"But you'll still be washing dishes." I forced myself to project a calmness I did not feel. "This other job is a chance for you guys to get into a really big company, with good benefits and a chance to move up into better jobs later on. Maybe even work full-time after graduation. It's a real opportunity."

"Maybe," Raul said, "but we're making more money now."

"If you get the job, I'll pay you the difference. I'll pay both of you." I could feel the color burning up the back of my neck. "You give me your pay slips and I'll pay you fifty cents for every hour you work to make up the difference until you get a raise."

Gusmaro laughed. "You're crazy, Miss J. Besides, we know teachers be poor."

"Yeah." Raul pointed out the window. "Look at that old junky car you gotta drive." I never could convince them that a twenty-year-old Fiat was a valuable collector's item. "And I seen them little bitty lunches you be eating every day. Carrots and apples and shit like that."

Gusmaro moved sideways, closer to Raul, and shook his head. "We can't take your money." He stuck his hands into the back pockets of his jeans. Raul mimicked the move.

"Come on, guys," I said.

"Can we think about it for a couple days?" Raul asked.

"Sorry. They're interviewing tomorrow."

Both boys moved back, a step closer to the door.

"Well," Gusmaro said, "maybe you could send some other guys who don't already got jobs." He turned away, then turned back. "Thanks anyway, though."

"Yeah," Raul said, clearly relieved that the issue was settled and lunch was imminent. "Check you later, Miss J."

They turned to leave, but I sidestepped them and stood in the doorway, one hand on each side of the door frame, blocking their exit.

"What if I get them to raise the salary?" I asked. The accountants at Sun would think I was crazy, but I thought they might agree to let me pay the additional fifty cents per hour.

"Aw, I don't know, Miss J. Let us think about it."

"Think about it now. I need to send two kids for interviews tomorrow."

Gusmaro traced a pattern on the tile floor with the toe of his sneaker. Raul stared straight ahead, his eyes glazed, looking at nothing, waiting for this torture to end. I wanted to scream: THIS IS YOUR CHANCE TO MOVE OUT OF YOUR POVERTY-STRICKEN NEIGHBORHOOD, TO LEAVE THE VIOLENCE AND DRUGS AND GANGS BEHIND, TO MAKE A DECENT LIFE. DON'T BE SUCH FOOLS!!!

But I didn't scream. I couldn't insult their families who worked hard to buy their ramshackle houses in the only neighborhood they could afford to live in. I thought about threatening to flunk them if they didn't take the interviews, but Gusmaro was just stubborn enough to take the F, and Raul had so many F's already on his transcript from his freshman year that one more wouldn't make much difference.

Finally it dawned on me that it might not be simple stubbornness. I moved one foot forward and bumped the toe of Gusmaro's sneaker. "What's the real problem?" I asked softly.

Gusmaro looked up, only for a split second, but I saw the fear in his eyes before he forced it down. He shrugged. "I kinda like working with my homies. You know we hang together, look out for each other's back. And everybody at Wilbur is Mexican, except Emilio, but he's cool."

"It's probably fun to work with your friends," I said.

"Yeah," Gusmaro said, warming up. "Nobody gets on us for speaking Spanish, and we don't gotta wear all them fancy clothes and stuff."

"But you aren't going to marry your friends, are you?" I asked. "Shouldn't you start thinking about making your own life for your own family someday? What kind of future do you have at Wilbur?"

Gusmaro stepped back, out of my reach, and gave me a look. "My friends will always be my friends. We hang together. Besides, we get raises all the time."

"There are other factors to consider besides money," I said. "Do you want to wash dishes all your life? And where do you go from there? There isn't anyplace to move up. You could be the head dishwasher. But I don't care how well you wash dishes, you're going to hit the pay ceiling soon. They are never going to pay you fifteen dollars an hour to wash dishes."

I dropped my hands and moved out of their way. Relieved, they started past me.

"Every other day you decide you don't want to go to college, so I'm trying to give you a chance for a job and a future you can be proud of. Something you might like to do for twenty or thirty years. So I won't have to worry about you being able to take care of your wives and children."

Raul kept walking, but Gusmaro stopped dead. I knew he had cut my class one day the previous week to take his girlfriend to the clinic for a pregnancy test. It was a false alarm, but it had made him much more conscious of the future looming in his face.

"Come on," I urged him. "I'll drive you there. I'll go in with you. I'll hold your hand and give you moral support. Do it for me, please. I'm an old woman. This may be my last wish."

Gusmaro rolled his eyes to the ceiling and sighed. From outside the doorway, Raul shook his head, but he was smiling.

"You don't play fair, Miss J," Raul said.

"I'm old," I said. "This is killing me."

"All right," Gusmaro said, "we'll go."

They turned down my offer to drive them to the interview but promised to let me know every detail. The following day, when I asked them about it, both pleaded previous engagements and raced from the room. A few minutes later, I found out why. The personnel manager called to ask me whether I had accidentally written down the wrong time and date for the interviews. Raul and Gusmaro had never arrived.

"We did so go," Raul insisted, when I tracked them down and cornered them outside the boys' locker room.

"Then why did that woman tell me you didn't go? Do you think she's lying?"

"Well, we went in the building, but then we left."

"Why?"

"They had all these fancy leather furnitures and expensive-looking paintings hanging all over the place," Raul explained.

"Yeah," Gusmaro said, "and the floor was real shiny and it was real, real quiet like a church or something. And everybody was wearing them three-pieced suits that cost a million dollars or something. There wasn't no Mexicans in there. Even the janitors was white guys. We figured Mexicans probably aren't even allowed to go in there or something. And we was just standing there looking around and the receptionist looked at us hard and asked could she help us, so we just left and went home."

Questions for Discussion and Debate

1. Why do Raul and Gusmaro decide not to take advantage of the interviews at Sun Microsystems? Point out all of the characteristics of the corporate environment that they mention.

2. Once these disadvantaged students have the skills and knowledge to "swim upstream," are there ways for teachers like Johnson to help them overcome the fears and discomforts that accompany their feeling of being "fish out of water?" What curricular ideas would you suggest?

3. In this excerpt, Johnson exhibits passion and humor, two characteristics without which a teacher can't function in stressful environments. Cite examples of *her* passion and humor and discuss where you have witnessed these qualities in classrooms, as a student or as an observer. Debate which of the two qualities is most important—or is there another, more important quality?

Activities and Projects

1. LouAnne Johnson notes in her Introduction to the book from which this excerpt is taken that she worked in the Academy Program, a school within a school, with a team of truly dedicated teachers and administrators who held high expectations for these students that many people had said the students couldn't meet. Johnson writes, "We asked our students to come to school every single day, to stay away from drugs and alcohol, to change their bad habits . . . resist the pressure to join gangs . . . clean up their language . . . and they gave us everything they had" (p. x).

   Watch the film, *Stand and Deliver* (1988), based on the true story of Jaime Escalante, a math teacher at Garfield High School in Los Angeles, who confronts similar environmental influences and yet brings his students academic success. How does he do this? Are his techniques unusual? Can his techniques, and Johnson's, be taught to all teachers and applied by all teachers? Answer and debate these questions in a roundtable discussion after viewing the film.

2. In groups of three, role-play the scenario portrayed in this excerpt. Feel free to play Johnson differently, however. Then compare and contrast the ways in which each group chose to portray Johnson. Reach a consensus on which "Johnson" was most effective, and why.

5.7 | *Up the Down Staircase* (1966)

Bel Kaufman

Former English teacher Bel Kaufman captures the rhythms and beat of an urban classroom in her best-selling novel, *Up the Down Staircase,* which saw 47 paperback printings and was translated into 16 languages. In 1988, the book was reissued again after 25 years, likely because the environment she described still exists. As she noted in an interview (Rose, 1988), the more the schools change, the more they stay the same. Clerical work, inadequate facilities, heavy teaching loads, and more bureaucracy continue to plague teachers today. In this excerpt, Kaufman cleverly conveys all of these problems through the verbal interactions between her leading character, Sylvia Barrett, and the students in her homeroom.

However, Kaufman herself believes that the problems lie not so much with the school environment, the shabbiness of a building or its structure, as with the societal problems, poverty, drugs, broken families, and unmanageable cities. Children who come to school, she says, come from the social setting first. "School used to be a refuge and now the outside has come in" (Kaufman, in Rose, 1988). This environmental issue, Kaufman believes, is what makes it so difficult for talented teachers to establish close relationships with students. Nevertheless, as she portrays in her novel, such relationships are still possible despite the obstacles.

Notice the *physical* feelings that you have as you read this excerpt or that you have by the end of the excerpt. What do your feelings reveal about the nature of teaching in an overcrowded urban environment?

Hi, teach!
Looka *her!* She's a teacher?
Who she?
Is this 304? Are you Mr. Barringer?
No. I'm Miss Barrett.
I'm supposed to have Mr. Barringer.
I'm Miss Barrett.
You the teacher? You so young.
Hey she's cute! Hey, teach, can I be in your class?
Please don't block the doorway. Please come in.
Good afternoon, Miss Barnet.
Miss Barrett. My name is on the blackboard. Good morning.
O, no! A *dame* for homeroom?

You want I should slug him, teach?
Is this homeroom period?
Yes. Sit down, please.
I don't belong here.
We gonna have you all term? Are you a regular or a sub?
There's not enough chairs!
Take any seat at all.
Hey, where do we sit?
Is this 309?
Someone swiped the pass. Can I have a pass?
What's your name?
My name is on the board.
I can't read your writing.
I gotta go to the nurse. I'm dying.

Don't believe him, teach. He ain't dying!

Can I sharpen my pencil in the office?

Why don't you leave the teacher alone, you bums?

Can we sit on the radiator? That's what we did last term.

Hi, teach! You the homeroom?

Pipe down, your morons! Don't you see the teacher's trying to say something?

Please sit down. I'd like to—

Hey, the bell just rung!

How come Mrs. Singer's not here? She was in this room last term.

When do we go home?

The first day of school, he wants to go home already!

That bell is your signal to come to order. Will you please—

Can I have a pass to a drink of water?

You want me to alphabetize for you?

What room is this?

This is room 304. My name is on the board: Miss Barrett. I'll have you for homeroom all term, and I hope to meet some of you in my English classes. Now, someone once said that first impressions—

English! No wonder!

Who needs it?

You give homework?

First impressions, they say, are lasting. What do we base our first—Yes? Do you belong in this class?

No. Mr. McHabe wants Ferone right away.

Who?

McHabe.

Whom does he want?

Joe Ferone.

Is Joe Ferone here?

Him? That's a laugh!

He'll show up when he feels like it.

Put down that window-pole, please. We all know that first impressions—Yes?

Is this 304?

Yes. You're late.

I'm not late. I'm absent.

You are?

I was absent all last term.

Well—sit down.

I can't. I'm dropping out. You're supposed to sign my Book Clearance from last term.

Do you owe any books?

I'm not on the Blacklist! That's a yellow slip. This here is a green!

Hey, isn't the pass back yet?

Quit your shoving!

He started it, teach!

I'd like you to come to order, please. I'm afraid we won't have time for the discussion on first impressions I had planned. I'm passing out—

Hey, she's passing out!

Give her air!

—Delaney cards. You are to fill them out at once while I take attendance from the Roll Book. Standees—line up in back of the room; you may lean on the wall to write. Print, in ink, your last name first, your parent's name, your date of birth, your address, my name—it's on the board—and the same upside down. I'll make out a seating plan in the Delaney Book. Any questions?

In ink or pencil?

I got no ink—can I use pencil? Who's got a pencil to loan me?

I don't remember when I was born.

Don't mind him—he's a comic.

Print or write?

When do we go to lunch?

I can't write upside down!

Ha-ha. He kills me laughing!

What do you need my address for? My father can't come.

Someone robbed my ball-point!

I can't do it—I lost my glasses.

Are these going to be our regular seats—the *radiator?*

I don't know my address—we're moving.

Where are you moving?

I don't know where.

Where do you live?

I don't live no place.

Any place. You, young man, why are you late?

I'm not even here. I'm in Mr. Loomis. My uncle's in this class. He forgot his lunch. Hi, Tony—catch!

Please don't throw—Yes, what is it?

This Mrs. Singer's room?

Yes. No. Not anymore.

Anyone find a sneaker from last term?

Hey, teach, can we use a pencil?

You want these filled out *now*?

There's chewing gum on my seat!

First name last or last name first?

I *gotta* have a pass to the Men's Room. I know my rights; this is a democracy, ain't it?

Isn't. What's the trouble now?

There's glass all over my desk from the window.

Please don't do that. Don't touch that broken window. It should be reported to the custodian. Does anyone—

I'll go!

Me! Let *me* go! That's Mr. Grayson—I know where he is in the basement!

All right. Tell him it's urgent. And who are you?

I'm sorry I'm late. I was in Detention.

The what?

The Late Room. Where they make you sit to make up your lateness when you come late.

All right, sit down. I mean, stand up—over there, against the wall.

For parent's name, can I use my aunt?

Put down your mother's name.

I got no mother.

Well—do the best you can. Yes, young lady?

The office sent me. Read this to your class and sign here.

May I have your attention, please. Please, class! There's been a change in today's assembly schedule. Listen carefully:

PLEASE IGNORE PREVIOUS INSTRUCTIONS IN CIRCULAR #3, PARAGRAPHS 5 AND 6, AND FOLLOW THE FOLLOWING:

THIS MORNING THERE WILL BE A LONG HOMEROOM PERIOD EXTENDING INTO THE FIRST HALF OF THE SECOND PERIOD. ALL X2 SECTIONS ARE TO REPORT TO ASSEMBLY THE SECOND HALF OF THE SECOND PERIOD. FIRST PERIOD CLASSES WILL BEGIN THE FOURTH PERIOD, SECOND PERIOD CLASSES WILL BEGIN THE FIFTH PERIOD, THIRD PERIOD CLASSES WILL BEGIN THE SIXTH PERIOD, AND SO ON, SUBJECT CLASSES BEING SHORTENED TO 23 MINUTES IN LENGTH, EXCEPT LUNCH, WHICH WILL BE NORMAL.

I can't hear you—what did you say?

They're drilling on the street!

Close the window.

I can't—I'll suffocate!

This is a long homeroom?

What's today's date?

It's September, stupid!

Your attention, please. I'm not finished:

SINCE IT IS DIFFICULT TO PROVIDE ADEQUATE SEATING SPACE FOR ALL STUDENTS UNDER EXISTING FACILITIES, THE OVERFLOW IS TO STAND IN THE AISLES UNTIL THE SALUTE TO THE FLAG AND THE STAR-SPANGLED BANNER ARE COMPLETED, AFTER WHICH THE OVERFLOW MAY NOT REMAIN STANDING IN THE AISLES UNLESS SO DIRECTED FROM THE PLATFORM. THIS IS A FIRE LAW. DR. CLARKE WILL EXTEND A WARM WELCOME TO ALL NEW STUDENTS; HIS TOPIC

WILL BE "OUR CULTURAL HER-
ITAGE." ANY STUDENT FOUND
TALKING OR EATING LUNCH IN
ASSEMBLY IS TO BE REPORTED AT
ONCE TO MR. McHABE.

Water! I gotta have water! My throat is
parching!
He thinks he's funny!
May I have your attention?
No!

TOMORROW ALL Y2 SECTIONS
WILL FOLLOW TODAY'S PROGRAM
FOR X2 SECTIONS WHILE ALL X2
SECTIONS WILL FOLLOW TODAY'S
PROGRAM FOR Y2 SECTIONS.

Where do we go?
What period is this?
The two boys in the back—stop throwing that
board eraser. Please come to order; there's more: . . .

Questions for Discussion and Debate

1. Make a list of the problems that are revealed
   in the verbal give-and-take between Miss
   Barrett and her homeroom students. Clas-
   sify the problems under the headings
   Clerical Work, Inadequate Facilities, Inane
   Bureaucracy, and any others you may deem
   appropriate. Discuss whether or not these
   problems are surmountable. If so, how? If
   not, what steps can a teacher take to change
   the situation?

2. After reading this excerpt, one might wonder
   how any real teaching can take place in such
   an environment. Perhaps whatever teaching
   does take place is a result of teacher perseverance. What evidence is there in this excerpt
   of Miss Barrett's perseverance? Debate the
   role of perseverance in a teacher's life.

3. Identify your favorite segment in this
   excerpt and explain why it "speaks" to you.

4. Miss Barrett had prepared a lovely activity
   for her homeroom that would enable them
   to get to know her and she them. She
   begins: "Now, someone once said that first
   impressions. . . . " She is interrupted, and
   each time she tries again to implement her
   plan, she is again interrupted. Discuss what
   you would do if circumstances prevented
   you from carrying out your perfectly written
   lesson plan. How does a teacher learn to
   switch gears, think on her or his feet, and
   meet the interruptions so common in the
   life of a typical lesson?

Activities and Projects

1. The novel *Up the Down Staircase* was
   adapted as a film of the same name (1967),
   starring the late Sandy Dennis. Watch the
   opening scenes of the film. Then compare
   and contrast the way in which the film

portrays the inspired lunacy of a New York
City high-school classroom with the way it
is conveyed in this excerpt from Kaufman's
book.

2. Visit classrooms in a city environment and note the particular ways in which teachers manage their classrooms. Bring back to class the classroom management techniques you observe and express your own views about their effectiveness. Are the management techniques that work in an urban environment the same as those that would work in a rural environment? A small private-school environment? Explain.

Note the similarities that exist between the classroom in this excerpt and the classrooms in which you have personally observed.

3. Read the excerpt aloud with your peers, with "Miss Barrett" reading the italicized words. Do the reading at a fast pace. Discuss any changes in your perception of her situation that occur as a result of reading the piece aloud.

5.8   *Seasoned Timber* (1939)

Dorothy Canfield

Timothy C. Hulme is the principal of the fictional Clifford Academy in Clifford, Vermont, in this excerpt from the novel by Dorothy Canfield (Fisher). Hulme wears many hats: He is administrator, teacher, and admissions director dealing directly with parents seeking to place their children in the academy. In this excerpt, Hulme meets with the McCanns in their New York City apartment. Ironically, Mr. McCann is a public high-school teacher, and his wife a librarian. Their explanation for wanting their daughter Jane to go to a country academy offers a rather detailed picture of the ills of the urban school environment. Hulme, on the other hand, counters this dismal picture with his own dubious description of Clifford Academy!

In reality, such academies exist and play a crucial role in rural New England (Burge, 1997, pp. B1, B7). Kathleen Burge's report on these academies led this editor to believe that the Clifford Academy in *Seasoned Timber* was based on St. Johnsbury Academy in St. Johnsbury, Vermont. Burge writes that St. Johnsbury is "not a high school this town of 7600 could afford to run. It is a private academy, founded in 1842. But as the only high school in the area, it also plays the role of a public high school. Its admissions office accepts everyone—although it is not required to do so . . . " (pp. B1, B7). Most of its students are day students who do not pay tuition. Burge notes that there are 17 other private high schools in New England that also function as local public high schools. Clifford Academy is much like St. Johnsbury in that it functions like a private school. Its trustees come from around the country, students must adhere to a dress code, the academy has no contract with the local school board, and admissions officials deal directly with parents (p. B7).

These hybrids can offer lessons on both the benefits and the problems of charter schools, a recent innovation in some states. Charter schools are public schools established by individuals who want to try some innovative educational structures and strategies without the usual strings attached. The 17 private academies mentioned previously share certain similarities with charter schools: They are insulated from the public scrutiny and politics that often afflict school boards; local residents have little influence over how the school is run; trustees are usually appointed rather than elected; and they have the power to determine their own curriculum, whom to hire, and, in the case of the academies only, how much to charge for tuition. Also in the case of the academies only, endowments and private fund-raising subsidize taxpayer's tuition payments.

Although Clifford Academy appears to be struggling to get the money it needs, the contemporary academies Burge refers to appear to be better able to pay for materials and furnishings than taxpayers alone could be. And, of course, there are the elite rural private schools—not the hybrids Burge refers to—that are usually able to provide the very best facilities, from tennis courts to computers to very small classes: but for a hefty tuition that most people can't afford. The hybrid academies would seem to be, among other things, a wonderful way for students from different socioeconomic levels to mingle as they do in many public schools. As you read this excerpt, weigh the advantages and disadvantages of the urban public school and the rural academy. In which environment would you prefer to teach? Why?

His next appointment was with a Mr. and Mrs. McCann, parents of a prospective student. The address was in the upper East Eighties, probably an old brownstone house made into an apartment. He wondered why people with an adolescent daughter were not in the suburbs. Well, how should he, this time, manage this recurrent big-city business of getting himself from where he was to somewhere else? He had had enough of the subway for one day, and marched off across town towards the Madison Avenue bus line, passing great plate-glass show-windows filled with handsome objects for sale, being passed by towering trucks loaded with things for sale, turning and veering on the crowded sidewalks to avoid collision with the men hurrying to sell, the women hurrying to buy.

Mr. McCann, the father of Jane, turned out to be a public high-school teacher, and Mrs. McCann to be a librarian in a branch of the public library. They were a pleasant, tired couple with a pleasant gawky daughter of fifteen whose front teeth were being straightened. Their apartment was, as he had expected, the second floor of an old brownstone house. From one look at the long, narrow frontroom where they received him, he knew, anyone would have known, just what quarters they had:—this room, another like it in the back, between them a kitchenette made out of the old washroom, and across the hall something or other for the little girl's bedroom. Or perhaps she slept on the couch where she and her mother now sat. And when she was sick—he remembered the cluttered, dirty, hall bedroom where he and Downer had slept and eaten and washed and cooked and been sick.

He was rather surprised to see that the child did not look sickly. The usual reason for sending a student to a country school was health. The father said, "No, Jane's not a delicate child. Not at all. But you know—or *do* you?—what a New York public high school is like."

The Vermont teacher said he had taught for a while in one, many years ago, but had not seen one for some time. So the city teacher told him:—six thousand students in one building, the corridors between classes as jammed, pushing, and dangerous as the subway in rush hour, the lunchroom a yelling mob snatching at platefuls of hastily slammed-down food, the long lines waiting for a chance at the drinking fountain, the constant need to keep your possessions in sight or locked up because of incessant thieving, one of Jane's teachers a paranoiac, kept in her place by political influence: all of the teachers, even the best of them, sunk by numbers. "Do you know how often Jane recites? Two minutes, twice a week. Do you know how the teachers correct English compositions? Well, you teach English: just think for yourself what would happen if you had two hundred and fifty in your classes, writing compositions. How many would you throw away unread and uncorrected? And do you know what happens sometimes in the toilet rooms when the crowd is so thick that . . ."

"I see," said Timothy Hulme. "But, listen, you're a colleague of mine—do *you* know what a beggarly country school in a poor mountain town is like?"

"We've read your catalogue from cover to cover," said McCann, and his wife added earnestly, "We *like* your ideas about discussion groups and assignments by the week, and Domestic Science that teaches young people to use what they have."

Jane's father said, "We can hardly believe there's a school within our means where Jane'll have somebody really trying to teach her something, not just trying to keep hell from breaking loose. She won't know how to act!"

The Principal of Clifford Academy laughed ironically. "Didn't you ever read any other school catalogues? Don't you know what is left out of a catalogue—by intention? I'll just tell you some of the things left out of ours. Our gymnasium is an old barn, heated by a wood stove. And we'll probably never have anything else. Some of the seats in our classrooms were there during the Civil War. I mean literally. Our heating plant is forty years old. The woodwork hasn't been painted since—since the American Revolution! Our edition of the Britannica is the 1911 one. Our teachers are frightfully underpaid—and not very well trained. One of them is worn out and only hanging on because there's no provision for pensions. Many of our students come clumping in straight from the farm and lots of them use the double negative when they first appear at the Academy. We haven't had a new . . . "

"How many in your classes?"

"From twelve to twenty."

The McCanns looked at each other, exulting. "Do the students have a chance to see anything of the teachers outside the classrooms? Would Jane, for instance, be in personal touch with you?"

"Oh, as to that, yes. Everybody in a small school and a small town sees everybody else all the time. The house where I live is at one end of the Main Building."

"Let me tell you a story, Mr. Hulme," said the father of Jane, "to give you some idea of the size of our building, and the kind of life the children have. At the beginning of our last term, a teacher in our department reported one of the Freshman boys absent from her class four days in succession, where he was by her list due to be present. We looked up his record and found he'd been at school those days, so I sent for him to come to the office. He turned out to be an anxious little kid, twelve or thirteen years old, whose family had just moved in from up-state somewhere. And he said the trouble was he couldn't *find* his English section. 'I have a gym period just before my English,' he told me, 'and when I leave that to go to my English class, I can't find the way. The first day I came out on the roof. And the next day in the basement. After I'd been miles up and down the halls every direction I could, I thought, "Well, I know how to get to that English class from the front door. If I went out and came in from outside I could get to it." So I went out a side door but when I tried to come in the front door the big boys wouldn't let me. . . . '"

Mrs. McCann broke in to explain, "That's the squad of Seniors stationed there to keep the tardy students from slipping into their classes without reporting."

Her husband went on, "The kid ended up, 'If I could only find Benny he could take me to that class. Benny knows the way. But he's got a different gym period from mine, and I never see him any more.'"

"Poor child!" said Mrs. McCann compassionately.

"Well, yes, I get your point," admitted Timothy, "but I'm afraid you'll only find it like St. Lawrence asking to be turned over on his griddle."

"That edition of the Britannica is really better than the latest one," said the librarian mother, evidently presenting this fact as a symbol.

"Let's see Jane's report cards," said Timothy.

They were all right. Jane was all right. She was, in fact, it seemed to the Principal, like any one of hundreds of nice little girls with gold bands on their teeth who had passed through his classes. The question of tuition came up. The McCanns did not ask for a reduction of tuition, but they laid their family budget before him and inquired if there was any fair way in which Jane's living-expenses might be lessened. Mr. McCann's salary was considerably more than that of the Principal of Clifford Academy: and in addition there was the pay of Mrs. McCann—although T.C. was shocked by the meager salary given librarians by the great and rich city. Their combined income came to more than half as much again as his own.

Questions for Discussion and Debate

1. List the problems Mr. McCann cites about the urban high school. Then list the problems Mr. Hulme cites about Clifford Academy. Look at the advantages and disadvantages of each environment and list them. In which environment would you prefer to teach, and why?

   Divide your class in half and hold a debate in which one side argues in favor of the urban option and the other argues for the rural.

2. Reread the introduction to this excerpt and then summarize the connection between the 17 existing rural academies in New England and Clifford. How are they the same or different? What are the positive and negative aspects of Clifford (St. Johnsbury)?

3. What are the similarities and differences between charter schools and these rural academies or "hybrids"? (See the introduction to this excerpt.)

Activities and Projects

1. Mr. McCann tells the story about poor Benny and the largeness of his urban school. What is your reaction to this tale? Make up an equivalent story—a rural version—that *Hulme* might have told. Share a tale from your own school experience that conveys a problem related to that particular environment. Is the use of such stories to illustrate problems more effective than simply detailing the problems statistically? Why, or why not?

2. You have read in this chapter several references to the problems of rural and urban school environments: Canfield's story comes out of the 1930s, Brown's and Kaufman's out of the 1950s and 1960s, and Johnson's out of the 1990s. What conclusions can you draw from their stories and the time periods they cover? Can you make some comparisons? Relationships? Generalizations? (Check back to the introduction to Selection 5.7 to reread Bel Kaufman's relevant quote.)

3. Do research on urban education and, if possible, shed an optimistic light on the situation by locating people and projects that are working to make significant changes in what has historically been a rather pessimistic picture.

4. Suburbia differs in many ways from urban and rural environments, and subsequently the problems faced by suburban school systems as well as their advantages are unique. Find out about the ways in which suburban environments influence the nature of schools and how these schools differ from those in other areas.

5. Continue the story this excerpt tells by writing what could possibly be the next page of the piece. Or write a short story about the first day of Jane McCann's life as a student at Clifford using data from the excerpt.

6. Charter schools resemble rural academies in certain ways but are far more controversial. Ever since the charter-school movement began over a decade ago, it has "attracted charlatans as well as champions" (Nathan, 2002, p. 32). Find out more about charter schools and then hold a debate on this resolution: Charter schools unfairly use funds that regular public schools could use to enact similar or other innovations. (As the legislation is currently written, when a charter school opens, there is less money available per pupil for the regular public schools in the district.)

7. Dorothy Canfield (Fisher) has written several books related to education. Research her work and life. Prepare a summary of your findings about the connection between this excerpt and her other work.

5.9 ▏▎▏▎ *The Miracle Worker* **(1956)**

William Gibson

Annie Sullivan (1866–1936) is the miracle worker, and playwright William Gibson explains why in this excerpt from his outstanding play based on the relationship between teacher Annie Sullivan and her most famous pupil, Helen Keller (1880–1968). There is no question that Keller's life has received far more attention than Sullivan's because of her extraordinary productivity, prolific body of writing, and hundreds of public appearances both here and abroad. Sullivan's claim to fame, on the other hand, was her role in unlocking—through the sense of touch—Keller's incredible potential for greatness. Thus it is to Gibson's credit that he gives the teacher center stage. Keller herself wrote a book, *Teacher* (1955), in which she tells of Anne Sullivan Macy's life and how, in addition to their earlier relationship, she stayed with Helen through her years at Radcliffe College, helping her to interpret lectures and class discussions. Though Anne married, she remained with Helen until her own death. In the 1950s, several years after Sullivan's death, when Keller traveled to Egypt, Brazil, and other countries to visit and speak at schools for the blind, she said that Sullivan's virtue and power of communication traveled with her and "nerved me to endure and persevere" (Keller, 1955, p. 247).

Perkins School for the Blind, where both Annie and Helen were educated, and similar schools today provide an environment in which students receive an education geared to their particular needs. With the movement toward inclusion, many students with impairments similar to Helen's and Annie's are being mainstreamed into regular classes in public schools and are often provided with an in-class aide. As you read this excerpt, think about the kind of preparation a classroom teacher would need to teach these students effectively. You will, no doubt, be moved by the scene in which Annie makes the miraculous connection to Helen. It has become one of the most memorable moments in teacher–student history! Have you witnessed any such miracles in the classroom?

(She [KATE] *holds* HELEN *struggling until we hear from the child her first sound so far, an inarticulate weird noise in her throat such as an animal in a trap might make; and* KATE *releases her. The second she is free* HELEN *blunders away, collides violently with a chair, falls, and sits weeping.* KATE *comes to her, embraces, caresses, soothes her, and buries her own face in her hair, until she can control her voice.)*

[KATE:] Every day she slips further away. And I don't know how to call her back.

AUNT EV: Oh, I've a mind to take her up to Baltimore myself. If that doctor can't help her, maybe he'll know who can.

KELLER [PRESENTLY, HEAVILY]: I'll write the man, Katie.

(He stands with the baby in his clasp, staring at HELEN'S *head, hanging down on* KATE'S *arm.*

The lights dim out, except the one on KATE *and* HELEN. *In the twilight,* JAMES, AUNT EV, *and* KELLER *move off slowly, formally, in separate directions;* KATE *with* HELEN *in her arms remains, motionless, in an image which overlaps into the next scene and fades only when it is well under way.*

Without pause, from the dark down left we hear a man's voice with a Greek accent speaking:)

ANAGNOS: —who could do nothing for the girl, of course. It was Dr. Bell who thought she might somehow be taught. I have written the family only that a suitable governess, Miss Annie Sullivan, has been found here in Boston—

(The lights begin to come up, down left, on a long table and chair. The table contains equipment for teaching the blind by touch—a small replica of the human skeleton, stuffed animals, models of flowers and plants, piles of books. The chair contains a girl of 20, ANNIE SULLIVAN, *with a face which in repose is grave and rather obstinate, and when active is impudent, combative, twinkling with all the life that is lacking in* HELEN'S, *and handsome; there is a crude vitality to her. Her suitcase is at her knee,* ANAGNOS, *a stocky bearded man, comes into the light only towards the end of his speech.)*

ANAGNOS: —and will come. It will no doubt be difficult for you there, Annie. But it has been difficult for you at our school too, hm? Gratifying, yes, when you came to us and could not spell your name, to accomplish so much here in a few years, but always an Irish battle. For independence.

(He studies ANNIE, *humorously; she does not open her eyes.)*

This is my last time to counsel you, Annie, and you do lack some—by some I mean *all*—what, tact or talent to bend. To others. And what has saved you on more than one occasion here at Perkins is that there was nowhere to expel you to. Your eyes hurt?

ANNIE: My ears, Mr. Anagnos.

(And now she has opened her eyes; they are inflamed, vague, slightly crossed, clouded by the granular growth of trachoma, and she often keeps them closed to shut out the pain of light.)

ANAGNOS [SEVERELY]: Nowhere but back to Tewksbury, where children learn to be saucy. Annie, I know how dreadful it was there, but that battle is dead and done with, why not let it stay buried?

ANNIE [CHEERILY]: I think God must owe me a resurrection.

ANAGNOS [A BIT SHOCKED]: What?

ANNIE [TAPS HER BROW]: Well, He keeps digging up that battle!

ANAGNOS: That is not a proper thing to say, Annie. It is what I mean.

ANNIE [MEEKLY]: Yes. But I know what I'm like, what's this child like?

ANAGNOS: Like?

ANNIE: Well—Bright or dull, to start off.

ANAGNOS: No one knows. And if she is dull, you have no patience with this?

ANNIE: Oh, in grownups you have to, Mr. Anagnos. I mean in children it just seems a little—precocious, can I use that word?

ANAGNOS: Only if you can spell it.

ANNIE: Premature. So I hope at least she's a bright one.

ANAGNOS: Deaf, blind, mute—who knows? She is like a little safe, locked, that no one can open. Perhaps there is a treasure inside.

ANNIE: Maybe it's empty, too?

ANAGNOS: Possible. I should warn you, she is much given to tantrums.

ANNIE: Means something is inside. Well, so am I, if I believe all I hear. Maybe you should warn *them*.

ANAGNOS [FROWNS]: Annie. I wrote them no word of your history. You will find yourself among strangers now, who know nothing of it.

ANNIE: Well, we'll keep them in a state of blessed ignorance.

ANAGNOS: Perhaps *you* should tell it?

ANNIE [BRISTLING]: Why? I have enough trouble with people who don't know.

ANAGNOS: So they will understand. When you have trouble.

ANNIE: The only time I have trouble is when I'm right.

(But she is amused at herself, as is ANAGNOS.*)*

Is it my fault it's so often? I won't give them trouble, Mr. Anagnos, I'll be so ladylike they won't notice I've come.

ANAGNOS: Annie, be—humble. It is not as if you have so many offers to pick and choose. You will need their affection, working with this child.

ANNIE [HUMOROUSLY]: I hope I won't need their pity.

ANAGNOS: Oh, we can all use some pity.

(Crisply)

So. You are no longer our pupil, we throw you into the world, a teacher. *If* the child can be taught. No one expects you to work miracles, even for twenty-five dollars a month. Now, in this envelope a loan, for the railroad, which you will repay me when you have a bank account. But in this box, a gift. With our love.

(ANNIE opens the small box he extends, and sees a garnet ring. She looks up, blinking, and down.)

I think other friends are ready to say goodbye.

(He moves as though to open doors.)

ANNIE: Mr. Anagnos.

(Her voice is trembling.)

Dear Mr. Anagnos, I—

(But she swallows over getting the ring on her finger, and cannot continue until she finds a woebegone joke.)

Well, what should I say, I'm an ignorant opinionated girl, and everything I am I owe to you?

ANAGNOS [SMILES]: That is only half true, Annie.

ANNIE: Which half? I crawled in here like a drowned rat, I thought I died when Jimmie died, that I'd never again—come alive. Well, you say with love so easy, and I haven't *loved* a soul since and I never will, I suppose, but this place gave me more than my eyes back. Or taught me how to spell, which I'll never learn anyway, but with all the fights and the trouble I've been here it taught me what help is, and how to live again, and I don't want to say goodbye. Don't open the door, I'm crying.

ANAGNOS [GENTLY]: They will not see.

(He moves again as though opening doors, and in comes a group of girls, 8-year-olds to 17-year-olds; as they walk we see they are blind. ANAGNOS *shepherds them in with a hand.)* . . .

• • •

KATE [A PAUSE]: It's a very special day.

ANNIE [GRIMLY]: It will be, when I give in to that.

(She tries to disengage HELEN'S *hand;* KATE *lays hers on* ANNIE'S.*)*

KATE: Please. I've hardly had a chance to welcome her home—

ANNIE: Captain Keller.

KELLER [EMBARRASSED]: Oh. Katie, we—had a little talk, Miss Annie feels that if we indulge Helen in these—

AUNT EV: But what's the child done?

ANNIE: She's learned not to throw things on the floor and kick. It took us the best part of two weeks and—

AUNT EV: But only a napkin, it's not as if it were breakable!

ANNIE: And everything she's learned *is*? Mrs. Keller, I don't think we should—play tug-of-war for her, either give her to me or you keep her from kicking.

KATE: What do you wish to do?

ANNIE: Let me take her from the table.

AUNT EV: Oh, let her stay, my goodness, she's only a child, she doesn't have to wear a napkin if she doesn't want to her first evening—

ANNIE [LEVEL]: And ask outsiders not to interfere.

AUNT EV [ASTONISHED]: Out—outsi—I'm the child's *aunt*!

KATE [DISTRESSED]: Will once hurt so much, Miss Annie? I've—made all Helen's favorite foods, tonight.

(A pause)

KELLER [GENTLY]: It's a homecoming party, Miss Annie.

*(*ANNIE *after a moment releases* HELEN. *But she cannot accept it, at her own chair she shakes her head and turns back, intent on* KATE.*)*

ANNIE: She's testing you. You realize?

JAMES [TO ANNIE]: She's testing you.

KELLER: Jimmie, be quiet.

*(*JAMES *sits, tense.)*

Now she's home, naturally she—

ANNIE: And wants to see what will happen. At your hands. I said it was my main worry, is this what you promised me not half an hour ago?

KELLER [REASONABLY]: But she's *not* kicking, now—

ANNIE: And not learning not to. Mrs. Keller, teaching her is bound to be painful, to everyone. I know it hurts to watch, but she'll live up to just what you demand of her, and no more.

JAMES [PALELY]: She's testing *you*.

KELLER [TESTILY]: Jimmie.

JAMES: I have an opinion, I think I should—

KELLER: No one's interested in hearing your opinion.

ANNIE: *I'm* interested, of course she's testing me. Let me keep her to what she's learned and she'll go on learning from me. Take her out of my hands and it all comes apart.

*(*KATE *closes her eyes, digesting it;* ANNIE *sits again, with a brief comment for her.)*

Be bountiful, it's at her expense.

(She turns to JAMES, *flatly.)*

Please pass me more of—her favorite foods.

(Then KATE *lifts* HELEN'S *hand, and turning her toward* ANNIE, *surrenders her;* HELEN *makes for her own chair.)*

KATE [LOW]: Take her, Miss Annie.

ANNIE [THEN]: Thank you.

(But the moment ANNIE *rising reaches for her hand,* HELEN *begins to fight and kick, clutching to the tablecloth, and uttering laments.* ANNIE *again tries to loosen her hand, and* KELLER *rises.)*

KELLER [TOLERANT]: I'm afraid you're the difficulty, Miss Annie. Now I'll keep her to what she's learned, you're quite right there—

(*He takes* HELEN'S *hands from* ANNIE, *pats them;* HELEN *quiets down.*)

—but I don't see that we need send her from the table, after all, she's the guest of honor. Bring her plate back.

ANNIE: If she was a seeing child, none of you would tolerate one—

KELLER: Well, she's not, I think some compromise is called for. Bring her plate, please.

(ANNIE'S *jaw sets, but she restores the plate, while* KELLER *fastens the napkin around* HELEN'S *neck; she permits it.*)

There. It's not unnatural, most of us take some aversion to our teachers, and occasionally another hand can smooth things out.

(*He puts a fork in* HELEN'S *hand;* HELEN *takes it. Genially:*)

Now. Shall we start all over?

(*He goes back around the table, and sits.* ANNIE *stands watching.* HELEN *is motionless, thinking things through, until with a wicked glee she deliberately flings the fork on the floor. After another moment she plunges her hand into her food, and crams a fistful into her mouth.*)

JAMES [WEARILY]: I think we've started all over—

(KELLER *shoots a glare at him, as* HELEN *plunges her other hand into* ANNIE'S *plate.* ANNIE *at once moves in, to grasp her wrist, and* HELEN *flinging out a hand encounters the pitcher; she swings with it at* ANNIE; ANNIE

falling back blocks it with an elbow, but the water flies over her dress. ANNIE *gets her breath, then snatches the pitcher away in one hand, hoists* HELEN *up bodily under the other arm, and starts to carry her out, kicking.* KELLER *stands.*)

ANNIE [SAVAGELY POLITE]: Don't get up!

KELLER: Where are you going?

ANNIE: Don't smooth anything else out for me, don't interfere in any way! I treat her like a seeing child because I *ask* her to see, I *expect* her to see, don't undo what I do!

KELLER: Where are you taking her?

ANNIE: To make her fill this pitcher again!

(*She thrusts out with* HELEN *under her arm, but* HELEN *escapes up the stairs and* ANNIE *runs after her.* KELLER *stands rigid.* AUNT EV *is astounded.*)

AUNT EV: You let her speak to you like that, Arthur? A creature who *works* for you?

KELLER [ANGRILY]: No, Don't.

(*He is starting after* ANNIE *when* JAMES, *on his feet with shaky resolve, interposes his chair between them in* KELLER'S *path.*)

JAMES: Let her go.

KELLER: What!

JAMES [A SWALLOW]: I said—let her go. She's right.

(KELLER *glares at the chair and him.* JAMES *takes a deep breath, then headlong:*)

She's right, Kate's right, I'm right, and you're wrong. If you drive her away from here it will be over my dead—chair, has it never occurred to you that on one occasion you might be consummately wrong?

(KELLER'S *stare is unbelieving, even a little fascinated.* KATE *rises in trepidation, to mediate.*)

KATE: Captain.

(KELLER *stops her with his raised hand; his eyes stay on* JAMES' *pale face, for a long hold. When he finally finds his voice, it is gruff.*)

KELLER: Sit down, everyone.

(*He sits.* KATE *sits.* JAMES *holds onto his chair.* KELLER *speaks mildly.*)

Please sit down, Jimmie.

(JAMES *sits, and a moveless silence prevails;* KELLER'S *eyes do not leave him.*

ANNIE *has pulled* HELEN *downstairs again by one hand, the pitcher in her other hand, down the porch steps, and across the yard to the pump. She puts* HELEN'S *hand on the pump handle, grimly.*)

ANNIE: All right. Pump.

(HELEN *touches her cheek, waits uncertainly.*)

No, she's not here. Pump!

(*She forces* HELEN'S *hand to work the handle, then lets go. And* HELEN *obeys. She pumps till the water comes, then* ANNIE *puts the pitcher in her other hand and guides it under the spout, and the water tumbling half into and half around the pitcher douses* HELEN'S *hand.* ANNIE *takes over the handle to keep water coming, and does automatically what she has done so many times before, spells into* HELEN'S *free palm:*)

Water. W, a, t, e, r. *Water.* It has a—*name*—

(*And now the miracle happens.* HELEN *drops the pitcher on the slab under the spout, it shatters. She stands transfixed.* ANNIE *freezes on the pump handle: there is a change in the sundown light, and with it a change in* HELEN'S *face, some light coming into it we have never seen there, some struggle in the depths behind it; and her lips tremble, trying to remember*

something the muscles around them once knew, till at last it finds its way out, painfully, a baby sound buried under the debris of years of dumbness.)

HELEN: Wah. Wah.

(*And again, with great effort*)

Wah. Wah.

(HELEN *plunges her hand into the dwindling water, spells into her own palm. Then she gropes frantically,* ANNIE *reaches for her hand, and* HELEN *spells into* ANNIE'S *hand.*)

ANNIE [WHISPERING]: Yes.

(HELEN *spells into it again.*)

Yes!

(HELEN *grabs at the handle, pumps for more water, plunges her hand into its spurt and grabs* ANNIE'S *to spell it again.*)

Yes! Oh, my dear—

(*She falls to her knees to clasp* HELEN'S *hand, but* HELEN *pulls it free, stands almost bewildered, then drops to the ground, pats it swiftly, holds up her palm, imperious.* ANNIE *spells into it:*)

Ground.

(HELEN *spells it back.*)

Yes!

(HELEN *whirls to the pump, pats it, holds up her palm, and* ANNIE *spells into it.*)

Pump.

(HELEN *spells it back.*)

Yes! Yes!

(*Now* HELEN *is in such an excitement she is possessed, wild, trembling, cannot be still, turns, runs, falls on the porch step, claps it, reaches out her palm, and* ANNIE *is at it instantly to spell:)*

Step.

*(*HELEN *has no time to spell back now, she whirls groping, to touch anything, encounters the trellis, shakes it, thrusts out her palm, and* ANNIE *while spelling to her cries wildly at the house.)*

Trellis. Mrs. Keller! *Mrs. Keller*!

(Inside, KATE *starts to her feet.* HELEN *scrambles back onto the porch, groping, and finds the bell string, tugs it; the bell rings, the distant chimes begin tolling the hour, all the bells in town seem to break into speech while* HELEN *reaches out and* ANNIE *spells feverishly into her hand.* KATE *hurries out, with* KELLER *after her;* AUNT EV *is on her feet, to peer out the window; only* JAMES *remains at the table, and with a napkin wipes his damp brow. From up right and left the servants—* VINEY, *the two Negro children, the other servant—*run in, and stand watching from a distance as HELEN, *ringing the bell, with her other hand encounters her mother's skirt; when she throws a hand out,* ANNIE *spells into it:)*

Mother.

*(*KELLER *now seizes* HELEN'S *hand, she touches him, gestures a hand, and* ANNIE *again spells:)*

Papa—She *knows*!

*(*KATE *and* KELLER *go to their knees, stammering, clutching* HELEN *to them, and* ANNIE *steps unsteadily back to watch the threesome,* HELEN *spelling widly into* KATE'S *hand, then into* KELLER'S, KATE *spelling back into* HELEN'S; *they cannot keep their hands off her, and rock her in their clasp.*

Then HELEN *gropes, feels nothing, turns all around, pulls free, and comes with both hands groping, to find* ANNIE. *She encounters* ANNIE'S *thighs,* ANNIE *kneels to her,* HELEN'S *hand pats* ANNIE'S *cheek impatiently, points a finger, and waits; and* ANNIE *spells into it:)*

Teacher.

*(*HELEN *spells it back, slowly;* ANNIE *nods.)*

Teacher.

(She holds HELEN'S *hand to her cheek. Presently* HELEN *withdraws it, not jerkily, only with reserve, and retreats a step. She stands thinking it over, then turns again and stumbles back to her parents. They try to embrace her, but she has something else in mind, it is to get the keys, and she hits* KATE'S *pocket until* KATE *digs them out for her.*

ANNIE *with her own load of emotion has retreated, her back turned, toward the pump, to sit;* KATE *moves to* HELEN, *touches her hand questioningly, and* HELEN *spells a word to her.* KATE *comprehends it, their first act of verbal communication, and she can hardly utter the word aloud, in wonder, gratitude, and deprivation; it is a moment in which she simultaneously finds and loses a child.)*

KATE: Teacher?

*(*ANNIE *turns; and* KATE, *facing* HELEN *in her direction by the shoulders, holds her back, holds her back, and then relinquishes her.* HELEN *feels her way across the yard, rather shyly, and when her moving hands touch* ANNIE'S *skirt she stops. Then she holds out the keys and places them in* ANNIE'S *hand. For a moment neither of them moves. Then* HELEN *slides into* ANNIE'S *arms, and lifting away her smoked glasses, kisses her on the cheek.* ANNIE *gathers her in.*

KATE *torn both ways turns from this, gestures the servants off, and makes her way into the house, on* KELLER'S *arm. The servants go, in separate directions.*

The lights are half down now, except over the pump. ANNIE *and* HELEN *are here, alone in the yard.* ANNIE *has found* HELEN'S *hand, almost without knowing it, and she spells slowly into it, her voice unsteady, whispering:)*

ANNIE: I, love, Helen.

(She clutches the child to her, tight this time, not spelling, whispering into her hair.)

Forever, and—

(She stops. The lights over the pump are taking on the color of the past, and it brings ANNIE'S *head up, her eyes opening, in fear; and as slowly as though drawn she rises, to listen, with her hands on* HELEN'S *shoulders. She waits, waits, listening with ears and eyes both,*

slowly here, slowly there: and hears only silence. There are no voices. The color passes on, and when her eyes come back to* HELEN *she can breathe the end of her phrase without fear:)*

—ever.

(In the family room KATE *has stood over the table, staring at* HELEN'S *plate, with* KELLER *at her shoulder; now* JAMES *takes a step to move her chair in, and* KATE *sits, with head erect, and* KELLER *inclines his head to* JAMES; *so it is* AUNT EV, *hesitant, and rather humble, who moves to the door.*

Outside HELEN *tugs at* ANNIE'S *hand and* ANNIE *comes with it.* HELEN *pulls her toward the house; and hand in hand, they cross the yard, and ascend the porch steps, in the rising lights, to where* AUNT EV *is holding the door open for them.*

The curtain ends the play.)

▄▄▄▄▄▄▄▄▄ Questions for Discussion and Debate ▄▄▄▄▄▄▄▄▄

1. Who was Annie Sullivan? Do a one-paragraph personality sketch of Annie based on the various clues to her character and demeanor throughout the excerpt. What adjectives would you use to describe Annie? Discuss with the class how her personality would or would not be effective in a more traditional setting. Compare *yourself* to the sketch you wrote about Annie.

2. Make a "place line" much like a time line, except instead of placing dates on the line, write down all the locations that are mentioned in the excerpt, from the first to the last page. Next to each place that you put on the place line, briefly write down who was there and what happened. (This place line

can be an effective way of summarizing the origins of and eventual relationship between Annie and Helen.)

3. What were Helen's multiple disabilities and problems? What were Annie's?

4. Metaphorically speaking, Annie, the teacher, provided the key with which Helen was able to unlock the door that had kept her from using her native intelligence and becoming a learner. That goal, of course, is what all teachers set for themselves. Describe in your own words how Annie made the miracle of communication happen in that most touching scene. Then discuss other metaphors that you think accurately represent the role of teacher.

Activities and Projects

1. Survey the area in which you are living to document what special schools are there. Are there any schools for hearing-impaired, visually impaired, special-needs, emotionally disturbed, or other special students? Try to visit one or more of these schools. Compare them with the public schools in the area. What are the similarities and differences between them? Prepare a presentation on your findings.

   Along with your exploration of special schools, interview a cross section of teachers about whether or not special students should be mainstreamed into the regular classroom. Debate the pros and cons of mainstreaming after researching studies on the subject. This activity might become a cooperative learning project by dividing up the tasks among members of the class.

2. Perform the scenes in this excerpt by taking roles and doing them as a radio play. Then discuss whether or not this activity enabled you to identify more closely with the people in these scenes. What other feelings did you have? What moved you?

3. Do research on Helen Keller and Annie Sullivan. Perhaps committees could be formed and each group could read a different biography or autobiography. After completing the research, have the groups share what they learned about the education of each woman and how they were the same or different. Include discussions of the frame of reference of each author and its influence on the nature of the book. In particular, how does each author portray the different environments in which Annie and Helen lived?

4. Watch the film *The Miracle Worker* (1962) as a class and discuss the pedagogical approaches used by Annie Sullivan. Which techniques are appropriate or adaptable to teaching in more traditional environments? (This activity could be done by just one individual, who might do a report on the movie and the question indicated here.)

5. Mark Medoff's Tony Award-winning play, *Children of a Lesser God* (1980), takes place in a school for hearing-impaired students and was also made into a movie (1986), starring William Hurt and Marlee Matlin. It centers around the love that grows between a teacher of the hearing-impaired and a deaf woman, a former student at the school. In the film the teacher implements a number of innovative and creative teaching techniques.

   The play emphasizes the active protest by students to get the administration of the school to hire more deaf teachers. Both the play and the film convey the problem of stereotyping, not just of the deaf by hearing people, but of hearing people by the deaf.

   Watch this film, in addition to *The Miracle Worker* or on its own, and, using a VCR, show the class clips of the film(s), stopping intermittently to discuss the environment of the school(s) and the problems and the techniques being used therein.

5.10 ▓▓▓ *Horace's Compromise* (1985)

Theodore Sizer

Horace is a composite character. He is you and me and every teacher who has ever experienced the frustrations of teaching in an environment characterized by assembly-line routines. He is every teacher who has ever had to compromise his or her standards to survive in an environment where teaching is undervalued, the class size is too large, and order is the goal, where each day is fragmented, the curriculum is fragmented, and the teacher's focus is fragmented.

Ted Sizer grapples with Horace's (our) dilemma. In this excerpt he attempts to define how reforming school environments may help teachers like Horace solve their dilemma.

Sizer is best known for establishing the Coalition for Essential Schools in 1984 at Brown University, where he was a member of the faculty. Though he retired as head of the Coalition in the spring of 1998, he continues to speak and write about the need for reform—both curricular and environmental. The criteria he prescribes in this excerpt guide more than 1,022 schools that are associated with the Coalition. Although Sizer designates Horace a high-school teacher, his discussion of the criteria and "conditions of a good school" are applicable to all grade levels and schools.

Do the criteria he presents and the rationale for implementing these conditions make sense to you? Evaluate each one as you read, and think about whether or not such favorable conditions exist in the schools where you are working or observing.

Most American families grapple in March and April with income tax returns. Most of those family members who assemble the materials and do the calculations need quiet, enough space to spread out the papers, sufficient hassle-free time to get the job done correctly, good enough light to read the fine print, and sympathetic husbands, wives, or children, who say, "You poor, poor thing for having to do that terrible job," and periodically bring coffee and brownies. Of course, not all tax-return assemblers are alike: some work well with a jumble of papers around, others need neat piles; some want total quiet, others want a "white sound"— Muzak—behind them; some prefer bourbon to coffee. In fact, no two of us efficiently complete this annual democratic chore in precisely the same way.

It is so with learners in schools. The environment is important. If it jangles the mind, or interrupts or demeans or frightens, there cannot be the kind of focused, sustained intellectual activity that is required to write a clear and graceful paragraph or accurately complete a Form 1040. One's flanks need be secure so that one can focus on some central object. Covered flanks require trust (I know I won't be interrupted by these people, because they understand my need to concentrate), predictability (I know I can count on the next

---

thirty minutes for this), and adequate resources (I know I have the tools to do this job).

It does not take much to ruin a class, to break the thread of thought. So it was in a social studies lesson in a small-town public high school. The classroom contained thirteen seniors. They chatted amiably among themselves and with Jim Gerry, the teacher, for a few minutes after the bell, an obviously necessary exercise, as five more students came in late, one by one, each in turn whispering to Gerry and handing him an excuse slip. He nodded pleasantly to each, and the student then found a chair, unloaded an armful of books in a tumble on the floor, and, once seated, stretched and looked expectantly at the movie projector that was set up at the center of the room.

This was a seniors' social studies elective, called sociology. Gerry told the students that he was going to open the class with a movie on the 1960s. He reminded them that they had seen it before, in tenth grade, but he said that it made sense to screen it again, because it was a fine film and was closely related to the current course's topic of "cultural change." Several of the students mentioned remembering it.

Gerry turned off the lights, asked several students on his right to pull down the shades, and started the film. It was a collage of newsreel and film clips taken during the sixties, with a sound track of speeches, Vietnam, the crowds outside the Chicago Democratic Party convention, the Beatles, Dr. King, the Kennedys, Bull Connor, the Newark riots, and more. It was an excellent production, as Gerry had promised, gripping the students, who had been born in the middle of the decade, almost as much as it did Gerry and his visitor, who as adults had lived through it. The piece opened with President Kennedy's inaugural speech and returned to it periodically, sometimes in irony, sometimes in pathos. At one of the ironic moments, well into the film, the public address system

rasped on. Gerry cut the film. Four announcements were made, on a wrestling camp, on freshman summer programs, on a meeting of the National Honor Society, and no tryouts for the swing choir. The blare extinguished itself as abruptly as it had erupted. Gerry turned on the film again, the sound track swooping back into audibility. Kennedy, before a living figure, was now papier-mâché.

Public address systems are the most malevolent intruder into the thinking taking place in public school classrooms since the invention of the flickering fluorescent light. In the name of efficient management, they regularly eviscerate good teaching. They are a symbol of misplaced priorities of schools that fail to value conditions for serious intellectual activity. Their cousins—the intruding messenger from the office and the extracurricular or public relations exercise on behalf of the school system that pre-empts class time—are no better. They all signal the low priority that routine teaching may hold, and they certainly puzzle students who on one occasion observe the school casually canceling some classes to make time for a Mr. and Miss Junior America Assembly and on another severely admonishing individuals not to miss any classes at all.

A good school should be a place of unanxious expectation. Although some expectations certainly are *angst*-producing, a good school's standards are challenging, not threatening, energy-producing rather than defense-producing. Neither a casual school, where no one does anything except that which seems to titillate him at a given moment, nor a tyrannical school, where cruel jockeying for position, involving both students and teachers, is the answer. Casual schools practice the Conspiracy—I'll not hassle you, Mr. Teacher, if you don't push me, the Student. Tyrannical schools simply scare people, whether by shakedowns in the lavatories, humiliation in classrooms, or the psychological warfare that some bigger, older, rougher, whiter, or blacker people impose by treating others as dirt, non-people, or worse.

Learning involves exposure—the exhibition of things not known, skills poorly developed, ideas ill formed. One learns to get things right by revealing where one is wrong. Such a display of incompetence, however well intentioned, makes one vulnerable, easily marked. Good schools promote displays of incompetence (strange though that may sound) in order to help students find their way to competence. A test that one fails may be a far more helpful test from which to learn than one on which one gets a perfect score. In a word, good schools make it O.K. to exhibit one's lack of learning and make it safe to do so—safe in the sense that ridicule will have no part in the process, even as correction does.

At the same time, a good school has standards, expectations about what students (and teachers—all the adults working there) can and should do. There is a difference between good effort and good performance, and evidence of the first, while it should be recognized and encouraged, should play no part in the fair assessment of the second. An adverb is an adverb, however nice, well-meaning, and hard-working the student is who insists that it is an adjective. Good teachers and wise students know how to separate performance (you flunked) from person (you're O.K.). Making a child feel stupid is itself stupid and cruel, but pretending that $2 + 2 = 5$ in order to massage the student's ego is cruel, and dishonest in addition.

Unanxious expectation applies as well to less subtle things. If anyone—student or teacher—is anxious about actual physical violence, little useful learning can take place in the school. Safe schools are essential, but in some strained communities may be difficult to attain.

Expensive retinues of security guards, police, and aides, in school merely to protect students from each other and from hostile parties from the outside, are unfortunate but necessary. That they are visible and active, with their walkie-talkies blaring, is no cause for embarrassment. It is simply an unequivocal statement that this place will be *safe*. No other priority can or should precede that. Nearly all students and teachers value it.

A good school is a stable school. One does not learn well in snippets, a bit snatched here and a morsel nibbled there. The processes of trial and error, of practice, of building up a repertoire of skills and a body of knowledge, take time. Rapid changes in routines, groups, settings, and expectations are confusing, and cause the very students who most need help to make fewer commitments. Why should I listen carefully to this teacher if he may not be here in four weeks? Why struggle with this material if I don't know whether anyone is going to be sympathetic and helpful next term? It is the same issue for the teachers: Why put hours into this demoralized child if he is absent half the time and will be transferred to another school in two months?

Governing authorities persistently underrate the importance of stability. For dozens of other pressing reasons, student school assignments are shuffled, often late in the summer. Teachers will be assigned abruptly, and reassigned during the year. Principals scream at "downtown": You can't do this! The program will be gutted! The answer is always: We know, but these other issues are paramount. Keeping a school together, keeping it stable, is clearly a low priority compared with other issues.

Part of stability is predictability: one is *sure* of certain things—times, policies, attitudes. A fetish can be made of this, of course. Some of the schoolkeepers' passion for punctuality, for example, is anal tidiness. No, Sally, you can't do that, because it says right here that you can't. The trick, of course, is to temper orderliness with flexibility, never an easy task.

Other qualities of good schools are as obvious as they are often difficult to practice. Good schools are clear on their mission (which is unsurprising: we tend to show up at places when we know the way to them). They are fair. Very simply, they are decent places, deserving loyalty. They are demanding, but not threatening, places of unanxious expectation.

Human factors rather than physical ones most shape the climate of a school. As one thorough research study reported, the "differences in outcome between schools were *not* due to such physical factors as the size of the school, the age of the buildings or the space available; nor were they due to broad differences in administrative status or organization. It was entirely possible for schools to obtain good outcomes in spite of initially rather unpromising and unprepossessing school premises." In a memorandum, prepared for our study, on the influence of physical environment on student achievement, Betsy Parsons, a secondary school teacher from Portland, Maine, pointed out the well-known fact that "we all know stories of brilliant teaching under the most adverse conditions." She went on, "Among my favorites are the tales of an Irish friend of mine, a high school literature teacher and incidentally a nun, who did her most inspired teaching and witnessed her students' most inspired learning in a cold, windy, yawning airplane hangar with the dust blowing on the class in biting sheets."

Be this as it may, physical conditions can yet have substantial effect. I visited a social studies class in a suburban high school built within the last twenty years. It was a large school—some twenty-two hundred students—and classes were held in a cluster of large steel-and-cinderblock prefabricated buildings. These had been intended for "open plan" teaching; the social studies block I visited had three classes going on simultaneously, separated by acoustical curtains. Two of these three classes were to be joined on the day of my visit, so the curtains between them were drawn back. The sounds of the lecture in the curtained-off third class were fully audible, however.

One class of thirty-five students, crowded together in tablet-arm desks, faced east. At their northeastern front, which was one corner of the building, there was an overhead projector and screen. One of the two teachers manned this station. The other class of thirty-five students faced north, toward a blackboard, desk, and lectern where the second teacher held forth. These students could swivel in their seats, or lean, to see the screen, and their colleagues in the first group could swivel to see the blackboard.

The class started with one teacher asking for votes for the basketball homecoming king and queen. This provoked giggling and gossiping. One of the teachers efficiently orchestrated the collection of votes himself. The other turned the process over to a student, who, confused, took far longer to complete the poll. Low-order chaos resulted, especially in the first group, which had completed its balloting.

The class continued with an assigned exercise, the preparation of a job application for a famous figure. Copies of such an application for Harry S. Truman were distributed, a clever piece of brief biography. Each student was to select his or her own "important figure" and prepare a similar sketch, and the teachers passed out an "Application for Employment" to assist them in the exercise.

When this brief written exercise was completed, the teacher next to the overhead projector started the formal lesson, a study of the American West—"number nine on your vocabulary sheet." This sheet, which some but not all of the almost seventy students present now rustled up, was a study guide, "what you'll be held accountable for." The lecturer continued, with attention now on "the American Indian and . . . the conflict between them [sic] and us." After a review of some of the points that were outlined in the study guide, the task of teaching swung to the second instructor, who picked up the lecture. The students swiveled to watch him. He told the story of Sutter's Mill. Then the thread went back to teacher number one. Students swiveled. Then back, to talk of "Pikers' [sic] Peak." We learned that the reason that Chinese were brought to the United States in the mid-nineteenth century was that it was cheaper to bring them here than to keep sending dirty laundry all the way across the Pacific. Back to teacher number one . . . The performance was like Ping-Pong (played occasionally with a very faulty ball), the students twisting back and forth, moderately entertained but as confused as I. No notes were taken, no additions made to the orderly study guide the teachers had prepared. The students near the third classroom were privy to the conversation in that class as well. For most of the students, the fifty minutes spent in that overcrowded, bewildering, acoustically calamitous place were not valuable, in any important educational sense. (The school's principal, attending the session with me, must have sensed my dismay; leaning over, he said that the students did not find this arrangement as bad as I obviously did.)

This is, perhaps, an extreme example. For some purposes—for example, a large lecture for all three social studies sections or for some kinds of classroom group work—the space so disastrously used on the day I visited could be functional. Lectures are well served by orderly rows of chairs for the listeners, each with a good view of the teacher. A seminar needs a smaller space. As argument among the participants requires excellent communication, students and teachers ideally should be seated at a round or oval table. (Since people like the psychological protection of an object between them and others, as well as a place to park their books, a table is preferable to an open circle, where "exposure" is total.) Recitation may suffer in the round; recitation is dialogue between the teacher and one particular student, with the other students to be kept as much as possible at a psychological, if not a physical, distance. Recitations are best served by small rooms with chairs in rows. There can be other configurations, varying with the teachers' tactics of instruction, the needs of the subjects, and the characteristics of the students. Form follows function, and different functions require different spaces, levels of quiet, and equipment.

Space teaches. A trenchant example was found in a Southern high school, one that had been founded over thirty years ago for an all-white student body. Today, it is an all-black school. It was shabbily maintained. Responsibility for upkeep lay "downtown." The principal could only send in requisitions to the central office and plead, curse, and pray. He could not get any of the work, even obviously needed simple painting, done on his own—even by himself—because that would breach contracts with the system's unionized and overscheduled painters. (His own ruse, a clever one, was to have hallway walls covered with murals by art classes—that was "education" rather than "maintenance," and he controlled the former.)

The students and staff got the message, as did the principal: no one really cared whether the school was a dump, and that showed that no one really cared about them as people. Most telling were the photographs on a long, third-story corridor. Starting in the 1940s, each graduating class had had a framed plaque hung on the walls, one that included the graduation photograph of each student, along with a group picture. These large photographic collages still hung on their wires, covered with grime, some dangling awry, with rows of white smiling faces. A close look found two or three black faces in the mid-1960s, more by the late sixties—and then no more plaques. Ghosts and questions hovered around those dusty frames. Every student must have noticed them.

Most middle- and upper-income Americans would be both shocked by and afraid of some of the places where the young citizens of the poor are now at school. They would be indignant about the Byzantine politics that entangle most understaffed and underfinanced maintenance operations. I have seen a sad poster on the walls of many tattered schools, one that is a poor substitute for the simple courtesies of decently maintained places for learning. It says, simply: "I *am* somebody because God don't make no junk."

Good schools expect no child to be junk. That expectation includes a commitment to provide each child with an education in a place that is attractive and free of fear. It is a pity that some schools, especially those serving the poor, fall so far short.

Questions for Discussion and Debate

1. What are the conditions Sizer cites of a favorable school environment? List them.

   - Next to each one, write the rationale for establishing that condition.

   - Then rank-order them, placing a "1" next to the most important condition, in your opinion, and so on.

   - Hold a debate in which you support your priorities with evidence and sound reasoning.

   - Refer often to the excerpt itself in your exchanges with the class.

   - Finally, feel free to add to Sizer's conditions if you believe that an important aspect of a school's environment is missing from his discussion.

     You might want to categorize your list into "Human," "Physical," and "Other" conditions, or use similar labels.

2. Try to express in one sentence what you think Sizer believes is *the* most important environmental condition in a school. Refer to the excerpt in explaining your conclusion.

Activities and Projects

1. Sizer (1985) says that the evidence about the size of a school in terms of establishing a favorable learning environment is inconclusive (p. 254). Some big schools "feel" small. He also quotes a survey done on the advantages and disadvantages of different school sizes and cites its major finding: Conclusions are "mixed." He notes that "the authors imply that size is a lesser concern than the 'principal's leadership, community support, and the qualities of the staff' " (p. 255).

   Interview a cross section of teachers, and after collating their views on the effects of school size on the overall teaching and learning environment, see if they are similar to the "mixed" conclusions of the research survey just described.

Refer back to the Brief Background to this chapter where Deborah Meier's quote appears (p. 261). Do research on CPESS to discuss whether, indeed, her school is an example of the validity of Sizer's perception that big schools can feel small.

2. Visit a school that is a member of Sizer's Coalition for Essential Schools. Bring with you the list you made of Sizer's environmental criteria (discussion question 1 above). Observe classes in the school to see how, or if, these criteria are met. Share your findings.

3. There are several school environments besides those addressed in this chapter's selections. Among them are charter schools, magnet schools, vocational schools, suburban schools, parochial schools, and single-sex private schools. Investigate some of these schools. Visit a few if possible and evaluate them using Sizer's environmental criteria as the measuring stick. What lessons, if any, can be learned from the ways in which these schools function?

4. Design your conception of the ideal school from an architectural and physical perspective. Does your design reflect any one of the philosophies listed in the Brief Background to chapter 3? Share your design and the rationale behind it with your peers.

5. Often the best way to see the truth of an issue is by nonexample. Therefore, think of the very *worst* school environment you have ever been in or personally seen. Describe it to your peers and then discuss with them what the problems were and how they could have been rectified. (While you may recall these environments with some trepidation, you might also find some humor in them in retrospect!)

6. In the spring of 1998, Theodore Sizer and his wife Nancy agreed to become coprincipals of the Francis W. Parker Charter Essential School in Harvard, Massachusetts. The school was established in 1995 according to the progressive principles espoused by the Coalition for Essential Schools, which Sizer directed until the spring of 1998. In taking this new position, Sizer returned to a "real-school" environment for the first time since leaving it in 1981 to enter the ivory tower of the university and to do research and write. Discuss the challenges Sizer might have faced in adjusting to, and operating in, the environment of this combined junior and senior charter high school. Base your discussion on your observation of and participation in the public-school environment *and* the college or university environment. What are the key differences between these two environments? Should either one consider reforming in the direction of the other? (Refer also to the discussion of charter schools presented in the prelude to Selection 5.8.)

Chapter References

Apple, M. W. (1979). *Ideology and curriculum.* Boston: Routledge and Kegan Paul.

Apple, M. W. (1988). Hidden curriculum. In R. A. Gorton, G. T. Schneider, & S. J. C. Fischer (Eds.), *Encyclopedia of school administration.* Phoenix, AZ: Onyx Press.

Ayers, W., & Ford, P. (Eds.). (1996). *City kids, city teachers. Reports from the front row.* New York: New Press.

Brown, C. (1965). *Manchild in the promised land.* New York: New American Library.

Burge, K. (1997, February 26). Schools with public spirit. *The Boston Globe,* pp. B1, B7.

Campbell, R. F., Cunningham, L. L., Nystrand, R. O., & Usdan, M. D. (1985). *The organization and control of American schools* (5th ed.). Columbus, OH: Merrill.

Canfield, D. (1939). *Seasoned timber.* New York: Harcourt, Brace.

Conant, J. B. (1959). *The American high school today.* New York: McGraw–Hill.

Cullen, C. (1970). Incident. In F. S. Freedman (Ed.), *The black American experience.* New York: Bantam.

Foxfire Fund. (1990). *The Foxfire approach: Perspectives and core practices.* Rabun Gap, GA: Foxfire Fund.

Friedland, N. (1995, May–June). Unschooling. *Home Education Magazine, 12*(3), 19–21.

Gibson, W. (1980). *The miracle worker.* New York: Alfred A. Knopf.

Holt, J. (1997). *Growing without schooling: A record of a grass roots movement.* Cambridge, MA: Holt Association.

Illich, I. (1971). *Deschooling society.* New York: Harper and Row.

Johnson, L. (1992). *My posse don't do homework.* New York: St. Martin's Press.

Johnson, L. (1995). *The girls in the back of the class.* New York: St. Martin's Press.

Kaufman, B. (1991). *Up the down staircase.* New York: Harper Perennial.

Keller, H. (1955). *Teacher.* Garden City, NY: Doubleday.

Marling, K. A. (1997). *Norman Rockwell.* New York: Harry N. Abrams.

Marshall, C. (1976). *Christy.* New York: Avon.

Medoff, M. (1980). *Children of a lesser God.* New York: Westmark Productions.

Moffat, L. N. (1986). *Norman Rockwell, a definitive catalogue.* Stockbridge, MA: The Norman Rockwell Museum at Stockbridge.

Nathan, J. (2002, May 29). A charter school decade. *Education Week,* pp. 32, 35.

Postman, N. (1979). *Teaching as a conserving activity.* New York: Delta.

Roorbach, B. (1997, February 2). Mommy, what's a classroom? *The New York Times Magazine,* Sect. 6, pp. 30–37.

Rose, M. (1988, October). The "Staircase" revisited, an interview with Bel Kaufman. *On Campus.*

Sanoff, A. P., et al. (1987, September 28). What Americans should know. *U.S. News and World Report,* 86–95.

Sher, J. P., & Tompkins, R. B. (1976). *Economy, efficiency and equality: The myths of rural school and district consolidation.* Washington, DC: National Institute of Education, U.S. Department of Health, Education and Welfare.

Sizer, T. R. (1985). *Horace's compromise.* Boston: Houghton Mifflin.

Takanishi, R. (Ed.). (1994). *Adolescence in the 1990s: Risk and opportunity.* New York: Teachers College Press, Columbia University.

Additional Readings

ERIC Clearinghouse on Educational Management. (1982, February). School size: A reassessment of the small school. *Research Action Brief,* No. 2.

Frymier, J. (1984). *One hundred good schools.* West Lafayette, IN: Kappa Delta Pi.

Goodlad, J. (1984). *A place called school.* New York: McGraw–Hill.

Knowles, J. G., Marlow, S. E., & Muchmore, J. A. (1992). From pedagogy to ideology: Origins and phases of home education in the United States, 1970–1990. *American Journal of Education, 100,* 195–235.

Kotlowitz, A. (1991). *There are no children here.* New York: Doubleday.

Lewis, A. C. (1993, October). The payoff from a quality preschool. *Phi Delta Kappan, 74.*

O'Gorman, N. (1970). *The storefront.* New York: Harper and Row.

Schwitzer, A. M., et al. (2001). *Promoting student learning and student development at a distance. Student affairs, concepts and practices for televised instruction and other forms of distance.* Lanham, MD: University Press of America.

Sizer, T. (1996). *Horace's hope: what works for the American high school.* New York: Houghton Mifflin.

Smith, J. D. (1995). *Pieces of purgatory: Mental retardation, in and out of institutions.* Pacific Grove, CA: Brooks/Cole.

Stevens, M. (2001). *Kingdom of children. Culture and controversy in the homeschooling movement.* Princeton, NJ: Princeton University Press.

Web Sites

Atlas Communities:
http://www.edc.org/ATLAS
Charter schools:
http://www.csr.syr.edu/index.html
Coalition of Essential schools:
http://essentialschools.org
ERIC Clearing House in Urban Education:
http://eric-web.tc.columbia.edu
Expeditionary Learning Outward Bound:
http://www.elob.org
Homeschooling:
http://www.teelfamily.com/education/education
Rural school environments:
http://www.nces.ed.gov/surveys/rural/ed
Urban school environments:
http://eric-web.tc.columbia.edu

Chapter 6

Living and Learning in a Diverse Society

Sociology of Education

America's strength is in its diversity.
President Bill Clinton (Second Inaugural Speech, January 1996)

America, from its very inception, has been characterized by diversity. Even before the 17th century, when Western Europeans—a majority of whom, by the way, were from *different* Protestant denominations—came here to settle, there was tremendous variation among Native Americans in terms of physical characteristics, customs, and language. And the diversity trend continues.

The question that faces educators today in light of America's historically diverse past and present is how best to help students—through education—live and learn in such a society. What should take precedence in the curriculum: multiculturalism or the cultural norms rooted in Western traditions?

Diverse responses to this question have been forthcoming since the 1960s when civil rights movements grew up among African Americans, women, Native

Americans, the poor, and other groups who demanded a place not only in society but also in textbooks, after years of unequal treatment both in and outside of the classroom. Public schools, in fact, became one of the major sites at which the struggle for equity took place, and several of the groups fighting for equal access to public education made gains. For example, Asians and Latinos are now served by bilingual and English-as-a-Second Language (ESL) programs. School integration was achieved in 1954 in the *Brown* v. *Board of Education* decision. Native American culture has been recognized by a number of textbook publishers and history departments. The women's movement continues the fight for enforcement of Title IX, and the disabled community struggles aggressively for full inclusion (Rofes, 1997, pp. 5–6). The latest movement, to end discrimination against gay and lesbian youth, has been trying to combat attacks from the right wing and certain religious groups and to offer a proactive progressive agenda for education; they have met with some success. In 1993, Massachusetts became the first state to pass a law protecting homosexual students in public schools, and concerned organizations, among them teacher organizations such as the National Education Association and the American Federation of Teachers, are continuing the struggle (p. 6). Individual teachers are also taking steps to correct past discrimination. "Understanding that multiculturalism might move beyond race/ethnicity to include groups defined by religion (Jews, Sikhs, Moslems) and culture (deaf people, lesbians, and gays, poor people), some teachers are valiantly creating rich . . . curricula which truly aim to teach 'respect for all'" (p. 6).

But not everyone agrees with such sentiments. In academic circles, views cover the entire political spectrum, from those on the right who oppose the emphasis on multicultural and diversity education to those on the left who believe that children should be taught to embrace and celebrate diversity.

In terms of the narrower use of the term *culture*—the one reflected in most of this chapter, which refers to racial, religious, and ethnic cultures—some of the participants in the so-called culture wars, such as Ira Shor (1987), contend that the movement toward reasserting cultural norms and Eurocentrism is the means by which conservative political forces intend to establish power. He believes, as do Banks and McGee Banks (1997) and others (Bigelow et al., 1995; Gollnick, 1998; Grant & Gomez, 1996; Takaki, 1993), that multicultural curriculum presents a more realistic reflection of America's pluralistic experience and a more comprehensive understanding of American history.

Participants in the intellectual backlash against cultural diversity, such as William J. Bennett (1992), express concern about the loss of those cultural norms that were the means by which new groups could move up the social and economic ladder. He and others who favor an emphasis on cultural commonalities (A. Bloom, 1987; H. Bloom, 1994; Cheney, 1995; D'Souza, 1992; Hirsch, 1987) argue that multiculturalism is divisive, fragments an otherwise united country, and undermines traditional American values. They accuse liberals of political correctness, a perspective characterized by sensitivity and tolerance toward differences. Because some, in their zeal for such tolerance, have appeared to be intolerant themselves, this perspective has taken on negative connotations: "PC" is how the right wing labels this otherwise constructive attitude that favors strengthening and affirming America's democratic principle of liberty and justice for all. A case in point is the controversy that arose across the country as a result of the decision by the Oakland, California, school board to recognize Black English, or Ebonics, as a distinct language that should be taught along with languages recognized in traditional bilingual programs. Supporters of the school board were accused of being politically correct to a fault. The dispute in February and March of 1997 exemplified a "volatile mix of politics, pedagogy and social issues" (Applebome, 1997, p. 10). In reality, the issue reflected the overall frustration many African Americans felt with the resources allotted to their children. The real question, according to the reporting journalist, was not about whether Black English is a distinct language, but about how best to educate children of diverse backgrounds (Applebome, 1997).

It appears that such culture wars will not be going away in the near-future, and the education establishment will need to continue addressing such questions as, To what extent should the curriculum include diversity? How should teachers be educated so as to face their own prejudices and develop a "culturally responsive pedagogy" (Villegas, 1991)? and, finally, What are the best approaches for educating children from diverse cultures, particularly in schools that serve as many as 40 cultures in one building (Yardley, 1997, p. 1)?

Brief Background

Because of America's history as a land of immigrants, author John Steinbeck (1996) proclaimed the motto of the United States—*E Pluribus Unum* (From Many One)—to be "a fact" (p. 12). Immigrants built the country and became "Americans—a new breed, rooted in all races, stained and tinted with all colors, a seeming ethnic anarchy . . . [and yet] each ethnic group has clicked into place in the Union without losing the pluribus" (pp. 12–13). Thus the question now—and probably for some time to come—is how schools should address both dimensions (*unum* and *pluribus*) of the nation's motto (Takaki, 1993).

Public education has historically dealt with this dilemma by providing a common language and a sense of common purpose to unify and strengthen the country. Albert Shanker (1928–1997), known for raising the economic and social status of teachers during his time as president of New York City's United Federation of Teachers and its parent organization, the American Federation of Teachers, wrote that "we have not outgrown our need for this; far from it" (1997, p. 6). Shanker was thankful for the role that the public schools played in holding this nation of diverse peoples together. Although minorities often experience the violence of prejudice within public schools, many, like Shanker, an immigrant himself, have also reaped the rewards of schools as sources of upward mobility where they could learn with and about students from many backgrounds. Interestingly, even before the late Brazilian educator Paulo Freire (1993) and others made popular the notion that "critical pedagogy" could empower oppressed peoples and that education could be used as a political tool for raising their consciousness, some public schools in America had been playing—and still play—that role for many minorities. And hopefully some day a consensus will exist about public education's role in developing pride in one's culture *as well as* pride in belonging to the larger whole.

Historically, minority groups have responded to this country and the public education it offered them in one of three ways: by assimilating, as Shanker's experience reflects; by living according to the idea of cultural pluralism; or by separating themselves from the mainstream.

The first response, *assimilation,* was particularly apparent after the massive influx of European immigrants between 1890 and 1920. Many of these immigrants believed that learning English, dropping their native garb, and, in some cases, changing their names—in essence melting into the American way of life—would spare them the pain of discrimination and help them move up and out of their isolating, yet protective ghettos. The schools generally agreed that their role was to act as the path to that "melting pot."

The second response to and by newcomers—one that philosopher and reformer John Dewey supported—was to learn about and acquire the common culture while at the same time maintaining aspects of their native cultures. This is the practice of *cultural pluralism,* which rejects the melting-pot metaphor in favor of the mosaic or tossed salad, in which Americans are enriched by the diverse qualities of other cultures.

The third historical response to diversity, clearly a more extreme position, was *separation* from the mainstream, a response either forced upon certain minorities, by the bigots who preferred not to mingle with the foreign or minority influence, or freely chosen by some groups. For example, there are Black Muslims, Hasidic Jews, and, more recently, some gay and lesbian students and young women who believe that such separation is liberating and can protect them from the low expectations and/or unequal treatment they receive in traditional settings. In the case of the religious minorities, separation is also viewed as the means for preserving and practicing their particular cultural beliefs or identities (Gilligan, Lyons, & Hanmer, 1990; Green, 1991; Sadker and Sadker, 1994). And, interestingly, the question of how best to educate their children has been an internal debate among African Americans ever since the well-documented dispute between Booker T. Washington and W. E. B. DuBois. The two differed in their views on the type of curriculum that would be most beneficial for African American students. Washington (1907) held to the idea that practical vocational skills would be best, and DuBois (1904) argued that academic and intellectual development was even more important for succeeding in American society.

Finally, schools have demonstrated all three of these responses in dealing with the education of groups that differ in ability. There is still little agreement among educators about how best to educate students with special needs, with different ability levels, and with different styles of learning (Gardner, 1983; Knapp & Shields, 1991; Lewis & Doorlag, 1995). Some educators favor assimilation for special-needs students, that is, inclusion within the mainstream classroom; others—the pluralists, one might call them—see room for both options, that is, inclusion for part of the day, depending on the needs of the students; and still others support some kind of separation, either through the establishment of resource rooms or by tracking. Unfortunately, the tracking option often relegates students to separate rooms based less on their ability level and more on their socioeconomic class or behavior. This kind of discrimination often goes unchallenged unless parents recognize how such decisions will affect their child's education.

Clearly any consensus among educators and the diverse minority groups themselves about what constitutes the best approach to education will remain elusive. The traditional approaches—assimilation, pluralism, and separation—will likely remain options, and the debate about their viability will continue.

On the other hand, sometimes consensus can be found among the folks who represent "public opinion" on the question of multiculturalism versus traditional American values. According to a study and survey conducted in 1994 by Public Agenda, a nonpartisan research education organization, Americans supported what appeared to be multicultural curricular perspectives, but with conditions. "[They rejected] . . . sharply negative critiques of American society" (Johnson & Immerwahr, 1994–1995, p. 44), indicating a desire for harmony and civility. The report concludes that Americans want the public school system to continue to play its historic role "in enabling diverse Americans to learn about each other and live together," particularly because "prejudice, anger, misunderstanding and distrust continue to divide the country along racial and ethnic lines" (p. 45). There was little indication that the public was aware of or concerned about the above-cited culture wars going on within the academic community. However, they did express a desire for schools both to teach respect for differences and to provide every child with a meaningful education. Perhaps this children's song best sums up their sentiments:

I'm proud to be me, but I also see
You're just as proud to be you.
We might look at things a bit differently
But lots of good people do.
That's just human nature, so why should I hate ya
For being as human as I.
We'll get as we give, if we live and let live
And we'll both get along if we try.
I'm proud to be me but I also see
You're just as proud to be you, it's true—
You're just as proud to be you!
(Zaret & Singer, 1957)

The theme of this chapter, diversity, clearly overlaps ideas contained in the previous five chapters, which is not surprising since most of the readings in the text carry interdisciplinary perspectives. For instance, in terms of the history of American education (chapter 2), there has always been tension between the one and the many, between the majority and the minority. That's why amendments to the Bill of Rights were needed: to bring minority rights in line with the majority. Chapter 2 contains excerpts that are, indeed, relevant to the diversity issue. Two of them (Douglass, Selection 2.7; Nock, Selection 2.8) recall the unequal treatment of African Americans and women, respectively. And another excerpt (Taylor, Selection 2.4) captures an immigrant family's desire both to assimilate *and* to maintain some of their unique traditions.

In terms of school environments (chapter 5), the issue of diversity is becoming more and more relevant in all areas of the United States, rural as well as urban, and within private as well as public education. Several excerpts in chapter 5 are connected to living and learning in a diverse society, including Brown's work (Selection 5.2) about his move from the streets to the reformatory and eventually to law school; Friedland's piece (Selection 5.4) about opting to separate from public school in favor of homeschooling; and Johnson's narrative (Selection 5.6) about her work with Hispanic students, which points out the difficulties for some of assimilating into the mainstream.

Politically (chapter 4), there is, among others, the affirmative action issue, reflected in the Bakke decision (Selection 4.9), which is still being debated. Some states, for example, have decided to repeal their affirmative action policy and others have voted to continue it in light of ongoing prejudice. That excerpt as well as the Rockwell painting (Selection 4.1), Conroy's work (Selection 4.3), and Trott's work (Selection 4.10) depict multiculturalism and the resistance that exists to cultural pluralism in its broadest sense.

In philosophical and curricular terms (chapter 3), the perennialists are clearly the supporters of the Western canon in emphasizing commonalities, whereas the social reconstructionists are the multiculturalists. Calderon's poem (Selection 3.4) conveys his view that pluralism within the curriculum can enhance learning for minority students, and Salzman (Selection 3.12) learns about cultural differences firsthand from his Chinese students.

Finally, here in chapter 6, certain sociological questions are raised that relate to the nature, status, and treatment of different groups in American society, many of whom have already been portrayed in the readings throughout this book.

Selections

The painting and the readings in this chapter have sociological implications since they provide you with an opportunity to ask the kinds of questions a sociologist might put to the field of education. For example, what are the similarities and differences within and among America's diverse groups? How can we best educate all children in light of this diversity? How do the beliefs, values, and status of these groups influence their learning styles and attitudes toward education and the treatment they receive within school environments? And how will changes in the population affect the educational status quo? For example, how will schools be affected by the fact that minority populations continue to grow? According to some predictions, by 2056, most Americans will trace their descent to "Africa, Asia, the Hispanic world, the Pacific Islands, Arabia—almost anywhere but White Europe" (Henry, 1990, pp. 28–31). It would be impossible, of course, to include in a volume of this kind enough readings to answer all of these questions, but these selections can provide a beginning.

This chapter contains excerpts from a wide variety of genres including fiction, nonfiction, poetry, and song and reflects the perspectives of people from diverse backgrounds. Embedded in Norman Rockwell's portrait of people from various cultures is the belief that diversity can enrich us if everyone practices *The Golden Rule*. Three of the pieces are autobiographies, one by journalist Russell Baker (*Growing Up*), who recalls his ethnic childhood peers, both friend and foe, and the other two by African American women, the Delany sisters and Maya Angelou, who all achieved professional success in different fields despite the prejudices they faced along the way. A poem, "Warning to Children," by Robert Graves, challenges learners to explore the wonders of their diverse world, while a satirical song ("National Brotherhood Week") mocks the hypocrisy of those who pretend to accept diversity. A novel, *The Chosen*, by Chaim Potok, reveals the often overlooked reality that there are variations of belief—even prejudices—*within* the same minority group, just as there are within the larger culture. In this case, differences in belief exist between two Orthodox Jewish boys who eventually are able to overcome those differences. Teachers speak out in three of the excerpts. Two of them share their views on methods; in one account a native of France (Jacques Barzun) talks about teaching foreign language, and in the other account, a New Zealander (Sylvia Ashton-Warner) describes her method of teaching reading to young Maoris, the native culture in New Zealand. A third teacher, Mike Rose (*Lives on the Boundary*), tells of his roots as a poor Italian American boy growing up "on the boundary," a phrase that also refers to the lives of people he eventually chooses to teach. And, finally, in an excerpt from a children's book (*Willow and Twig*), a young girl learns how to help others understand the disabilities of the little brother she loves.

As you read these selections, note the cultural backgrounds of the authors. Think about what motivated them to write their works. Do they seem to share a common purpose? If so, what might that purpose be? Consider how you might use some of these pieces in your own classroom or how they might influence the way in which you teach and interact with your students.

6.1   Work of Art: *The Golden Rule* (1961)

Norman Rockwell

Norman Rockwell explained why he painted *The Golden Rule* ("Do unto others as you would have them do unto you") for one of his *Saturday Evening Post* covers (April 1, 1961): "Like everyone else, I'm concerned about the world situation, and, like everyone else, I'd like to contribute something to help. The only way I can contribute is through my pictures. So for a long time I had been trying to think of a subject that might be of some help" (*The Norman Rockwell Album* [*NRA*], 1961, p. 182). This painting conveys Rockwell's humanitarian viewpoint.

Rockwell tells about how he brought his 10-foot-long unfinished charcoal drawing of his United Nations picture up from his cellar. He had depicted all the peoples of the world gathered together, and viewing the drawing again, he realized that that was exactly what he wanted to express about the Golden Rule. While it took him more than 5 months to complete, he "never stopped thinking that it was worthwhile" (*NRA*, 1961, p. 182). He finished the painting on January 8, 1961.

The painting does, indeed, capture the diversity of the world's peoples and Rockwell's hope that, despite the differences, they can come together in peace. Notice what he placed to both left and right of the center in the painting. Wrote Rockwell, "The two mothers holding their children seemed to express exactly what I was trying to say about the Golden Rule. Using them as the basis of my composition, I introduced new figures" (*NRA*, 1961, p. 183). "I wanted to include people of every race, creed and color, depicting them with dignity and respect" (p. 184). "Of the twenty-eight heads in the finished painting, eight were taken from the United Nations charcoal" (p. 183).

The Golden Rule is common to all religions and appears with varied phrasings in the Bible (Christianity), the Talmud (Judaism), the Udanavarga (Buddhism), the Analects (Confucianism), the Mahabharata (Hinduism), Traditions (Islam), Yogashastra (Jainism), the Kabir (Sikhism), the T'ai Shang Kan Ying P'ien (Taoism), and the Dadistan-I-dinik (Zoroastrianism) (*NRA*, 1961, p. 190). Today the painting hangs appropriately in the United Nations, the organization comprised of peoples from these and other religions as well as people who, though they may not believe in a religion, likely concur that the Golden Rule prescribes a rational basis for interaction among different peoples. The goal of the United Nations, of course, is to help nations practice what they preach.

In terms of this painting, Rockwell struggled to give each head a character of its own while having each one contribute to the overall conception, achieving in effect a representation of the motto, From Many One (*E Pluribus Unum*), in this case standing not just for American culture but for the whole human race. He wrote about working out the subtle relationships of color and tone to achieve this goal (*NRA*, 1961, p. 189). The concept of tone refers to "the effect produced by the combination of light, shades, and color" (*Webster's New World Dictionary*, 1984, p. 1497). Do you think Rockwell's *tone* achieves his goal of giving each head a characteristic of its own while having each contribute to the whole? Do your responses to each individual head differ from your response to the whole? Study the painting and reflect on its connection to the theme of this chapter, "Living and Learning in a Diverse Society," and to the readings herein.

DO UNTO OTHERS
AS YOU WOULD HAVE THEM
DO UNTO YOU

Questions for Discussion and Debate

1. What is your response to this painting? What does it say to you about diversity?

2. Study the painting in which Rockwell said he tried to depict people of all races, religions, and colors. Which ones can you identify? Notice not only the heads but the clothing and items in the hands of several of the people.

   Discuss with your peers *where* in the world many of these representative peoples live. Do you think some or all of these peoples are also represented in the United States? How would you find out?

3. Do you think Rockwell achieved his goal of giving each head a character of its own while having each one contribute to the overall conception? If so, discuss how he was able to achieve that balance *and* integrity.

4. Do you have a different response to each individual head? Why, or why not? Does your response to each head differ from your response to the whole painting?

5. In many ways the United States is a microcosm of the world, for Americans have come from nearly every country in the world. Discuss how a painting of a composite of American society would differ from this painting.

Activities and Projects

1. Peruse the excerpts in both this chapter *and* the other chapters. Which excerpts do you think are reflected in Rockwell's painting? Why? Share your findings with the class.

2. How is this painting the same as or different from the other paintings in this text in terms of both style (more or less realistic, for example) and content, purpose, and mood?

3. What are some ways you could integrate the Golden Rule into the behavior management aspects of your teaching and into the actual subject matter students are studying? Consider going into a number of classrooms and talking with teachers about their use of the Golden Rule or a related policy, such as character education.

4. Bring the painting with you to classes in the school where you are teaching or, if you are not in a practicum, locate classrooms where you can share this painting with students.

Ask them what they see, what they believe the artist's purpose is, and whether or not they like it and why. Do they notice the details? Do they agree with the message? Record the responses you get and share them with your peers.

5. Do research on the different ways people from different cultures greet one another. For example, in America, people frequently shake hands upon meeting. Report back to class and demonstrate the differences you were able to find. Then discuss what other differences among cultures teachers should be aware of so as not to insult or miscommunicate with diverse students in their classes. Finally, as a group locate the sources from which you can learn about such cultural differences such as the meaning of certain hand signals, head movements, and other gestures.

6. Try your artistic hand at portraying the Golden Rule in a different manner—or, short of that, discuss with peers other ways the same message might be depicted. Try locating paintings or photographs that appear to convey the same message. How are these pictures more or less effective than words in conveying the message of tolerance and respect for diversity?

7. Art is one way in which underserviced children can express their frustrations as well as give shape to their dreams. One model of such a program, in Germantown, New York, is offered with the help of New York State's migrant education outreach program and a federal grant to the Rural and Migrant Ministry, which also offers advocacy, academic support, and summer programs. The afterschool art program enables children of migrant workers, most of whom are Mexican American, to form bonds to the school and their teachers, bonds that are often sorely missing from these children's lives because of their frequent movement from one school to another (Saunders, 1997, p. 28). Look for other examples of art programs for minority students that help to strengthen the quality of the education they now receive. Share your findings. Do you think you could design such a program if you taught in an area where there were children in danger of becoming alienated from the rest of the system? Try developing such a program with a small group of your peers.

6.2   *Teacher* (1963)

Sylvia Ashton-Warner

Sylvia Ashton-Warner (1912–1984) was a novelist, musician, and artist, but most of all she was a teacher whose pioneering work in culturally diverse schools in New Zealand she described in *Teacher,* which *Time* magazine called the "best book on education" of 1963.

While others have been given the credit for originally developing the whole-language approach to teaching reading, it is Ashton-Warner who should be called the "mother of whole language." This student-centered approach to the language arts is characterized by integrating the skills of reading, writing, speaking, and listening with stories chosen or produced by the student or chosen by the teacher for their literary qualities. These original or chosen works become the student's primary sources for learning to read and write.

Many of the 5-year-olds Ashton-Warner taught were Maori, the minority Polynesian culture that lived in New Zealand for a thousand years before the Europeans. Ashton-Warner was challenged with motivating these children to read, speak, and write in English so they could be successful within the larger Anglo or *pokeha* culture, where many had experienced prejudice and failure by European standards. Her theory was that the best way to teach them to read was to use an organic strategy that involved releasing the native imagery of the children, drawing it out somehow, and then using it as "working material." One part of the method was to discover what she called their key vocabulary, words that had relevance and meaning for the children, not only words that crossed cultures, like *mother* and *father,* but also words that were particularly connected to Maori culture (Ashton-Warner, 1958, 1963, 1972, 1979). She then wrote down their stories using their key vocabulary; she illustrated the stories with appropriate images, thus producing what she called "big books," which she and the children read together.

Initially Ashton-Warner's "scheme," as she called it, was rejected by New Zealand publishers and even by some of her administrators; ironically this rejection led to her self-inflicted exile from New Zealand and stays in America, Israel, and other parts of the world where her approach was welcomed (Ashton-Warner, 1972, 1979). Toward the end of her life, however, her native land embraced her and honored her for her contribution to education, for creating a whole-language approach to teaching reading to minority children and, indeed, all children around the world.

In this excerpt, Ashton-Warner draws you into her way of reaching each child as an individual within a multicultural setting. As you read her words, think about how her strategy of individualizing not only meets the children's need for learning how to read, but also helps to raise their self-esteem while promoting more positive attitudes toward their native culture.

Children have two visions, the inner and the outer. Of the two the inner vision is brighter.

I hear that in other infant rooms widespread illustration is used to introduce the reading vocabulary to a five-year-old, a vocabulary chosen by adult educationists. I use pictures, too, to introduce the reading vocabulary, but they are pictures of the inner vision and the captions are chosen by the children themselves. True, the picture of the outer, adult-chosen pictures can be meaningful and delightful to children; but it is the captions of the mind pictures that have the power and the light. For whereas the illustrations perceived by the outer eye cannot be other than interesting, the illustrations seen by the inner eye are organic, and it is the captioning of these that I call the "Key Vocabulary."

I see the mind of a five-year-old as a volcano with two vents; destructiveness and creativeness. And I see that to the extent that we widen the creative channel, we atrophy the destructive one. And it seems to me that since these words of the key vocabulary are no less than the captions of the dynamic life itself, they course out through the creative channel, making their contribution to the drying up of the destructive vent. From all of which I am constrained to see it as creative reading and to count it among the arts.

First words must mean something to a child.

First words must have intense meaning for a child. They must be part of his being.

How much hangs on the love of reading, the instinctive inclination to hold a book! *Instinctive.* That's what it must be. The reaching out for a book needs to become an organic action, which can happen at this yet formative age. Pleasant words won't do. Respectable words won't do. They must be words organically tied up, organically born from the dynamic life itself. They must be words that are already part of the child's being. "A child," reads a recent publication on the approach of the American books, "can be led to feel that Janet and John are friends." *Can be led to feel.* Why lead him to feel or try to lead him to feel that these strangers are friends? What about the passionate feeling he has already for his own friends? To me it is inorganic to overlook this step. To me it is an offence against art. I see it as an interruption in the natural expansion of life of which Erich Fromm speaks. How would New Zealand children get on if all their reading material were built from the life of African blacks? It's little enough to ask that a Maori child should begin his reading from a book of his own colour and culture. This is the formative age where habits are born and established. An aversion to the written word is a habit I have seen born under my own eyes in my own infant room on occasion.

It's not beauty to abruptly halt the growth of a young mind and to overlay it with the frame of an imposed culture. There are ways of training and grafting young growth. The true conception of beauty is the shape of organic life and that is the very thing at stake in the transition from one culture to another. If this transition took place at a later age when the security of a person was already established there would not be the same need for care. But in this country it happens that the transition takes place at a tender and vulnerable age, which is the reason why we all try to work delicately.

Back to these first words. To these first books. They must be made out of the stuff of the child itself. I reach a hand into the mind of the child, bring out a handful of the stuff I find there, and use that as our first working material. Whether it is good or bad stuff, violent or placid stuff, coloured or dun. To effect an unbroken beginning. And in this dynamic material, within the familiarity and security of it, the Maori finds that words have intense meaning to him, from which cannot help but arise a love of reading. For it's here, right in this first word, that the love of reading is born, and the longer his reading is organic the stronger it becomes, until by the time he arrives at the books of the new culture, he receives them as another joy rather than as a labour. I know all this because I've done it.

> *First words must have an intense meaning.*
> *First words must be already part of the dynamic life.*
> *First books must be made of the stuff of the child himself, whatever and wherever the child.*

The words, which I write on large tough cards and give to the children to read, prove to be one-look words if they are accurately enough chosen. And they are plain enough in conversation. It's the conversation that has to be got. However, if it can't be, I find that whatever a child chooses to make in the creative period may quite likely be such a word. But if the vocabulary of a child is still inaccessible, one can always begin him on the general Key Vocabulary, common to any child in any race, a set of words bound up with security that experiments, and later on their creative writing, show to be organically associated with the inner world: "Mummy," "Daddy," "kiss," "frightened," "ghost."

"Mohi," I ask a new five, an undisciplined Maori, "what word do you want?"

"Jet!"

I smile and write it on a strong little card and give it to him. "What is it again?"

"Jet!"

"You can bring it back in the morning. What do you want, Gay?"

Gay is the classic overdisciplined, bullied victim of the respectable mother.

"House," she whispers. So I write that, too, and give it into her eager hand.

"What do you want, Seven?" Seven is a violent Maori.

"Bomb! Bomb! I want bomb!"

So Seven gets his word "bomb" and challenges anyone to take it from him.

And so on through the rest of them. They ask for a new word each morning and never have I to repeat to them what it is. And if you saw the condition of these tough little cards the next morning you'd know why they need to be of tough cardboard or heavy drawing paper rather than thin paper.

When each has the nucleus of a reading vocabulary and I know they are at peace with me I show them the word "frightened" and at once all together they burst out with what they are frightened of. Nearly all the Maoris say "the ghost!" a matter which has a racial and cultural origin, while the Europeans name some animal they have never seen, "tiger" or "alligator," using it symbolically for the unnameable fear that we all have.

"I not frightened of anysing!" shouts my future murderer, Seven.

"Aren't you?"

"No, I stick my knife into it all!"

"What will you stick your knife into?"

"I stick my knife into the tigers!"

"Tigers" is usually a word from the European children but here is a Maori with it. So I give him "tigers" and never have I to repeat this word to him, and in the morning the little card shows the dirt and disrepair of passionate usage.

"Come in," cry the children to a knock at the door, but as no one does come in we all go out. And here we find in the porch, humble with natural dignity, a barefooted, tattooed Maori woman.

"I see my little Seven?" she says.

"Is Seven your little boy?"

"I bring him up. Now he five. I bring him home to his real family for school eh. I see my little boy?"

The children willingly produce Seven, and here we have in the porch, within a ring of sympathetic brown and blue eyes, a reunion.

"Where did you bring him up?" I ask over the many heads.

"Way back on those hill. All by heeself. You remember your ol' Mummy?" she begs Seven.

I see.

Later, standing watching Seven grinding his chalk to dust on his blackboard as usual, I do see. "Whom do you want, Seven? Your old Mummy or your new Mummy?"

"My old Mummy."

"What do your brothers do?"

"They all hits me."

"Old Mummy" and "new Mummy" and "hit" and "brothers" are all one-look words added to his vocabulary, and now and again I see some shape breaking through the chalk-ravage. And I wish I could make a good story of it and say he is no longer violent. . . .

"Who's that crying!" I accuse, lifting my nose like an old war horse.

"Seven he breaking Gay's neck."

So the good story, I say to my junior, must stand by for a while. But I can say he is picking up his words now. Fast.

Questions for Discussion and Debate

1. What does Sylvia Ashton-Warner mean when she uses the term *organic* in relation to teaching reading? Describe her organic method. Describe her "scheme."

2. What does she mean by *Key Vocabulary*? And what are some examples of the children's key vocabulary, Maori examples as well as those words that transcend cultures?

3. Ashton-Warner's motives for developing her method were not simply to help her students read and love reading, but also, she often wrote, to channel their aggressive behaviors into more peaceful activities. Do you agree or disagree that there is a connection among teacher method, the curriculum, *and* student behavior? If you agree, then why is there a need for discipline strategies? Debate this resolution: If teachers constructed curriculum and instruction, content, and method that were sound and motivating, there would be no need for concern about managing students' behavior.

4. Have you seen the whole-language approach being implemented in a classroom? If so, share your observations.

5. Debate whether or not big books written and published by textbook publishers have the same kind of usefulness as those produced by the children.

6. Debate whether or not Ashton-Warner's scheme could also be adapted in high-school classrooms in all subject areas.

Activities and Projects

1. Locate some of Ashton-Warner's other books (see chapter references). Read one or more of them and then report to the class on other aspects of Ashton-Warner's philosophy as well as on the successes and difficulties she faced teaching in a multicultural environment. Try to locate the film, *Sylvia*, based on her autobiography.

2. Do research on the whole-language approach to teaching reading. Prepare a report on this strategy. Then do research on the use of phonics to teach reading. Address the question of whether these two methods can be used together to teach reading. (There has been an ongoing debate about this question in which devout whole-language advocates deplore the use of phonics, while advocates of phonics accuse whole-language devotees of depriving children of an important tool for unlocking the magic of reading.) Lead a discussion of both methods and their strengths and weaknesses.

3. Visit one or more classrooms where the teacher uses a whole-language approach. First prepare a checklist of teacher and student behaviors that you will be trying to observe. Share your findings with the class.

4. Locate teacher texts in which the whole-language approach is described and taught. If possible, try out one or more of the strategies—either within a practicum situation or with peers. Critique your experience with your cooperating teacher or with your peers.

5. Find some examples of the big books that have been produced by publishers or within classrooms. Share them with your peers. Try writing one with children if you are now working in a classroom.

6. Ashton-Warner utilized art, music, literature, and drama in her attempts to unlock her students' particular paths to learning. More recently those "particular paths to learning" have been described in terms of multiple intelligences. Howard Gardner of Harvard University has written extensively about the importance of recognizing that some students possess other types of intelligence, for example, musical intelligence, as opposed to the more traditional verbal or

mathematical intelligences. Do research on Gardner's (1983) ideas and evaluate to what extent his work reflects not only Ashton-Warner's contributions to teaching but the theories of others whose ideas are contained in this anthology.

7. In Harper Lee's *To Kill a Mockingbird,* there is a scene in a classroom in which the teacher, Miss Caroline, tells Scout, "Now you tell your father not to teach you anymore. It's best to begin reading with a fresh mind." This kind of advice flies in the face of studies that show that children who are brought up surrounded by books, who are read to, and, yes, who are exposed to printed material on a daily basis will come to school ready to read or to learn. Children without such exposure are at a disadvantage. Consult these studies. Find out about government programs such as Head Start that were created to assist low-income children. Visit a Head Start program in your community and observe the ways in which children are prepared for reading. Share your observations with the class.

6.3 *Teacher in America* (1945)

Jacques Barzun

Clearly, this excerpt from Jacques Barzun's book, *Teacher in America,* is a plea for teaching foreign languages that would enable students to move beyond their own cultures and immerse themselves in a world that has gotten even smaller since his book was published.

Even though most of us are hyphenated Americans (Irish-, Jewish-, African-, and so on), and may already have some connection to languages besides the English that unites us, Americans have tended to be somewhat ethnocentric about the need to learn other languages. Barzun, a native of France, was himself personally aware of the value of speaking more than one language.

In 1943–1944, he took a sabbatical leave from his position as history professor at Columbia University in New York City and traveled throughout the United States observing teachers and teaching in several locations. What he learned as a result of his brief sabbatical "entangled itself in [his] own experience as a teacher, a parent, and a learner" (Barzun, 1945, p. 6). Even before World War II had ended, Barzun felt compelled to share his observations about language teaching and other aspects of curricular reform that still have relevance today.

The end of World War II and the establishment of the United Nations had, of course, given rise to a great deal of thinking about America's connections to the rest of the world and the need for international understanding, especially as a preventive to future wars. Learning languages, Barzun believed, was one of the means of reaching

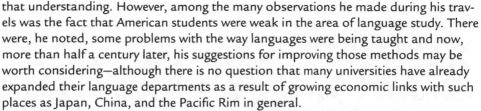

that understanding. However, among the many observations he made during his travels was the fact that American students were weak in the area of language study. There were, he noted, some problems with the way languages were being taught and now, more than half a century later, his suggestions for improving those methods may be worth considering—although there is no question that many universities have already expanded their language departments as a result of growing economic links with such places as Japan, China, and the Pacific Rim in general.

Before reading this excerpt, recall your own experiences with learning a language(s). Were the methods effective? In what ways do you think the methods could have been improved? After reflecting on these questions, read Barzun's piece and compare his ideas to your own experiences. Reflect also on how learning a foreign language can help to build bridges among the many cultures of the world as well as the cultures within this country.

10. TONGUES AND AREAS

"Is a Frenchman a man?"
"Yes,"
"Well den! Dad blame it, why doan' he talk *like a man? You answer me dat!"*

— JIM AND HUCKLEBERRY FINN

Shortly before setting foot in the United States, I tried to learn something about the country from an old guidebook which had been around the house for years. With my imperfect command of the language, one sentence near the beginning, I remember, filled me with apprehension:—

The European tongues are taught in the high schools all over the country, but the instruction is purely theoretical, and the number who can talk French, German, or Italian is very small. Tourists who wish to travel among the remoter districts of New England should be well acquainted with the language, which is the English of Elizabeth with a few local idioms.[1]

Having no idea whether I should be called upon to travel in the "remoter districts of New England," much less what was meant by the "English of Elizabeth," I pinned all my faith on this "theoretical instruction" of American youth in European tongues. I now know what it means. It means that boys and girls "take" French or Spanish or German (never Italian: the guidebook is wrong) for three, four, or five years before entering college, only to discover there that they cannot read, speak, or understand it. The word for this type of instruction is not "theoretical" but "hypothetical." Its principle is "*If* it were possible to learn a foreign language in the way I have been taught it, I should now know that language. . . ."

The ultimate educational value of knowing a foreign language is that it lets you into the workings of other human minds, like *and* unlike your own. It takes you out of your narrow local self and points out ways of seeing and feeling that cannot be perceived apart from the alien words that record the perception. The reason educated people in every country find themselves using foreign phrases in the midst of their own speech is that these expressions point to real things but are untranslatable: *gemütlich, raison d'être, dolce far niente, high life,* and so on. And if snobs ape the habit merely to show off, the imitation only proves that there is a real thing to imitate.

---

[1]*New England: A Handbook for Travellers,* James R. Osgood, Boston, 1873.

These locutions—whether expressive of feelings or ideas or objects—are the signs of the bigger ones, represented by a nation's literature, philosophy, or contributions to science and religion. This being so, the study of a language becomes the study of a people, and the notion of a language as a tool destroys itself: a tool is a dead, unchanging thing; a language lives. A tool is for some ulterior purpose; a language exists as a world in itself. Is the ulterior purpose perhaps to read foreign books? But the books *are* the language or a part of it. To speak to the cabman in Naples? But what he says and what you say are not "tools" with which to manufacture understanding, they are meanings—or they fail as meanings—in the instant of utterance. In short, words are not clothing for an idea, they are its incarnation.

This should give us a clue to the better teaching of language in the schools. The scholastic assumption has been that the pupil studies vocabulary and grammar, after which, like the journalist in *Pickwick* who had to write on Chinese Metaphysics and looked up first China, then Metaphysics, he "combines his information." After vocabulary and "forms" come those practice sentences about books being under the table and umbrellas belonging to every member of the family in turn.[2] So far, no meaning has raised its head anywhere. The teacher does not really speak, he repeats the inane remarks in the book; the pupils write this nonsense at home, write it on the board, chant it in unison, and hate it at sight.

As against all this, it is invariably found that a successful language teacher dramatizes his class hour by involving his students in the exchange of purposeful ideas. He talks to them about the day's news or the football season or their own delinquencies—something close to their life in common, yet not manufactured hokum. To do this easily and naturally, the teacher should be a native or a thoroughly fluent speaker; he ought not have to grimace to utter umlaut *ü*. He should bring to class with him foreign books, newspapers, and posters, as well as maps of the country whose language he teaches. He ought to have friends who are natives and invite them to address the group very briefly or to join in refreshments after recess. Preferably these guests should come from varying walks in life, speaking in different accents about different things. Each visit will then yield matter for weeks of argument, analysis, and criticism.

For more than any other subject, language must be learned close to its living sources. Other things can stand being made "academic" through language, but language itself is an activity which just as soon as possible should become transparent, unnoticeable, that is to say, communicative. This does not mean that the language teacher should ignore words and rules. These on the contrary become interesting from the moment one begins to see them in the perspective of their own language. Even young pupils can be made to feel the humor or incoherence of word groupings that are theoretically possible but actually contrary to idiom.[3]

All this means that speaking, reading, writing, and thinking in the alien speech must unite into a single fluency. . . .

There remains one human obstacle to cope with. The teacher must conquer the shy pupils' reluctance to make with their mouths what they feel is affected sounds. On this

[2]Joseph Conrad called this type of language "Ollendorff" from the name of a well-known publisher of language manuals. The term deserves to live, because so many novels and other works are couched in this idiom.

[3]I am indebted to Mr. Enno Franzius for many of these suggestions. As a linguist, globe trotter, and teacher of languages he gives the authority of practice and successful experience to this one and only method.

point, majority pressure can be gently applied. When everybody acts the fool to produce a continental "I," the few who hold out are the eccentrics. A language can only be learned by plunging into it, making mistakes, and rushing on unabashed. You simply cannot learn to skate or talk French without making yourself ridiculous. . . .

Questions for Discussion and Debate

1. Share with your peers your experiences related to learning languages in school. Discuss in what ways the methods used were or were not effective.

   Which of Barzun's comments struck you as "so true?" Why? Did you find that learning a language brought you closer to other cultures? Explain.

2. What are *all* the values of learning a foreign language, according to Barzun?

3. First consider the unsuccessful methods of teaching language. Then list the techniques Barzun discusses as those used by "a successful language teacher."

4. Debate whether or not you think the "one human obstacle" teachers must cope with can ever be overcome? Include in your support for your position examples and observations from your own experience.

5. Debate this question: At what age should students begin to be taught foreign languages in school?

6. Bilingual education programs have been the source of tremendous controversy and their value will likely continue to be debated. Divide the class into two sides and, after doing some research on the issue, debate the question: Are bilingual education programs beneficial to immigrant students? (The California state school board voted in 1998 to end their bilingual education program.)

Activities and Projects

1. Another current controversial issue concerns whether or not English should be declared the national language of the United States. There are, of course, powerful implications for both points of view. Find out about the reasoning of both positions. Then debate the question, with one side arguing the affirmative and the other the negative.

2. Interview one or more foreign-language teachers, noting, in particular, (a) why they think teaching language is important and (b) their most successful methods. Share your findings with the class.

3. Find out at what age students in the school system in your (college) community begin to learn languages. Try to observe foreign-language teaching at more than one level. Share your observations with the class and, together, evaluate the techniques you observed and their effects. Reach a consensus on the issue of when it is best to begin teaching students a second language.

4. Do research on this question: In what ways does teaching foreign languages have the effect of building multicultural awareness and tolerance within America itself?

5. Find out about ESL (English as a Second Language) programs. Explain their purpose and what methods they use to assist students in learning English. If possible, interview an ESL teacher about his or her work and what type of education preparation is needed to teach ESL.

6. With growing recognition of the world as a "global village," there has been a prolifera-tion of global education curricula across the disciplines. However, there is some question as to both the quality of these materials and the extent to which school systems have integrated them consistently.

Establish criteria for investigating global education resources. If possible, evaluate several global education projects. Describe in detail a curriculum that met your criteria.

6.4   *I Know Why the Caged Bird Sings* (1983)

Maya Angelou

Maya Angelou stood on the podium during the presidential inauguration ceremony for Bill Clinton in 1993 and read the poem, "On the Pulse of Morning," that she had writ-ten especially for the occasion.

> There is true yearning to respond to
> The singing river and the wise rock.
> So say the Asian, the Hispanic, the Jew
> The African and the Native American, the Sioux,
> The Catholic, the Muslim, the French, the Greek
> The Irish, the Rabbi, the Priest, the Sheikh,
> The Gay, the Straight, the Preacher,
> The Privileged, the Homeless, the Teacher.
> They hear. They all hear
> The speaking of the Tree.

She had come long and far in her life for an African American woman raised in the segregated South in an educational environment dramatically different for Black and for White students. Her school, Lafayette County Training School, in Stamps, Arkansas, was set on a dirt hill. To the left was an expanse used for sports activity and some rusty hoops on swaying poles. The White high school, on the other hand, had a lawn, hedges, a tennis court, and climbing ivy; a multicultural South with two major cultures separate and unequal.

In this excerpt from her autobiography, Angelou recalls how pleased and excited she was as she anticipated her graduation with honors from high school (1940). De-spite the educational inequities, she and her family were proud. She would be "one of the first called in the graduating ceremonies" (Angelou, 1983, p. 145). But something happens during the ceremonies that reminds her of her place in society as a Negro, the term then commonly used for African Americans. And her joy turns to anger, seething vengeful anger. Only at the very end of the ceremony does something else happen that reminds her of two things: that her people have a rich and beautiful culture and that she and her fellow graduates, among them the valedictorian of the class, have intellectual gifts that will continue to bring pride to their community.

Put yourself in Angelou's place as you read this excerpt and then compare your graduation experience to hers. What are the differences between your experience and hers? Do you think there are still people with the same kind of insensitivity as demonstrated by Mr. Donleavy, the local politician and main speaker?

The school band struck up a march and all classes filed in as had been rehearsed. We stood in front of our seats, as assigned, and on a signal from the choir director, we sat. No sooner had this been accomplished than the band started to play the national anthem. We rose again and sang the song, after which we recited the pledge of allegiance. We remained standing for a brief minute before the choir director and the principal signaled to us, rather desperately I thought, to take our seats. The command was so unusual that our carefully rehearsed and smooth-running machine was thrown off. For a full minute we fumbled for our chairs and bumped into each other awkwardly. Habits change or solidify under pressure, so in our state of nervous tension we had been ready to follow our usual assembly pattern: the American national anthem, then the pledge of allegiance, then the song every Black person I knew called the Negro National Anthem. All done in the same key, with the same passion and most often standing on the same foot.

Finding my seat at last, I was overcome with a presentiment of worse things to come. Something unrehearsed, unplanned, was going to happen, and we were going to be made to look bad. I distinctly remember being explicit in the choice of pronoun. It was "we," the graduating class, the unit, that concerned me then.

The principal welcomed "parents and friends" and asked the Baptist minister to lead us in prayer. His invocation was brief and punchy, and for a second I thought we were getting back on the high road to right action. When the principal came back to the dais, however, his voice had changed. Sounds always affected me profoundly and the principal's voice was one of my favorites. During assembly it melted and lowed weakly into the audience. It had not been in my plan to listen to him, but my curiosity was piqued and I straightened up to give him my attention.

He was talking about Booker T. Washington, our "late great leader," who said we can be as close as the fingers on the hand, etc. . . . Then he said a few vague things about friendship and the friendship of kindly people to those less fortunate than themselves. With that his voice nearly faded, thin, away. Like a river diminishing to a stream and then to a trickle. But he cleared his throat and said, "Our speaker tonight, who is also our friend, came from Texarkana to deliver the commencement address, but due to the irregularity of the train schedule, he's going to, as they say, 'speak and run.'" He said that we understood and wanted the man to know that we were most grateful for the time he was able to give us and then something about how we were willing always to adjust to another's program, and without more ado—"I give you Mr. Edward Donleavy."

Not one but two white men came through the door offstage. The shorter one walked to the speaker's platform, and the tall one moved over to the center seat and sat down. But that was our principal's seat, and already occupied. The dislodged gentleman bounced around for a long breath or two before the Baptist minister gave him his chair, then with more dignity than the situation deserved, the minister walked off the stage.

Donleavy looked at the audience once (on reflection, I'm sure that he wanted only to reassure himself that we were really there), adjusted his glasses and began to read from a sheaf of papers.

He was glad "to be here and to see the work going on just as it was in the other schools."

At the first "Amen" from the audience I willed the offender to immediate death by choking on the word. But Amens and Yes, sir's began to fall around the room like rain through a ragged umbrella.

He told us of the wonderful changes we children in Stamps had in store. The Central School (naturally, the white school was Central) had already been granted improvements that would be in use in the fall. A well-known artist was coming from Little Rock to teach art to them. They were going to have the newest microscopes and chemistry equipment for their laboratory. Mr. Donleavy didn't leave us long in the dark over who made these improvements available to Central High. Nor were we to be ignored in the general betterment scheme he had in mind.

He said that he had pointed out to people at a very high level that one of the first-line football tacklers at Arkansas Agricultural and Mechanical College had graduated from good old Lafayette County Training School. Here fewer Amen's were heard. Those few that did break through lay dully in the air with the heaviness of habit.

He went on to praise us. He went on to say how he had bragged that "one of the best basketball players at Fisk sank his first ball right here at Lafayette County Training School."

The white kids were going to have a chance to become Galileos and Madame Curies and Edisons and Gauguins, and our boys (the girls weren't even in on it) would try to be Jesse Owenses and Joe Louises.

Owens and the Brown Bomber were great heroes in our world, but what school official in the white-goddom of Little Rock had the right to decide that those two men must be our only heroes? Who decided that for Henry Reed to become a scientist he had to work like George Washington Carver, as a bootblack, to buy a lousy microscope? Bailey was obviously always going to be too small to be an athlete, so which concrete angel glued to what country seat had decided that if my brother wanted to become a lawyer he had to first pay penance for his skin by picking cotton and hoeing corn and studying correspondence books at night for twenty years?

The man's dead words fell like bricks around the auditorium and too many settled in my belly. Constrained by hard-learned manners I couldn't look behind me, but to my left and right the proud graduating class of 1940 had dropped their heads. Every girl in my row had found something new to do with her handkerchief. Some folded the tiny squares into love knots, some into triangles, but most were wadding them, then pressing them flat on their yellow laps.

On the dais, the ancient tragedy was being replayed. Professor Parsons sat, a sculptor's reject, rigid. His large, heavy body seemed devoid of will or willingness, and his eyes said he was no longer with us. The other teachers examined the flag (which was draped stage right) or their notes, or the windows which opened on our now-famous playing diamond.

Graduation, the hush-hush magic time of frills and gifts and congratulations and diplomas, was finished for me before my name was called. The accomplishment was nothing. The meticulous maps, drawn in three colors of ink, learning and spelling decasyllabic words, memorizing the whole of *The Rape of Lucrece*—it was for nothing. Donleavy had exposed us.

We were maids and farmers, handymen and washerwomen, and anything higher that we aspired to was farcical and presumptuous.

Then I wished that Gabriel Prosser and Nat Turner had killed all whitefolks in their beds and that Abraham Lincoln had been assassinated before the signing of the Emancipation Proclamation, and that Harriet Tubman had been killed by that blow on her head and Christopher Columbus had drowned in the *Santa María*.

It was awful to be Negro and have no control over my life. It was brutal to be young and already trained to sit quietly and listen to charges brought against my color with no chance of defense. We should all be dead. I thought I should like to see us all dead, one on top of the other. A pyramid of flesh with the whitefolks on the bottom, as the broad base, then the Indians with their silly tomahawks and teepees and wigwams and treaties, the Negroes with their mops and recipes and cotton sacks and spirituals sticking out of their mouths. The Dutch children should all stumble in their wooden shoes and break their necks. The French should choke to death on the Louisiana Purchase (1803) while silkworms ate all the Chinese with their stupid pigtails. As a species, we were an abomination. All of us. . . .

. . . There was shuffling and rustling around me, then Henry Reed was giving his valedictory address, "To Be or Not to Be." Hadn't he heard the whitefolks? We couldn't *be,* so the question was a waste of time. Henry's voice came out clear and strong. I feared to look at him. Hadn't he got the message? There was no "nobler in the mind" for Negroes because the world didn't think we had minds, and they let us know it. "Outrageous

fortune"? Now, that was a joke. When the ceremony was over I had to tell Henry Reed some things. That is, if I still cared. Not "rub," Henry, "erase." "Ah, there's the erase." Us. . . .

I had been listening and silently rebutting each sentence with my eyes closed; then there was a hush, which in an audience warns that something unplanned is happening. I looked up and saw Henry Reed, the conservative, the proper, the A student, turn his back to the audience and turn to us (the proud graduating class of 1940) and sing, nearly speaking,

"Lift ev'ry voice and sing
Till earth and heaven ring
Ring with the harmonies of Liberty . . ."

It was the poem written by James Weldon Johnson.

It was the music composed by J. Rosamond Johnson.

It was the Negro national anthem. Out of habit we were singing it.

Our mothers and fathers stood in the dark hall and joined the hymn of encouragement. A kindergarten teacher led the small children onto the stage and the buttercups and daisies and bunny rabbits marked time and tried to follow:

"Stony the road we trod
Bitter the chastening rod
Felt in the days when hope, unborn, had died.
Yet with a steady beat
Have not our weary feet
Come to the place for which our fathers sighed?"

Every child I knew had learned that song with his ABC's and along with "Jesus Loves Me This I Know." But I personally had never heard it before. Never heard the words, despite

---

"Lift Ev'ry Voice and Sing"—words by James Weldon Johnson and music by J. Rosamond Johnson. Copyright by Edward B. Marks Music Corporation. Used by permission.

the thousands of times I had sung them. Never thought they had anything to do with me.

On the other hand, the words of Patrick Henry had made such an impression on me that I had been able to stretch myself tall and trembling and say, "I know not what course others may take, but as for me, give me liberty or give me death."

And now I heard, really for the first time:

"We have come over a way that with tears has been watered,
We have come, treading our path through the blood of the slaughtered."

While echoes of the song shivered in the air, Henry Reed bowed his head, said "Thank you," and returned to his place in the line. The tears that slipped down many faces were not wiped away in shame.

We were on top again. As always, again. We survived. The depths had been icy and dark, but now a bright sun spoke to our souls. I was no longer simply a member of the proud graduating class of 1940; I was a proud member of the wonderful, beautiful Negro race.

═══════ Questions for Discussion and Debate ═══════

1. This excerpt begins and ends with references to the Negro National Anthem by poet James Weldon Johnson and J. Rosamond Johnson. What role did its initial omission from the ceremony play? And what role did the song ultimately play at the end?

2. This excerpt also shows just how powerful a role the stereotypical words of a bigot can play in destroying a minority culture and the self-esteem of its children. On the other hand, the excerpt also conveys the power of words and music in restoring some of that which was injured. Discuss the ideas that Donleavy, the local politician, delivered at

the graduation and all that they represent. Then summarize the sentiments in the Johnson poem and what they represent. Compare the two, then debate which one has the greater power in terms of affecting the self-esteem of minority children. Essentially, this debate is about whether or not the scars of prejudice can ever be removed or healed.

3. Angelou, in her anger, makes disparaging references to many other minority groups, even her own people. Why do you think she does this? What is her conclusion about human nature? Do you agree? Why, or why not?

═══════ Activities and Projects ═══════

1. Angelou's intense anger is directed against others whom she views as her people's oppressors. However, some members of minority groups turn their rage inward and commit suicide. There are more suicides among Native American teenagers than within other minorities. Statistics between

1980 and 1995 show that suicide rates for African American males have risen dramatically, and homosexual students are twice as likely to attempt suicide than are heterosexual teenagers (Green, 1991). Find out about organizations that are trying to help prevent minority students—whether based on race or sexual orientation—from turning to suicide.

2. Locate a recording of the Negro National Anthem or visit a Black church where it might be sung. What emotional feelings does this song elicit? Does the "Star-Spangled Banner" elicit the same feelings for you? Explain. Can the ideas in the two anthems stand together without canceling each other out? Discuss these questions with your peers.

3. Do research on the *Brown* v. *Board of Education* (1954) decision, in which the Supreme Court decided that separate schools were inherently unequal *even if* all physical characteristics (books, buildings) were the same. Find out about psychologist Kenneth Clark's interviews with African American children during the hearings that influenced the court's decision. (Scenes based on these interviews appear in the 1991 film *Separate but Equal,* starring Sidney Poitier as Thurgood Marshall, who argued the case in front of the Supreme Court. He eventually was appointed to the Court.)

4. Do additional research on the psychology of prejudice and how it affects children's ability to learn. Consult the work of the late Harvard psychologist Gordon Allport (*The Nature of Prejudice,* 1958) and the documentary film, *Eye of the Storm,* about teacher Jane Elliot's lesson on prejudice in her third-grade classroom, a lesson often referred to as "the brown eyes, blue eyes experiment."

5. In her book, *I Know Why the Caged Bird Sings* (1983), from which this excerpt is taken, Angelou notes her multicultural heritage, which includes a nearly White grandmother raised in a German family, who spoke German fluently, and a grandfather from the West Indies (p. 50). How multicultural are *your* roots? Research your cultural heritage and see how many places on the map your family can be located. Try to discover any stories that might exist about the early problems and successes of family members who first came to America. How did *your* ancestors deal with the problems they faced? How is their and your story different from or the same as Maya Angelou's?

6.5 | *Lives on the Boundary* (1989)

Mike Rose

Mike Rose grew up poor and isolated in South Los Angeles. The culture of working-class ethnic Americans, in this case, Italian Americans, is not so different from that of other minorities in this country in terms of the alienation that develops because of glaring differences between their socioeconomic circumstances and the promise of the American Dream. Rose, in the end, is more fortunate than most.

In the 1960s Rose appeared to be headed for failure at Loyola University, a Catholic institution in Los Angeles that was, at that time, a school for mostly White middle- and upper-class males. (Interestingly, now Loyola is coeducational and has an

Asian Pacific Students Association, a Black Student Alliance, and a Chinese Resource Center.) He was one of those people to whom he refers in the title of his book; his own life was "on the boundary." However, he had a high-school teacher who recognized his intelligence and looked out for him even after he graduated. Jack MacFarland stepped in to help Rose and some of his other former students gain an opportunity to follow a curricular alternative that would enable them to use their talents and gradually acquire skills for which they had not been adequately prepared.

In this excerpt from chapter 3, "Entering the Conversation," Rose describes that turning point, after which he was able to make use of the resources at his disposal and cross the cultural boundary, in other words, enter the conversation, and benefit from a quality education that would enable him to become a teacher and writer. Because he believes that all underprepared, underserved students deserve the same, he chose to teach men, women, and children with "lives on the boundary." In his book Rose describes many of those people as well as the techniques he used to help them enter the mainstream.

Have you ever considered poverty to be a cultural classification? The culture of poverty, of course, transcends racial, ethnic, and religious categories. As you read the excerpt, note the similarities as well as the differences between Rose's difficulties and those experienced by racial minorities as revealed in the excerpts by Angelou (Selection 6.4) and Ashton-Warner (Selection 6.2) in this chapter and others: Marshall (Selection 5.5) Conroy (Selection 4.3), and Kozol (Selection 4.5).

It is an unfortunate fact of our psychic lives that the images that surround us as we grow up—no matter how much we may scorn them later—give shape to our deepest needs and longings. Every year Loyola men elected a homecoming queen. The queen and her princesses were students at the Catholic sister schools: Marymount, Mount St. Mary's, St. Vincent's. They had names like Corinne and Cathy, and they came from the Sullivan family or the Mitchells or the Ryans. They were taught to stand with toe to heel, their smiles were inviting, and the photographer's flash illuminated their eyes. Loyola men met them at fraternity parties and mixers and "CoEd Day," met them according to rules of manner and affiliation and parental connection as elaborate as a Balinese dance. John and I drew mustaches on their photographs, but something about them reached far back into my life.

Growing up in South L.A. was certainly not a conscious misery. My neighborhood had

its diversions and its mysteries, and I felt loved and needed at home. But all in all there was a dreary impotence to the years, and isolation, and a deep sadness about my father. I protected myself from the harsher side of it all through a life of the mind. And while that interior life included spaceships and pink chemicals and music and the planetary moons, it also held the myriad television images of the good life that were piped into my home: Robert Young sitting down to dinner, Ozzie Nelson tossing the football with his sons, the blond in a Prell commercial turning toward the camera. The images couldn't have been more trivial—all sentimental phosphorescence—but as a child tucked away on South Vermont, they were just about the only images I had of what life would be without illness and dead ends. I didn't realize how completely their message had seeped into my being, what loneliness and sorrow was being held at bay—didn't realize it until I found myself in the middle of Loyola's social life without a guidebook, feeling just beyond the superficial touch of the queen and her princesses, those smiling incarnations of a television promise. I scorned the whole silly show and ached to be embraced by one of these mythic females under the muted light of a paper moon.

So I went to school and sat in class and memorized more than understood and whistled past the academic graveyard. I vacillated between the false potency of scorn and feelings of ineptitude. John and I would get in his car and enjoy the warmth of each other and laugh and head down the long strip of Manchester Boulevard, away from Loyola, away from the palms and green, green lawns, back to South L.A. We'd throw the ball in the alley or lag pennies on Vermont or hit Marty's Liquor. We'd leave much later for a movie or a football game at Mercy High or the terrible safety of downtown Los Angeles. Walking, then, past the *discotecas* and pawnshops, past the windows full of fried chicken and yellow lamps, past the New Follies, walking through hustlers and lost drunks and prostitutes and transvestites with rouge the color of bacon—stopping, finally, before the musty opening of a bar where two silhouettes moved around a pool table as though they were underwater.

I don't know what I would have found if the flow of events hadn't changed dramatically. Two things happened. Jack MacFarland privately influenced my course of study at Loyola, and death once again ripped through our small family.

The coterie of MacFarland's students—Art Mitz, Mark Dever, and me—were still visiting our rumpled mentor. We would stop by his office or his apartment to mock our classes and the teachers and all that " 'Loyola man' bullshit." Nobody had more appreciation for burlesque than Jack MacFarland, but I suppose he saw beneath our caustic performances and knew we were headed for trouble. Without telling us, he

started making phone calls to some of his old teachers at Loyola—primarily to Dr. Frank Carothers, the chairman of the English Department—and, I guess, explained that these kids needed to be slapped alongside the head with a good novel. Dr. Carothers volunteered to look out for us and agreed to some special studies courses that we could substitute for a few of the more traditional requirements, courses that would enable us to read and write a lot under the close supervision of a faculty member. In fact, what he promised were tutorials—and that was exceptional, even for a small college. All this would start up when we returned from summer vacation. Our sophomore year, Jack MacFarland finally revealed, would be different.

When Lou Minton [his mother's friend] rewired the trailer, he rigged a phone line from the front house: A few digits and we could call each other. One night during the summer after my freshman year, the phone rang while I was reading. It was my mother and she was screaming. I ran into the house to find her standing in the kitchen hysterical—both hands pressed to her face—and all I could make out was Lou's name. I didn't see him in the front of the house, so I ran back through the kitchen to the bedroom. He had fallen back across the bed, a hole right at his sideburn, his jaw still quivering. They had a fight, and some ugly depth of pain convulsed within him. He left the table and walked to the bedroom. My mother heard the light slam of a .22. Nothing more.

That summer seems vague and distant. I can't remember any specifics, though I had to take care of my mother and handle the affairs of the house. I probably made do by blunting a good deal of what I saw and navigating with intuitive quadrants. But though I cannot remember details, I do recall feelings and recognitions: Lou's suicide came to represent the sadness and dead time I had protected myself against, the personal as well as public oppressiveness of life in South

Los Angeles. I began to see that my escape to the trailer and my isolationist fantasies of the demi-monde would yield another kind of death, a surrender to the culture's lost core. An alternative was somehow starting to take shape around school and knowledge. Knowledge seemed . . . was it empowering? No, that's a word I would use now. Then I felt freed, as if I were untying fetters. There simply were times when the pain and confusion of that summer would give way to something I felt more than I knew: a lightness to my body, an ease in breathing. Three or four months later I took an art history course, and one day during a slide show on Gothic architecture I felt myself rising up within the interior light of Mont-Saint-Michel. I wanted to be released from the despair that surrounded me on South Vermont and from my own troubled sense of exclusion.

Jack MacFarland had saved me at one juncture—caught my fancy and revitalized my mind—what I felt now was something further, some tentative recognition that an engagement with ideas could foster competence and lead me out into the world. But all this was very new and fragile, and given what I know now, I realize how easily it could have been crushed. My mother, for as long as I can remember, always added onto any statement of intention—hers or others—the phrase *se vuol Dio,* if God wants it. The fulfillment of desire, no matter how trivial, required the blessing of the gods, for the world was filled with threat. "I'll plant the seeds this weekend," I might say. "Se vuol Dio," she would add. *Se vuol Dio.* The phrase expressed several lifetimes of ravaged hope: my grandfather's lost leg, the failure of the Rose Spaghetti House, my father laid low, Lou Minton, the landscapes of South L.A. *Se vuol Dio.* For those who live their lives on South Vermont, tomorrow doesn't beckon to be defined from a benign future. It's up to the gods, not you, if any old thing turns out right. I carried within me no history of assurances that what I was feeling would lead to anything.

Because of its size and because of the kind of teacher who is drawn to small liberal arts colleges, Loyola would turn out to be a very good place for me. For even with MacFarland's yearlong tour through ideas and language, I was unprepared. English prose written before the twentieth century was difficult, sometimes impossible, for me to comprehend. The kind of reasoning I found in logic was very foreign. My writing was okay, but I couldn't hold a candle to Art Mitz or Mark Dever or to those boys who came from good schools. And my fears about science and mathematics prevailed: Pereira Hall, the Math and Engineering Building, was only forty to fifty yards from the rear entrance to the English Department but seemed an unfriendly mirage, a malevolent castle floating in the haze of a mescaline dream.

We live, in America, with so many platitudes about motivation and self-reliance and individualism—and myths spun from them, like those of Horatio Alger—that we find it hard to accept the fact that they are serious nonsense. To live your early life on the streets of South L.A.—or Homewood or Spanish Harlem or Chicago's South Side or any one of hundreds of other depressed communities—and to journey up through the top levels of the American educational system will call for support and guidance at many, many points along the way. You'll need people to guide you into conversations that seem foreign and threatening. You'll need models, lots of them, to show you how to get at what you don't know. You'll need people to help you center yourself in your own developing ideas. You'll need people to watch out for you. There is much talk these days about the value of a classical humanistic education, a call for an immersion in the humanities, a return to the great books. These appeals raise lots of suspicions, for such curricula have traditionally served to exclude working-class people from the classroom. It doesn't, of necessity, have to be that way. The teachers that fate and Jack MacFarland's crisis intervention sent my way worked at making the humanities truly human. What transpired between us was the essence of humane liberal education, and it enabled me to move far beyond the cognitive charade of my freshman year.

Questions for Discussion and Debate

1. Describe the environment in which Mike Rose grew up. What influences could have prevented his gaining a college education? What variables existed that led to his perseverance and positive attitude?

2. Compare South Los Angeles to the area in which you went to school. Were you exposed to any influences that might have led you away from a higher education? If so, how did you overcome those obstacles?

3. Much of what constitutes higher education—and "a classical humanistic education"—is meaningless and irrelevant to students who lack the proper preparation. Debate the following resolution with your peers: A classical education—the Great Books (for example, Plato, Dewey, Locke, Shakespeare)—is relevant to all peoples no matter what their socioeconomic or cultural identity.

Activities and Projects

1. Rose refers to images on television that portrayed for him the American Dream, the good life, which seemed very far from his life in South Los Angeles but showed him that alternatives lay beyond the "illness and dead ends" of his experience. Do a survey of the prime-time television programs from which the students of today are getting their images of America. What are those images? Do they serve to offer alternative desirable futures to which young people might aspire? Bring your findings to class for discussion.

2. Walk around the town or city in which you are now living. Locate the neighborhoods where working-class ethnic Americans like Mike Rose's family live. Prepare a summary of your observations of the physical characteristics of the area, the influences you notice, and the resources available to that community. How are these areas different from the middle- and upper-class areas and the areas with racial minorities? You might want to document your observations with photographs.

3. Visit classrooms where working-class students are enrolled. Talk with their teachers. Are these students underserviced? Prepare a position paper in which you recommend policies and practices that will ensure that these students receive the kind of attention and curriculum they need to succeed. Note also the positive programs that exist to help these children maintain pride while providing them access to the "conversation" and to the next rung on the socioeconomic ladder.

4. This particular excerpt expands the concept of cultural diversity beyond the narrower references to ethnic, religious, and racial

cultures. Further expansion of the concept might also encompass lesbian and gay culture, the culture of the disabled, and even differences based on age. Divide the class into research groups for the purpose of exploring the nature of discrimination within schools against the different groups mentioned here.

In addition to finding out about the prejudices that exist, identify any legislation or programs that have been established to provide these groups equal educational opportunities. (See the chart in Activities and Projects, item 6, following Selection 6.10.)

6.6 "National Brotherhood Week" (1981)

Tom Lehrer

Tom Lehrer, a teacher of mathematics, was nominated for *Entertainment Weekly*'s Humor Hall of Fame as one of the 50 funniest people of all time. No, the nomination is not related to his math teaching! Lehrer is best known for his songs of musical parody and political satire, 40 of which were released between 1953 and 1965. (Tauber, 1997, p. 50). There are Lehrer fans today who can, believe it or not, recite or sing every one of them.

After producing compilations of his work, *Too Many Songs by Tom Lehrer* (1981), Lehrer has chosen not to continue writing musical satire even though his well-wishers are "constantly suggesting hilarious subject matter, such as the gradual destruction of the environment, or recent presidents, etc." (p. 7).

Lehrer noted in a *New York Times* interview that he was not a comedian but a songwriter: "I was much more interested in getting the audience to think about the material" (cited in Tauber, 1977, p. 50). And that's precisely what this satirical song, "National Brotherhood Week" makes the listener do. In fact for a song that *sounds* light-hearted, its content is serious and thought-provoking. Lehrer wrote it during the volatile 1960s when civil rights movements were making history, and like most of his songs, this one is a parody of those current events. For example, his reference to "Lena Horne and Sheriff Clark dancing cheek to cheek," was indeed a most unlikely and unimaginable scenario, because Lena Horne is an African American singer and Sheriff Clark was the man who ordered hoses and dogs to be turned on a crowd of African Americans during a nonviolent civil rights march.

This scenario in song is a good example of what Lehrer says he tries to do with satire: "Avoid what the listener has provisionally guessed" about the song from the tune and title. Avoid predictability: "That's what is creative, the surprise" (cited in Tauber, 1997, p. 50). As you read or sing this song, note all of those surprises, those unpredictable phrases and words that Lehrer has joyfully but instructively created. Has he achieved his goal of making clear his point of view on "brotherhood" and the status of tolerance in our world today? Is satire an effective way of expressing protest?

National Brotherhood Week

Words and Music by Tom Lehrer

Questions for Discussion and Debate

1. Does this song successfully fulfill its role as satire? Explain by referring to parts of the song.

2. Go through each verse and list the conflicts and/or the attitudes that Lehrer has cited. Discuss these conflicts and attitudes, sharing whatever you already know about them. Discuss also your personal experiences with these particular examples of intolerance.

3. Lehrer also alludes to the hypocrisy that exists with regard to cultural pluralism (i.e., "It's fun to eulogize the people you despise"). Discuss examples of hypocrisy that you have observed in the schools and/or in relation to the educational goals and ideals espoused by people you have encountered. In other words, are there local examples of the issues raised by Lehrer in this song?

4. This satirical song uses humor in teaching tolerance. Share examples of humor in the classroom that you have memories of experiencing. What role can humor play in the classroom? What, if anything, should teachers beware of in using humor?

5. Debate this question: Does emphasis on multiculturalism in schools and in the world of music and other venues lead to fragmentation of an otherwise unified society?

Activities and Projects

1. Did you know that for many years there was a National Brotherhood Week? Do research on this celebration: when it began, who initiated it, and why it is a thing of the past. Find out what, if any, comparable celebrations now exist.

2. Divide the class into groups and have each group do research on one of the various prejudices or conflicts that Lehrer alludes to in the song. Then discuss what each group discovers to be the status of that conflict today (i.e., Hindus and Moslems and their current relationship, especially in India and Pakistan; Protestants and Catholics, especially in Northern Ireland; anti-Semitism; and so on).

3. In groups or individually identify a current controversial issue within the schools related to multicultural or global curricula or attitudes (i.e., bilingual education, Eurocentric curricula, Ebonics, others). Then try your hand at writing a political satire—musical or poetic, in the style of Tom Lehrer—in which you express *your* position on that issue.

6.7 *The Chosen* (1967)

Chaim Potok

In the novel, *The Chosen,* Chaim Potok (1929–2002) takes the reader to the Williamsburg section of Brooklyn, New York, both during and after World War II to observe the diversity within Jewish tradition. In doing so, however, he reaches peoples of *all* cultural persuasions because of his use of universal themes such as love between fathers and sons and crises around cultural identity. For example, his story raises the question, What is it like to be a young Jew (or Protestant or Muslim, etc.) and find yourself baffled by a heritage and an environment that surround and envelop you? How do young people deal with the difficulties that come with the struggle to make sense of the contradictions and differences *within* their own culture and in a diverse world? Potok's words speak both to those who have experienced that struggle and to those outside of the struggle who need to understand and empathize. We learn that minorities suffer not only from the ignorance or intolerance that exists outside of their culture but also from the ignorance within it.

Reuven is the young man telling the story of his struggle, which includes the complexities of his friendship with Danny Saunders. Both are Orthodox Jews, but Danny is a member of a more Orthodox Hasidic sect, which, like his father Reb Saunders, views less religious Jews as *apikorsim,* a disparaging term implying that such Jews are nonbelievers. On the other hand, many of the less Orthodox Jews as well as non-Jews in the area tend to lump all of the Hasidic Jews together as fanatics. The story revolves around the tolerance that both boys develop as a result of an incident on the baseball field.

Reuven conjures up a fanatical image of Danny when he hears that Danny has called his team *apikorsim*. He believes that Danny's team is literally out to kill them. When Danny's pitch hits Reuven in the eye, Reuven is convinced of it. Danny visits Reuven in the hospital where he is recovering from the incident and tells him he is sorry. He then explains that it was only by telling his father that "we [have] a duty to beat [the] apikorsim" (p. 71) that his father would allow them to form a team in the first place. For Danny's father, baseball was an "evil waste of time, a spawn of the potentially assimilationist English portion of the Yeshiva [Jewish school] day" (p. 12).

During the course of their conversation, the two boys come to learn about the bases of their motivations in life and how their behavior is inextricably linked to their cultural heritage and biases. They also learn about their aspirations. That visit is the beginning of their friendship and serves as an example of one way to overcome prejudice: sharing with others *your* cultural perspective and belief and tolerating another's. Then the dialogue can begin.

The scene in this excerpt takes place in the hospital where Reuven's father (*abba* in Hebrew), sick with worry about his son, comes to visit Reuven, who shares his ward with Billy and a boxer, Mr. Savo, whose eye was injured in a fight. What can you learn about commonality and difference from this scene? And what forms do tolerance and intolerance take?

My father came in a few minutes later, looking worse than he had the day before. His cheeks were sunken, his eyes were red, and his face was ashen. He coughed a great deal and kept telling me it was his cold. He sat down on the bed and told me he had talked to Dr. Snydman on the phone. "He will look at your eye Friday morning, and you will probably be able to come home Friday afternoon. I will come to pick you up when I am through teaching."

"That's wonderful!" I said.

"You will not be able to read for about ten days. He told me he will know by then about the scar tissue."

"I'll be happy to be out of this hospital," I said. "I walked around a little today and saw the people on the street outside."

My father looked at me and didn't say anything.

"I wish I was outside now," I said. "I envy them being able to walk around like that. They don't know how lucky they are."

"No one knows he is fortunate until he becomes unfortunate," my father said quietly. "That is the way the world is."

"It'll be good to be home again. At least I won't have to spend a Shabbat here."

"We'll have a nice Shabbat together," my father said. "A quiet Shabbat where we can talk and not be disturbed. We will sit and drink tea and talk." He coughed a little and put the handkerchief to his mouth. He took off his spectacles and wiped his eyes. Then he put them back on and sat on the bed, looking at me. He seemed so tired and pale, as if all his strength had been drained from him.

"I didn't tell you yet, abba. Danny Saunders came to see me today."

My father did not seem surprised. "Ah," he said. "And?"

"He's a very nice person. I like him."

"So? All of a sudden you like him." He was smiling. "What did he say?"

I told him everything I could remember of my conversation with Danny Saunders. Once, as I talked, he began to cough, and I stopped and watched helplessly as his thin frame bent and shook. Then he wiped his lips and eyes, and told me to continue. He listened intently. When I told him that Danny Saunders had wanted to kill me, his eyes went wide, but he didn't interrupt. When I told him about Danny Saunders' photographic mind, he nodded as if he had known about that all along. When I described as best I could what we had said about our careers, he smiled indulgently. And when I explained why Danny Saunders had told his team that they would kill us apikorsim, he stared at me and I could see the same look of absorption come into his eyes that I had seen earlier in the eyes of Danny Saunders. Then my father nodded. "People are not always what

they seem to be," he said softly. "That is the way the world is, Reuven."

"He's going to come visit me again tomorrow, abba."

"Ah," my father murmured. He was silent for a moment. Then he said quietly, "Reuven, listen to me. The Talmud says that a person should do two things for himself. One is to acquire a teacher. Do you remember the other?"

"Choose a friend," I said.

"Yes. You know what a friend is, Reuven? A Greek philosopher said that two people who are true friends are like two bodies with one soul."

I nodded.

"Reuven, if you can, make Danny Saunders your friend."

"I like him a lot, abba."

"No. Listen to me. I am not talking only about liking him. I am telling you to make him your friend and to let him make you his friend. I think—" He stopped and broke into another cough. He coughed a long time. Then he sat quietly on the bed, his hand on his chest, breathing hard. "Make him your friend," he said again, and cleared his throat noisily.

"Even though he's a Hasid?" I asked, smiling.

"Make him your friend," my father repeated. "We will see."

"The way he acts and talks doesn't seem to fit what he wears and the way he looks," I said. "It's like two different people."

My father nodded slowly but was silent. He looked over at Billy, who was still asleep.

"How is your little neighbor?" he asked me.

"He's very nice. There's a new kind of operation they'll be doing on his eyes. He was in an auto accident, and his mother was killed."

My father looked at Billy and shook his head. He sighed and stood up, then bent and kissed me on the forehead.

"I will be back to see you tomorrow. Is there anything you need?"

"No, abba."

"Are you able to use your tefillin?"

"Yes. I can't read though. I pray by heart."

He smiled at he. "I did not think of that. My baseball player. I will see you again tomorrow, Reuven."

"Yes, abba."

I watched him walk quickly up the aisle.

"That your father, kid?" I heard Mr. Savo ask me.

I turned to him and nodded. He was still playing his game of cards.

"Nice-looking man. Very dignified. What's he do?"

"He teaches."

"Yeah? Well, that's real nice, kid. My old man worked a pushcart. Down near Norfolk Street, it was. Worked like a dog. You're a lucky kid. What's he teach?"

"Talmud," I said. "Jewish law."

"No kidding? He in a Jewish school?"

"Yes," I said. "A high school."

Mr. Savo frowned at a card he had just pulled from the deck. "Damn," he muttered. "No luck nowhere. Story of my life." He tucked the card into a row on the blanket. "You looked kind of chummy there with your clopper, boy. You making friends with him?"

"He's a nice person," I said.

"Yeah? Well, you watch guys like that, kid. You watch them real good, you hear? Anyone clops you, he's got a thing going. Old Tony knows. You watch them."

"It was really an accident," I said.

"Yeah?"

"I could have ducked the ball."

Mr. Savo looked at me. His face was dark with the growth of beard, and his left eye seemed a little swollen and bloodshot. The black patch that covered his right eye looked like a huge skin mole. "Anyone out to clop you doesn't want you to duck, kid. I know."

"It wasn't really like that, Mr. Savo."

"Sure, kid. Sure. Old Tony doesn't like fanatics, that's all."

"I don't think he's a fanatic."

"No? What's he go around in those clothes for?"

"They all wear those clothes. It's part of their religion."

"Sure, kid. But listen. You're a good kid. So I'm telling you, watch out for those fanatics. They're the worse cloppers around." He looked at a card in his hands, then threw it down. "Lousy game. No luck." He scooped up the cards, patted them into a deck, and put them on the night table. He lay back on his pillow. "Long day," he said, talking almost to himself. "Like waiting for a big fight." He closed his left eye.

Questions for Discussion and Debate

1. Reuven is caught between two adult perspectives, his father's and Mr. Savo's. What are the two perspectives, and why do you think each adult believes as he does?

2. How does this scene demonstrate the *commonalities* that exist among people from different cultures? What are these commonalities?

3. Discuss your own experiences with situations or people who were "not always what they seemed to be."

4. What did *you* learn about Jewish culture from this excerpt? Had you any preconceived ideas?

5. Why does Reuven's father tell him to make "Danny Saunders your friend"? What implications does this advice have for the future, not just Reuven's and Danny's future? What implications does it have for classroom cultures and curriculum?

<hr>

Activities and Projects

1. Most of Potok's book portrays people who are responding in different ways to their identities as Jews, but overall the book can speak to people from many backgrounds, because seeking one's identity is a universal theme. Identify an author whose writing reflects *your* cultural heritage? Read some of that author's work to (a) learn more about your heritage, (b) discover whether or not he or she also deals with the ignorance that often exists within the same group, (c) share your cultural heritage and this author's work with your colleagues, and (d) consider and discuss classroom contexts in which the author's work could be used.

2. Brainstorm with your peers about all of the ways in which tolerance can be taught. From those ideas develop a lesson or mini-unit on tolerance that would make sense *within the context* of your discipline or subject area and grade level. Use excerpts from and/or references to literature that will further illustrate the objectives of your lesson or unit. Share with your peers, and, if possible, implement your lesson with students. (The Southern Poverty Law Center in Montgomery, Alabama, publishes a free quarterly journal called *Teaching Tolerance*. To locate or send for copies, contact *Teaching Tolerance*, 400 Washington Avenue, Montgomery, AL 36104; www.teachingtolerance.org.)

3. Read this excerpt aloud, with people taking the roles of Reuven, his father, and Mr. Savo. Does this dramatization add in any way to your initial response to this excerpt? Then look again at the description of Danny's visit to Reuven in the hospital given in the introduction to this excerpt. Try improvising that scene with two people assuming their roles.

6.8 "Warning to Children" (1961)

Robert Graves

Poetry has the capacity to convey important messages in a very compact but rhythmic format. In addition, poets like Robert Graves, in "Warning to Children," use repetition and metaphors, enabling you to picture their messages, to take hold of them, turn them around, and inspect them so you can nearly see their shapes. And Graves's poem

<hr>

"Warning to Children" by Robert Graves. From COMPLETE POEMS by Robert Graves.

has many shapes and colors. Notice how he begins and ends the poem with similar phrases. Notice also how he repeats six lines of the poem three times, changing the tense and/or sequence of the words to create a kind of crescendo that gives the reader a hint of what the children he is speaking to should and will do. Should they untie the string around the parcel? Why? What do all of his metaphors represent? Do you, as a teacher, have any influence on those children sitting with "a brown paper parcel on their laps"? What are the consequences of leaving the parcel untied?

Consider all of these questions as you read this poem through several times. Have fun imagining what the other metaphors represent. Enjoy.

Children, if you dare to think
Of the greatness, rareness, muchness,
Fewness of this precious only
Endless world in which you say
You live, you think of things like this:
Blocks of slate enclosing dappled
Red and green, enclosing tawny
Yellow nets, enclosing white
And black acres of dominoes,
Where a neat brown paper parcel
Tempts you to untie the string.
In the parcel a small island,
On the island a large tree,
On the tree a husky fruit.
Strip the husk and cut the rind off:
In the centre you will see
Blocks of slate enclosed by dappled
Red and green, enclosed by tawny
Yellow nets, enclosed by white

And black acres of dominoes,
Where the same brown paper parcel—
Children, leave the string untied!
For who dares undo the parcel
Finds himself at once inside it,
On the island, in the fruit,
Blocks of slate about his head,
Finds himself enclosed by dappled
Green and red, enclosed by yellow
Tawny nets, enclosed by black
And white acres of dominoes,
But the same brown paper parcel
Still untied upon his knee.
And, if he then should dare to think
Of the fewness, muchness, rareness,
Greatness of this endless only
Precious world in which he says
He lives—he then unties the string.

Questions for Discussion and Debate

1. What is the warning that Graves is trying to convey in this poem? What are the consequences of *not* untying the string? Do you agree with Graves? And if the children *do* decide to untie the string, what challenges face them? How would you suggest they meet the challenge(s)?

2. What metaphors does Graves use throughout the poem, and what does each represent? (You and your peers may not all agree on the meanings of each metaphor, which is fine as long as you try to defend reasonably your hypothesis about their meanings.)

3. What phrases are repeated? Discuss the effects of this repetition on the meaning and emotion derived from the poem.

Activities and Projects

1. Share the poem with children, possibly a class with which you are now working. Ask them if they like it—or ask them what they *see* and, also, what the poem means to them. Have the students illustrate the poem.

2. Illustrate the poem as *you* interpret its message. Share with peers.

3. This poem integrates the colors we associate with the visual arts, the rhythm we associate with music, and the phrasing we, of course, associate with poetry. Because you will likely have students in your classes whose native intelligence lies within the musical or artistic realms, poetry may be the best way to help them make meaningful connections to your lessons in general. Therefore, do research and try to locate poems that you could use to make your lessons more meaningful and memorable. Share your discoveries and explain the context in which you would use each poem.

4. This editor remembers when bagels were something you could get only in New York City's Lower East Side or another Jewish neighborhood, and tacos were something served only in Mexican restaurants. Now McDonald's and other fast-food eateries have assimilated these foods into the *American* cuisine! With your class, brainstorm all of the foods from different cultures that are truly gifts to American culture. What are the implications of this phenomenon in the debate between the multiculturalists and the traditionalists noted in the Brief Background to this chapter?

5. Do a closet inventory by looking at all of the labels on your clothing, shoes, hats, and so on. Make a list of the items and, next to each, the places where they were made. Have you discovered the world in your closet? Again, what are the implications of this phenomenon? Is this activity appropriate for children? Discuss its potential; maybe even try it out with children. Relate the activity to this poem. Could Graves' poetic use of color possibly signify diverse cultures?

6.9   *Growing Up* (1982)

Russell Baker

Russell Baker (1925–) is a political satirist whose syndicated columns have appeared in *The New York Times* and hundreds of other newspapers. Check out one of his columns so you can see for yourself how he put his wit to observations of life's trials and triumphs, which he also has done in recalling the details of his own life. *Growing Up,* his autobiography, received praise for the warmth and humor with which Baker portrayed his coming of age during the Depression years and World War II. This editor views the book as an archetypal story of a poor American boy, a White Anglo-Saxon Protestant who refuses to isolate himself from the diversity in both his immediate and his larger surroundings. The reader is able to learn alongside Baker the lessons he learns: about the power of both poverty and its antidote, education; about how to recognize where one's talents lie—and don't; and about how historical circumstances and family members—some quite quirky—can play a significant role in shaping identity, in Baker's case, as a writer.

This excerpt details an episode from Baker's early teenage years when he and his mother were living temporarily in Belleville, New Jersey, with his Uncle Allen and Aunt Pat, until his mother could set up a home of their own. His father had died, his body wasted by drinking, leaving them with so little that his mother was forced to give up Russell's younger sister to a relative. He did, however, have role models to emulate, and they are mentioned in the first part of this excerpt. In the main segment, however, you meet some of the boys that Russell went to school with, children from different ethnic and religious backgrounds who become good friends in most cases, despite their differences and the traditional prejudices of their parents.

As you read this excerpt, notice the interesting fact that it is *because* Russell is so different from his Italian American friends in terms of personality and native ability that they are attracted to each other. There is mutual respect for those differences; note also how the child becomes the parent when Russell's tolerance begins to work away at his mother's hypocrisy. What lessons for you as a teacher are contained in this excerpt from *Growing Up*?

At this time I had decided the only thing I was fit for was to be a writer, and this notion rested solely on my suspicion that I would never be fit for real work, and that writing didn't require any. My mother didn't try to discourage me, though writing was not a career just then that many ambitious parents encouraged their children to plan for.

"Writing runs in the family," she said. And it seemed to. Her mother had written poetry in the manner of Tennyson. One of her uncles had written for the *Baltimore American;* with a little more luck Uncle Charlie might have had a career on the *Brooklyn Eagle;* and Cousin Edwin was proof that writing, when done for newspapers, could make a man as rich as Midas.

"Look where Edwin James is today. If Edwin could do it, you can do it." I heard those words again and again while we toiled together over

seventh-grade English homework. She pounced like a tigress if she spotted an error in spelling or grammar, and she spotted many. I was not a sparkling writer. Once, assigned to write a composition about farm produce, I chose to write about wheat. In seventh grade they were always assigning you to write about things like farm produce. I chose to write about wheat, maybe because it seemed less boring than turnips and was easier to spell than rutabagas. My mother examined the finished product in despair.

"You can do better than this, Buddy," she said.

I didn't know how. Wheat was not Carl Hubbell pitching against Dizzy Dean at the Polo Grounds or James Cagney walking the last mile to the electric chair—subjects which fascinated me. Wheat was just—wheat. But she was insistent. She found an old geography book preserved from her teaching days for just such an emergency as this. It contained a fine discussion of wheat. I cribbed it furiously, but still failed to satisfy her. She scratched out lines, changed words, added a paragraph or two of her own, then had me rewrite it neatly. The result contained hardly a word or thought from my version.

The teacher was delighted with it. She read it aloud to my classmates. They were unmoved, but I preened shamelessly in the honor of having it read aloud as my own work. The teacher was so pleased she sent it to the *Belleville News* for possible publication as an example of the fine work being done in the school system. Several weeks later, buried inside the newspaper under the one-word headline WHEAT, this composition ran on for five or six paragraphs. At the top were the words "By Russell Baker." It was my first appearance in print. It had been ghost-written by my mother. She bought several copies of the paper, clipped out "Wheat," put a few copies of it in the mail to distant relatives, and stored two in her trunk. She had produced a budding contender for Cousin Edwin's crown of glory.

"Look where Edwin James is today—"

I did look now and then. Edwin was in New York, and from certain places in Belleville I could look out and see the top of the New York skyline piercing the far horizon. I lacked artistic inclination and had no eye for beauty, but, making my magazine rounds on roller skates, when I reached a hilltop vista which looked far out over the Hackensack Meadows, I loved to sit and stare at that fantasy rising miles and miles away through the mists. From that distance it seemed to me as dreamlike as the Emerald City of Oz. I was sitting there daydreaming late one autumn afternoon when Walter came along to beat me up.

I had been beaten up three or four times in the past by Walter for not being Irish. On the

first occasion he'd caught me on St. Patrick's Day not wearing a green necktie and bruised my ribs. Since then he'd fallen into the habit of beating me up whenever our paths crossed. The second time, figuring he hated me for not being Irish, I tried to buy peace by telling him my Aunt Pat was Irish, but it didn't satisfy him. He seemed to feel a patriotic Hibernian duty to bully me whenever we accidentally met. The result was I hated Walter and had begun to hate everything Irish, though I made an exception for Aunt Pat.

The strange thing about Walter was that he was an absolute loner. Usually you didn't have to worry about being beaten up unless you ran afoul of a whole gang. Gangs seemed to lust for battle, but a boy you didn't know never gave any trouble if he was traveling alone. Except for Walter. Walter always traveled alone. He hadn't a friend in the world so far as I could make out. I never saw him playing with a crowd on an empty lot or heading off to the movies with a pal. He went to the Catholic school in Belleville, and I had some friends there too, but I never saw them in company with Walter. Short, red-haired, not much taller than a fireplug but just as solid, he prowled the streets, taciturn and alone, looking for blood. Now, finding me sitting on the hilltop admiring the Manhattan skyline, he said, "Get up and fight."

It was no use trying to jolly Walter out of it. I'd tried that, too, but genial talk didn't interest him. He didn't seem to have any talk in him, just grunts and a few basic lines he'd picked up from movies about tough guys. Still, I didn't get up off the ground. It was dishonorable to hit a man while he was on the ground.

I tried wheedling. "What'd'ya always want to fight for?"

"I don't like your looks," he said.

This was a line I recognized from many tough-guy movies.

"I got skates on," I said. "You can't fight with skates on."

Walter bent over, grabbed me by my shirt, pulled me upright, and punched me in the stomach, and I went down again. Since he had now knocked me down from the standing position he was entitled to fall on me and pummel away, and he did, but only around my ribs and stomach. Walter had never punched me in the jaw, nose, or face, which was another strange thing about him. Most street fighters wanted to blacken your eye or bloody your nose. Not Walter. He preferred punishing the torso. I concentrated on trying to push him off me, but he was solid rock. Suddenly I felt his weight being lifted away.

Looking up, I saw my three best friends—Frankie, Nino, and Jerry—taking Walter in hand.

"What's the idea hitting a guy with skates on?" Frankie demanded. "You ought to have your teeth knocked out for that kind of fighting."

Any one of them could have done it, too, even to Walter. Or so I thought, for I envied their rippling muscularity. Sons of Italian immigrants, they'd befriended me in the classroom, taken me home to meet their parents, placed me under their protection in the schoolyard, and even engineered my election as president of our homeroom class. Aunt Pat referred to them when they weren't around as "Russell's beloved wops." The slur angered me toward her, but it was true that the affection I felt for them was close to love. Their friendship had brought me to a love of all things Italian, as Walter's bullying had caused me to hate all things Irish.

Just now, though, I had a serious problem. Although they had Walter under restraint, there was no possibility they would do what I wished they'd do and beat him senseless. This would violate the code of honor, just as Walter had violated it by hitting me with my skates on. Frankie, Nino, and Jerry weren't there to avenge me by pounding Walter black and blue but to see that the rules of honor were observed.

"We'll hold him while you get your skates off, then we'll see if he can fight clean," Frankie announced.

This was grim news. I knew too well how effectively Walter could fight, even fighting clean. I didn't mind being beaten, I was used to that with Walter, but I hated the idea of being humiliated in front of my friends. Still, Frankie was our leader, and his decision was law. I didn't dare let him see I was too timid to fight Walter.

The truth was, I was always too timid to fight. I hated fighting and did it badly because I lacked the appetite for inflicting pain. I couldn't bear to cause pain. This weakness went back to my earliest childhood in Morrisonville, when, climbing on the backyard fence one day, I stepped to the ground without looking and crushed a newborn chick under my foot. I'd screamed at the horror of it and wept for an hour in spite of my mother's assurances that it was all right, I didn't mean to do it, there were plenty of other new chicks, it happened all the time.

I'd developed a loathing for violence that made me an easy victim for the world's Walters. Now Frankie's interference meant I would have to go at Walter with the violence necessary to make it a good fight or be thought a sissy by my friends. Hating Walter's taciturn Irish stupidity for getting me into this, I unstrapped my skates, got to my feet, and balled my hands into fists.

"You ready now?" Frankie asked.

"Yeah, let him loose."

Frankie shoved Walter at me and stepped back. Freed, Walter raised his fists and started to circle as we'd seen actors do in movies about boxers. Then he dropped his fists.

"Not fair fighting four against one," Walter said.

"We're not fighting" Nino said.

"We're just watching" Frankie said.

Walter looked at the three of them.

"It's not fair watching," he said.

"Fight!" Frankie commanded, and gave him another push.

"Watching's not fair," Walter howled.

"What'r'ya, yella?" Jerry shouted.

"Not yellow," said Walter, and he got his fists up again and looked at me with an expression I'd never seen before when he was calmly beating me. Then we had been punisher and victim locked silently in idiot's solitude. Now he was plainly scared as sick as I was.

We circled each other listlessly, and one of them—Nino or Jerry—yelled to me, "Hit him! He's yellow!" and for the first time I knew the pleasure of feeling like the brute in battle. I lunged forward and swung as hard as I could at Walter's face. My fist caught him across the mouth and nose. He cried out. There was blood on his mouth and chin.

"All right," he shouted, "all right," and dropped his fists in the recognized signal of surrender. Still, certain words had to be spoken.

"You give up?" I asked.

"Give up," he said.

The code also required certain civilities once the fight was over.

"Somebody give him a handkerchief," Frankie said. "His nose is bleeding."

I gave him mine. Walter clamped it over his nose and walked off the field alone and silent. I didn't tell Frankie, but I knew Walter could have whipped me easily if they hadn't destroyed his solitude. After that, though, he never way-laid me again.

My mother didn't like my being so close to Italian boys. For one thing, friendship with Italians wasn't likely to help me make something of myself, since in Belleville Italians stood at the bottom of society. Their community, clustered on "The Hill" at the top of the town, was made up mostly of poor immigrants from southern Italy and Sicily. Though most of my classmates were native-born Americans and spoke English in the streets, they spoke Italian in their homes to parents who clung to the dialects of Naples, Calabria, and Palermo. When I first began to be accepted on The Hill, I marveled that people could talk and understand each other in sounds as meaningless to me as hen cackles. It seemed wonderful that Frankie and Nino could shift so easily from English into a language that was totally beyond me. To my mother this was not a miracle but cause for alarm.

"My God, Russell, they don't even speak the English language up there," she said once when I told her I'd been visiting on The Hill.

We quarreled off and on about the Italian problem. She never forbade me to run with Frankie or Nino or Jerry or Carmen or Joe, but for the longest time she tried by wily arts to break those friendships.

If I was off to the Saturday movies with Frankie and Nino she might say, "Why don't you ever go with any nice boys?"

I knew what she meant by "nice boys"— boys who were not Italian—and the sly knife-thrust of her bigotry infuriated me. Still, I was not cheeky enough to come back at her with the question that had formed in my mind: "How can you go to church every Sunday and talk about loving your neighbor when you hate my friends because they're Italian?"

Instead I took the mild tack—"I'm sorry you don't like my friends"—which produced another twist of the knife:

"I'm not saying I don't like your friends, Buddy. You've got a right to pick your own friends, but remember—a man is known by the company he keeps."

Most likely she didn't actually hate my friends because they were Italian; she was probably just angry at me for choosing friends who couldn't pass muster in the world of people who had made something of themselves. Maybe, in a way she didn't understand, she was angry at them, too, for being as poor as we were and so far down on the social ladder. In this quarrel, though, I had detected for the first time a flaw in her character. I didn't know the word "hypocrisy," but this was the crime I silently charged her with. She insisted we go to church to improve my character, and it angered me that she should slip disgracefully from the gospel of brotherly love after the Sunday singing and praying were over and brotherly love was put to the test of daily life. Until now she had done all the improving on me; now I tried my hand on her. Determined to bring her around on the Italian question, I found ways of luring my friends to the New Street house when I knew she'd be home. This was not easy, but gradually I persuaded Nino and Frankie to come by and sit on our porch steps, and after a while I got them to enter the house.

Their introduction to my mother was a triumph. Frankie, whose manly power to charm women was always impressive, received the highest accolade in my mother's power. "He's just like Tom Sawyer," she said. Frankie had won her over by telling her I was the smartest person in school.

Questions for Discussion and Debate

1. Identify the influences that steered Russell in the direction of becoming a writer. (Note both the internal and the external influences.) Relate these kinds of influences to your choice to become a teacher, if, indeed, teaching is your goal. Share with the class those influences that affected *your* decision.

2. Describe the kinds of boys with whom Russell hung out. How were they the same as and different from him? Recall the friends you had in elementary and middle school. Did you also find yourself with friends who differed from you in some ways? Discuss the influence of schools in terms of whom we befriend. Do schools play a role in bringing people of different backgrounds together?

3. You have likely heard the expression, "You've got to be carefully taught," as it relates to prejudice as an attitude children learn from their environment and families. The expression is the title of a song in the Rodgers and Hammerstein musical, *South Pacific*, in which discrimination against Asians is an issue. However, Russell doesn't share his mother's views of his ethnic friends. Why doesn't he? Discuss why you think his mother harbors such attitudes. Why do you think some children learn all too well the prejudices of their parents, while others do not?

4. What is hypocrisy? In what way is Baker's mother hypocritical? Discuss your own experiences with hypocrisy. Have you seen it among teachers? Others? Have you seen its effects? Explain.

5. The initial insecurity, fear, and poverty of new immigrants to this country have frequently resulted in their taking out their frustrations on the next wave of immigrants. Debate this question: Is this pattern inevitable and unavoidable?

6. Describe yourself in terms of the categories of race, ethnicity, religion, class, and so on. How has your identity affected your life? Explain.

Activities and Projects

1. The violence portrayed in this excerpt is child's play compared to the violence of gangs who have replaced fists with guns. In addition to the victims of gang warfare who are themselves members of gangs, hundreds of innocent children in inner cities are killed in crossfire nearly every week. Indeed, the culture of the gang has in many cases replaced the role usually played by one's native or adopted culture, within which certain traditions and beliefs can provide security and an identity. Many teenagers who choose to belong to gangs have had difficulties straddling two cultures. Alienation often results when a person is in limbo between two cultures, connected to one and not feeling welcomed into the other. Teenagers in this situation seek out the gang, where they will be accepted and offered a concrete identity. Inner-city African American, Hispanic, and other students who are surrounded by the frustrations of poverty, discrimination, and the ever-present gang culture often find it hard to resist the pressure to belong. Gun violence is now the leading cause of death among African American teenagers, who are five times more likely than European American males to be gunshot victims (Children's Defense Fund, 1996, pp. 1–2).

   Do research on the culture of gangs. Share what you find out about their origins and their role within certain ethnic groups.

2. Others in class could do research on programs that have been created to deal with gangs, programs that help steer at-risk teenagers into more constructive options. Have any of these programs been successful? If so, why? If not, why not?

3. Biographies and autobiographies, like Baker's, are excellent sources for learning about the famous people within *your* subject area who are from diverse as well as more traditional backgrounds. For example, if you are teaching mathematics or science, have your students read a biography of a mathematician or scientist. This method is one of the best ways to make a subject come alive, to bring across the point that there is flesh and blood in their studies. Share with the class a biography or autobiography that inspired you or that they might use in the classroom.

4. This excerpt is ripe for dramatization. Write scenarios based on it or improvise Baker's episode. Again, think about such an activity for *your* students after they read a biography or autobiography of someone related to the subject they're studying. Have them act out a significant scene—perhaps the turning point—in the person's life. And, again, try to select biographies of relevant people from diverse backgrounds.

5. What are some strategies for teachers who want to ensure that the cultural differences among their students have positive effects on student learning?

6.10 | Having Our Say: The Delany Sisters' First 100 Years (1993)

Sadie and Bessie Delany

Sadie Delany was a New York City schoolteacher, one of the first African American teachers at Theodore Roosevelt High School, or as she would put it, one of the first "colored" teachers, since that term usually was not considered offensive during the first part of the 20th century. Her sister Bessie was also a pioneer, becoming the first African American female dentist. In 1993 when their book was published, they were 103 and 101, respectively. "Their story traced the rise of the Black middle class and their determination to join the ranks of the first African American professional women" (Saunders, 1997).

The success of their book was followed by a play based on the book and then a second best-seller, *The Delany Sisters' Book of Everyday Wisdom*. After Bessie died in 1996 at age 104, Sadie wrote another book, *On My Own at 107* (1997), in which she described her life since her sister's death. Sadie Delany died in January 1999 at age 109.

In this summary of Chapter 18 ("Sadie," pp. 116–121) of *Having Our Say*, Sarah, or Sadie as she refers to herself, recounts how she became a public schoolteacher and achieved self-respect despite the many obstacles she faced, mostly on account of her color. Her disposition, feistiness, and intelligence played a role in achieving her goals. But she attributed her ability to work within the system and tolerate abuse to her father, who modeled for her how to cope with institutional racism. He told her simply that the way to succeed was "to be better at what you did than any of your white competition," without being smug about it (p. 116). He had done just that and in 1918 had earned the respected position of bishop within his church.

As you read this summary, note other factors that may have provided Sadie with the means of overcoming prejudice. Have times changed much since Sadie was a teacher? What questions would you haved liked to ask her?

Sadie got her first teaching job in a "mostly colored" elementary school, P.S. 119, in Harlem in 1920. Black teachers were not wanted in White schools because parents usually objected. The principals kept Black teachers out of their schools by saying that hiring teachers with Southern accents could damage the children, and, of course, "most of us colored teachers at the time had Southern accents" (p. 118). But Sadie, armed with the wisdom of her father, found a way around that and began taking elocution lessons from a white woman, even though each time she would go to the woman's apartment, the doorman made her take the freight elevator.

She was an enterprising young woman, and to make some additional money—her annual teaching salary was $1500—she made cakes and candy, "Delany's Delights," and sold them

From *Having Our Say, the Delany Sisters' First 100 Years* by Sarah and A. Elizabeth Delany with Amy Hill Hearth. New York: Kodansha International, 1993, pp. 116–121.

all over New York, including at Abraham and Straus, a popular department store.

Eventually Sadie decided that she wanted to teach high school, which paid better and was considered a promotion, but again, there were "brick walls set up for colored folks" (p. 119). Once more, though, she got around the obstacles. After waiting 3 years to get to the top of the seniority list, Sadie received a letter from the Board of Education saying that they wished to meet her in person. She knew, however, that if she showed up and they saw that she was colored, they would find some reason for not hiring her, so she didn't go. Instead, Sadie sent the Board a letter making up some excuse for her absence and—because of the way bureaucracies work or, rather, don't work—she decided that it was worth taking the chance of just showing up on the first day of school. In the fall, when she arrived at the all-White Theodore Roosevelt High School, "they just about died. . . . A colored woman!" (p. 120). But her name was, indeed, on the list and it was too late for them to replace her. "Once I was in," she reported, "they couldn't figure out how to get rid of me" (p. 120).

So Sarah Delany became the "first colored teacher in the New York City system to teach domestic science on the high school level" (p. 120). And for the rest of her career she taught at three other excellent high schools including a night job teaching adults at Washington Irving High School in lower Manhattan. She got that job by being more dependable and cooperative than the woman for whom she had been substituting. "But that's the way you get ahead, child," Amy Hill Hearth records Sadie as saying (p. 120).

Sarah Delany completed her master's degree in education at Columbia in 1925 and continued to enjoy teaching, though, she said, as a colored teacher she was always given the toughest kids. And, she notes, she often got lonely, being the only colored teacher in her school. Even though the White teachers were friendly, she couldn't count on their real friendship. For example, she recalled one teacher who befriended her, then snubbed her one day and went off with her White friends, leaving Sadie standing there to watch them go off together. The woman had not wanted the others to know she had a colored friend. But just as her father before her, Sadie recognized the hypocrisy but didn't let it get her down. She even remained on good terms with the woman. Had it been her sister, Bessie, on the other hand, well, Bessie "'wouldn't have had nothing more to do with her this side of Glory!' Bessie would have given her a piece of her mind. Sure, it annoyed me. But I didn't let it ruin my day. Life is short, and it's up to you to make it sweet" (p. 121).

Sadie Delany said she owed her attitude and her comfort with who she was to her parents; she was bewildered by the discomfort others had with who they were, for example, the Negro ladies who got their hair straightened and the White ladies who got their hair curled. She had no desire to change who she was, and it was with this philosophy that she became for others—as her father had been for her—a model of how, gently and slowly, to make true progress for herself and her people.

Questions for Discussion and Debate

1. What obstacles faced Sadie as she strove to become a respected teacher? Cite all of the examples of prejudice she faced, all of which potentially could have led her to give up her goals. How did she deal with each obstacle?

2. What personality characteristics and behaviors did Sadie possess that got her through difficult times?

3. Sadie says, "If I can get ahead, doesn't that help my people?" This gives us some insight into the unusual weight that minority members carry through life: Rather than being judged as individuals they are seen as representatives of a group. Discuss this phenomenon and its potential effects on someone in Sadie's situation or in an even less advantageous position.

4. In terms of dealing with White people like the woman who snubs Sadie because of her color, whose approach do you think is preferable, Sadie's or Bessie's? Why?

5. Educators often debate about which level is more demanding in terms of teaching. Sadie says that the high-school schedule is more demanding than the elementary-school schedule. Is this true? Is so, why? If not, why not? (Try to talk with teachers who have taught at both levels.)

6. This summary reveals the obstacles Sadie faced not only as a Black person but also as a woman. Historically, women weren't even considered for high-school positions, and once they were hired, many school systems actually paid them less money than men earned for the same work. Does discrimination or sexism still exist in the teaching profession? Explore this question by talking with teachers at all levels.

7. Is there an argument to be made for or against affirmative action based on Sadie's story? Explain.

8. If you had the chance to talk to Sadie, what questions would you like to ask her?

Activities and Projects

1. Sadie and Bessie were young adults during the 1920s and 1930s, the period of the Harlem Renaissance. Do research on this time period. What was the Harlem Renaissance, and how did it affect the status of African Americans in New York and in the rest of the country? Did you learn about this historic period in school? Would including this period in the history, English, and arts curricula be appropriate? Why? Why not? Hold a discussion about the implications of such curricula for changing preconceived biased attitudes. What other topics can serve a similar purpose?

2. In a video store, locate the film *White Man's Burden* and watch it with your class. The film depicts a role reversal, with Whites being the underclass and African Americans the middle and upper class who wield power over Whites. What is your reaction to the film? What do you learn from it? Discuss it with your peers. Can such films teach tolerance? What other films would be useful? The class could be divided into groups, with one researching appropriate films for teaching tolerance to young children; another, films for upper-elementary and middle-school students; and the third, such films for high-school students.

3. Find out what colleges and state education departments are doing, if anything, to recruit more minorities into teaching. Do you believe this recruitment is necessary? Why or why not?

4. Sadie's story about being snubbed by the White teacher in favor of her White girlfriends brings to mind what is commonly

seen in lunchrooms, playgrounds, and multiracial classrooms: Whites tending to cluster with Whites, and Blacks with Blacks. Why does this happen? Is it necessarily a sign of intolerance? Should teachers try to change this phenomenon? Interview students and teachers about this situation and report the results of your survey.

5. Eliot Abramson was a teacher who was concerned about the stereotyping and segregation that continued within classrooms even after integration was achieved in 1954. He discovered that in heterogeneous, multiracial classrooms with students on different socioeconomic levels, attitudes toward the minorities were still stereotypical. So he developed a strategy that he called the *jigsaw approach* to cooperative learning. The teacher establishes groups made up of diverse students in which every student in the class is able to become an expert on a fixed portion of the topic under study. Having received the support of their smaller group in learning the fixed portion, students then join another group in which they teach peers what they have mastered. Abramson observed that children who once had been stereotyped as not being smart were succeeding, and as a result, peer attitudes toward them were also changing. Find out more about the jigsaw approach and other cooperative learning methods that could be useful in developing an appreciation among students for the diversity in their midst.

6. Including women in the curriculum is, believe it or not, a rather recent phenomenon, and therefore, the following names may not be as familiar to you as the names of their male counterparts. How many of these American women do you know, and when and how did you learn about them? Circle the names of the women whose contributions you *can* identify.

a. Divide the names on the list among the class so that they and you can locate information about some of these women and their contributions. Consult history texts and other sources.

b. Bring the information you gather about your portion of the list to class, and decide with your peers which of the women's contributions should be better integrated into textbooks.

c. Discuss the reasons why many of the women on the list were not known to you and the class before you did the research (i.e., Who wrote most of the history books? What laws existed that deprived women of equal rights? What attitudes still remain?).

1. Betty Friedan
2. Louisa May Alcott
3. Florence Nightingale
4. Rachel Carson
5. Martha Graham
6. Clara Barton
7. Margaret Fuller
8. Helen Keller
9. Barbara Fritchie
10. Annie Sullivan
11. Elizabeth Peabody
12. Mary Lyons
13. Emma Willard
14. Jane Addams
15. Anna Howard Shaw
16. Dorothea Dix
17. Mother Jones
18. Gertrude Stein
19. Phyllis Wheatley
20. Beverly Sills
21. Sojourner Truth
22. Francis Perkins
23. Margaret Sanger
24. Harriet Tubman
25. Bessie Smith

26. Lillian Wald
27. Julia Lathrop
28. Florence Sabin
29. Lydia Maria Child
30. Mary Elizabeth Lease
31. Sandra Day O'Connor
32. Sacajawea
33. Elizabeth Cady Stanton
34. Lucretia Mott
35. Lucy Stone
36. Susan B. Anthony
37. Ma Rainey
38. Lucy Parsons
39. Emma Goldman
40. Mary Mcleod Bethune
41. Dorothea Lange
42. Sarah Winnemucca
43. Dolores Huerta
44. Emily Dickinson
45. Mary Cassatt
46. Mildred Didrickson Zaharias (Babe)
47. Elizabeth Gurley Flynn
48. Eleanor Roosevelt
49. Alice Paul
50. Elizabeth Blackwell
51. Amelia Earhart
52. Margaret Mead
53. Althea Gibson
54. Rosa Parks
55. Martha Berry
56. Deborah Sampson
57. Mahalia Jackson
58. Jeanette Rankin
59. Bessie Coleman
60. Nellie Bly
61. Eleanor Holmes Norton
62. Maria Mitchell
63. Buffy Ste. Marie
64. Anne Hutchinson
65. Janet Guthrie
66. Sally Ride
67. Margaret Bourke-White

68. Annie Smith Peck
69. Nancy Lopez
70. Ida Tarbell
71. Victoria Woodhull
72. Maria Martinez
73. Shirley Chisholm
74. Maria Tallchief
75. Annie Wauneka
76. Grimke Sisters
77. Elizabeth Kübler-Ross
78. Joan Baez
79. Ella Grasso
80. Mumbet
81. Fanny Kemble
82. Edith Wharton
83. Catherine Sedgwick
84. Madeline Kunin
85. Florence Kelley
86. Dorothy Day
87. Anna Louise Strong
88. Abigail Adams
89. Mother Seton
90. Helen Hayes
91. Marion Anderson
92. Margaret Chase
93. Ida Wells
94. Juliette Low
95. Golda Meir
96. Carrie Chapman Catt
97. Belva Lockwood
98. Emma Lazarus
99. Julia Ward Howe
100. Harriet Beecher Stowe

7. Study the chart on p. 366 and write a paragraph in which you explain the overall messages it conveys. Then find out what reforms have been made to bring about more equality and place those reforms in the appropriate columns at the bottom of the chart.

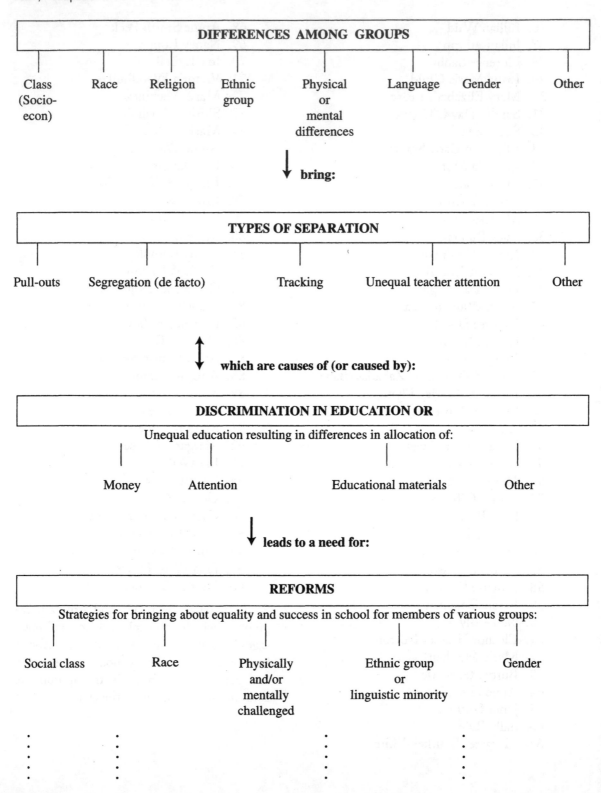

DIFFERENCES AMONG GROUPS

Class (Socio-econ)   Race   Religion   Ethnic group   Physical or mental differences   Language   Gender   Other

↓ bring:

TYPES OF SEPARATION

Pull-outs   Segregation (de facto)   Tracking   Unequal teacher attention   Other

↕ which are causes of (or caused by):

DISCRIMINATION IN EDUCATION OR

Unequal education resulting in differences in allocation of:

Money   Attention   Educational materials   Other

↓ leads to a need for:

REFORMS

Strategies for bringing about equality and success in school for members of various groups:

Social class   Race   Physically and/or mentally challenged   Ethnic group or linguistic minority   Gender

6.11 *Willow and Twig* (2000)

Jean Little

Calvin, or Twig, as he is called, is 4 years old and hearing impaired, a result of the physical abuse he experienced when he was 2 years old. Some people think he is "re-tarded" or "demented" when he starts to scream and kick (Little, 2000, p. 201). His sister, Willow, is the only one who can comfort him, but his grandmother, Gram, is learning fast. In this children's book by Jean Little, a prize-winning Canadian author, who is herself visually impaired, a brother and sister are deserted on the streets of Vancouver by their addicted mother. They make their way to Ontario, where they test the patience and love of their grandmother, their sometimes hostile Aunt Constance, and their eccentric Uncle Hum, who, in the following excerpt appears to be a very wise man.

Exceptional children and adolescents have experienced many of the same forms of discrimination as the culturally diverse people you have read about in this chapter, and for similar reasons: They differ in some way from the majority, many among the major-ity are ignorant about those differences, and ignorance leads to fear. While such atti-tudes persist to some extent, legislation has provided exceptional learners with many of the opportunities they were denied for decades. For example, with the Education of the Handicapped Law, Public Law 94-142, Part B, known as the Mainstreaming Law (1975), come provisions that protect the rights of the disabled, including the right to a "free and appropriate education." (The 1990 Individuals with Disabilities Education Act [IDEA] amended the former law by changing the term *handicapped* to *with disabilities*.)

The lesson that schools—and the general public—can learn both from this book and from such legislation is that diversity is a *natural* part of our environment. Jean Little—in a scene at the end of the book—describes how Twig and his neighbor, Matthew Marr, "knew each other very well and took their differences for granted" (p. 200).

In the following excerpt, Willow's uncle helps her to understand that she can do her part to offset fear and ignorance by talking to her new friend, Sabrina Marr, about Twig's disabilities. Willow is reluctant to do so because she doesn't know how her friend will respond. Have you ever had to gather the courage to tell a difficult truth? Is Willow's uncle asking her to do the right thing? Perhaps before reading the excerpt, members of the class might discuss their own experiences working and playing with exceptional children and/or what it has been like for those in the class who, like Twig, have special needs.

"Willow, have you talked to Sabrina about Twig?"

. . . "What about Twig?"

"Have you told her he has a hearing disability? Have you talked with her about your life before you came here?"

"No."

He said nothing, just let the silence grow.

"I . . . I don't know what to say. I mean, she thinks he's weird."

"Well, face it, child. You'd think he was pretty strange yourself if you knew nothing about what makes him the way he is. Are you ashamed of him?"

Willow stopped walking, anger blazing up in her.

"No, Goddamnit!" she yelled. "Of course not. Why should I be? I love him. He's my brother."

Uncle Hum amazed her by chuckling.

"Con's my sister and I love her but I have to admit I find myself embarrassed by her often," he said. "I think you owe it to your brother to talk openly about his disabilities and abilities. Matthew Marr and he might be friends. He needs children to play with, you know. You've been his mother and his teacher and his rock, all rolled into one. You'll always be closer to him than anyone else, I think, but everybody needs more than one other person."

Silence came again as Willow struggled with her muddled feelings. At last, she said feebly, "How will I begin?"

"Just plunge in. If you stick to the truth, you can't go wrong. I suspect rumours will be winging around Ponsonby School about your brother and it's always best to scotch a rumour before it's loose and there's no catching up with it. We could talk a bit about what you might say, if you like?"

Willow nodded and then remembered he couldn't see.

"Yes," she said hurriedly. "I don't know how much to tell."

"What matters is that he has a severe hearing loss in one ear and a moderate loss in the other. He is also ADHD, we think. It means Attention Deficit Hyperactivity Disorder."

"What?" Willow interrupted, startled. "Say that again. Slowly."

Uncle Hum did and went on to explain.

"It's why he has trouble sitting still, has difficulty focusing his attention on things in which he isn't intensely interested. It's why he finds it very hard switching from one activity to another."

"Why is he like that? Is it . . . Was it the drugs?"

"Probably. You were born before your mother got hooked but Twig spent eleven months dependent on drugs."

"Eleven months . . ."

"When he was in the womb, every time she had a fix, so did he. If she hallucinated, he shared it somehow. . . .

"It may not have been the drugs," he went on when she did not speak. "Sometimes it just happens for no known reason. Twig's frustration with his struggles sets him screaming sometimes. I'm sure the Marrs have heard him once in a while and been anxious. To tell the truth, that's what set me on to talk this over with you. Sabrina's mother inquired, ever so hesitantly, what was wrong with the little boy when Sirius and I went over to get eggs. She knew we couldn't be abusing him but she'd never heard such a prolonged rumpus, I guess."

Willow went stiff with fury and then forced herself to relax. If she had lived next door, she'd have wondered too. So Sabrina must be dying of curiosity. She'd done well to keep quiet this long. It must be killing her.

Uncle Hum laughed. "I can feel you wanting to screech yourself," he said. "But curiosity is an admirable trait really. The thing you must do is open up to Sabrina and do your best to keep calm while you're doing it. It's nothing to be ashamed of; it's something to be understood. My blindness is like Twig's deafness. We have nothing to be ashamed of but we both need special help sometimes. As he gets older, you'll have to help him know how to tell people about himself."

They went on talking even after they were home again, until Willow felt she could handle discussing her brother calmly. She even knew it would be a relief. . . .

Questions for Discussion and Debate

1. What advice does Uncle Hum give Willow? What is his rationale? Do you agree with him? What is Willow's response to his advice?

2. What are the characteristics of ADHD according to Uncle Hum? Have you encountered children or adults with ADHD? If so, share your observations with the rest of the class.

3. The controversial drug, Ritalin, is often prescribed to counter the behavior of children with ADHD. Debate the use of this drug.

(First read some of the studies that have been carried out on its use and/or talk to parents and teachers who are familiar with Ritalin.)

4. Discuss with your peers any information you have learned thus far in courses dealing with the teaching of children and adolescents with special needs. Together make a list of questions you *still* have about how best to serve the special-needs students you will be teaching within your classes.

Activities and Projects

1. Reread the excerpt from *The Miracle Worker* (Selection 5.9) and item 1 under Activities and Projects there, which suggests that you survey the area in which you live or attend school to see what special schools exist and what the local attitudes toward mainstreaming are. If you have not already done so, consider carrying out this project.

2. There are more than 5 million exceptional learners in America (U.S. Department of Education, 1995), who fall into categories such as gifted and talented students and students with special needs, that is, mentally retarded, sensory-impaired, physically disabled, and learning-disabled students and

those with emotional and behavioral disorders, attention deficit disorders, and communication disorders. Within each of these categories are subgroups indicating still other characteristics that require careful diagnosis. While determining which students fall within a particular group may be a useful process in securing an appropriate IEP (Individual Education Plan), such labeling might also have negative effects, that is, discriminatory or pejorative connotations. To minimize this possibility, the terminology related to exceptional learners has changed periodically. For example, the term *handicapped* is currently unacceptable in some circles.

a. Analyze the reasons for the changes in terminology and discuss whether or not such changes do, in fact, decrease negativity.

b. Who are the people and groups playing a role in making these changes?

c. Discuss the pros and cons of applying labels in the first place.

3. Do research on the legislation and court decisions related to the rights of students with special needs. Share with the class *three* of the most significant laws or decisions and, together, assess whether or not there is need for additional reform. (Gather related information by visiting the web site, http://www.ld.org. Organizations such as the National Center for Learning Disabilities can be accessed via this site.)

4. In the novel, *Willow and Twig,* Jean Little implies that there are difficult questions to address even after a child's condition has been diagnosed. For example, in Twig's case, there was the question of what setting would best address his needs, a regular classroom or a separate therapeutic environment? Once the best environment is selected, then there is the issue of the best methods to employ. In Twig's case, was sign language a better method than lip reading? Imagine that you are teaching a class in which you have several children with special needs. Do research or interviews with teachers of special-needs children to find out what criteria *they* use in deciding which methods are most appropriate. Share your findings with the class.

Chapter References

Allport, G. (1958). *The nature of prejudice.* Garden City, NY: Doubleday.

Angelou, M. (1971). *I know why the caged bird sings.* New York: Bantam.

Another book for the over-100 set. (1997, May 5). *New York Teacher,* 11.

Applebome, P. (1997, March 1). Dispute over Ebonics reflects a volatile mix that roils urban education. *The New York Times,* p. 10.

Ashton-Warner, S. (1958). *Spinster.* New York: Simon & Schuster.

Ashton-Warner, S. (1963). *Teacher.* New York: Simon & Schuster.

Ashton-Warner, S. (1972). *Spearpoint: "Teacher" in America.* New York: Alfred A. Knopf.

Ashton-Warner, S. (1979). *I passed this way.* New York: Alfred A. Knopf.

Baker, R. (1982). *Growing up.* New York: New American Library.

Banks, J. A., & McGee Banks, C. A. (Eds.). (1997). *Multicultural education: Issues and perspectives* (3rd ed.). Boston: Allyn & Bacon.

Barzun, J. (1955). *Teacher in America.* New York: Doubleday.

Bennett, W. J. (1992). *The devaluing of America: The fight for our culture and our children.* New York: Simon & Schuster.

Bigelow, B., et al. (Eds.). (1995). *Rethinking our classrooms: Teaching for equity and justice.* Wisconsin: Rethinking Schools.

Bloom, A. (1987). *The closing of the American mind.* New York: Simon & Schuster.

Bloom, H. (1994). *The western Canon. The books and the school of the ages.* New York: Harcourt Brace.

Brown v. Board of Education of Topeka, Kansas. (1955). 349 U.S. 294, 75 S.Ct. 753.

Cheney, L. V. (1995). *Telling the truth: Why our schools, culture and country have stopped making sense and what we can do about it.* New York: Simon & Schuster.

Children's Defense Fund. (1992). *The state of America's children, 1992.* Washington, DC: Author.

Delany, S. (1997). *On my own at 107.* New York: HarperCollins.

Delany, S., & Delany, A. E., with Hearth, A. H. (1993). *Having our say, the Delaney sisters' first 100 years.* New York: Kodansha International.

D'Souza, D. (1992). *Illiberal education: The politics of race and sex on campus.* New York: Random House.

DuBois, W. E. B. (1904). *The souls of black folk.* Chicago: A. C. McClurg.

Freire, P. (1993). *Pedagogy of the oppressed.* New York: Continuum.

Gardner, H. (1983). *Frames of mind: The theory of multiple intelligences.* New York: Basic Books.

Gilligan, C., Lyons, N., & Hanmer, T. (Eds.). (1990). *Making connections: The relational worlds of adolescent girls at Emma Willard School.* Cambridge, MA: Harvard University Press.

Gollnick, D. M., & Chinn, P. C. (1998). *Multicultural education in a pluralistic society.* Columbus, OH: Merrill.

Grant, C. A., & Gomez, M. L. (1996). *Making schooling multicultural: Campus and classroom.* Upper Saddle River, NJ: Prentice Hall.

Graves, R. (1961). Warning to children [Poem]. In O. Williams (Ed.), *A pocket book of modern verse.* New York: Washington Square Press.

Green, J. (1991, October 13). This school is out: At Harvey Milk, a high school for gay students, lessons are taught in grammar, algebra, and survival." *The New York Times Magazine.* p. 32.

Henry, W. A., III. (1990, April 9). *Beyond the melting pot. Time, 135*(15), 28–31.

Hirsch, E. D. (1987). *Cultural literacy: What every American needs to know.* Boston: Houghton Mifflin.

Johnson, J., & Immerwahr, J. (1994–1995). First things first: What Americans expect from the public schools. *American Educator, 18*(4), 4–6, 8, 11–13, 44–45.

Knapp, M. S., & Shields, P. M. (Eds.). (1990). *Better schooling for the children of poverty: Alternatives to conventional wisdom.* Berkeley, CA: McCutchan.

Lehrer, T. (1981). National brotherhood week [Song]. In *Too many songs by Tom Lehrer.* New York: Pantheon Books.

Lewis, R. B., & Doorlag, D. H. (1995). *Teaching special students in the mainstream.* Columbus, OH: Merrill.

Little, J. (2000). *Willow and twig.* Toronto, Ontario, Canada: Penguin.

The Norman Rockwell album. (1961). Garden City, NY: Doubleday.

Potok, C. (1967). *The chosen.* New York: Fawcett.

Rofes, E. (1997). Gay issues, schools, and the right-wing backlash. *Rethinking Schools, 11*(3), 1, 4–6.

Rose, M. (1989). *Lives on the boundary.* New York: Free Press.

Sadker, D. M., & Sadker, M. (1994). *Failing at fairness: How America's schools cheat girls.* New York: Macmillan.

Saunders, S. (1997, November 17). After-school program helps students forge bonds and other masterpieces. *New York Teacher, 39*(6), 28.

Shanker, A. (1997, March 24). Keeping public education together. *New York Teacher,* 6.

Shor, I. (1987). *Culture wars: School and society in the conservative restoration. 1969–1984.* New York: Routledge.

Steinbeck, J. (1966). *America and Americans.* New York: Viking.

Takaki, R. (1993). *A different mirror: A history of multicultural America.* New York: Little, Brown.

Tauber, P. (1997, November 2). The cynic who never soured [Tom Lehrer]. *The New York Times Magazine,* p. 50.

U.S. Department of Education. (1996). *Digest of education statistics 1995.* Washington, DC: U.S. Government Printing Office.

Villegas, A. M. (1991). *Culturally responsive pedagogy for the 1990s and beyond.* Princeton, NJ: Educational Testing Service.

Washington, B. T. (1907). *The future of the American Negro.* Boston: Small, Maynard.

Yardley, J. (1997, November 16). School sheds stigma and renews dedication. *The New York Times, 147*(50), p. 1.

Zaret, H. & Singer, L. (1957). *Little songs on big subjects.* New York: Argosy Music.

Additional Readings

Anderson, C. C., with Nicklas, S., & Crawford, A. (1998). *Global understandings: A framework for teaching and learning.* Alexandria, VA: Association for Supervision and Curriculum Development.

Banks, J. A., & Banks, C. A. (Eds.). (1995). *Handbook of research on multicultural education.* New York: Macmillan.

Chartock, R. K. (1991). Identifying local links to the world. *Educational Leadership, 48*(7), 50–52.

Colangelo, N., Dustin, D., & Foxley, C. (Eds.). (1985). *Multicultural nonsexist education: A human relations approach.* Dubuque, IA: Kendall–Hunt.

Cruz, G., Jordan, S., Melendez, J., Ostrowski, S., & Purves, A. C. (1997). *Beyond the culture tours. Studies in teaching and learning with culturally diverse texts.* Mahwah, NJ: Lawrence Erlbaum Associates.

Friend, M., & Bursuck, W. D. (1996). *Including students with special needs: A practical guide for classroom teachers.* Boston: Allyn & Bacon.

Gay, G. (2000). *Culturally responsive teaching: Theory, research, and practice.* New York: Teachers College Press.

Greene, M. (1993). *Freedom's plow: Teaching in the multicultural classroom.* New York: Routledge.

Harbeck, K. (1997). *Gay and lesbian educators: Personal freedom, public constraints.* Malden, MA: Amethyst Press.

Hollins, E. R. (Ed.). (1996). *Transforming curriculum for a culturally diverse society.* Mahwah, NJ: Lawrence Erlbaum Associates.

Kleinfeld, J. (1995). *Guide to foundations in action: Videocases: Teaching and learning in multicultural settings.* Boston: Allyn & Bacon.

Lazear, D. (1992). *Seven ways of teaching: The artistry of teaching with multiple intelligences.* Palatine, IL: IRI/Skylight.

McAdams, R. (1993). *Lessons from abroad: How other countries educate their children.* Lancaster, PA: Technomic.

McCarty, T. L. (2002). *A place to be Navajo. Rough Rock and the struggle for self-determination in indigenous schooling.* Mahwah, NJ: Lawrence Erlbaum Associates.

McIntyre, A. (1996). *Making meaning of whiteness: Exploring racial identity with white teachers.* Albany: State University of New York Press.

Nieto, S. (1992). *Affirming diversity: The sociopolitical context of multicultural education.* New York: Longman.

Shimahara, N. K., et al. (2002). *Ethnicity, race, and nationality in education.* Mahwah, NJ: Lawrence Erlbaum Associates.

Shulman, J. H., & Mesa-Bains, A. (Eds.). (1994). *Diversity in the classroom. A casebook for teachers and teacher educators.* Mahwah, NJ: Lawrence Erlbaum Associates.

Sleeter, C. E., & Grant, C. (1988). *Making choices for multicultural education: Five approaches to race, class and gender.* Columbus, OH: Merrill.

Valenzuela, A. (1999). *Subtractive schooling: U.S.–Mexican youth and the politics of caring.* Albany: State University of New York Press.

Walsh, C. E. (Ed.). (1996). *Education reform and social change. Multicultural voices, struggles and visions.* Mahwah, NJ: Lawrence Erlbaum Associates.

Weinberg, M. (1997). *Asian-American education. Historical background and current realities.* Mahwah, NJ: Lawrence Erlbaum Associates.

Women's Educational Media. (1996). *It's elementary: Talking about gay issues in school* [Video]. (Available from Women's Educational Media, 2180 Bryant Street, No. 203, San Francisco, CA 94110 [415-641-4632].)

Web Sites

American Forum for Global Education: www.globaled.org

The Civil Rights Project, Harvard University: www.law.harvard.edu/civilrights

Education for Social Responsibility: www.esrnational.org

Gender Issues (American Association of University Women): http://www.aauw.org

National Center for Education Statistics: http://nces.ed.gov/pubsearch

Public Law 94-142 (law governing education for students with special needs): http://www. ridgewater.mnscu.edu

Teaching Children About Democratic Values Through Literature: www.foxberry.net/rbutler/dept/bio.html

Teaching Tolerance: www.teachingtolerance. org

United Nations Report on Education Efforts Around the World: www.unesco.org/education/efa/monitoring/pdf/monitoring-report_en.pdf

---

Concluding Activity

You have just completed a text in which you learned about education and teaching from the creative works of outstanding individuals past and present, including writers, artists, philosophers, and others. You also hopefully expanded your knowledge of education by completing the questions and activities that followed each of the works.

Now, in this concluding activity, you have an opportunity to reflect on what you have learned and to express that learning in a creation of your own, perhaps using one of the formats included in the text. In addition to drawing on these sources for inspiration, think about your experiences as a student and future teacher. You could, for example, write a short story about a fictional student or teacher whose actions convey a belief about education that you hold, in much the same way that Conroy, Hilton, or Smith did in their novels. Or you could write an essay or poem in which you express your conception of curriculum or of teaching just as Montessori, Emerson, and Whitman did in their writing. Or if you are artistically inclined, you might paint a scene from which a viewer could derive your perspective on one or more aspects of education. Whatever you decide to do, try to identify which of the contents in this text influenced you the most, since there may be ways to integrate those influences or that wisdom into your own work.

Before carrying out this concluding activity, try brainstorming. Jot down the first voices from this book and from your own educational experiences that come to your mind. Then reflect on the beliefs you now hold. Finally, use all of this raw material to shape a personal expression that can teach something to others. Consider submitting your work for publication in a journal or another appropriate periodical.

Enjoy the process, and it is my hope that you discover the satisfaction that comes with teaching and making a difference in the lives of students. Perhaps you already have.

Appendix A

Debate Format

Learning through Teamwork and Formal Argument

Parts of a Debate

Constructive Speeches: By all four speakers—two affirmative, two negative.

Cross-Examinations: Follow each speech—done by member of opposition.

Rebuttals: Closing remarks by one member of each side.

Speakers are permitted to use notecards and reference materials during their presentations.

What Is a Constructive Speech?

All speakers begin their speeches with this:

We of the affirmative/negative team believe/do not believe that (state the resolution)....

- Speaker 1 on the affirmative side defines the terms of the resolution and makes a strong case for the resolution by providing evidence and data in support of resolution.
- Speaker 1 on the negative side does the same for his or her side.
- Speaker 2 on the affirmative side proposes a detailed plan by which the resolution can effectively be carried out.
- Speaker 2 on the negative side knocks down the affirmative plan point by point.

What Is the Nature of Cross-Examination?

When a team member cross-examines the opposition, he or she must only question and not continue making his or her case. The examiner, however, has the power to point out weaknesses in the opposition by asking selective questions and limiting the time the opposition has to answer.

What Is a Rebuttal?

A rebuttal is the final opportunity for each side both to restate main points and to put down the opposition's major arguments.

Debate Sequence

Symbols: #1 = First speaker
#2 = Second speaker
CS = Constructive speech
CE = Cross-examination
A = Affirmative
N = Negative

Constructive speeches are often 5 minutes long and cross-examinations are often 3 minutes. Plan according to the length of the class session. A whole debate can be carried out in less than 1 hour. A less formal structure could also be considered using a similar sequence.

You will need a timekeeper.

Sequence

Speaker or element	Activity and/or time
1. Affirmative #1	CS: 5 minutes
2. Negative #1	CE of A#1: 3 minutes
3. Negative #1	CS: 5 minutes
4. Affirmative #1	CE of N#1: 3 minutes
5. Affirmative #2	CS: 5 minutes
6. Negative #2	CE of A#2: 3 minutes
7. Negative #2	CS: 5 minutes
8. Affirmative #2	CE of N#2: 3 minutes
9. Preparation of rebuttals	3 minutes

A#1 and A#2/N#1 and N#2 go to respective "corners" to plan rebuttal; only one speaker from each side will speak.

During the preparation of rebuttals, the "judges"—the class—fill out their assessment sheets (see next page) individually. They consider ways to provide constructive critiques for the debaters.

10. Rebuttal by A (#1 or #2)	3 minutes
11. Rebuttal by N (#1 or #2)	3 minutes
12. Critique of debate	10 minutes or more

13. If there is time, the class can express their views on the resolution.

Evaluating the Debate (for Critiquing the
Debaters Constructively)

Resolution: THAT _____

_____

Affirmative (in favor of resolution) (Names):   **Negative** (Against the resolution)(Names):

Speaker 1. _____   Speaker 1. _____

Speaker 2. _____   Speaker 2. _____

CRITERIA FOR JUDGING (Optional: Judging can be qualitative not quantitative): Points assigned from 5 (excellent) to 4 (very good) to 3 (good) to 2 (fair).

Parts of the Debate

CONSTRUCTIVE ARGUMENT:

- Presented sufficient facts, including documentation to support them (A#1, N#1).
- Proposed a plan by which to implement the resolution (A#2).
- Refuted the plan point by point (N#2).

Speaker 1. _____   Speaker 1. _____

Speaker 2. _____   Speaker 2. _____

DELIVERY: Clearly expressed, audible, and grammatically correct.

Speaker 1. _____   Speaker 1. _____

Speaker 2. _____   Speaker 2. _____

CROSS-EXAMINATION: Good questions and/or answers.

Speaker 1. _____   Speaker 1. _____

Speaker 2. _____   Speaker 2. _____

REBUTTAL or CLOSING REMARKS: Emphasized main points and why opposition is weak.

Speaker: _____   Speaker: _____

Judge's Name: _____

Additional Comments: _____

Appendix B

How to Use This Text: Two Suggested Approaches

The following ideas are suggestions only. Instructors should consider adapting these ideas in ways that will facilitate their personal instructional style.

Approach#1: Using *Educational Foundations: An Anthology* as the *Primary* Text

Below is an outline of suggested assignments and activities based on 3-week cycles that would enable students to complete all six chapters in the anthology during one semester.

A. *First Week of a Chapter* (Students work on these assignments during the same week that they are sharing their projects from the previous chapter.) *Students will:*
   1. Read the introduction to the chapter and outline it in their notebook or journal.
   2. Read all or several of the selections in the chapter including the remarks that precede them.
   3. (You might want to alternate having the students do one of the following assignments in connection with the selections.)
      a. *Summary/Response:* Summarize the selections in writing and then write half-page reactions to each one, i.e., Did you like it? Why, or why not? Does the selection relate to ideas or experiences you have had, seen, wondered about? (A formal reaction paper is another alternative assignment.) — or —
      b. Answer some or all of the Questions for Discussion and Debate that follow each selection.
   4. (Optional): Begin to do research for a debate or position paper. (Each student could be assigned one or the other for each chapter. Suggested debate and position paper topics are listed by chapter at the end of this section.) The *position paper* is a three-part paper, two to three pages long, in which the student summarizes both the pro and the con positions on the assigned question and then takes a position and defends it using outside resources including education journals and the Internet. These papers are submitted to the instructor. The debaters—on that same question—would simply be evaluated through observation. Following the debate and the critique of the debate, all of the students can discuss the issue together. (See Appendix A.)
   5. Peruse the Activities and Projects sections and decide on the two on which they want to work (or the instructor will assign them).

B. *Second Week of a Chapter*
   Students will:
   1. Work on the two projects they selected or were assigned from the lists in the chapter's Activities and Projects. Record findings in their journals.
   2. In class—in small or large discussion groups—either compare their *summaries and responses* to the selections or compare their *answers to the questions,* depending on which of those assignments was required. (Another approach could be to have the class read four or five selections. Then have pairs of students lead a class discussion of the selections. Still another approach would be to call on students to read aloud their written summaries and responses to a selection and then compare and contrast them.)

C. *Third Week of a Chapter*
   Students will:
   1. *Begin* doing the reading and written responses related to the next chapter. (See Section A above.)
   2. Share one of their projects with members of a small group or with the whole class. (The instructor will check journals and, if possible, meet with each student to discuss his or her projects.)
   3. Hold a debate in front of the class on one of the suggested topics listed below. (The rest of the class submits their position papers on that same question.)

Possible Topics for Debates and Position Papers

Chapter 1: *Teacher Behavior, Teacher Roles*

1. Tenure is a necessary policy for teachers on all levels.
2. Teachers' personal lives should be a reflection of the professional roles they are expected to fill.
3. Principals should continue to teach at least one class or carry out some kind of instructional role along with their administrative responsibilities.
4. Student teachers should be allowed more autonomy within their practica.

Chapter 2: *Historical Perspectives*

1. Religion should play a role in America's public schools.
2. There is nothing new under the (educational) sun.
3. Schools and schooling have changed very little during the last 150 years.
4. Teachers should be risk-takers (as opposed to preservers of the status quo).

Chapter 3: *Philosophical Foundations*

1. A spiritual component within the curriculum can improve public education.

2. Classical music and the arts should be considered as important as reading and math in the school curriculum.
3. Approaches to curriculum development and instruction based on the traditional separation of the disciplines are more effective than interdisciplinary approaches.
4. Student-centered teaching is more effective than teacher-centered teaching.
5. Students should have the major role in selecting their curriculum.

Chapter 4: *The Politics of Education*

1. Local property taxes remain the best and fairest source of funding for schools.
2. School choice and vouchers should be available to parents who want to send their children to private or parochial schools.
3. There is a need for a Department of Education on the federal level.
4. Affirmative action is necessary to prevent discrimination in education.
5. Alternative routes into the teaching profession should be increased.
6. Teachers' academic freedom should take precedence over the community's values.
7. Standardized tests are effective assessment tools.

Chapter 5: *School Environments*

1. Homeschooling is an effective learning alternative.
2. Charter schools are a fair use of public funds.
3. Mainstreaming children with special needs is a sound educational policy.
4. Home visits by teachers should be required as a way of increasing parental involvement in children's education.

Chapter 6: *Living and Learning in a Diverse Society*

1. Tracking—or ability grouping—enables students at all levels to achieve success.
2. Emphasis on multicultural curriculum is beneficial, not divisive.
3. A classical education (i.e., the Great Books of Plato, Shakespeare, Locke) is relevant to all students no matter what their socioeconomic identity or plans for the future.
4. Assimilation (over pluralism) should be the goal of America's public school curriculum.
5. Bilingual programs are beneficial to immigrant children.

The following chart can facilitate your use of Approach#1. The *only* information you need to insert is the *due dates* of the assignments that are listed at the top of the chart.

Chapter No. and name	Due dates		
	1. Outline of chapter introduction 2. Questions or summaries/reactions 3. Start working on ————————▶	Paper or debate	Projects
Chapter 1: Teacher Roles			
Chapter 2: Historical Perspectives			
Chapter 3: Philosophical Foundations			
Chapter 4: Politics of Education			
Chapter 5: School Environments			
Chapter 6: Sociology of Education			

Approach#2: Using the Anthology as a Supplementary Text

If you choose to use this anthology as a supplementary text, the following suggestions may be helpful.

Suggestion 1   After identifying which chapter in the anthology corresponds to a chapter in your primary text, have students read the Brief Background to that anthology chapter and *outline* it in a journal. They could also read the introductory remarks for each selection in the chapter and answer the questions that appear at the end of those remarks, just prior to the excerpts themselves.

Offer students *extra credit* for reading a selection and doing any of the Activities and Projects that follow it. If there is time, have them share their project with the class.

When appropriate, use some of the projects as assignments for the whole class.

Suggestion 2   In addition to or instead of Suggestion 1, assign the reading of one or more of the selections in a chapter. Have students answer the Questions for Discussion and Debate that follow the selection(s) and write their responses in a journal. Then, in small groups or with the whole class, have them compare and discuss their answers. They should incorporate data from their primary text in their discussion and answers.

Suggestion 3 This approach is referred to as the *jigsaw approach* and is also described in chapter 6 (in item 5 of the Activities and Projects following Selection 6.10)

a. Divide the class into small groups (called *T-groups* or *teaching groups*). Assign each member of the same T-group a *different* selection to read and answer questions about. (Do this for each T-group. Thus a *total* of four or five selections could be covered, depending on the size of the groups.)

b. During the next class session, have the students from the different T-groups who read the *same* selection form *E-groups* or *expert groups*, in which they discuss the same selection so they can become experts on its content and relevant questions.

c. Then have each *"expert"* return to his or her original group (the T-group) and teach the members of that group about the selection they read.

Appendix C

Lesson Plan: Outline and Sample Plan

Parts of a Lesson Plan

1. Teacher name
2. Date of lesson
3. Subject and grade level
4. Unit title and major concept
5. Purpose of the lesson (instructional goal)
6. Rationale (why the lesson is important)
7. Behavioral objectives (in three domains: knowledge, attitudes, and skills)
8. Methods of teacher and student activities and responses
   a. Motivation (the "hook")
   b. Development of the lesson
   c. Closure (review of content; what's next)
9. Resources and materials
10. Evaluation procedures

A Sample Lesson Plan (High-School Social Studies)

Teacher: Elizabeth O'Connor

Date of Lesson: December 6, 1993

Subject: Contemporary America

Grade: Twelfth

Name of Unit: Contemporary issues from the weekly *Time* magazine

Concept: Castro's Cuba: Cuba in a post-Soviet Union world

Purpose of Lesson: To explore with students the changing economic, social, and political changes in Cuba today

Rationale: The economic, social, and political changes in Cuba as a result of the demise of the Soviet Union have potential important social and economic implications for the United States.

A. Behavioral Objectives

By the completion of this lesson, students will be able to:

1. Identify and explain the main factors contributing to the economic conditions in Cuba today.

2. Describe Cuba's past economic and political links with the former Soviet Union.

3. Describe the relationship between the United States and Cuba and place that relationship in its proper historical context.

4. Relate the recent defection of Cuban athletes to the United States to the Cuban social, economic, and political climate.

B. Methods of the Teacher (Implementation)   Student Activity and Response

1. *Motivation*

Methods of the Teacher	Student Activity and Response
• Ask students to write what they know about Cuba.	• Write what they know about Cuba.
• Discuss what they have written.	• Discuss with teacher what they have written.
• Give students a map to show Cuba's geographical relationship to the United States.	• Observe on map Cuba's geographical relationship to the United States.

2. *Development*

Methods of the Teacher	Student Activity and Response
• Give students a time line of Cuba's modern history.	• Read time line.
• Give students a brief overview of Cuba's history.	• Listen to overview.
• Give students a political cartoon depicting Castro's relationship with the former Soviet Union.	• Read political cartoon and analyze it in writing.
• Give students a brief biographical sketch of Fidel Castro.	• Listen to overview.
• Summarize the *Time* article.	• Listen to overview.
• Pass out the article from *The Berkshire Eagle* newspaper.	• Students read article and summarize it.
• Break the class into small groups.	
• Ask students to find evidence to support the claims of the defecting Cuban athletes.	• Find evidence in *Time* article to support the claims of the defecting Cuban athletes. (*Eagle* article)
• Bring the class back together to discuss their findings.	• Discuss their findings with the teacher.

3. *Closure*

Methods of the Teacher	Student Activity and Response
• Review the major points of the lesson.	• Respond to review.
• Ask for questions.	• Ask questions.

- Review with students why the
  lesson is important.

- Ask students to write three things   • Write three things they
  about Cuba they learned from the   learned from the lesson.
  lesson.

- Ask students to find another article about   • Homework.
  Cuba and write a summary. Compare
  its content to that of the recent
  article in the lesson.

C. Resources and Materials

1. Cuban athletes defect in droves (1993, December 2). *The Berkshire Eagle,* pp. A1, A8.

2. McGeary, J., & Booth, C. (1993, December 6). Cuba alone. *Time,* 42–54.

3. Sanford, W. R., & Green, C. R. (1992). *Basic principles of American government* (2nd ed.). New York: AMSCO School Publications.

4. Ward, F. (1978). *Inside Cuba Today.* New York: Crown.

D. Evaluation Procedures

1. Oral questions.

2. Small-group discussion.

3. Full-class discussion.

4. Writing a paragraph, cartoon analysis and writing a list of three things they learned from the lesson.

Web Site

Information on lesson planning: http://www.ericsp.org

Name Index

Subject Index

Tolerance

Different
Ideas/Views

Accepting
Showing Respect
Working Alongside

Ultimate Frisbee
A class
— Varying talent
Disabilities